Questions and Answers
on Real Estate

Questions and Answers

on Real Estate

ROBERT W. SEMENOW, B.S. in Econ., Litt.M., J.D., L.L.D. —EXECUTIVE VICE-PRESIDENT, NATIONAL ASSOCIATION OF REAL ESTATE LICENSE LAW OFFICIALS • HONORARY LIFE MEMBER, GREATER PITTSBURGH BOARD OF REALTORS • FORMERLY PROFESSOR OF URBAN LAND STUDIES, UNIVERSITY OF PITTSBURGH, AND DIRECTOR OF PENNSYLVANIA REAL ESTATE BROKER'S LICENSE LAW • AUTHOR, SELECTED CASES IN REAL ESTATE (PRENTICE-HALL, INC., 1964)

Sixth Edition

Englewood Cliffs, N. J.

Published by PRENTICE-HALL, INC.

PRENTICE-HALL INTERNATIONAL, INC., *London*
PRENTICE-HALL OF AUSTRALIA, PTY. LTD., *Sydney*
PRENTICE-HALL OF CANADA, LTD., *Toronto*
PRENTICE-HALL OF INDIA PRIVATE LTD., *New Delhi*
PRENTICE-HALL OF JAPAN, INC., *Tokyo*

SIXTH EDITION

LIBRARY OF CONGRESS
CATALOG CARD NUMBER: 69-13131

Third Printing.....April, 1970

NOTE:

THE FORMS CONTAINED IN THIS BOOK HAVE BEEN CAREFULLY SELECTED IN ORDER TO COVER THE SITUATIONS AND PROBLEMS OF THE SUBJECT MATTER AS COMPLETELY AS POSSIBLE. THEY WILL BE USEFUL FOR ADAPTATION TO SPECIFIC SITUATIONS IN CONNECTION WITH WHICH THEY ARE TO BE USED. LAYMEN WILL FIND THEM INFORMATIVE ON THE CONTINGENCIES AND PROBLEMS THAT SHOULD BE CONSIDERED, BUT SHOULD CONSULT THEIR OWN LEGAL COUNSEL BEFORE ENTERING INTO ANY CONTRACT OR BUSINESS ARRANGEMENT BASED ON THESE FORMS.

B&P

THIS BOOK is respectfully dedicated to the many license law officials in this country and Canada, who, by their conscientious application to duty in the administration and enforcement of license laws and in the promotion of educational courses, institutes, and clinics, are doing so much to safeguard the interests of the public, protect the legitimate broker, and elevate the standards of real estate.

Preface

Today, every state in this country, the District of Columbia, five Canadian Provinces and the Virgin Islands require a person to be licensed in order to engage in the real estate business, as broker or salesman. More than 800,000 persons are so licensed. With the progress of the real estate business towards a professional level, increased emphasis has been placed by the industry and by Real Estate Commissions upon the importance of education in this connection. A state examination is a prerequisite for a license in every state.

The publication of this *Sixth* Edition of *Questions and Answers on Real Estate* is an eloquent testimonial to the popularity and value of preceding editions to the applicant for a license. The present edition contains more than 3,500 questions and answers on real estate. It provides an applicant for license the best proven study aid in preparing for an examination. It also raises his competency to a high level, when he commences his real estate career. All questions are similar to those found in state examinations.

The book is also a ready, reliable reference guide to the real estate practitioner in meeting every day problems. The text material in such basic areas as agreements of sale, brokerage, deeds, and other subjects, has been expanded. Likewise, the definitions of real estate terms, and the section on arithmetic problems (with answers) related to the real estate business, have been enlarged. Salient provisions of the important 1968 Federal Housing Act, with questions and answers, are included.

The encouragement, cooperation and advice of the following license law officials are here most gratefully acknowledged.

Mary J. Thompson, Alabama; J. Fred Talley, Arizona; Erwin E. Barger, Arkansas; Burton E. Smith, California and John E. Hempel, California; Keith T. Koske, Colorado; James F. Carey, Connecticut; William R. Downing, District of Columbia; M. M. Smith, Jr., Florida; Annelle S. Johnson, Edward A. Isakson, Georgia; Robert E. Bekeart, Hawaii; Marion J. Voorhees, Idaho; William H. Robinson, Illinois; T. C. Dickson, Indiana; C. R. Galvin, Iowa; John C. Ball and Helen Edgerton, Kansas; Joseph Glass, Esq., Kentucky;

H. D. Ruffin, Louisiana; Leo M. Carignan, Maine; Samuel T. Abrams, Maryland; Charles E. Harmon, Michigan; Ralph Heaton, Minnesota; Bonnie Collier, Mississippi; Marvin W. Camp, Missouri; Paul Quinlan, Nebraska; G. D. Don McNelley, Nevada; Andrew W. McCabe, Jr., New Jersey; Paul R. Brown, New Mexico; Elia J. Malara, New York; Joseph F. Schweidler, North Carolina; Dennis D. Schulz, North Dakota; Ira McCauley, Ohio; Joseph T. Frizzell, Oklahoma; Walter J. Kucherepa, Ontario; John E. Black, Oregon and William E. Healy, Oregon; Ann Z. Bennett, Pennsylvania; Ralph H. Baer, Jr., South Carolina; Jack C. Burchill, South Dakota; Ann Blount, Tennessee; Andy James, Texas; Nelda G. Rossi, Vermont; Turner N. Burton, Virginia; Alan Tonnon, Washington; Donald E. Portis, West Virginia; Roy E. Hays, Wisconsin; Glenn J. Hertzler, Jr., Wyoming. I am grateful to H. Bemis Lawrence, Esq., Louisville, Ky., for his generous assistance over the years. In particular, a special debt is owed to my close friend and former law partner, Roger I. Harris, Esq., Vice-President and Chief Counsel, General Dynamics Corporation, who gave untiringly of his time and advice in the preparation of the license law material.

R. W. S.

Table of Contents

Table of Cases

Index to Forms

Introduction

IT IS of fundamental importance to know that the extent of the right which a man acquires in property can be no greater than that enjoyed by his predecessor in title. This is a principle very frequently met with in connection with deeds and mortgages. Very often an owner will be heard to exclaim: "What do you mean I do not own this property? I have a deed to it." Yet if the previous owner did not own the entire tract or there was some encumbrance against it, it follows that his purchaser received no better title than he had. Therefore, a cautious and prudent purchaser will have the title examined in order to ascertain the extent of the present owner's interest in the property. And so, it is often necessary to trace the title through a long line of previous owners, in order to ascertain the extent of the original owner's interest in the subject property.

From time to time, a state will pass "curative" acts intended to correct defects in the title, such as validating improper acknowledgments or executions. In the few states where registered titles pertain under the Torrens system, a purchaser relies upon the registered title, without further search.

By way of further introduction, it should be noted that the rights a person has in real estate are determined and protected by the law. The purpose of law it may be said, is to define and to assert legal rights and, as collateral thereto, to prevent and punish legal wrongs. Blackstone defines law as "a rule of civil conduct prescribed by the supreme power in the State, commanding what is right and prohibiting what is wrong." In the widest sense of the word, law may be said to be a "rule of action prescribed by a superior which an inferior is bound to obey." The social concept of law is that it consists of rules for the guidance of man in his relations to his fellow man and to organized society as well. There are two types of law: (1) the unwritten law; (2) the written law. By the unwritten law we mean the customs of a community. Custom is not to be confused with usage. Custom has the force of law whereas usage is merely a fact. There may be usage without custom, but there can be no custom without usage. "Usage," it is said, "consists merely of the repeti-

xix

tion of acts, while custom is created out of their repetition." The common law is a set of cases establishing principles of law. Written law embraces constitutions, statutes, and court decisions. The Federal Constitution is the fundamental law of the land and is representative of a system of laws and customs. A statute is a law enacted by the legislative body of the state or by the Federal Congress. A court is a body in the government to which is delegated the public administration of justice. Civil courts are created by statutes which define their composition and jurisdiction. Courts of law are not law-making bodies. They have the very important function, which sometimes closely approaches legislation, of interpreting the Constitution of the United States, the laws passed by Congress, the state constitutions, and state statutes. If a constitutional question is involved, for example, the deprivation of property without due process of law, recourse, by appeal, may be had to the United States Supreme Court, the court of last resort. Thus, it can be seen that the decisions of the courts are of the utmost importance as the source of all law. The body of the Federal law applies generally throughout the country, but each state, by reason of its particular development and the peculiar conditions and influences which prevail, has its own laws based upon its own constitution, court decisions, and customs. Court decisions, as well as statutes, may be tempered by the social needs of the society within the confines of the particular state. In most of the states in the eastern part of the country, the common law as introduced from England predominates, whereas in the South, codified law, resulting from French and Spanish influence, is the rule. It must be realized that there is no body of real estate law applicable to all of the states or even to a majority, but that the laws relating to deeds, mortgages, landlord and tenant, and other subjects differ materially even from one state to its immediate neighbor. Fundamental concepts and principles, however, are applicable to practically all the states, so that attention and discussion are directed, in the main, to the fundamentals of the law as it applies to each subject discussed. The same approach is true of the problems, questions, and answers included in this work.

Questions and Answers
on Real Estate

Definitions of Real Estate Terms

Absolute fee simple title
One that is unqualified; it is the best title one can obtain.

Abstract of title
A condensed history of the title, consisting of a summary of the various links in the chain of title, together with a statement of all liens, charges, or encumbrances affecting a particular property.

Acceleration clause
A clause in a mortgage, land purchase contract or lease stating that, upon default of a payment due, the balance of the obligation should at once become due and payable.

Access right
The right of an owner to have ingress and egress to and from his property.

Accretion
Addition to the land through natural causes—usually by change in water flow.

Acknowledgment
A formal declaration made before a notary public or other person empowered to perform the service, by the signatory to the instrument, as to the genuineness of the signature.

Acre
A measure of land, 160 square rods (4,840 square yards; 43,560 square feet).

Administrator
A person appointed by court to administer the estate of a deceased person who left no will; that is, who died intestate.

Advance fee
A fee paid in advance of any service rendered in the sale of a property or in obtaining a loan.

Ad Valorem
A tax according to valuation.

Adverse possession
The right of an occupant of land to acquire title against the real owner, where possession has been actual, continuous, hostile, visible, and distinct for the statutory period.

1

Affidavit
A statement of declaration reduced to writing, and sworn or affirmed to before some officer who has authority to administer an oath or affirmation.

Agent
One who represents another from whom he has derived authority.

Agreement of sale
A written agreement whereby the purchaser agrees to buy certain real estate and the seller agrees to sell upon terms and conditions set forth therein.

Air rights
The ownership of the right to use, control or occupy the air space over a designated property.

Alienation
The transfer of real property by one person to another.

Alluvion
Also alluvium. Soil deposited by accretion; increase in land on shore or bank of river due to change in flow of stream.

Amortization
The liquidation of a financial obligation on an installment basis.

Annuity
A sum of money or its equivalent that constitutes one of a series of periodic payments.

Appellant
The party who takes an appeal to a higher court.

Appellee
The party against whom the appeal is taken to a higher court.

Appraisal
An estimate of quantity, quality, or value. The process through which conclusions of property value are obtained; also refers to the report setting forth the estimate and conclusion of value.

Appraisal by capitalization
An estimate of value by capitalization of productivity and income.

Appraisal by comparison
Comparability to the sale prices of other similar properties.

Appraisal by summation
Adding together of parts of a property separately appraised to form the whole: for example, value of the land considered as vacant added to the cost of reproduction of the building, less depreciation.

Appurtenance
That which belongs to something else; something which passes as an incident to land, such as a right of way.

Architect
A person whose profession is designing buildings, drawing up plans, and generally supervising construction of the building.

Arpen
French measurement term, being ⅞ of one acre.

Assessed valuation
Assessment of real estate by a unit of government for taxation purposes.

Assessment
A charge against real estate made by a unit of government to cover the proportionate cost of an improvement, such as a street or sewer.

Assignee
The person to whom an agreement or contract is assigned.

Assignment
The method or manner by which a right, a specialty, or contract is transferred from one person to another.

Associate broker
A person who has qualified as a real estate broker, but works for a broker named in the associate broker's license.

Avulsion
Removal of land from one owner to another when a stream suddenly changes its channel.

Backfill
The replacement of excavated earth into a hole or against a structure.

Balustrade
A small supporting column for a handrail.

Bargain and sale deed
Deed which conveys the property for a consideration, but without any warranties.

Barge board
A wide trim board placed on the ends of a gable roof.

Base and meridian
Imaginary lines used by surveyors to find and describe the location of lands.

Baseboard
The board skirting the walls of a room at the floor line.

Basement floor
The lowest floor level in a building.

Bench marks
A location indicated on a durable marker by surveyors.

Bilateral contract
Both parties expressly enter into mutual engagements (reciprocal).

Binder
An agreement to cover a down payment for the purchase of real estate as evidence of good faith on the part of the purchaser; in insurance: a temporary agreement given to one having an insurable interest, and who desires insurance subject to the same conditions which will apply if, as, and when a policy is issued.

Blanket mortgage
A single mortgage which covers more than one piece of real estate.

Bona fide
In good faith, without fraud.

Bond
Any obligation under seal. A real estate bond is a written obligation, usually issued on security of a mortgage or a trust deed.

Bridging
Small wood or metal pieces used to brace floor joists.

Broker
One employed by another, for a fee, to carry on any of the activities listed in the license law definition of the word.

B.T.U.
British thermal unit. The quantity of heat required to raise the temperature of one pound of water one degree Fahrenheit.

Building code
Regulating the construction of buildings within a municipality by ordinance or law.

Building line
A line fixed at a certain distance from the front and/or sides of a lot, beyond which no building can project.

Bundle of legal rights
Establishes real estate ownership, consists of right to sell, to mortgage, to lease, to will, to regain possession at end of a lease (reversion); to build and remove improvements; to control use within the law.

Business chance broker
One who negotiates the sale of a mercantile business for another for a fee.

Caveat Emptor
"Let the purchaser beware"; the buyer is duty-bound to examine the property he is purchasing and he assumes conditions which are readily ascertainable upon view.

Certificate of no defense
An instrument, executed by the mortgagor, upon the sale of the mortgage, to the assignee, as to the validity of the full mortgage debt.

Chain
Unit of land measurement—66 feet.

Chattel
Personal property, such as household goods or removable fixtures.

Chimney cap
The finishing course at the top of the chimney.

Closing statement
An accounting of funds in a real estate sale made by a broker to the seller and buyer, respectively.

Cloud on the title
An outstanding claim or encumbrance which, if valid, would affect or impair the owner's title; a judgment, or dower interest.

Cognovit note
Note authorizing confession of judgment.

Color of title
That which appears to be good title, but as a matter of fact, is not good title.

Commission
Sum due a real estate broker for services in that capacity; the administrative and enforcement tribunal of real estate license laws.

Common law
Body of law that grew up from custom and decided cases (English law) rather than from codified law (Roman law).

Community property
Property accumulated through joint efforts of husband and wife living together.

Condemnation
Taking private property for public use, with compensation to the owner, under the right of eminent domain.

Condominium
Individual ownership units in a multi-family structure, combined with joint ownership of common areas of the building and ground.

Constructive eviction
Breach of a covenant of warranty or quiet enjoyment; for example, the inability of a purchaser or lessee to obtain possession by reason of a paramount outstanding title.

Constructive notice
Notice given by the public records.

Contract for sale
See Agreement of sale.

Conveyance
The means or medium by which title to real estate is transferred.

Cornice

An ornamental projection at the top of a wall.

Covenant

An agreement between two or more persons, by deed, whereby one of the parties promises the performance or nonperformance of certain acts, or that a given state of things does or does not exist.

Cubage

Front or width of building multiplied by depth of building and by the height, figured from basement floor to the outer surfaces of walls and roof.

Cul de sac

A passage way with one outlet; a blind alley.

Curtesy

The right which a husband has in his wife's estate at her death.

Curtilage

Area of land occupied by a building and its yard and outbuildings, actually enclosed or considered enclosed.

Damnum Absque Injuria

A loss which does not give rise to an action for damages against the person causing it.

Declaration of no set-off

See Certificate of no defense.

Decree of Foreclosure

Decree by a court upon the completion of foreclosure of a mortgage, lien or contract.

Dedication

An appropriation of land by an owner to some public use together with acceptance for such use by or on behalf of the public.

Deed

A writing by which lands, tenements, and hereditaments are transferred, which writing is signed, sealed, and delivered by the grantor.

Default

The nonperformance of a duty, whether arising under a contract, or otherwise; failure to meet an obligation when due.

Defeasance

An instrument which nullifies the effect of some other deed or of an estate.

Deficiency judgment

The difference between the indebtedness sued upon and the sale price or market value of the real estate at the foreclosure sale.

Depreciation

Loss in value, brought about by deterioration through ordinary wear and tear, action of the elements, or functional or economic obsolescence.

Devise
A gift of real estate by will or last testament.

Dispossess
To deprive one of the use of real estate.

Dower
The right which a wife has in her husband's estate at his death.

Duplex
A single two-story structure designed for two-family occupancy.

Duress
Unlawful constraint exercised upon a person, whereby he is forced to perform some act, or to sign an instrument, against his will.

Earnest money
Down payment made by a purchaser of real estate as evidence of good faith.

Easement
The right, liberty, advantage or privilege which one individual has in lands of another (a right of way).

Economic life
The period over which a property may be profitably utilized.

Ejectment
A form of action to regain possession of real property, with damages for the unlawful retention.

Eminent domain
The right of the people or government to take private property for public use upon payment of compensation.

Encroachment
A building, part of building, or obstruction which intrudes upon or invades a highway or sidewalk or trespasses upon property of another.

Encumbrance
A claim, lien, charge, or liability attached to and binding upon real property, such as a judgment, unpaid taxes, or a right of way; defined in law as any right to, or interest in, land which may subsist in another to the diminution of its value, but consistent with the passing of the fee.

Equity
The interest or value which an owner has in real estate over and above the mortgage against it; system of legal rules administered by courts of chancery.

Equity of redemption
Right of original owner to reclaim property sold through fore-

closure proceedings on a mortgage, by payment of debt, interest, and costs.

Erosion
The wearing away of land through processes of nature as by streams and winds.

Escheat
Reversion of property to the sovereign state owing to lack of any heirs capable of inheriting.

Escrow
A deed delivered to a third person for the grantee to be held by him until the fulfillment or performance of some act or condition.

Estate
The degree, quantity, nature and extent of interest which a person has in real property.

Estate in reversion
The residue of an estate left in the grantor, to commence in possession after the termination of some particular estate granted by him. In a lease, the lessor has the estate in reversion after the lease is terminated.

Estoppel certificate
See Certificate of no defense.

Ethics
That branch of moral science, which treats of the duties which a member of a profession or craft owes to the public, to his client, and to the other members of the profession.

Et ux.
Abbreviation for *et uxor,* meaning "and wife."

Eviction
A violation of some covenant in a lease by the landlord, usually the covenant for quiet enjoyment; also refers to process instituted to oust a person from possession of real estate.

Exclusive agency
The appointment of one real estate broker as sole agent for the sale of a property for a designated period of time.

Execution
A writ issued by a court to the sheriff directing him to sell property to satisfy a debt.

Executor
A person named in a will to carry out its provisions.

"Fannie Mae"
The secondary mortgage market. It provides a market for mortgages held by primary lenders, such as banks and savings and loan associations and provides the primary market with a ready market

for mortgages, so as to permit a greater turnover of money for loans.

F.H.A.
Federal Housing Authority; an agency of the Federal Government that insures real estate loans.

Fee simple
The largest estate or ownership in real property; free from all manner of conditions or encumbrances.

Finder's fee
A fee or commission paid to a broker for obtaining a mortgage loan for a client or for referring a mortgage loan to a broker. It may also refer to a commission paid to a broker for locating a property.

Fixture
An article that was once personalty, but has become real estate by reason of its permanent attachment in or to the improvement.

Firm commitment
A commitment by the F.H.A. to insure a mortgage on specified property with a specified mortgagor.

Flashing
Metal strips placed around roof openings to provide water tightness.

Foreclosure
A court process instituted by a mortgagee or lien creditor to defeat any interest or redemption which the debtor-owner may have in the property.

Foreshore
Land between high-water mark and low-water mark.

Foundation
The walls of a building below the first or ground floor.

Fraud
The intentional and successful employment of any cunning, deception, collusion, or artifice, used to circumvent, cheat or deceive another person, whereby that person acts upon it, to his detriment, loss, or disadvantage.

Freehold
An estate in fee simple or for life.

Front foot
A standard of measurement, one foot wide, extending from street line for a depth, generally conceded to be 100 feet.

Gable roof
A pitched roof with sloping sides.

G.I. loan
Loan guaranteed by the Veterans Administration under Service-

men's Readjustment Act of 1944, as amended; only honorably
discharged veterans and their widows are eligible.

General warranty
A covenant in the deed whereby the grantor agrees to protect the
grantee against the world.

Grantee
A person to whom real estate is conveyed; the buyer.

Grantor
A person who conveys real estate by deed; the seller.

Gross lease
A lease of property whereby lessor is to meet all property charges
regularly incurred through ownership.

Ground rent
A rent reserved by a grantor to himself, his heirs and assigns in
conveying land in fee.

Habendum clause
The "To Have and To Hold" clause which defines or limits the
quantity of the estate granted in the premises of the deed.

Hand money
Same as an earnest money deposit.

Hereditaments
The largest classification of property; includes lands, tenements,
and incorporeal property, such as rights of way.

Holdover tenant
A tenant who remains in possession of leased property after the
expiration of the lease term.

Homestead
Real estate occupied by the owner as a home; the owner enjoys
special rights and privileges.

Housing for the Elderly
A project designed specially for older persons (62 years or over)
which provides living unit accommodations, and common social
and activities space, and facilities for health and nursing services
for residents.

H.U.D.
Department of Housing and Urban Development.

Indenture
A formal written instrument made between two or more persons
in different interests; name comes from practice of indenting or
cutting the deed on the top or side in a waving line.

Installment contract
Purchase of real estate upon an installment basis; upon default,
payments are forfeited.

Ipso facto
By the fact itself.

Irrigation district
Quasi-political districts created under special laws to provide for water services to property owners in the district.

Jalousie
A kind of blind or shutter made with slats fixed at an angle.

Joint tenancy
Property held by two or more persons together with the distinct character of survivorship.

Judgment
Decree of court declaring that one individual is indebted to another and fixing the amount of such indebtedness.

Judgment d. s. b.
D. s. b. is the abbreviation for the Latin *debitum sine brevi*, which means "debt without writ." It is a judgment confessed by authority of the language in the instrument.

Junior mortgage
A mortgage second in lien to a previous mortgage.

Laches
Delay or negligence in asserting one's rights.

Land contract
A contract for the purchase of real estate upon an installment basis; upon payment of last installment, deed is delivered to purchaser.

Land economics
Branch of the science of economics which deals with the classification, ownership, and utilization of land and buildings erected thereon.

Landlord
One who rents property to another.

Lease
A contract, written or oral, for the possession of lands and tenements on the one hand and a recompense of rent or other income, on the other hand.

Leasehold
An estate in realty held under a lease.

Legal description
A description recognized by law, which is sufficient to locate and identify the property without oral testimony.

Lessee
A person to whom property is rented under a lease.

Lessor
See Landlord.

License
A privilege or right granted by the State to operate as a real estate

broker or salesman. An authority to go upon or use another person's land or property, without possessing any estate therein.

License year
Period specified in license law for license; usually different from calendar year.

Lien
A hold or claim which one person has upon property of another as security for a debt or charge; judgments, mortgages, taxes.

Life estate
An estate or interest held during the term of some certain person's life.

Lis Pendens
Suit pending; usually recorded so as to give constructive notice of pending litigation.

Listing
Oral or written employment of broker by owner to sell or lease real estate.

Littoral
Belonging to shore as of sea or Great Lakes; corresponds to riparian rights.

Louver
A domed turret with lateral openings in a roof.

Mansard roof
A roof with two slopes on each of the four sides, the lower steeper than the upper.

Market value
The highest price which a buyer, willing but not compelled to buy, would pay, and the lowest a seller, willing but not compelled to sell, would accept.

Marketable title
Such a title as a court would compel a purchaser to accept; it is free from any encumbrances or clouds.

Marshalling
Where a creditor has two or more funds out of which to satisfy a debt, he cannot so elect as to deprive another individual, who has but one fund, of his security.

Mechanic's lien
A species of lien created by statute which exists in favor of persons who have performed work or furnished materials in the erection or repair of a building.

Meeting of minds
A mutual intention of two persons to enter into a contract affecting their legal status based on agreed-upon terms.

Merchantable title
(*See* Marketable title)

Messuage
Dwelling house and adjacent land and outbuildings.

Metes and bounds
A description in a deed of the land location, in which the boundaries are defined by directions and distances.

Mill
One-tenth of one cent; the measure used to state the property tax rate. That is, a tax rate of one mill on the dollar is the same as a rate of one-tenth of one per cent of the assessed value of the property.

Mortgage
A conditional transfer of real property as security for the payment of a debt or the fulfillment of some obligation.

Mortgagee
A person to whom property is conveyed as security for a loan made by such person (the creditor).

Mortgagee in possession
A mortgage creditor who takes over the income from the mortgaged property upon a default on the mortgage by the debtor.

Mortgagor
An owner who conveys his property as security for a loan (the debtor).

Multiple listing
The arrangement among real estate board or exchange members whereby each broker brings his listings to the attention of the other members so that if a sale results, the commission is divided between the broker bringing the listing and the broker making the sale, with a small percentage going to the board or exchange.

NAREB
National Association of Real Estate Boards.

Net listing
A price, which must be expressly agreed upon, below which the owner will not sell the property and at which price the broker will not receive a commission; the broker receives the excess over and above the net listing as his commission.

N.S.F. check
Not sufficient funds check—(not honored by bank).

Obsolescence
Impairment of desirability and usefulness brought about by physical, economic, fashion or other changes.

Open listing
An oral or general listing.

Option

The right to purchase or lease a property at a certain price for a certain designated period, for which right a consideration is paid.

Over-improvement

An improvement which is not the highest and best use for the site on which it is placed by reason of excess in size or cost.

Partition

A division made of real property among those who own it in undivided shares.

Party wall

A wall erected on the line between two adjoining properties, belonging to different persons, for use of both properties.

Patent

Conveyance of title to government land.

Percentage lease

A lease of property in which the rental is based upon the volume of sales made upon the leased premises.

Perch

A unit of land measurement; 16½ feet.

Percolation test

A soil test to determine if soil will take sufficient water seepage for use of a septic tank.

Personalty

All articles or property that are not real estate.

Plat book

A public record of various recorded plans in the municipality or county.

Plottage

Increment in unity value of a plot of land created by assembling smaller ownerships into one ownership.

Pocket license card

Evidence of licensure, which should be carried by the licensee at all times and presented when requested by any person with whom the licensee is dealing in regard to real estate.

Police power

The inherent rights of a government to pass such legislation as may be necessary to protect the public health and safety and/or to promote the general welfare.

Postponement of lien

The subordination of a presently prior lien to a subsequent judgment or mortgage.

Principal

The employer of an agent; the person who is ordinarily liable primarily.

Principal note
The promissory note which is secured by the mortgage or trust deed.

Property
The right or interest which an individual has in lands and chattels to the exclusion of all others.

Prospectus
A printed advertisement for a new enterprise, such as rural property or subdivision.

Public policy
That principle of the law, which holds that no person can lawfully do that which has a tendency to be injurious to the public or against the public good.

Public trustee
A person appointed or required by law to execute a trust.

Purchase money mortgage
A mortgage given by a grantee to the grantor in part payment of the purchase price of real estate.

Quiet enjoyment
The right of an owner to the use of property without interference of possession.

Quiet title
A court action brought to establish title and to remove a cloud on the title.

Quit claim deed
A deed given when the grantee already has, or claims, complete or partial title to the premises and the grantor has a possible interest that otherwise would constitute a cloud upon the title.

Range
A strip of land six miles wide determined by government survey, running in a north-south direction.

Realtor
A coined word used to designate an active member of a local real estate board affiliated with the National Association of Real Estate Boards.

Redemption
The right of a mortgagor to redeem the property by paying the debt after the expiration date; the right of an owner to reclaim his property after a sale for taxes.

Reformation
An action to correct a mistake in a deed or other instrument.

Release
The relinquishment of some right or benefit to a person who already has some interest in the property.

Release of lien
The discharge of certain property from the lien of a judgment, mortgage, or claim.

Remainder estate
An estate in property created at the same time and by the same instrument as another estate and limited to arise immediately upon the termination of the other estate.

Reproduction cost
Normal cost of exact duplication of a property, as of a certain date.

Restriction
A device in a deed for controlling the use of land for the benefit of the land.

Restriction covenant
A clause in a deed limiting the use of the property conveyed for a certain period of time.

Reversion
The residue of an estate left to the grantor, to commence after the determination of some particular estate granted out by him.

Right of way
An easement over another's land—also used to describe strip of land used as a roadbed by a railroad or other public utility for a public purpose.

Riparian
Pertaining to the banks of a river, stream, waterway, and so forth.

Riparian owner
One who owns lands bounding upon a river or water course.

Satisfaction piece
An instrument for recording and acknowledging payment of an indebtedness secured by a mortgage.

Section
A section of land established by government survey and containing 640 acres.

Seizin
Possession of real estate by one entitled thereto.

Separate property
Property owned by a husband or wife which is not community property; acquired by either spouse prior to marriage or by gift or devise after marriage.

Septic tank system
Private sewage disposal section for an individual home.

Setback
The distance from curb or other established line, within which no building may be erected.

Severalty ownership
Real property owned by one person only; sole ownership.
Siding
Finish covering on exterior walls.
Simple listing
Listing property with a broker for sale or rent other than through exclusive agency or an exclusive right-to-sell contract; an open listing, usually verbal.
Sky lease
Lease for a long period of time of space above a piece of real estate; upper stories of a building to be erected by the tenant; upon the termination of lease, the improvement belongs to the lessor.
Special warranty deed
A deed wherein the grantor limits his liability to the grantee to anyone claiming, by, from, through or under him, the grantor.
Specific performance
A remedy in a court of equity compelling the defendant to carry out the terms of the agreement or contract which was executed.
Statute of frauds
Requires certain contracts relating to real estate, such as agreements of sale, to be in writing, in order to be enforceable.
Subdivison
A tract of land divided into lots suitable for home-building purposes.
Subletting
A leasing by a tenant to another, who holds under the tenant.
Subordination clause
A clause in a mortgage or lease, stating that rights of the holder shall be secondary or subordinate to a subsequent encumbrance.
Sump pump
An automatic water pump used in basements to raise water to the sewer level.
Surrender
The cancellation of a lease by mutual consent of lessor and lessee.
Survey
The process by which a parcel of land is measured and its area ascertained.
Tax
A charge assessed against persons or property for public purposes.
Tax deed
A deed for property sold at public sale by a political subdivision, such as a city, for nonpayment of taxes by the owner.

Tenancy at will
A license to use or occupy lands and tenements at the will of the owner.

Tenancy in common
Form of estate held by two or more persons, each of whom is considered as being possessed of the whole of an undivided part.

Tenant
A person who holds real estate under a lease (lessee).

Tenant at sufferance
One who comes into possession of lands by lawful title and keeps it afterwards without any title at all.

Tenement
Everything of a permanent nature which may be holden.

Terre tenant
One who has the actual possession of land.

Title
Evidence of ownership, which refers to the quality of the estate.

Title by adverse possession
Acquired by occupation and recognized as against the paper title owner.

Title insurance
A policy of insurance which indemnifies the holder for any loss sustained by reason of defects in the title.

Torrens system
A system of title records provided by state law.

Tort
An actionable wrong.

Township
A territorial subdivision, six miles long, six miles wide, and containing 36 sections, each one mile square.

Trust deed
A conveyance of real estate to a third person to be held for the benefit of a cestuique trust (beneficiary).

Unearned increment
An increase in value of real estate due to no effort on the part of the owner; often due to increase in population.

Unilateral contract
One in which one party makes an express undertaking, without receiving in return any promise of performance from the other.

Usury
Charging more than the legal rate of interest for the use of money.

V.A. loan
(*See* G.I. loan)

Vara

Spanish term of measurement, being 33⅓ inches.

Vendee

The purchaser of real estate under an agreement.

Vendor

The seller of real estate, usually referred to as the party of the first part in an agreement of sale.

Waiver

The renunciation, abandonment, or surrender of some claim, right, or privilege.

Warranty deed

One that contains a covenant that the grantor will protect the grantee against any claimant.

Water table

Distance from surface of ground to a depth at which natural ground water is found.

Windowsill

The lower or base framing of a window opening.

Writ of execution

A writ which authorizes and directs the proper officer of the court (usually the sheriff) to carry into effect the judgment or decree of the court.

Zoning ordinance

Exercise of police power of a municipality in regulating and controlling the character and use of property.

Chapter I

BROKERAGE

Real estate commissions stem, in the main, from brokerage in the sale and rental of real property. In 1969, more than 800,000 persons in the United States and Canada were licensed to perform brokerage services. In return for such service as an intermediary in bringing the seller and buyer, or owner and tenant, to an agreement, the licensee performs a valuable service, and is entitled to a commission. Before the licensee can qualify for a commission, he must be employed by one of the parties in the transaction, to whom he looks for compensation. Usually, it is the owner-seller who employs the broker, by listing the property with him. Thus, commissions depend upon listings and listings may be said to be the heart of the real estate business. In order to recover a commission, in a court of law, it is necessary for the broker to prove that:

1. He was properly licensed
2. He had a contract of employment
3. He was the efficient and procuring cause of the sale

In the Wisconsin case of *Kemmerer v. Roscher*, 100 N.W. 2d 314 (Wis. 1960), the Supreme Court held that it was necessary for a broker to be licensed, not only at the time when the agreements of sale were signed, but from the very inception of the transaction, i.e., when the listing was obtained.

The United States Circuit Court of Appeals took an opposite view in another case, involving a similar issue. In the case of *Schreibman v. L. I. Combs and Sons, Inc., et al.*, 377 F. 2d 410 (1964), the plaintiff broker, licensed in New York, obtained a license in Indiana, *after* he secured a listing in Indiana. He was licensed at the time the agreements of sale were signed between the owner and the buyer procured by him. The Federal Appellate Court held that since the plaintiff was licensed at the time the cause of action arose (when the agreements were signed), the District Court was in error in dismissing the suit. The case was returned to the District Court for hearing on its merits.

The case of *Rosenthal et al. v. Art Metals, Inc., et al.*, N.J. (1968) also involved the same provision in the New Jersey license law as to "the time the cause of action arose." The court decided against the broker, since negotiations were carried on before he received his broker's license, although prior to the execution of the contract of sale: *Benedell v. De Dominicis* 251 N.Y. 305.

In spite of declaring that it shall be unlawful for a person to engage in the real estate business without a license, most states provide, as in Indiana, that recovery of a commission depends upon whether the broker was licensed *at the time the cause of action arose.* The Illinois law requires a license "prior to the time of offering to perform any such act or service or procuring any promise or contract for the payment of compensation for any such contemplated act or service." The same is true of the Maryland law. It is important to remember that prompt renewal of a license is a *must,* including bond renewal, where the state requires a bond, in order not to prejudice or jeopardize an earned commission.

Fee splitting between brokers

In associating with a real estate broker from another state, the licensee should make sure that the other broker is properly licensed in the latter's state. Even so, the licensee should also examine the license law and the Rules and Regulations in his own state, to ascertain whether he can share his commission legally with the non-resident broker. Apropos of the matter is the case of *Wheaton v. Ramsey* 436 P. 2d 248 (Idaho) (1968). Ramsey was a licensed broker in Montana; Wheaton was licensed in South Dakota. At the time of the suit for a share in the commission, Ramsey was a resident of Idaho and for that reason suit was brought in that state. In late 1963, Wheaton, appellant, contacted defendant, Ramsey, concerning her ranch listings in Montana and obtained from her information concerning the Goat Mountain Ranch. The parties discussed the possible joint sale of the property and agreed that in such event, they would split the real estate commission. In October 1963, appellant traveled to Montana with prospective purchasers, Mr. and Mrs. O. W. McPherson, and spent several days showing them the ranch. He also showed the property to other prospects. In December 1963, the McPhersons agreed with the defendant to purchase the ranch for $275,000. Upon completion of the sale in January 1964, the defendant received a five per cent commission of $13,750. Ramsey refused to pay to appellant any share of the commission on the ground that her own Montana real estate license would be jeopardized, since Wheaton was not licensed in Montana. The Court said:

The principal issue is whether by Montana law the understanding between appellant and respondent Ramsey constituted an illegal agreement, inasmuch as appellant was unlicensed in Montana, so that such agreement cannot now be enforced. Both parties concur that an agreement between real estate brokers to share a commission is not within the statute of frauds and may be made orally. *Reilly v. Maw* 146 Mont. 145 (1965), *Iusi v. Chase,* 169 Cal. App. 2d 83 (1959). The controlling statute is Montana's Real Estate Licensing Act of 1963. . . . It provides that ". . . it is unlawful for any licensed broker to employ or compensate directly or indirectly any person for performing any of the acts regulated by this Act, who is not a licensed broker or licensed salesman; provided, however, *that a licensed broker may pay a commission to a licensed broker of another state so long as such non-resident broker has not conducted and does not conduct in this state any service for which a fee, compensation or commission is paid . . .*" (emphasis supplied)

Appellant's argument might be persuasive were it not for the definitive Montana statute, which deals precisely with the situation at bar. Both parties agree that appellant, in showing the Goat Mountain Ranch to McPherson and other prospective purchasers, performed acts and services within Montana for which a fee, compensation or commission is normally paid a real estate broker. Such being the fact, (the statute) is dispositive of appellant's complaint; it would be unlawful for respondent Ramsey to compensate appellant directly or indirectly pursuant to the fee-splitting arrangement. The agreement, therefore, is unenforceable . . .

In the case of *Provisor v. Haas Realty, Inc.,* 256 A.C.A. 5 (1968), the California Appellate Court denied the plaintiff, an attorney, claiming compensation on a real estate transaction, because he was not a licensed real estate broker.

The plaintiff represented the purchaser of property and participated in the negotiations in behalf of the purchaser. For this activity he requested, or imposed, the requirement of the defendant broker to agree to split the commission. The broker agreed in writing to do this. When escrow opened, plaintiff was asked for his real estate license number. When he didn't show that he was licensed, the defendant broker refused to share any portion of the commission.

The Court sustained the defendant broker's position that the payment to the plaintiff, an attorney but not a real estate broker, would be an unlawful payment of compensation, for the reason that the plaintiff did not come within the exemption provision of Section 10133, in that he did not perform any legal service for the broker.

Employment

Employment is an important prerequisite to the recovery of a commission in a court of law. The cases are legion where a broker was unsuccessful in recovering a commission, because he could not prove a contract of employment. It is regrettable that the law in every state does not require a broker's employment to be in writing. At the present time, fifteen states do require a broker's employment to be in writing (Arizona, California, Hawaii, Idaho, Kentucky,

Louisiana, Michigan, Nebraska, New Jersey, New Mexico, Oregon, Texas, Utah, Washington, and Wisconsin—also the District of Columbia and the Province of Ontario). These states also require a definite expiration date in exclusive listing contracts. A number of states require a definite expiration date by rule and regulation of the Commission. A written listing eliminates misunderstanding and curtails litigation. In the long run, it inures to the benefit of the licensee, because it is strong evidence of employment.

Where the law requires the listing to be in writing, it should contain a description of the property, terms of the sale, amount of commission to be paid, the expiration date and signature by the party to be charged.

In states where an oral listing is valid, many owners are full of curiosity; in an active market, they may be just curious to see what they could get for their property or they entertain a half-hearted idea that they want to sell it. If a buyer is obtained, they have a change of mind. In a suit, there is a complete variance as to the facts; whereas, if there were a written employment, the writing would speak for itself. In the Missouri case of *Windsor v. International Life Ins. Co.*, 29 S.W. 2d 1112 (1930), where a broker, unsolicited, visited defendant and offered to exchange a business building for farm lands, the defendant said he was not interested, but would be interested in exchanging farm lands for high class apartment properties. The broker said he would see what he could do. Nothing was said about commission. Later, broker sued for commission. Court held that there was no employment, so no recovery.

In the case of *Yurgelin v. Emery* 282 Mass. 571 (1933), the Court held that a single inquiry by the owner as to the amount of commission a broker would charge, was insufficient to warrant a finding that the owner expressly or impliedly contracted with the broker to find a purchaser.

A writing authorizing an agent to sell "property described on the reverse side of this card," was held sufficiently signed where the owner's signature appeared at the end of the face side of card: *Kelley v. J. R. Rice Realty Co.* 235 Ky. 643 (1930).

In the case of *Svoboda v. De Wald* 159 Neb. 594 (1955) the court held that the broker's name on the agreement of sale constituted a written listing.

A sign on a property reading "SEE YOUR BROKER" does not create employment. The Pennsylvania Supreme Court so held in the case of Appeal of *Lancaster Farmers National Bank* 219. A. 2d 647 (1966), reversing an award in favor of a broker by a lower court. The testimony tended to show that appellee (broker) had no specific contract to sell and that he was never contacted by the appellant (seller) and given authority to sell the subject property. The broker contacted the Bank to ascertain whether the particular property was available *after* he learned that the Millers were interested in purchasing it. The Bank had placed a sign on the property indicating that it was for sale and directing interested parties *to contact their brokers*. The plaintiff broker had previously dealt with the Bank, having sold a property for it and having received a commission in the sale. The Court said:

The fact that a broker has previously made a sale and received a commission does not entitle him to a commission on a subsequent sale made by him for the same vendor, if he has not been employed to effect that sale. Thus, the previous transaction, not being sufficiently probative in itself, to create a subsequent agency, did not entitle appellee to a commission. Neither was the sign directing prospective purchasers to contact their brokers an offer of employment. In *Lanard and Axilbund v. Thomson Printing Co.*, 84 Pa. Super. 199 (1924), defendant notified approximately one hundred real estate brokers by postal card that it had property to rent. The Superior Court there held that: "The postal card amounted to no more than a notice that defendant had a property to rent. It did not authorize plaintiffs to secure a tenant." The sign in the instant case also was nothing more than a notice that the property was available. It created no agency.

When appellee contacted the appellant to determine if the property was still for sale, no agency was created, since this conduct was as consistent with the broker's agency to the purchaser as it was to his agency to the vendor. . . . Here, as a matter of law, there was insufficient facts to create an employment or to give appellant notice of appellee's claim for a commission from it on the sale, and there can be no adoption or ratification of an unknown obligation.

A case in the same area of law, in which one broker sued another broker successfully, is the case of *Levit v. Bowers*, 2 Ill. App. 2d 343 (1954). In that case, the defendant, a Realtor, held an exclusive agency for the sale of a large plot of ground in Chicago. In June 1949, he mailed a letter to about one thousand real estate brokers in the Chicago Loop, offering to pay a full commission to a broker who "successfully negotiates a sale" of all or a portion of the property. The plaintiff broker recovered a verdict for $4,200 and the defendant broker appealed. It appears from the facts that on May 17, 1950, the plaintiff submitted an all cash offer of $84,000 for the subject property. This offer was accepted and defendant stated that he would give the plaintiff the name of the attorney for the seller so that the attorney could draft the necessary agreement. On June 5, he called the defendant by telephone telling him the offer was still open and asking the name of the attorney immediately. The defendant did not furnish the attorney's name, nor did he take any steps to close the deal, and the negotiation was terminated. It was the defendant's contention that the words "successfully negotiating sale" meant that no commission would be paid unless the sale was consummated. In regard to the meaning of the words in controversy, the Court said:

The letter in question was prepared and signed by a Realtor and sent to one thousand real estate brokers—men who make their living as agents for buyers and sellers of real estate. The final transfer was beyond their control. . . . If a sale had to be consummated before the broker was entitled to his commission, then the solicitation by the defendant of the services of a thousand Realtors in the Chicago Loop was hardly more than a snare and a delusion. . . . The property being vacant and the transaction being for cash and was left no matter of substance to be decided.

In the case of *Sackett v. Ford*, 1 Tenn. 506, the court held that where a broker asks an owner the price of his house, and introduces him to a customer who subsequently purchases it, he is not entitled to a commission, unless he was employed by the owner to make the sale, although he may have, to some extent, influenced the sale.

No particular form of words is necessary to employ a broker although a mere statement to a broker of the price at which the owner will sell is not, in itself, sufficient to imply a contract of employment. The broker must act with the consent of the principal, whether such consent be given by written instrument, orally, or by implication from the conduct of the parties. (*Greenwald v. Marcus*, 3 Ill. App. 2d 495 (1954).

In Corpus Juris Secundum, 32 Section 12, it is said:

. . . the mere leaving of a description of the property at the office of a broker, by the owner or his agent, with the request that the broker sell the property at a designated price and upon designated terms, amounts to an employment of the broker; but the mere fact that a broker asks and obtains from the owner the price at which he is willing to sell does not of itself establish the relation of principal and agent between them.

It is important that the broker have a definite understanding with the owner *that he will be paid a commission*, if the broker obtains a buyer upon the seller's terms.

In the case of *Tenbusch v. R.K.N. Realty Co.*, 107 Ohio App. 133 (1958), a jury found in favor of a broker for $5,750 as a commission. The appellate court reversed, stating:

There is no evidence in the record here that the defendant consented to this plaintiff's acting as its agent, the testimony only relating to the price of the property and that a commission was discussed. A broker can derive no authority by voluntarily thrusting his services upon another without the latter's consent.

In the Kentucky case of *O. L. Hamilton v. Booth*, 332 S.W. 2d 252 (1960), a broker sued for a $750 commission. The only question involved was whether the contract of sale between the owner and the buyer constituted a *written* contract of employment between the owner and the broker, as required under Kentucky law. The Court said:

This sales agreement between the defendant and the purchaser of his property has no resemblance of a contractual arrangement between the defendant and plaintiff. It recites that the property was sold through Bud's Hamilton Realty Auction Co., (this is a printed form) but these words standing alone are meaningless. If plaintiff was to recover on the basis of this writing, it should show an agreement with him and the terms of the agreement. It fails to show either. The plaintiff, therefore, had no claim based on this writing as a contract.

The cases are legion where a commission has been refused, because the broker could not establish affirmatively that he was actually employed. Thus, a *written* contract of employment, required by law, would obviate this situation. However, where a broker has merely discussed the possibility of selling the property of an owner, and *feels* that he has been employed, but entertains some doubt on that score, he can protect himself, in some measure, by putting the owner on notice that he is employed. A letter, in following form, might well be used in this connection:

April 26, 1969

Dear Mr. and Mrs. Tom Morgan:

In accordance with our conversation today, we are pleased to list your property at 2715 Murray Avenue, Pittsburgh, Pennsylvania, for sale. We will endeavor to obtain a purchaser at your suggested price of $20,500 and, of course, will expect the usual commission of 7%.

If you decide at a future date not to sell and to terminate our employment or if you decide to change the selling price, please notify us immediately.

We hope to be able to obtain a purchaser upon your terms and to your complete satisfaction.

Thanking you for this business, we are,

Sincerely yours,

MODERN REAL ESTATE COMPANY

By Frank W. Smith
President

Upon receipt of such a notice, the owner, if he does not want to sell, will undoubtedly notify the broker to that effect. In this event, the broker will not waste any time or money in attempting to obtain a purchaser.

Authority of person listing property

Where the owner is listed with the broker by a person who is not the owner, the broker should make careful inquiry as to such person's authority to list the property. Often a son or daughter of foreign parents, or of persons of little business experience, will do the negotiating with the broker. Should he obtain a buyer upon the terms requested, he may find that the old folks have changed their minds and want to continue in the neighborhood where they have lived for many years. A suit for commission is futile unless the broker can prove that the child was the authorized agent of the parents. Agency is often a difficult burden for a claimant to establish, as the affirmative burden of proof rests upon the plaintiff broker. The broker would have a cause of action against the child, but a judgment would probably be uncollectible.

Where a broker obtains a listing from a husband and knows that the wife, who is also an owner, will not sign a contract of sale, so that the buyer cannot obtain good title, the broker cannot collect a commission, if he obtains a buyer. The marital relationship does not make one spouse the agent for the other, per se. It is important to obtain authority to sell from both parties: *Ginn v. MacAluso,* 310 P. 2d, 1034 (N.M. 1957). Where husband and wife own property jointly and they are living separate and apart, a cautious broker will accept a listing signed only by both parties. In dealing with a corporate owner, through an officer, the burden is upon the broker to establish that the officer was the authorized agent of the corporation.

In the case of *Virginia M. Pepper, appellant, v. J. C. Chatel, appellee,* No. 30561, Municipal Court of Appeals for the District of Columbia (1962), the appellant had inherited certain property prior to her marriage, which she listed with the broker under her maiden name. The broker produced a buyer the next day and a contract was immediately executed by appellant under her maiden name. At settlement, however, appellant's husband refused to join in the conveyance and the sale was not consummated.

Appellant testified that at the time of signing, she was unaware that her husband had to join in the conveyance, and that the broker failed to so advise her, although he knew at the time that she was married. The broker testified that he did not learn of her marriage until after the contract was executed. The Court said:

In the case before us appellant testified that she was unaware of the necessity of having her husband join in the conveyance. Nevertheless, we are of the opinion that the evidence supports the conclusion that the broker is entitled to his commission. It is clear from the finding that the broker did not learn appellant was married until after the contract was executed, and that he acted in good faith when he procured a purchaser acceptable to appellant. Perhaps the result would be different if the broker had known not only that appellant was married but also that her husband was unwilling to join in the conveyance. A broker should not be permitted to impose upon his principal an expense he knows to be useless, but appellant did not even attempt to establish that the broker possessed such knowledge.

In the case of *Cohen v. Garlick* 344 Mass. 654 (1962), an auctioneer firm was hired by an owner of real estate to sell it at auction. The auctioneer announced in effect that "broker participation" would be "allowed" to a broker representing the successful bidder at the time of his purchase if the broker had registered his "client" with "us," and would be "paid by us after settlement." A broker for the successful bidder had duly registered him on a form stating that if "my client" were the successful bidder "I am to receive" such commission, "payable to me upon settlement." The Court held that the facts did not permit an inference that the owner of the property had authorized the auctioneer firm to bind him to pay such commission nor justify a ruling that the owner was liable to the successful bidder's broker therefor.

It should be kept in mind that there are two separate contracts involved in connection with brokerage. The first is the employment contract between owner and broker. It prescribes the terms of the broker's employment. Its object is for the agent to procure a buyer, who will enter into a contract with the owner to purchase the property upon the seller's terms. This contract is between the seller and buyer. If the broker procures a bona fide buyer upon the seller's terms, the broker has discharged his contract of employment with the seller, and he is entitled to his commission. This is true even though the seller refuses to sign the agreement of sale.

The law imposes a number of important duties upon one who undertakes to act as an agent in a real estate transaction.

Broker's duty of loyalty

If a real estate broker is to discharge creditably the duties which devolve upon his office, it is necessary that he have a knowledge of certain cardinal and fundamental principles of law which affect the everyday practice of his business. Real estate brokerage represents a combination of the principles of the law of principal and agent and the law of contracts. A real estate broker is an agent in the fullest sense of the word, in that he represents another from whom he has derived his authority. The interests of three persons are thereby involved: that of the owner, of the broker, and of the purchaser with whom the broker negotiates. A knowledge of the law of principal and agent is essential in order to determine accurately the respective rights and liabilities of these three parties to the contract. A broker occupies a position of trust and confidence toward his principal, and there are certain important duties that every agent owes to his principal. The first of these is that he must be loyal to his trust. This duty embraces substantially all the others. To be loyal to his trust, an agent cannot so exercise his duties as to garner a profit for himself at the expense of his principal. The courts have decided that in order for a broker to be loyal to his trust he must not sell to himself, purchase for himself, or purchase from himself. Where a property is listed with a broker for sale, it is the duty of the broker to determine a fair market value for that property and list it at that price. A broker will not be permitted to purchase a property which has been listed with him for sale where he feels that the list price is below the normal market price and purchases it either in his own name or in the name of another person in trust for himself, and then resells the property at a profit. The reason for this rule is interestingly given in a New Jersey case in which the Court said as follows:

Owing to the greed and selfishness of human nature there must, in the great mass of transactions, be a strong antagonism between the interest of the seller and the buyer, and universal experience shows that the average man, when his interests conflict with his employer's, will not look upon his employer's interests as more important and entitled to more consideration than his own.

In discussing a broker's duty of loyalty, the Supreme Court of Minnesota said in the case of *Kingsley v. Wheeler*, 95 Minn. 360 (1905) that:

An agent to sell land does not fulfill the measure of legal requirements by merely carrying out his specific instructions. He owes the duty of making a full, fair and prompt disclosure of all facts affecting the principal's rights or interests, or pertaining to the sale of land by him. He is denied the right to profit at the expense of his principal by concealment of facts which he ought to have revealed.

So also, the Supreme Court held in the case of *Franck v. Blazier*, 66 Ore. 377 that a broker employed to sell cannot become interested in the purchase without the knowledge and consent of his principal, but he may openly and fairly buy the property at the price fixed by the principal, if the latter has full knowledge of the facts.

In the Missouri case of *Blakeley v. Bradley et al.*, 281 S.W. (2d) 835, (1955) the Supreme Court extended the principle that a broker should not purchase a property listed with him unless this fact is made known to his principal in advance, to include also the broker's employees and their near relatives. In a case where it appeared that the property in question was purchased by the mother of one of the broker's employees, the Court held there was sufficient indication of fraud to rescind the deed and to put the parties back in their original positions.

Broker is a fiduciary

The cases are legion in holding that a broker occupies a fiduciary relationship to the owner, and the law exacts a high degree of loyalty and fidelity from the agent.

In construing loyalty, the courts in this country have uniformly held that a real estate broker may not have a secret personal interest in the subject matter of his employment or make a secret profit or commission or become the purchaser of his principal's property unless he discloses to the principal everything within his knowledge which might affect the principal's rights or interests or influence his action in relation to the subject matter of the employment: 8 Am. Jur. Secs. 89, 152. He cannot sell to himself, purchase for himself, or from himself, without making full disclosure to his principal. This rule has been held to extend to employees, partners and near relatives: Corpus Juris Secundum, 42, p. 103.

In the case of *Cox v. Bryant*, 347 S.W. 2d 861 (Mo. 1961), a farm was listed with a broker at $40,000. A salesman, Cox, thought he had a purchaser, but the sale did not materialize. Cox then decided to buy the farm at the listed price of $40,000 and agreements were signed to that effect. The agreement provided, among other things, that the sellers were to pay the broker firm five per cent commission and also, that if either party defaulted, said party would pay to the other party $4,000, as liquidated damages. Before the deal was closed, the Bryants, sellers, changed their minds, wanted to get out of the deal, and were willing to pay the agreed upon $4,000, as liquidated damages. Cox, the salesman-buyer, refused and insisted that the Bryants go through with the deal. He instituted an action for specific performance, in an effort to accomplish this end. At the trial of the case, it developed that Cox was to receive 60 per cent of the commission to be paid his broker in the transaction. This fact was fatal to Cox's cause of action. The Court said:

In this case, before Cox could properly become the purchaser, it was his duty to terminate all agency relationships with the Bryants and thus place himself in the character and position of a purchaser. When this

relation existed it must be held to have continued until the agent, in dealing with the principal's property, notifies the principal that he is no
longer dealing, as an agent, *but desires to deal at arm's length as a purchaser,* and had disclosed all the facts and information acquired by him
to the principal that relates to the subject matter of the contract while
the agency existed. . . . Among the facts that Cox should have disclosed
to the Bryants was the fact that he was to receive a $1,200 commission
for a sale to himself. . . .

The case of *Nutter, appellant, v. Becktel,* 433 P. 2d 993 (Ariz.
1967), is of a similar tenor.

The courts throughout this country have adhered strictly to the
principle of law that a broker is a fiduciary in the strictest sense of
the word and owes a high degree of loyalty to his principal. In the
case of *Cochrane v. Wittbold,* 102 N.W. 2d 459 (Mich. 1960), a
saleswoman employed by a broker caused her parents to purchase
for her land listed for sale with her employer. She collected a commission on the sale, without disclosing identity of true purchasers
to seller, and almost immediately resold it to another for a profit.
Such conduct, the Court held, was violative of the State Corporation and Securities Commissions rules, prohibiting a broker from
purchasing property listed with him, without making full disclosure
to listing owner. Such action was also contrary to public policy of
the state.

In the case of *King v. Pruitt,* 288 S.W. 2d 923 (Mo. 1956), where
the agent knowingly failed to disclose the name of the true purchaser, which was a material fact affecting the purchase price, the
broker was not entitled to a commission.

It was held in *Simone v. McKee,* 298 P. 2d 667 (1956) that a
broker retained by owner to sell realty, owed owner affirmative duty
to disclose second offer to purchaser, and failure to disclose was
equivalent to affirmative representation that no other offer existed.

In the case of *Haymes v. Rogers,* 219 P. 2d 339 (Ariz. 1950), the
plaintiff, a broker, sued to recover a commission. From a verdict in
favor of the broker, the owner appealed. After failing to sell the
property at $9,500, the price originally listed with the broker, he
stated to the purchaser his belief that the property could be bought
for $8,500. After sale of property for $8,500, the broker sued to
recover commission. The appellate court held, *as a matter of law,*
plaintiff could not recover as there was a breach of fiduciary relationship. A Louisiana case is squarely opposed: *Wolf v. Casamento,* 185
So. 537 (1939). Other cases are in harmony with the Arizona
decision, although other circumstances entered into the case, as
where broker acted in his own interest, or withheld information

from his principal. Most cases hold a broker liable where he not only misrepresents to the purchaser the owner's minimum price but also *misrepresents himself to be the owner's agent.*

In the case of *Heard, et al. v. Miles,* 32 Tenn. 410 (1949), two real estate brokers claimed a commission. The owner recognized the efforts of Joyner-Heard Realty Co. as the procuring cause, but paid the money into court, since there were two claims. The unsuccessful broker, Marx & Bensdorf, Inc., had negotiated three leases on the subject property. This broker also had negotiated several forbearance agreements on an existing mortgage. The last lease contained a *new* clause that a commission would be paid "on any subsequent agreement to sell or exchange, made with or through Lessee." The property was sold to the tenant. No one ever called the owner's attention to the added clause. Although the court pointed out that the broker was not guilty of any fraud, intentional bad faith or unfairness, it could not recover because it was the *duty* of the broker here to disclose to its principal the provision in the renewal lease for the benefit of the broker. The principle of disclosure, the court said, "is one of prevention, not remedial justice, which operates however fair the transaction may have been—however free from every taint of moral wrong."

Where the broker makes full disclosure of his interest, the law does not prevent him from purchasing property listed with him for sale and making a profit. In the case of *Sylvester v. Beck,* 406 Pa. 607 (1962), the plaintiff sued a real estate broker for damages alleging a breach of trust in the purchase and resale of real estate. The plaintiffs won a jury verdict in the amount of $9,000. The lower court entered judgment in favor of the broker, notwithstanding the verdict. (Judgment N.O.V.) The plaintiffs appealed. The defendant was authorized to sell the property for $15,000 and he displayed his broker's "for sale" sign on the property. Later the plaintiffs agreed to sell the property to the broker for $14,000. Within one month, the broker sold the property for $25,000. A few weeks later, both deals were closed on the same day. Subesquently, when the plaintiffs learned that the defendant had realized a huge profit in a quick resale of the property, they entered suit. The Court said:

> The fact that the defendant entered into a contract to resell the property twenty-seven days after he had contracted to purchase it and did not disclose this particular fact to the plaintiffs until after final settlement does not, in itself, entitle the plaintiffs to damages. The agency having ended when the plaintiffs agreed to sell, the agent was under no obligation to furnish his former principal with the details of events that took place subsequent to the termination of their relationship of principal and agent.

Agent must obey instructions

The second fundamental duty that an agent owes to his principal is that he must obey the instructions that are given him by his principal. If a broker undertakes to judge that he may depart from the instructions of the owner, and that such variation would not be material, he does so at his own peril, and should any loss result by reason of the agent's deviation from his given instructions, he will be personally liable. For example, where a broker is engaged to sell property on a cash basis but instead accepts notes which are later declared invalid, the agent will be held personally responsible for the resulting loss. The owner, however, must be specific in his instructions.

A real estate broker is a *special* agent with *limited* authority. A broker is employed for the specific purpose of negotiating a sale. When he accomplishes that purpose, his authority as agent ends. He has no authority, once the agreements of sale are signed, to permit the purchaser to take possession of the premises prior to the closing of the deal, or to enter to make repairs or to decorate the premises. If the deal fails to be consummated through no fault of the buyer, the broker could be held personally responsible for the buyer's expense. The Iowa Supreme Court held that a real estate agent who contracted for a new well, and who was not authorized by actual owners to represent them in doing so, was liable for the cost of drilling the new well; *Cryder Well Co. v. Brown, et al.*, 136 N.W. 2d 519 (1965). If a buyer requests some special privilege or consideration, the request should be referred to the owner.

Agent must not be negligent

The third duty which every agent owes to his principal is that he must not be negligent in acting in the interests of his principal. An agent should not be dormant, but should actively and aggressively assert his employer's interests. An agent who is grossly negligent in the interests of his principal will be personally liable for any loss which the principal may sustain by reason of such negligence. An attorney failing to disclose an encumbrance of record against a property which his principal is purchasing will be personally responsible to his principal for any damage sustained by the latter.

Where a broker accepts a note from the purchaser for a deposit, in lieu of cash funds, the broker would be liable to his principal, if the transaction was not consummated and the buyer failed to pay the note. Other situations which would be tantamount to negligence could be where the broker held a check for the earnest money for an unduly long period of time, at the request of a buyer, or where he accepted a post dated check, unless, in each of these situations, he advised his principal of the *facts* and the principal approved. It is common real estate practice for a broker to accept a check instead of cash, as an earnest money deposit. Where the broker deposits such check promptly and should the bank upon which it is drawn refuse payment because of insufficient funds, no liability can be visited upon the broker on that account. Likewise, if the buyer dies before the bank honors the check, the broker would not be personally responsible.

Act in person

Fourth, an agent must perform acts in person. He cannot delegate the authority which he has received from his principal to another. An owner employs a broker because of the confidence that he has in the ability and integrity of that particular person, and so a broker has no right to delegate his authority to another without consent or request of his principal, except as to matters which are of a purely ministerial or mechanical character, and where such delegation does not involve discretion, confidence, or skill.

In the South Dakota case of *Croughaw v. Gerlach,* 68 S.D. 93 (1941), a broker sued for commission. The defendant was a resident of Minnesota and owned a farm in Moody County, South Dakota. One, Dwight Lloyd, an attorney at Flandreau had authority to find a purchaser for the land and was acting as defendant's agent for that purpose. The plaintiff broker contacted the attorney and contends that Lloyd agreed that if the plaintiff found a purchaser, a commission would be paid to him. Later, the broker obtained a prospect and negotiations were conducted with Lloyd but no sale resulted. Later, the same prospect saw Lloyd and rented the property for one year with an option to purchase. He later bought it. The court held that Lloyd was not authorized to employ a subagent to sell the farm at the expense of the defendant. There was nothing to show that defendant had any knowledge that the plaintiff was the inducing cause of the sale, so that there was no ratification by the seller. A delegation of his authority may, however, be permitted by the usages of the trade. Where a nonresident owner of land employs an agent, also a nonresident, to sell his land, it will be presumed that such agent has authority to appoint a subagent in the locality where the land is located in order to facilitate the sale of such land. Where, however, an owner knows that a broker employed by him to sell land has secured the services of a subagent by promising the subagent half commission from the owner and the owner assents thereto either expressly or by remaining silent when it is his duty to object if he has any objection, the owner is directly liable to the subagent for his share of the commission.

Stopping payment on check

A prospect may sign an agreement of sale on Friday, giving the broker a check as the earnest money deposit. Over the weekend, he turns the deal over in his mind and decides he has made a mistake. Monday morning, he hurries to his bank and stops payment on the check. Two questions arise: (1) what is his liability for the amount of the check; (2) what effect does the stop-payment order on the check, have on the validity of the agreement of sale? An examination of the agreement of sale is necessary, in order to determine what remedies are afforded, upon failure of the buyer to perform. A typical clause in this connection, is found in the Michigan case of *Duncan v. Baskin,* 154 N.W. 2d 617 (Mich. 1967). Plaintiffs Duncan executed a listing agreement authorizing plaintiff Frank & Grossman, a licensed real estate broker, to arrange a sale of their home, in which case a six per cent commission would be paid the broker. Thereafter the broker procured from defendants a signed offer to purchase under the terms of which defendants were to make a deposit of $5,000—$1,000 to be paid immediately and the balance on the offer to purchase and on the same day defendants delivered to the broker two checks in the amounts of $1,000 and $4,000 respectively. Three days later defendants stopped payment on the checks and declined to consummate the transaction.

Paragraph three of the offer to purchase, signed by all the parties, provides that in the event of default by the purchasers the sellers may elect to enforce the terms of the agreement or declare a forfeiture and retain the deposit as liquidated damages. It is provided on the listing agreement between the Duncans and the broker, and on the offer to purchase, that if a forfeiture is declared the broker will receive one-half the deposit.

. . . We think that the dismissal was proper only as to plaintiffs Duncan. The only rights which they had to assert were under the written agreement, and recovery may not be had under the common counts for breach of a written agreement, *Mitchell v. Reolds Farms Co.,* 268 Mich. 301 (1934). It was improper to grant the motion to dismiss as to plaintiff broker because upon dishonor, and subject to any notice of dishonor or protest, the holder of a check has an immediate right of recourse against the drawer. Production of the checks entitled the broker to recover on them without submitting further proof of damages, subject to whatever proper defenses defendants raise. The checks are evidence of a promise to pay a sum certain in money and the consideration for that promise was shown. That being the case, recovery may properly be had under the common counts.

In view of the foregoing the judgment is set aside and the cause remanded with instructions to the trial court to reinstate plaintiff broker's cause of action and to proceed to hear proof of any defenses advanced by defendants.

In the case of *Beazell v. Kane* 127 Cal. App. 2d 593 (1954), the court held that a real estate broker who obtains a purchaser with whom the owner enters into a valid contract of sale is entitled to recover a commission from the owner, even if the purchaser stops payment on the check given for the deposit. It would follow that the broker would likewise be entitled to his commission where he accepts a note as a deposit, with the consent of the owner and the note is not paid by the purchaser at maturity. The payee of the note would have a collateral independent right to recover proceeds of the note in a court action.

In the ordinary contract of sale, the broker's right to his commission cannot be defeated by the owner's decision not to enforce the contract: *Johnson v. Smith* 43 Wash. 2d 603 (1953); *Callopy v. Stevenson* 125 Kan. 703 (1928).

Account for money and property

Lastly, an agent must account for money and property of his principal. Money and property entrusted to his care should, in all cases, be kept separate and apart from his own funds. If a broker carelessly mingles his employer's funds with his own, and the bank in which the funds are on deposit should fail, the broker will be personally responsible for the loss. Most state license laws provide the commingling of trust funds with a broker's personal funds shall constitute grounds for suspension or revocation of license. The account of the employer's funds should be kept as a trustee account, and so long as the agent exercises due care and caution in selecting a safe depository for such funds, he will not be personally responsible for any later loss. This matter is of particular importance because not infrequently a real estate broker, by agreement between the parties, retains the deposit money until such time as the deal is consummated. One trust account is sufficient for all trust funds coming into the broker's hands.

Broker's responsibility for deposit money

The seller and buyer are the two prime parties to the contract of sale, or earnest money contract. The broker is not a party to it. Thus, when the agreement recites "$1,000 earnest money, upon the signing of these agreements, receipt whereof is hereby acknowledged," the owner can refuse to sign the agreement unless he receives the earnest money deposit. It should be noted that where the broker has a written contract of employment, it should include a clause: "The owner hereby agrees that all deposit money paid upon the consideration price shall be retained by the within broker, in escrow, until the transaction is consummated or terminated."

With such a clause in the listing agreement, the broker can prevail upon the seller to permit him to hold the deposit money in escrow.

The question of who is entitled to the earnest money or down payment frequently arises when the buyer defaults in performance. The broker mistakenly believes that, if he holds the hand money, he is entitled to his commission out of this fund. It must be remembered that the broker is acting in a representative capacity, as agent for his principal, the owner. It thus appears that the money belongs to his principal. Under his employment by the owner, the broker has contracted to produce a purchaser, *ready, able,* and *willing* to buy. It would not appear that the agent has met his legal responsibilities if his purchaser is unwilling to complete the deal. It may be contended that, when the owner signs the agreement, he has placed his stamp of approval upon the purchaser, accepted him, and, upon the latter's default, must pursue him in a court of law for performance. The question is highly controversial although there are court decisions recognizing the broker's rights to his commission out of the deposit money held by him. If the buyer is pecuniarily unable to complete the transaction, litigation is futile, and the broker has not earned a commission.

It has been the general rule of law that a broker is entitled to his commission when the contract of sale is signed by buyer and seller. In accepting the purchaser, the seller has approved the buyer, and should the latter later refuse to consummate the deal, the burden is upon the seller to enter suit to compel the buyer to perform. A case of great importance, which rejects the premise that the owner is liable to the broker for commission, where the buyer defaults, is the case of *Ellsworth Dobbs, Inc. v. Johnson (owner) and Iarussi (buyer),* 50 N.J. 528 (1967). In joining the buyer as defendant, the broker charged the buyer with breach of an implied agreement to pay the commission if he failed to complete the purchase and thus deprived the broker of commission from the seller. The trial judge held, *as a matter of law,* that the broker's commission vested upon execution of the contract of sale, and the commission was not dependent upon the closing of title. The jury found for the buyer in the amount of $15,000 against the owner. The appellate court reversed.

In the Ohio case of *McGarry Realty Co., et al. v. McCrone, et al.,* 97 Ohio App. 543 (1954), the plaintiff negotiated the sale of certain property and the plaintiff knew that the funds necessary to purchase the property were to be provided by the buyers' relatives. The day following the execution of the agreements of sale, the purchasers called the plaintiff and told him they could not get the money. The Court said:

We find no Ohio case where this question has been clearly presented, but no principle of law has been more clearly affirmed by the courts of this state than that an agent should not be permitted to benefit by his own failure to perform his full duty in representing his principal . . .

It would appear, then, in these circumstances that a broker should have the agreements of sale signed by the persons who will furnish the funds necessary for the purchase. After the deal is closed, such person (the relative) can transfer the property to the party, for whom the property is desired.

In most states, a broker who receives an earnest money deposit is required to deposit such earnest money in a trust or escrow account until the transaction is consummated or terminated. Many brokers desire to hold the deposit money in order to guarantee payment of their commission. Where the broker receives a substantial portion of the consideration price, without authorization, and the seller defalcates, the broker would be liable to the buyer for his resulting loss.

Forfeiture of deposit money when commission is payable

Many listing contracts in current use provide: "A deposit made, if forfeited by the buyer, shall first apply to the broker's commission; the balance, if any, shall belong to the owner."

While a broker is certainly entitled to a return for his efforts, good conscience requires that it shall not be at the expense of an innocent principal. Suppose the clause in question is used and the broker obtains a purchaser for a property at $10,000, and collects a deposit of $500. Later, the buyer defaults and forfeits the deposit money. Should the broker be permitted to retain the *entire* deposit as commission on the ground that the owner has a legal right to sue the defaulting buyer, even though litigation may prove futile? It is scarcely ethical that the broker should keep all the money paid on account of the purchase of the owner's property, and the latter required to pursue litigation, entailing additional expense of costs and attorney's fees, for recovery of a judgment which may be uncollectible. In addition, the property may be "tied up" for a considerable period of time from the date when the agreements were signed. Fair dealing requires that the down payment be divided equally between broker and owner, up to an amount where the broker receives full payment of his commission. A *fair* provision in the agreement of sale relative to the earnest money would read:

Should the buyer fail to make settlement, as herein provided, the sum or sums paid on account of the purchase price, at the option of the seller, may be retained by the seller, either on account of the purchase price, the resale price, or as liquidated damages. In the latter case, the contract shall become null and void. In the latter event, all monies paid on account shall be divided equally between the seller and the broker, but in no event shall the sum paid to the broker be in excess of the standard rate of commission due him according to the schedule of the Greater Pittsburgh Board of Realtors.

Other cases are of a similar note. In *Hersh v. Kelman*, 104 N.E. 2d 35 (1951), plaintiff obtained a purchaser and a $200 deposit on an "open listing." Before the owner would sign the agreement, he had the broker write into the agreement "commission to be paid when deal is consummated." The buyer moved to Detroit and defaulted. The seller sold the property through another broker and paid a commission. The first broker sued for a commission. The lower court decided in favor of the broker. The appellate court reversed. The Court said:

Failure of the prospective purchasers to consummate the deal, without any fault on the part of the seller, relieved the seller completely under the special terms of the contract from liability for the payment of any commission.

In the case of *Jones v. Palace Realty Co.*, 226 N.C. 303 (1946), the North Carolina Supreme Court held that it was the event of closing the deal and not the date of its expected or contemplated happening that made the promise to pay enforceable. In the case of *Bechtel Properties, Inc. v. Blanken*, 299 F. 2d 928 (D.C. 1962), the agreement provided that "if the purchaser shall fail to make full settlement, the deposit herein provided for may be forfeited at the option of the seller. . . ." The agreement further provided that:

The entire deposit shall be held by Sam Blanken & Co. until settlement hereunder is made or until the deposit is forfeited. . . .

The broker had obtained a purchaser, who had shown himself ready, able and willing to perform. Certain matters arose which could not be resolved and the lower court said: "Apparently the transaction was just abandoned by the parties when the property was resold by the defendant." The appellate court said:

In view of the fact that the contract was not settled, through no fault of the agent, and apparently by mutual agreement of the seller and the purchaser (or, if not by mutual agreement, at least with the acquiescence of the seller), the commission agreement could not be performed in accordance with its terms. This is not to say, however, that the agent is to be deprived, by that reason, of his commission, which was in the total amount of $7,000. Certainly, if the agent is entitled to the commission—and we hold that he is, in the circumstances shown—he is not to be deprived of it because of the impossibility of payment in the exact terms of the commission agreement. We think he was entitled to be paid, and in cash, when his receipt of payment in the manner prescribed by the agreement was rendered impossible, through no fault of his.

Rate of commission

If, in the contract of employment, nothing is said in regard to the rate of commission, then the broker is entitled to a reasonable rate of compensation, this rate being the one used generally in the business in the particular locality in which the property is situated. It is assumed here, of course, that the broker is licensed. Since an owner entrusts his property for sale to a person whose ordinary business it is to sell real estate on a commission basis, the law presumes, in the absence of any agreement to the contrary, that commission or compensation is to be paid for the services rendered. The rate is not fixed by any statute, but is a matter of custom or trade usage. The broker can recover on a "quantum meruit" basis what he deserves, or what his services are worth. In order to avoid any controversy or future litigation, it is always desirable that the rate of compensation should be agreed upon in advance, at the time of the employment. There is no provision in any license law regulating or attempting to regulate the rate of commission to be charged. It is one of voluntary agreement between the parties.

Minimum net sale price

Where the owner has fixed a minimum net price, below which the agent may not sell the property, the question frequently arises as to whether or not the broker is entitled to any excess realized over and above the net price. In other words, assume that an owner has left property for sale with a broker, with the understanding that the property is not to be sold for less than $10,000, and the broker negotiates a sale at a price of $12,000. The question arises as to the distribution of the $2,000 excess. It must be remembered here that the first duty that an agent owes to his principal is that he must do everything possible to assert and protect his principal's interest; and so the courts have held that under the circumstances which have just been outlined, the $2,000 belongs to the owner. This is so unless it is *expressly* stipulated that the broker is to retain the excess as his commission. While net listings are used frequently, they are not looked upon with favor in good real estate circles. Since the property belongs to the owner, he should receive the highest possible price for it and the broker should look to his compensation upon a basis commensurate with his services. A broker who receives $1,000 commission upon a $20,000 sale has, usually, earned a fair return.

Where a property is listed at $30,000 and the broker is able to obtain an offer of $37,500, it seems unconscionable that the broker will earn 25 per cent on the deal. Net listings, further, are conducive to fraud in that a broker is often sorely tempted to employ a straw purchaser and then resell the property at a handsome profit. Alabama, British Columbia, California, Georgia, Maryland, Michigan, Ontario, Tennessee, and Utah prohibit or regulate net listings.

In order for a broker to recover commission under an express contract requiring a net price to the owner, he must procure a purchaser at a price sufficiently in excess of the net price to cover commissions. An owner listed with a broker for sale certain real estate, which consisted of 13 houses. The owner wrote the broker: "I think you might proceed and sell the entire 13 houses separately for $50,000 net cash to me. Your commission of 3% to come out of the last sale made." The houses were sold for the aggregate of $50,000. The owner refused to pay a commission and the broker sued for $1,500. The broker could not collect, because, as the Court stated: [1]

Where one states to a broker that he will sell land for a certain sum 'net' to him, the broker, on procuring a purchaser, is entitled to no commission unless the sum received exceeds the 'net' price, the word 'net' meaning that which remains after deducting all charges and outlay. We see no weakening of the effect of the word 'net' by the words used in the communication which the prospective vendor sent to the broker, quoted above, that the commission was to come out of the last sale made. The agreement was in writing and there is nothing in the case which would justify a departure from the evident purpose of the agreement that the vendor was to get $50,000 net cash, clear and above any commissions.

Employment of several brokers

It has become a common practice for an owner to leave property for sale with a number of real estate brokers. When this is done, the rule of law is that they possess concurrent authority to sell, and that the sale of the property by one of them terminates the agencies of the others by removing the subject matter of the contract. It is advisable for an owner listing a property for sale with a number of real estate brokers to inform each broker that the property has been listed for sale with other concerns, and that upon the sale of the property by one, the employment of the others shall auto-

---

[1] Fink v. Dougherty, 90 Pa. Super. 443 (1927).

matically cease. In Virginia, the law is that if two or more brokers, knowing of one another's employment, are employed to sell the same land, the owner, if he shows no favoritism, may sell to the purchaser who is first produced and the broker producing such purchaser is the one entitled to commission.[2]

A serious difficulty, where a property has been listed with a number of real estate offices, is that frequently a single purchaser is the prospect of a number of brokers. When a sale results to that purchaser, which broker is entitled to the commission? The test for recovery is determining which broker was the efficient and procuring cause of the sale. Suppose, for example, a large industrial property is on the market. In June, 1965, Allen, a broker, interests Taylor in the property. In October, 1965, broker Barnes submits the same property to Taylor. Signed agreements by Taylor are procured by Chase, a broker, in January, 1966. Who is entitled to the commission? It would appear that the broker, Chase, was the one who brought the deal to a "head" and, seemingly, is the one entitled to the commission. However, either Allen or Barnes may have a claim, depending upon how effective or instrumental each broker was in "selling" the property. If Barnes did the essential "spade work" and convinced Taylor of the desirability of the plot for Taylor's purposes, Barnes is not to be deprived of the fruits of his commission merely because Chase stepped in at the last minute and induced Taylor to sign the agreement. If the owner had no knowledge or notice of the activities of Allen or Barnes, these brokers would be pursuing a lost cause in a quest for the commission. It is most important, then, for a broker, in order to protect his rights to a commission, that he acquaint the owner with the identity of every prospect to whom he submits the property. One good-sized commission, as a result of such notice, will adequately compensate a broker for the detail work entailed. It is not to be inferred that a broker may merely submit the name of a prospect and then sit idly by and await the fortuitous circumstance of a sale ultimately occurring. He cannot be guilty of abandonment and then claim compensation because a sale is made to his original prospect. He must activate the sale although the mere introduction of the principals may suffice, and if that sets in motion a series of events which culminate in a sale, a commission is earned. The rule is well stated by the West Virginia Court[3] to be: "If a broker sets in motion machinery by which sale is made, which without break in its continuity, was procuring cause of sale, he is entitled to commission, although

---

[2] Cannon v. Bates, 115 Va. 711 (1914).
[3] Averill v. Hart & O'Farrell, 101 W. V. 411 (1926).

he does not conduct *all* negotiations." In the case of *Dobson v. Wolf,*
54 N.W. 2d 469 (South Dakota, 1952), the Court said:

If a broker does not have the exclusive sale of property, he does not
become entitled to a commission merely by showing the property to
the person who eventually buys it, but a personal introduction of the
purchaser to the owner if not essential and it is sufficient if, through
the efforts of the broker, the parties are brought into communication
with each other. *It is not enough that a broker's efforts may have contributed to the negotiations resulting in the Sale.* "If this were the rule,"
says the court in *Carney v. John Hancock Oil Co.*, 187 Minnesota 293,
"no owner desiring to sell could safely employ more than one broker,
for in the event of each of several being able to convince a jury that
he had contributed anything to a sale, the principal might be held for
as many commissions as there were brokers employed. The law contemplates no such absurdity."

To the same effect is *Vreeland v. Vetterlein,* 33 New Jersey 247
(1869), in which it is said:

Where the property is openly put in the hands of more than one
broker, each of such agents is aware that he is subject to the arts and
chances of competition. If he finds a person who is likely to buy, and
quits him without having effected a sale, he is aware that he runs the
risk of such persons falling under the influence of his competitor—and
in such case, he may lose his labor. This is a part of the inevitable risk
of the business he has undertaken.

Where claims for commissions have been advanced by several
brokers, who claim to have produced the same purchaser for the
owner's property, an owner should hesitate in voluntarily paying
such commissions. There have been many instances where an
owner has voluntarily paid a commission to one broker, and a court
and jury have subsequently decided that the sale resulted from the
efforts of a second broker, so that the owner was compelled to pay
a second commission. Where the owner is in doubt regarding which
broker's efforts produced the sale, he should pay the amount of
commission into court and there have the matter settled by a court
of law without any further liability to himself.

In the case of *Julius Heller Realty Co. v. Jefferson Gravoco Bank,*
144 S.W. 2d 174, 176 (Mo. 1940), the Court succinctly quoted the
law as follows:

In other words in these cases where an owner appoints more than
one broker to procure a purchaser for his property, the rule is to the
effect that he "who sows the seed and tills the crop is entitled to reap
the harvest—rather than one who volunteers to assist in tilling a crop,
the seed for which he has not sown." The question of whether the plaintiff

was procuring cause of the sale was for the jury to determine. Verdict in favor of owner affirmed.

In the case of *Watts v. Barker*, 275 Ky. 411 (1938), the Court said that where a property has been listed for sale with more than one broker, the owner is liable for only one commission, even if more than one broker had dealings with the ultimate purchaser; the broker who succeeds in bringing the seller and buyer together and induces them to enter into the contract is the one who earns the commission, regardless of which broker first introduced seller and purchaser. The Court further stated that the seller would not be liable to brokers with whom she had listed real estate, if trade was closed through another broker with whom she had also listed realty and the owner had not been advised by a first broker that the purchaser was her customer, until after the sale had been completed.

Of course, all parties must act in good faith. A purchaser cannot accept the services of a broker, and when the deal is imminent, arbitrarily or capriciously dismiss the broker and refuse to do business with him. Nor can he circumvent the broker by using a third person as the purchaser for him. In *Orr v. Woolfolk*, 250 Ky. 279 (1933), the Court said, "Where a broker's prospect interests another who becomes the eventual purchaser of property which the owner had listed with broker for sale, the broker is entitled to his commission." This does not mean that where a broker negotiates the sale of a property in a subdivision to a purchaser and the buyer interests a friend in an adjoining house, who buys directly from the owner, that the broker is entitled to a commission on the second sale.

In *Beougher v. Clark*, 81 Kan. 250 (1909), the Court has stated the principle of law as follows:

> The law will not permit one broker who has been entrusted with the sale of land and is working with a customer whom he has found, to be deprived of his commission by another agent stepping in and selling the land to the customer so found by the first broker. The utmost good faith must be exercised between the principal and the broker.

To the same effect is *Greshman v. Lee*, 152 Ga. 829 (1921).

Must be efficient and procuring cause of sale

To determine which of several brokers is entitled to the commission, where each claims to have found the same purchaser, is often a problem of no little difficulty. Where all the brokers are employed independently, at least, it would seem that the ordinary rule applicable to the case of the employment of a single broker would apply; that is, that the broker who was the efficient procuring cause of the sale is entitled to the commission and that this right cannot be affected because the principal in person, or by another agent, takes into his own hands and completes the transaction which the broker has inaugurated.

Where an owner is confronted with two or more claims for a commission, he should hesitate to honor any of them. Admitting liability, the owner should invite a suit and then pay the money into court. If he voluntarily pays one broker, that fact is not admissible in evidence in a suit brought by a second broker.

Where two or more brokers are employed, there is no implied contract to pay more than one commission, and it therefore becomes necessary to lay down a rule for determining which one of different possible claimants is entitled to be paid. Where several brokers have each endeavored to bring about a sale which is finally consummated, it may happen that each has contributed something without which the result would not have been reached. One may have found the customer, who otherwise would not have been found, and yet the customer may refuse to conclude the bargain through his agency; and another broker may succeed where the first has failed. In such a case, in the absence of any express contract, the one only is entitled to a commission who can show that his services were the really effective means of bringing about the sale, or "the predominating efficient cause."

Where several brokers are openly and avowedly employed so that each can be said to have undertaken the employment on that basis, it is held in many cases that the entire duty of the principal is performed by remaining neutral between them and that he has a right to sell to the buyer who is first produced by any of them without being called upon to decide which of the several brokers was the primary cause of the sale.

Other cases state the rule somewhat less broadly, and it is everywhere agreed that in order to be entitled to the benefit of it the principal must in fact have remained neutral, and he certainly must not knowingly permit, much less aid in or connive at, the appropriation by one man of the rewards of what was really the result of another man's efforts. However, payment of a commission to one broker by an owner is not admissible as evidence in a suit by a second broker for a commission claimed in the sale to the same prospect.[4]

The general rule of law throughout the country is well stated in the case of *Trent Trust Co. v. Mac Farlane*, 21 Hawaii 435 (1913), where the Court held that a broker is not entitled to a commission

---

[4] Walker v. Randall, 85 Pa. Super. 443 (1925).

on a sale effected through another broker, even though a purchaser was introduced by the first broker or even though the sale may be aided by the first broker's previous efforts, provided the owner acts in good faith.

If one of several brokers gives notice to his principal that he cannot effect a sale, he will not be entitled to commissions because another broker, who is informed by the first that the property is for sale, succeeds in finding a purchaser. So, if two brokers are employed, and one of them enters into negotiations with a purchaser, which fail and are abandoned, he will not be entitled to commissions because another broker subsequently succeeds, wholly through his own efforts, in making a sale to the same person and upon substantially the same terms as those proposed by the first broker. The same result will follow where one broker has not been able within a reasonable time to effect a sale, and another broker afterwards succeeds in selling to a purchaser first approached by the former broker. The principal, acting in good faith, and with no intention of defeating the broker's claim, may revoke his authority, while his efforts are yet unsuccessful, even though the principal in person or through another broker subsequently sells to a purchaser to whom the first broker endeavored to sell.

A number of courts have pronounced the rule that sale of the property by one of the brokers *terminates the authority of the brokers* immediately, *although they have no actual notice of the sale: Hunt v. Judd*, 225 Ill. App. 395 (1922); *Kennedy v. Vance*, 201 Okla. 80 (1949).

Abandonment of effort

Clearly, if one broker abandons his efforts, he cannot later claim a commission if a sale is made by the owner, or through another broker, to his original prospect. For example:

Broker "A" had an open listing on a property of $30,000.00. He showed it to a prospect, Mrs. White, who was interested but did not make up her mind to buy it. Broker "B" showed Mrs. White various properties. He did not show the subject property, but mentioned it to her. She said she had already seen it through Broker "A." About two weeks later she called Broker "A" and stated that she wanted to go through the house again with her husband but he told her it was too late—"the house is sold." A few days later she called Broker "B" and when she mentioned that the house she was interested in was sold, he expressed surprise because he had had no notice of cancellation of the listing. He called the owner, who referred him to her attorney. The attorney told Broker "B" that there was a signed agreement from a buyer, but it was subject to the buyer's selling his present home and that he was going to advise his client, the owner, not to accept the deal, whereupon, the owner accepted the deal with Mrs. White. Now, Broker "A" is claiming a commission, as is also Broker "B." Here, "A" is not entitled to any commission as there was an abandonment of negotiations when "A" told Mrs. White, "the house is sold, you are too late," and did nothing more.

In the case of *Mammen v. Snodgrass,* 13 Ill. App. 2d 538 (1957), the Court said:

The law is well settled in this state that the fact that the seller consummates a sale or that it is made upon different terms from those proposed to the broker, does not necessarily deprive the broker of compensation. If he is the efficient procuring cause of the transaction, he is entitled to his commission.

But that a sale is finally brought about by the efforts of the principal with a person with whom the broker had previously negotiated without success, does not furnish a basis for commission, if it appears that the broker has for a long time ceased negotiation with the purchaser and abandoned the property. A time must necessarily arrive after a prospective purchaser has declined to purchase when the owner may treat the negotiation at an end and begin an entirely new and independent solicitation. . . .

In the North Carolina case of *Jackson v. Northwestern Life Insurance Co.,* 133 F. 2d 111, the Court held that a broker was not entitled to a commission where he had failed to effect an agreement and abandoned his efforts, even though he may have introduced to each other parties who otherwise would never have met. The plaintiff broker did nothing for fourteen mouths and the deal was closed through another broker.

Introducing purchaser to owner may be sufficient

Mere introduction of the purchaser to the owner by the broker may be sufficient performance of the broker's contract of employment with the owner, depending, of course, upon the facts in the particular case. If negotiations are taken up from the point of introduction by the buyer and seller without the aid or intervention of the broker and a sale results, the broker is entitled to his commission. The question is: "Did the broker set in motion a series of circumstances, which, without interruption, culminated in a sale?" If the introduction did that, the broker is considered the efficient and procuring cause of the sale, and he can recover.

It is not a question of how much work a broker did in a particular transaction, but, rather, how effective his work was. If he did the "spade work," by obtaining a prospective purchaser, the owner cannot then take the purchaser, deal with him directly, and turn the broker out of doors. In other words, after the broker has shaken the tree and dislodged the fruit, as it were, the owner may not pick the fruit and avoid a claim for commission. The law is well settled that if the broker sets in motion a series of events which, without interruption, culminate in a sale, he is entitled to his commission. Nor can the owner take the matter into his own hands and complete the sale, either above or below the listing price, and then refuse to pay a commission.

The general rule of law is that, where there has been no direct communication between the broker and the purchaser, it must be shown affirmatively that the latter was induced to enter into the negotiations which resulted in the purchase through the means employed by the broker for that purpose. If the broker employed other persons to aid him, whether under pay or not, or if he put up maps, signs, notices, or otherwise advertised the property, and if by means of these measures, a person was induced to open negotiations with the owner which resulted in his buying the property, the sale may be said to have been effected through the broker's instrumentality. But it must be made to appear that what the broker did was the immediate and efficient cause of such negotiations. If the broker merely talked about the property with different persons and one of them, on his own accord and not in behalf of the broker, mentioned to another that the property was for sale and such last mentioned person thereupon looked into the matter and finally became the purchaser, the agency of the broker in inducing the sale was not sufficiently direct to entitle him to a commission.

Duration of employment

Where no time is fixed for the duration of a broker's employment, either party, acting in good faith, may terminate the contract at will. Ordinarily, the contract continues for a reasonable time. What is a reasonable time depends upon the circumstances in the particular case.[5] In the matter of the sale of the ordinary dwelling house, a few months might be said to be a reasonable time within which the broker should procure a customer. Where a broker was put in charge of selling 250 lots under an agreement which specified no particular duration, and the broker had sold only two lots in four months, it was held that he had demonstrated his inability to perform even

---

[5] Richter v. First National Bank of Cincinnati, 82 Ohio App. 421 (1947); Roudebush Realty Co. v. Toby, 135 N.E. 2d 270 (1955).

though he was entitled to a reasonable time within which to do so. For that reason the owner was justified in terminating the contract by notice to the broker.

A previous sale of the property revokes the agent's authority, and no notice to the broker of the sale is necessary.

In the case of *Hunt v. Judd* 225, Ill. App. 395, the Court held that where several real estate brokers are employed to sell a property, sale of the property by one of the brokers terminates authority of the others at once, although they have no actual notice of the sale. To the same effect is *Kennedy, et al. v. Vance*, 201 Okla. 80 (1949), in which the Court said:

Since the plaintiffs were not given an exclusive right to sell, they assumed the risk of knowing that the land might be sold by the owner or another agent before they could find a purchaser, ready, able and willing to buy on the terms specified and that such a sale would ipso facto revoke their agency, *Mecham on Agency* (Second Edition) Page 625.

Ordinary courtesy would dictate, however, that notice be given to the broker. A broker must produce a buyer while the premises are still on the market. In terminating employment an owner must act in good faith. Where an owner gives a second broker an exclusive listing agency, while an open listing is still in existence, the open listing given to a broker earlier is not automatically terminated. The owner must give notice of cancellation of employment to the first broker. A broker is not entitled to compensation for merely procuring a customer to take an option which has never been exercised.

To avoid any presumption that the employment of the broker is to continue until a sale is effected, the owner should take some action to notify the broker that his employment is terminated.

Owner's right to terminate agency

Where a broker is employed to sell lands for his principal and there is no stipulation in the contract as to the duration of the broker's employment, the courts have held that the principal may terminate the agency at any time and discharge the broker, subject to the rule, however, that the purpose of the revocation cannot be to deprive the broker of an earned commission. In other words, it must be in good faith. It may be in writing, oral, or implied from the circumstances. Smith employed Brown to sell real estate for him. No time was fixed for the duration of Brown's employment. Before Brown had an opportunity to sell the land, Smith revoked his employment and took the sale of the land out of Brown's hands. Brown then sued Smith for breach of contract. The court decided that the owner was within his rights in terminating the employment and that Brown was without any legal redress. An agency once terminated is not revived by subsequent acts.

If, however, the purchaser is found within the time limited, it is immaterial that the actual sale was not fully consummated until afterwards. Where no time has been fixed, performance within a reasonable time will be sufficient, unless the offer to the broker has been withdrawn earlier. Where no time is fixed, a sale made within a reasonable time is sufficient. A lapse of three years does not necessarily terminate the broker's authority, but the authority continues until revoked, and the lapse of time is merely one fact to be considered by the jury in determining whether the authority has been revoked.

A broker may recover any expenses incurred in connection with the agency, previous to the revocation of his authority. Barnes employed Adams to sell real estate. In an action in assumpsit by Adams against Barnes to recover damages for a breach of contract, it appeared that Adams had agreed to sell a tract of land belonging to Barnes, which had been laid out in 449 building lots, for which Adams was to receive as compensation $100 for the sale of each lot. Adams erected a temporary office upon the land and incurred expenses amounting to $230. After Adams had sold two of the lots, it was found that Barnes' wife would not join in the deeds, and thereupon Barnes notified Adams that he was unable to carry out the agreement. The Court directed a verdict for Adams for the amount of his expenses.

Where there is an open listing and a broker has a sale imminent, the owner is liable for a commission, even though he sells the property two days later to another party, without the assistance of a broker. In the case of *Romine v. Greene*, 13 N.J. Super. 261 (1951), the Court held that the broker was entitled to a commission, where the defendant accepted an offer to sell two days after the broker procured purchaser at same price. Since the broker had no notification of sale prior to his performance, the owner was liable for commission "unless he could prove a binding agreement for sale made so short a time before plaintiff's performance that reasonable opportunity to notify plaintiff was not afforded under the circumstance." Citing *Mecham on Agency* (Second Edition) Page 625, *Kennedy and Kennedy v. Vance*, 202 P. 2d 214 (Okla. 1949), the Court stated as a general rule of law that the prior sale (by owner) itself acts as a revocation of the power, if insufficient time has elapsed between such sale and performance by the broker to give reasonable opportunity, under all the circumstances of the case, for notification of the prior sale to the broker. However, a broker who obtains a buyer cannot be deprived of his commission merely because the owner is negotiating for the sale on his own account, even though such negotiations materialize into a sale at a later date. Mere preliminary discussion or negotiation is not enough. There must be a binding agreement for the sale: *Hartig v. Schrader*, 190 Ky. 511 (1921); *Hawks v. Moore*, 27 Ga. App. 555 (1921). A New Jersey Court held that the owner was liable to the broker for a commission, "unless he can prove a binding agreement for sale made so short a time before the broker's performance that reasonable opportunity to notify the broker was not afforded under the circumstances."

Agency coupled with an interest

Where the employment is coupled with an interest of the broker in the subject matter of the employment, the owner cannot arbitrarily terminate the broker's employment. Such an employment is irrevocable even after death. The Arizona Supreme Court so held in the case of *Phoenix Title and Trust Co. v. Grimes*, 416 P. 2d 979 (1966). In this case a broker joined with others in the purchase, subdividing, development and resale of desert land for their mutual benefit. The broker was given the exclusive right to sell the property. He performed all conditions of his contract for three years, prior to his death. The defendants then served notice upon the broker's executor that they refused to permit the executor to carry on, in performing the terms of the agreement. The court held that:

If the agency or power of the agent is coupled with an interest in the subject matter of the agency, the power so coupled will survive to the personal representative of the agent upon the death. Although contracts to perform personal acts which can only be performed by the particular person contracted with are discharged by death of the person who is to perform said acts, this rule does not apply where the services were such that they could be performed by others acting on behalf of the personal representatives of the decedent. In re Burke's Estate 198 Cal. 163, 244 Pac. 340. We are convinced here that the executor could hire qualified, licensed real estate agents to carry on the agency herein, which was coupled with an interest.

When broker's commission is earned

A broker has earned his commission when he has procured a purchaser ready, able and willing to buy the property upon the seller's terms. This is so, even if the owner refuses to sign the agreement of sale for the property. And it is likewise true, if the seller cannot convey good title. Where the owner and buyer have signed an agreement of sale and later agree to cancel the agreement, upon forfeiture of the deposit money by the buyer, the broker is entitled to his commission upon the consideration price stated in the deed, and not merely upon the deposit money forfeited: *Stewart Realty Co. v. Brock,* 60 N.M. 216 (1955). Of course, a written listing contract between owner and broker may provide otherwise.

Commission dependent upon transfer of title

A broker may, by special agreement with his principal, contract to make his compensation depend upon the actual signing of the contract, or upon the actual passing of title, or other contingencies. Even under these conditions, a broker may recover his commissions at the time fixed in the contract of sale if it develops that the negotiations fall through by reason of some defect in the title of the seller, or upon the arbitrary refusal of the seller to go through with the deal. The owner is not permitted to plead that the failure to consummate the transaction will operate to deprive the broker of his commission.

Where the default or failure is on the part of the seller, the courts generally hold that the broker may recover the commission agreed upon. Where the failure or default is attributable to the purchaser, the rule is different. Ordinarily, the signing of an agreement of sale for the property in question by the owner and prospective purchaser gives to the broker in the transaction a right to his commission. The execution of the agreement of sale by the owner is an admission on his part of the acceptability of the prospective purchaser produced by the broker and ordinarily will entitle the broker to his commission.

In every case the fundamental doctrine, under varying forms of expression, is that the duty assumed by the broker is to bring the minds of the buyer and seller to an agreement on a sale and on the price and terms upon which it is to be made and that, until this is done, his right to commissions does not accrue. A broker is not entitled to commissions when the customer through no fault of the seller refuses to complete the contract; but it is different when the customer has entered into a contract binding upon both parties or into an agreement to pay a stipulated sum as damages in case of refusal to complete the contract.

A broker who has fully earned his commission is generally not bound by any subsequent agreement that no commission is to be paid until the deed passes, for such an agreement is without consideration and cannot affect the obligation of the owner to the broker; and the agreement is not more binding when it recites a nominal consideration or good and valuable consideration when in fact, none passed. The fact that the seller refused to make the contract unless the broker agreed to wait for his commission until the deal was closed has been said not to furnish sufficient consideration. If the agreement of sale provides that the broker's commission is to be paid *at settlement,* the contract means exactly what it states, and if the settlement does not materialize, the broker is not entitled to commission, nor is this clause to be interpreted to mean that commission is to be paid when settlement *should have* taken place.

In the case of *Jones v. Palace Realty Co.,* 226 N.C. 303 (1946), the Court held under contract for payment of commission to broker out of sales price of property:

when the deal is closed up, he could not recover when the deal was never closed due to inability of purchaser to comply. It was the actual event of closing the deal and not the date of its expected or contemplated happening that made the promise to pay enforceable.

To the same effect is the Michigan case of *Kostan v. Glasier,* 60 N.W. 2d, 283 (1953), where commission was "payable only when and if deal is finally closed."

The law is general that in the absence of a special agreement, a broker earns his commission when he produces a purchaser able and willing to buy the property upon the seller's terms. This is so, if the seller accepts the broker's customer and enters into a binding contract with him, even though it develops that the buyer is financially unable to close the deal: 12 C.J.S. Brokers, 85, p. 188. However, the broker and owner may, by express language, make the broker's right to a commission depend upon a future happening, such as the actual passage of title from seller to buyer. If the contingency does not materialize, it is fatal to the broker's claim for a commission: *Amies v. Wesnofske,* 174 N.E. 436 (N.Y. 1931).

In the case of *Richard v. Falletti,* 13 N.J. Sup. 534 (1951), suit was brought by broker to recover unpaid half of a broker's commission earned on sale of defendant's land. The lower court rendered judgment for defendants on ground that plaintiff's right was contingent on delivery of deed, which had not taken place. The Superior Court, Appellate Division, reversed, holding that obligation to pay full commission was not contingent on delivery of deed, and that broker completed performance, and earned commission, when he induced purchaser to sign sales agreement.

Procuring cause of sale is a question of fact for a jury to decide. Whether a broker is the efficient and procuring cause of the sale is a question of fact, which falls within the province of a jury to determine. It is not a question as to how much a broker does in a deal, but how *effective* is what he does. The case of *Mehlberg v. Redlin*, 96 N.W. 2d 399 (S.D., 1959), is in point. The Court made the significant observation:

As background of the events of Friday, April 26, 1957, it should be noted that theretofore plaintiff had devoted time, effort and expense in establishing a market place to which both vendors and purchasers of real estate would be induced to resort. It was this preliminary activity of plaintiff which brought both Redlin and Rev. Schumann to that office. These facts suggest that to conclude plaintiff's only contribution toward bringing Redlin and the synod together, was the answering of a single telephone call, is to ignore an important part of her activities.

Exclusive listings

Most brokers prefer a written exclusive listing contract and some real estate offices will not accept a verbal listing, particularly, if the office belongs to a multi-list association. In an exclusive listing, the broker is assured that he will have the unrivaled right for a named period of time to negotiate the sale of the property in question. In return for this protection, the broker will usually advertise the property and make an added effort to sell the property. It should be remembered that there is an important distinction between an exclusive agency contract and an exclusive right to sell contract. They are not the same. In an exclusive agency contract, the broker is protected during the period specified against a sale of the same property by *another broker.* He is not protected if the owner himself sells the property during the exclusive period, unless the broker has a purchaser already available for the property upon the owner's terms. Under an exclusive right to sell contract, the broker is protected if the owner sells the property during the exclusive period. Such words as "I hereby grant and give to you the sole and exclusive right to sell said property"; "upon its sale or exchange by whomsoever the same may be made or effected" are necessary. In *Flynn v. LaSalle National Bank*, 9 Ill. 2d 129 (1958), the Court held that where there is an "exclusive agency" to sell realty, the owner is not precluded from selling the realty himself, but is only barred from appointing another agent; but where there is an "exclusive right" to sell the realty, the owner is liable for commission even if he effects the sale himself.

In an exclusive listing contract, the duration of the employment is fixed by the contract, but it may run on indefinitely unless the owner gives the broker notice of termination. For example—the period stated may be 90 days, but the contract provides that it shall continue thereafter indefinitely, until the owner gives the broker 30 days' written notice of termination. A number of State Real Estate

Commissions frown upon this type of contract and 24 states require a *definite* expiration date by provisions of the licensing act or by a rule and regulation of the Commission. Good ethics would require a definite expiration date in all written listing contracts.

Many brokers mistakenly believe that they have an exclusive agency for an indefinite period, where the owner gives no notice to terminate, when they do not have such protection at all. For example, the following form is in general use:

The undersigned hereby employs Stanley Sims as the sole and exclusive agent for the sale of the property described on the reverse hereof for a term of three (3) months and agrees to pay to the said agent a commission of five (5) per cent on the gross consideration upon its sale or exchange, by whomsoever the same may be made or effected.

The agent's authority hereunder may be revoked by the owner at any time after the expiration of the above term when no negotiations are pending for the sale and exchange of the property, but only upon and after 30 days' notice in writing to that effect given to the agent. And if, subsequently to such revocation, the property should be sold or exchanged to anyone with whom the agent had heretofore been negotiating the said commissions will be paid to said agent.

Suppose that a few days before the expiration of the three-month period, the broker showed the property to a prospective purchaser, who purchased the property 20 days after the three-month period expired, directly from the owner, who had given no notice to terminate the agency. The case poses two questions: (1) Was the exclusive agency still in effect? (2) Was the sale made to one with whom the broker "had heretofore been negotiating"? The law is now well established that the contract above does *not* confer an exclusive agency after its original term and until it is revoked by 30 days' written notice from the owner. *The exclusive character prevails only during the original term.* After that, the agency continues as only an open or general listing, until revoked. During the original period the broker can recover commission no matter who makes the sale; in order to recover after the expiration of the original three-month period, the broker must prove that he was the procuring cause of the sale. *Negotiating* means more than introducing or pointing out the property to the prospective purchaser. To negotiate means to discuss and arrange the details. Merely to call attention to the property without further discussing the details which necessarily follow for the consummation of the sale cannot be called a negotiation. On the other hand suppose that an owner, Ashworth, employed a broker, Bonwit, to sell his property under the following agreement:

The undersigned owner hereby employs Bonwit as the sole and exclusive agent for the term of three (3) months from the date hereof, and solely and exclusively thereafter until the expiration of thirty (30) days after written notice has been given to the broker by the owner.

The contract provides for a 5 per cent commission on the selling price, in event of a sale, whether made by another broker or by the owner himself. The contract of employment is dated January 3, 1969. No notice of termination is given by Ashworth to Bonwit, but on May 19, 1969, Ashworth, himself, sells the property to Crane. Bonwit now claims a commission. In this case the broker could recover, because the *exclusive* character of the employment has been continued by express agreement between the parties.

Exclusive right to sell

A distinction should be observed between a broker's exclusive agency and an exclusive right to sell. In an exclusive agency, the broker is given protection only against the competition of another broker during the period of the contract. If the owner himself sells the property, not through the efforts of a second broker, no commission would be due. On the other hand, if the broker holds an exclusive right to sell contract, and a sale is made by the owner during its term, the broker could recover. The distinction lies in the words "by *whomsoever* made" or "effected by you or by myself or by any other person."

It has been held in some cases, where the parties had executed a contract in which it was expressly covenanted that the broker should be paid a stipulated commission in the event of a sale within the time specified, no matter whether it was effected by the broker, or by the principal, or by any other person; that the commission could be recovered when the sale was made; and that it was immaterial who made it. These cases announce no new rule of law. They are simply declaratory of a fundamental maxim which is that the parties are bound by the terms of their own contract. If an owner of real estate chooses to make a contract with a broker in which it is stipulated that the broker shall have the exclusive right to sell the property within a specified time and that he shall be entitled to receive a certain commission if the sale be made within the time designated, no matter who makes it, he is bound by its terms and cannot be relieved from a bad bargain because his agreement may have been foolish or improvident. Our cases have gone thus far and no further.

Assume that an owner has signed a prepared listing contract. The contract is signed on February 2, 1957. The exclusive listing is for two months. It may be surprising to know that the contract could be terminated by the owner on February 3, 1957. Certainly, the broker has a cause of action, but what is the measure of damages? It is not the amount of commission which the broker might have earned on the deal, but rather the damages and expenses which he has actually sustained *at the date of the breach*. This amount is usually negligible. The Supreme Court of Arkansas so held in the case of *Nance v. McDougald,* 211 Ark. 800 (1947).

Where a principal revokes the broker's agency before the expiration of the listing period, he renders himself liable, unless such revocation is for cause, for such damages as are the proximate result of the termination of the employment contract: *Linden v. Loabs,* 30 Wis. 2d 618 (1966). There were mutual promises, constituting consideration (a bilateral contract). Even where obligations are imposed upon one party (a unilateral contract), nevertheless the owner may not breach it, where there has been substantial performance by the broker, such as advertising and obtaining interested prospects. Clearly, considerations of practical justice warrant and require that where there has been part or substantial justice on the part of the broker, the owner cannot arbitrarily cancel the employment before its expiration date: *Hutchinson v. Dobson-Bainbridge Realty Co.,* 31 Tenn. App. 490. If a broker has a bona fide purchaser, *before* the revocation was communicated to him, he would be entitled to recover his commission.

Furnish owner with copy of listing

Good ethics require that a broker voluntarily furnish the owner with a fully completed copy of the listing of the contract at the time it is signed. Some brokers are reluctant to give the owner a copy of the listing because they do not want him to know, perhaps, that it runs on indefinitely, unless written notice of cancellation (usually 30 days) is given to the broker.

To obviate this practice, which is considered unethical in good real estate circles, many Commissions, by statute or Rule and Regulation, require a *definite* expiration date in listing contracts. Since there is often controversy as to whether the broker actually furnished the owner with a copy of the listing, it is a good precaution to have the owner sign his name on the original copy retained by the broker, under a clause: "I hereby acknowledge receipt of a fully completed copy of this Listing Contract." The clause should be in prominent type. Failure to furnish the owner with a copy of the listing may constitute grounds for suspension or revocation of license. However, in the case of *Fleetham v. Schneekloth,* 52 Wash. 2d 176

(1958), the court held that failure to furnish a copy of the listing to the owner was not a fatal bar to a recovery of commission in a law suit against the owner. Some states, by Rule or Regulation, require that the original period for an exclusive listing shall not exceed one year. In the case of *Schlechter v. Foltz*, 179 Pa. Superior Ct. 119 (1955), the court held that a listing for the period "until sold" was not void, but was valid for a *reasonable time*.

Termination of exclusive contracts

Two final questions arise in regard to exclusive listings as follows:

1. Can such a contract be terminated before the expiration date?
2. Is the broker entitled to a commission upon a sale to a prospect procured by him, who signs an agreement by sale subsequent to the expiration date in the listing?

In Missouri, the cases make a distinction in listing contracts as to whether they are unilateral or bilateral. In a unilateral contract, where the broker does not in any way *obligate* himself to advance the sale of the property in the interest of the owner, then what has been previously stated in regard to the owner writing a cancellation of employment applies. A unilateral listing contract imposes a duty only upon the owner to pay a commission if the broker obtains a buyer; it imposes no duty upon the broker to endeavor to get a buyer. However, in a bilateral contract where the broker expressly obligates himself to advance the cause of his principal's property, then, the owner may not captiously or arbitrarily terminate the employment without being liable for the commission as damages to the broker. Such a clause creating a bilateral listing contract may read:

I acknowledge that the listing of this property, and your endeavor and efforts to procure a purchaser, through advertising, co-brokers, or otherwise, shall constitute a good and sufficient consideration for this agreement.

In the Missouri case of *Chamberlain v. Grisham*, 230 S.W. 2d 721, the Court held that after brokers listed the property and endeavored to procure a purchaser, contract became a bilateral one and was no longer revocable by owner at will. In other words, if there is substantial performance, the listing cannot be withdrawn. The listing contract must impose some duty or obligation upon the broker, as well as the owner, in order to give it a bilteral character. In the State of Hawaii, brokers use a form which recites, "In consideration of $1, receipt whereof is hereby acknowledged, etc.," which gives the contract good consideration. A provision that the broker will promptly relist the property with the members of his multi-list association, of which he is a member, makes the listing contract a bilateral one.

This listing contract should be signed by both *broker* and owner.

It is also well to provide a clause in the listing agreement that if the owner rescinds the contract before its expiration, or is guilty of a breach, he agrees to pay to the broker a designated sum, which may well be the amount of the commission, as *liquidated damages,* and call it "liquidated damages." The contract of employment should be under seal.

Next, is the broker entitled to commission upon a sale to a prospect procured by him, who signed an agreement of sale subsequent to the expiration date in the listing? Listing contracts, commonly used, provide:

> In the event that . . . during your employment you place me in contact with a buyer, to or through whom at any time within 90 days after the termination of said employment I may sell or convey said property, I hereby agree to pay you, etc.

This clause is often referred to as the "hold over" or "carry over" clause. Many different words are used in an endeavor to make the broker's claim for entitlement to a commission, effective. Other clauses provide "if the property is sold to anyone to whom the said property was *submitted* by the said broker, or his representatives within three (3) months from the termination date hereof," etc.; "if property is *shown*," etc.; or "to any person to whom the broker had *introduced* the property," etc. A number of listing contracts provide in the hold over clause that if a sale takes place within six months after the expiration date to any person with whom the broker had *negotiated* during the original term and whose names are filed with me (owner) in writing, prior to the termination of this contract: *E. M. Boerke Inc. v. Williams,* 28 Wis. 2d 627 (1966). The listing contract involved in *Bonn v. Summers,* 249 N.C. 357 (1950), required names of prospects shown the property to be filed within three days after the listing expired.

The general rule of law in this connection is stated in the case of *Everson v. Phelps,* 115 Oregon 523, where a broker in Tillamock sued for commission upon a sale made several days after the exclusive agency had expired. The claim was refused. The Court said: "Where there is no fraud or bad faith on the part of the employer and the broker does not perform within the time limit, the employer, after the expiration thereof, may contract with a customer introduced by the broker within the period for performance, either upon the same terms or upon others more or less favorable than those the broker was authorized, without receiving any liability to compensate the latter for his services."

In the case of *Schmidt, Inc. v. Brock,* 97 Ohio App. 469 (1953), the plaintiff alleged that it had a buyer, but defendant waited until exclusive expired and then sold it the next day to the buyer. The Court held that the broker could not recover as the plaintiff showed that no bad faith or any unjustifiable conduct by the defendant prevented the sale by him.

In the case, *McGuire v. Sinnett,* 158 Ore. 390 (1938), a broker had a listing contract which expired on August 23, 1936. A salesman for the broker showed the property to a prospect before the written listing expired. A second broker advertised the property after the listing expired and on September 1, 1936, the same prospect made an offer to purchase the property through the second broker and the deal was closed. The first broker sued the owner for a commission, contending that he was protected for 90 days under a clause in his listing contract which provided that the owner would pay the broker a commission if the broker placed the owner "in touch with a buyer to or through whom, within ninety (90) days after the expiration hereof, I (Seller), may sell, exchange or convey said property." The Supreme Court permitted the broker to recover, stating:

> In the case before us, the broker is entitled to his commission in one of the three following instances: (1) If he found a buyer ready and willing to enter into a contract with the defendant on terms and price agreed to by the defendant; (2) if he placed the defendant in touch with a buyer to whom the defendant sold the property during the life of the contract or within ninety days after the expiration thereof; or (3) if he was the procuring cause of the sale.

The broker was entitled to a commission upon proving that he placed a purchaser in touch with the seller during the term of the listing and the buyer consummated the deal within ninety days from the expiration date of the listing. The language of the listing contract is important. "In touch with," or "in contact with" is far different from "with whom the broker has been negotiating." To negotiate means more than merely submitting or showing the property to a prospective purchaser. In the Ohio case of *Kalna v. Fialko,* 125 N.E. 2d 565 (1955), the court held that "to negotiate" means to transact business, to procure, to induce, to treat with another respecting a purchase and sale. In a 1968 case, *King v. Dean* 238 N.C. 2d 828, the court stated that "negotiation is not a single act, but a process. It involves a dialogue or back-and-forth communication with a purpose; in this case, to sell real estate."

The case of *Nichols v. Pendley*, 331 S.W. 2d 673 (Mo. 1960), involved a suit for a real estate commission. On March 2, 1958, the parties entered into a written contract whereby, the owners appointed the broker as an exclusive agent for a period of two weeks to sell their residence at a price of $8,750. The contract further provided that "if this property is sold during the time this agreement is in force, or if sold to anyone to whom said property was submitted by Nichols Agency within three months from the termination date hereof, then in that event the undersigned shall pay to said Nichols Agency, broker, 5 per cent of the sales price as his commission due." It is admitted that within the two weeks exclusive period, a salesman of the broker offered the property to Woolevers for sale and took them through the house. They made no offer. The owners were present at the time. A sale was made to the Woolevers during the 90-day period following the expiration of the original term. The case turned up the interpretation of the word "submitted." The Court stated that:

The defendants contend that the word 'submitted' means that the efforts of the broker must have proceeded to the point where the Woolevers were 'likely purchasers.' Other cases cited referred to 'negotiating.' It has been held generally that 'negotiating' implies a situation where the interest of the buyer has been aroused to the point that the purchaser may be considered a likely purchaser. Negotiation implies a discussion of terms, a bargaining. It is generally used in connection with the *consummation* of business matters. The word 'submitted' means 'to leave or commit to the discretion of another.'

The Court further stated:

It is a close question. The acts of the plaintiff went far enough to fulfill the terms of the contract. But we are of the opinion that under the facts of this case the plaintiff 'submitted' the property to the purchasers within the exclusive period when he offered defendant's property to the Woolevers for sale and took them through the house in the presence of the defendants. The broker recovered.

Broker's option to purchase

Exclusive listing contracts sometimes contain a provision that the broker himself shall have the option of purchasing the property at the price stated. This type of contract is questionable as to good ethics, for it permits a broker to adopt a dual relationship to his principal. However, an agent may lawfully purchase from his principal if, before the transaction, there is a full disclosure of all the pertinent facts: *Sylvester v. Beck*, 406 Pa. 607 (1962).

Purchaser may be liable for deceit

It sometimes happens that a broker brings a property to the buyer's attention and then the latter deals with the owner direct. Many brokers have had instances where they show the outside of a dwelling listed and the prospect disclaims any interest and will not even make an inspection of the interior. Later on, the broker finds that the prospect has purchased the property. If the broker had previously notified the owner as to the identity of the prospect, he would have a good cause of action for commission. Clearly, if the owner is unaware of the interest of the broker's prospect or identity, the difficulty of recovering a commission is apparent. A *purchaser* may lay himself open to a lawsuit for commission by the broker, after the broker has submitted the property to him, by stating to the owner that there is no broker in the deal. A cautious or prudent seller, who has listed his property with one or more brokers for sale, will include a clause in the agreement of sale to the effect that the purchaser warrants that there is no broker involved in the sale. In the case of *McCue v. Deppert,* 21 N.J. Sup. 591 (1952), a broker, McCue of Rumson, New Jersey, sued a purchaser, Peter C. Deppert, under these very facts. There the property was listed at $30,000, and a McCue salesman showed Deppert the property. He said he would return with his wife. Instead, he went directly to the owner, Kramer, who lived at Lakewood, and bought the property for $25,000, "because there was no broker charge." The broker sued the buyer. The lower court decided against the broker, but upon appeal, the Superior Court held that the buyer could not "rely on his wrongful acts, in preventing the plaintiff from meeting the condition of procuring a ready, able and willing purchaser." The Court said:

From the proofs, it was open to the jury to find that the defendant Deppert became interested in the property through plaintiff's efforts, determined to buy it, and, but for Deppert's representation to the owner that no broker was involved, it was reasonably probable that plaintiff would have consummated the deal. It was also open to the jury to find that this representation was untrue and made with the intention of eliminating plaintiff from the transaction to the defendant's financial gain.

Another similar case was decided by a lower court in Ohio in 1952, in the case of *Schlesinger v. Zeilengold,* where the broker sued the buyer in an action of deceit and recovered a verdict of $2,800.00. The case involved a commercial property in Lyndhurst, Ohio. There the buyer secured from the broker certain pertinent information

about the property and then used it on his own. He then professed
to be totally uninterested in the property and refused to enter into
any discussion with the broker about its purchase. The buyer at the
time was in direct negotiation with the owner. The Court's decision
holds, in effect, that a prospective purchaser who perpetrates a
fraud upon a broker thereby preventing the broker from pursuing
his lawful and legitimate rights under his employment contract,
commits an actionable wrong in tort.

Acting as broker for buyer and seller

It is a generally accepted rule that a broker cannot act as the agent
for both parties in the same transaction. Each is entitled to his
undivided efforts and to the unimpaired use of his skill, knowledge,
and experience. It is not possible for a broker to fulfill these requirements if he is at the same time giving an equivalent service to the
other party to the contract. The interests of buyer and seller are
diametrically opposed to each other. The seller is interested in get-
ting as high a price for his property as he possibly can, while the
purchaser is naturally interested in obtaining the property at as low
a price as possible, and so it is impossible for an agent to represent
justly these conflicting interests. An agent cannot serve two masters.
The agent must not, in other words, occupy the position of a judge,
impartially weighing the merits of both sides. He has been engaged
by a principal to present in as convincing a manner as he can the
claims of his principal, and it is therefore imperative that the broker
do all in his power to secure the most favorable price possible under
the circumstances. He is neither interested in nor must he take any
heed of the wishes of the other party in the transaction to the prejudice of his principal. In other words, his employment by one is
incompatible with his employment by the other. This is so whether
the sale is for cash or whether there is an exchange of property
involved. This general rule has been followed strictly in most states.

The case of *Hughes v. Robbins, et al.*, 164 N.E. 2d 469 (1959),
involved a suit by a broker for commissions, against both seller and
buyer in an exchange deal. The plaintiff claimed that both parties
knew of the dual agency and there was no unfairness, double dealing, fraud, or damage to the parties. Hood, a defendant, testified
that he knew of the double employment. Robbins, the other defendant, emphatically denied knowledge. The Court denied a recovery. The Court said:

We find that all of such evidence as was submitted is not sufficient to
justify a finding that the defendants, Mr. and Mrs. Robbins, knew of,

consented to, or acquiesced in the dual agency. . . . It should be further observed that even if the defendants Hood were aware of this dual agency, and the defendants Robbins were not so aware still the broker cannot recover from either of the defendants, his principals—the rule being that the broker cannot recover from either of his principals unless both with knowledge of, consented to and acquiesced in such double employment . . .

An agent cannot ethically fulfill his duties to both employers.

It has been well written that "no servant can serve two masters, for either he will hate the one and love the other or else he will hold to the one and despise the other."

The fact that no actual damage resulted from the conduct of the broker here cannot prevent the application of this general rule, which is intended not as a remedy for the actual wrong, but, preventive of the possibility of it.

Under certain circumstances broker may recover

Under certain extenuating circumstances, however, there has been a divergence from this principle of law. Even though the transaction is an exchange, the broker cannot recover commissions if he is entrusted with any discretion and has an agreement to receive any commission from the other side without the knowledge of both parties. The rule, however, does not apply to an exchange of property where the broker has no discretion but is simply to bring the parties together. In such case the broker is merely a middleman. It may be said that an owner might reasonably assume that in an exchange of property, a broker receives commissions from both sides.

However, a broker who is vested with discretion or upon whom his employer has a right to rely for the benefit of his skill or judgment loses his right to compensation if he agrees to act in a similar capacity for the other party. A broker who is employed to sell property and whose duty it is not only to find a purchaser but to negotiate the sale cannot accept any compensation from any other than his employer; if he does make an agreement to be paid by the purchaser or if he assumes a position with reference to the transaction where his duty and interest might clash, he loses all right to his commission from his employer.

In summing up the law it may be stated that a broker may only recover commission from both parties to the same transaction when (1) he merely brings the parties together, (2) nothing is left to his discretion, (3) no special confidence reposes in him, (4) the fact that he is acting in a dual capacity is known to both parties, and (5) he is employed by both parties.

Broker's right to commission where agreement or a lease recognizes him as broker in the deal

Many real estate brokers specialize in the field of management and their livelihood is derived from commissions in regard to the leasing of residential, commercial, industrial and vacant properties. There is no prescribed rate of commission for services rendered in this area, as the matter is one of agreement between the broker and the owner. In many areas, it is suggested that a broker charge one-half of the first month's rent for a lease of one year or less, plus 3% of the total gross rental for the term in excess of one year, payable at the time of execution of the lease.

The question has frequently arisen where a broker has negotiated a sale or a lease whether he has an action in court for a commission when the agreement of sale or the lease includes a clause recognizing the broker as the one who negotiated the deal.

In the Pennsylvania case of *Richard B. Herman and Company v. Stern,* 419 Pa. 272 (1965), the plaintiff broker sued for a commission on the sale of a certain business property, upon a clause in the lease negotiated by the broker that in the event that the property were sold to the tenant, the broker would be entitled to a commission.

In a majority opinion (4 to 3), the Court said: (Opinion by Mr. Justice Henry X. O'Brien)

Appellant (Stern) obligates himself in clear and unambiguous language, for a recited consideration from the broker, under seal, to pay specific commissions. That this particular agreement is contained in the lease agreement between the lessor, appellant and lessee, Sailor, is neither unusual nor legally objectionable. Its presence in the document can be only to create a binding agreement between principal, appellant and agent, appellee, who signed as agent, for those commissions. Otherwise, its existence cannot be rationally explained. There is no legal or logical reason for prohibiting the inclusion of such promise. It is a practical manner of handling an every-day business matter in an efficient and legally effective manner, avoiding the necessity of other separate contracts. The simple matter is that the lessor, appellant, adopts the lease agreement prepared by his agent with the lessee as his own contract with the agent. The adoption of the contract in clear, unambiguous language, under seal, for the purpose for which it was executed, cannot be denied. This situation is a fundamental problem in ordinary contract law. There are many instances in which a party not a signatory to the writing may recover on the instrument, e.g., a payee of a check or note, a grantee under a deed. In these instances, only the maker or grantor signs the writing. Here, the action is on the appellant's promise to pay commissions as determined by that portion of the lease agreement between

appellant and lessee and signed under seal by appellant. He is the party
to be charged, and his signature to that promise is sufficient.

To the same effect is the case of *W. D. Nelson & Co., Inc., v.
Taylor Heights Development Corp.*, 207 Va. 386 (1966).

Care in making representations

If a broker is authorized to sell property for his principal as well
as to initiate negotiations, it is very important that the broker be
circumspect in the representations which he makes to prospective
purchasers concerning the property for sale. Representations include not only actual statements made by the broker, but also any
impression or belief that his conduct is calculated to produce in the
mind of the other party as to the facts. The law holds the broker
responsible for his representations in almost the same manner as if
he were acting for himself. Not only will the broker lose his right
to commission when he has been guilty of misrepresentation, but,
in addition, he may find himself the defendant in an action brought
by the disappointed purchaser, such as a fruitless action against the
principal in the contract, for any damages or expenses incurred by
the disappointed purchaser.

Even more important, the broker may find himself the defendant
in an action before the Real Estate Commission for violation of the
license law.

The general rule of law is well stated by the Nebraska Supreme
Court [6] as follows: "A person is justified in relying on a representation made to him in all cases where the representation is a positive
statement of fact and where an investigation would be required to
discover the truth."

To answer an inquiry regarding termites by saying, "There are no
termites in this house," is a statement of fact. But to say, "I have
seen no termites," is not a misrepresentation, although there are
termites, but the broker was unaware of that fact.

Puffing of goods

There is also a doctrine of law to be noted here known as "puffing
of goods." Where the broker makes extraordinary and extravagant
statements regarding the property for sale, as, "It is the most beauti-
ful spot in the world," and, "The sun shines daily," and where there
is no serious intent to include in the contract for sale that the property possesses all the magical powers and charms claimed for it, the

---

[6] Martin v. Hutton, 90 Neb. 34 (1912).

deluded victim has only his pains for his trouble and no remedy at law. A principal selling property is presumed to know whether the representations he makes concerning it are true or false, and if he knows them to be false, then he commits a positive fraud. If he does not know whether his representations are true or false, then his actions constitute gross negligence, and in contemplation of law, a representation founded on a mistake resulting from such negligence is fraud. The purchaser confides in the information furnished him by the owner upon the assumption that an owner knows his own property, and it is consequently immaterial to the purchaser whether the misrepresentation proceeded from a mistake or fraud. The injury to him in both cases is the same, whatever may have been the motive of the seller.

The law imposes the same obligations upon an agent acting for the owner of the property. He must be just as scrupulous in the statements which he makes concerning it as the principal would be were he conducting the negotiations personally. If the misrepresentations made by the broker were made upon the information supplied by the owner, the broker is entitled to his commission from the owner if he procures a purchaser, and he is not liable to buyer for damages.

Not liable for honest mistakes

A real estate broker is not personally responsible for an error or mistake which he honestly makes, unless he has been careless, grossly negligent, or has gone contrary to his honest convictions and beliefs.

It sometimes happens that a broker acts for an undisclosed principal, and the prospective purchaser deals exclusively with the agent as owner of the property. In such case the agent is as liable as if he were the principal. It is the duty of the agent, if he desires to avoid personal liability on the contract, not only to disclose the fact that he is acting in a representative capacity but also to disclose the identity of his principal. If he fails to do so, it must be taken that he assumes and intends to bind himself. It is important that a broker obtain full information concerning the listed property, and preferably, have the owner *sign* the reverse side of the listing contract, where such detailed information and data should be written.

Broker's liability for earnest money

The retention of deposit money, paid by a buyer on account of the purchase price, will be discussed in connection with agreements of sale. The subject is also pertinent to brokerage. We have already indicated that most state license laws *require* a broker to deposit earnest money in a trust or escrow account until the transaction is consummated or terminated. Failure to do so constitutes grounds for suspension or revocation of license. Where there is a written listing, signed by the owner, it is important that it should contain a clause to the effect that the broker should hold all deposits of earnest money in escrow until the transaction is consummated or terminated. Under such authority, the broker should encounter no difficulty in convincing his owner that the broker should hold the earnest money deposit. Of course, money paid the broker by a purchaser can be recovered by the purchaser where the owner refuses to execute the agreement or is guilty of a breach of the agreement. This is so even though the agreement provides that "It is understood that the broker is acting as agent only and will in no case whatever be held liable to either party for the performance of any term or covenant of this agreement or for damages for nonperformance thereof." This clause is not really necessary where the broker's principal is disclosed, since the action generally will be directed against the owner. But the buyer can sue the broker if the broker retains the deposit money, provided the buyer has a right of action against the owner.

It is also well to include in the listing contract a provision that if the buyer defaults, and the deposit money is forfeited, that the deposit money shall be divided equally between the owner and the broker, up to the amount of the broker's commission. The owner receives any excess.

Commission upon cancellation of lease

The question frequently arises as to a broker's right to collect commission upon the unexpired term of a lease negotiated by the broker where the lease is terminated by a sale or where the management of the property is taken out of the broker's hands before the expiration of the lease term. Thus, two different situations are presented. In the first case assume that a lease has been negotiated by a broker for a three-year term and the lease contains a provision that it can be terminated in event of sale of the property upon the owner giving the tenant 60 days' notice in writing to that effect. Suppose, at the end of one year, the owner makes a bona fide sale and gives the tenant the required 60 days' notice. The broker is obviously not entitled to a commission on the rent for the remaining 22 months since he negotiated the lease and is cognizant of the sales clause and his commission upon the lease term is necessarily contingent upon the tenant remaining in possession during the *entire* three-year period. In the second case, where no sales clause is contained in the lease and the owner sells the property subject to the existing lease, the situation is different. Upon negotiation of the lease by the broker, he becomes entitled to a commission for the full period of the lease. Where the new owner takes the property out of the broker's hands, his rights against the original owner continue unabridged. However, custom, as evidenced by the practice among brokers or under the rules of a real estate board, may permit a reduction of the full amount of commission claimed under these circumstances.

Broker's right to sign agreement of sale

A broker's contract of employment is separate, apart, and independent of the sales contract between the owner and the purchaser, and ordinarily, a broker cannot execute an agreement of sale, which is binding upon his principal. He is employed to bring about a contract of sale between his principal and a third party, who is the buyer. However, a number of listing contracts executed by an owner and used in various parts of the country, expressly confer authority upon a broker to execute a binding contract of sale. For example ". . . and to execute a binding contract on our behalf." "I hereby authorize you to sell or contract with purchaser for the sale and conveyance by warranty deed of said premises." There may be extenuating circumstances where such broad authority is necessary, as where an owner who is listing property for sale with a broker intends to leave the city for an extended period of time. Ordinarily, however, such authority is foreign to the broker's employment by the owner and, generally, the owner does not understand nor intend to give such broad power to his agent. It has been held that the employment of a broker "to sell" real estate for an owner does not give the broker authority to execute a binding contract of sale.

In the case of *Gallant v. Todd, et al.,* 111 S.E. 2d 779 (S.C. 1960), a purchaser brought an action against the owner for specific performance of certain land under a contract of sale, signed by the broker. The defense was that the broker had no authority to sell. The action was based upon a writing dated June 12, 1958, as follows:

I hereby authorize Horton Bros. Co., Inc., Anderson, South Carolina, to sell for me the below described property of which I am the owner, making them my sole agent for that purpose, and in case sale of said property is made by them or by anyone else, I do hereby contract and agree to pay them 5 per cent commission on $60,000 or price accepted for said property and to give good and sufficient title to same.

A written contract of sale was entered into by Horton Bros. Co.,

Inc. as seller's agent at $60,000, with a $3,000 down payment. The Court said:

It is well settled that a real estate broker, under the ordinary contract of employment has no implied authority to execute a contract of sale in behalf of his principal. He is generally a special agent, with limited powers, whose usual duty is simply to find a purchaser, ready, able, and willing to enter into a contract upon the terms and conditions fixed by the owner . . . must ascertain the *intention* of the parties . . . Even though Mrs. Todd had confirmed the fact that she was willing to sell for $60,000, that cannot be construed as creating an agency with power to contract for the sale of the property.

In concluding the subject of brokerage, it is important to note that a broker, in order to protect his right to a commission, should always acquaint the owner with the identity of every prospect to whom the owner's property has been submitted. In some real estate offices, it is the practice to send the owner a form letter immediately upon the submission of his property to a prospect. This is a wise policy. The average owner would be hesitant to honor a second broker's efforts when the same prospect is involved, once he has been advised of the prospective purchaser's identity by the first broker. Such a notice is made up in duplicate, the copy is retained by the broker. In fact, a third copy for the salesman is advisable. The notice reads:

HUSS BROTHERS, Realtors
REAL ESTATE and INSURANCE
5972 Baum Blvd., Pittsburgh, Pa.

MONTROSE 4700

Date........ *JAN. 7* ...., 19 *62*

M R. *HUGO CHRISTOPHER*

Street *3629 BENNETT ST., PITTSBURGH, PA.*

Please be advised that today we submitted to.... *CHAS. WHEELER;*

MRS. GRACE LYNNHURST ....your property listed with this office, located

at *1610 ROSS AVE., WILKINSBURG, PA.*

Price quoted *$27,900 —* .... We will endeavor to interest this prospect further. If they return to examine same, or call by phone, please notify us at once, as your co-operation will greatly assist in the sale of your property.

HUSS BROTHERS

By........ *PHIL DONNELLY* ....Salesman

NOTE:—If any change has taken place since your property has been listed with this office, we would appreciate word from you at once.

Questions on Brokerage

1. Q. C. D. Sloan owns a vacant commercial building in a downtown area. He places a large sign reading "For Sale or For Rent, Call 261-1225" or "SEE YOUR BROKER." Randolph, a prospect, contacts a broker, Marlin, who calls Sloan and obtains the terms of sale. Later, a sale is made by Sloan to Randolph at $72,000. Marlin claims the usual commission of 7 per cent in that area. Can he recover?

   A. No. The statement "See Your Broker" does not establish a contract of employment between Sloan and Marlin. In states requiring a listing contract to be in writing, Marlin, of course, could not recover.

2. Q. Adams employed the Boston Auction Company to sell his residence at auction. The auctioneer announced that "broker participation" would be allowed if the broker had registered his client with "us," if his party was the successful bidder. A broker, Clark, registered the successful bidder with the auctioneer, who refused to pay any commission. Clark sued Adams. Can he recover?

   A. No. There was no privity of contract between Adams and Clark. The auctioneer had no authority to bind the owner.

3. Q. Broker Jones secures an oral listing from seller, MacDonald, to sell his house for $17,500; agreement to terminate in 30 days, commission to be 6%. Jones secures a buyer for the property at $17,500. The owner refused to permit broker to complete sale and completes it himself. Jones demands his commission. Can broker recover?

   A. In those states which require a listing contract to be in writing, he could not recover. In the other states, he could recover.

4. Q. A broker is employed by a wife to sell her real estate; he secures a buyer on her terms; the husband refuses to sign the contract of sale and the deal falls through. Is the broker entitled to a commission from the wife?

   A. Yes. He has fully performed his contract of employment since he produced a purchaser, ready, able, and willing to buy. However, if he had good reason to believe that the husband would not join in the contract of sale the decision would be different.

5. Q. An owner gives an exclusive listing to broker Abel for a six months period. During the exclusive period, he gives a non-exclusive listing to Kane, who produces a buyer. What is the owner's liability for commission?

A. He is obligated to pay full commission to both Abel and Kane.

6. Q. A salesman is assisted in a deal by another salesman employed by another broker. The first salesman pays one-half of his commission to the salesman who assisted him. Is this legal?

A. No; the salesman has no right to recognize anyone other than his employing broker. The latter should deal and recognize the other broker and not the other broker's salesman.

7. Q. Why does an exclusive right to sell listing contract afford the broker more protection than an exclusive listing?

A. Full commission is asured the broker, regardless of who sells the property during the term of the listing.

8. Q. Assuming you are a broker and discover you have obtained an Exclusive Right to Sell contract from a property owner who is incompetent. What are your rights in enforcing this contract?

A. None. Contract is void.

9. Q. If you have a property listed for sale and find a prospect who is willing to take an option on the same at the terms offered, are you entitled to your commission?

A. No. An option does not bind the purchaser to buy, and the broker is entitled to his commission only if he produces a ready buyer.

10. Q. If you listed a house for sale, which had wall to wall carpeting in the living room and hall, would you make reference to the carpeting in your listing?

A. Yes. A statement in listing may save argument and perhaps loss of sale later.

11. Q. Name at least five methods by which an agency may be terminated.

A. 1. By agreement between principal and agent.
2. By expiration of the term.
3. By extinction of subject matter.
4. By death of either principal or agent.
5. By incapacity of either principal or agent.
6. By renunciation by either agent or principal.

12. Q. A broker is employed by the son of A and B, husband and wife, to sell the parents' real property. The mother has authorized the son to list the property but the father has not. The broker secures a buyer on the exact terms of the listing; the father refuses to sign an agreement of sale and the deal falls through. Can the broker recover a commission?

A. The broker can recover from the mother since the son was her authorized agent. The broker could also sue the son, who gave the listing, as he represented he was duly authorized to do so. He could not recover from the father.

13. Q. A broker claimed a commission for procuring a purchaser for an owner's property. He obtained a buyer. When the deal was closed, title was taken in the name of the father of the purchaser

and the property leased to the son. Can the broker recover a commission?

A. Yes, the broker clearly made the deal and the arrangement for taking title would not defeat his earned commission.

14. Q. William Rushton, a broker, had an exclusive listing on Albert Doty's home, which expired on August 30, 1968. Before the listing expired Rushton procured Frank Stone as a prospect. On August 15, 1968, Doty *leased* the property to Stone for six months and on December 6, signed an agreement to sell him the property. Is Rushton entitled to a commission?

A. Yes; it appears that the lease was merely an arrangement to circumvent the commission claim and that the parties to it did not act in good faith.

15. Q. The National Insurance Company owned a farm. Wilson, a broker, offered to trade an apartment house, listed with him for sale, for the farm. He dealt with Alberts, treasurer of the Company. The treasurer stated: "We want high class apartment property." The broker replied "All right, sir, I will see what I can do." An exchange was made through another broker. Wilson unsuccessfully sued the other broker for a commission. Can he recover against National Insurance Company?

A. No. There is no express or implied contract of employment. It would appear that plaintiff was representing the apartment building owner, since the Insurance Company had not listed the farm with him.

16. Q. Where Ash lists property for sale with broker, Burns, who procures a purchaser, Cohn, can Burns collect a commission if the agreements are made between Ash and Drew, the father-in-law of Cohn?

A. Yes, if Cohn is the real purchaser and takes possession of the premises. It is immaterial that title is taken in Drew's name or even whether he furnishes the money. It is assumed that Ash knew of the relationship between Cohn and Drew, or should have known from the circumstances in the case.

17. Q. Ahern lists property for sale with Brett, a broker, at $6,000. Brett purchases the property in Cobb's name and sells it to Simmons for $7,500. Brett collects a commission from Ahern of $300. Later Ahern discovers the real facts. What redress does he have?

A. He can recover the $1,500 profit and, in addition, can recover the $300 commission paid to Brett. The broker forfeits his right to a commission because of his duplicity.

18. Q. Aiken lists property for sale with Benson, a broker, at $8,000, the broker to receive a commission of five per cent. Benson procures a buyer who refuses to pay more than $7,500. Two months later the deal is made at $7,500 and Benson claims $375 as commission. Aiken refuses to pay claiming the listing was at $8,000. Can Benson recover?

A. Yes. The courts will not permit an owner to take advantage of a broker's efforts and then turn him "out of doors." The agent here was still the efficient and procuring cause of the sale.

19. Q. Bowles, a broker, was employed by Archer to sell three lots for him. It was not an exclusive agency. Bowles procured Mrs. Crane who was acting for herself and her husband. Each purchased one lot, as did Drake, whom Mrs. Crane had informed that the lots in question were for sale. Bowles sued Archer for a commission on the sale of all three lots. Can he recover?

A. Bowles can recover commissions only upon the sale of the two lots to the Cranes. The broker was in no way directly connected with the sale of the lot to Drake. The law deals only with proximate and not remote causes.

20. Q. The plaintiff broker, Bender, "worked upon" one Collins and induced him to look at property owned by Allen, listed with Bender for sale. Collins finally decided not to buy himself, but upon Collins' advice, Collins' brother bought directly from the owner, Allen. Is Bender entitled to a commission on the sale?

A. No. In the absence of collusion or fraud, the plaintiff was not the procuring cause of the sale to Collins' brother.

21. Q. Jones gave Peters an exclusive listing upon his property at $9,000. The agreement was for a term of 3 months at 5 per cent commission. The agreement provided for termination after the term upon 30 days' written notice from the owner. "In default of such notice, this exclusive contract shall renew itself from term to term as an exclusive contract . . . until notice herein provided shall be given to terminate." The agreement was dated November 28, 1967. Notice of termination was given on May 16, 1968. The property was sold by the owner, Jones, on July 26, 1968. Is the broker entitled to his commission?

A. Yes. The written notice of termination given May 16, 1968 was too late to terminate the contract during the term in which it was given. It operated to terminate the listing as of August 28, 1968. Inasmuch as the property was sold on July 26, 1968, Peters was entitled to his commission.

22. Q. Smith, a minor, employs Black to sell a piece of real estate which he owns. Black, dubious as to Smith's age, makes inquiry. Smith misrepresents his age to be 25 years. After Black sells the property, Smith disaffirms the contract of employment and refuses to pay Black any commission. Can Black recover?

A. No. Black's suit in assumpsit (upon a contract) is against an infant upon a *voidable* contract. Smith cannot make himself of age by misrepresenting his age. He is still an infant in fact and the law permits him to plead infancy as a defense. An infant is liable for deceit, which is tort (an actionable wrong) action. Black could sue Smith in a trespass action upon the tort.

23. Q. Andrews, an owner, wrote Burns, a broker, "You might proceed

and sell the entire 13 houses separately for $50,000 net cash to me. Your commission of 3% to come out of the last sale made." The houses were sold by Burns for an aggregate amount of $50,-000. Andrews refuses to pay any commission. Can Burns recover?

A. No. The broker is not entitled to any commission unless the sum received exceeds the specified "net" price, the word "net" meaning that which remains after deducting all charges such as commission.

24. Q. Flynn, a broker, asks Dubbs, an owner, the price of his house, and introduces him to a client, who subsequently purchases it. Can he recover a commission?

A. No. Even though he may have, to some extent, influenced the sale, he cannot recover, because he cannot prove an employment. "See what you can get," or, "How much do you want for it?" does not constitute employment.

25. Q. On March 28, 1969, Bunn, a broker, was employed by the defendant, Cox, to negotiate certain investment real estate for $72,000. The price of the property was held at $76,000. The owner, Ash, had listed the property for sale with Bunn at the latter figure. Bunn testified that he did not expect a commission from owner, Ash, and had not received any commission. Can Bunn recover from the purchaser, Cox?

A. No. Having accepted employment as agent for the seller, Bunn could not secretly become agent for the buyer. Employment by one is incompatible with employment by the other. A servant cannot serve two masters.

26. Q. Arthur listed property for sale with Blaine at $12,000. Blaine negotiated a sale to Clancy, who paid $1,000 down. After the agreement of sale is signed, Arthur obtains a memorandum from Blaine that "commission is to be paid at the time of settlement." Settlement is never made due to default by Clancy, and Arthur refuses to sue Clancy upon the contract. Can Blaine recover from Arthur for commission?

A. Yes. There was no legal consideration for the promise to wait for his commission until the date of settlement. If the promise had been made *prior* to the signing of the agreement of sale, the broker could not recover.

27. Q. Woods mails a description of his property to Talley, a broker, with a request that he sell it at $18,500 cash. Nothing is said about commission. The broker obtains a buyer at $18,500 cash. There is an argument about paying a commission. Can Talley recover?

A. Yes. There is an implied promise to pay the usual commission, since the broker obtained a satisfactory buyer upon the seller's terms. He could recover on a "quantum meruit" basis, what he deserves.

28. Q. Albert gave Ross a written listing for the sale of property at $29,-

000. It read ". . . to procure a bona fide purchaser at the stipulated price of $29,000 cash subject to the balance due the First National Bank." The mortgage was for $21,000 and had about one year to run. Ross procured Collins as a purchaser for $29,-000 cash. The bank refused to accept payment of the mortgage unless paid interest in advance, amounting to about $1,000. Albert and Collins both refuse to pay the interest. Is Ross entitled to a commission?

A. No. The case turns upon the exclusive listing provision "subject to the balance due" and so forth. Any ambiguity would be construed against the broker who prepared the listing. It certainly could not mean $29,000 cash *plus* the $21,000 mortgage. It could only mean *subject* to the mortgage and the balance in cash. The cash terms of the proposed sale were at variance with the listing contract and Ross could not recover.

29. Q. Young is a tenant of Fox for certain premises used as a variety store. Young lists the business for sale with Boone, a real estate broker. Boone advertises the business for sale and interests Dunn, a prospective purchaser. Dunn and Young call upon Fox for the purpose of transferring the lease, but Fox refuses, and as a result Dunn purchases the building from Fox. Can the broker, Boone, recover a commission from Fox?

A. No. In the first place Boone cannot establish a contract of employment with Fox, and, in the second place, Boone was not the direct proximate cause of the real estate sale.

30. Q. Benson, a broker, obtained an inquiry from Mann for certain industrial real estate, at a purchase price of $20,000. Benson had the same property listed with him by Ambers, the owner, at $14,000. Benson informed Ambers that he himself would purchase the property at Ambers' price. Agreements were signed and Benson assigned the agreements to Mann. Ambers sues Benson for $6,000. Can Ambers recover? Is Benson entitled to a commission on the $20,000 deal?

A. Ambers can recover. Benson is not entitled to any commission. An agent is a fiduciary. He owes a high degree of loyalty to his principal. He cannot make a secret profit at the expense of his principal. Since Benson offered to buy the property *after* he had a purchaser at a higher price, he forfeits his rights to a commission.

31. Q. Peters gave Brent an exclusive agency to sell his real estate for $8,500. The contract is dated February 28, 1969. It runs for 6 months and then indefinitely as an *exclusive agency* unless terminated by 30 days' written notice from the owner. After procuring a few prospects in the spring of 1969, nothing is done by Brent upon the listing. Peters sells the property in December 1969 through another broker, Kane, to whom he pays the usual commission. Can Brent collect a commission?

A. Yes. Although his right would appear unconscionable, the exclusive listing "ran on" until Peters took the necessary steps to cancel it, by giving Brent written notice to that effect.

32. Q. Jones lists his property for sale verbally with three real estate offices. Brown, a broker, shows the property to Neil. Later Neil calls at the office of a second broker, Clark, who shows him several properties, including Jones's property. Neil tells Clark that he has already seen the property but Clark insists that he make another inspection. Clark calls Neil's attention to the construction, fixtures, and appointments. Neil is impressed and several days later calls at the house alone and gives Jones a check for $500 on the purchase. The deal is closed. Jones pays Brown a one-half commission and pays Clark a one-half commission. Both Brown and Clark sue Jones. Who will win?

A. Clark appears to be the broker who actually effected the sale. But the question of which broker is the efficient and procuring cause of the sale is a question of fact. One jury might hold that the first broker, Brown, was the efficient cause as he put in motion a series of events, which, without interruption, culminated in a sale. In claims from more than one broker, an owner should pay the money into court, so as to confine his liability to the payment of a single commission.

33. Q. A broker holds a license expiring on June 30, 1968. On July 2, 1968, he has not renewed his license. On that date, he negotiates the sale of property of an owner. Indicate by check-mark, which of the following will apply.

A. He is still registered _____.
The sale is illegal _____.   √
The broker forfeits his commission _____.
The registration of the broker may be revoked _____.
The seller may sue the broker for any expenses he incurred _____.

The purchaser may sue the broker for all sums paid to the broker _____.

34. Q. Name two persons to whom a broker may lawfully pay compensation for services in a real estate transaction.

A. His licensed real estate salesman.
A licensed real estate broker.

35. Q. In obtaining a listing of a residence for sale, name at least ten factors in regard to the property, which a broker should include on his listing card data.

A. Construction and design; layout of rooms and sizes; types of floors; baths; heating system; age of building; roof construction and spouting; size of lot; garage; taxes and mortgage data; amount of assessment; screens; weather-stripping; type of plumbing; special features.

36. Q. What is the legal terminology of the relationship between a broker and his client?

A. Agency.

37. Q. Are these three reasons why a broker should obtain an exclusive listing?

A. (a) Guarantees a broker he will earn a commission—Yes__. No X.

(b) Protects against other brokers stealing his prospects—Yes X. No__.

(c) Causes the broker to feel more secure—Yes X. No__.

38. Q If a listing does not state a definite expiration date, it may nevertheless be terminated in several ways. Name them.

A. Performance, lapse of time, revocation, abandonment, renunciation. (In some states, listing is void.)

39. Q. Broker Smith gives you information concerning one of his listings and you sell the property. Should you negotiate through Smith or directly with the owner? Why?

A. With Smith, because he has the only legally enforceable contract of agency employment.

40. Q. What is the difference between a "Realtor" and a "Real Estate Broker"?

A. A "Realtor" is a member of the local, state, and national real estate association. A "Real Estate Broker" is any licensed broker.

41. Q. Ash lists a property for sale with Burns on Jan. 16, 1969. Ash leaves for a 2-month vacation but dies while he is away. Burns, unaware of Ash's death, obtained a signed agreement for the property from Johnson upon Ash's terms. Ash's heirs refuse to honor it or to pay Burns a claimed commission. Can Burns recover?

A. No. Ash's death automatically cancelled Burns's employment. The fact that Burns was unaware of Ash's death is immaterial.

42. Q. Ahern lists his porperty for sale with Brown by telephone. Brown calls Foster's attention to the property by phone. Ahern and Foster are friends, and Foster has visited Ahern's home a number of times. When Brown calls Ahern's attention to Foster as a prospect, Ahern replies, "Oh, I talked to him about buying my property years ago." Later Ahern sells to Foster. Is Brown entitled to a commission?

A. Yes. He has brought the parties to an agreement. Although his services, measured in time, may not have amounted to much, yet he was responsible in bringing the parties together, which resulted in the agreement.

43. Q. A broker has been authorized by all parties involved to negotiate an exchange of certain properties. Would he be entitled to commission on all the properties in the transaction?

A. Yes. His dual employment is known and recognized by the parties involved.

44. Q. Jane Thomas, who generally conducted her father's (Tom Thomas's) affairs, gave Fair the sole agency for the sale of a

lot. He placed his sign on it. This was done with the father's knowledge, and without objection. Jane referred a prospect to the broker, stating that the matter was entirely out of her hands. Can Fair recover from Thomas upon a sale to the prospect?

A. Yes. Under the doctrine of estoppel, the father is prevented from denying the authority of the daughter to list the property with the broker.

45. Q. Allen employed Black, a broker, to sell some investment property for him. Black obtained Clay as a purchaser. At the time of closing the deal it developed that the property did not have the rental income claimed by Allen, whereupon Clay refused to go through with the deal. Is Black entitled to a commission?

A. Yes. He complied with his contract of employment with Allen.

46. Q. A minor, Young, employed Bell to sell his property. Bell obtained a purchaser, Cooper, upon Young's terms, and Cooper made a substantial down payment. Young refused to accept the offer, stating that he had changed his mind. Can the broker collect a commission?

A. No. Who deals with an infant does so at his peril. The contract is voidable and may be disaffirmed by the minor.

47. Q. Miss Agatha Vebler listed property, which she had inherited, with Smith-Jones Realty Company. The next day, the firm produced a purchaser and Miss Vebler signed the contract of sale. Prior thereto, Miss Vebler married Anthony Taylor. At the closing, the husband refused to join in the deed and the deal fell through. Can the plaintiff broker recover a commission?

A. Yes. The broker acted in good faith, without any knowledge that the owner was married when she signed the contract of sale.

48. Q. A principal directs a broker to sell his property for $50,000. The broker might have obtained $50,000, but by collusion with the purchaser he sells it to him for $40,000, with the consent of the owner, who knows nothing of the collusive agreement and is anxious to sell at any price. The owner, later learning of the broker's infidelity, refuses to pay him any commission. What are the rights of the parties?

A. The broker cannot collect any commission and the owner can recover from the broker any secret profit, which the broker may have made in the transaction. The broker has violated his duty of loyalty to his principal and forfeits his rights to any compensation.

49. Q. Axford employs Bird, a licensed broker, to sell property for which he is to receive a specified sum as his commission. Without informing Axford, Bird also acts for the buyer, who also promises him a commission. When Axford discovers that Bird is acting for both parties, he goes through with the deal but refuses to pay the broker's commission. Bird sues. Can he recover?

A. No. A broker cannot represent both parties in the same transaction. The law does not permit a servant to serve two masters. The broker's employment by the seller is incompatible with his similar employment by the buyer since the seller is interested in obtaining the highest price possible for his property and the buyer is anxious to purchase it at the lowest price possible.

50. Q. Under what circumstances, if any, may a seller impose the condition on a broker that he is to receive commission only in the event that the sale is consummated by the execution and the delivery of the deed?

A. Only if the condition is agreed upon before the broker has procured a bona fide purchaser for the property and a properly executed agreement of sale.

51. Q. Barnes, a broker employed by Arthur, procures an agreement of sale signed by Clark and upon the owner's terms of sale. However, the agreement provides for closing the deal ninety days hence. Arthur has another purchaser for the property at the same price with the closing fixed for thirty days. Arthur refuses to sign Barnes' agreement. Is Barnes entitled to a commission?

A. No. Ninety days is an unreasonable length of time for the closing, and Arthur is within his rights in objecting to the delay.

52. Q. Brett, a licensed real estate broker, obtained from Ash, an owner, the terms upon which Ash would be willing to sell his property. Brett submitted these terms to Connor, a prospective purchaser. Brett did nothing more. Ash and Connor thereafter and without Brett's knowledge, entered into an agreement of sale for the property upon the original terms. Brett sued for commission. The Court held that Brett was not entitled to the commission. What were the reasons for the Court's finding?

A. Brett was not the efficient and procuring cause of the sale. There is no evidence in the facts stated that Brett brought the parties together, or that Brett disclosed Connor's identity to Ash.

53. Q. A real estate broker is forced to sue to collect a commission that is due him. In addition to the facts setting forth his cause of action, what fact does the License Law require him to allege in his complaint and prove on the trial of his case?

A. That he was properly *licensed* as a real estate broker at the time the real estate deal was negotiated.

54. Q. A contract for the sale of real estate provides as follows: "The seller agrees that John Doe brought about this sale and agrees to pay him the broker's commission of five hundred dollars." Subsequent to the execution of the contract, John Doe, in a conversation with the seller, states that he will not claim his commission unless title is actually closed. Thereafter, and prior to the date set for the closing of the title, John Doe demands his commission from the seller who refuses to pay, claiming that

John Doe was not entitled to a commission until the actual closing of title. Who will win?

A. John Doe, the broker, will win as his commission was earned when he produced a purchaser ready, able, and willing to buy upon the seller's terms upon the execution of the sales agreement. There was *no* consideration for Doe's promise to wait until the closing for his commission.

55. Q. What protection does a written listing give an owner?

A. The terms of the contract, such as expiration date and commission, are clearly defined so that controversy and litigation can be avoided.

56. Q. May a real estate broker or salesman pay a portion of his commission to an unlicensed person for his assistance in a sale?

A. No. It is unlawful.

57. Q. Broker Carroll has an exclusive listing on certain property from an owner and receives an unsolicited bona fide offer from Broker Woodruff. He refuses to submit the offer to the owner on the grounds that his exclusive agency does not obligate him to deal with or through any other broker, and that the prospect must deal with him directly and not through any other broker. Is he correct?

A. No. The broker is obligated to submit any offer or information which he may have regarding the subject of the agency. While Carroll may refuse to split a commission, his duty to his principal requires him to divulge the offer through Woodruff. The owner may decide to pay each broker a full commission.

58. Q. Abel listed his property with broker Berm at $15,500. Berm receives an offer of $10,500 from a prospect. Should he ignore the offer or obtain a deposit from the prospect and communicate it to Abel?

A. He should accept the deposit and advise Abel of *all* information which has come to his knowledge.

59. Q. If the broker or salesman selling a property is the owner thereof or has an ownership interest therein, should that fact be disclosed to the purchaser before the latter obligates himself to buy?

A. Yes. A broker or salesman is not permitted to act as an undisclosed principal in a real estate transaction, whether it be as purchaser or seller.

60. Q. Smith is employed as a real estate salesman by Brown, a broker. While so employed, he attempts to sell Albert's property to Cox. A few days later, Smith and Brown "fall out" and Smith resigns from Brown's employ. Smith's license is returned to the Real Estate Commission for cancellation. He then makes a connection with the real estate office of Edwards. After applying for a transfer of license to Edwards, but before the new license has been issued, Smith negotiates and concludes the sale of Albert's

property to Cox. Is Brown, Smith or Edwards entitled to a commission?

A. No one is entitled to a commission under the law. Since Smith's contract with Brown was terminated, he had no license in force when the deal with Cox was made. Smith had no assurance that the transfer of license to Edwards would be made. The salesman must be licensed whenever negotiations for the sale of real estate are carried on.

61. Q. A salesman in the employ of a real estate broker put through a sale. He demanded commission on behalf of his firm and the seller refused to pay it. His employing broker refused to be involved in litigation regardless of the merits of his claim. Thereupon the salesman sued the seller in his own name. Can he recover?

A. No. A salesman usually has no standing in a court of law; an action for commission must be instituted in the name of the broker employed by owner.

62. Q. Adams employed Bell, a broker, to sell his property. Parker employed Cross, a second broker, to buy property in the neighborhood. Parker contacted Bell and persuaded Bell to help him buy Adams' property, Bell to "put the pressure" on Adams. Bell was to receive a commission from Parker and to split the commission which Parker paid Cross. Adams signed the agreement of sale. When Adams discovered these facts, he refused to perform the contract. Will he succeed?

A. Yes. The collusion between the purchaser and Bell to take an unfair advantage of Adams will defeat any rights that Bell might otherwise have against Adams. The broker, Bell, forefeits any claim to commission.

63. Q. Jones gives you an exclusive listing on a home; you procure a buyer, ready, willing, and able. You now discover that Jones does not own the house but that his brother does. May you recover your commission from Jones?

A. Yes. You have fulfilled the terms of your contract with Jones. By holding himself out as the owner, Jones is liable.

64. Q. Blake, a broker, sells a parcel of real estate for Young, an infant, aged 20 years and 10 months. When Young becomes of age, he disaffirms the contract of sale. The broker demands that Young pay him the commission and upon Young's refusal institutes suit for payment. Can Blake recover?

A. No. The contract was voidable at Young's option, and he was, therefore, within his legal rights in disaffirming it.

65. Q. Harris, broker, obtained a purchaser, and a $500 deposit, on an "open" listing. The listing was for $12,000 and the buyer agreed to pay $11,200. Before the owner, Grant, would sign the agreement, he had Harris write in, "Commission to be paid when deal is consummated." The buyer moved to Detroit and defaulted.

Grant sold the property through another broker. Can Harris recover?

A. No. Failure of the buyer to close the deal, without any fault of the seller, relieved the seller under the special terms of the contract from liability for the commission.

66. Q. Enumerate five duties which an agent owes to his principal.

A. 1. Loyalty to his trust.
   2. Must obey instructions.
   3. Must account for money and property.
   4. Must not be negligent.
   5. Must act in person.

67. Q. Under what circumstances, if any, may a broker recover a commission from both buyer and seller?

A. A broker can recover a commission from both parties when:
   1. He is employed by both parties.
   2. He merely brings the parties together.
   3. Nothing is left to his discretion.
   4. No special confidence is reposed in him.
   5. The fact that he is acting in a dual capacity is known to both parties.

68. Q. The listing contract provided for a six months' "carry over" clause —if property was sold for $65,000 to a buyer procured by the broker, he was entitled to a commission. During the six-month period, the property was sold for $45,000 through another broker. It was established that the plaintiff broker presented no offer to the owner, but he had submitted the property to the ultimate purchaser during the original term of the listing; but, who did not offer $65,000. Can the broker recover?

A. No. The broker did not *procure* an acceptable buyer. He cannot recover a commission for an independent sale at a later date to the prospect for a substantially lower amount than that quoted by the broker.

69. Q. Fordham desires to list his property for sale with you at $38,000. Before accepting the listing, you make a careful appraisal of the property and it amounts to $29,500. You offer to list it at $30,000. The owner insists on listing it and advertising it at $38,000, and agrees to pay the advertising costs. Should you accept the listing?

A. No. An unrealistic listing will not sell and the broker will save time and effort by not accepting the listing.

70. Q. List the requirements, before you can legally enforce the payment of a real estate commission.

A. 1. Be licensed as a broker.
   2. Be employed by the owner.
   3. Obtain a purchaser, ready, willing, and able to buy upon the owner's terms.

71. Q. What points should an exclusive listing cover?

    A. Description of property, price, terms, encumbrances, definite period for which listing is binding, agreement to pay a commission in case of sale, and witnessed signatures of owners.

72. Q. How, if at all, should a broker go about negotiating a sale of property listed exclusively by another broker?

    A. Contact the listing broker and operate through him only.

73. Q. A broker holding a listing on a property secures from a prospect a deposit and a signed agreement to purchase. What two steps should he take next?

    A. 1. Deliver three signed copies to seller for acceptance.

        2. If accepted, leave one signed copy with the seller, deliver one copy (signed) to buyer and retain one for himself.

74. Q. What is the difference, if any, between a "client" and a "customer"?

    A. A customer transacts business with a real estate broker but does not retain his services.

    A client is one who retains services of broker to represent his interest in real estate.

75. Q. A broker fails to renew his license by July 1, 1968. Then he continues to operate and does not renew his license until July 14, 1968. On July 5 he completes a transaction and retains his commission. The owner of the property demands that he receive the full amount including that portion retained by the broker for his commission. Can a broker collect a commission under these circumstances?

    A. No. He was not licensed and not legally operating as a licensed broker at the date the sale was made.

76. Q. Tucker, a broker, sees a "For Sale" sign on Boyer's home and brings Davis, a prospective purchaser, to the property and introduces him to Boyer. Davis buys the property and Tucker claims a commission. Will he recover?

    A. No. Tucker is a "volunteer" and cannot show a contract of employment with the owner. Buyer may well believe that Tucker was the representative of Davis.

77. Q. Smith, a broker, has a customer for a warehouse. He contacts an official of a manufacturing building and inquires if the company will consider the sale of one of its buildings. The officer replies in the affirmative and states a price of $30,000. Smith introduces his customer to the official and later a sale is made. Is the broker entitled to commission from the company?

    A. No. The broker is unable to establish that he was employed by the seller, which is a prerequisite to recovery.

78. Q. In the general function of an appointed property manager are a number of specific duties. List briefly the specific duties which you consider the most important.

    A. 1. Determine proper schedule of rents.

        2. Secure desirable tenants.

3. Collect rentals.

4. Render service; provide for building maintenance and repairs.

5. Keep adequate accounts.

6. Study to increase efficiency.

7. Assist in planning space, etc.

79. Q. A broker obtained a written contract of employment from an owner on January 3, 1968, which provided: "This agency shall continue 30 days from date hereof and thereafter until three days have elapsed after receipt of written notice from the Owner, terminating this agency, sent by registered mail, or delivered in person to said agent." On June 8, 1968, the legislature passed an act which provided that the practice of demanding or receiving a fee under agreements which contain no definite termination date is ground for revocation of a license. The question arose whether the act was retroactive so as to invalidate the agency employment. Decide.

A. The act is operative. The general rule is that the legislature cannot pass a law which impairs the obligation of a contract. The California appellate court held that it is equally well settled that the legislature, in the exercise of its police power, may regulate the conduct of business, and every contract is made in subordination to that authority and must yield to its control.

80. Q. What is a listing?

A. A detailed record of property listed with a broker for sale or rent.

81. Q. A prospect desires to purchase property listed with a broker at $26,000 and proposes two offers, one at $23,000 and the second for the full price of $26,000. The second offer is to be submitted, however, only in the event that the owner rejects the first offer. Should the broker take two offers in this matter?

A. No. He must be loyal to his principal and should inform the prospective purchaser that he can only submit the offer at $26,000.

82. Q. Why should a broker purchasing a property from an owner disclose his personal purchase?

A. Acting as a principal is incompatible with a broker's employment as an agent in a fiduciary capacity.

83. Q. A broker has a 30-day exclusive listing. He advertises the property extensively at his own expense, but is unable to produce a buyer within 30 days. Two days after the exclusive expires, the seller negotiates a deal direct. The broker sues for a commission on the grounds that the deal had been made as a result of his advertising. Can he recover?

A. No. This is a risk which the broker assumes when he advertises and is unable to obtain a buyer during the period of his exclusive agency.

84. Q. Adams gives Bair a written exclusive listing for 60 days. Adams dies during the 60-day period. Is the agency cancelled?

   A. Yes. Death automatically cancels the agency, unless it is coupled with an interest.

85. Q. Adam Blake is licensed as an individual broker. He obtains a listing from Joe P. Brown on January 4, 1969. He then decides to incorporate. A charter is granted on February 18, 1969 and all of the assets of Blake (including listings) are transferred to the corporation, Enterprise Realty Co. A sale of the subject property is made on March 15, 1969 and a license is issued to the corporation on March 17, 1969. Brown refuses to pay any commission. Can Blake, individually, or the corporation recover?

   A. No; the corporation, not Blake, made the sale. The corporation was not licensed when the sale was made.

86. Q. Is it good practice to include the "carry over" clause in a listing contract that "if the property is sold within 6 months to any person to whom the broker showed the property," the broker is entitled to a commission?

   A. No. The broker might be the procuring cause of the sale without ever actually showing the property to a prospect.

87. Q. If the listing contract is ambiguous, how will the courts construe it?

   A. Most strongly against the broker, because he prepared it.

88. Q. In the "carry over" clause in a listing, various terms are used such as "any person with whom you had negotiations," "submitted the property to," "had contact with," "showed the property to," "on information given, received, or obtained through this agency," "to any prospect secured by you," or "to any person with whom you have been dealing." Which of the above terms are acceptable from the standpoint of fair practice?

   A. "With whom you had negotiations."

89. Q. Kentucky requires a listing contract to be in writing. Plaintiff broker sued for a $750 commission and relied on a sales agreement signed by the seller and buyer, which contained a printed clause that the property was sold "through Bud's Hamilton Realty Auction Co." Could the plaintiff recover on this writing as a contract?

   A. In the case of *Hamilton v. Booth*, 332 S.W. 2d 252 (Ky. 1960), the Court held that broker could not recover on this writing between seller and buyer.

90. Q. Nebraska requires a listing contract to be in writing. A contract of sale contained a clause "I further agree to pay the above named agent the cash commission agreed upon in the amount of $3,500." At the bottom left-hand side, underneath Witness, broker signed "Bill B. Svoboda." Does the broker have a written contract of employment?

A. Lower court held against broker. The Supreme Court reversed: *Svoboda v. DeWald*, 159 Neb. 594 (1955). The appellate court found that the writing complied with the requirements of the Statute, in that 1. it was in writing; 2. contained a description of the property; 3. commission to be paid; and 4. it was signed by the parties.

91. Q. A property is listed with a broker at $12,000. He feels it is a bargain and after one week, he has an agreement of sale signed by his wife's mother. The broker has no buyer in mind at that time. Six months after the deal is closed, the broker sells the property for $14,000. Is the broker guilty of misconduct?

A. Yes; in failing to disclose his true interest in the transaction. There is nothing wrong in a broker buying property listed with him for sale, if he feels it is a good buy, so long as he acts "above board" and lets the owner know his true position in the situation.

92. Q. Steiner owned a property upon which there was a mortgage, delinquent in a large amount. He gave an exclusive listing on the property to Stoner for 90 days, hoping to salvage something from a sale. During the 90-day period, the owner and the mortgagee resolved their differences by having the owner give the mortgagee a voluntary deed in return for a cash payment of $500. The broker claimed a commission on the value of the property (listing price). Could he recover?

A. Yes; the Court held that it was a voluntary sale based upon a valuable consideration, so that the broker was entitled to his commission.

93. Q. Woodruff gave a six months' exclusive listing on his property to Woodring. During the exclusive period, the state instituted condemnation proceedings against the property and made an award of $40,000. Is the broker entitled to a commission?

A. No; it was an involuntary sale, for which the owner was in no way responsible.

94. Q. Hoyle lists his property for sale with Doyle, a good friend who is a member of a multi-list association. It is sold by Boyle, a fellow member. Upon Hoyle's refusal to pay the commission, Boyle sues him. Can he recover?

A. No. There is no privity of contract (employment) between Hoyle and Boyle.

95. Q. What is meant by the "carry over" clause in an exclusive contract?

A. It is the clause which reads, in effect, that if a sale or exchange is made within six (6) months after the exclusive period has expired, to any person with whom the broker had been negotiating or "dealing," he is entitled to his commission.

96. Q. Would it be proper for a real estate salesman to negotiate for the sale of property with the parents of minors who are lawful owners?

A. No. The proper party with whom to negotiate would be the guardian of the minors; who may also be the parents.

97. Q. On or about April 26, 1969, the owner listed his property for sale exclusively (orally) until "on or about the 15th day of June" on which date defendant anticipated removing with his family to Miami, Florida. Plaintiff advertised the property and showed the property. On May 20th, it was sold through another broker. Is the plaintiff entitled to recover a commission?

A. Yes. (*Werder v. Browne*, 78 GA. App. 587.) The Court held that the alleged date on which the contract was to come to an end was not so vague and indefinite as to render the contract void and unenforceable. The date of removing to Miami was a definite time capable of being sustained by proof.

98. Q. Plaintiff broker sued for $2625 commission in connection with the sale of a motor court on U. S. Highway, south of Savannah. The broker failed to plead that he was a licensed broker. Was this fatal to his claim?

A. Yes. (*Lynes Realty Co. v. Mays*, 80 Ga. App. 4.)

99. Q. Should a listing contract authorize a broker to execute a binding contract of sale for the owner?

A. No.

100. Q. An exclusive listing of a house is obtained by Adam Boyer and/or Fairplay Realty Company, a corporation, on April 2, 1969. Boyer is licensed at the time but the corporation (Boyer, President) is not licensed until May 13, 1969. The property was sold during the period of the exclusive listing. Boyer sued for commission on the sale. Can he recover? Reasons.

A. No; the listing is *several* and since the corporation was not licensed when the deal started, neither the corporation nor Boyer can recover.

101. Q. A licensed broker sued an owner for a commission upon an employment contract that the seller was to obtain "$125,000 cash or better, or $125,000 with *reasonable* financing." The broker obtained a responsible buyer who was willing to pay $55,000 cash and execute a $70,000 purchase money mortgage, payable within 10 years, with interest at 5%. The seller refused to accept the deal. Is the broker entitled to his commission? Discuss.

A. Yes; broker's deal would constitute "reasonable financing." Contract did not say "satisfactory financing," therefore, the broker can recover.

102. Q. An owner gave an exclusive listing to a licensed broker to sell his property for $100,000, with a cash payment of $29,000 and "terms to suit." The broker produced a buyer who agreed to pay $5,000 down, $24,000 in cash at the closing, "10 lots to be released from the purchase money mortgage for the balance; thereafter lots to be released in groups of 10 for additional payments of $4,900, until the full purchase price has been paid."

The owner refused to sign the agreement and the broker sued for commission. Can broker recover commission?

A. No; terms are "to suit" seller. He need not be satisfied with any deal broker negotiates. The contract is too indefinite. Broker cannot recover.

103. Q. Fred Lane signs a written exclusive right to sell listing with the Rucker Agency on April 9, 1969 for a period of three months. During the exclusive period, Lane sells the property himself. Rucker sues for a commission. Lane defends on the grounds that it was verbally agreed between him and Rucker that if he sold the property himself during the exclusive period, no commission would be due Rucker. Is this a good defense?

A. No. Under the Parol Evidence Rule, oral testimony cannot be introduced to vary or contradict a written instrument, except for fraud, accident or mistake. Lane would have to allege and prove that the oral understanding was fraudulently omitted from the written listing.

104. Q. Stone, a broker, sues both the seller, Adams, and the buyer, Baker, for commissions in an exchange deal. Baker admitted that he knew of the dual employment. Adams emphatically denied knowledge. The broker claimed that both parties knew of the dual agency and there was no unfairness, double dealing, fraud or damages to the parties. Can the broker recover from Adams; can he recover from Baker?

A. He cannot recover from either. The rule of law is that a broker cannot recover from either of his principals unless *both* with knowledge of, consented to and acquiesced in such employment.

105. Q. Broker Hayes negotiated a deal between Stevens, seller, and Todd, buyer. After the agreements were signed, Hayes gave Todd permission to fill in some of the subject property, which was to be used for parking. The deal fell through and Todd now sues Hayes for $725, cost of fill in and paving. Can he recover?

A. Yes. Hayes is a special agent, with only limited authority to obtain a buyer. He exceeded his authority when he authorized the buyer to fill in and pave the lot. He is personally liable for the buyer's expense.

106. Q. Eaton lists his property for sale with Foster for $15,000. After some efforts, Foster is unable to sell the property and he then offers to buy the property at $14,000. Eaton agrees to sell at that price. Within three weeks, and before the deal is closed, Foster sells the property for $24,000. After both deals are closed, Eaton learns of the $24,000 sale, and sues Foster for the profit. He claims that the broker made an unconscionable profit, was guilty of bad faith and breached his duty of loyalty to his principal. Can he recover?

A. No. The parties acted as principals. So long as the agent did not conceal anything from his principal while he was acting as an agent, he owes no duty to the former owner after he acquires ownership in good faith.

107. Q. Beatty lists certain property with Coleman for sale at $40,000. He informs the broker that the property contains 3.5 acres. Coleman obtains a signed offer from Dixon at that price, which Beatty accepts. The agreement states 3.5 acres "more or less." The recorded deed description measures 2.5 acres. This is confirmed by a survey. Dixon demands a refund of his deposit money. Beatty refuses, relying on the "more or less" clause in the agreement. Decide.

A. Dixon will win. "More or less" is no defense, where there is a substantial difference in the acreage. A one acre discrepancy in a three and one-half tract is substantial.

108. Q. Alberts owned a vacant tract of land. He arranged with Bates, a broker, that the latter would have the engineering work done to lay out the land into a 40 lot subdivision. Bates was to have the exclusive sale of the lots for a three year period. At the end of the first year, few lots have been sold and Alberts desires to terminate the agency. Can he do so?

A. No. The agency is coupled with an interest and cannot be revoked; even if Alberts died during the three year period, the agency would still continue.

True and False

1. The broker generally pays for advertising a property for sale. **T** F
2. If a broker has an exclusive agency listing, he can recover a commission if the owner sells the property himself during the term of the listing. T **F**
3. A broker managing real estate is entitled to any secret rebates, so long as he does not pay more than the market price for any item. T **F**
4. The contract giving employment to the broker is known as the listing contract. **T** F
5. A salesman, who leaves his broker, may take all of his listings to his new broker. T **F**
6. A licensed salesman may divide his commission with another licensed salesman with his broker's consent. T **F**
7. He could, with the *other* broker's consent. T **F**
8. A listing contract which authorizes the broker to sign a contract of sale for the seller is unusual. **T** F
9. A broker employing 10 or more salesmen must have a sales manager. T **F**
10. The principal in a listing contract is the seller. **T** F
11. The State Real Estate Board or Commission has authority to fix 6 per cent as the rate of commission on real estate. T **F**
12. A broker is obligated to advise a seller of his responsibility

to pay such loan discount (points) as is imposed when the sales contract calls for F.H.A. or G.I. financing. **T** F

13. A listing contract without a definite expiration date is not valid in all states. **T** F

14. The duration of a listing contract, in the absence of a specified period, is determined by the Statute of Frauds. T **F**

15. "Earnest money" is the commission which the broker receives in the deal. T **F**

16. "Realtor" is the term used by a broker after he successfully negotiates a deal. T **F**

17. A contract between two brokers to cooperate on a real estate deal need not be in writing. **T** F

18. A broker may pay compensation only to his salesmen and to licensed brokers. **T** F

19. A straight salary may be paid by a broker to an unlicensed person who only solicits listings. T **F**

20. All listing contracts should be made in triplicate so that there are copies for the buyer, seller and broker. T **F**

21. The broker generally pays the fee for recording a deed. T **F**

22. The Real Estate Commission determines the rate of commission to be charged for selling real property. T **F**

23. A listing contract is ended if the salesman who obtained the listing dies. T **F**

24. An open listing is a listing in which the sales price is not set. T **F**

25. An "exclusive" listing is preferable to an "open listing." **T** F

26. A broker should close the deals negotiated by his salesmen. **T** F

27. An exclusive listing contract on real property would not be valid for a period longer than six months. T **F**

28. A seller can refuse to pay a broker an earned commission when he discovers that the buyer is also paying the broker a commission. **T** F

29. A salesman should understand the law of principal and agent. **T** F

30. A salesman, who solicits listings, but does not sell, is not required to have a real estate license. T **F**

31. There is no statutory lien for a broker's unpaid commission. **T** F

32. The usual "open listing" provides for the payment of a commission to the broker who lists the property first and an additional compensation to the broker who sells it. T **F**

33. A broker should deliver voluntarily a copy of the authorization-to-sell contract to the owner who signed. **T** F

34. A broker who has not been employed by the owner can recover a commission, if he obtains a buyer whom the owner accepts. T **F**

35. A salesman may not divide his commissions with the salesman of another broker. **T** F

36. A listing contract might be renewed after its expiration date. **T** F

37. A broker may not represent more than one party to a transaction unless he so advises both of them and has their consent. **T** F
38. A broker who asks for a listing "until sold" offends good real estate ethics. **T** F
39. A listing contract is terminated by the death of the owner. **T** F
40. If a real estate broker has no written listing, he may collect a commission if he can produce two witnesses to the transaction. T **F**
41. The fact that the person who signed the listing did not own the property is no defense in an action for a real estate commission. **T** F
42. It is not important to specify the amount of commission to be charged for the sale of property because that is fixed by law. T **F**
43. It is unlawful to charge a commission for the sale of improved real estate in excess of 6 per cent of the sale price. T **F**
44. Commission for sale of real estate is determined by agreement between the parties. **T** F
45. Procuring listings by house to house solicitation is beneath the dignity of a broker. **T** F
46. It is unlawful for a real estate salesman to receive compensation for the sale of property from anyone except the broker with whom he is licensed. **T** F
47. A salesman should advertise the sale of real estate in his own name. T **F**
48. Placing "Sold" signs on property sold by a broker is one of the best ways of securing new listings. **T** F
49. It is best that a broker accept nothing but exclusive listings. **T** F
50. An exclusive agency is preferable to an exclusive right-to-sell contract. T **F**
51. The law obligates every agent to act in and for the best interest of his employer. **T** F
52. A salesman selling his own property or that of the broker by whom he is employed should inform the prospective buyer of that fact. **T** F
53. A person who answers the broker's ad and looks at the real estate with idea of purchasing same is the broker's client. T **F**
54. Employment of a broker to find a tenant for real estate need not be in writing to be enforceable. **T** F
55. An agreement employing a real estate broker is terminated by the death of the owner prior to procuring a purchaser, ready, able, and willing to buy on owner's terms. **T** F
56. A real estate broker is required to use ordinary diligence to keep his employer advised of his actions in the course of his agency. **T** F
57. It is lawful for a broker to agree with the tenant of a house, which the broker has for sale, to pay the tenant a part of the

commission if the tenant will show the property to any prospect of the broker who later buys the property.   T **F**

58. An exclusive listing and a net listing are the same and the terms may be used interchangeably.   T **F**

59. If an oral listing agreed upon has no expiration date, it remains in effect a reasonable time.   **T** F

60. If a broker has an exclusive agent agreement, he may recover a commission from the owner if the owner sells the property himself during the term of the listing.   T **F**

61. An "exclusive listing" means one confined to a single piece of real estate.   T **F**

62. An owner cannot refuse to sign a sales agreement when the broker employed by him obtains a buyer upon the seller's terms.   T **F**

63. A salesman cannot collect a commission in his own name and divide it with his broker.   **T** F

64. A real estate broker and a real estate salesman may not enter into a partnership.   **T** F

65. A principal is the employer of a broker.   **T** F

66. A broker's client and a broker's prospect are one and the same.   T **F**

67. A defrauded client has no right of court action against a broker but must sue the surety company, if the broker is bonded.   T **F**

68. Commission rates to be charged on real property sales are limited to a certain scale by the legislature.   T **F**

69. If a broker has real estate for sale and finds a prospect willing to take an option to purchase the property at the price stated, the broker is entitled to a commission.   T **F**

70. Commission rates are usually fixed by the local real estate board.   **T** F

71. A salesman licensed under one broker may deal directly with another broker and obtain a commission from the second broker.   T **F**

72. Under no circumstances can a broker collect a commission from the buyer.   T **F**

73. Solicitations of listing by house to house canvas is unethical. **T** F

74. An exclusive listing refers to a single tract of land.   T **F**

75. From the owner's standpoint, an exclusive agency contract is preferable to an exclusive right to sell listing.   **T** F

76. It is unlawful for a broker to give part of his commission to the buyer for the purchase of a new electric range.   **T** F

77. A real estate broker under an agency acts in a fiduciary relationship to his principal.   **T** F

78. In real estate a broker usually acts for and on behalf of the owner or seller.   **T** F

79. If you have real estate listed for sale and find a prospect

ready, willing, and able to take an option to purchase the property on the terms at which the property is offered, you have earned and are entitled to a commission. **T F**

80. The use of a listing form which also contains an option agreement between owner (seller) and broker is not considered good practice. **T** F

81. A net listing or an exclusive contract to sell a parcel of real estate at a net price to the owner makes the broker an optionee. **T F**

82. A broker accepting a net listing to sell a piece of real property should not accept any compensation from the purchaser unless he reveals this fact to the seller. **T** F

83. An exclusive listing contract on real property would not be valid for a period longer than 90 days. **T F**

84. An agent is the "alter ego" of his principal. **T** F

85. It is proper for a broker to buy an interest in a property listed with him without making the fact known to the listing owner. **T F**

86. It is unlawful for a broker to purchase property listed with him in the name of a "straw" man. **T** F

87. An owner should always be given a copy of the exclusive contract he signs. **T** F

88. An agreement between brokers to split a commission need not be in writing. **T** F

89. A broker usually acts for and in behalf of the purchaser. **T F**

90. When no rate of commission is stated in a listing, and the property is sold, the usual or customary rate which is charged in that locality is used. **T** F

91. A listing obtained exclusively by one firm only for a limited period of time is called an exclusive listing. **T** F

92. If a salesman's name is used in advertising property for sale, the ad should also contain the name and address of the broker. **T** F

93. A real estate broker holding a 60-day exclusive agency to sell a parcel of real estate, may continue his efforts to sell such property even though the owner died during the 60-day period. **T F**

94. A real estate salesman, having consummated a sale of real property, has the choice of demanding his share of the commissions earned, either from the broker employing him or the seller, who for some personal reason refuses to pay the broker. **T F**

95. A real estate broker holding a 60-day exclusive agency to sell a parcel of real property may, without disclosing the relationships, sell the property to his wife and receive a commission for such sale. **T F**

96. A real estate broker is entitled to a commission for the con-

summation of a sale of real property upon the asking price
set by the seller even though he was in a position to obtain
another purchaser willing to pay more than the asking price. T **F**

97. An owner is under no obligation to pay a commission to the
broker when it is ascertained, after the execution of the
contract of purchase, that the purchaser was induced to
enter into the contract of purchase because of some misrepresentations made by the broker.   **T** F

98. Where a broker introduces a purchaser to an owner, whose
property is listed with the broker, the broker is entitled to
a commission if a sale follows through direct negotiations
between the principals.   **T** F

99. Where the property is listed at a price of $25,000 or higher,
the broker's employment must be in writing.   T **F**

100. A broker cannot collect a commission unless he obtains a
contract signed by the buyer.   T **F**

101. The broker who first calls the buyer's attention to the property is the one entitled to the commission.   T **F**

102. When deposit money is received by the broker, he may use
such money for his personal account up to the amount of
his commission as soon as it seems reasonable to expect the
closing of the deal.   T **F**

103. Brokers employing salesmen are relieved of all responsibility
for the acts of the salesmen if the salesmen are bonded.   T **F**

104. The real estate salesman should not be concerned with the
restrictions attaching to a property while attempting to ne-
gotiate its sale.   T **F**

105. A salesman transferring to another broker is entitled to take
with him the listings which he obtained personally while
working for the first broker.   T **F**

106. All brokers are members of the National Association of Real
Estate Brokers.   T **F**

107. A real estate salesman must be at least 21 years of age.   **T** **F**

108. Listings obtained by a real estate salesman are considered
to be the salesman's own personal property.   T **F**

109. In an integrated association, every licensed broker would
be a member of the state real estate association.   **T** F

110. A real estate listing may be taken in the name of a salesman
so long as the transaction is closed in the name of the broker. T **F**

111. A broker employed to obtain a purchaser can sign an agree-
ment of sale for the owner, which would be enforceable.   T **F**

112. A broker is entitled to a commission under a properly drawn
"exclusive right-to-sell listing," if the owner sells the prop-
erty himself during the term of the listing.   **T** F

113. If owner and broker have not expressly agreed upon the rate
of commission, the broker is entitled to recover on a "quan-
tum meruit" basis, if he makes the deal.   **T** F

114. A salesman may deduct his share of the commission from a down payment before turning it over to the broker. T **F**

115. The commission rate for selling real property is usually at the same rate as for leasing. T **F**

116. Where an owner lists a property for sale with a broker "at a sale for not less than $5,000," the broker is entitled to $1,000 commission if he sells the property for $6,000. T **F**

117. If an owner lists a property for sale with one broker, he cannot employ another broker to sell the same property unless the first broker withdraws. T **F**

118. An agency to sell real estate usually comes under the Statute of Frauds. T **F**

119. Where a property is listed for sale with the broker at $7,000, and a sale is made to the broker's prospect at $5,000, the broker is entitled to a commission. **T** F

120. Every real estate contract negotiated by a broker should contain a clause recognizing the broker as the procuring cause of the sale. **T** F

121. A broker who initiates a deal is entitled to a commission if, a year later, a sale is made by the parties direct without the assistance of the broker. T **F**

122. A broker is the "efficient and procuring" cause of a sale when he procures a buyer, ready, able, and willing to buy. **T** F

123. A broker can compel the payment of his commission out of the proceeds of the deal at the time it is closed. T **F**

124. A broker may file a lien against the owner's real estate for an unpaid commission. T **F**

125. A listing contract containing a confession of judgment clause for the broker's commission is considered bad practice. **T** F

126. A commission agreed upon by broker and buyer will prevent the broker from collecting a commission from the seller. **T** F

127. Whether a broker is the efficient cause of a sale is a question of law and not of fact. T **F**

128. An exclusive agency contract permits the owner to sell without liability for a commission to the broker. **T** F

129. An unlicensed broker may collect a commission in the sale of real estate, by court action, if he has a signed exclusive listing from the seller. T **F**

130. A "post dated check" given for a deposit has the same effect as a N.S.F. check. T **F**

131. The broker who obtains the buyer's signature on the "dotted line" is the one entitled to a commission. T **F**

132. A broker has the legal right to render an opinion on the validity of title to real estate. T **F**

133. The commission to be charged for the sale of real estate is determined by the license law. T **F**

134. If you, a licensed real estate salesman, obtained a real estate

listing, and subsequently located a buyer for your listing, you would be within your rights under the real estate license law to close the transaction, so long as your broker received his rightful share of the commission.   T   **F**

135. It is lawful to charge more than five per cent commission in a real estate deal.   **T**   F

136. A broker may collect a commission from both parties in an exchange deal with their knowledge and consent.   **T**   F

137. In some cases, an owner may have so conducted himself as to be liable to two brokers in one real estate sale.   **T**   F

138. Where two brokers claim a commission in the sale of a house, the owner should pay the broker who makes the first claim.   T   **F**

139. Where two or more brokers claim a commission for the sale of the same property, the owner should pay the money into court.   **T**   F

140. A contract accompanied by hand money is not always *conclusive* evidence that the broker is entitled to the commission.   **T**   F

141. Where a broker obtains a signed agreement of sale and has an exclusive right to sell contract, the owner must sign the agreement of sale.   T   **F**

142. Most prospects are alert to observe misrepresentations of salesmen and brokers.   **T**   F

143. A satisfied customer for a home represents economic justification for a broker.   **T**   F

144. In order to protect his commission, it is advisable for a broker to draw up a contract of sale.   **T**   F

145. A contract of employment which cannot be completed in one year must be in writing.   T   **F**

146. A broker may be held responsible for representing property as "the most quiet spot in the world."   T   **F**

147. Placing a "For Sale" sign upon vacant property without the owner's authority constitutes unethical conduct.   **T**   F

148. In order to secure a listing of property to sell, it would be permissible to give a friend a ten dollar bill to assist you in securing the listing.   T   **F**

149. A broker is entitled to his commission if he produces a buyer ready, willing, and able to meet the terms proposed by the seller in his listing, even if the owner refuses to go through with the deal.   **T**   F

150. A broker usually does not require the signatures of both husband and wife on an "authorization to sell" their community property.   T   **F**

151. A "key lot" is the most desirable lot on which to build a residence in any subdivision.   T   **F**

152. Quantum Meruit means the reasonable value of a broker's services.   **T**   F

153. In a suit upon a "quantum meruit" basis, the broker seeks to recover the usual or prevailing rate of commission. **T** F

154. An escrow company may be fined for paying commissions to any unlicensed person. **T** F

155. The data on the reverse side of a listing contract constitutes a part of the employment contract. **T** F

156. Failure to give an owner a copy of the listing contract prevents the broker from recovering his commission. T **F**

157. A broker may purchase property listed with him for sale if he informs the seller he is acting as a principal. **T** F

158. A broker who has been refused a commission can block a sale if he notifies the title company or escrow company, in writing, of his commission claim. T **F**

159. A broker has a right to file a Mechanic's Lien for his unpaid commission. T **F**

160. A salesman cannot sue an owner direct for his share of the commission. **T** F

161. A bilateral listing contract is preferable to a unilateral contract from the broker's standpoint. **T** F

162. A broker who has failed to show the buyer the property listed with him, cannot recover a commission. T **F**

163. A broker is a nonproductive element of goods in our society. T **F**

164. Inquiry of a seller as to price and availability for sale does not constitute a contract of employment. **T** F

165. Three different actions may be brought against a broker who makes a secret profit at the expense of his principal. **T** F

166. Where two real estate closings occur at the same time, the broker may close one deal and his salesman the other. T **F**

167. A broker is a special agent and not a general agent of his principal. **T** F

168. A real estate broker's commission is deemed to have been earned by him at the closing of title. T **F**

169. Open listing means the price is not set. T **F**

170. Experts agree that an advertising budget should not exceed 10% of gross commission. **T** F

171. A real estate broker holding a sixty-day exclusive agency to sell a parcel of real property should discontinue his efforts to sell such property if the owner dies during the sixty-day period. **T** F

172. When the sales contract calls for FHA or GI financing, the broker is required to advise the seller that he is obligated to pay discount points on the loan. **T** F

173. All full time brokers are Realtors. T **F**

174. Whenever a broker is authorized to negotiate for the sale of property, he is also authorized to accept a deposit. T **F**

175. If a real estate broker failed to disclose the identity of his prospective customer, and if the negotiations failed, and the

purchaser sought out the owner and consummated the deal
direct, the broker would not be entitled to his commission.   **T**   F
176. A real estate broker should never act as an escrow holder
in transactions covering property in which he personally
owns an interest.   **T**   F
177. A real estate broker is entitled to a commission for the consummation of a sale of real property for the asking price
set by the seller, even though he was in a position to obtain another purchaser willing to pay more than the asking
price.   T   **F**
178. It is unethical for a licensee to advise that the asking price
of the seller is too high or too low.   T   **F**
179. A broker should not bother an owner by submitting an offer
which the broker considers ridiculously low.   T   **F**
180. The listing employment contract should be signed by the
salesman who obtained the listing.   T   **F**
181. A Real Estate Commission may sell real estate without a
license.   T   **F**
182. "Puffing of goods" as applied to real estate means extravagant
statements regarding the desirability of the property.   **T**   F
183. A gives B, a broker, an exclusive listing on March 21, 1969
for 90 days. B dies on April 24, 1969. The listing is cancelled. **T**   F
184. A listing by a minor is voidable by him.   **T**   F
185. A listing which provides for a 15 per cent commission is void. T   **F**
186. The National Association of Real Estate Boards regulates the
rate of commission to be charged.   T   **F**
187. In a multi-list association, the listing broker and the selling
broker usually receive an equal amount of the commission.   T   **F**
188. "Caveat emptor" relieves an owner or broker from any misrepresentation.   T   **F**
189. In a multi-list association, the selling broker generally has no
right to sue the owner for a commission.   **T**   F
190. A selling broker is a subagent of the listing broker.   **T**   F
191. A broker's suit for commission is based on privity of contract
with the owner.   **T**   F
192. Brokerage is the most profitable segment of the ordinary
licensee's business.   **T**   F
193. The usual listing contract, employing the broker "to sell" the
property, authorizes the broker to sign the contract of sale. T   **F**
194. An owner-builder of more than 20 houses requires a broker's
license.   T   **F**
195. The penalty for selling real estate without a license is the
same as paying a commission to an unlicensed person.   T   **F**
196. The law does not require a person to obtain a license for
negotiating a sale until the contract is signed by the parties. T   **F**
197. A person may call himself a Realtor once he passes the state
licensing examination.   T   **F**

198. A salesman owes a prospect the duty to disclose the lowest price the seller will take, if it is considerably less than the listing price.　　T **F**

199. A property is listed at $15,000. The broker tells the buyer that he knows the owner will accept $13,000. The prospect offers $13,000, which is accepted. The broker has violated his duty to the owner.　　**T** F

200. A salesman negotiates a deal and witnesses the signatures of buyer and seller. The seller's prime duty is to pay the salesman the commission.　　T **F**

201. The salesman should close the deal negotiated by him, since he has dealt with both buyer and seller.　　T **F**

Multiple Choice

1. A salesman receiving a deposit should
   ( ) Place it in his "Special Account."
   ( ) Place it in the broker's general account.
   (x) Turn it over to his broker.

2. Two rival brokers claim the commission in a real estate deal. Broker "A" sues the owner. The owner should
   ( ) pay the broker with whom the property was listed.
   (x) pay the money into court (interpleader).
   ( ) pay each broker one half.

3. In listing property for sale, which item is *not* necessary for a valid exclusive listing agreement?
   ( ) Date of listing.
   ( ) Address of property.
   (x) Legal description.
   ( ) Listing period.

4. Another broker has a listing on a property you desire to show a prospect. Which one of the following should you do?
   ( ) Call the local Real Estate Board.
   ( ) Wait until the other broker's listing expires.
   (x) Get in touch with the other broker and ask his permission to show the property.
   ( ) Show your prospect the property and then call the owner for a listing.

5. A real estate listing is
   ( ) A list of all property held by one owner.
   (x) Employment of a broker by owner to sell or lease real property.
   ( ) A written list of improvements on the land.
   ( ) A rendition of property for taxation.

6. An agent is one employed by a
   ( ) Salesman.
   (x) Principal.
   ( ) Master.

( ) Broker.
7. All real estate listed for sale by a broker should be advertised in the name of the
   ( ) seller.
   ( ) salesman who obtains listing.
   ( ) salesman on the premises.
   (x) principal licensed broker.
8. What is the maximum commission rate that a broker may charge on the sale of improved property?
   ( ) 6%.
   ( ) 5%.
   ( ) 10%.
   (x) Any rate agreed upon by agent and principal.
9. An agency coupled with an interest is one
   (x) that cannot be terminated before its expiration date.
   ( ) where broker makes a secret profit at the expense of his principal.
   ( ) where broker receives interest-bearing note in payment of his commission.
   ( ) where a suit is filed for commission, which constitutes a lien on the real estate.
10. It is possible for an owner to have more than one agent in a certain situation, such as
   ( ) an open listing contract.
   (x) multiple listing.
   ( ) a non-exclusive listing.
   ( ) a general listing.
11. The first step necessary for a licensed broker to recover a commission is to
   ( ) find a buyer.
   ( ) find a seller.
   (x) have a contract of employment.
   ( ) advertise the property for sale.
12. In the real estate business another term for principal is
   ( ) customer.
   ( ) prospect.
   (x) client.
   ( ) alter ego.
13. The relationship of a licensed real estate broker to his principal is that of a
   ( ) trustee.
   ( ) salesman.
   (x) fiduciary.
   ( ) beneficiary.
14. A contract authorizing the sale of real property which is signed by a minor is
   (x) Voidable.

( ) Terminated.
( ) Void.
( ) Valid.

15. A valid listing on community property must be given by
( ) Agent and buyer.
(x) Husband and wife.
( ) Buyer and seller.
( ) Broker and salesman.

16. A prospect, to whom a broker shows the property, ordinarily has a right to rely upon the broker's representations as to
( ) Title.
( ) Future prospects.
( ) All statements made by the broker regarding the property.
(x) Past rentals of the property.

17. Which one of the following funds should not be placed in the real estate trustee account?
( ) Earnest monies.
( ) Rental collections.
( ) Installment land contract collections.
(x) Insurance premiums.

18. A broker is holding an earnest money deposit, equal to the amount of his commission. The seller, at the closing, not only refuses to pay the broker a commission but demands that the broker pay him the entire deposit money. The broker should
( ) refuse to permit the closing of the deal.
( ) retain the earnest money as his commission.
( ) file a complaint with the Real Estate Commission.
(x) pay the earnest money to the seller and then sue, if necessary, for his commission.

19. In the absence of a prior agreement as to when the broker's commission is earned, such commission is earned at
( ) consummation of the deal.
(x) meeting of the minds of buyer and seller.
( ) time broker introduced buyer to seller.
( ) when deed is delivered.

20. An owner lists a property for sale with a broker at $10,000, who finds a purchaser who is willing to pay $11,500 for the property. The broker should
( ) report the sale to the owner on the basis of the $10,000 listing and keep the $1,500 as his commission.
(x) report the sales price to the owner and take commission on the $11,500.
( ) figur his commission on $10,000 and divide the $1,500 excess equally between owner and himself.
( ) buy the property himself at $10,000 and resell it to his buyer at $11,500.

21. A broker receiving a deposit from a purchaser should

( ) Give it to the owner.
( ) Deposit it immediately in his general office checking account.
( ) Deposit it in his personal account.
(x) Deposit it in a trust account at a bank.

22. Real estate listed for sale with a broker should be advertised in the name of
( ) The owner.
( ) The licensed broker.
( ) The salesman to whom the listing has been assigned.
(x) The broker and the salesman to whom assigned.

23. The amount of commission to be paid to a broker is fixed by
( ) law.
( ) State Real Estate Department.
(x) agreement of the parties.
( ) the local real estate board.

24. A real estate broker must bring an action in the courts to recover real estate commission within
( ) one year.
( ) four years.
(x) six years.
( ) ten years.

25. A contract which provides for the payment of a commission to a broker even though the owner makes a sale without the aid of the broker is called an
( ) exclusive listing.
( ) open listing.
( ) option.
(x) exclusive right to sell.

26. If an owner refuses to pay the broker a commission, the broker may
( ) file a complaint with the Real Estate Commission.
( ) file a lien against the real estate sold.
(x) bring court action.
( ) take out a bond.

27. When broker and salesman have a dispute over the commission upon a deal, they should
( ) complain to the owner.
(x) bring action in court.
( ) file a joint complaint to the Commission.
( ) compel arbitration.

28. An owner employs a broker to sell his real estate and promises to pay a commission; the broker brings about a sale on terms orally accepted by the owner so that the sale is fully consummated; under such circumstances the broker's employment is
(x) valid.
( ) void.
( ) voidable.

29. If a broker receives more than one worthy, bona fide offer for the same property at approximately the same time, he should

( ) submit only the highest offer.

(x) submit all offers to the owner.

( ) submit only the one he considers for the seller's best interest.

30. A broker is entitled to his commission when

   ( ) he lists the property.

   ( ) he has shown the property to several prospects.

   (x) he brings together a willing buyer upon the seller's terms.

31. To be enforceable a listing must be signed by

   ( ) broker.

   (x) seller.

   ( ) buyer.

   ( ) tenant.

32. The broker's fiduciary relationship with the client requires that

   ( ) he act as a reasonable and prudent person.

   ( ) he discuss all angles of each deal with his salesmen.

   (x) act in the highest and best interests of his client.

   ( ) he act commensurate with his compensation.

33. A broker receives an offer to purchase upon a form, which states: "This offer shall remain open irrevocably for a period of five days." On the third day, the prospective buyer notifies the broker he does not want the property and requests the return of his $500 deposit. The broker should:

   (x) return the deposit to the buyer.

   ( ) inform the buyer he must wait the full five days to see if the seller accepts.

   ( ) notify buyer he must go through with the deal.

34. "Ethics" most nearly means

   ( ) observing usual closing hours of other businesses.

   ( ) belonging to the proper civic clubs and community projects.

   (x) observing duties to clients, colleagues and public.

35. An exclusive listing is

   ( ) a listing given to several brokers.

   ( ) an implied listing.

   ( ) a listing on an exclusive or elegant property.

   ( ) a net listing.

   (x) a listing given to one broker only with an agreement not to list with other brokers during the term of the listing.

36. There are two ways of determining the amount of compensation a broker is to receive. One of these is

   ( ) by overage.

   ( ) by time and effort.

   ( ) by provisions of the real estate license law.

   ( ) by diligence.

   (x) by agreement.

37. A broker, Burns, represents and lists property of Adams for $5,000 cash sale. The broker finds a customer, Cox, who is willing to pay $6,500 cash. Burns should

   ( ) report the sale to the owner on the basis of the $5,000 listing and keep the $1,500 for his commission.

( ) provide a dummy purchaser, Drew, to purchase at the net price and then resell from Drew to Cox.

(x) report the total offer to owner and take commission on the $6,500.

( ) turn the offer down.

( ) buy the property himself at the net price and resell to Cox.

38. A broker, upon showing a client's property to a prospect, should

( ) make an office memorandum.

( ) confirm the interview by a memo to the buyer.

(x) notify the seller as to the prospect's identity.

( ) wait until the prospect makes the deal with the owner.

39. Which type of contract affords the broker the greatest protection?

( ) An open listing.

( ) An exclusive listing.

( ) A written listing.

(x) An exclusive right-to-sell listing.

40. A broker, who sells a property to a purchaser recommended by a friend, should

(x) thank the friend.

( ) buy the friend a suitable gift.

( ) give the friend half the commission.

( ) pay the friend 5 per cent of the commission.

41. An example of fiduciary relationship is that which exists between

( ) broker and prospect.

( ) broker and anyone he talks to about real estate.

(x) broker and client.

( ) broker and the Real Estate Commission.

( ) broker and salesman's prospect.

42. The broker must obey all instructions made known to him by his principal. Should the principal instruct the broker to violate the law, the broker should

( ) do as instructed.

( ) not do as instructed.

(x) withdraw from the transaction.

( ) sue the principal.

( ) do nothing.

43. Ash gives a written listing on certain property to broker, Brown, for sale on stipulated price and terms. Ash does not list this property with any other broker for 90 days.

(a) Brown has an exclusive listing.   T **F**

(b) Ash cannot sell the property to a buyer obtained through his own efforts.   T **F**

(c) If Ash sold this property to a purchaser produced by another broker, he would have to pay Brown a commission.   T F

(d) This listing does not create a fiduciary relation between Ash and Brown.   T **F**

44. A salesman obtains a binding offer in writing and is given a deposit of earnest money.
    (a) He should immediately turn contract and deposit over to the employing broker. **T** F
    (b) Should the offer not be accepted by the owner, the money should be returned to the prospective buyer. **T** F
    (c) If the offer is accepted by the owner and the owner thereafter refuses to or cannot deliver title, the broker should keep the deposit, or part of it, to pay him for his trouble. T **F**
    (d) Should the owner accept the offer and the prospective buyer fail to complete the sale for reasons of his own, the money should be divided equally between the broker and owner up to the amount of what the broker's commission would have been had the sale been completed. **T** F
    (e) If the face amount of the offer is considerably larger than the price in the listing, only the price stated in the listing should be offered the owner. The balance should be divided between the salesman and broker. T **F**

45. A broker may lawfully receive a commission from
    (a) the owner. **T** F
    (b) a co-broker. **T** F
    (c) both buyer and seller. T **F**

46. A contract which provides for the payment of a commission to a broker, even though the owner makes a sale without the aid of the broker, is called
    ( ) general listing.
    ( ) unilateral contract.
    ( ) bilateral contract.
    ( ) multiple listing.
    (x) exclusive right to sell.

47. A listing may be brought to an end in several ways. One of these is included in the following:
    ( ) regulation.
    ( ) reneging.
    ( ) regurgitation.
    (x) renunciation.

48. An authorization to a person to act for and in behalf of another in a real estate transaction is called
    ( ) an option.
    (x) a power of attorney.
    ( ) a reconveyance.
    ( ) an exclusive right of sale.

49. An unlicensed salesman negotiated the sale of real estate. The commission is payable to
    ( ) the broker.
    ( ) the salesman.

(x) no one.

( ) an escrow holder.

50. An attorney-in-fact is the holder of

( ) a certificate as an attorney-at-law.

(x) power of attorney.

( ) appointment by order of court.

( ) deed from a trustee under a will.

51. Two rival brokers claim the commission in a real estate transaction. It should be paid to

( ) the broker with whom the property was first listed.

(x) the broker who was the procuring cause.

52. A salesman may lawfully obtain listings when

( ) He obtains a broker who will employ him.

( ) The salesman's application has been filed.

(x) The broker receives the salesman's license from the Commission.

( ) The salesman has passed his examination.

53. A broker finds a purchaser, acceptable to his owner. After the agreements are signed, the buyer and seller agree not to consummate the deal. The broker

( ) Is not entitled to a commission.

( ) Is entitled to commission only upon the earnest money deposited.

( ) Is entitled to a full commission from the buyer.

(x) Can collect full commission from the seller.

54. An owner, who employs more than one broker at the same time, has given each broker

( ) Unilateral listing.

( ) A multiple listing.

(x) An open listing.

( ) An exclusive listing.

55. A broker's relation to an owner is governed by

( ) the law of equity.

(x) law of agency.

( ) respondent superior.

( ) investiture.

56. A printed advertisement for a new development, such as a subdivision is called a

( ) reservation.

(x) prospectus.

( ) nomenclature.

( ) origination.

57. A real estate salesman may lawfully accept an extra commission in a difficult sale from

( ) An appreciative seller.

( ) A thankful buyer.

(x) The broker-employer.

( ) The mortgage finance company.

58. A real estate listing is
   ( ) Real estate held for sale by auction.
   ( ) A list of all property held by one person for tax purposes.
   (x) Employment of a broker by an owner to sell or lease his property.
   ( ) An offer to buy property owned by a political subdivision.
59. A real estate salesman may lawfully pay a part of his commission to
   ( ) Any person.
   ( ) As a refund to the buyer.
   ( ) As a bonus to the seller for selling.
   ( ) Another licensee.
   (x) No one.
60. Salesman Sloan is licensed under broker Klaus but wants to work for broker Fair, so he
   ( ) May start selling for Fair as soon as he places his license on display in Fair's office.
   ( ) May start selling as soon as he notifies the Real Estate Commission of the change.
   ( ) May start selling if Klaus writes the Commission that he has no objection to the change.
   (x) May start selling for Fair as soon as the Real Estate Commission reissues his license to Fair.
61. An example of fiduciary relationship is that which exists between
   ( ) Broker and prospect.
   (x) Broker and client.
   ( ) Broker and his salesman's prospect.
   ( ) Broker and anyone.
62. Rose gave a written listing on certain property to broker Harris. Rose did not list this property for sale with any other broker for 90 days
   (x) Harris had an open listing.
   ( ) Harris had an exclusive listing for 90 days.
   ( ) Rose cannot sell the property himself for 90 days.
   ( ) If Rose sold the property through another broker during the 90 day period, he would have to pay Harris a commission.
63. The Realtor Code of Ethics recommends an
   ( ) Open listing.
   (x) Exclusive listing.
   ( ) Net listing.
   ( ) Parol listing.
64. When a broker shows a prospect a house listed with him for sale, he should
   ( ) Telephone the owner.
   ( ) Post the premises.
   (x) Give the owner written notice of prospect's identity.
   ( ) Send written notice to prospect.
65. A salesman can buy property listed for sale with his broker, where

( ) He takes title in name of another person.
( ) He takes title in name of his broker, in trust for the salesman.
(x) He discloses his intention to the owner.
( ) Notifies the Real Estate Commission in advance.

66. Under the usual employment contract, a broker is entitled to his commission when
( ) The deal is consummated.
(x) He produces a ready and willing buyer, upon seller's terms, even though the seller refuses to sign the agreement of sale.
(x) He produces a ready and willing buyer at the listing price of the property.

67. If a prospective seller asks a salesman at what price he should list his property for sale, the salesman should reply
( ) We will list at whatever price you suggest.
( ) At two and one-half times the assessed value.
(x) I will ask my broker to appraise it for you and list it at that figure.
( ) List it at 30 per cent above the present mortgage.

68. Whether to forfeit the deposit money, resell the property, or sue the buyer for performance, where the buyer defaults, is a matter for whom to decide?
( ) Broker.
(x) Vendor.
( ) Salesman.
( ) Independent agency.

Chapter 2

AGREEMENTS OF SALE

THE FUNCTION of a broker is to negotiate a valid contract of sale between his principal, the owner, and the buyer. In this connection the broker prepares the agreement of sale, which, to a large extent, makes the law by which seller and buyer are governed.

It is important that a real estate broker or salesman be fully cognizant of the responsibilities which he assumes in undertaking to draw an agreement of sale. The instrument fixes legal rights and obligations of the seller and the buyer. It must adequately protect his principal, the seller, and at the same time, protect the buyer, who may be engaging in his first real estate venture. A poorly drawn agreement of sale may not only lead to dissatisfaction and controversy, but to expensive litigation as well. In addition, the broker, who prepared the faulty agreement of sale, may find himself the defendant, not only in an action at law, but also in proceedings for revocation or suspension of license, on the grounds of incompetency. In many respects, the agreement of sale is more important than the deed because it dictates and determines what goes into the deed. If there is any ambiguity as to the meaning, interpretation or construction of the language in the agreement, it will be construed most strongly against the owner because the agreement was prepared by the owner's agent—the broker.

The broker is a special agent, with limited authority. He is employed to obtain a purchaser for the owner. This employment, generally, cannot be enlarged to authorize the agent to execute a valid agreement of sale, binding upon the owner.[1] In the case of *Gallant v. Todd, et al.* 111 S.E. 2d 779 (S.C. 1960), a buyer sought to compel the owner to convey certain real estate to him, based upon an agreement of sale, signed by the broker, as agent for the owner. The Court said:

It is well settled that a real estate broker, under the ordinary contract of employment has no implied authority to execute a contract of sale in behalf of his principal. He is generally a special agent, with limited powers, whose usual duty is simply to find a purchaser, ready, able and

---

[1] Peters v. Windmiller, 314 Ill. 496.

willing to enter into a contract upon the terms, and conditions fixed by the owner. . . .

Likewise, an agent exceeds his authority when he permits a purchaser to take possession of the premises before the deal is closed; or permits the buyer to enter the premises for the purpose of doing some painting or decorating, or to make minor repairs. Where the deal fails to materialize, the broker may find himself the defendant in an action by the disappointed purchaser to recover his expenses and damages. If the buyer desires some special privilege before closing the deal, the broker should refer him to the owner for permission.

An agreement of sale is a contract in writing whereby one party agrees to sell and another to buy certain real estate under such terms and conditions as are therein set forth. It must be remembered that an agreement of sale is a contract. Hence, all the essential elements of a valid contract must be present; these are (1) offer and acceptance, (2) seal or consideration, (3) capacity of parties, (4) reality of consent, and (5) legality of object. Since the contract relates to real estate, an additional element, special formality, is also required. Offer and acceptance means there must be a "meeting of minds" upon the subject matter and terms of the contract. The terms of the contract must be precise and definite. It is the responsibility of the broker who undertakes to prepare the agreements to see to it that the form and substance of the contract will meet any legal challenge. Offer and acceptance may, and often do, arise from correspondence between the parties, so that a formal contract is never signed.

It is often difficult to determine whether a writing is a mere receipt or a sufficient agreement under the Statute of Frauds. If the memorandum contains the names of the parties and a definite enough description to identify the property and the terms of the sale, it will suffice.

Sometimes, a broker will have the parties sign a preliminary agreement, such as an offer to purchase, although the advisability of using two separate instruments to do a single job is questionable when one is sufficient. Where there are conflicting clauses in the two papers, trouble may ensue, and it does not always follow that the terms of the preliminary agreement are carried over into the later one.

The case of *Tomkins v. France*, 21 Ill. App. 2d 227 (1959), is pertinent. In that case, the preliminary agreement provided that the parties would execute the usual Chicago Real Estate Board sales contract form, embodying the terms, within five days. The contract submitted was not on the Chicago Board form and called for an earnest money deposit of $4,950, instead of $2,000, stated in the preliminary agreement to purchase. The court held that the buyer did not need to perform and he was entitled to a refund of his $2,000 deposit.

No particular form is necessary for an agreement of sale. It need only be signed by the vendor and need not be under seal. The memorandum or writing should contain the following information: (1) the names of the parties; (2) terms of the sale; (3) a description sufficient to identify the property; (4) the purchase price to be paid. A receipt for hand money which embodies this data would suffice. Where the vendor is married, it is good practice to have the wife also sign even though the property is held in the name of the husband alone. This is true even if her name does not appear in the body of the agreement.

The case of *Boekelheide v. Snyder,* 71 S.D. 470 (1947) was an action for specific performance by the buyer. The writing, upon which the action was based, read:

> Received of H. H. Boekelheide $50 to apply
> on purchase of house and property of the old
> Young house. Balance $650.
>   Margaret Snyder

Does this memorandum satisfy the Statute of Frauds, as a written contract of sale? The Court held the writing insufficient. It must be complete in itself, containing all the terms of the contract. Oral evidence is not admissible to suply defects in a written contract, which must be in writing under the Statute of Frauds. Payment of $50 did not constitute part performance.

The offer and acceptance must be definite. In a certain case, a broker prepared an agreement of sale, and the buyer paid $1,000 hand money, which was turned over to the seller. The buyer then sued the seller for the return of the money, claiming that the agreement of sale was inadequate, incomplete and ineffective. The provision in controversy related to a mortgage. The agreement said simply, "Subject to purchaser obtaining mortgage." It was silent as to the amount of the mortgage and all the related terms, such as the rate of interest, the duration of the mortgage, the size of monthly payments to be required, and whether or not the mortgagor had the right of anticipation. Clearly, the agreement lacked *definiteness,* the first essential in a meeting of the minds. It would have been preferable to have stated, "Vendee will pay cash to highest loan obtainable at 6 per cent." In this connection, a broker should be alert as to the responsibilities which he assumes when he, independently, represents or warrants to the buyer that he will obtain the necessary financing. If the broker is unable to produce the required mortgage with the result that the deal falls through and the buyer's hand money is lost, the buyer has the legal right to sue the broker upon the latter's broken promise to produce the mortgage. It is considered unethical practice to require that the buyer finance the property through the broker *alone,* so that the buyer cannot look where he pleases for funds.

The same is true of the situation where the broker knows that the buyer must sell his present home in order to obtain funds necessary in the purchase of the new home. The broker, in good faith, may promise to sell the buyer's present home before the sale is consummated for the new home. If he fails to perform, the buyer can sue the broker, upon the latter's independent promise, for any loss he sustained. If the deal is contingent upon the buyer obtaining a mortgage or sale of his present home, the broker should write the contingency into the contract of sale, so that the owner will know that he has only a conditional sale, which may not materialize.

In connection with the necessary financing of a purchased dwelling, attention is called to a rather extensive and dangerous practice in real estate circles. It is the use of dual contracts, sometimes referred to as "kiting" or "ballooning." This is the situation where a purchase contract is executed by buyer and seller for the true consideration price of $16,000. Buyer requires a mortgage of $15,000. A second set of purchase contracts are then executed by the seller and buyer at a fictitious consideration price of $18,000. It is the $18,000 agreement which is submitted to the lending institution for a loan of $15,000. Very often the dual agreements are suggested by the real estate broker with the assurance to the parties that "it's done all the time."

Not only is this practice considered unethical and violative of the Realtor's Code of Ethics, but it constitutes a material violation of the license law, and is a criminal offense, as well. The broker, buyer, and seller and lending institution officer are all subject to criminal prosecution. Texas and Colorado make such practice a misdemeanor under State law. The Federal Act of June 25, 1948 makes it a federal crime for any person to make a false statement in applying for F.H.A. mortgage insurance, or *"to aid or abet"* such action.

Offer may be revoked

An offer is not irrevocable. It can be withdrawn at any time before acceptance. An objection to a preliminary offer to purchase contract is that it usually provides that the seller is to have a certain period of time within which to accept the offer—three, five, seven or ten days. The prospective buyer is not bound to keep his offer open for the designated period of time. He can withdraw the offer at any time. It simply means that the offer will *automatically* expire at the expiration of the named period, if the seller does not accept. Also, where a formal agreement of sale is prepared, which the buyer signs, it is still only a naked offer, which can be withdrawn at any time before acceptance. Thus, a broker should act promptly in seeing to it that his owner signs the agreement as soon as possible.

It is also important that a broker deliver the seller's signed agreement to the buyer as soon as possible. In other words, it is not only necessary that the seller accept the buyer's offer by signing the agreement, but the acceptance must be *communicated* to the buyer. Until the acceptance has been communicated, the buyer can withdraw his offer of purchase, even though he has signed the agreement of sale.

In the case of *Reynolds v. Hancock*, 53 Wash. 2d 682 (1959), a broker sued the buyer for a commission on the strength of a clause in an offer to purchase, which read:

This offer is made subject to approval of the seller by midnight of March 27, 1957. In consideration of agent submitting this offer to seller, purchaser agrees with the agent not to withdraw this offer during said period or until earlier rejection thereof by seller.

After signing the offer to purchase, the buyer, prior to midnight of March 27, 1957, notified the seller, in California, that the offer was withdrawn. The Court held that there was no consideration to the buyers from the broker not to withdraw the offer prior to its expiration date. The broker could not recover. In Arizona, a number of brokers use the following clause in an offer to purchase:

In consideration of the Broker refraining from offering said premises for sale to any other person, the Buyer agrees not to withdraw this offer during said period, or unless earlier rejected by the Seller.

The offer must be accepted in order to have a binding contract. Anson on Contracts has compared an offer to a train of gunpowder. Once the match is applied, it produces something which cannot be undone or recalled, unless the gunpowder has lain until it has become damp, or the man who laid the train removes it before the match is applied; so an offer, once it is accepted, cannot be undone or recalled, but the offer may lapse through passage of time, or the man who made the offer may withdraw it *at any time* before acceptance. Thus a broker should stress to his owner the importance of signing the agreement upon his terms, as soon as possible. A counter-proposition is a rejection of the offer and an offer, once rejected, is gone forever unless the offeror reinstates it.

Where the buyer withdraws his offer before acceptance by the owner, he is entitled to a full refund of his earnest money or deposit, without any "strings" or conditions attached whatsoever. In one case, before returning the earnest money, the broker sought to have the buyer sign a memorandum that if he *ever* bought a property in the future, it would be through that broker. The memorandum is unethical and clearly unenforceable. In 8 Amer. Juris. 1060, Sec. 130, it is said:

> If earnest money is paid to a broker, and the contract is broken by the principal, the broker, notwithstanding that he has disclosed his principal, is liable to the buyer for a refund of the deposit money, unless he has in good faith paid it over to his principal. The fact that a broker has a claim against his principal is no justification for his refusal to return the deposit money. (*Gosslin v. Martin,* 56 Ore. 281, 107 P. 957.) (*Perry v. Thorpe Bros., Inc.* 267 Minn. 29 (1963).)

If the agreement of sale is under seal, it is not necessary to inquire as to the consideration which passed between the parties. A seal is said to be a substitute for a consideration. In the ordinary transaction there is sufficient and acceptable consideration present. The concurrent mutual promises of seller and buyer constitute the necessary consideration. The transfer of the property by the seller at a definite future date, and the payment of a monetary value by the buyer at that time, satisfy the requirement of consideration. While no deposit money is essential for the validity of the contract, it is the invariable practice to require a down payment from the buyer as evidence of his good faith and as a financial protection to the seller in case the buyer defaults. The size of the down payment should be commensurate with the amount of the consideration price for the property. A 10% earnest money requirement upon the signing of the agreement of sale is reasonable. The time for closing is also a factor to be considered in connection with the size of the hand money deposit. If the deal is to be closed more than 30 days from the date of the agreements, a larger down payment should be obtained as a protection to the seller, since the real estate market might change in that period. It often happens in real estate practice that a buyer does not have cash funds available for a 10% deposit, or even a 5% deposit. For example, in the purchase of a home for $17,500, the buyer does not have ready cash available for more than $200. It would be satisfactory for the broker to prepare a contract of sale at $17,500, with a cash deposit of $200, upon the signing of the contract. However, he should further provide that the buyer agrees to pay an additional sum of $800 or $1,500 within thirty days thereafter, *which date is of the essence of the agreement.*

Down payment

The agreement should provide that the down payment or hand money may be retained as liquidated damages at the seller's option in case the buyer fails to go through with the deal. Thus, ". . . five hundred ($500.00) dollars, upon the signing of this agreement, receipt whereof is hereby acknowledged and which sum may, at the option of the party of the first part [vendor] be retained as liquidated damages in event of breach of any of the conditions contained herein by the said party of the second part [vendee], or applied on any loss on a resale of the property." The agreement should stipulate that the balance of the consideration should be payable at the settlement, *in cash.* The seller can then elect to accept a certified or bank check.

In contrast to the above clause, many brokers merely provide relative to the deposit money, as follows: ". . . five hundred ($500.00) dollars, upon the signing of this agreement, receipt whereof is hereby acknowledged and the balance of nine thousand five hundred ($9,500) dollars upon delivery of deed." The general rule of law is to the effect that the vendor may keep the down payment if the purchaser defaults. The law has been aptly stated in a New Jersey case as follows: "The rule is entirely settled that a part payment of the purchase money cannot be recovered by a purchaser if he refuses to execute his contract without cause." Each case necessarily depends upon its particular facts. Where an agreement of sale provides for more than a single initial down payment, then *all* payments should be forfeited, and the sales agreement should so provide.

Deposit money in escrow account

Most states, by law, or by rule and regulation of the Commission, require that the broker keep all deposit monies in an escrow or trustee account. This does not mean that a broker must open a new account every time he receives an earnest money deposit. One trustee or escrow account will suffice. Such funds should be held inviolate until the deal is closed. A broker is not entitled to use such funds for personal uses. The theory that he may properly do so up to the amount of his commission in the particular deal, pending the final closing, conclusion or settlement of the transaction does not apply.

Broker's responsibility for deposit money

The seller and buyer are the two prime parties to the contract of sale, or earnest money contract. The broker is not a party to it. Thus, when the agreement recites "$1,000 earnest money, upon the signing of these agreements, receipt whereof is hereby acknowledged," the owner can refuse to sign the agreement unless he receives the earnest money deposit. It should be noted that where the broker has a written contract of employment, it should include a clause: "The owner hereby agress that all deposit money paid upon the consideration price shall be retained by the within broker, in escrow, until the transaction is consummated or terminated."

It is the general rule of law that a purchaser of real estate who is in default cannot recover a portion of the down payment, and where the purchaser has notified the seller of his refusal to go through with the deal, the seller is not required to make tender of a deed.

The question of who is entitled to the earnest money or down payment frequently arises when the buyer defaults in performance. The broker mistakenly believes that, if he holds the deposit money, he is entitled to his commission out of this fund. It must be remembered that the broker is acting in a representative capacity, as agent for his principal, the owner. It thus appears that the money belongs to his principal. Under his employment by the owner, the broker has contracted to produce a purchaser, *ready, able,* and *willing* to buy. It would not appear that the agent has met his legal responsibilities if his purchaser is unwilling to complete the deal. It may be contended that, when the owner signs the agreement, he has placed his stamp of approval upon the purchaser, accepted him, and, upon the latter's default, must pursue him in a court of law for performance. The question is highly controversial although there are court decisions recognizing the broker's rights to his commission out of the deposit money held by him. However, if the buyer is pecuniarily unable to complete the transaction, litigation is futile, and the broker has not earned a commission. Where the agreement provides that the broker is to be paid his commission *upon delivery of deed,* he is not entitled to any sum under the circumstances outlined. Such a clause reads: "It is understood that Packer & Co. are the sole moving cause of this sale, and the vendors agree to pay said Packer & Co. a commission of five per cent of the full purchase price, said commission to be payable upon delivery of deed." The clause identifying the broker (Packer & Co.) as the broker negotiating the deed protects the broker against *both* buyer and seller, if the deal is completed, since it constitutes a *warranty* by both principals that Packer & Co. brought about the sale.

Many listing contracts in current use provide: "A deposit made, if forfeited by the buyer, shall first apply to the broker's commission; the balance, if any, shall belong to the owner."

While a broker is certainly entitled to a return for his efforts, good conscience requires that it shall not be at the expense of an innocent principal. Suppose the clause in question is used and the broker obtains a purchaser for a property at $10,000, and collects a deposit of $500. Later, the buyer defaults and forfeits the deposit money. Should the broker be permitted to retain the *entire* deposit as commission on the ground that the owner has a legal right to sue the defaulting buyer, even though litigation may prove futile? It is scarcely ethical that the broker should keep all the money paid on account of the purchase of the owner's property, and the latter required to pursue litigation, entailing additional expense of costs and attorney's fees, for recovery of a judgment which may be uncollectible. In addition, the property may be "tied up" for a considerable period of time from the date when the agreements were signed. Fair dealing requires that the down payment be divided equally between broker and owner, up to an amount where the broker receives full payment of his commission. A *fair* provision in the agreement of sale relative to the earnest money would read:

Should the buyer fail to make settlement, as herein provided, the sum or sums paid on account of the purchase price, at the option of the seller, may be retained by the seller, either on account of the purchase price, the resale price, or as liquidated damages. In the latter case, the contract shall become null and void. In the latter event, all monies paid on account shall be divided equally between the seller and the broker, but in no event shall the sum paid to the broker be in excess of the standard rate of commission due him according to the schedule of the Greater Pittsburgh Board of Realtors.

An agreement of sale sometimes provides: "It is understood that the broker is acting as agent only and will in no case whatever be held liable to either party for the performance of any term or covenant of this agreement or for damages for nonperformance thereof." This clause is not really necessary where the broker's principal is disclosed, since the broker, as agent, would not be liable in any event unless he exceeds his authority.

Handling of deposit money has been a prime source of complaints to Real Estate Commissions in recent years. As a result, states, by statute, rule or regulation, or both, regulate the subject. Guide rules laid down, require:

1. Broker must retain deposit money in a separate custodial account until transaction is consummated or terminated.
2. Every real estate salesman must promptly turn over deposit money received by him to his broker.
3. Under no circumstances shall a broker permit any advance payment of funds to be deposited in his business or personal account, or be commingled with any funds he may have on deposit.
4. Custodial or trust fund account must provide for withdrawal of funds without previous notice.
5. Must keep complete records, showing the date and from whom he received deposit money, the date deposited, the dates of withdrawal and other pertinent information.
6. Broker executes a consent to bank permitting Commission representative to examine bank records.
7. Salesman cannot receive an advance on commission but must wait for closing.

Postdated checks for down payment

It should be noted that the sales agreement acknowledges that the buyer has paid so much money as a down payment, "receipt whereof is hereby acknowledged." Sometimes a broker will accept a "postdated check" (bears a date subsequent to its delivery) which is not honored upon presentation to the bank. Unless the owner has consented to the acceptance of the check, the broker has violated his fiduciary responsibility to his principal and again jeopardizes not only his commission, but his license, which means his livelihood. A broker is within his rights in accepting an ordinary check for earnest money, even though the buyer immediately stops payment on the check because it is everyday business custom to accept a check in lieu of cash; but the broker who receives a check is duty-bound to deposit it *promptly* for payment. A postdated check, which is dishonored, or a check upon which payment has been stopped, has no effect upon the validity of the agreement of sale, if the seller takes action against the buyer to enforce it. Sometimes, instead of cash, the buyer will give the broker a short-term promissory note. A broker is guilty of bad faith and jeopardizes his license when he accepts a note instead of cash without disclosing this fact to his principal. The agreement is not void because of the default upon the note.

In the case of *Witherspoon v. Pusch,* 136 P. 2d 137 (Colo. 1960), suit by an owner for breach of written contract to purchase realty and to recover on check for down payment on which payment had been stopped. The Supreme Court held that parol testimony of buyer as to understanding with owner's *broker* that the offer to pur-

chase was not a firm offer and that check for down payment was to
be held until buyer had opportunity to investigate zoning restrictions and adaptability of the property to intended use, was admissible to show that there was no contract, and was not an attempt to
vary terms of writen contract. The plaintiff relied upon signed
contract, and check for $1,500 marked "Payment Stopped." The
Court said:

The check itself stands or falls upon the existence of a good and sufficient contract between the parties. It is also the rule that its being
honored or paid can be upon conditions and that it is not a binding
obligation if given with the understanding that it is to be used or deposited until the happening of a certain event. In this case, Mrs. Pusch
(buyer) testified that the signing of the offer and the giving of the check
was a convenience which would make it unnecessary for the parties to
meet again, if she found upon the investigation that everything was
satisfactory as to zoning classification, adaptability of the plumbing for
conversion of the building into apartments made by the City and County
of Denver.

The plaintiff contended that if these conditions were made between
Mrs. Pusch and the broker, they were not binding upon her because the broker was not a party to the contract. The Court held
that the broker was the agent of the owner and, therefore, there
could be no recovery.

Where a broker accepted a note instead of cash, as recited in the
agreement of sale, he was precluded from recovering a commission
in the case of *Slusser v. Brillhart,* 159 N.E. 2d 480 (Ohio, 1958).
Mrs. Brillhart, the defendant, signed a sales agreement on July 26,
1956, which recited that Mr. and Mrs. Roberts had paid to the
broker $1,500 in cash, which sum was designated in the purchase
agreement as "cash herewith." The fact was that the broker had
$200 in cash and a note due two weeks after July 19, 1956 for $1,300,
signed by Mr. Roberts. The note was paid to the broker on or about
September 28, 1956. On August 17, 1956, Mrs. Brillhart wrote the
Roberts that she did not desire to sell her property. They purchased
other property. Is the broker entitled to a commission?

Mrs. Brillhart denied that she owed a commission on the ground
that her signature was obtained by the broker on his representation
that he had received a $1,500 cash deposit. The lower court directed
a verdict for the broker. Upon appeal, the higher court said that
the lower court committed prejudicial error in granting plaintiff's
motion for judgment for the commission, quoting *Mecklenborg v.
Niehaus,* 85 Ohio App. 271, where the Court said:

An agent owes a duty to his principal to inform him of all facts relating to the subject matter of the agency that would affect the principal's interest.

The facts should have been submitted to a jury to decide.

Where a broker signs a receipt for earnest money, which contains a notation that check is to be returned if purchaser cannot get a mortgage to cover balance (price of farm $4,200; balance $3,780), and no mention is made of the mortgage condition in the formal agreement of sale signed by seller and buyer, the broker is held personally responsible for the return of the down payment, if the mortgage is unobtainable: *Wartman v. Schockley,* 154 Pa. Superior Ct. 196 (1943).

A broker authorized to negotiate a sale of property has implied authority to accept the initial down payment but no implied authority to accept subsequent payments made on account of the purchase price. In the case of *Gerig v. Russ,* 200 Ore. 196 (1954), a broker in Salem negotiated the sale of 103 acres of land at $23,500 for Russ to Gerig. The earnest money receipt read:

Received of David Gerig and Ellen I. Gerig the sum of $500.00 as earnest money on the following described property: Approximately 103 acres and building located east of Parkersville School. Purchase price, $21,500.00. Terms ½ down payment in cash, balance to be arranged by loan.

Between June 23, 1949 and July 22, 1949, the purchasers paid to the broker various sums, totalling $11,500.00 without the knowledge or consent of the sellers. The buyers brought suit for specific performance, tendering balance of $9,500.00. Sellers demanded balance of $21,000.00. The Court said:

There is nothing in the language itself, "Terms: ½ down payment in cash, balance to be arranged by loan" implying the authority of the broker to receive such down payment . . . it was the duty of the purchasers to make the payments direct to the sellers rather than to the broker, and when they turned the money over to the broker, they did so at their own risk.

Broker entitled to commission when agreements are signed

Once the agreements of sale are signed, the broker is generally entitled to his commission at that point. It is the burden of the owner, in a commission suit, to prove *affirmatively* that the purchaser produced by the owner is not financially able, in order to avoid payment of a commission.[1] This means that it is necessary for the owner to sue the buyer to prove that the latter is not "financially

---

[1] See Ellsworth Dobbs, Inc. v. Johnson et al, 50 N.J. 528, on page 38.

able." It is noteworthy to observe in the case of *Simmons v. Libbey,* 53 N.M. 36 (1949), the Court stated that:

The agent is not concerned as to the ability of the purchaser to buy, for the seller relieves him in that respect when he accepts the purchaser as satisfactory and a binding contract is made, citing a Texas case, *Seidel v. Walker,* 173 S.W. 1170.

However, it has been held that a broker could not recover a commission where the agreement of sale was signed by a young couple and the broker knew that the necessary funds would be supplied by a relative, who was not a party to the agreement: *McGarry Realty Co. v. McCrane, et al.,* 97 Ohio App. 543 (1954).

Where the buyer causelessly defaults, the seller may forfeit the earnest money deposit and the broker is entitled to his commission. Where a seller and buyer, after execution of the agreement of sale, mutually agree to cancel the agreement, the broker is entitled to his commission upon the full consideration price. Stewart Realty Company v. Brock 60 N.M. 216 (1955). In the case of *Huber v. Gerahman,* 300 S.W. 2d 501 (Mo. 1957), the Court held that the broker was entitled to his commission where buyer and seller mutually rescinded an executed contract for the sale of a theatre. $2,500 deposit had been paid. The sales contract provided:

Earnest deposit to be retained by Listing Agent, without interest; if sale is closed, earnest money to apply on sale commission. Forfeited earnest money shall go first toward reimbursing expenses of agent, and balance to go one-half to seller and one-half to agent.

The Court said:

In these circumstances, the contracting parties were not free to direct the return of the $2,500 to the purchaser and ignore the contract rights of the broker in the earnest money deposit.

To avoid any question as to the broker's rights, it is advisable to provide in the listing agreement *and* in the agreement of sale, that in case any hand money is forfeited, it will be divided equally between the seller and the broker, up to the amount of the broker's commission.

CAPACITY OF PARTIES

Minors

Not all persons have *full* contractual capacity. Persons with limited capacity include infants, married women, insane persons, corporations, and aliens. In most states, an infant does not become of age until he reaches 21 years of age. During his minority, most contracts entered into by him are voidable at his option. Only contracts for necessaries are binding upon him. There is no hard and fast rule to define necessaries. They include more than those articles required for bare subsistence. Items which are useful and suitable to his station in life are included as necessaries. Certainly maintenance, food, clothing, *lodging*, medical attention, and education in a reasonable amount, are included in the term. A voidable contract may be disaffirmed by the minor at any time during his minority or within a reasonable time after he attains his majority. Infancy is a defense personal to the infant alone. It cannot be pleaded by the other party to the contract as grounds for avoidance of his contractual liability. The appointment of an agent by an infant is generally void. In dealing with an infant owner of real estate, the other party should require the appointment of a guardian for the infant and deal with the guardian. A broker employed by an infant to sell property would be unable to collect his earned commission if the infant changed his mind and repudiated the contract of employment. It makes no difference that the sale arranged by the broker is advantageous to the infant. An infant may appear to be of full age, but this has no bearing upon his liability or freedom from liability in a contract. Even if he wrongfully misrepresents his age, the rule of law is the same, for he cannot make himself *sui juris* (of legal age) by falsifying his age. The infant could still disaffirm his contract. However, the injured party could sue the infant in a *tort* action of deceit.

An infant who elects to disaffirm his voidable contract must do so *in toto*. He cannot elect to ratify as much of the contract as will benefit him and reject that portion which operates to his disadvantage. For example, an infant who agreed to purchase a commercial property for $10,000 by paying $2,500 cash and giving the owner a purchase money mortgage for $7,500 could not compel the seller to deed the property to him upon payment of the $2,500 cash and then disaffirm his obligation to execute the $7,500 mortgage.

Insane persons

The law also protects persons mentally incompetent from their imprudent contracts. Mentally incompetent persons include insane persons and drunkards. To affect the contractual ability, the degree of mental derangement must be such as to render the person incapable of reasoning from cause to effect and thus understanding the effects of his acts. A person, mentally incompetent, is nevertheless liable for necessaries furnished himself, his wife, or children. Other contracts, if yet to be performed (executory), are voidable by him.

The weight of authority is to the effect that where the contract has been executed so that the insane person has had the benefit and the parties cannot be restored to their former position, unaccompanied by any proof that the other knew or ought to have known of the insanity, the contract will not be voided. If the insane party has received no benefit, he may void the contract and recover what he has paid notwithstanding the other party's good faith. To be on the safe side, a guardian or committee for the estate of the incompetent should be appointed by the court and the sale of real estate made under the direction of said court. The test of whether a guardian should be appointed for the estate of a person is the degree of his mental unsoundness; if he is incapable of conducting the ordinary affairs of life so that to leave property in his possession and control would render him liable to become the victim of his own folly or designing persons, a guardian should be appointed.

Drunkards

An habitual drunkard may be regarded as an insane person and his capacity to contract is likewise limited. When a man loses his mind, he is entitled to legal protection whether such loss is occasioned by his own imprudence or otherwise. This is true even though the intoxication be voluntary and not procured by the intervention of another party.

Married women

The contractual powers of a married woman are based upon statute. Today a married woman is almost completely emancipated in her capacity to contract. She may generally transact business in the same manner as a single woman (a feme sole trader). In states where she cannot sell her own real estate without the joinder of her husband, he should join in the execution of an agreement of sale. Even in these states, if a woman, before marriage, enters into an agreement to sell her real estate and marries before the deal is consummated and the deed delivered, the courts will honor her agreement of sale and compel her husband to join in the deed.

Corporations

The contractual powers of most corporations are defined and limited by their charters and by the constitution and laws of the states where they are formed. They have those powers expressly stated in their charters and such implied powers as may be necessary and incidental to carry out those expressed powers. Where a corporation exceeds its powers, the act is *ultra vires* and unenforceable. An agreement for the sale of real estate by a corporation should be executed in pursuance of a resolution by the board of directors authorizing and directing the particular conveyance. When the agreement is made under a general resolution authorizing the officers to execute deeds for any property which they may sell, it is doubtful whether such a sale is valid since the price and terms are left to the discretion of the officers. Reference here is made to business and manufacturing corporations. Where the corporation is formed for the express purpose of dealing in real estate, requisite authority may be conferred upon its officers by general resolution to execute proper agreements and deeds as the occasions arise.

Aliens

In general, foreigners, whether citizens of another state or another nation, have full contractual authority. However, under the Federal law prohibiting trading with an enemy, an affidavit by the parties to a real estate deal should be executed stating that they are not enemy aliens.

REALITY OF CONSENT

Mistake

A contract must be free from mistake, misrepresentation, fraud, duress, and undue influence. In other words, the consent to the contract must be *real*. To avoid a contract on the ground of mistake, the mistake must be mutual and substantial; that is, it must go to the heart of the agreement. Thus, where parties use ambiguous language and each has in mind an entirely different subject matter as the basis of the agreement, there is no contract. Where Ash owned considerable real estate, some of which was located on Jackson Street in Pittsburgh while another parcel was located on Jacksonia Street in the same city, an agreement was prepared for a parcel of real estate on Jackson Street. Due to the similarity in name, the buyer thought he was purchasing and intended to buy the tract on Jacksonia Street. The contract could be set aside on the grounds of mistake.

Misrepresentation and fraud

Misrepresentation and fraud are often confused. Misrepresentation is an innocent misstatement of a material fact, without intent to deceive, but which induces the contract. If Jones should sell Smith certain building lots and represent that the lots were on high ground and it later developed that they were not above tide level, Jones could not hold Smith to the contract even though he were honest in his representation. However, if the party to whom the misrepresentation was made did not rely upon it and made his own independent examination, he could not claim that the misrepresentation induced his contract. Misrepresentation must be as to fact and not a mere expression of opinion. If a broker represents to a customer that certain real estate *cost* $10,000 to build and it only *cost* $7,000, there is fraudulent misrepresentation present. Where the broker states, instead, that the property is *worth* $10,000, that is mere expression of an opinion and does not constitute misrepresentation.

If the following representations were untrue, they would constitute grounds for recision of the agreement of sale: that heating plant, plumbing, and electric wiring were in good condition; that an adjoining dilapidated house had been condemned by the city and would shortly be torn down; that there was sufficient land to sell a 60-foot lot off the property, for which lot an offer of $2,000 had already been made; that the cellar was dry and in good condition; and that the roof was in good repair. These representations are such that the truth cannot be readily determined from an inspection of the premises by one not skilled in the knowledge of home construction and plumbing. It has been held that plumbing, electric wiring, and heating are not generally ascertainable on viewing. The same is true of a roof. A sale is not dependent upon the fortuitous circumstance that a purchaser be available when rain or snow is falling so that he can inspect the roof and determine whether it is watertight and that the cellar is dry. An owner or broker must be circumspect in regard to the statements he makes.[2]

Whereas misrepresentation may be set up as grounds for the avoidance of a contract, it does not lay any basis for an action for damages, but only for actual incurred expenses. Fraud is a misstatement of a material fact made with intent to deceive or made with reckless disregard of the truth, which actually does deceive. It may also arise where a party conceals a material fact, disclosure of which is a duty. Fraud is a tort as well as a ground for avoiding a contract and will sustain an action for damages. *Caveat emptor* is the ordinary rule of contracts; i.e., "let the purchaser beware." The buyer's eyes are supposed to see his bargain. Unless the seller does something to conceal a defect or throw him off the inquiry, the buyer

---

2 Lake v. Thompson, 366 Pa. 352 (1950).

has only himself to blame if the purchase turns out less valuable than he anticipated. An owner, in selling a vacant lot to a person who desires to purchase it for the erection of a home, is not bound to disclose that the lot is "filled in" land unless the buyer makes inquiry and the owner, by word or deed, does something to disarm his suspicions and steer him away from the inquiry. By the same token, a buyer in negotiating the purchase of farm land, is not bound to disclose the presence of underlying coal land which is motivating the purchase in question. The parties deal "at arms length." It is wise to permit a prospective purchaser to make a thorough examination of the premises under consideration and then to insert a clause in the agreement of sale to the effect that the purchase is being made as a result of the buyer's inspection; or that he is buying the property "as is." As a general rule, the buyer takes the property subject to *patent* defects, *i.e.* those which are ascertainable upon view, or a reasonable inspection of the property; the buyer can rescind the contract, where he later discovers *latent* (hidden or concealed) defects which were not readily ascertainable upon view, such as a defective septic tank, plumbing or electrical lines.

Where the broker relies upon representations made to him by the owner, which he relays to a prospect, the broker is not personally responsible, unless his experience and training in real estate would make him doubt the owner's statements. Since there are so many law suits involving misrepresentations, it is advisable for a broker in accepting a written listing, to have the seller certify, over his signature, that the data and information furnished concerning the subject property, are true and correct. In *Smith v. Badlain*, 112 Vt. 143 (1941), the defendant, a real estate broker, interested the plaintiff in an orchard. The broker told the prospect that there were 3,500 apple trees of different varieties. The plaintiff asked for an inventory and in a few days, the defendant broker gave him a paper listing the different varieties with the total 3,500. The defendant knew nothing about the number of trees except what the owner, Anderson, told him. The owner also told the plaintiff there were 3,500 trees. The defendant testified that he did not know whether the inventory he gave the plaintiff was true or false. Verdict for defendant. The Court said:

> In view of the fact that the defendant represented a known principal, it cannot reasonably be inferred that the plaintiff understood that the defendant made the statements and inventory as of his own knowledge. An agent is not liable because of the misrepresentations of the principal or of another agent unless he should know of them.

The case of *Wallo v. Rosenberg, et al.*, 331 S.W. 2d 8 (Mo. 1960), was an action to rescind the purchase of a motel in Kansas City for $51,000. The broker represented to the buyers that the weekly rental was $386.00, that the owner had the record books, and that seven apartments were occupied, but could not be seen, because the tenants had the keys. It was found that the rental was $184.00 per week and that the seven units were unoccupied and in bad repair. The agreement of sale provided: "the undersigned to accept the property in present condition and upon own investigation." The Court held that the owner was bound by the broker's misrepresentations made, and being bound by them "cannot escape their legal effect on the ground that the buyer should have made a more thorough investigation or that the contract contained the mentioned clause."

In the case of *Becker v. Lagerquist Bros., Inc.*, 348 Pac. 2d 423 (Wash. 1960), suit was brought by buyer against seller for cost of paving property on W. 105th St. in a subdivision adjacent to the City of Seattle. Defendant advertised it would pave street in the subdivision and the court found that purchases were made in response to direct oral promises to them by defendant's agent that the street in question would be paved. The sales agreement contained a clause, as follows: "There are no verbal or other agreements which modify or affect this agreement." The Court held that

the agreement to pave the street in no wise conflicts with anything in the earnest money receipt. It is entirely consistent with it. Indeed, there was no reason to deal with the subject at all in the receipt. It was a material inducement to the contract.

The majority opinion pointed out that parol evidence of false and fraudulent representations inducing one to enter into a written contract is admissible notwithstanding the contract contains an express recital that there have been no representations, or that all oral representations should be inoperative.

In the case of *Gronlund v. Andersson*, 38 Wash. 2d 60 (1951), a similar clause, as above, was not in the contract of sale, but it was in the earnest money receipt. The broker represented that the property had an adequate water supply. The Court held that

an agreement concerning the adequacy of the water supply would not vary or modify such a contract in any sense, and in fact would have nothing whatever to do with it.

In the case of *Shapiro v. Kornick*, 103 Ohio App. 49 (1959), where in reply to the question, "Did you use the best materials and build this house well?" the builder replied, "I have the sort of reputation so that I can't afford to build a bad house." It was held not to constitute an express warranty.

Where a lot was represented to be 70 feet by 123 feet and actually was only 58 feet front and 116 feet deep, the Court held it to be a material misrepresentation sufficient to avoid the contract, and that it was not necessary for the buyer to check the distance by his own measurement: *Young v. Price*, 98 Pgh. Leg. J. 177. A misrepresentation by vendors of boundary line of lot and fraudulent description in deed as 50 foot instead of 55 foot frontage, giving purchasers no space on one side of house past eaves, held sufficiently material to warrant recision by purchaser: *Williams v. Reinert*, 251, Ky. 344 (1933).

In the case of *Russo v. Williams*, 160 Neb. 564 (1955), the Court held that in view of the nature of termites, purchasers of motels were not estopped by their inspection and examination before entering into contract, from saying they had relied on vendor's representation that property was in good condition and free from termites. However, the buyers went into possession in April 1952 and did not complain until September. The case was decided against the buyers because they had waited too long to complain (laches).

In the case of *Berger v. Pittsburgh Auto Equipment Co.*, 387 Pa. 61 (1956), it was decided that a representation stating that a warehouse floor would support weights of 300 pounds and upwards per square foot, but was subsequently found to be incapable of withstanding even the minimum of 125 pounds as required by the city building code, was material and constituted grounds for cancellation of a contract to lease.

In the case of *Schuler v. Humphrey*, 198 Ore. 458 (1953), a contract of sale described the ranch as 430 acres, more or less, but it consisted of 407 and the 23 acres omitted from the ranch was river bottom land, on which alfalfa was growing; variance was held material and as grounds for recision of the contract.

In the case of *Peoples Furniture and Appliance Co. v. Healy*, 113 N.W. 2d 802 (Mich. 1962), a buyer sued for the return of a $5,000 deposit, when the buyer elected not to complete the deal, upon discovering there was a possibility of flooding. Plaintiff was unable to obtain flood insurance. The Supreme Court held that representation of agent with regard to slight possibility of flooding was material. The Court held that "the fact that plaintiff might have ascertained the situation from others is no defense if plaintiff had a right to rely on defendant's representation."

A statement that the property was in good or sound condition did not constitute misrepresentation, when buyer later discovered termite damage: *Pywell v. Haldane*, 186 A 2d 623 (D.C. 1962).

Undue influence

Undue influence is a mixture of fraud and force. Sometimes a person will enter into a contract in order to get rid of a persistent salesman. The mere fact that consent was obtained through nagging and importunity is insufficient to avoid the consequences of a contract. However, where the mind is enfeebled by old age, disease, or great distress, undue influence may be readily proved. Force is opposed to freedom. Free consent is the essence of every agreement. The question to be determined is whether the party was deprived of the exercise of his free will power.

Duress

Duress may be defined as that degree of constraint or danger, either actually inflicted or threatened and impending, which is sufficient in severity to overcome the mind of a person of ordinary firmness. Mere threat of imprisonment or of a law suit is insufficient.

Legality of object

The object of the contract must be legal. If the purpose contravenes the Constitution, a statute, or a Federal treaty, the contract is void. Likewise a contract which tends to interfere with the public government or is injurious to the public at large, such as the perpetration of a nuisance, is unenforceable.

Oral agreement to purchase

It has been previously stated that a contract for the sale of real estate must be in writing in order to be enforceable. Under certain circumstances, where the purchaser has gone into possession under an oral agreement of sale, paid part of the purchase price, and made improvements, a decree of specific performance will be entered; that is, the seller will be ordered and directed by the court to execute a proper deed to the purchaser for the property. It should be noted that an oral agreement of sale is *not* void; it simply will not sustain an action for specific performance. The disappointed party may sue for damages for breach of the contract. But monetary damages may not adequately compensate a purchaser for the loss of his bargain. He may have had his heart set on acquiring the particular real estate for personal or business reasons. A court of equity would not compel specific performance of his claim because the agreement was verbal. If the contract is in writing, duly executed, a court of equity would decree specific performance. An oral agreement of sale subsequently reduced to writing is effective as of the date of the oral agreement. However, if a signed agreement of sale to another party intervenes, a different result would follow. An owner, Andrews, a widower, listed certain property for sale with several brokers. Barnes, a broker, procured Cohen, a purchaser, on March 22, 1966, Cohen and Barnes orally agreed upon the terms of sale. On March 25, 1966, Andrews signed an agreement to sell the same property to Dugan, who prepared an informal writing. No broker was involved. On March 26, 1966, Andrews, under the importunities of Barnes, signed an agreement of sale to Cohen, which agreement was recorded immediately. In a contest between Cohen and Dugan for the property, Dugan's written agreement having been executed first, would have priority.

The written requirement for a real estate contract of sale is for the protection of the seller and inures to his benefit alone. The seller may be held for damages in an action by the buyer upon a verbal contract.

"Dummy" purchaser

Where the seller is accepting a mortgage in part payment of the purchase price, he should insist upon the real buyer signing the agreement. If the agreement is signed by a "straw" man or "dummy," the purchase money mortgage and accompanying note or bond add no value to the property security. In case of foreclosure at a future date, the seller would be unable to recoup any loss sustained between the sale price of the property at foreclosure and his debt.

Conditions in agreement

Where the broker prepares the agreement of sale, he should ascertain from the owner's deed whether there are any conditions in the title which might affect the transferability of the property. Reference is made to oil, gas, coal and mining rights, rights of way, building restrictions, driveways, and the like. The agreement should be made subject to grants, rights, easements, covenants, and restrictions contained in prior deeds of record. If there is some question of encroachment or overlapping, the agreement description should be made subject to actual conditions shown by survey. These items, unless excepted, constitute encumbrances within the meaning of the term. Since the seller covenants that he will convey clear title, the buyer could refuse to consummate the deal and look to the seller for damages, unless the encumbrance in question was specifically excepted. A *definite* date for closing must be inserted in the agreement. If no date is specified for closing, the courts may well consider that the parties *intended* a reasonable time and would be governed accordingly.

A broker should be circumspect not to change or alter an agreement of sale after it has been executed, unless both parties agree *in writing*. The alterations may appear harmless but turn out differently. Suppose that, at the instance of four adult sellers who sign the agreement *after* execution by the buyer, the broker types in "subject to approval of guardian" for two minor owners. The buyer could very well avoid the agreement because of the alteration and the broker would not be entitled to a commission.

An elderly seller agreed to sell his farm for $19,000—$1,000 earnest money deposit, $1,500 when the deal was closed, and the balance of $16,500 in a purchase money mortgage at the rate of $100 per month. The broker prepared the agreement of sale accordingly. The buyer inserted three small words "not less than" in front of "$100 per month." The seller refused to deal, because he wanted a monthly income in his old age and the buyer under the "not less than" clause could pay the entire mortgage or a substantial part of it at any time. The deal fell through and the broker lost a commission.

Date—essence of the agreement

If either party wants to insist that the closing be held absolutely upon the date specified, the date must be made a vital and material part of the agreement; thus, ". . . on April 2, 1969, which date and time is of the *essence* of this agreement." If the date for closing is not made the essence of the agreement, both parties have a *reasonable* time after the date specified within which to close. There is no hard and fast rule to determine what constitutes a reasonable time. It depends upon a variety of circumstances—the activity of the real estate market, type of property involved, time of year, and the like. Thirty or sixty days in most cases would constitute a reasonable time. The situation frequently arises where a seller signs an agreement of sale that is conditional upon his ability to purchase other quarters. For example, an agreement of sale executed in May, 1948, provided that possession to a certain thirty-acre farm was "to be given as soon as legally possible after . . . (the sellers) . . . have found a suitable place to live." Although the buyers from time to time asked the sellers to complete the deal, the sellers never tendered a deed. In the fall of 1950, the purchasers sued for specific performance. The sellers contended that the contract was too indefinite because the contract did not set forth the time when the conveyance was to be made. The courts have repeatedly held that where no time is fixed for delivery of deed, it is presumed that a reasonable time was intended. The lapse of more than two years was held to be a reasonable time for the sellers to find other quarters so that a decree of specific performance was entered and the sellers were compelled to execute a deed. However, in the above case, if the buyers had elected to rescind the deal and recover the down payment, the buyers could recover because of the long lapse of time. To put the buyer in default the seller must make a *tender* of the deed and *demand* for performance.

Tender and demand

Tender may be excused where the buyer has expressed unequivocally an intention of renouncing the agreement. This is known as anticipatory repudiation. Tender would be a futile and meaningless gesture, but evidence of repudiation should be readily available before tender is omitted. The seller may sue immediately without waiting for the time of performance. Tender of a deed is unnecessary if there has been a repudiation by the vendee. Of course, the owner can sue the buyer for the balance of the consideration price under the contract. Where the more comprehensive type clause is used, with the *option* clause, the seller has a choice of three actions; (1) he may sue on the contract for the balance of the purchase price; (2) he may resell the property at public or private sale and sue the buyer for the difference, if any, between the contract price and price realized at the resale; or (3) he may keep the earnest money as liquidated damages. Ordinarily, an owner will elect the last option, especially so, if he believes he will be able to sell the property advantageously at a later date. Often, nothing is done until months later when a new buyer is obtained for the property. It may then be too late to make a tender and demand upon the first buyer in order to put him into default. Tender should have been made within a *reasonable* time after the date specified for closing. The first buyer might well recover his hand money, under the circumstances. Note that it is dangerous to permit a buyer to take possession of premises under an agreement of sale which has not yet been consummated. In the absence of a *lease*, the buyer would be under no obligation to pay rent while in possession, if the deal were not consummated. When a buyer is allowed possession before the deal is closed, he should be required to execute a short-term lease. The rental might well be increased substantially from month to month. The same precaution should be taken when the seller is permitted to remain in possession after the deal is closed. A broker should keep in mind the distinction between a specific date for closing and "at the time of the delivery of deed." Thus if taxes are to be apportioned as of the date specified—e.g., October 1, 1968—the buyer has the obligation for taxes from that date on even though the transaction is not closed until November 15, 1968, whereas, if taxes are apportioned as of the date of delivery of deed, the buyer's responsibility for taxes would not accrue until November 15, 1968.

Acknowledgment

It is not necessary to have the agreement of sale acknowledged. From the standpoint of the buyer, it is a good precaution to have the agreement acknowledged by the seller, particularly if a considerable time is to elapse before the deal is closed. Acknowledgment permits the agreement to be recorded and thus constitutes a cloud upon the title until the agreement is merged into a deed or stricken from the record by some voluntary action upon the part of the buyer or by order of court.

In practically every case, a disappointed purchaser is the one who seeks to have the agreement of sale recorded, and, unless the seller has acknowledged the agreement at the time of its execution, the buyer has a practical difficulty in recording the agreement. For this reason, it is good practice for a broker to have the agreement signed by the seller, witnessed by two persons. It is permissible for the broker himself to be one of the witnessing parties. This is true because in many jurisdictions, in order to have the agreement recorded, it is necessary for two witnesses to make affidavit that they were present and did see the seller sign the instrument. Where the parties to the agreement subsequently desire to remove the agreement from record, it may be done by an agreement of extinguishment duly recorded. However, if the property is subsequently sold to the purchaser in the recorded agreement, then an ordinary deed will suffice to remove the cloud from the title.

With the signing of an agreement of sale the equitable ownership of the property is transferred to the vendee. The vendee should protect this interest by insurance against loss by fire, casualty, or accident because, in most states, *the risk of loss now falls upon him.*

Since September 1947, the Vendor and Purchaser Risk Act has been adopted in California. The Act provides (Section 1662 of California Civil Code):

Any contract hereafter made in this State for the purchase and sale of real property shall be interpreted as including an agreement that the parties shall have the following rights and duties, unless the contract expressly provides otherwise:

(a) If, when neither the legal title nor the possession of the subject matter of the contract has been transferred, all or a material part thereof is destroyed without fault of the purchaser or is taken by eminent domain, the vendor cannot enforce the contract, and the purchaser is entitled to recover any portion of the price that he has paid;

(b) If, when either the legal title or the possession of the subject matter of the contract has been transferred, all or any part thereof is destroyed without fault of the vendor or is taken by eminent domain, the purchaser is not thereby relieved from a duty to pay the price, nor is he entitled to recover any portion thereof that he has paid.

Assignment of leases

If possession is to be given by assignment of leases, the leases should be checked for parties, terms, and *expiration* date before the agreement of sale is signed. A provision should be incorporated in the agreement stating the expiration date in question. The leases should be properly assigned to the grantee at the closing, as well as the insurance policies which are to be assumed by the new owner, and the consent of the companies to the transfer endorsed thereon.

Personal property

The agreement of sale should recite in detail the specific articles of personal property which are included in the sale. These articles frequently include lighting fixtures, curtains, curtain rods, awnings, storm doors, screens, shrubbery, ranges, gas stoves, refrigerators, air conditioning units, carpets, mirrors attached to walls, coal, oil, and fireplace accessories. In the contract the vendor should warrant that he has good title to the articles in question. At the closing the seller should execute a bill of sale for such personal property.

Assignability

Ordinarily, an agreement of sale is assignable by the vendee without any special notation to that effect. Very often a purchaser engages to buy a property without any intention of taking title but with the expectation that he will be able to sell (assign) the agreements at a higher price to a new buyer and pocket the difference. The seller cannot refuse to deed the property to the new purchaser unless he has agreed to take back a mortgage from the original purchaser in part payment of the purchase price, or unless the original buyer has assumed and agreed to pay an existing mortgage.

This is based on the theory that a person has a right to select his debtor. It may make considerable difference to the seller whether the vendee, a person of financial stability, is indebted to him, or whether he must look to the vendee's assignee, a person financially irresponsible, for payment. If the owner desires to deal exclusively with the original buyer in any event, then he should stipulate that "rights under the within agreement of sale are not assignable." In this connection, a person preparing an agreement of sale should be fully cognizant of the legal effect of several clauses used in regard to an existing mortgage. Let us assume that Adams is selling a property to Black for $10,000 and there is at present a mortgage against the property for $7,000 executed by Adams to the mortgagee, Crane, three years earlier. From Adams's standpoint it is to his advantage to insist that the buyer, Black, pay all cash or provide his own financing so that Adams's mortgage to Crane can be paid and satisfied. This is the only certain way that Adams can be relieved of any further obligation under the mortgage. If Black is to take the property, however, subject to the mortgage, caution must be exercised to see that the buyer, Black, not only takes the premises subject to the existing mortgage in favor of Crane, but also that he *assumes and agrees to pay it*. If a short form clause—such as "Under and subject, nevertheless, to a certain unpaid mortgage in the amount of $7,000 given by Adams to Crane, which mortgage dated November 1, 1968, is recorded in the office of the Recorder of Deeds of Blank County in Mortgage Book Vol. 2139 P. 422"—is used, the buyer is simply purchasing whatever equity there is in the property over and above the mortgage debt. If the property should subsequently be sold for default on the mortgage, Black would lose what money he has already paid on the property and no more.

Assumption of mortgage

Should the property at foreclosure sale be sold for less or be less valuable than the amount of Crane's claim, Black would not be liable for the deficiency of the mortgagee. Crane would have to look to Adams alone for payment. On the other hand, if the clause referring to the mortgage read exactly as it appears above, with this addition, "which mortgage the vendee expressly assumes and agrees to pay as part of the consideration herein," Crane, in event of a deficiency judgment, could look to Adams or Black, or both, for payment. If Crane collected the full deficiency from Adams, then Adams, in turn, could look to Black for reimbursement, by reason of the mortgage *assumption* clause. Of course, it is necessary that the same clause be inserted in the *deed* from Adams to Black.

Seller's damages for breach by buyer

If the seller intends to sue the buyer for damages resulting from the latter's breach, he should first attempt to receive a bona fide offer for the same property from another buyer. He should then notify the defaulting buyer as to the best price offered and advise the buyer that unless he can get the seller a higher price, the property will be sold at that price and the buyer will be held responsible in damages for the difference between the contract price and the best price that the seller could obtain.

Buyer's damages for breach by seller

Where the seller breaches an agreement of sale, the buyer's measure of damages depends upon whether the seller is guilty of fraud in the breach. If no fraud is present, the buyer can recover only his down payment and actual expenses. Where a borough ordinance is discovered, which provides for widening of the street upon which the property abuts, the buyer could rescind his contract to purchase and recover the deposit money and actual expenses. The same result would follow where a lot is of less width than contracted for, even though slight, and the buyer viewed the premises. False statements of value, or cost of the building, or the seller's arbitrary refusal to perform would constitute fraud and the buyer could then recover the full value of his bargain.

Options

An option is a contract. It may be defined as an agreement, in writing, whereby the owner (optionor) gives to another (optionee) the exclusive right *for a limited period of time* to purchase (or lease) his real estate upon certain terms and conditions. The option requires a consideration to support it, or it may be under seal. The consideration may be nominal, that is, $1.00. If the option recites a $1.00 consideration, that is sufficient, even though it has not actually been paid. Time is the very *essence* of an option agreement, and if not exercised prior to the expiration date, it automatically expires. Unlike an agreement of sale, there is no period of grace for performance beyond the expiration date. Where the owner is married, the wife's signature should be obtained to the option agreement of sale if the optionee exercises his rights under the option, so that if the optionee exercises the option, the wife of the optionor can be compelled to join in the agreement of sale. Death of the owner during the term of the option would not affect the optionee's rights under the agreement. Where the option is extended or renewed for an additional term, there *must* be additional consideration for the added term. An option is assignable in the same manner as the ordinary agreement of sale. The purpose of the option is to give the holder, in return for the consideration paid, a period of time to make up his mind whether he will elect to purchase the property in question. During the specified time, the property is withdrawn from other purchasers. If the optionee does not exercise the option, the money paid for the option is forfeited. However, the option agreement may specify that if the option is exercised, the money paid for the option shall be credited to the purchase price of the property.

Installment land contracts

In the promotion of subdivision tracts, many lots are sold on an installment basis. In depression years, considerable improved real estate is sold in the same manner. This means that the purchaser makes an initial down payment and then certain monthly payments until the full consideration price is paid, when he receives a deed. This method permits a modest wage earner to acquire land or a home through periodic payments out of income. Upon signing the installment contract, the buyer acquires an equitable interest in the real estate. The monthly payments are usually first applied to interest upon the unpaid balance of the consideration and to taxes as they become due, and the balance to the unpaid principal indebtedness. Many installment contracts, or, as they are sometimes called, land contracts, provide that upon payment of a certain amount of the consideration price (often 50 per cent), the vendee will receive a deed for the property. He, in turn, will then execute a mortgage to the seller for the balance of the purchase price. The contract usually provides that in event the purchaser defaults, the money paid on account shall be forfeited to the seller. There is often a provision, too, that upon default, the balance of the purchase price, at the option of the seller, shall become payable forthwith. A clause may even be included which would permit the seller to confess judgment against the buyer for the full amount unpaid. An inherent danger in the installment contract, from the standpoint of the buyer, is that judgments may be entered against the seller during the long term the contract has to run. Such judgments, of course, would be a lien against the property.

Questions on Agreements of Sale

1. Q. Define an agreement of sale.
   A. A written contract whereby the purchaser agrees to buy certain real estate and the seller agrees to sell upon terms set forth therein.
2. Q. When a broker receives an earnest money deposit from a buyer, may he keep the money on file in his office pending the closing of the deal?
   A. No; he should deposit it immediately in his trust or escrow account.
3. Q. What recourse would a seller have against the broker, if the buyer backed out of the transaction before it was closed?
   A. None; the broker is not responsible for the buyer's default.
4. Q. Allen offers Burns a tract of ground for $10,000. The offer is in writing dated October 4, 1968 and provides, *inter alia,* "this offer to remain open until October 25, 1968." On October 11, 1968 Allen notifies Burns that the offer is withdrawn. Burns writes Allen on October 14, 1968, accepting the offer. Is there a contract for the sale of the land?
   A. No. Burns did not have an option, merely an offer to him. The offeror had a right to withdraw the offer at any time before acceptance. The October 25th date simply meant that the offer would automatically expire on that date, but it could be withdrawn prior thereto.
5. Q. Anthony gives Benson, a broker, a written exclusive contract to sell his property at $5,000. Benson procures Clark as a purchaser upon Anthony's terms. Clark signs an agreement but Anthony, the owner, refuses to sign. Does Clark have any right of action against Anthony?
   A. No. Anthony did not sign the agreement of sale. Anthony is not liable to Clark but would be liable to Benson for a commission.
6. Q. Wilson and Peters execute an agreement of sale for Wilson's property at $9,000, under and subject to a mortgage of $5,000 which Peters assumes and agrees to pay. Peters assigns the agreements to Crane. Wilson refuses to recognize Crane. Can Crane compel Wilson to execute a deed to him?
   A. No. Ordinarily an agreement of sale is assignable. However, where the financial responsibility of the buyer is involved, as here, the seller has a right to select his debtor.
7. Q. What conditions must be met in a memorandum in writing to comply with the Statute of Frauds?

A. The writing must name the consideration, the property to be sold, and the terms, and it must be signed by the seller or by his lawful agent authorized in writing to do so.

8. Q. Assume that after a sales contract has been written and executed, a slight change is made in the terms or conditions, and that the broker, in the presence of the interested parties, alters the writing to conform to the new agreement: what precaution should the broker take to protect himself against any future controversy?

A. He should have all parties to the contract place their signature or initials in the margin opposite or nearest the alterations.

9. Q. Arnold agrees to sell a property to Winters for $10,000—$500 down and the balance in cash. Winters is unable to complete the deal and he obtains Summers, to whom the agreements are assigned. Two days later Summers finds that his wife disapproves the purchase, and he assigns the agreements to Davidson. Arnold, a business competitor of Davidson, refuses to execute a deed to him. Who will win?

A. Davidson can compel Arnold to execute a deed to him as the agreement of sale was assignable.

10. Q. An agreement of sale is made out between Alfred Sims, vendor and Don Cosgrove, vendee. It is signed, however, by Alfred Sims and Elsie Sims, his wife, as well as by Don Cosgrove. The wife refuses to execute the deed on the grounds that she is not named as a party in the agreement proper. Must she join in the deed?

A. Yes. Her signature is sufficient to show an intention on her part to be bound.

11. Q. Abrams signs an agreement to purchase Bell's property at $10,-000 and pays $500 as hand money. Later Abrams fails to complete the deal and Bell keeps the deposit money. Three months later Bell sells the same property to Clark for $9,000 and now sues Abrams for an additional $500. Can he recover?

A. No. When Abrams failed to perform, Bell could have sued for the purchase price. Since he elected to keep the $500 as liquidated damages, he has no other remedy.

12. Q. A buyer asks the broker not to deposit his earnest money check of $1,000 for ten days. The check is later deposited and returned on account of insufficient funds. The buyer fails to complete the transaction. Is the broker liable to the owner?

A. Yes. The broker is required to deposit the earnest money promptly, unless the owner knew and agreed to the delayed deposit.

13. Q. A broker negotiated the sale of a property for $40,000, his commission to be 6 per cent. The buyer deposited $4,000 as earnest money. Before the deal was closed, buyer and seller mutually agreed to call the deal off, the owner to keep the $4,000 de-

posit. The owner offers the broker a commission of 6% on the $4,000 deposit. The broker claims $2,400. Decide.

A. The broker is entitled to $2,400 as he fully performed his contract with the owner in obtaining a purchaser acceptable to the owner.

14. Q. How should a down payment clause be worded to protect the seller fully?

A. "$500 upon the signing of these agreements, receipt of which is hereby acknowledged, and which sum may, *at the option* of the party of the first part, be retained as liquidated damages in event of breach of any of the conditions contained herein by the party of the second part, and the balance of $9,500, in cash, upon delivery of deed."

15. Q. How large a down payment should the seller require?

A. At least 10 per cent of the purchase price; a larger amount if the closing is at a date pretty far in the future or the responsibility of the buyer is questionable.

16. Q. An agreement of sale calls for the closing on May 1, 1969. The buyer is unable to close at that time. Will he forfeit his earnest money (down payment) if he fails to close on May 1?

A. No. The buyer has a reasonable time after May 1, 1969 to close the deal. What is a reasonable time depends upon the circumstances of each case. 30 days is certainly a reasonable time.

17. Q. Suppose, in the preceding case, the seller has certain commitments on May 1, 1969 and wants to be certain the deal will be closed on that date. How can the seller protect himself?

A. By providing that the date of closing is "of the essence" of the agreement.

18. Q. When a buyer defaults, what steps should a seller take?

A. Make a formal *tender* of the deed and *demand* of the consideration price.

19. Q. When is tender excused?

A. Tender is unnecessary where there is an anticipatory repudiation by the buyer; where the buyer has notified the seller before the closing that he will not go through with the deal.

20. Q. Is it necessary to have an agreement of sale acknowledged?

A. No. If acknowledged, the agreement can be recorded. The unexecuted agreement would then constitute a cloud upon the title.

21. Q. If the agreement of sale makes no provision for the apportionment of taxes, whose responsibility is the taxes?

A. The seller's unless local custom dictates otherwise.

22. Q. Bunt agreed to sell certain land to Judd, a purchaser, brought by Rice, a broker. The terms as written in the sales contract were "Selling price $5,000; ½ cash balance 1 to 4 years, with interest at 6%." Is the contract enforceable?

A. No; it is too vague and indefinite to be enforced, on account of the 1 to 4 year provision.

23. Q. What fixtures pass with the sale of real estate under an agreement of sale?
    A. Only those articles which may be considered as constituting a part of the freehold (real estate).

24. Q. Under what circumstances may an agent sign for his principal an agreement or contract required to be in writing?
    A. When he has a power of attorney duly recorded.

25. Q. Must an agreement for the sale of real estate be in writing?
    A. Yes, unless the purchaser has gone into possession, paid part of the purchase price, and made improvements.

26. Q. What should a broker do with down payments or earnest money that he has received?
    A. Deposit them in a trust account.

27. Q. Why is it important that a broker have the seller sign an agreement of sale and deliver a signed copy to the buyer?
    A. Because the purchaser may revoke his offer to purchase prior to the communication to him of the seller's acceptance of the offer.

28. Q. Can a contract for the sale of real estate be enforced if the description is not sufficient to identify the property?
    A. No.

29. Q. What is meant by a so-called "scavenger sale"?
    A. A sale of property which has reverted to the state because of nonpayment of taxes.

30. Q. Reed signs an agreement of sale to purchase certain real property from King on February 1, 1969 for $17,500. He pays $1,000 as a down payment and with King's consent, Reed moves in on February 15th. The deal was to be closed on March 15, 1969, but differences arose due to a faulty septic tank. The deal is not closed and Reed remains in possession until May 1, 1969. King claims a rental of $100 per month from February 15th to May 1st for use and occupancy. Can he recover?
    A. No. Reed did not move in under an express or implied *lease*. He simply took possession under the sales agreement and King cannot recover for use and occupancy. (Moral: If vendee is to take possession, have him sign a tight form lease for one month, with renewal on a monthly basis.)

31. Q. An offer to purchase is signed by a purchaser on January 28, 1969, and he pays $1,000 as a deposit at that time. It contains a clause to the effect that the buyer agrees to keep the offer open without fail for 5 days, within which the seller may accept the offer. On January 29, 1969, the buyer notifies the owner that he is withdrawing the offer and demands the return of his $1,000. Can he do so?
    A. Yes; he can withdraw the offer at any time before it is accepted. The five days simply means that the offer will automatically

expire at the end of that period unless accepted or previously withdrawn.

32. Q. What is the purpose of keeping a purchaser's deposit separate and apart from your own?

    A. The money does not belong to the broker. It is being held by him for the account of the owner and should therefore be treated as trust funds.

33. Q. A broker holding a listing on a property secures from a prospect a deposit and a signed agreement to purchase. What two steps should be taken next?

    A. He must leave one copy with the buyer, take three copies to the seller and have him sign all three copies. He leaves one copy with the seller, delivers one copy bearing the seller's signatures to the buyer, and keeps one copy for his own file.

34. Q. Should a broker deduct his commission from a deposit for the purchase of property if the offer of purchase is declined by the owner?

    A. No. There has been no binding contract of sale. Any commission due the broker should be paid by the seller.

35. Q. What is a "binder" in real estate?

    A. Earnest money paid to show good faith until the sale is closed.

36. Q. What are the essentials of a valid contract for the sale of real estate?

    A. The date, names of the parties, description of the property, terms of the sale, and signatures of the parties.

37. Q. In a contract for the sale of real property, by what term is the party known who (1) is selling the property? (2) is buying the property?

    A. (1) Vendor. (2) Vendee.

38. Q. If you, as broker, sell a property for your client and he takes back a purchase money mortgage in part payment, is he a mortgagor or mortgagee?

    A. Mortgagee.

39. Q. If a vendor signs an agreement of sale for real estate and transmits it by messenger to a notary public, can the notary legally take the acknowledgment of the signature?

    A. No. The person making the acknowledgment (the affiant) must appear in person.

40. Q. What is meant by the clause commonly found in contracts for the sale of real property reading "rents, taxes, interest on mortgages, and all premiums on insurance policies in force at date hereof are apportioned"?

    A. The items are prorated between buyer and seller as of the date of closing.

41. Q. A contract is made for the sale of real estate. Before taking title to the property and not being certain of the boundaries, the purchaser causes a (1) _____ to be made. Upon inspection of this document he discovers that telephone poles are situated on the plot of land and that for this reason the telephone company has a (2) _____ on the seller's land. He also discovers that one of the walls of a garage built on the rear portion of the land is situated on the adjoining property and this constitutes an (3) _____ on the adjoining property. Disturbed by these physical facts of the property he is about to buy, the purchaser orders an (4) _____ for the purpose of ascertaining the soundness of the title of the property.

A. (1) survey.
   (2) right of way.
   (3) encroachment.
   (4) abstract of title.

42. Q. A broker receives a $1,000 earnest money deposit. The parties have a controversy at the closing and the deal is not consummated. Buyer and seller demand the $1,000 deposit. Who is entitled to it?

A. Neither buyer nor seller. The broker is required to hold the deposit until the transaction is consummated or terminated. Since the matter may result in litigation, the broker should retain the money until court action is instituted. Then he should pay the money into court (interpleader) and enter a claim for his commission with the court.

43. Q. A broker had a $5,000 bond filed when he obtained his real estate license. The broker is sued on a furniture claim and the creditor recovers a judgment for $1,700. Can the creditor recover on the broker's real estate bond?

A. No. The claim did not result from a real estate transaction.

44. Q. (1) Why is it advisable from the standpoint of the purchaser to have inserted in the real estate contract that he is taking the property subject to an existing mortgage, rather than that he is assuming payment of the mortgage indebtedness? (2) If the purchaser does assume the mortgage indebtedness, does that relieve the original mortgagor of this obligation?

A. (1) Under this type mortgage clause (the short form) the purchaser is not liable to the mortgagee for payment of the mortgage indebtedness. The buyer can lose the property upon a mortgage default, but the mortgagee cannot collect a deficiency judgment from the purchaser of the property.

(2) Even though the purchaser does assume and agree to pay the mortgage debt (under long-form clause), the original mortgagor is not relieved from the mortgage obligation.

45. Q. In relation to real property, in what instances are the following terms employed? (1) "time is of the essence of this contract." (2) "to apportion as of the date of delivery of deed."

A. (1) Provision in agreement of sale which specifies the date for closing and makes it mandatory for the parties to perform on said date.

(2) Refers to prorating of taxes, rents, interest, and insurance.

46. Q. What is meant by an action of "specific performance"?

A. Court action to compel vendor to execute a deed in accordance with the terms of the agreement of sale.

47. Q. Keeping in mind the printed forms of real estate agreements of sale commonly used, list six of the items of information which should be inserted in the blank spaces.

A. 1. Name of the parties.
2. Date of closing.
3. Description.
4. Terms of the sale.
5. Apportionments of taxes, rent, interest, and insurance.
6. Date of possession.

48. Q. John Steele owns certain real estate clear of any mortgages or unpaid taxes. Name three other types of encumbrances which might cloud the title.

A. 1. Judgments.
2. A lease.
3. A right of way.

49. Q. Can the seller refuse to sign an agreement of sale when the broker insists upon retaining his commission out of the down payment?

A. Yes. The broker should deposit the money in an escrow account.

50. Q. In arranging for the closing of a real estate deal, enumerate at least ten items that a broker should look after or check.

A. 1. Have a copy of the agreement of sale at the closing.
2. See that tax receipts and water rent receipts are available.
3. Leases properly assigned to purchaser.
4. Endorsements for transfer of insurance policies.
5. Statement from mortgagee as to exact balance due upon mortgage; also receipt for last payment of mortgage interest.
6. Seller's old deed available for checking description in new deed.
7. Survey, if available.
8. Bill of sale for any personal property.
9. New deed to buyer.
10. Estimate of closing expense.
11. Purchaser has certified funds.
12. Transfer of keys.

51. Q. Harris, owner of certain premises, executed an exclusive listing contract on January 2, 1969, in favor of Stewart, a broker, for a period of three months, with power "for me and in my name to sell and execute contracts of sale" for the property in question. Stewart signed an agreement of sale with Snyder, deal to be closed on May 1, 1969. Harris refused to convey the property, contending that where the principal-agent relationship is limited to time, the agent is without authority to enter into a contract to be performed subsequent to the expiration of the agency contract. Snyder brought suit for specific performance. Who will win?

A. Snyder will win. Under the listing contract, Stewart is authorized to execute a binding agreement of sale for the owner, Harris. It is of no consequence that the agreement of sale will be consummated subsequent to the expiration of the listing contract.

52. Q. Name five items which are usually adjusted at the closing of a real estate transaction between seller and buyer.

A. 1. Taxes.
   2. Water rents.
   3. Fire insurance premiums.
   4. Rents.
   5. Interest on mortgage.

53. Q. What is meant by proration and what items are usually pro-rated?

A. Proration is the apportionment of certain items as of the date of closing the deal between seller and buyer. The items usually pro-rated are stated in the preceding answer.

54. Q. A and B sign a binder for the sale of a parcel of real property, with the provision that a formal contract would be signed the next day. The following day A refused to complete the transaction. Can B force A to go through with the transaction since no formal contract was signed?

A. No, since the terms of the contract have not yet been agreed upon. Courts do not make contracts for the parties.

55. Q. You have obtained an offer to purchase and have an earnest money receipt signed by the prospective purchaser. You find that the property is owned by John Brown and Mary Brown, his wife, and Martha Brown, the mother of John Brown. The offer is acceptable to the Browns. Who would you have sign the earnest money receipt?

A. John Brown and Mary Brown, his wife, and Martha Brown, the mother.

56. Q. In the above case you find upon contact with the owners of the property that Martha Brown, the mother, is away on a trip to California and not readily available. You, therefore, have the earnest money receipt signed by John and Mary Brown. Later, before any further steps are taken, the purchaser decides to cancel the deal and asks for his money back. Are you required to refund the earnest money deposit?

A. Yes; the offer has not been accepted by all parties who hold title.

57. Q. Suppose in the case above-cited it develops that the mother,

Martha Brown, will not sign the deed transferring the property to the prospective purchaser. You have a buyer ready, willing, and able but cannot deliver. Can you collect a commission? If so, from whom?

A. Yes. You can sue John Brown and Mary Brown.

58. Q. The following earnest money receipt was submitted as evidence:

> May 10, 1969. Received from John Doe $80.00 Eighty Dollars earnest money on lot and house number 960 Union Street. Price $5,000.00 Five Thousand and balance of $4,920.00 to be paid when papers and title insurance are completed. It is understood this deal would be closed and house vacated on or before June the 10th. All furniture except personal belongings included in this transaction.

Is this document binding upon the parties?

A. No; agreement is incomplete as it contemplates a subsequent instrument. In Oregon, omission of city considered fatal; in Pennsylvania, parol (oral) evidence permitted for purpose of giving a more precise description.

59. Q. An agreement of sale is made out between Ben Sharp, vendor, and Charles Lang. However, the agreement is signed by Ben Sharp and his wife, Myrtle Sharp. The wife, later, refuses to sign the deed. Can she be compelled to join in the deed?

A. Yes. Although her name does not appear in the body of the agreement, she has indicated an intention to be bound by the agreement by signing it.

60. Q. If a broker accepts a check for $1,000 from a buyer, who signs an agreement of sale, which is also executed by the seller, and then the buyer stops payment on the check, is the agreement of sale void?

A. No; the contract came into being when the agreement of sale was signed by both principal parties. The check is incidental or collateral to the contract and has no effect upon its validity.

61. Q. A broker prepared an agreement of sale, which recites a $1,000 cash deposit received. Actually, he received a 10-day promissory note to his order, which is unpaid at maturity. Upon ascertaining these facts, the seller decides to renounce the deal. Can he do so?

A. No; the buyer can hold the seller to the agreement so long as the buyer fully performs his part of the deal at the closing.

62. Q. A broker negotiates a real estate deal upon his oral promise that he will find "suitable or comparable" quarters for the seller. He fails to do so. Is he liable on his oral promise which is not contained in the agreement of sale?

A. Yes; the broker is personally responsible in damages to the seller for his failure to perform his promise.

63. Q. In order to prevent the assignment of an agreement of sale, what clause should be included?

A. "It is hereby agreed that rights under the within agreement are not assignable."

64. Q. A recorded agreement of sale constitutes a cloud on the title. How may it be removed?

A. 1. By a deed from vendor to vendee.

2. By a quit claim deed from vendee to vendor or vendor's purchaser.

3. By court decree.

4. By instrument of extinguishment.

65. Q. What is meant by equity when used in connection with real estate transactions?

A. The margin of value which the owner possesses between the market price of the property and the indebtedness against it.

66. Q. A broker obtained a written offer to purchase certain property at $20,500. The seller agrees to sell at $21,200 and signs a contract at that price. This price is unacceptable to the buyer. Two days later, the seller signs acceptance of the original offer at $20,500. The buyer now refuses to buy the property. Is there a valid contract?

A. No; when the seller offered to sell at $21,200, it was a counter-proposition and constituted a rejection of the original offer. An offer once rejected is gone forever unless the offeror elects to revive it.

67. Q. Identify the following, whether realty or personalty: (1) growing corn, (2) cut logs, (3) growing wheat, (4) growing meadow grass, (5) nursery trees, (6) window shades, (7) electric chandeliers, (8) linoleum glued to floor, (9) potted plants, (10) gas grate setting in fireplace.

A. 1-2-3-5-6-9-10 are personalty; 4-7-8 are realty.

68. Q. Where an offer has been mailed to the seller, is there a contract if the seller mails his acceptance, and due to some delay in the mail service, it does not reach the buyer for 15 days?

A. Yes. The contract came into being when the letter of acceptance was mailed. The mail service is considered the agent of the buyer since he used that medium in communicating the offer.

69. Q. What effect does an alteration to an agreement of sale by the broker or seller, after execution by buyer, have upon the instrument?

A. The buyer could repudiate the contract. Even if the alteration appears harmless, it may have some effect as to the buyer's desires or prejudice his purposes.

70. Q. What is the difference between cancellation and rescission of a contract of sale?

A. Cancellation is by mutual consent; rescission is by court action.

71. Q. Does a counter proposition enjoy the same rights of withdrawal (before acceptance) as the original offer to purchase?

A. Yes, since a counter proposition constitutes a new offer.

72. Q. D. Smith makes a written offer to purchase R. Lincoln's property for $18,000, with $1,000 down, $1,000 in 30 days and balance in 90 days. Lincoln makes a counter proposition to sell for $19,000 with terms of $2,000 down and balance in 60 days. This proposition is refused by Smith. Lincoln then agrees to accept Smith's original proposition, but Smith now refuses to deal. Is there a valid contract?

A. No. A counter proposition is the same as a rejection. An offer, once rejected, is gone forever, unless the other party is willing to reinstate it.

73. Q. To whose advantage is it to prorate taxes and rent from an income property as of the possession rate, rather than the closing date?

A. Seller. He will continue to receive rents, which should exceed taxes and expenses.

74. Q. A husband and wife buy a home and take title, as such. Shortly afterwards, the husband leaves and his whereabouts are unknown. The wife cannot afford to keep up the payments. Can she sell the property?

A. No; unless she has him declared legally dead after the years specified in the statute.

75. Q. If a broker has good reason to doubt the competency of his owner, due to age and senility, and the owner wishes to sell, what protective steps can the broker take to avoid difficulty with some members of owner's family?

A. Have an interested party petition the court to appoint a guardian for the owner and have guardian sign agreement.

76. Q. In selling a home, can the seller take with him the bedroom unit air-conditioner, or does it belong to buyer?

A. The unit is considered the personal property of the seller.

77. Q. John Davis, 21 years of age, signs an agreement to purchase a house. He is drafted before the deal is closed. He writes the owner to cancel the deal. Will he succeed?

A. Yes; as a practical matter. He is protected by law from any court proceeding on the contract during his military service. Rather than tie up the property indefinitely, the owner's interests would be served by selling the property to another party.

78. Q. An agreement of sale recites that the Friend Real Estate Co. is the broker in the deal and the owner agrees to pay him a commission of 7 per cent. Can Friend maintain a court action for a commission on the strength of this clause?

A. Yes; recent court decisions in Pennsylvania and Virginia have so held.

79. Q. A listing agreement, dated May 2, 1969 is given to a broker for 90 days. Will it expire in three months?

A. No. It will expire at midnight on the 90th day from May 2.

80. Q. Can a salesman be held liable for earnest money that was turned over to his broker, who dies insolvent?

A. No. The salesman is required to turn over all deposit money to his employing broker.

81. Q. Clayton lists property with Moore Realty for $15,000. He obtains a prospect at $13,700. Clayton uses the offer of $13,700 to sell the property to his own prospect at $14,200. Is the broker entitled to a commission?

A. No. This is one of the "risks of the trade."

82. Q. Under what circumstances can a broker represent a buyer?

A. There is nothing to prevent a broker from representing a buyer and look to the *buyer* for a commission. However, he cannot, at the same time, represent the seller, unless both parties know it and agree to it.

83. Q. Should a broker quote any price other than the listing price to a prospect?

A. No. He can entertain a lower price offered by a prospect and submit it to the owner and thus negotiate.

84. Q. Can there be a verbal exclusive listing contract?

A. Yes; but it is difficult to prove and very unsatisfactory. In states requiring listings to be in writing, the answer is No.

85. Q. Is an agreement between salesman and broker legal that states that if salesman leaves the broker's employ, he will never again engage in the real estate business in that state?

A. No. Contracts in restraint of trade must be reasonable as to area and as to time.

86. Q. Is it improper for a broker to loan his commission to the buyer for use as the down payment?

A. Yes. The practice would be unethical and cast doubts that he has an "able" buyer.

True and False

1. A buyer is entitled to the prompt refund of his deposit money if he withdraws his offer before the owner accepts it.   **T** F

2. The licensee can rely upon the seller's statement that the city will build a public garage next door within one year and repeats this to a prospect.   T **F**

3. A purchaser under a land contract usually takes possession of the premises.   **T** F

4. In any real estate transaction, the broker is empowered to sign a contract of sale for the seller.   T **F**

5. A contract for the purchase of real estate for cash may be assigned to another.   **T** F

6. A vendor of real estate is sometimes called the seller.   **T** F

7. Federal Revenue Stamps are not required on a deed.   **T** F

8. Either the salesman or broker must witness the purchase contract to make it valid.   T **F**

9. The terms "option" and "listing" have the same meaning.   T **F**

10. Title insurance offers protection against loss by fire if property is destroyed before the deal is closed.   T **F**

11. An option contract must be bound by a consideration.   **T** F

12. Conditional land contracts of sale may be assigned.   **T** F

13. Chattel and personal property mean the same thing.   **T** F

14. Deposit money held by a broker must be kept in a fireproof safe.   T **F**

15. The amount of the consideration determines the amount of the earnest money deposit.   T **F**

16. Provided the broker and the buyer agree, it is permissible not to cash the check for the deposit money until the closing.   T **F**

17. A real estate broker is not required to give the buyer a copy of the closing statement until the deed is recorded.   T **F**

18. The earnest money check should be made payable to broker instead of to seller.   **T** F

19. A broker has authority to acknowledge a purchase agreement since he is a neutral party.   T **F**

20. Where the sole owner is a married woman, the husband's signature is necessary on a contract of sale.   **T** F

21. Land divided into 6 parcels for purpose of sale is known as a subdivision.   **T** F

22. Chattel is another name for a wife's interest in her husband's property.   T **F**

23. Marginal land is land on the edge of a real estate development.   T **F**

24. In an option, the optionor has the right to collect rents on the property during the life of the option.   **T** F

25. A broker should close the deals negotiated by his salesmen.   **T** F

26. The full consideration in any real estate deal must always be in legal tender.   T **F**

27. A person, other than an attorney at law, may be given power of attorney.   **T** F

28. Contracts to exchange real property need not be in writing to be enforceable.   T **F**

29. A sales agreement must be acknowledged in order to be valid.   T **F**

30. The purchaser cannot rescind the deal and get his earnest money back after the seller has orally approved the deal.   T **F**

31. Real estate sold on "conditional sale contract" or "land contract" can be subject to liens for indebtedness of the seller.   **T** F

32. There is no difference between a void and a voidable contract.   T **F**

33. Any alteration to an executed contract of sale is proper, if it is initialed by all the parties.   **T** F

34. It is important that the broker sign the contract of sale for real estate.   T **F**

35. A sales agreement must be acknowledged in order to be recorded.   **T** F

36. When a prospect submits to a broker an offer to buy real estate, the prospect cannot withdraw his offer until the owner has had an opportunity to act upon it. **T** **F̲**

37. Both parties to an agreement of sale should receive signed copies of the agreement. **T̲** F

38. An agreement of sale to be valid and binding must
    1. be entered into by competent parties. **T̲** F
    2. be bound by a consideration. **T̲** F
    3. possess mutuality. **T̲** F
    4. represent an actual meeting of minds. **T̲** F
    5. cover a legal and moral act. **T̲** F
    6. be oral. T **F̲**

39. A seller under an agreement of sale is known as the vendee. T **F̲**

40. One who has taken an option on certain real estate is bound to complete the purchase of property. T **F̲**

41. A contract of sale must be accompanied by a deposit to bind the transaction. T **F̲**

42. It is essential that a deal be closed on the date specified in the agreement. T **F̲**

43. The real estate broker is not a principal party to an agreement of sale. **T̲** F

44. An agreement of sale need only be signed by the vendor if the vendee pays a deposit. **T̲** F

45. A contract for the exchange of real estate must be in writing. **T̲** F

46. There must be at least three persons and a witness to form a binding agreement of sale. T **F̲**

47. An agreement of sale must be acknowledged by the vendor in order to be binding. T **F̲**

48. Upon the sale of a piece of property, the seller may remove and take with him:
    1. the gas range in the kitchen. **T̲** F
    2. a chandelier. T **F̲**
    3. shrubbery bordering the walk. T **F̲**
    4. the hall carpet. **T̲** F
    5. the furnace shovel and poker. **T̲** F
    6. the living room lamp. **T̲** F
    7. the awnings (specially fitted). T **F̲**
    8. gas or electric water heater. T **F̲**

49. An option should always be signed by the optionee. T **F̲**

50. A "bill of sale" is the instrument by which title to real estate is conveyed. T **F̲**

51. Once an agreement of sale is signed, the broker may file a lien for his commission, if not paid. T **F̲**

52. An attorney-in-fact who signs an agreement of sale must be an attorney at law. T **F̲**

53. Restrictions as to the use of property in an agreement are encumbrances but are not liens. **T̲** F

54. Fence posts are personal property. T **F̲**

55. An "abstract of title" guarantees a clear title.   T **F**
56. An equity represents the actual amount of money a purchaser has paid on the property.   **T** F
57. An option for which no consideration is given is not enforceable.   **T** F
58. A power of attorney to sign an agreement of sale can be given only to duly qualified attorneys at law.   T **F**
59. If a prospective purchaser revokes his offer in writing before he has received an accepted copy, signed by the seller, of the offer to purchase, he is entitled to the return of his deposit.   **T** F
60. The sale of a property for cash automatically cancels a lease for less than one year.   T **F**
61. An oral agreement for the sale of real estate, never reduced to writing, usually cannot be enforced.   **T** F
62. When a prospect submits to a broker an offer to buy real estate, the prospect cannot withdraw his offer until the owner has had an opportunity to accept or reject it.   T **F**
63. Where money is actually paid as consideration for an option, the option cannot be assigned by the holder thereof.   T **F**
64. A purchaser cannot rescind the deal and get his earnest money back after the seller has orally approved the deal.   T **F**
65. If the earnest money received by a broker is represented by a note, it is essential that the earnest money receipt show that fact.   **T** F
66. A tractor used to till a farm is considered real estate.   T **F**
67. If a seller is married, it is the duty of the broker to procure the signature of the seller's husband or wife on the agreement of sale.   **T** F
68. If a slight alteration is made in the earnest money receipt after it is signed by the purchaser, this does not invalidate the earnest money receipt.   T **F**
69. Permanent buildings on real estate are not personalty.   **T** F
70. Once the owner accepts an offer to purchase even on different terms from those contained in the offer, there is a binding contract.   T **F**
71. The seller should pay for the continuation of an abstract of title.   **T** F
72. The buyer should pay for an attorney's examination of the title.   **T** F
73. The sale of land does not include buildings unless expressly stated.   T **F**
74. A purchaser buying real estate under a land contract does not usually have title to the property.   **T** F
75. A valid written sales contract is binding even if the seller dies.   **T** F
76. A real estate transaction completed on Sunday is enforceable.   T **F**
77. If a person signs a joint and several note with other persons,

it is possible that he may become liable for the entire sum of the note. **T** F

78. A contract of sale must be accompanied by a deposit to bind the transaction. **T** **F**

79. "Trade fixtures" mean the brands, labels, names of products and the good will of a business. **T** **F**

80. When a property is sold, all insurance policies then in effect should be immediately cancelled and new policies written. **T** **F**

81. An agreement of sale, which requires the purchaser to place his mortgage through the broker who negotiated the deed, is contrary to good ethics. **T** F

82. One who has taken an option on certain real estate may refuse to complete the purchase of the property. **T** F

83. If property is held by husband and wife as tenants by the entirety, neither may agree to sell to a third party his or her interest separately. **T** F

84. The reason for securing a deposit on the sale of real property is to guarantee the broker his commission in the event of a sale. **T** **F**

85. Unless expressly released in writing by the vendor, the vendee making an assignment of his interest in a land contract is not released from his liability for the unpaid balance of the contract. **T** F

86. When a husband is buying real property, it is not necessary for the wife to sign the contract to purchase as the husband's signature binds both of them. **T** **F**

87. Apportionment of taxes means prorating taxes between vendor and vendee as of time of closing. **T** F

88. All rights under an agreement of sale are merged in the subsequent deed. **T** F

89. The seller is always entitled to keep the earnest money if the buyer defaults without cause. **T** F

90. A tender of deed and demand for payment of the consideration is necessary in order to place the buyer in default. **T** F

91. Any items of movable or immovable property other than real estate is called a chattel. **T** F

92. There is a difference between a void and a voidable contract. **T** F

93. When title to real property is transferred, the insurance policies on the property are usually prorated at the closing. **T** F

94. An owner can refuse to sign a sales agreement unless the deposit money is turned over to him. **T** F

95. A listing agreement should provide that deposit money shall be held by the broker in escrow. **T** F

96. Once the seller signs the sales agreement, he cannot later demand that the down payment be turned over to him. **T** F

97. A broker is not liable for any misstatements that he makes because he is not a party of the sales agreement. **T** **F**

98. A broker is personally responsible, if he promises the buyer
that he will procure a mortgage and is unable to do so. **T** F

99. If the sale is contingent upon buyer selling his present home,
the broker should include that fact in sales contract. **T** F

100. A broker is within his rights in accepting a "postdated"
check even if sales agreement acknowledges cash. T **F**

101. It is acceptable practice for a broker to tell a salesman to attend the closing in his stead, even if the salesman did not
negotiate the deal. T **F**

102. The broker attends the closing only to receive the commission or balance due him. T **F**

103. The broker attends the closing to settle any disputes that
may arise between seller and buyer. T **F**

104. A broker should not compromise his commission claim in
order to resolve a financial dispute between seller and
buyer. **T** F

105. A broker cannot collect an earned commission if it is contingent upon a settlement, which does not materialize. **T** F

106. An offer-to-buy may be withdrawn after the prospective purchaser and the seller have signed the writing, but before the
seller's signed copy is delivered to the buyer. **T** F

107. An habitual drunkard is considered insincere and his contractual capacity limited accordingly. **T** F

108. An oral contract to sell real estate is not void but unenforceable. **T** F

109. If a buyer defaults upon a contract of sale, the broker should
turn the entire earnest money deposit over to the seller
forthwith. T **F**

110. Where the seller and buyer have a dispute as to the terms of
a contract of sale and the deal is not closed, the broker should
pay the earnest money deposit into court. **T** F

111. A broker should not advise a buyer as to his legal rights
where there is a dispute between buyer and seller. **T** F

112. A listing agreement must be signed by both buyer and seller
in order to be enforceable. T **F**

113. Hand money, deposit money and earnest money mean the
same thing. **T** F

114. The sale of lands does not include buildings unless specifically
stated. T **F**

115. Every state has a statute of frauds which requires real estate
contracts to be in writing in order to be enforceable. **T** F

116. An acceptance of an offer to purchase, after expiration of the
time limit of the offer constitutes a "counter proposition." T **F**

117. The salesman who made the sale, rather than his broker,
should attend the closing. T **F**

118. Where the buyer withdraws his offer after he has signed a
contract of sale, he is liable to the broker for his commission. T **F**

119. If an agreement of sale does not have a date specified for closing, it is void. **T** **F**
120. Where the description in the contract of sale gives a street address and number, but no city, it is void. **T** F
121. Where a single woman, who is engaged to be married, executes a sales contract for her own property, it is necessary to have her fiancé join. **T** **F**
122. An inmate of a home for the aged cannot execute a real estate sales contract without an order of court. **T** **F**
123. A land purchase contract is generally used to purchase real estate by people of limited means. **T** F
124. A buyer may rescind an agreement of sale, where the broker, without authority of the seller, has misrepresented the property. **T** F
125. Where the broker knows the property is infested with termites, and fails to disclose that hidden fact from the buyer, the latter can rescind the contract. **T** F
126. Rescission or avoidance of a contract is addressed to the equity side of the court. **T** F
127. A judgment or cognovit note, payable on demand, is the same as a cash earnest money deposit. **T** **F**
128. At the closing of a real estate, the seller can refuse to accept the buyer's personal check in payment of the consideration price. **T** F
129. A check on a building and loan association account is acceptable as an earnest money deposit. **T** **F**
130. A broker should place a "SOLD" sign on a property when the agreement of sale is signed by both buyer and seller. **T** **F**
131. The vendee pays the cost of preparing the mortgage or deed of trust papers. **T** F
132. A broker is entitled to a fee for preparing the mortgage papers. **T** **F**
133. Action by a buyer for specific performance of a contract of sale must be brought within two years from the specified date for performance. **T** **F**
134. Where the closing date in a sales agreement is more than three months in advance, the broker should insist upon a much larger down payment than usual. **T** F
135. The deposit money is necessary in order to enforce an agreement. **T** F
136. If the date in an agreement of sale is missing, the contract is void. **T** **F**
137. In signing a binder, the purchaser does not obligate himself for a future purchase agreement. **T** F
138. A broker can accept a note as a deposit so long as he is willing to make up the note, if unpaid. **T** **F**
139. An article can change from personalty to realty and then back to personalty. **T** F

140. Earnest money is money paid to close a real estate transaction.   T **F**
141. In a land contract, the purchaser receives a deed and takes
possession immediately.   T **F**
142. The listing contract is usually the first instrument the buyer
signs in purchasing property.   T **F**
143. Trade fixtures are usually so affixed to the property that they
become part of the property and may not be removed.   T **F**
144. Property classed as real property can become personal property.   **T** F
145. A thirty-day month is usually used in prorating all real
estate transactions.   **T** F
146. A purchaser usually takes possession under a land contract.   **T** F
147. Where a conflict arises, the written part of a contract usually
prevails over the printed part.   **T** F
148. The sale of land does not include the buildings unless expressly stated.   T **F**
149. When rugs and drapes are included in the sale of a residence,
title to these articles is usually transferred by a chattel
mortgage.   T **F**
150. A salesman receiving a deposit of earnest money should turn
it over to the owner.   T **F**
151. A buyer under a land contract who erects improvements may
remove the same if he defaults on his contract.   T **F**
152. An escrow holder is considered the agent for both the buyer
and the seller.   **T** F
153. Fixtures, shelves, counters and merchandise in a grocery store
do not pass with a transfer of the property.   **T** F
154. A bill of sale is used to convey title to appurtenances.   T **F**
155. Hand money paid upon the signing of a contract of sale is
called an option.   T **F**
156. An acceptance of an offer after the expiration of the time limit
on the offer constitutes a counter proposition.   **T** F
157. Under a land contract, the seller retains title until certain
stipulated conditions are performed.   **T** F
158. "Good will" has value but is never carried as an asset.   T **F**
159. The salesman who negotiated the deal should attend the closing in order to collect the commission.   T **F**
160. Under an exclusive right-to-sell listing contract, the broker
has authority to sign an agreement of sale for the owner.   T **F**
161. The consideration for a deed must always be shown in
dollars and cents.   T **F**
162. The sale of land does not include the buildings unless expressly stated.   T **F**
163. The buyer pays for the abstract examination.   T **F**
164. The broker pays for the loan closing costs.   **T** F
165. An agreement of sale that requires the buyer to place his

fire insurance through the selling broker as long as he owns the property would be considered unethical.   **T** F

166. A contract of sale involving financial responsibility is not assignable.   **T** F

167. A contract calling for a May 1, 1969 closing date must be closed on that date or the buyer forfeits his deposit money.   T **F**

168. After terms of an escrow are agreed upon, they may not be later modified.   T **F**

169. A quit claim deed from vendee to vendor may be used to extinguish an agreement of sale.   **T** F

170. A land instrument contract and an option are the same.   T **F**

171. It is not necessary for all parties in a partnership to sign an agreement to sell real property.   **T** F

172. Ordinarily, an optionee may collect rents on the optioned property, during the life of the option.   T **F**

173. A purchaser may rescind the transaction and recover his earnest money even after the seller orally approved the sale.   **T** F

174. The optionor can enforce the terms of an option contract by legal action.   T **F**

175. $1 is sufficient consideration to support an option to purchase a property worth $1,000,000.   **T** F

176. Under an installment land purchase contract, the seller can enter judgment for the balance of the purchase price.   **T** F

177. When a buyer signs an agreement of sale, he can void it by stopping payment on the check for the deposit money.   T **F**

178. An agreement of sale controls the contents of the deed.   **T** F

179. The first instrument a buyer signs in a real estate transaction is usually the agreement of sale.   **T** F

180. Good consideration is always in monetary terms.   T **F**

181. In order to make a joint tenancy deed, it is necessary for the agreement of sale to so provide.   **T** F

182. An agreement of sale may be enforceable by court action, even if no earnest money deposit is paid.   **T** F

183. Acceptance is to an offer what a lighted match is to a charge of gun powder, in that it produces something which cannot be undone or recalled.   **T** F

184. There is a difference between fraud and misrepresentation. **T** F

185. Co-insurance means that husband and wife are co-owners of an insurance policy.   T **F**

186. A good way for a broker to obtain listings is to advertise free appraisals.   T **F**

187. A licensed broker has the legal right to render an opinion on the validity of title to real estate.   T **F**

188. If a sale is contingent upon a buyer selling his present home, this fact should not be included in the agreement of sale. T **F**

189. If the buyer is to obtain a mortgage, the agreement should
specify amount, interest and term.   T   F

Multiple Choice

1. Once an agreement of sale is signed, the purchaser has
   ( ) legal title.
   (x) equitable title.
   ( ) ostensible title.
   ( ) naked title.
2. A charge against a property owner to cover the proportionate cause
   of a street paving is
   ( ) an ad valorem tax.
   ( ) a county tax.
   (x) an assessment.
   ( ) equitable obligation.
3. Whenever all parties agree to the terms of a real estate contract,
   there has been
   ( ) legality of object.
   (x) meeting of the minds.
   ( ) reality of consent.
   ( ) bilateral consideration.
4. At the time a buyer indicates he is ready to execute an agreement,
   the broker should obtain a
   ( ) trust deed.
   ( ) negotiable note.
   (x) deposit.
   ( ) surety.
5. Unless there is a stipulation to the contrary, when real estate
   under a lease is sold, the lease
   ( ) must be renewed.
   ( ) is immediately cancelled.
   (x) remains binding on the new owner.
   ( ) becomes a tenancy from month to month.
6. A real estate salesman, after receiving a deposit of earnest money,
   should immediately
   ( ) turn it over to the seller.
   ( ) deposit it in his personal account until the closing.
   (x) give it to his broker to deposit in a trustee account.
   ( ) turn it over to seller's attorney.
7. Ames, a prospective purchaser, writes a letter to Brown on January 7, 1969, offering to buy certain described real estate owned by
   Brown for $20,000. Brown replies promptly by letter stating "I ac-
   cept your offer contained in letter of January 7, 1969." Which of
   the following describes the situation?
   ( ) There is an offer but no acceptance.
   (x) There is a valid contract between Ames and Brown.

   ( ) There is an acceptance but no offer.
   ( ) There is no contract between the parties.

8. One who has the right to sign the name of his principal to a contract of sale is
   ( ) a special agent.
   ( ) an optionee.
   (x) an attorney-in-fact.
   ( ) an attorney at law.

9. When real property is sold on an installment contract, and a warranty deed to be delivered at a future date, the warranty deed should be placed in the custody of
   ( ) the real estate broker.
   ( ) the seller.
   ( ) the buyer.
   (x) an escrow agent.

10. A seller, upon signing a contract of sale, has
   ( ) equitable title.
   (x) naked title.
   ( ) beneficial title.
   ( ) reversionary title.

11. Which of the following instruments is not delivered to the buyer at the closing of the sale?
   ( ) Deed.
   ( ) Lease.
   ( ) Affidavit of title.
   (x) Mortgage.

12. Under the usual form agreement of sale, the option to declare the deposit money forfeited belongs to
   (x) Seller.
   ( ) Broker.
   ( ) Buyer.
   ( ) Real Estate Commission.

13. A contract by which the owner agrees with another person that he shall have a right to buy the property at a fixed price within a certain time is called
   ( ) an escrow agreement.
   ( ) an exclusive.
   (x) an option.
   ( ) the first right of refusal.

14. A purchaser's part ownership or interest in a parcel of real estate is called an
   ( ) equality.
   (x) equity.
   ( ) inheritance.
   ( ) fee.

15. To each sales agreement there must be
   (x) an offer and an acceptance.

( ) earnest money payment.
( ) notarial acknowledgment.
( ) a recordation.
16. The tax on a given piece of real property is always determined by multiplying the tax rate by the
    ( ) selling price.
    (x) assessed valuation of the property.
    ( ) appraised valuation of the property.
17. When the contract for the sale of real property includes the sale of certain removable fixtures, such as, refrigerators and radiator covers, upon delivery of the deed, the seller should also deliver a
    (x) bill of sale.
    ( ) estoppel certificate.
    ( ) chattel mortgage.
    ( ) satisfaction piece.
18. A broker, receiving a deposit of earnest money, should
    ( ) tender it to the owner.
    ( ) keep it, pending final closing of the deal.
    ( ) use it to cover expenses on the sale.
    (x) deposit it in a trust account at the bank.
19. An option contract differs from a contract of sale in that
    (x) the option need not be consummated.
    ( ) the option needs no consideration.
    ( ) the contract of sale is enforceable on either party to it.
    ( ) the contract of sale requires consideration.
20. An owner delivers to Smith an option to purchase certain real estate upon Smith's payment of $10,000 within 30 days; the option recites that it is given in consideration of one dollar, the receipt of which the owner acknowledges; as a matter of fact, *nothing* is paid for the option. Under these circumstances the option is generally
    (x) valid.
    ( ) void.
    ( ) voidable.
21. A contract of purchase or sale of real property should be signed by
    ( ) the broker.
    ( ) the agent and seller.
    ( ) the seller only.
    (x) the buyer and seller.
22. Tender of deed is unnecessary where
    ( ) time is of the essence.
    ( ) the earnest money is less than 5 per cent.
    ( ) date for performance has expired.
    (x) there is an anticipatory repudiation by buyer.
23. The amount of deposit money is
    ( ) fixed by the real estate license act.
    (x) agreement of the parties.
    ( ) a minimum of 5 per cent of consideration price.

( ) determined by broker.
24. Where the seller defaults, the hand money or earnest payment
    ( ) belongs to the broker.
    (x) should be returned to the buyer.
    ( ) should be placed in an escrow fund.
25. An oral agreement of sale may be enforced where
    ( ) the consideration price is less than $2,500.
    ( ) there is a down payment of 20 per cent of the consideration.
    (x) the purchaser has gone into possession, paid part of the purchase price, and made improvements.
    ( ) the broker guarantees performance.
26. Breach of an oral agreement of sale gives rise to
    ( ) an action for specific performance.
    (x) an action for damages.
    ( ) a suit by broker against buyer for commission.
    ( ) a suit for a written agreement of sale.
27. Upon the signing of agreements of sale
    ( ) the legal title passes to purchaser.
    (x) the equitable title passes to purchaser.
    ( ) no title to the real estate passes.
28. Anything that is fastened or attached to real property permanently is considered to be
    ( ) personal property.
    (x) real property.
    ( ) private property.
    ( ) separate property.
29. A sewage disposal bill is a
    ( ) easement.
    ( ) lien.
    ( ) encumbrance.
    (x) charge.
30. A contract based on an illegal consideration is
    ( ) valid.
    (x) void.
    ( ) legal.
    ( ) enforceable.
31. The seller of real estate is sometimes called the
    ( ) vendee.
    (x) vendor.
    ( ) lessee.
    ( ) lessor.
32. Where a property is destroyed by fire after the agreement of sale is signed, the loss usually falls upon
    ( ) the seller.
    (x) the buyer.
    ( ) the broker.
33. When a purchaser withdraws his offer to purchase before it has

been accepted by the seller, the broker should dispose of any hand
money received from the would-be purchaser in the following
manner:

( ) give it to the seller.

(x) give it to the buyer.

( ) keep it as his commission.

( ) pay it into court.

34. An option without a valid consideration is

( ) valid.

(x) void.

( ) revocable.

( ) enforceable.

35. A payment made to bind a seller to the sale of real estate for a
period of time is

( ) a binder.

( ) a bond.

( ) an escrow agreement.

(x) an option.

36. Hand money paid upon the signing of an agreement of sale is called

( ) an option.

( ) a recognizance

(x) earnest money.

( ) a freehold estate.

37. The description of land sold under an agreement of sale should

( ) give the house number and street.

(x) give a full legal description.

( ) describe the improvements.

38. If, upon receipt of an offer to purchase under certain terms, the
seller makes a counter offer, the prospective purchaser is

( ) bound by his original offer.

( ) bound to accept the counter offer.

( ) bound by the agent's decision.

(x) relieved of his original offer.

39. Insurance policy premiums on real property are prorated in escrow
from the date the policy was

( ) written.

( ) recorded.

(x) transferred.

( ) cancelled.

40. Which of the following instruments would not belong in the same
escrow with the others?

( ) Mortgage.

( ) Escrow instructions.

( ) Warranty deed.

(x) Deed of trust note.

41. When speaking of "improvements" regarding real estate, we mean

( ) fences, wells, drains, roadways, etc.

(x) everything except the land.

( ) additions to the original house.

42. An owner delivers to a party an option to purchase certain real estate upon payment of $5,000 within thirty days; the option states that it is given in consideration of one dollar, the receipt of which the owner acknowledges; as a matter of fact, nothing is paid for the option. Under these circumstances, the option is generally

(x) valid.

( ) void.

( ) renewable.

( ) not enforceable.

43. A sales agreement which provides that the broker involved should have the exclusive right to place the fire insurance upon the property during the life of the building is

( ) allowed only if the broker is also licensed as an insurance agent.

(x) contrary to public policy.

( ) in the best interests of all.

( ) allowed if a copy is filed with the State Insurance Department.

44. It is necessary to set forth in a land contract

( ) the date the final payment is due.

(x) the purchase price and terms of agreement.

( ) amount of commission received by broker.

45. A tract of land described as the NE¼ of NW¼ of NW¼ of NW¼ contains:

( ) 20 acres.

( ) 10 acres.

( ) 5 acres.

(x) 2½ acres.

46. The document which conditionally conveys title to real estate is a

(x) mortgage.

( ) land installment contract.

( ) chattel mortgage.

( ) conditional bailment lease.

47. A financing arrangement by which the buyer does not become the owner of record would be by a

( ) trust deed.

(x) land contract.

( ) purchase money mortgage.

( ) quit claim deed.

48. An option cannot legally be sold or assigned if the original consideration for the option was

( ) money.

( ) a promissory note.

(x) love and affection.

( ) a personal check.

49. A licensed real estate broker selling a property on which he holds
    an option must notify the purchaser that he is the
    (x) optionee.
    ( ) optionor.
    ( ) tenant.
    ( ) lessee.
50. To determine the reasonable limit a man of ordinary income might
    be expected to pay for a home, his annual income is multiplied by
    ( ) 1.
    (x) 2½.
    ( ) 5.
    ( ) 10.
51. A bill of sale is used to convey title to
    ( ) an easement.
    (x) personal property.
    ( ) life estate in real estate.
    ( ) real property.
52. A state deed transfer tax should be paid by the
    (x) seller.
    ( ) buyer.
    ( ) broker.
    ( ) mortgagee.
53. A contract which has no force or effect is said to be
    ( ) valid.
    (x) void.
    ( ) voidable.
    ( ) revoked.
54. An item of personal property may be called a
    ( ) freehold.
    ( ) realty.
    ( ) tenure.
    (x) chattel.
55. A statement that property is not termite-infested constitutes
    ( ) puffing of goods.
    ( ) sales talk.
    (x) misrepresentation.
    ( ) caveat emptor.
56. Where a broker accepts a note in lieu of cash, as down payment in
    a real estate deal, and the note is unpaid, the owner can
    ( ) declare the contract void.
    ( ) bring a criminal action against the buyer.
    (x) hold the broker responsible.
    ( ) file a complaint with the local credit bureau.
57. A purchaser should be notified by the broker, who has an option
    on the property being sold that he, the broker, is the
    (x) optionee.
    ( ) optionor.

( ) escrowee.

( ) lessee.

58. A broker should prepare how many copies of the agreement to purchase?

( ) Two.

(x) Four.

( ) Three.

( ) Five.

59. After an agreement to purchase has been prepared by the broker and signed by the buyer, the seller insists upon a slightly higher price and slightly different terms. The broker should

( ) delete the objectionable terms and insert the new terms, and then have the seller sign the contract.

( ) delete the objectionable terms, insert the new terms and have buyer and seller write their initials in margin.

(x) prepare a new contract and have buyer and seller sign.

( ) have seller sign contract as originally drawn and send a memorandum to buyer as to changes.

60. Adams signs an offer to purchase Baker's property at $7,000. The broker with whom the property is listed at $7,500 submits the offer to Baker, but Baker wants $7,350. The broker prepares a new contract at $7,350. Adams refuses to sign. Baker then accepts Adams' offer at $7,000, but Adams has changed his mind about buying. There is

( ) a contract.

(x) no contract.

( ) due a commission by the seller to the broker.

( ) due a commission by the buyer to the broker.

61. The description of property sold under a contract of sale should

( ) state the size of lot in terms of feet—60 × 150 feet.

( ) give the house number and street.

( ) give location by approximation.

(x) give a full legal description.

62. Land that is divided into five or more parcels of lots for purpose of sale is defined as

( ) plottage.

(x) subdivision.

( ) a section.

( ) a hereditament.

63. An oral contract for the sale of real property is unenforceable because of

( ) laws of agency.

( ) statute of limitation.

(x) statute of frauds.

( ) licensing law.

64. Where a broker holds an option on a property and desires to sell the property, he must disclose that he is the

( ) optionor.
( ) trustor.
(x) optionee.
( ) assignee.

65. Which of the following is an element necessary to establish fraud or misrepresentation?
( ) the broker knows the truth.
(x) the party to whom the statement is made relies upon it to his detriment.
( ) the property is worth so much money.
( ) the property will resell at a certain price.

66. Under a land contract, who retains legal title until certain specific conditions are fulfilled?
( ) vendee.
(x) vendor.
( ) public trustee.
( ) recorder of deeds.

67. "A" conveyed a vacant one acre tract of land to "B." He received
(x) 43,560 sq. ft.
( ) 5,280 sq. ft.
( ) 43,650 sq. ft.
( ) 22,350 sq. ft.

68. The law which requires contracts for the sale of real estate is known as the
(x) statute of frauds.
( ) statute of limitations.
( ) adverse possession law.
( ) parol evidence rule.

69. The term "sui juris" means
(x) legal capacity to enter into a contract.
( ) trial without a jury.
( ) the acknowledgment to a legal instrument.
( ) legal right to execute a will.

70. An agreement of sale is not enforceable if
( ) it is unilateral.
(x) there was fraud in its inducement.
( ) it is unilateral and bilateral.

71. Marginal real estate is
( ) yielding farm land.
( ) waste land due to erosion, swamps and the like.
(x) land which barely repays cost of operation.
( ) the end lot in a subdivision.

72. Insurance policy premiums are prorated in escrow from the date the policy was
( ) written.
( ) recorded.
(x) assigned.

( ) cancelled.

73. A check is generally called a
    ( ) time draft.
    ( ) note payable.
    (x) negotiable instrument.
    ( ) bill of attainder.

74. An option contract differs from an agreement of sale in that
    ( ) the option needs no consideration to support it.
    ( ) the agreement of sale needs no consideration to support it.
    (x) the option need not be consummated.
    ( ) the option automatically renews itself.

75. An owner may sell the property to a second buyer where the first buyer has indicated
    ( ) that he will receive funds after the date fixed for closing.
    ( ) where buyer complains dwelling is in disrepair.
    (x) the buyer has declared an anticipatory repudiation.
    ( ) buyer's credit rating is sub-par.

76. In order to take advantage of a capital gains tax on a real estate purchase and sale, the property must be held for at least
    (x) six months.
    ( ) one year.
    ( ) three months.
    ( ) 30 days.

77. Zone R 1 usually refers to
    ( ) hospitals.
    (x) single family dwellings.
    ( ) light industrial.
    ( ) commercial.

78. If there is ambiguity as to the meaning of any term in an agreement of sale, prepared by a broker, and signed by seller and buyer, it will be construed most strongly against
    ( ) broker.
    (x) seller.
    ( ) buyer.
    ( ) lending institution.

79. Escrows are opened for protection of
    ( ) broker's commission.
    ( ) public.
    (x) buyer and seller.
    ( ) mortgagee.

80. When real property is sold on an installment contract and a warranty deed is to be delivered at a future date, the deed should be placed in custody of
    ( ) the broker.
    ( ) the seller.
    ( ) the public trustee.
    (x) an escrow agent.

81. An option given without an active consideration is
    ( ) enforceable.
    ( ) revocable.
    ( ) assignable.
    (x) invalid.
82. When a real estate deal includes the sale of removal fixtures, such as
    a refrigerator, gas stove, etc., the seller should give to the buyer a
    (x) bill of sale.
    ( ) chattel mortgage.
    ( ) chattel deed of trust.
    ( ) release.
83. A buyer made an initial deposit of $500 on a $10,000 house. He with-
    draws the offer before it is accepted by seller. The broker should
    dispose of the buyer's earnest money by
    ( ) turning it over to the seller.
    ( ) paying it into court.
    (x) returning it to the buyer.
    ( ) keeping it for his commission.
84. When a seller accepts an offer to purchase, a salesman should deliver
    a copy of the signed acceptance to the
    ( ) lending institution.
    (x) buyer.
    ( ) escrow agent.
    ( ) employing broker.
85. An option to purchase real estate is valid for how many days after
    the specified date
    ( ) thirty days.
    ( ) one month.
    (x) none.
    ( ) ten days.
86. If a buyer fails to consummate a real estate deal, forfeiture of the
    deposit money is at the option of the
    (x) seller.
    ( ) buyer.
    ( ) broker.
    ( ) salesman.
87. When a purchaser withdraws his offer to purchase before acceptance
    by seller, he is entitled to a refund of his deposit at what time
    (x) immediately.
    ( ) after seller has had opportunity to accept agreement and
        declines.
    ( ) after broker keeps his commission.
    ( ) after buyer obtains court decree.
88. A sales agreement to be enforceable must have
    ( ) signature of wife of married seller.
    ( ) an earnest money deposit.
    (x) competent parties.
    ( ) an attestation by a disinterested party.

89. An installment purchase contract does not give the buyer
    ( ) possession.
    ( ) right to lease the property.
    (x) title to the property.
    ( ) right to devise the property.
90. When real estate is sold on a land contract and a warranty deed is to be delivered at a future date, the warranty deed should be placed in the hands of
    ( ) the broker.
    (x) escrow agent.
    ( ) buyer.
    ( ) no one.
91. Where a broker accepts a note, in lieu of cash, as a down payment on a real estate deal and the note is unpaid, the owner can
    (x) hold the broker responsible.
    ( ) declare the deal void.
    ( ) bring a criminal action against buyer.
    ( ) file a complaint with the Real Estate Commission.
92. In fire insurance the most widely used coinsurance clause is
    ( ) 60%.
    ( ) 70%.
    (x) 80%.
    ( ) 90%.

Chapter 3

DEEDS

Real Property and Personalty Distinguished

AT THE OUTSET, it is important to remember that certain words and phrases in connection with real estate have a technical meaning and a different interpretation than is generally attributed to them by the average layman. The all-inclusive term "property" may be said to be the rights or interest which a person has in lands and chattels to the exclusion of all others. Blackstone defines land as comprehending all things of a permanent substantial nature. *Estate* means quantity of ownership, and *title* is the evidence of ownership. Estate stands for quantity and title refers to quality. Lands are *realty;* chattels are *personalty*. All property of whatever kind and description that is capable of being owned must fall into one of these two classes—realty or personalty. Realty, in turn, includes a twofold classification, *corporeal* realty and *incorporeal* realty. Personalty, likewise, may be divided into two groups, *tangible* (a desk) and *intangible* (chose in action). "Corporeal" is derived from the Latin word *corpus,* meaning body. Corporeal realty, like

land, a building, or a tree, can be seen and felt. In other words, real property includes land and almost anything built upon, growing or affixed to the soil. Incorporeal realty includes rights issuing out of, annexed to, or exercisable within land, such as a right of way. It is frequently stated that realty includes lands, tenements, and hereditaments. The relationship of these three classes may be represented by three concentric circles. The smallest circle embraces lands; the next, tenements. Tenements, therefore, include lands

170

and certain things which are realty but which cannot be described as land, such as a building or messuage. The largest circle contains whatever may be classed or inherited as realty. Hereditaments embrace lands, tenements, and certain other things, usually of an incorporeal nature, such as a right of way.

A tree growing upon land is real estate. When the tree is severed from the soil and cut into so many feet of boards, the lumber is personalty, and, when the lumber is fashioned into a dwelling, the lumber becomes real estate again. So too, when clay is part of the soil, it is realty. When it is removed and made into bricks, it becomes personalty. When these bricks are put together to form a building, they become realty again. Thus, many articles may change from realty to personalty and back again. When they are solidly fixed to land or to the structures built upon land, generally they are realty. However, there are many fixtures solidly fastened to buildings, such as heavy machinery bolted to a floor, which remain personalty. Then, there may be articles which have been annexed to the realty and were accidentally or wrongfully removed, which, nevertheless, retain their character of realty. Suppose that a storm blows down a garage or tree. The garage or tree may be no longer connected with the land, but it remains realty until the owner shows an intention to treat it as personalty. The key to a house is such a necessary part of the improvement that it would properly be considered realty.

As a rule, articles that have been brought upon land in order that they may become part of the improvement are not transformed from personalty to realty until they become an integral part of the improvement. For example, lumber and millwork delivered to a building job are not realty and would be subject to seizure as the contractor's personal property while deposited on an adjoining lot.

Realty and personalty distinguished

Thus, the distinction between realty and personalty is an important one because the law applicable to the two classes of property is radically different. The distinction is also a practical one, readily apparent in the sale of a house when a controversy arises between the interested parties as to whether certain articles, such as stoves, screens, wall mirrors, shrubbery, refrigerator, gas ranges, and other equipment, pass with the sale of the house. Certain apparatus which was a constituent part of a rolling mill was held to be realty, although temporarily detached from the mill. The mere fact that the machinery could be unscrewed or otherwise removed without injury to the building would not constitute it personal property. The greater or less facility with which the removal could be accomplished would be too vague a test; the slightest tack or fastening would be sufficient to convert personalty into realty. If the possibility of removing an article without damaging the real estate were the test, the results would also be unsatisfactory. For example, an owner who sold a residence might lift the window shutter off the hinges without any damage to the building, but, in all fairness, it would seem that the shutters are a permanent part of the real estate and should pass with the sale. In the absence of an express stipulation in the agreement, the issue of realty or personalty may be determined finally only by recourse to the courts. The true test for determining whether an article, fixture, or piece of equipment or machinery is realty or personalty is the *intention* with which the article is affixed to the property, considered in the light of what is fair and reasonable under all the surrounding circumstances. In other words, each case must stand upon its own particular facts, but the main feature is "the intention" as disclosed by words or conduct of the owner when the installation was made, with due regard given to existing custom, if established. Custom plays an important part in determining what articles are realty and which are personalty. Most persons would be greatly surprised if the seller should detach and remove the chandeliers and radiators in a house. We have come to look upon such fixtures as an essential part of the premises, as are doors and windows. It is a broker's obligation to prepare a comprehensive and satisfactory agreement defining what shall pass with the conveyance of the premises.

Chattels which are distinctly furniture, as distinguished from improvements, and not particularly fitted or fastened to the property with which they are used, remain personalty. Chattels which, although physically connected with the real estate, are so affixed as to be removable without destroying or materially injuring the fixtures or the property to which they are annexed become part of the realty or retain their character as personalty, depending upon the intention of the parties at the time of the annexation. Chattels which are so annexed to the property that they cannot be removed without material injury to the real estate or to themselves are realty even if there is an expressed intention that they should be considered personalty.

Transfer of Title to Real Estate

TITLE TO real estate, the evidence of ownership, passes generally in several ways: (1) by purchase, through delivery of deed and (2) by descent, through a will or by inheritance. As will be seen later, title may also be obtained (3) through adverse possession and (4) by eminent domain.

Origin of title

It is of fundamental importance to know that the extent of the right which a person acquires in property can be no greater than that enjoyed by his predecessor in title. This means that one cannot buy more from the former owner than the latter had, despite the fact that he may give what purports to be a valid deed. If an owner gives a deed for a tract of land, 110 feet in depth, but he only owned 100 feet, it follows that the buyer obtains title only to 100 feet. Thus, in order to determine the exact extent of the rights of a present owner of property, a diligent and thorough search must be made in order to ascertain the rights which were handed down to him through a long line of former owners, and in many cases, it is necessary to trace the title back to its origin so as to ascertain the extent of the original grant which was made. This general principle, of course, is subject to certain modifications, for many laws have been passed, intended to cure or remedy defects in titles produced through carelessness or blunders. Title to a property has a very long life, extending back to the beginning of private ownership. Technically, titles emanated from a sovereign power or government, the exact source varying in the different sections of the country. For example, in New Jersey and Delaware, it is Lord Baltimore; in New York, it is the Duke of York, or his successor, the State of New York; in Pennsylvania, it is William Penn. In Kansas and Nebraska, it is the United States government, which secured title to the Great Western Domain through grants made by the thirteen original states, and subsequent negotiations with France for the purchase of the Louisiana Territory. A prudent purchaser of land, anywhere, will insist upon an Abstract of Title and opinion of title, or have the title insured by a title company, in order to obtain protection as to the quality of title to the land purchased.

Formality of title transfer—by deed

The law has always regarded the transfer of real estate as one of the most solemn acts in which an individual can engage and thus a great deal of formality attends its transfer. In the early days of land tenure, transfer was accomplished by "livery of seizin," which, literally, means transfer of possession. The seller and buyer would go upon the land in question and there, in the presence of witnesses, the seller would take a clod of turf or a twig from a tree and hand it over to the buyer as a symbol or token of the transfer. The transfer was then made a matter of record by having the scrivener (the person in the community who could write) write out the transfer upon parchment or other durable matter, in order to prevent erasure or alteration; the scrivener wrote the name of the grantor (seller), and the latter affixed his personal seal. With the development of education, the emphasis has shifted, so that the signature is the all-important feature in the execution of a deed and the seal only incidental, usually printed upon the deed form. Although a deed is a contract between the grantor and grantee (buyer), it is not necessary for the latter to sign it, and, in fact, this would be unusual. The acceptance of the deed consummates the contract. It should be kept in mind that a deed is a contract and, therefore, all the essential elements of a valid contract must be present. It is also necessary to have special formality—that is, the deed must be in writing. There can be no such thing as an *oral* transfer of real estate. Under Spanish law, an oral deed, coupled with transfer of possession, was effective to pass title. A deed represents the formal completion of an agreement of sale previously executed by the parties.

Deeds—definition

Transfer of title by *deed* is the most common method of passing title to real estate. Blackstone defines a deed as a "writing or instrument under seal, containing some contract of agreement, and which has been delivered by the parties." Thus the word "deed," in a legal sense, may mean any sealed contract or instrument, such as a lease, mortgage, or bond. The popular sense restricts it to a conveyance of property. A deed may then be defined as a writing by which lands, tenements, and hereditaments are conveyed, which writing is signed, sealed, and delivered by the parties. The ordinary common warranty deed contains a number of clauses that have an important bearing upon the rights of the parties.

For purposes of study, a deed may be divided into three component parts—the premises, the habendum and the testimonium. The Premises includes the date, parties, consideration, granting clause, description, recital and appurtenances. The Habendum et Tenendum (to have and to hold clause) includes this clause and the Under and Subject or Mortgage clause. The Testimonium clause includes the Warranty and "In Witness Whereof," etc. This outline is valuable to remember so that a person may check a deed to ascertain that all clauses are included and, also, as an aid in preparing a proper deed. Now for a fuller discussion of the various parts.

Date

The date usually comes first but is not essential to the validity of a deed. When inserted, it indicates the time when the title passed; that is, when the deed was delivered; but it is only *prima facie* evidence, and the presumption of time of delivery may be rebutted by convincing testimony to the contrary. A deed dated on Sunday but delivered on a week day is good. A deed without a date or a date subsequent to that in the acknowledgment affidavit would not be void, but the party accepting the deed would have the burden, in case of litigation, of proving when the deed was actually delivered. If the date in the acknowledgment antedates the date in the deed, a technical examiner may require a new acknowledgment and re-recordation. If the grantor is dead or cannot be located, difficulty in this connection is readily apparent. Great care should therefore be exercised to examine the dates in the deed in order to avoid difficulty at a later date. If the date is inserted, the grantee would have the presumption in his favor that the deed was delivered on the date specified and the burden would then be upon the opponent of the deed to prove otherwise.

Parties

The names and residences of the parties to the deed immediately follow the date. The party selling the property is known as the *grantor;* the purchaser of the property is known as the *grantee.* Any uncertainty as to the persons intended would render the deed void. Where the parties have a middle initial, it should be inserted. A deed must be made to some certain person or else it is void. A deed to a fictitious or unincorporated community or corporation which has no legal existence is void. Thus a deed to the Ajax Printing Company, which is a partnership consisting of two members, is void. The deed should have been made in the names of the two partners. A deed "to the employers of the school at Plum Creek" would also be invalid. Where a corporation is a party to a deed, a slight mistake in setting out its name will not vitiate the deed, if it is clearly apparent from the face of it that one certain corporation was intended. Thus, a deed written in the name of Boulevard Land and Development Company, Inc., would be upheld where the name of the corporation actually was Boulevard Land Development Company, Inc.

Deed of bargain and sale—consideration

A deed of bargain and sale, which is the instrument adopted in most states to transfer real estate, requires consideration for the deed, although it need not be necessarily expressed. Consideration in the deed may be either good or valuable. A good consideration proceeds from love and affection or the like, and has no pecuniary measure of value. A valuable consideration is money or its equivalent, anything capable of being measured by a monetary standard. The practice of inserting a dollar as consideration is sufficient for the requirements of the law. Courts do not inquire into the adequacy of the consideration. The slightest consideration is sufficient to support the most onerous obligation. Thus a $1.00 consideration will support the transfer of a property worth $1,000,000. If the title is being transferred to a relative without any cash consideration, as from father to son, the deed should recite for "$1.00 and other good consideration." A deed made by an insolvent owner to a close relative or friend with the intent to disturb, delay, hinder or defraud creditors is void against a creditor. Deeds from fiduciaries, such as trust companies, should recite the true consideration price rather than a nominal consideration. An error in stating the true amount of consideration will not affect the validity of the deed.

Deed transfer stamps

Prior to January 1, 1968, it was necessary for the seller to affix United States Internal Revenue stamps to the deed, at the rate of $.55 per $500, or part thereof, based upon the consideration price. Since repeal of the federal tax, a number of states have passed laws, requiring state stamps on the deed at the same rate as the repealed federal documentary tax. It is not necessary to affix any stamps where no consideration passes, as in the case of a deed from a husband to himself and wife, or in a gift deed from a parent to child. Examination of the state law is necessary in order to ascertain whether stamps must be affixed for the full consideration, where the purchaser assumes an existing mortgage. In some states, documentary stamps *may* only be necessary for the difference between the consideration price and the mortgage granting clause or operative words.

Granting clause or operative words

The words used in the deed that transfer the estate from the grantor to the grantee constitute the granting clause and are termed the "operative words." These words are generally "grant and convey" or "grant, bargain, and sell." They usually precede the description but may be placed in any part of the deed. The necessity for technical words is no longer felt, and any words indicating an intention to convey will operate to transfer title. Following the grant and immediately preceding the description of the property are the words of limitation denoting the quantity of estate intended to be granted. The words ordinarily employed to pass a fee simple title are "heirs and assigns." A fee simple estate is the greatest estate which may be held in property, and at common law the words "heirs and assigns" were absolutely essential to pass a fee. Without the word "heirs" only an estate for life passes. It would not suffice to say that the "grantee is to have and to hold forever" or "to the grantee and his assigns forever," for this does not mean that the issue of the grantee acquire any vested interest in the land. The word "heirs" is said to be a word of *limitation*, rather than a word of *purchase*, and indicates a complete title of perpetual duration with power to sell to anybody; it does not give the issue or heirs of the grantee any rights in the property after his death. Today, the operative words in a deed, *"grant and convey,"* or either of them will generally be held to be effective to convey a fee simple title if the grantor had such title.

Fee simple title

A fee simple title is the highest and most complete ownership or enjoyment in real estate. It is sometimes referred to as ownership in fee or fee absolute. Where such owner executes a lease, he does not part with title. The person to whom the property is leased acquires a lesser, or leasehold estate. Likewise, if a person acquires a property for life, by deed, or will, he does not become a fee simple owner, but rather the owner of a transitory life estate, which ceases at his death. The person who succeeds to the title when the life estate terminates is known as the remainderman.

Description

The intent of the description in a deed is to identify sufficiently the land to be conveyed, and no deed will be operative which does not contain a description sufficient for an exact identification of the property. The description need not necessarily be technically accurate but must be sufficiently precise to enable a surveyor to locate the boundaries. If the description is not sufficiently full, the deed will fail; verbal testimony will not be admitted to supply the deficiency unless such deficiency is the result of fraud, accident, or mistake, in which case the courts permit a reformation of the deed description.

Parol evidence rule

The parol evidence rule generally applies. The rule is that verbal testimony cannot be introduced to vary, contradict, add to, or subtract from a written instrument, or to change its legal import, unless fraud, accident, or mistake is pleaded. However, should the deed refer to some other instrument, such as a previous deed, which accurately describes the premises, the new deed will be valid. All directions expressed as "northward" or "westward" mean due north and due west. There are four types of descriptions generally used:

1. Rectangular survey descriptions.
2. Lot number on plot or map.
3. Metes and bounds descriptions.
4. Monuments.

Rectangular survey

The rectangular survey was adopted by Congress as early as May 20, 1785, and is used outside of the original thirteen states. In the *Real Estate Primer* issued by the State of Iowa * (1961 edition), the rectangular survey is explained and illustrated as follows:

This [rectangular survey] refers to a grid of north and south (meridians) and east and west (parallels) lines surveyed by the government. Identification of property is east or west so many ranges or vertical rows of checks from the north and south line called a "principal meridian" and so many horizontal rows of tiers or townships north of an east and west line called the "base line."

---

* Permission of George M. Clarkson, Director.

Distance between the parallels and meridians is twenty-four miles and the area contained therein is called a check. In this area are sixteen townships and the townships are further divided into thirty-six sections of a mile square each. The section is further divided into halves, quarters and smaller subdivisions.

Fractional sections on the north and west side of a township are due to corrections made of the survey lines for the curvature of the earth. This results in these sections having more or less 640 acres, depending

SUBDIVISION OF A CHECK

upon corrections. In describing these sections the words "fractional sections" should be used.

In reading rectangular descriptions, for convenience one reads backwards from the general part of the description to the specific part at the beginning. The general part of the description refers to the range and township and the specific to that part of a section.

Lot number

The lot number is used in urban centers where there has been a concentrated development of land. A property is transformed from farm or vacant land into a subdivision laid out in numbered lots. The plan, if approved, is accepted by the municipality and recorded. The property would then be identified as "Being all of Lot #162 in the Bower Hill Plan of Lots as laid out, and recorded in the office of the Recorder of Deeds of Dauphin County in Plan Book Volume 18, Page 113, being designated as Block 14J Lot 44 in the records of the Dauphin County Deed Registry Office."

SUBDIVISION OF TOWNSHIPS INTO SECTIONS

36	31	32	33	34	35	36	31
1	6	5	4	3	2	1	6
12	7	8	9	10	11	12	7
13	18	17	16	15	14	13	18
24	19	20	21	22	23	24	19
25	30	29	28	27	26	25	30
36	31	32	33	34	35	36	31
1	6	5	4	3	2	1	6

Adjoining sections are shown to give numbering.

Corrections for convergence are ordinarily made in sections 1, 2, 3, 4, 5, 6, 7, 18, 19, 30 and 31.

Metes and bounds

The oldest method of describing land is by "metes and bounds." Metes are measurements of length—feet, inches, perches (1 perch = 16½ ft.); bounds are artificial and natural boundaries such as streets, roads, adjoining farms, roads and streams. Metes determine the certain quantity of land (acreage) while bounds confine that quantity within certain fixed limits. Such a description should have a definitely ascertained starting point, such as so many feet distant from the nearest cross street or at a definite lot dividing line, and then proceed clockwise, tracing the lines by directions and distances back to the point of beginning. A deed would be void in which the starting point was given as "a point on Bowman Street at the dividing line of property of B. Davidson" and a search of the

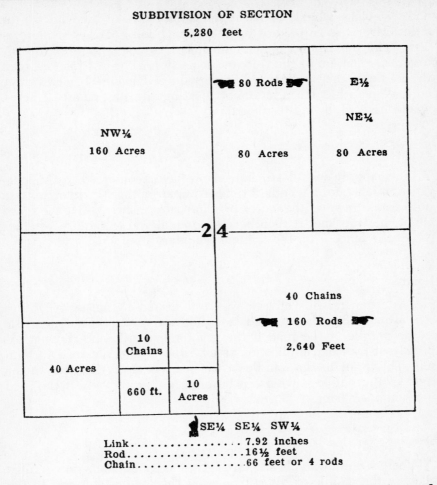

SUBDIVISION OF SECTION

5,280 feet

80 Rods

NW¼
160 Acres

80 Acres

E½

NE¼

80 Acres

2 4

40 Chains

160 Rods

2,640 Feet

40 Acres

10
Chains

660 ft.

10
Acres

SE¼ SE¼ SW¼

Link............... 7.92 inches
Rod...............16½ feet
Chain...............66 feet or 4 rods

title failed to locate any property owned or occupied by the said Davidson. The principle is well established that the courses and distances in a deed always give way to the boundary markers found on the ground or supplied by proof of their former existence when the marks or monuments are gone. Thus, a deed description "from said point, 40° 30′ west a distance of 220 feet to the Revolutionary chestnut tree" would give the purchaser 230 feet, if that was the actual distance to the tree in question. This rule is to be used only in reconciling discrepancies.

Monuments

In rural areas, descriptions by monuments are still frequently used. Land is cheap, and a survey to determine the exact courses and distances would be of appreciable cost. At the end of the description it is customary to insert "containing 64 acres, more or less." The description by monuments does not lend itself readily to an examination of the title, particularly for one not familiar with the locale of the property. A description conveying "10 acres more or less" of other lands, and not locating the particular 10 acres, would be void, owing to uncertainty.

Fences

When the owners of adjoining land have acquiesced in the location of a fence for a length of time required by the statute of adverse possession, they are thereafter precluded from saying that the fence is not the true line. It then becomes immaterial to inquire whether or not the fence is on the original boundary line.

Roads

It is a general rule of law, well established by authority, that a conveyance of lands bounded by a highway gives the grantee title to the middle of the road if the grantor had title and did not expressly or by clear implication reserve the bed of the road to himself. This right to the middle of the road is always subject to the right of the public. Ownership becomes important only if the road is abandoned later.

Streams

Where a nonnavigable stream is given as a boundary, the grantee takes to the middle of the stream as in the case of a street. In the case of a navigable stream, the grantee takes absolutely to high water mark and, in a qualified sense, to low water mark. That is to say, in the area between high and low water, his rights are subject to the rights of the public for navigation purposes, which include all privileges necessary for such purposes. A navigable stream in law is one which is navigable in fact. The land between high and low water mark is known as flat land. A description in a deed read "five acres of marsh meadow *bounded by the River S.*" The boundary of the firm land *by the river* carried with it the adjacent flat land. The fact that the description states that the land is bounded "by" a stream or that it runs "along" a stream and names a monument on the shore does not necessarily show an intention to exclude the stream, and this is regarded merely as a statement of the point at which the boundary strikes the stream. It is impractical to place a marker in the stream proper.

An individual property owner has no absolute riparian rights of ownership in a navigable stream and to the land *below* high water mark, nor does he have littoral rights of ownership to land covered and uncovered by the flow and ebb of the sea tide. It has been held by the United States Supreme Court [1] that even the State of California has no title to the submerged land between the shoreline and the three-mile limit, but that title is in the Federal Government. The question of ownership is highly important because of valuable underlying oil deposits.

When a map, plan, or other survey is referred to in a deed, it becomes a material and essential part of the conveyance and is to have the same force and effect as if copied in it. Where there is a deed reference to a map of a highway to be dedicated in the future, there are two opposing rules. The New York rule holds that such a reference to an unopened highway raises a presumption of an intention to convey the land to the middle of the proposed highway as if the highway actually existed. The Massachusetts rule, on the other hand, states that the roadbed of the proposed highway is not included and the boundary is fixed at the side of the proposed highway. In Pennsylvania the law seems to be that where the street is merely plotted upon the plan, the grantee takes only to the edge of the street, but when the street is opened, the grantee's title jumps to the middle of the street.

Calls in a deed are always to be controlled by lines on the ground. If the sale is made by lines staked and marked on the ground, such lines on the ground govern, if in conflict with the deed description.

Recital

The recital is a statement of facts interesting, or necessary, for persons examining a title to know. It tells how the grantor acquired title, or the reason why the deed is made, or some other explanatory remark. It usually follows the description, although when long, such as Trustee's and Executor's deeds made under an Order of Court, it usually comes after the names of the parties and commences with the word "Whereas." It can hardly be regarded as an essential part of the deed unless it contains something of a contractual nature between the parties to the instrument.

---

[1] United States v. California, 332 U.S. 19 (1947).

Appurtenances

The deed may contain the phrase "with the appurtenances and all the estate and right of the party of the first part [grantor] in and to said premises."

The right to the appurtenances goes with the property as a matter of law, so there is no real need for the above clause. All easements, rights, and incidents, which belong to the property conveyed and are necessary to its full enjoyment, pass as "appurtenances" without mention of them. What is merely convenient to the enjoyment does not. These include alleyways, water courses, light, and air. Thus, the deed should specify "together with" followed by a description of the rights intended to pass. What is appurtenant to a piece of land is appurtenant to every part thereof. Where a right of way is granted as appurtenant to a tract of land and the tract is later subdivided into smaller lots, each of the lot purchasers would be entitled to the same right of way. Also, where a property, bounded by a private alley is sold, and the alley is necessary to the premises sold, the right to use it passes as an appurtenance to the property unless there is something in the conveyance restricting the use solely to the grantor or expressly excepting the alley from the grant.

Habendum clause

The habendum clause (to have and to hold), where used, operates to define the quantity of estate which the grantee is said to have in the property granted. The habendum is not absolutely necessary. The estate granted may be limited in the earlier part of the deed and if the habendum contradicts the earlier limitation, it will have no effect. If the two can be reconciled, then effect will be given to both. Where the limitation in the premises is in general terms, as to Jones and his heirs generally, and the habendum limits the estate to Jones for and during the term of his natural life, the grantee takes a life estate.

Warranties

A seller, in conveying property, makes certain representations to the purchaser. He warrants that he has a fee simple title, that he has the right and power to convey it, and that there is no lien or encumbrance against the property. The seller is placed in the position where he personally guarantees the truthfulness of these statements and may be held personally responsible for them in case any of the statements are later proven false. Under the covenant of warranty the grantee may hold the grantor for any damage he has sustained. The three covenants of title relating to the ownership of a fee simple— the owner of the property in fee, the right to convey, and the freedom of the property from encumbrances—are known as covenants *in prae- senti* (as of the present). The grantor also warrants that the grantee will quietly enjoy and that the grantor will make further assurances. These two warranties are known as covenants *in futuro* (as of the future). The quiet-enjoyment warranty means that the grantee will not be ousted by someone under a paramount title to his grantor. The further-assurances warranty provides that the grantor—if it is discovered at any time that, through an oversight or mistake in the deed, the grantee's title is imperfect—will voluntarily execute such instruments as are necessary to give the grantee the title which he thought he was receiving and which it was intended that he should receive. For example, a deed is improperly executed by the grantor. The grantee requests a new deed properly signed. The grantor cannot take the position that he is "through" with the deal and refuse to do anything more unless remunerated for doing so. Under the particular warranty the purchaser could enlist the aid of the court in compelling the seller to execute the necessary writing.

General and special warranty

The grantor also warrants the title and covenants to protect his grantee against any claimant. In a *general warranty* deed the grantor agrees with the grantee that he will "forever warrant and defend the property against every person or persons whomsoever lawfully claiming the same, or any part thereof." In other words, he agrees to protect or defend the buyer against the entire world.

The covenant of special warranty is not so sweeping in its grant. A man may not care to defend the title of a property against every- one. He may feel that he should be required to guarantee the title only against himself or anyone claiming under him. A *special war- ranty* is a promise or covenant on the part of the grantor to defend the grantee against all claims which may be brought by the grantor or his heirs, assigns, or anyone claiming under the grantor. The general warranty clause can be made into a special warranty by inserting the few words "by, from, through, or under him." If there are plural grantors, then use "them, or any of them." A purchaser of real estate has no right to expect a covenant of general warranty in his deed unless he bargains for it in the agreement of sale. He cannot refuse to take the deed merely because it contains a special warranty. Trustee deeds and deeds given in pursuance of an order of court are special warranty deeds. Where no warranty is expressed, the court will hold there is an implied special warranty in favor of the grantor.

Execution—power of attorney

A deed may be executed by the grantor himself, or through his proxy under a power of attorney. A power of attorney has been defined as "an instrument, in writing, under seal, by which the party executing it appoints another to be his attorney and empowers him to act for him, either generally in all matters of business, or especially to do some specified act or acts, in his name and behalf." The power of attorney must be acknowledged so that it may be recorded in the county where the property is located; it must be recorded so that a purchaser may know that the particular execution was properly authorized. Death of the person executing the power of attorney automatically revokes the power of attorney even if the agent has no notice of the death. An attorney-in-fact has no right to delegate his authority unless the instrument by which he is appointed expressly authorizes the substitution. The signature of a deed by an attorney-in-fact should read as follows:

> "John Steele
> by Adam Taylor
> his Attorney-in-fact"

However, the attorney or agent need not sign his own name; the name of the principal alone is sufficient. Better practice dictates the agent's name as well.

Signature

The object of a signature is to authenticate the genuineness of the document. It is not essential that the grantor himself should sign the deed. His mark, where he cannot write, or even where he can, if intended as a signature, will be sufficient. Signature by mark would be:

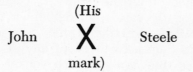

A signature by mark must be witnessed by two witnesses. Where the signing is done by a third person in the *presence* of the grantor and *at the direction* of the grantor, it amounts to a compliance with the requirements of the law. The ordinary situation is for property to stand in the name of one person. It is usual, however, where the title is in the name of the husband alone, to have the wife join in the execution of the deed. The wife joins for the purpose of extinguishing any claim which she may later have through her dower interest in the property.

Dower

Dower is the right which a wife has in her husband's estate *at his death*. It is an inchoate or potential right which does not vest unless she survives her husband. It is personal to the wife alone and can only be asserted by her. It sometimes develops that a seller's wife refuses to sign the deed. She cannot be compelled to do so, unless she has signed the agreement of sale. In that event, an action can be maintained in court for specific performance to compel her to sign the deed. Thus, it is wise to have the wife join in the agreement, even though the property is in the name of the husband alone. If she does not sign the agreement of sale and refuses to join in the deed, the land remains subject to her dower interests in it. However, a husband ordinarily can mortgage his own real estate without the joinder of his wife. Sometimes a mortgage to the buyer is used to circumvent the wife's dower interests. If the wife can show fraud upon her, the transaction could be set aside unless the rights of a bona fide purchaser, without notice of the fraud, have intervened. The wife cannot prevent the sale of real estate by her husband, and she does not have any right of action against the purchaser until after the death of her husband, and then only in the case that she survives him. It sometimes happens that a man and woman contemplating marriage will enter into an agreement determining their property rights after marriage. This is known as an ante-nuptial agreement and is frequently used where one or both of the contracting parties are advanced in years. Under this agreement, the wife-to-be may surrender her rights in her husband's real estate, and he, in turn, agrees to relinquish any claim to her real estate after her death. Such agreements are not contrary to public policy, and if fair and conscionable, will be enforced. Thus, if a wife, prior to marriage, has entered into an ante-nuptial agreement and after marriage refuses to join in the agreement of sale or the subsequent deed, she may be compelled to execute her joinder by virtue of her previous agreement.

Dower is an encumbrance within the meaning of the term. If the wife refuses to sign, a purchaser has two alternatives. First, he can refuse to accept the deed signed by the husband alone and demand damages for the expense to which he has been put. Second, he can accept the husband's deed, in which event he is required to pay the full purchase price. He then assumes the risk of the wife predeceasing her husband or, if she does not, of paying her dower claim.

Deed by married women

In some jurisdictions (Alabama, Indiana, North Carolina, Texas), a deed by a married woman for real estate held in her own name is void unless her husband joins in the conveyance or unless she has been declared a feme sole (single woman). For cause shown, as where the husband has deserted the wife or is a profligate, the court, upon application of the wife, may declare her a feme sole, as if she were unmarried. She could then execute a valid deed by her signature alone. In Arkansas, Oklahoma, and other states, a married woman can convey her separate real estate without the joinder of her husband.

Where property is owned by a single woman who enters into an agreement of sale and, before the consummation of the deal, marries, the purchaser can compel the wife and her newly acquired husband to join in a valid deed. Since the married woman, prior to marriage, had contracted to sell the property, she retained only the bare legal title after the agreement of sale was signed, and her marriage was ineffective to enlarge her interest or to impinge upon the equitable title obtained by the purchaser under the agreement.

Estates by the entireties

Where property is held in the name of husband *and* wife, it is known as a joint tenancy and in some states as an estate by the entireties. In the Tennessee case of *Ballard v. Farley*, 226 S.W. 544, the Court held that a conveyance to a named person "and wife," without naming her was sufficient to create an estate by the entireties. It exists only in favor of husband and wife and has certain advantages to recommend it. A deed from John Steele to Adam Taylor and Anna Mae Taylor, his wife, would automatically create such an estate. In most states, both signatures are absolutely essential in order to convey title. Upon the death of one, the property immediately and automatically vests in the surviving spouse; no court proceedings are necessary. The property is usually free from state inheritance taxes, and in most states a judgment against one of the parties would not be a lien against the property, unless the debtor spouse survived. Both parties can join in a good conveyance of the property, free and clear of the judgment against the one party. Although they can join in a clear deed to a purchaser, a mortgage executed by them would be taken subject to the judgment. The distinction here between a deed and a mortgage lies in the fact that a mortgage is only a temporary transfer of the property, and, when paid off, the property reverts to the entireties. Thus the judgment creditor may sell the property and have a prior lien over a mortgage if his debtor survives the other spouse. Holding property by the entireties is only recommended where the husband and wife enjoy a harmonious marital relationship and prospects of its permanency are good. Otherwise, divorce will not terminate the tenure and the property becomes a source of controversy where the paries go their separate ways and cannot agree upon a mutual partition of the premises. After divorce, either party may petition the court, in a partition proceedings, to have the property sold. By statute, as in Pennsylvania, the legislature may decree that after divorce, such property shall be held as tenants in common of equal one-half shares in value.

Where a conveyance is made to two married persons and their spouses and it is intended that each couple shall hold by the entireties, the names and status of the respective parties should be set forth as follows:

THIS DEED, made the 10th day of June, 1969, between JOHN T. STEELE and FRANCES L. STEELE, his wife, of the city of Miami, County of Dade, and State of Florida,

A
N
D

WILLIAM C. GRAY, JR., and THELMA T. GRAY, his wife, and CARL T. FRYE and ALICE L. FRYE, his wife, of the same place, AS TENANTS BY THE ENTIRETIES AS TO THE RESPECTIVE SHARE OF EACH HUSBAND AND WIFE AND AS TENANTS IN COMMON OF THE WHOLE.

Sometimes a man and woman take title to property as husband and wife, when they are not so in fact. Such a tenure is not void, but they will hold title as joint tenants or as tenants in common, depending upon what the court could determine as their *intention* from all of the facts.

Homestead

Homestead property resembles an estate by the entireties. Homestead laws exist in Alabama, Arkansas, California, Florida,

Georgia, Iowa, Louisiana, Missouri, Mississippi, Oklahoma, South
Dakota, Texas, Virginia, West Virginia, Wisconsin and Wyoming.
Property owned and occupied as a home, in a certain amount, is
known as the family homestead. Both husband and wife must join
in any deed or mortgage for this property. In the interests of public
policy for the preservation of the family, homestead property cannot be sold to satisfy a judgment against the husband. Certain
elements must be present to establish a homestead. There must be a
family of two or more persons living together under a family head
and actually occupying the land in question. The proper declaration must be filed that the property is actually occupied as a
homestead. The homestead laws provide maximum areas and values
of the homestead. In Arkansas, for example, the statute sets up two
types of homesteads: first, the rural homestead, outside of any urban
district, owned and occupied as a residence, consists of land not
exceeding 160 acres, but no less than 80 acres, and not exceeding
$2500 in value; second, the urban homestead, in a city, town or
village occupied as a residence, cannot exceed one acre of land, but
no less than ¼ acre, and not exceeding $2500 in value. It is not
necessary for a person to live on a homestead in order to claim
homestead rights, but there must always be an *intention* to return
to the homestead. In Texas, property upon which the head of the
family conducts his business is known as his "business homestead."
In California, the exemption from execution on homestead property
is $7500. In Florida, homestead exists as to 160 acres outside an
incorporated city or town, and as to one-half acre if located within
a city or town. In Wisconsin, not exceeding ¼ acre residential, 40
acres rural.

Community property

Property acquired during coverture (marriage) other than by
gift, devise, or descent is community property, and each spouse
owns an undivided one-half interest, and each is entitled to dispose
of his or her interest.

The basic concept of community property is that *whatever may
be acquired during marriage by the efforts of either spouse belongs,
on acquisition, in equal halves to both.* It was introduced into the
United States through the Spanish-influenced laws of Mexico and
Louisiana. The institution, by virtue of its Spanish origin, exists in
California, Louisiana, New Mexico, Texas, and Arizona. It has likewise been incorporated into the statutes of Nevada (1865), Idaho

(1867), Washington (1869), Oklahoma and Hawaii (1945), and Michigan, Nebraska, Oregon, and Pennsylvania (1947).[2]

Recent enactments were prompted by a desire to reduce Federal income taxes payable by the income-producing husband. Court decisions are not uniform as to the allocation of income received by each spouse from different sources. Texas cases hold that *all* income received during marriage is community property, including income from a trust in which one of the parties has a life estate. In California, the Supreme Court held to the contrary, maintaining that wife's income from her *separate* estate remained as her separate property.

Joint estates and estates in common

It has been stated previously that, where husband and wife own property together, the property is held by the entireties. In some states, as in Nebraska, it is termed a joint tenancy. Two or more persons may own property together; if they are not husband and wife, the ownership is joint or in common. In a joint tenancy, each party is possessed of an undivided part of the whole. In a tenancy in common, each is possessed of the whole of an undivided part. The language to create a joint tenancy must be clear and explicit; otherwise, the parties will be deemed to hold in common. In a joint ownership, a deceased party's interest in the property goes to the surviving owner or owners and not to the decedent's heirs or next of kin. A deed from Roger Harris to Carl Parsons and Edward F. Parsons, "as joint tenants, with the right of survivorship and not as tenants in common" would clearly create a joint estate. Upon the death of Carl Parsons, the property would vest absolutely in the surviving party, Edward F. Parsons, rather than in any surviving heirs or kin of Carl Parsons. If the conveyance from Harris were simply to "Carl Parsons and Edward F. Parsons," the grantees would hold as owners in common, and upon the death of Carl Parsons, his interest in the property would not go to the surviving party, Edward F. Parsons, but would vest in Carl's heirs. Where one joint owner dies, and there are two or more owners surviving, the property vests in all of the survivors until the last survivor, who succeeds to the entire estate. Joint owners must acquire ownership by a single deed. Husband and wife may hold property as tenants in common rather than by the entireties if the deed makes this clear.

---

[2] Pennsylvania Act declared unconstitutional in case of Wilcox v. Penn Mutual Life Ins. Co., 357 Pa. 581.

A deceased joint owner's interest in real estate is subject to inheritance and estate taxes. A sale by one of three joint owners of his interest would not destroy the joint ownership of the other two as joint owners.

A conveyance of a farm to Francis Lucas, a single man, and to Joseph and Matilda Lucas, husband and wife, raises the serious question whether each of the three grantees owns an undivided one-third interest, whether Francis owns a *one-half* interest, and Joseph and Matilda own the other half by the entireties, or whether Joseph owns a one-third interest and the married couple own the other two-thirds by the entireties. A broker preparing a deed is duty-bound to "spell out" the *intentions* of the parties, but he must first be cognizant of the applicable law under the circumstances. If the intention is not sufficiently manifested, a serious consequence may ensue. With no more language in the deed than indicated in the Lucas case above, Francis would own a *one-half* interest and Joseph and Matilda would own the other half interest by the entireties.[3]

The Uniform Partnership Act provides for a special form of tenancy called a "tenancy in partnership." Property owned by two or more persons as co-owners is not partnership property and real estate held by partners for *firm purposes* does not constitute a tenancy in common. The property must be purchased with *partnership* funds. Partnership property can be sold free of any dower claim of the wives of the individual partners. Likewise, a judgment against one of the partners would not constitute a lien against the partnership property. A deed must clearly indicate that the conveyance is to a partnership, *as such;* otherwise, the grantees will be considered to be tenants in common. The partnership realty, upon death of one partner, passes to the surviving partners, but payment of the deceased partner's interest must be made to the decedent's state.

Reading deed

Where a grantor signs a deed, he is presumed to have read it and to be familiar with its contents. Illiteracy is no defense to the validity of the instrument. If a person cannot read, the burden is upon him to have someone read the deed to him. A grantor cannot complain at a later date that the transaction has turned out differently than he anticipated, or that he was unaware of the full import of the deed, because he could not read. Where the illiterate grantor has been imposed upon and the deed content misrepresented to him, equity will grant relief and set the transfer aside.

---

3 Heatter v. Lucas, 397 Pa. 296 (1951).

Witnessing

Although it is not necessary to have the deed witnessed, it is a good precaution in the event that a dispute arises, for the subscribing witnesses may be procured to testify as to the deed execution. The witness attests nothing but the signing and delivery of the deed. The date and other contents of the deed are matters which he does not attest and to which he seldom attends.

Acknowledgment

In addition to signing, sealing, and witnessing a deed, it is customary for the grantor to acknowledge it. The acknowledgment is a formal declaration made before a notary public, justice of the peace, alderman, or other official empowered to perform this service, affirming the genuineness of the signature on the deed. The acknowledgment accomplishes two things: first, it establishes the deed as *prima facie* evidence in any legal proceeding; that is, the deed will be accepted as evidence without any further proof of its genuineness; and second, *it permits the recording of the deed*. The acknowledgment contains the venue or county in which it is executed— "State of Illinois, County of Cook"—, the date, the name of the grantor, and the signature, seal, and expiration date of the commission of the officer taking the acknowledgment. It should state that the affiant is personally known or satisfactorily proved to be the subscriber. The grantor's marital status should also be indicated —"John Steele, unmarried," or "John Steele and Mary Steele, his wife," or "John Steele, unmarried, and Helen Steele, unmarried." In most states, only one acknowledgment need be taken for both husband and wife. In some states—Alabama, New Jersey, North Carolina, South Carolina, and Texas—separate acknowledgments are necessary for husband and wife. The married woman's acknowledgment must be taken apart from her husband—that she signed the deed freely and voluntarily.

Delivery

Delivery is one of the most important steps in the transfer of title to real estate. A deed, signed, sealed, witnessed, and acknowledged, does not pass title until it is delivered by the grantor to the grantee, or to a third person for him. Thus Smith, a man 80 years of age, signed and acknowledged a deed to his nephew, Brown, and placed it in an old tin box which he kept in his room. He died shortly afterwards and the deed was then discovered. In the event of a contest between Brown and other heirs for the property, the heirs would win since there had been no delivery of the instrument. In most cases, there is a manual delivery of the deed directly from the grantor to the grantee and no question arises as to the transfer of title. When the deed is not "handed over," question of delivery arises. If delivery may be "presumed" from the circumstances, then title will pass. The question to be determined is the *intention* of the grantor. An executed deed, recorded by the *grantor,* would raise a strong presumption of delivery. Ordinarily, it may be said that retention of the deed by the grantor raises a strong presumption against delivery and possession by the grantee creates a presumption in favor of delivery. In both cases only a presumption is raised and is subject to rebuttal by proof.

Delivery absolute

There are two kinds of delivery, delivery absolute and delivery in escrow. Delivery absolute occurs when made to a grantee or his agent without any conditions or stipulations attached. This is the usual situation.

In escrow

A delivery in escrow occurs when the deed is delivered to a third person and will take effect only upon the performance of some condition by one of the parties or the happening of some event. In an escrow delivery, the grantor loses all control over the deed, and he is powerless to recall it. The condition of the escrow must be stated *at the time* the deed is turned over to the escrow holder and not at some later time. The *time* for performance of the escrow condition should be definitely stated and, also, what happens if the condition is not performed. Otherwise, the delivery will be considered absolute and the escrow holder as agent for the grantee. The escrow holder should require that the condition of delivery be in writing, signed by the interested parties. A deed delivered in escrow will pass no title if it is stolen or otherwise fraudulently procured by the grantee or if delivered to him without fulfillment of the escrow condition, but a bona fide purchaser from the grantee, without notice, will obtain good title.

It should be remembered that the escrow holder must be some disinterested or impartial third person and the principals or their legal counsel are not such disinterested parties within the contemplation of the law. Nor is a broker a disinterested third party, because he is the agent of the owner from whom he receives compensation for his services in the form of a commission. A bank, title company or an escrow company should preferably be used as the escrow holder. A deposit of earnest money with a real estate broker should not be confused with an escrow.

Recording

When the deed has been signed, sealed, and delivered, the transfer of title is complete. However, in order for the purchaser to protect himself in the ownership, the law requires him to take one additional step. This consists in recording or registering his deed in the office of the Recorder of Deeds, Registrar, or Register of Deeds in the county where the property is located. The recording of a deed consists in having it transcribed in a proper book and indexed, so that the public at large may have notice of the transfer of title. The deed should be recorded promptly in order to protect the grantee against a subsequent conveyance of the same property by his grantor, or against a mortgage or judgment entered against the same grantor. Green delivers a deed to White on December 6, 1968 which is not recorded until March 21, 1969. A judgment entered against Green on February 21, 1969 would be a lien against the real estate in question. So also, a bona fide purchaser of the same land from Green would have a preferred claim to the property if he had no actual or constructive notice of the transfer to White. Actual notice is express or direct knowledge gained in the course of the transaction.

Constructive notice

Thus, Cox's knowledge that Adams at one time had mortgaged property to Brown would not be of itself actual notice to Cox unless he learned of it in the course of his negotiations with Adams for the purchase of the particular property. In most cases, notice of an unrecorded deed must be made out from a statement of facts that existed at the time and from which notice would be presumed to have been given to a cautious purchaser. This is what is known as "constructive notice." The rule concerning constructive notice is that notice can be presumed to have been given where there are circumstances which would make a prudent man suspicious and which would cause him to inquire whether the seller had not previously parted with his title. The chief test of constructive notice concerns *who was in actual possession of the land at the time of the sale.* If the land is not in the possession of the man holding himself out to own it but is occupied by the holder of the prior deed, then a little inquiry from the party in possession would readily reveal the duplicity of the original owner.

Torrens system

A system of land registration was introduced in Australia in 1858 by Sir Robert Torrens. The system provided a permanent method of title registration with an assurance fund out of which losses due to title defects would be paid. Once the title is registered by an owner, subsequent transfers of the certificate of title registration could be readily effected at slight expense. The original Torrens system has not made any great inroad into the recording system in this country due to the initial expense involved, certain substantial objections inherent in the system, and the opposition of the title companies. Although adopted in varying forms in a number of states (California, Colorado, Georgia, Illinois, Massachusetts, Mississippi, Minnesota, Nebraska, New York, North Carolina, North Dakota, Ohio, Oregon, South Carolina, South Dakota, Tennessee, Utah, Virginia, and Washington), title searches are, in the main, still required. In Massachusetts and Illinois are found the most satisfactory applications of the Torrens system. Adaptations of the Torrens system require the registration of title ownership through court proceedings. The certificate of title issued by court authorization is conclusive insofar as the character of the title is concerned.

Quit claim deed

A *quit claim* deed is used to clear clouds upon the title as in the case of a recorded agreement of sale or the release of a life estate or a contingent remainder. The grantee in the quit claim deed may already have or may claim a complete or partial title to the premises and the grantor has a *possible* interest that might constitute a cloud upon the title. A deed of *confirmation* is similar, in effect, to a quit claim deed. The operative words are "remise, release, and quit claim." The warranty is omitted entirely, and the grantor forever quits whatever interest he might have in the property. A wife, who has not joined in the bargain and sale deed, may subsequently sign a quit claim deed barring her potential dower right in the property.

A quit claim deed may be used to extinguish a recorded agreement of sale. The vendee (purchaser) would be the grantor in this deed.

Condominiums

CONDOMINIUM OWNERSHIP represents a new concept of property ownership in this country. It is of old origin elsewhere, having been used in Rome since the sixth century B.C. It is well established in Puerto Rico and Latin America and has made gigantic strides in recent years in the United States. Basically, it is a form of cooperative ownership, having most of the advantages of a "co-op" and eliminating the major disadvantages. It has been described as "the individual ownership of single units in a multi-unit structure, with common ownership of halls, stairs, elevators, lobbies, driveways, parking area, etc. Condominiums may be bought, sold, mortgaged, and are taxed *separately*. Each owner's property is liable for his own mortgage debt. Another's default does not endanger his interests." In a sense, a condominium is a subdivision.

The California Horizontal Property Act provides (Section 4), inter alia, that ". . . an apartment in the building may be individually conveyed and encumbered and may be the subject of ownership, possession, or sale . . ."

Section 6 states that ". . . an apartment owner shall have an exclusive right to his apartment and shall have a common right to share with other co-owners, in the common elements of the property."

The Act defines in Section 2 what the common elements are, viz.: yards, gardens, roofs, basements, power, light, gas, water, refrigeration, reservoirs, elevators, garbage incinerators, parking facilities, etc.

The statute provides that the Master Deed shall express a description of the land, a general description and number of each apartment (unit), describing its area, location, and any other data necessary for its identification, and a description of the general common elements of the building.

The fact that the owner of a condominium unit is liable only for taxes assessed against his unit and for the separate mortgage created by him gives him the same security and safety as the owner of a private dwelling. It is important to remember that the owner of a condominium unit, like an owner of a private dwelling, owns it in fee simple and he enjoys a joint ownership with the other unit own-

197

ers as to the common areas and the land underneath. In the more common form of co-ops, the owner purchases stock in the corporation owner and his unit is held under a long-term renewable lease. Or the co-op may offer the purchaser a deed to an undivided interest in the whole with the right to occupy a particular unit apartment. Thus, if the operation consists of 20 units, he would own a 1/20 interest in the structure and all the facilities used by all owners in common. While some title companies are reluctant to insure condominium titles because of difficulty in describing accurately the subject premises, progress is being made in this area. With title insurance available, mortgage financing will be as readily obtained as in the case of a private dwelling. This will certainly broaden the market for lending institutions, since under a co-op of 200 units, there would be only one mortgage of say $3,000,000, whereas under the condominium, there would be 200 mortgages of $15,000 each. The condominium is the partial answer to scarcity of land and mounting land costs. The first F.H.A. insured condominium project in the country was built in Richmond, Virginia. The Hartshorn Homes offered a unit consisting of three bedrooms, one and one-half baths for $11,500, with a $350 down payment and monthly payments of $66.60 to cover principal, interest, taxes and insurance. To facilitate the use of condominium ownership, the Housing Act of 1961 added Section 234 to the National Housing Act. Section 234 authorizes the Federal Housing Administration to insure mortgages on "individually owned units in multi-family structures" *in states where real property title and ownership are established for such units.* Condominiums are also a possibility under the Veterans Administration Loan Guarantee Program.

The Federal Housing Administration is authorized to insure a first mortgagee of a condominium owner. Since 1961, the benefits of F.H.A. insurance are extended to a condominium mortgagee for amounts up to 97% of the value of the apartment unit, for a term up to 30 years, at a $5\frac{1}{4}\%$ interest rate.

All the co-owners agree, by contract among themselves, to share certain expenses common to the operation and maintenance of the improvement, through monthly assessment upon each unit owner, dependent upon their respective percentages of ownership in the common elements.

Under the F.H.A. program, the Administration points out the chief differences between condominium housing and cooperative housing, as follows:

1. In condominiums, individuals take title to their units; in cooperatives, individuals have a stock ownership in the cooperative and the right of occupancy to a specific unit.

2. In condominiums, individuals vote on a proportionate basis; in co-operatives, each individual has one vote regardless of the size of his unit.
3. In condominiums, individuals are taxed separately on their units; in cooperatives, individuals pay their share of taxes on the project in their monthly carrying charges.
4. In condominiums, individuals are responsible only for mortgage indebtedness and taxes involving their own property and have no mortgage indebtness or tax liability for the other properties; in cooperatives, each individual is dependent upon the solvency of the entire project.

Condominium ownership affords the owner certain important advantages. Interest paid on mortgages is an income tax deduction; other income tax benefits are depreciation; lower tax liability on the land since it is spread among a large number of owners. With the great exodus in recent years from urban to suburban areas in many of our larger cities, the condominium form of ownership will, to some measure, counteract this movement. One important advantage is that it will eliminate to some extent the pressures of commuting to work and marks a trend from suburban living back to the metropolitan area. Each owner of a condominium unit enjoys stock ownership in a corporation formed to provide for the common areas, such as landscaping, playground, utilities, parking facilities and maintenance.

Restrictive Covenants, Easements, Zoning

A COVENANT is generally defined as an agreement between two or more persons, entered into by deed, whereby one of the parties promises the performance or nonperformance of certain acts or that a given state of things does or does not exist. Covenants may arise by implication of law, from the conduct of the parties. They may be divided into two classes, personal covenants and restrictive covenants or covenants running with the land.

Restrictive covenants

Restrictive covenants, as the expression is generally understood, are covenants running with the land. They are sometimes called "negative" covenants. They may be created in a number of ways. First, the limitations on the use of land may be explicitly set forth in the deed instrument. Second, the restrictions may be contained in a separate written instrument recorded or determined from a printed plan of the proposed development of the property. Third, restrictive covenants may be brought into existence by estoppel through oral representations alone. Thus, where an owner sells part of a subdivision tract under representations that his entire plan is restricted to the same extent, he thereby restricts use of remaining portion of his land to that extent.

The owner of a tract of land divided into lots sometimes imposes restrictions on some of the lots as sold. Such restrictions are not to be defeated merely because similar restrictions are not imposed upon the remainder of the lots. Where an owner of lots conveys one of them by a deed containing building restrictions with a covenant that he will impose the same restrictions in the deeds for the remainder of the lots, the deed is recorded, and he subsequently conveys the remaining lots by deed without such restrictions, his later grantee is bound by the terms of the deed to the former grantee, although he has no actual notice of such terms. In examining the record he is bound to read the whole of the former deed and if he fails to do so, he is affected by notice of all that it contains. In reading the deed he will thus have notice of the restrictions affecting all of the lots.

It is a well-recognized principle of law that every owner of land has the right to restrain its use by his grantees and to limit its appropriation to purposes which would in any way impair or lessen the value of that portion which he retains. Restrictions will be enforced by a court of equity unless they are against public policy. They are enforceable, if reasonable, commensurate with the quality and character of the development. Where a tract of land is conveyed to a person with restrictions and he afterwards subdivides the land and conveys the several lots to third persons *without* restrictions, his several grantees or their purchasers would have no right to enforce, *inter se* (among themselves) the restrictions in the deed to their common grantor. Where the restrictions are common to all the lot purchasers, each has a right to enforce the covenants and enjoin their violation. When a man sells lots in a plan with a 25-foot building line, the restriction is mutual to the extent that any lot owner may enjoin the violation of the building line restriction by any other lot owner.

A personal covenant is one binding upon the original party (covenantor) only, and when he dies, or disposes of the property, the rectriction is at an end.

Restriction requirements

1. The language of a restriction must be clear as to its meaning. If ambiguous, it will be stricken down, for the courts are ever vigilant to protect the free alienation of property. Restrictions are strictly construed against persons seeking to enforce them and all doubts are resolved in favor of natural rights. All doubts must be resolved against the restriction and in favor of a free and unrestricted use of the property. Where the restriction limited an owner to one dwelling house upon a lot, the erection of a duplex dwelling was held not to be a violation. However, a restriction for the erection of a private dwelling house would prohibit the erection of an apartment building, housing a number of families. In the term "a private dwelling" the word "dwelling" restricts the character of building by eliminating all buildings for business or commercial purposes, such as stores, garages, warehouses, factories and the like. The word "private" further excludes buildings of a public character, such as hotels, dormitories, and apartment houses. A motion picture theatre was held not to violate a restriction against any building for "offensive occupation."

2. It is necessary to ascertain the *intention* of the grantor in order

to determine whether the restriction is for the personal benefit or protection of the grantor or runs with the land. Where Jones owns tracts 1 and 2, and sells tract 2 to Brown, reserving a right of way across the tract sold, the covenant would be personal to Jones alone and upon Jones's death or sale of tract 1 by him, the restriction would cease. However, if Jones reserved the right of way to himself, his heirs and assigns, the language used would clearly indicate an intention to create the right of way over tract 2 in favor of tract 1, regardless of the ownership of the latter. In this example, tract 2 would be the *servient tenement,* the tract upon which the burden or privilege is imposed, and tract 1 would be the *dominant tenement,* the tract to which the privilege attaches. Any subsequent owner of tract 1 could enjoy the right of way.

3. Restrictions should be limited as to time—20, 30, or 50 years. If not so limited, the restriction would be perpetual and could become ineffectual due to resistless evolution effecting a radical change in the character of the neighborhood. The restriction would be tempered to conform to the "change of neighborhood," even before the time limit has expired.

4. Care should be taken in ascertaining how the restriction is to operate. Prohibiting an erection of a commercial structure will not operate to prevent the *use* of a residence for a commercial purpose. In order to prevent erection *or* use, the restriction clause should read:

That no building on said lot, or any hereafter erected, shall be erected for or used or occupied for business, trade, commerce, manufacturing, or for any offensive or malodorous occupation, or be used for any purpose other than that of a private dwelling house with private garage.

5. The restriction must not be contrary to public policy. The courts have uniformly held that a prohibition by municipal *ordinance* effecting a racial restriction violates the Constitution and is invalid.

Enforcement

When considering relief by injunction against the breach of a restrictive covenant, the courts require due diligence upon the part of the plaintiff, and delay upon his part (laches) will ordinarily defeat his application; for instance, where an objector has permitted a violation to proceed without objection and the lot owner has incurred considerable expense in the building construction. Equity aids the vigilant and not the "sleeping." A person violating the restriction himself could not enjoin a similar violation by another owner. Where Jones converted a part of his residence into a store, in violation of a restrictive covenant, he would not succeed in enjoining Smith from using his building for a commercial purpose. Injunction is an extraordinary or special remedy addressed to the equity side of the court and "he who comes into equity must do so with clean hands." Injunction may be invoked or a building ordered to be torn down where a warning has not been heeded. Building restrictions are considered warranties rather than conditions. A breach generally gives rise to injunction or money damages rather than a forfeiture of the estate to the grantor as would be true if the restriction were construed as a condition. A sample form of simple restrictions would read as follows:

John STEELE, and
Mary K. STEELE, his wife

BUILDING RESTRICTIONS

Declaration and Agreement as to Covenants and Building Restrictions in Respect to Nomad Heights Plan of Lots Located in the City of Miami, County of Dade, State of Florida

THIS DECLARATION AND AGREEMENT, made and entered into this 2nd day of October, 1968 between John STEELE and Mary K. STEELE, his wife, Parties of the First Part, and all purchasers and their respective heirs and assigns of lots in the Nomad Heights Plan of Lots, Parties of the Second Part;

WHEREAS, the Parties of the First Part intend to sell and convey the lots in said Nomad Heights Plan by deeds referring to restrictive covenants on the part of purchasers contained in this Declaration and Agreement, and which is to be recorded to the end that the restrictive covenants herein imposed shall inure to the benefit of each and all of the purchasers of said lots:

THE PARTIES OF THE FIRST PART agree that all lots in said plan shall be sold subject to the respective covenants contained in the Declaration and Agreement, and all purchasers of lots in said plan, for themselves, their heirs and assigns, by the purchase of said lots, agree to be bound by the covenants herein contained, by reference in their respective deeds to the Volume and Page in the Recorder's Office where this Declaration and Agreement will be recorded.

The purchaser as to any lot in the said Nomad Heights Plan and with the intent to bind all persons with whom the title of said lot may hereafter vest, agrees to the following restrictive covenants:

1. THESE covenants are to run with the land and shall be binding on all parties and persons claiming under them until January 1, 1978, at which time said covenants shall automatically extend for an additional period of ten years, unless by vote of a majority of the then owners of the lots it is agreed to change said covenants in whole or in part.

2. If the parties hereto, or any of them, or their heirs and assigns, shall violate or attempt to violate any of the covenants herein mentioned, it shall be lawful for any other person or persons owning any real property situated in said development or subdivision to prosecute any proceedings at law or in equity against the person or persons violating or attempting to violate any such covenant, and either to prevent him or them from so doing or to recover damages or other dues for such violation.

3. All lots in the plan or tract shall be known and described as residential lots.

4. No structure shall be erected, altered, placed or permitted to remain on any residential building lot other than one semidetached single family dwelling, and a private garage for not more than two cars, and only one residence shall be permitted upon each numbered lot in the plan. No building shall be erected, placed, or altered on any building plot in this subdivision until the building plans, specification and plot plan showing the location of such building have been approved in writing by John

STEELE, as to conformity and harmony of external design with existing structures in the plant or proposed structure, the plans for which have been approved, and also as to the location of the building with respect to topography and finished ground elevation, which approval shall not be unreasonably withheld. In the event said John STEELE fails to approve or disapprove such design and location within thirty (30) days after said plans and specifications have been submitted to him or, in any event, if no suit to enjoin the erection of such building or alteration or construction has been commenced prior to the completion thereof, such approval will not be required, and this covenant will be deemed to have been fully complied with.

5. No building shall be located nearer to the front lot line or nearer to the side street line than the building setback line shown on the recorded plan. In any event, no building shall be located on any residential building plot nearer than thirty (30) feet to the front lot line, nor nearer than thirty (30) feet to any side street line. No building except a detached garage, or outbuilding located fifty (50) feet or more from the front road line, shall be located nearer than five (5) feet to any side line. No residence or attached appurtenance shall be erected on any lot farther than forty (40) feet from the front lot line.

6. No residential structure shall be erected or placed on any building plot, which plot has an area of less than five thousand (5000) square feet, or a width of less than fifty (50) feet at the front building setback line.

7. No trailer, basement, tent, shack, garage, barn, or other outbuilding erected in the tract shall at any time be used as a temporary or permanent residence, nor shall any structure of a temporary character be used as a residence.

8. No building costing less than nine thousand (9000) dollars shall be permitted on any lot in the tract, and the ground floor area of the main structure exclusively of one story open porches and garages shall be not less than six hundred fifty (650) square feet in the case of a one story structure, nor less than four hundred fifty (450) square feet in the case of a one and one-half or two story structure.

9. No noxious or offensive trade or activity shall be carried on upon any lot, nor shall anything be done thereon which may be or become a nuisance or annoyance to the neighborhood.

10. Invalidation of any of these covenants by judgment or court order shall in no wise affect any of the other provisions, which shall remain in full force and effect.

IN WITNESS WHEREOF, the parties hereto have affixed their hands and seals the day and year aforesaid.

John Steele   (SEAL)

Mary K. Steele   (SEAL)

Witnesses:

John N. Harkins

Earl A. Hart

STATE OF FLORIDA } ss.
COUNTY OF DADE }

On this 2nd day of October, 1968 before me, a notary public in and for said County and State, personally appeared John STEELE and Mary K. STEELE, his wife, known to me, who being duly sworn according to law doth acknowledge the foregoing to be their act and deed to the end that it may be recorded as such. Sworn to and subscribed before me this 2nd day of October, 1968.

James A. Herron

NOTARY PUBLIC
My Commission expires May 1, 1969

(NOTARIAL SEAL)

Easements

A restrictive covenant constitutes an incorporeal right. It is akin to an easement. An easement is defined as a liberty, privilege, or advantage which one proprietor may have in the lands of another, without profit in a material, physical sense. Easements may be classified as appurtenant—running with the land; and in gross—or personal to the individual owner, in the nature of a license. The best known easement is perhaps a right of way over another man's land. In origin, easements may be express or implied. Express easements are those which have been set forth in a deed or some supplementary writing, whereas the others arise as the result of a legal implication. With the opening up of the West, many situations arose where highways and boundaries between properties were laid down improperly, and, as a consequence, a man trespassed over other property in order to reach the main road. As a result, the courts invented the doctrine of implied easements, and this rule has been adopted throughout the country so that at the present time it is practically general.

Easement by necessity

An easement may be implied where the circumstances surrounding the case are such as to make such a course desirable in the interest of public policy. The implication under which the easement is created, however, must be based upon *necessity* and not mere *convenience*. It is difficult to lay down any general rule by which to judge the existence of necessity. The courts will judge that an easement is necessary in most cases where the facts show that an original arrangement, which is clearly in the nature of an easement, has existed and where the disturbance of this arrangement could be inequitable to the party claiming the right. Jones laid a gas line across the rear of White's property in 1952 in order to obtain fuel for domestic purposes. In 1961, White sold his property to Black. In 1967, due to personal differences between Jones and Black, the latter instructed Jones to remove the gas line from his property. Under the facts stated, and particularly since Black purchased the property with the gas line upon it, it is extremely doubtful that a court, after 15 years, would require its removal.

One of the most important things to remember concerning appurtenant easements is that they are not personal grants which die with the death of the person in whose favor they were made, or become extinguished when he parts with the property. They belong, instead, to the land, and pass with it to all subsequent holders, unless excepted by the express provisions of the deed. It is also important to remember that the right of an easement belongs to all and every part of the land. The holder of any portion of the original tract, no matter how small a tract, is entitled to all the rights that he would possess if he owned the entire tract. The courts will permit the burden to be made greater where the additional servitude is due to the more complete development of the dominant tenement. The right of way which one farm possesses over another may be used very seldom so long as the tract is used for farming; but, when the ground is subdivided into lots, it is readily seen that the burden of the servient tenement is considerably increased; however, so long as the use is confined to those who are holders of any part of the original property, the courts will not intervene to release the servient tenement of any part of the extra burden. This is so because the easement right belongs to the property and to limit the full use and development of the property would be contrary to public policy.

Implied easement

Another example of an implied easement is where the owner of two properties constructs a building upon one lot, and a cornice, roof, or spouting encroaches over the other parcel. If he sells the unimproved property to another, the purchaser takes it subject to the open, visible, permanent, and continuous servitude which has been placed upon it by the encroachment, and he cannot later demand the removal of the encroachment. It is necessary, however, in order to create an implied easement in favor of the improved property, to show that the advantage which is claimed satisfies these requirements: *open, visible, permanent,* and *continuous.* In other words, it is such a burden as could readily be seen by the intending purchaser before he has paid for the property and he thus takes the property subject to the existing encroachment. However, if the dwelling with the encroaching cornice burned down or was destroyed, the owner would not be permitted to rebuild so as to continue the encroachment. He would be required to contain the *entire* building within his own property limits. It should be noted, too, that an implied easement cannot be extended to include land. An owner of two lots erected a garage upon the premises at the rear of one lot so that a portion of the garage building extended onto the second lot. Later, the owner sold the two lots to different purchasers—the first lot, with the major portion of the garage to Arnold and the second lot with the lesser portion of the garage to Blake. The garage could be used only by Arnold. The purchaser, Blake, could compel the removal of the building from his lot, as Arnold would not have an implied easement. Otherwise, Arnold would obtain a property right to part of Blake's land in *fee,* rather than a mere incorporeal easement. The doctrine of implied easement will not be enlarged to deprive an owner of the right of use or possession of his property. Circumstances may temper this principle, as where the case involves a *slight* encroachment of a building upon or near the dividing line, or where the use of the encroachment upon land is claimed as a real necessity, the deprivation of which would cause a severe hardship.

Finally, it should be remembered that the easement does not in any way give its beneficiary title to the property which is subservient to it. It simply gives the right of use and not of possession. The owner of the servient tract can sell the land over which his neighbor has certain rights, in the same way as though those rights did not exist; and if, by mutual agreement, the easement is cancelled, it is not necessary that the strip which has been subject to the servitude be deeded back to the owner of the servient tenement since he already possesses title to it. An easement is an encumbrance and a purchaser could refuse to accept a deed subject to a right of way or other privilege unless the agreement of sale provided that the conveyance was to be subject to the right.

Usufructory right in water

Property rights in water and in the use and enjoyment of it are well established as rights in the soil over which it flows. But water, from its very nature, does not readily adapt itself to possession as does land so that a property right in water is really only a usufructory right, a right of use. If the natural channel of a watercourse lies along or through the lands of different owners, the water therein is the common and indivisible property of all. They have equal privileges to it in all respects insofar as a right to its use for domestic or business purposes. An upper owner, whose land is traversed by the stream, cannot so exercise his use as to deprive the lower owners of a similar enjoyment. That is to say, he cannot divert the water, dam it up, or interfere with its natural flow. If, however, in the ordinary, normal, and reasonable exercise of his right to use, the result is to prevent a subjacent owner of a similar use, the lower owner has no redress. This is the common law rule of the doctrine of riparian rights. A mining company would be liable if pollution of the stream results from an artificial diversion of the stream.

In a number of the western states the common law rule has been rejected, where, by reason of the arid condition of the land, the

necessities of the people compel a change in the rule. The policy
there permits a diversion of the stream water from its natural course
and protects the *first* appropriation as a recognized proprietary
right. Three elements must exist for a valid appropriation: (1)
intent to appropriate the water to some beneficial use existing at
the time or contemplated in the future; (2) an actual diversion
from the natural channel by means of a ditch, canal, or other con-
duit; and (3) the practical application of the water within a reasonable time to some useful industry. The appropriation, intention, the
use, and the beneficial purposes are the test by which the right to
divert a stream are determined.

The question of liability is frequently raised relative to the overflow of water from one property on to another. The law is clearly
established that the first owner may not obstruct a natural channel
for the flow of the water or a channel that has acquired the character of an *easement,* nor may he gather surface water into a body
and discharge it upon adjoining land. He may not act negligently
in directing the flow so as to do unnecessary damage to others.
But so far as he acts upon his right to the enjoyment of his own
property, any accidental damage to a neighbor is, in the eyes of the
law, *damnum absque injuria* (injury without wrong). In other words
the injured party has no legal remedy.

Zoning

Closely allied to building restrictions, which result from voluntary
agreement of the parties, are zoning restrictions.

We have already discussed the limitations upon a property
owner's free use of property through the medium of building restrictions contained in deeds and by special agreement. They are designed to insure the uniform character of a development. Further
restrictions upon the use of property may arise through zoning
regulation. Zoning is the creation by law of districts in which regulations, differing in various districts, prohibit injurious or unsuitable
structures and uses of structures and lands. Zoning, if reasonably
exercised, represents a valid exercise of the police power of the
state. The zoning, however, is not done by the state but by the
municipality in pursuance of an enabling act of the state, permitting
the municipalities within the state to adopt zoning codes or ordinances. The general purpose of zoning laws requires that such regulations shall be made in accordance with a comprehensive plan
—designed to lessen congestion in the streets, to secure safety from
fire, panic, and other dangers, to promote health and the general
welfare, to provide adequate light and air, to prevent the over-

crowding of land, to avoid undue concentration of population, or to facilitate the adequate provision of transportation, water, sewerage, schools, parks, and other public requirements. The regulations must be made with reasonable consideration, among other things, to the character of the district and its peculiar suitability for particular uses, and with a view to conserving the value of lands and buildings and encouraging the most appropriate use of land throughout the particular political subdivision. Regulation under the guise of zoning, which results in the destruction or confiscation of property, must necessarily fail. Courts, in the interests of justice and equity, may pertinently inquire into the valid or invalid exercise of the police power, keeping in mind whether the challenged ordinance is necessary *for the public health, safety, morals, or general welfare.* The reasonableness of the ordinance is for judicial determination. It is not the duty of the courts to fix district lines or to usurp the place of zoning authorities, but the work of such authorities is subject to review and, if its application is found, upon judicial examination, to be unreasonable and confiscatory, to be set aside. The United States Supreme Court has declared that: "the inclusion of private land in a residential district under a zoning ordinance with resulting inhibition of the use for business and industrial buildings to the serious damage of the owner, violates the Fourteenth Amendment, if the health, safety, convenience, or general welfare of the part of the city affected will not be promoted thereby."

Zoning ordinances will be held inoperative when based upon purely aesthetic considerations. They must have a substantial relation to the public good. Civic-minded real estate operators and brokers are in accord that reasonable zoning regulation is essential to maintain and promote the attractive character of a city or town. To permit the unbridled development or use of land in accordance with the selfish interest of an individual owner is bound to be reflected in the depreciated value of surrounding properties. Favored legislation in the form of "spot" zoning so that the zone of one particular property is changed is equally vicious and inimical to the community as a whole.

Nonconforming use

Zoning laws have no application to the location of properties or their use prior to the enactment of the zoning measure. This is known as a nonconforming use. A zoning ordinance is not an encumbrance within the meaning of the term, which would enable a purchaser to renounce his agreement of sale. However, a title insurance policy will except any existing zoning ordinance from the title insurance contract. A broker's responsibility to the prospective purchaser or lessee should require him to ascertain the use to which the property is to be put and whether the proposed use conforms to zoning provisions. Zoning ordinances excluding the use of property by certain races are clearly illegal. A broker should be ever cautious in locating a family in a plan or on a street where the entrance is offensive to the entire neighborhood. Where a zoning ordinance is in force, a property owner who desires to erect a structure must first obtain a building permit from the city building inspector or department. If the proposed building meets the requirements of the building code of the municipality and is not violative of any zoning restrictions, the desired permit will be issued and posted upon the property. Where the use contemplated does not adhere to the zone set up for the particular location, the permit will be refused. An appeal by any aggrieved party may then be taken to the board of adjustment, or as it is sometimes called, the zoning board. The board has power to hear and decide appeals where it is alleged there is error in the decision of an administrative official, to hear and decide special exceptions to the terms of the ordinance, and to authorize, in special cases, a variance from the terms of the zoning ordinance. The board can take cognizance of special conditions where a literal enforcement of the ordinance provisions will result in unnecessary hardship. Further appeal to court is permitted, and ordinarily an appeal from the decision of the board operates to stay the proceedings upon the decision appealed, but the court may, on application, grant a restraining order, upon cause shown and upon the petitioner posting a bond as in other cases seeking injunctive relief.

Zoning classifications

Municipalities follow different zoning classes, depending upon their requirements and the size and area of the municipality. All ordinances have classifications of residential, industrial, and commercial zones. A higher use classification is usually permissible in a lower use classification. In urban centers, industrial classification is divided into heavy and light industrial zones. Even under the lowest classification of heavy industrial zone, certain uses are sometimes prohibited. Prohibited uses would include abattoirs, manufacture of animal fertilizer, gun powder or explosive manufacture or storage, garbage disposal plants, or stockyards. Any of these operations would be offensive or dangerous to the population if carried on within the city limits. A dwelling, except living quarters for the use of watchmen employed upon the premises, could also be excluded. A commercial district can also be separated into classifications to take care of special needs in a neighborhood retail district as well as the downtown commercial zone. Residential zones are often classified into several districts. In a class "A" residence district, for example, one-family or more dwellings, including apartment buildings, are permitted, as well as educational or charitable institutions, churches, greenhouses, or schools. In a "B" residence district, multiple family (more than two) or apartment buildings would be prohibited, while in a "C" residential district, only a single family dwelling use might be permitted. A large part of zoning ordinances is devoted to height limitations and front, rear, and side yard areas.

In a metropolitan area, comprising many different municipal sub-divisions, civic planning is necessary in order to promote orderly development of the contiguous neighborhood as a whole.

Adverse Possession

O RDINARILY, AN owner of real estate relies upon a "paper" title to establish ownership; that is, by deed from his predecessor, and which, when traced back, shows a continuity of title ownership to the source of title in the particular state. An examination of the public records establishes a "chain of title" upon which the occupier of land relies to prove ownership. Technically, title emanates from a sovereign power or government, the exact source varying in the different sections of the country. However, a resident of land may claim title to property without any deed or color of title at all. He may rely upon adverse occupation. Such title may be superior to that of the holder of the "paper" title if certain statutory requirements are met. This is known as title by *adverse possession*. The law governing adverse possession is now universal, being enforced in practically every state of the country. The purposes of these laws are identical. They are prompted in the first place by the demands of public policy which hold that a statute of this kind is necessary to prevent the abandonment of any portion of the territory. The law provides that where an occupier holds land and maintains actual, continuous, hostile, notorious, distinct, and visible possession for the required period of time, he is deemed to have the legal title as against one who holds a deed for the same land. The period varies from seven to thirty years. In Utah, 7 years is the statutory period; Mississippi, Missouri, and Oregon, 10 years; Connecticut, Kansas, Kentucky, Minnesota, and Oklahoma, 15 years; Illinois, Massachusetts, Maine, New York, 20 years; Pennsylvania, 21 years; and, in some cases, 30 years. The Adverse Possession Act is in a sense a statute of limitations in that it bars the legal owner from asserting his claim to the land where he has remained silent and done nothing to oust the adverse occupant during the statutory period. The theory of the law is that "no person ought to be permitted to lie by while transactions can be fairly investigated and justly determined, until time has involved them in uncertainty and obscurity, and then ask for an inquiry." The incidents of adverse possession are actual, continuous, hostile, notorious, visible, and distinct.

Actual possession

Incidents which help establish actual possession include building a dwelling or other structure, clearing brush, sowing crops, pasturing cattle, erecting fences, cutting timber, irrigating the land, constructing drainage ditches, planting orchards, and paying taxes.

By actual possession is meant such a possession of the property as leaves no doubt in the mind of the ordinary person as to the nature of the occupancy. The law insists that the claimant must show the performance of adequate acts amounting to an open denial of the title of the recorded owner. It must not be inferred, however, that he is required to exercise force, as the law does not insist that a man should provoke a quarrel in order to demonstrate his ownership. Evidence of actual possession is to be taken from such facts as cultivating the land, erecting improvements upon it, fencing in the property, and payment of taxes. It has been said that the adverse claimant "must unfurl his flag on the land, and keep it flying, so that the owner may see, if he will, that an enemy has invaded his domains, and planted the standard of conquest." He must intend to hold the land for himself, and that intention must be made manifest by his acts. It is the intention that guides the entry and fixes its character. No particular act, or series of acts, is necessary to demonstrate an intention to claim ownership. Such a purpose is sufficiently shown where one goes upon the land and uses it openly and notoriously, as owners of similar lands use their property, to the exclusion of the true owner. The owner is, of course, chargeable with knowledge of what is openly done on his land and therefore calculated to attract attention. But a mere passive possession without intending to claim the property, is insufficient, regardless of the length of time it continues, or however open, notorious, or exclusive it may have been. (1 R.C.L. section 7, page 693.)

Thus, a tenant could never claim title by adverse possession no matter what improvements he might make nor how long he might be in possession, because he acknowledges the superior title of his lessor from the very beginning. Payment of taxes alone, without actual residence and dominion over the property, would be insufficient to prove adverse possession. Payment of taxes is entitled to some weight in proving the adverse claim, but it is a contributing factor, not the controlling one.

Constructive possession

It is not to be inferred that actual possession of a particular tract or area will cover a larger tract in its entirety. It is a well-recognized principle in the United States that a person having a "color of title"

—that is, anything in writing concerning the title which serves to define the extent of the claim, no matter how imperfect the paper title is—is to be regarded in constructive possession of the whole tract although he is in actual residence of only a part of it. The entry of the owner would be barred to the entire tract after the lapse of the statutory period. This rule is founded on the theory that the person claiming adverse possession under "color of title" has a notorious possession by reason of the written instrument. A realistic interpretation of this doctrine must be made. It is doubtful whether possession of a few acres out of a thousand purported to be conveyed by the invalid deed would be held to be constructive possession of the whole. The rule concerning constructive possession applies when possession is taken, first, under a conveyance which is invalid either for want of title or capacity in the grantor or for want of proper formalities in the execution of the instrument, and second, under a void or voidable decree of court. However, if the paper title under which a person claims is a nullity, the adverse occupier acquires title only to so much of the land as has been actually occupied. One who enters into possession of a part of a tract of land under "color of title" is immediately, by construction of the law, in actual possession of the whole tract. But one who enters without "color of title" is a trespasser and acquires title only to the area actually occupied. In some states, where there is color of title, the period of adverse occupancy is materially reduced.

Continuous possession

The next requirement is that a claimant must have exercised continuous and uninterrupted possession for the statutory period. Any abandonment of the property would defeat the title. A man claiming title to a wood lot by adverse possession will be defeated if he shows that the only occupancy of the property has been an occasional visit to it for the purpose of cutting fire wood or for fence material. Likewise, a man cannot claim title by adverse possession to a coal mine to which he made only sporadic visits for a supply of coal. In the case of farm land, where the rigors of winter prevent its cultivation and the claimant temporarily abandons it to follow his trade so that he can obtain funds for the purchase of necessary farm implements, the continuity of his possession would not be broken.

Tacking

Where the possession has been continued for a number of years and has been handed down from one to another without any break or interruption, for a valuable consideration, or by descent as from parent to child, it is in some measure respectable. The right which the adverse occupier has in the property, although it has not ripened into title, may be sold. The purchaser can "tack" his seller's period of occupation to his own possession in computing the necessary statutory period. The possession is *connected* by privity of contract or by descent. For example, Adams takes possession of certain land in 1945 and sells his interest to Bell in 1953. Bell remains in possession until 1968. Bell can claim title to the land through the necessary period of adverse possession.

In order to take advantage of "tacking," it is advisable to indicate in the deed that the grantor is transferring all rights to any portion of the tract claimed by adverse possession, to the grantee. Such a clause would read:

The parties of the first part hereby convey any title by adverse possession to any property adjacent to the above described premises.

In a certain case, Jones was the owner of a tract of land in 1915. Smith took possession adversely to Jones in that year and remained in possession until 1928, when he died. Previously, Smith had gone through a ceremony with Jane Brown, who was already married at the time. A child, David, was born to Smith and Jane. At Smith's death, Edward, a brother, was the only legal heir. David had resided with Smith until 1928, and continued in possession at all times since Smith's death. In 1932, Edward gave David a deed to the premises. In 1939, Jones brought ejectment against David. In the particular state, the adverse possession period is 21 years. If David is the legal heir of Smith, he could tack on Smith's previous occupancy as there would be privity of estate by descent. However, since Jane had a legally subsisting marriage at the time of her ceremony with Smith, she could not enter into a valid marriage. Thus David, the offspring, has no claim to legitimacy and would not be recognized as a legal heir to Smith. Nor does the deed from Edward, the legal heir of Smith, cure the defect, because Edward was never in possession of the tract. David must stand on his own feet, as it were, and since his own occupancy did not date until Smith's death in 1928, his adverse period falls short of the required term. Thus Jones, the original owner, would succeed in his claim to the property.

In Pennsylvania, where an *owner* of land is under a legal disability, an adverse claimant must occupy the land for 21 years *plus* the period of the owner's disability. But, by statute, an adverse occupier obtains legal title, where he remains in possession for 30 years, regardless of the owner's disability. Infants, married women, insane persons, and persons imprisoned or beyond the seas are considered

legally disabled in this connection. The disability must be in existence at the date the adverse occupation begins, in order to affect
the running of the regular statutory period.

Hostile or notorious possession

The next requirement is hostile or notorious possession. The claimant must show that his possession has been hostile to the holder of
the paper title, and not subordinate to it. The adverse possessor
"must keep his flag flying," which means that he must exercise all
the acts of dominion over the land, not only against the outside
world but also against the owner in case the opportunity presents
itself. If he recognizes the claim of the owner as superior to his
own, he defeats his own claim because the element of hostile possession is lacking. Where the owner is absent or cannot be found,
the question of hostility is purely one of invention. It may be said
that hostile merely means occupation *foreign* to the paper title.

The doctrine of hostility, however, varies in different states. The
Connecticut rule, frequently cited in other states, is that where two
owners had located a line between their properties in an inaccurate
manner, under an honest belief or mistake as to the exact boundary,
with the result that one of them had occupied a strip of land which
was, in reality, the property of the other, for the statutory period,
without interruption, he should be given title to it even though there
had been no intention to do wrong, or to exercise a hostile possession
against his neighbor. The courts have decided, in effect, that *ground
occupied under a mistaken belief is necessarily a hostile possession.*
Other states follow the rule laid down in Iowa. Under the same facts
the decision would be that the period of adverse possession would
not begin to run until the mistake was discovered by the one encroaching. The *intention* of the party who took it and occupied the
ground was the controlling factor. The intention could not arise
until the mistake was discovered.

Visible possession

Possession must be visible. This requirement would preclude
adverse possession to coal where the entrance took place beneath
the surface and the entry was not readily noticeable to the owner
or the public at large.

Distinct possession

The final requirement is that the possession of a claimant must
be distinct. He cannot establish his claim to the ground unless he

has laid claim to and exercised control over a definite piece of ground which can be sharply defined. He must exercise *exclusive* occupancy over it. Joint occupation would not satisfy the requirements.

Exceptions

The statute will not run against a remainderman until the termination of a precedent estate such as a life tenant. One owner in common could not claim adverse title against a co-owner. Neither will the statute run against the state nor against land owned by the United States Government, nor against any land used for a public purpose. In 1860 a railroad purchased a narrow strip of land, 700 feet in length by 75 feet in width. When the railroad attempted to make use of the land in 1911, it was found to be in possession of one Jones. An ejectment action was brought to recover possession. In the trial of the case the plaintiff railroad showed a *paper* title (deed) to the land in question. The defendant, in reply, set up a claim of the title by adverse possession in himself and his predecessors for more than 21 years. The pivotal question was whether title to land purchased by a railroad company outside its right of way for future railroad purposes can be acquired by adverse possession. Ordinarily, land used by a railroad as a right of way and for public purposes cannot be the subject of title by adverse possession. The same would be true insofar as land similarly used by any public utility. It is not true, however, where the land lies outside of the right of way. The railroad could not be heard to say, more than 40 years after the purchase, that it bought the land intending some day to use it for railroad purposes, but had not actively exercised this use. It was significant too, that the land in dispute was acquired by purchase rather than in the exercise of the company's right of eminent domain. The fact of condemnation, that is through eminent domain, indicates a public use, whereas in the case of a purchase, it indicates nothing and establishes nothing but title in the purchaser.[4]

Present-day significance

Where a person has complied with the adverse possession requirements, he obtains valid title to the land so occupied. While he has no deed to his property, yet he can give a deed to another. He can compel a purchaser from him to accept his deed. His rights and privileges differ in no respect from that of an ordinary owner.

---

[4] Delaware Lackawanna R.R. v. Tobyhanna Co., 228 Pa. 487.

Adverse possession has contemporary significance through many cases where fences, markers and buildings have been improperly located and the mistake not discovered for the period specified in the statute. Where the statutory period has expired, the claimant's subsequent abandonment of the property would not defeat his ownership unless some new occupier took over and maintained his occupation, in turn, for the necessary period.

Easements

An easement, such as a walk or right of way, can also be acquired by adverse use. It must be hostile in its inception in order to found a claim by adverse use. This is known as easement by prescription and the general rules of adverse possession apply. It is sometimes difficult to determine whether the land itself has been acquired adversely, or merely a right of way over it. The owner of the land, in order to prevent the easement, must take adequate measures to prohibit the unlicensed use of his property. If a physical barrier is not effectual, application to court for injunctive relief should be made. Notice or threat of legal proceedings will not defeat the statute.

Thus, it may be seen that title to real estate may be acquired through descent (by will), through purchase (by deed), and through occupation (by adverse possession). Title to real estate may also be acquired through the involuntary act of the owner (by eminent domain).

Eminent Domain

Eminent domain may be defined as the power of the state to take private property for public use. Under the 5th Amendment to the Constitution of the United States, the Federal Government is prohibited from taking private property for public use without just compensation and, under the "due process" clause of the 14th Amendment, the prohibition is extended to the several states. The right is expressly given to the state by constitutional provision. Even though the state constitution contained no such provision, the right could, nevertheless, be exercised by the state as eminent domain in an inherent attribute of state sovereignty. The state government is the supreme power in the state, and private rights are held under such supreme power and may be said to represent an indulgence by the sovereign power. The right of eminent domain exists not only in favor of the state but also for the benefit of any municipal subdivision of the state. In fact, any public corporation or any private corporation vested with a public use may exercise this extraordinary power when necessary for the public good. Appropriation of private property does not mean confiscation of such land, for the owner is entitled to fair and just compensation for the taking. Ordinarily, a public utility embarking upon a program of expansion, or a municipality in the development of a needed civic project, will endeavor to purchase the required properties for what is considered a fair consideration price. It is only when private bargaining fails that resort is made to condemnation through eminent domain proceedings. The court, upon failure of the interested parties to agree upon the sale price or to accept an award of court-appointed viewers, will then determine a just price for the property in question

If the right to eminent domain did not exist, a single obstructionist property owner in a key position for a planned improvement could successfully stay the betterment and progress of a whole community with his refusal to sell or his unwillingness to sell at any but a prohibitive price. Eminent domain frequently operates to the advantage of the property owner as it guarantees just compensation to him.

Frequently, a land owner will receive a higher price through court condemnation proceedings than was offered to him for a voluntary conveyance of the same land. Just compensation is held to be the fair market value of the land and the improvements thereon. Where, however, only a part of the owner's tract is condemned, differences and difficulties arise as to the amount of compensation. Certainly, the claimant is entitled to the fair market value of the part taken and it is equally well accepted that he is entitled, as an element of damage, to the depreciation in value, if any, caused by the improvement to the land retained by him. These two elements constitute his highest possible damage.

Benefits assessed against the taking

Should not the owner, by the same logic, be taxed for the benefit resulting to the remaining tract because of the improvement? The cases on this question are not uniform throughout the country. Sound logic would seem to dictate that *special benefits* received by the owner should be charged against the price paid to him. Lewis, on Eminent Domain, summarizes the law on benefits as follows (Sec. 687):

The law in regard to benefits is now pretty well settled in every State, either by the decisions of its courts, or by its statutes, or its constitution. While different and conflicting rules prevail in the different States under precisely the same constitutional provisions, it is evident that there can be but one absolutely correct rule. In taking private property for public use, the State acts rightfully and not as a wrongdoer. It guarantees just compensation and nothing more. In arriving at what is just compensation, the matter is to be viewed in the same light as though the State had bargained with the owner for a portion of his land and had agreed to make him just compensation therefor. It is self-evident that, where a part of a tract is taken, the just compensation cannot be determined without considering the manner in which the part is taken, the purpose for which it is taken, and the effect of the taking upon that which remains. All the authorities concede this so far as damages to the remainder are concerned, and the justice of so doing may be taken for granted. But what justice is there in considering the effect insofar only as it produces damage? If a railroad is constructed through a farm and drains a valuable spring whereby the remainder is depreciated five hundred dollars, it is conceded that just compensation must include this five hundred dollars. But if, instead of draining a valuable spring, it drains a marshy tract so as to make it worth five hundred dollars more for actual use, the same sense of justice requires that this five hundred dollars of benefits should be considered.

It is true, of course, that the entire municipality profits and benefits by the improvement of streets and other public services, and indirectly, the entire tax-paying population participates in the maintenance of the original improvement. But where, for example, a street which serves only a limited number of properties is changed from a dirt street to one of brick, it is fair that only the immediate properties benefited should be assessed for the improvement.

In recent years, special authorities were created by the Congress and the state legislative bodies for erecting public housing projects. These projects, intended to supply badly needed housing and to improve the standard of living for low income groups, have had an important effect upon the economic and social well-being of a large segment of our industrial population. In the fulfillment of the housing program, blighted areas have been condemned and destroyed and new structures erected. In this development, it is often necessary to resort to condemnation of an entire zone or district. This is known as *zone condemnation* and is the only practical and effective method of clearing slums. Zone condemnation is for a specific purpose. Even in public condemnation the cost is great, but the benefits of better health of the inhabitants and the elimination of crime are readily commensurate with the cost involved. The United States Government in the exercise of its broad war powers has, in the interests of flood control, condemned extensive areas throughout the country. Today state legislatures have created public authorities with the right of condemnation for housing, sanitation, parking, and public utility purposes.

Excess condemnation

Excess condemnation, as the name implies, is the taking of land in larger measure than actually necessary for the improvement proper. Special constitutional authority is necessary for exercising this extraordinary right. The earlier court decisions have held that statutes for excess condemnation, enacted under the general constitutional provision, were invalid. Recent social philosophy may well influence the judicial view that public use, liberally interpreted, may often permit excess condemnation. A street is laid out and land on each side of the proposed street is taken in excess of the area actually needed to confine the street. The control of the excess part by the municipality, whether in the case of a street, park, or other development, insures the usefulness of the improvement and is conducive to the better channelling of municipal growth. Better city planning is bound to ensue.

Title taken under the right of eminent domain ordinarily carries with it a fee simple title to the land, so that the condemnor has as absolute a title as if it were acquired by purchase. But land taken for roads is usually a base fee. It is governed by statute.

Federal Open Housing Legislation:
Anti-Discrimination

IN RECENT YEARS, repeated crises have plagued many of our large cities, and small ones, too. Riots, "sit-ins," racial incidents, dissatisfaction with the war in Vietnam, strikes by school teachers and public employees, together with other factors, have all contributed to some extent to crime, violence and disorders. Many books have already been written as to the underlying causes and suggested remedies. Poverty and discrimination are always given as basic causes, from which crime and violence erupt. City, state, and federal programs, combined, were found wanting as a cure to the nation's ills. Equally important as a basic cause of the nation's turbulent times is racial discrimination in the housing field, particularly, against Negro citizens, although other minority groups are also affected.

Under the President's Executive Order of November 20, 1962, housing, which related to or was aided by Federal assistance, came under an anti-discrimination mandate. The Order included new F.H.A. or V.A. mortgage construction, public housing, housing assisted through urban renewal, and Federally-owned housing. Since then, statutes have been passed in a number of states, augmented by ordinances in some cities, making it illegal to discriminate against a purchaser on the grounds of race, color, religion or national origin or background. These regulatory measures vary as to their provisions and effectiveness.

On April 11, 1968, President Johnson signed an open housing law that is vitally important for all those in the housing and mortgage business. The law prohibits racial discrimination by most sellers and renters of dwellings, and also bans discrimination by all those who make loans to buy or improve residential property. For sellers and renters, the law takes effect in three stages, but for lenders its effective date is January 1, 1969. The agency charged with administering and enforcing the law is the Department of Housing and Urban Development (HUD); the Department of Justice will also play a role in those instances where violations reach the courts.

It is important to note that, by some state statutes, or by amendment to existing state license laws, conviction of a real estate broker or salesman as being a party to a discriminatory act, constitutes grounds for disciplinary action by the Real Estate Commission.

The problem of housing is nationwide, and the states look to the Federal Government for leadership and guidance in alleviating the complex difficulties. The Congress acted and passed an Open Housing law, which was signed by the President on April 11, 1968. A capsule analysis of the important provisions of the law, follows, (taken from Prentice-Hall, Inc.,—*Federal Aids to Financing Report,* with permission):

The law prohibits discrimination on the grounds of race, color, religion, or national origin in the sale, rental, or financing of dwellings. This includes setting harsher terms, publishing discriminatory advertising, telling a person that a dwelling is not available for sale or rental when in fact it is, or "block-busting" (attempting to get a person to sell or rent by representations that people of a particular race, color, religion or national origin are entering or are about to enter the neighborhood).

The law becomes effective in three stages:

(1) In 1968, it bans discrimination in the sale or rental of housing insured or guaranteed by the Federal Government or located in a Federally assisted urban renewal or slum clearance project. The ban applies to all such housing backed by the Government after November 20, 1962 (the date of the Executive Order banning discrimination in government-backed housing), unless payment was made before the date of enactment, namely, April 11, 1968.

It also covers dwellings owned or operated by the Federal Government and dwellings built with the aid of loans, advances, grants, or contributions made by the Federal Government.

(2) Effective January 1, 1969, the ban applies to all dwelling units, no matter how financed, with these two exceptions:

(a) Single-family homes, provided the owner does not own more than three single-family homes at one time. If the owner is a non-occupant of a single-family home he sells, he gets the exemption for only one sale within a 24-month period. (b) One-to-four family dwellings, if the owner occupies one of the units.

Loans: Also effective January 1, 1969, banks, savings and loan agencies, mutual savings banks, insurance companies and other lenders cannot discriminate in making loans on apartment buildings or homes—whether for purchase, repairs, or construction. Also forbidden is discrimination in setting the terms of the loans, such as the amount of the mortgage, the interest rate, and so on.

Enforcement of the Act is in the Secretary of Housing and Urban

Development (HUD). The Secretary, or his assistant, is limited in his powers in handling complaints to "education, conciliation, and persuasion." In this connection, he can investigate complaints, issue subpoenas, and hold hearings, before issuing a final order. He cannot issue a "cease and desist order," nor fine an offender. For punitive damages for violation of the law, a complainant must file a suit in a Federal district court. If there is a "substantially equivalent" local or state fair housing law, the Federal Court generally will direct that a complaint be filed in the state or local forum.

The law gives the government the right to inspect the records of anyone charged with discrimination.

In addition to the enforcement provisions, the Attorney General can bring action in cases where there is a general pattern of discrimination or an issue of general public importance.

On June 17, 1968, the United States Supreme Court handed down its land mark decision on open housing, in the St. Louis case of *Jones v. Mayer Co.* 392 U.S. 409 (decided June 17, 1968), involving the purchase of a homesite in a subdivision called Paddock Woods. The Supreme Court held that an Act of Congress passed in 1866, forbade racial discrimination in the sale or rental of housing in the United States. In a majority (7-2) opinion, Mr. Justice Potter Stewart said, inter alia,

Negro citizens North and South, who won in the Thirteenth Amendment a promise of freedom—freedom to go and come at pleasure and to buy and sell when they please—would be left with a mere paper guarantee if Congress were powerless to assure that a dollar in the hands of a Negro will purchase the same thing as a dollar in the hands of a white man.

The Act of 1968 contains many exemptions, including specifically single-family residential units until sold without an agent. The Act of 1866 contains no such exemption and it lacks the federal enforcement machinery and other remedies available under the 1968 Act.

The law is comparatively new and it is not yet court tested as to any ambiguities or conflicts in its provisions, particularly, in its relationship to the Act of 1866 and the recent Supreme Court decision. A number of legal experts are in accord that the Supreme Court opinion in the Jones case has the effect of eliminating the several exceptions contained in the Act of 1968, without voiding the law itself. In support of this view, they call attention to the language of the 1866 Act, which states:

All citizens of the United States shall have the same right, in every state and territory, as is enjoyed by white citizens thereof to inherit, purchase, lease, sell, hold, and convey real and personal property.

It would appear that a party plaintiff could petition for injunctive relief in a federal district court, on the basis that there is no irreconcilable conflict between the Act of 1968 and the Act of 1866. The total effect of the Supreme Court decision is to bring all property, personal as well as real, under anti-discriminatory regulation. In real estate, the decision creates an "open housing" law throughout the country. However, it should be noted that buyers or renters can still be rejected for reasonable *cause*, but the grounds for rejection must apply equally to *all* persons.

Questions on Deeds

1. Q. What is meant by good and sufficient abstract of title?
   A. It must be marketable.
2. Q. What does real property include?
   A. Lands, tenements and hereditaments.
3. Q. What is meant by tenements and hereditaments?
   A. Tenements include land and anything affixed permanently to the land such as a building. Hereditaments include lands, tenements and things of an incorporeal nature, such as a right of way.
4. Q. Do all titles emanate by patent from the U. S. government?
   A. No. In the 13 original states, title originated from the Proprietor (under grants from the King of England) or from the sovereign states.
5. Q. Under a fee simple deed, what is the legal concept of land which a purchaser acquires?
   A. The surface land, to an indefinite extent upwards and down to the center of the earth.
6. Q. How would you define a "property right"?
   A. The right to enjoy lands and chattels to the exclusion of all others.
7. Q. Into what two classes is property divided?
   A. Realty and personalty.
8. Q. Into what two classes can realty be divided? Give examples.
   A. Corporeal realty (lands and buildings); incorporeal realty (right of way; an easement).
9. Q. Name four ways by which good title to real estate may be acquired.
   A. Deed, Will, Adverse Possession, Eminent Domain.
10. Q. What estate is of potentially indefinite duration and is fully transferable and inheritable?
    A. Fee simple.
11. Q. What is a deed?
    A. A deed is a writing by which lands, tenements and hereditaments are conveyed, which writing is signed, sealed and delivered between the parties.
12. Q. What is meant by a merchantable title?
    A. A title free from any clouds or defects.
13. Q. Name four types of legal description of land.
    A. 1. Rectangular survey. 2. Metes and bounds. 3. Monuments. 4. Recorded map—lot and block number.

14. Q. Name at least three classifications of estates.
   A. Inheritance, life, years, at will.
15. Q. When real estate is held in the husband's name, why is it necessary for the wife to join with the husband in deeding the property to another?
   A. In order to extinguish her dower right.
16. Q. What is meant by a Government Patent?
   A. Original and initial conveyance of real property from the United States Government to individuals, or from a state to an individual.
17. Q. What defect is there in the following property description:
   "Property next to Marvel Gasoline Station, City limits, Andrews County, Texas, official records in Recorder's Office of Andrews County, also known as the 500 block on Main Street in the City."
   A. The description is fatally defective because the name of the City does not appear.
18. Q. What are the requirements usually necessary in determining whether an article is a fixture?
   A. 1. Actual physical annexation to the realty.
      2. Application or adaptation to the use or purpose to which the realty is devoted.
      3. An intention on the part of the person making the annexation to make a permanent accession to the land.
19. Q. Who are the parties to a deed?
   A. The grantor and the grantee. The grantor is the one who sells the property and signs the deed. The grantee is the purchaser, who receives the deed.
20. Q. Real Estate ownership is said to consist of a "bundle of legal rights." Name six "rights."
   A. 1. To lease. 2. To sell. 3. To will. 4. To regain possession at end of lease—reversion. 5. To build thereon—destroy improvements —maintain—control use within law. 6. To mortgage.
21. Q. What is a quit claim deed?
   A. A deed used to clear clouds upon the title. The operative words are "remise, release, and quit claim." There is no warranty of title in this form of deed. A wife who has not joined in a warranty deed may sign a quit claim deed in order to bar her dower interest in the property.
22. Q. What does the word "title" mean when referring to property?
   A. Title is the evidence of ownership in land.
23. Q. Why is it necessary for a deed to be in writing?
   A. Statute of frauds passed in England in 1660 in order to prevent unscrupulous persons from swearing under oath that property had been deeded or leased for a long period of time at a ridiculously low rental. It requires contracts for the sale and transfer of real estate to be in writing. The statute of frauds has been adopted in the various states.

24. Q. For what purposes is a special warranty deed most generally used?

A. It is the usual form of conveying a tax title. It is also used by fiduciaries or trustees in conveying title to real estate.

25. Q. What are the principal types of deeds used in real property transfers?

A. General Warranty Bargain and Sale, Special Warranty, Quit Claim.

26. Q. Name five kinds of entries or instruments found in an "abstract of title."

A. 1. Deeds. 2. Mortgages. 3. Releases. 4. Foreclosures. 5. Delinquent Taxes.

27. Q. What are the two most common methods of title closing?

A. Escrow and delivery of deed.

28. Q. Is a date essential to the validity of a deed?

A. No. It indicates the time when the deed was delivered. It is only prima facie evidence; i.e., appears to be sufficient to establish the time of delivery but may be rebutted by stronger proof.

29. Q. Is a deed dated on Sunday void?

A. Not if delivered on a week day.

30. Q. Is consideration necessary in a deed?

A. Yes. Good or valuable consideration.

31. Q. What is good consideration?

A. Good consideration arises from love and affection and has no pecuniary value.

32. Q. What is understood by a valuable consideration?

A. Money or its equivalent measurable in monetary terms.

33. Q. Is a $1.00, or nominal, consideration valid?

A. Yes. Courts do not inquire into the adequacy or inadequacy of the consideration.

34. Q. What parties have limited or qualified right to contract?

A. Infants, insane persons, married women, corporations, and aliens.

35. Q. Name three types of deeds which may be executed to transfer the title to real estate.

A. 1. Deed of bargain and sale.
2. Quit claim.
3. Sheriff's deed as a result of foreclosure on a judgment or mortgage.

36. Q. Is a deed from husband to a wife valid where the husband has been made the defendant in a lawsuit involving a substantial sum of money?

A. No. Any conveyance made with intent to disturb, delay, hinder, or defraud creditors may be set aside as fraudulent.

37. Q. Is a joint estate the same as an estate by the entireties?

A. An estate by the entireties, which may be held only by husband and wife, enjoys advantages over a joint tenancy. In some states, as in Nebraska, husband and wife hold as joint tenants, similar to an estate by the entireties.

38. Q. What are "appurtenances" in a deed?
A. Rights which pass as incidental to the premises; anything necessary to the enjoyment of the property. Land ordinarily cannot pass as appurtenant to land, but a right in land may.

39. Q. What are a husband's rights in his wife's property called?
A. Curtesy.

40. Q. Is a deed by a married woman for her own property valid, void, or voidable?
A. Valid in most states, but void in others, unless she has been declared a "feme sole."

41. Q. Who is a "feme sole"?
A. A single woman. A married woman may be declared a feme sole by court decree where her husband has deserted her or is a drunkard, or there is other good cause.

42. Q. What is meant by "estate by the entireties"?
A. The ownership of property by husband and wife. The tenancy exists only in favor of husband and wife.

43. Q. What are the advantages of an estate by the entireties?
A. 1. Upon death of one party the property forthwith vests in the surviving spouse.
2. No probate or other court proceedings are necessary.
3. Not subject to state inheritance tax.
4. A judgment against one spouse will not be a lien.

44. Q. What is the main disadvantage of such an estate?
A. Unless both parties join in a deed, court action is necessary to partition the estate.

45. Q. What is the difference between "joint tenancy" and "tenancy in common"?
A. In joint tenancy, where one of the parties dies, the property vests in the surviving party or parties. In a tenancy in common, each of whom is considered as being possessed of the whole of an undivided part, upon death of one, his interest goes to his heirs.

46. Q. Brother and sister are purchasing a residence. Brother is a widower, with two children, and sister is a widow with no children. What kind of a deed should issue if she is to have a ⅓ interest and he is to have a ⅔ interest?
A. A deed as tenants in common.

47. Q. What are the purposes of the acknowledgment?
A. 1. The deed will be accepted as prima facie evidence in any court proceedings.
2. The deed may be recorded.

48. Q. Is it necessary for the grantee to acknowledge or sign the deed?
A. No.

49. Q. Jones conveys certain real estate to Brown and Smith as joint tenants, and not as tenants in common. Subsequently, Brown dies, and Smith claims the entire property. Brown's son claims title to the same property. Who will win?

A. Smith, the survivor. The deed to Brown and Smith expressly created a joint tenancy.

50. Q. Adams conveys certain real estate to Black, Carr, and Dean as tenants in common. Black later dies, and in a contest among Carr, Dean, and Black's widow for Black's share in the property, who will win?

A. The widow. The conveyance to Black, Carr, and Dean established a tenancy in common.

51. Q. White conveys property to Smith and Jones as joint tenants. Can Smith sell his interest to Green? If so, would Green then become a joint owner with Jones?

A. Smith can sell or alienate his interest in the property to Green. Green does not become a joint owner with Jones, but Green and Jones now hold the property as tenants in common. (Alabama, Indiana, North Carolina, Pennsylvania, Texas.)

52. Q. Various covenants designed to limit, restrict or prohibit the use, improvement or occupancy or real estate are sometimes incorporated in deeds to real estate. Name three different types.

A. Buildings must be of a certain height, they cannot be used as residential or commercial houses, liquor cannot be sold upon the premises and they cannot be used as rooming houses.

53. Q. What is a tax deed?

A. A deed issued for property which has been sold for taxes.

54. Q. Is a title that is acquired by purchase at a treasurer's sale for unpaid municipal taxes, good and marketable?

A. No, the owner still has right of redemption.

55. Q. Name three types of encumbrance which might cloud the title to real estate.

A. Unpaid taxes, judgments, a right of way.

56. Q. What is the meaning of the words "more or less" in many deed descriptions?

A. Intended to indicate that a slight variation in dimensions of the tract would not void the contract.

57. Q. What is a tax title?

A. Title by which one owns land purchased at a tax sale.

58. Q. Where are deeds to real estate officially recorded?

A. In the Office of the Recorder of Deeds, or Register of Deeds.

59. Q. Does an abstract of title guarantee a clear title?

A. No; it merely gives a summary as to the conditions of the title.

60. Q. What is the purpose of a correction deed?

A. A correction deed, often called a deed of conformation, is used to correct an error in a deed. This is usually done with a quit claim deed containing explanations.

61. Q. Is it correct to state that a lease on a property being sold constitutes an encumbrance on that property?

A. Yes.

62. Q. What are the dangers in not having a deed recorded promptly?

A. The deed may be destroyed or lost; judgments may be entered against the previous owner, which would constitute a lien against the property; the previous owner might deed or mortgage the property to someone else, who, by recording his instrument promptly, would have priority.

63. Q. What is included in the execution of a deed?

A. The execution includes the signing, sealing, and acknowledgment of the instrument.

64. Q. Is it necessary for the grantor himself to sign the deed?

A. Good practice requires the grantor's personal signature, but a deed signed by another for the grantor in the grantor's presence and at his direction would be a sufficient compliance with the requirement for signature.

65. Q. If the grantor cannot write, how should the deed be signed?

A. The grantor should make his mark in the presence of witnesses and the grantor's name should then be appended by someone for him. The signature would appear "John (his X mark) Steele." There must be two witnesses to the mark.

66. Q. Can a grantor later repudiate a deed because he is illiterate and could not read the instrument?

A. No. The burden is upon the grantor to have someone read the deed to him; unless fraud has been practiced on the grantor.

67. Q. Can a husband and wife make a single acknowledgment of a deed?

A. In most states, yes. In Alabama, New Jersey, North Carolina, South Carolina, and Texas, it is necessary to have separate acknowledgment of the wife.

68. Q. What information does the acknowledgment contain?

A. The venue, place where the acknowledgment is taken (state and county); the name of the grantor and his marital status, as John Steele, single; the signature of the person taking the acknowledgment, his official capacity, expiration date of his office, and official seal.

69. Q. Must the grantors appear in person before the officer taking the acknowledgment?

A. Yes. An acknowledgment should never be taken in absentia.

70. Q. Can a deed be executed by an agent under a power of attorney from the owner?

A. Yes. The power of attorney, however, must be recorded.

71. Q. When should a proxy or power of attorney be used?

A. Only in rare cases and under special circumstances as when the grantor is uncertain as to his whereabouts at the time of closing the deal and does not want to execute the deed beforehand. The attorney-in-fact should be a person in whom the grantor reposes the highest trust and confidence.

72. Q. When does title to the property pass?

A. When the deed is delivered to the grantee or his agent.

73. Q. What kinds of delivery are there?
   A. 1. Delivery absolute, where the deed is handed over to the purchaser without any conditions.
      2. Delivery in escrow, where the deed is delivered to a third person until the performance of some act or condition by one of the parties.

74. Q. Arthur delivers a deed in escrow to Cox until certain items in the title are cleared up. The purchaser, Bell, turns over the consideration price at the same time to the escrow agent, Cox. Two days later Arthur notifies Cox to return Bell's money to Bell and to return the deed to Arthur. Must Cox comply with these instructions?
   A. No. Once the deed is delivered to the escrow agent and the condition of delivery is specified, the grantor is powerless to recall it.

75. Q. Suppose that Abbot delivers a deed to Cooper in escrow for Brown, to be handed over to Brown once he has paid Cooper the balance of the consideration price. Later in the day, Brown visits Cooper's office during Cooper's absence and sees the deed on Cooper's desk. Brown takes the deed and records it. Does Brown get good title? Suppose that after recording the deed Brown conveys the property to Quinn for a valuable consideration. Will Quinn obtain a valid title?
   A. Brown will not obtain good title because of his fraudulent act, and Abbot could have the deed stricken off. However, Quinn, an innocent purchaser for value, would obtain good title, for he had no notice of Brown's fraud, assuming, of course, that the transfer from Brown to Quinn was made before Abbot took any legal proceedings to set Brown's deed aside.

76. Q. Anthony executes a deed to Burger and delivers it to Conway, to be delivered to Burger upon the death of Anthony. Will Burger get good title upon the death of Anthony?
   A. Yes. If the title does not pass until Anthony's death, it cannot do so at the death. This would seem to defeat Anthony's purpose. But the law comes to the rescue and considers the passing of title as "relating back to the date of direct delivery," which was, of course, prior to Anthony's death. This is known as the doctrine of relation. When finally delivered to the grantee, it operates as from the date of first delivery, which was, of course, prior to Anthony's death.

77. Q. Ash executes a deed to Burke and places it in his inside coat pocket. The coat is hung in Ash's cupboard. Ash is killed in an explosion that afternoon. The deed is intact. Does Burke obtain title to the real estate?
   A. No. The deed was not delivered.

78. Q. Jones executes a deed to Brown and records it. Later Jones

seeks to set the conveyance aside, claiming that there had been no delivery to Brown. Will he succeed?

A. No. In cases like this, delivery is presumed from recording.

79. Q. Is it necessary to have the deed recorded?

A. As concerns grantor and grantee, title passes upon delivery and it is not necessary to record it. However, in order to protect the grantor against a lien or a subsequent deed by the grantor for the same property, the law requires the grantee to record his deed.

80. Q. Adams delivers a deed to Black on December 6, 1968, which Black records on January 21, 1969. Adams deeds the same property to Clark on January 14, 1969; Clark records his deed the same day. Who owns the property?

A. Clark. The person who gets his deed on record first, providing he had no notice of a prior deed, is deemed the owner.

81. Q. Suppose that in the preceding case, Black took possession on December 6, 1968. Would the decision be the same?

A. No. Clark would have constructive notice of Black's ownership, and he would then be a purchaser with notice.

82. Q. Brown owns two adjoining tracts of land. He conveys one piece to Evans and reserves a right of way across the rear in order to reach a side street. Later he sells the other tract to Case. Subsequently, Evans and Case have differences, and Evans refuses to permit Case the use of the right of way across his land. Can Case enjoin Evans from interfering with his use?

A. No. The original right was personal to Brown, and when Brown conveyed the property, the right was extinguished. If Brown had reserved the right to himself, "his heirs and assigns," Case would be successful.

83. Q. Williams owns two parcels of real estate. A house is built upon one tract, with the cornice encroaching upon the other. Williams sells the second tract to James. Nothing is mentioned in the deed about the encroachment. Later, James, notifies Williams that he is trespassing by the encroachment and demands that he remove the objectionable cornice. Will James succeed?

A. No. Williams has an implied easement in James's land to the extent of the encroachment. The condition was open, visible, continuous, and permanent at the time James purchased the property and accordingly, he takes it subject to the existing condition. If the house were destroyed by fire or other cause, Williams could not rebuild so as to continue the encroachment.

84. Q. In 1969, Peters purchases land from Mack. The deed description states "subject to a 20-foot street as shown on the G.I. Coltart Plan." There is no recorded plan. The township, in which the property is located, now requires a minimum street width of 30 feet. Clark has been using the existing street or right of way for 24 years. It measures 12 feet in width. Clark

now attempts to compel Peters to permit him to use an adjoining 8 feet of Peters's land. Will Clark succeed?

A. No. Since the plan is not recorded and the 20-foot street has never been dedicated to a public use, all Clark has is a right of way within its present confines of 12 feet.

85. Q. Smith's deed to a farm is made subject to a right of way in favor of Jones's farm. The latter, 12 years later, is subdivided into lots. The lot owners attempt to use the same right of way and Smith objects to the increase of use. Will Smith succeed?

A. No. The right of way exists for the benefit of every part of Jones's farm and the increased use represents a normal and logical development of the farm.

86. Q. Adams, without Black's consent, uses a shortcut across Black's farm. From time to time, Black places an obstruction across the path, which Adams removes. The use, under these conditions, continues for more than 21 years. Black now "digs in" a fence across the path and Adams takes legal action to prevent Black's interference with his use of the right of way. Who will win?

A. Adams. In order to defeat the statute of adverse possession, Black's interference or objection must be effective. Since the barriers during the 21-year period were not effective in preventing the use, Adams will win. Black should have obtained a court decree enjoining the trespass.

87. Q. As used in legal descriptions of real estate, what is (a) a section, (b) a township, (c) a range, (d) the 3rd Principal Meridian? Where is this meridian?

A. Refer to definitions and index.

88. Q. What is the "Torrens system"?

A. It is a system of land registration introduced in Australia by Sir Robert Torerns about 1858. It is a system for the registration of land titles whereby the state of the title, showing ownership and encumbrances, can be readily ascertained from an inspection of the "register of titles" without the necessity of a search of the public records. It is used to a modified extent in some states in this country.

89. Q. In 1955, an owner made a contract with the owner of an adjoining residence for the joint use of an automobile driveway, half of which lay on each lot. In 1968, the owner made a contract to sell and convey his lot free of all encumbrances. When the title was searched, the joint users' agreement, which had been recorded, came to light. Under such circumstances, would the buyer have had the right to refuse to go through with the deal?

A. Yes. The joint driveway is an easement, constituting an encumbrance within the meaning of the term.

90. Q. Upon the closing of title to real property, where the pur-

chaser, as part of the purchase price, gave a purchase money mortgage, the seller, upon the receipt of said purchase money mortgage, and the buyer, upon the receipt of the deed, have each taken the respective two documents and placed them in a bank safe deposit vault for safe keeping. By doing so, have the two individuals committed anything detrimental to their interests with respect to the two documents? Why?

A. Both grantor and grantee have taken an unwarranted risk. The mortgage and deed should be recorded so that the grantee will be protected against a subsequent deed or mortgage for the same property given by the grantor and so that the grantor will be protected against a subsequent mortgage or lien given or suffered by the grantee before the deed is recorded, such as taxes.

91. Q. Would you prefer a general warranty deed with merchantable title or a court deed?

A. A general warranty deed with merchantable title. The court deed would not guarantee the title.

92. Q. Adams, residing in Dade County, Florida, owns a lot in Broward County. Adams asks where he must legally record the deed to his lot.

A. Broward County. Recordation of the deed must be in the county where the property is located.

93. Q. Harris conveys certain real estate to his son, John, "for and during the grantee's life." What kind of an estate does John obtain?

A. John obtains a *life estate* only.

94. Q. A deed is executed by Alfred Sims to the First Presbyterian Church, of which he is a member. The Church is not an incorporated body. Does the Church obtain good title to the property?

A. No; the deed is void because the grantee is incapable of taking title to real estate.

95. Q. What is meant by a homestead?

A. The homestead consists of the dwelling house in which the claimant resides, together with outbuildings, and the land on which the same are situated. Declaration of homestead must be filed in the Recorder's Office.

96. Q. What information must be given in the declaration filed?

A. 1. A statement showing that the claimant is the head of a family.
   2. If claimant is married, the name of the other spouse.
   3. That claimant is residing on the premises and claims them as a homestead.
   4. A full description of the premises.
   5. An estimate of their actual cash value.

97. Q. What advantages accrue to homestead property?

A. Such property is protected from execution and foreclosure sale against most creditors.

98. Q. What claims will not be defeated by a homestead?

A. 1. Judgments which became liens before the declaration was recorded.

2. Mechanics' liens for work or materials furnished upon the premises.

3. Mortgages and trust deeds executed and acknowledged by husband and wife or by an unmarried owner.

4. Mortgages and trust deeds recorded before the declaration was recorded.

99. Q. How may a homestead be terminated?

A. By a conveyance or by recorded instrument of abandonment.

100. Q. Does removal from the premises effect an abandonment of a homestead?

A. No.

101. Q. Wherein does a sale of real estate differ from a sale of personal property?

A. A sale of real estate is effected by a formal deed, duly signed, acknowledged, delivered, and recorded. A sale of personalty is effected by a bill of sale delivered to the purchaser.

102. Q. What federal income tax advantage do residents of community property states have?

A. The husband's income may be divided equally between husband and wife for income tax purposes. The income tax law permits this division of income in all the states which have community property.

103. Q. What is the difference between (1) an abstract of title, (2) a certificate of title, and (3) a title insurance policy?

A. 1. An abstract of title is a document setting forth a brief synopsis of all matters of record affecting the title to the real estate in question.

2. A certificate of title gives the net result of the examination of title, showing the name of the owner and the encumbrances and defects of title as of the date of the certificate.

3. A title insurance policy insures the title in a given name, subject to noted exceptions and encumbrances listed in the policy and renders the insurer liable to compensate the insured for loss arising from errors of search and legal interpretation, in an amount not exceeding that stated in the policy.

104. Q. What is the purpose of recording a deed?

A. To give notice to the public of the transfer of title, thus protecting a subsequent purchaser or mortgagee from the same grantor.

105. Q. John Lake has been designated by William Gardner as his attorney in-fact. Indicate how Lake would sign a deed on behalf of Gardner.

A. William Gardner (Seal)

By his attorney-in-fact,
John Lake   (Seal)

> The power of attorney must be recorded.

106. Q. Paul Simon conveys a lot in the Holliday Plan to Miles Jones. The deed recites a number of building restrictions and a provision to the effect that all other lots in the plan will be sold subject to the same restrictions. Without any mention of the restrictions, Simon sells a lot to Woodruff who attempts to erect a store. Jones files suit to enjoin the violation.

A. Jones will win. Woodruff is bound to examine the deeds of record and has notice of the restrictions in Jones' deed. Jones has an implied easement to the extent that the same restrictions apply to all lots in the plan, which he can enforce.

107. Q. Helen is married to Michael. The property is only in Michael's name. Should Helen sign the agreement and deed?

A. Yes; she should sign the agreement so that she can be compelled to sign the deed. She should sign the deed in order to extinguish her dower right.

108. Q. What is the bulk sales law and what is its purpose?

A. It is a law which requires that the seller of certain personal property give a list of all outstanding obligations prior to the completion of the sale and that the creditors be notified of the sale. It is intended to protect the purchaser of certain types of personal property, such as merchandise purchased in bulk, and arises frequently in connection with sale of business opportunities.

109. Q. What is the size of a Section of Land?

A. One square mile or 640 acres.

110. Q. How many sections of land in a Township?

A. Thirty-six.

111. Q. How many acres of land in SE¼?

A. One hundred sixty.

112. Q. For the purpose of legal description of urban real estate, how is land usually divided?

A. In lots, blocks, and plan of lots.

113. Q. Is the street address of a property one and the same thing as "legal description"?

A. No.

114. Q. Are town lots any part of a Section, Township, or Range?

A. Yes.

115. Q. Point out three *errors* in the following description:
"Beginning at the North-West Quarter of lot numbered Eleven in Blank addition to the City of Poe, Roe County, Missouri; thence running South a distance of 202 feet; thence West a distance of 300 feet; thence North a distance of 202 feet to the point of beginning, containing five acres more or less."

A. 1. Beginning at North-West Quarter is wrong; should be North-West *corner*.
2. Tract does not close out—should go East 300 feet.
3. Size of tract is considerably less than five acres. Tract 202 x 300 feet would total only 60,600 square feet.

116. Q. Adams owns a tract of land which is traversed by a stream of water. The source of the stream is a spring-fed lake about two miles distant. Baker owns land between the lake and Adams's tract. Baker diverts the stream in order to make a pond about a quarter mile away from the stream channel. Adams learns of Baker's intention and gets an injunction against Baker prohibiting him from diverting the stream. Will the injunction stand? If so, why?

A. Yes; an upper owner merely has a usufructory right (right to use). He may not divert the stream from its natural channel so as to deprive a lower owner of his right to use the stream.

117. Q. *A*, who owns a house and lot, has contracted to sell it to *B*. He wishes to remove the following articles from the premises. Indicate which of the following items will pass as real estate.

A. (x) Small evergreen trees and bushes.
( ) The coal range in the kitchen.
(x) The living room chandelier.
( ) The furnace shovel and poker.
( ) The living room lamp which is attached to a wall plug.
( ) The stair carpet.
( ) Awnings.

118. Q. An electric light company has the right to erect its poles and run its lines along the rear five feet of a lot. What sort of a property right is this?

A. An easement.

119. Q. There are a number of restrictions usually found in deeds to property in high class subdivisions. Name two of these and state the reason for such restriction.

A. 1. Floor space restriction which determines minimum house which can be built.
2. Price restriction which determines minimum amount which can be spent for dwelling.

120. Q. Lawrence conveys the coal under his farm to the Acme Coal Company. Finney purchases the farm and lays out a subdivision. Later, Finney sells a lot to Jordan giving a general warranty deed and no mention is made of the coal conveyance. Jordan builds and subsequently attempts to sell to Reed who refuses to complete the deal because of the coal conveyance. Does Jordan have any claim against Finney?

A. Yes, since Finney gave Jordan a general warranty deed, he warranted that title was absolute and complete and guaranteed the purchaser against all claimants.

121. Q. Watson conveys certain real estate to Lee "subject to coal and mining rights conveyed by prior deeds of record." Later, damage is caused to the house because of a surface cave-in due to the removal of the coal by the Ajax Coal Company. Does Lee have any action for damages?

A. He would not have any right of action against Watson because the deed to Lee was made subject to coal mining rights previously conveyed. It depends upon the language of the deed to the coal company whether he would have any cause of action against the Ajax Coal Company. The general rule of law is that all property in this country is held under the implied obligation that the owner's use of it shall not be injurious to the community. Thus, failure of the mineral owner to render support to the surface will make him liable to the surface owner. However, the United States Supreme Court has held (260 U. S. 392) that the owner may relinquish, by deed or agreement, his right to surface support. Most coal deeds now provide, "WITHOUT LIABILITY UNDER ANY CIRCUMSTANCES WHATEVER FOR DAMAGES DONE TO THE SURFACE OF SAID LOT OR TO THE IMPROVEMENTS NOW ERECTED OR HEREAFTER TO BE ERECTED THEREON."

122. Q. William McKee and Fred Starr are partners doing business as McKee and Starr. They have acquired real estate for the firm purposes with partnership funds. Subsequently, the property is sold to Lowell Baker. Both McKee and Starr are married. Is it necessary for their wives to join in the deed?

A. No. Since the real estate was partnership property and held *as such*, the joinder of the wives is unnecessary.

123. Q. A tract of land was settled by Miller who lived on it for nine consecutive years. Dut to conditions of health, he moved away for a six-year period. He then moved back to the same land and occupied it for six years. At the end of this period, or twenty-one years from his first occupancy, he claimed title by adverse possession. Will he succeed?

A. No. The possession must be continuous. Since he moved away for six years, the continuity has been broken, which is fatal to his claim. His adverse occupation has continued only for the last six years.

124. Q. Dolan owns certain real estate, upon which there is a mortgage held by Walsh. The mortgage is in default and in lieu of foreclosure, the mortgagee agrees to accept a voluntary deed from Dolan.

1. Does Walsh get a good title?
2. Is the mortgage extinguished?

A. 1. Walsh gets no better title than Dolan has. If there are judgments against Dolan, they will continue as liens against the property.

2. The deed, per se, does not extinguish the mortgage. The deed should recite the *intention* of the parties—that the mortgage is cancelled.

125. Q. A deed of farm land describes the land as running from a certain defined point nine hundred feet to the Revolutionary chestnut tree. The tree in question has long been identified and known in the neighborhood as such. The actual distance to this tree is 987 feet. Is the purchaser entitled to 987 feet or 900 feet?

A. 987 feet. In reconciling distances in a deed with distances shown by monuments upon the ground, the latter govern.

126. Q. Where a single woman owns real estate and sells the property after marriage, how should the deed refer to her as the grantor?

A. "Mary Steele, formerly Mary Sone." The notarial acknowledgment should read the same way.

127. Q. Is an oral deed, accompanied by occupancy by buyer, valid?

A. No.

128. Q. If a property is encumbered by a mortgage, would it be a merchantable title?

A. No.

129. Q. What is "escheat" in reference to lands?

A. The lapsing or reverting of land to the state, which occurs usually for failure of heirs or want of legal ownership.

130. Q. What type of deed is preferable from the buyer's standpoint?

A. A general warranty deed, because the grantor warrants to protect the grantee against any claimant.

131. Q. Local planning commissions have an area of jurisdiction, in addition to the most common ones—land use through zoning, community subdivision, design and flood control. Name at least three of these other fields.

A. 1. recreation 2. streets and highways 3. sewage disposal and drainage.

132. Q. Name four different ways in which an owner of real estate may have secured title to it.

A. Purchase, gift, inheritance, adverse possession.

133. Q. If a warranty deed has been executed and delivered to a purchaser, is it necessary to have it recorded in order to make it a valid conveyance?

A. No.

134. Q. What is the danger in not recording a deed promptly?

A. Judgments may be filed against previous owner; also, previous owner may sell or mortgage the property to someone else.

135. Q. May a life estate be sold?

A. Yes; purchaser would hold during the life of his grantor (per Auter Vie).

136. Q. Who is the legal owner of a piece of property when the deed to it is delivered but not recorded?

A. The grantee (purchaser).

137. Q. What is a Condominium?

A. An individual ownership of a single unit in a multi-family structure.

138. Q. How does it differ from ownership in a co-operative apartment?
 A. A condominium can be bought, sold or mortgaged and is taxed separately. In a co-op, the owner usually purchases stock in the corporation and holds possession under a long-term, renewable lease.

139. Q. Smith conveys one-half of a tract of land to Ellis, reserving to himself a right of way across the rear ten feet. On April 24, 1969, Smith sells his one-half to Lawrence. Later Ellis attempts to restrain Lawrence from using the right of way. Will he succeed?
 A. Yes. The right of way was reserved to Smith as a personal covenant. To permit Lawrence to use it, the reservation should have been made to Smith, "his heirs and assigns."

140. Q. Is it necessary to affix United States Revenue Stamps to a deed?
 A. No. Not since January 1, 1968.

141. Q. Is there a difference in making a deed "under and subject to a mortgage" and in making deed "under and subject to a mortgage, which the grantee assumes and agrees to pay"?
 A. Yes. In the first clause, the grantee does not *personally* assume any obligation to pay the debt; in the second clause, he does and he would be personally liable for any deficiency judgment, i.e., the difference between the amount of the debt and the amount realized at a foreclosure sale.

142. Q. A deed is signed in blank by the owner and left with a broker, with the request that broker make the best deal possible. The broker deeds the property to a friend at a price lower than the market price. Is the deed valid?
 A. Yes. The deed is good unless there was some "connivance" between broker and buyer. The broker can be held accountable to the owner for his lack of good faith.

143. Q. At a closing, a seller refuses to pay a broker's commission and demands that the deal be closed. Can the closing officer ignore the broker's claim and disburse the funds?
 A. Yes; the broker has a collateral claim to the deal between buyer and seller.

144. Q. One year after a closing, an unpaid special assessment of $540 is discovered. Is the broker or owner responsible to the buyer, or neither?
 A. The owner is responsible to the buyer for the assessment, and costs, under a general warranty deed.

True and False

1. A deed to real estate cannot be assigned. **T** F
2. An abstract of title guarantees clear title. T **F**

3. The full consideration in any real estate transaction must always be in legal tender. T **F**

4. In a tenancy in common, one person may own ⅕th interest and another person may own a ⅘th interest. **T** F

5. When the tide water is a boundary in the deed, title to the ordinary high water mark is conveyed. **T** F

6. The passing of title to real estate or an interest therein from one person to another is called a conveyance. **T** F

7. Escrow is another name for a husband's interest in his wife's estate. T **F**

8. Constructive notice is knowledge charged by law to one who has no actual knowledge **T** F

9. A warranty deed to real estate may be assigned. **T** **F**

10. Recorded restrictions in a deed may be enforced by any citizen of the community. T **F**

11. The cost of extending an abstract is generally paid for by the purchasers. T **F**

12. Urban real estate is always described by sections. **T** **F**

13. A deed should state the marital status of parties. **T** F

14. Recording of a deed is a proper charge against the seller. T **F**

15. A conveyance of the title to property for the duration of the life of the grantee is called a life estate. **T** F

16. A deed cannot be recorded unless it is signed by the grantee. T **F**

17. A quit claim deed ordinarily conveys a good and merchantable title. T **F**

18. A special warranty deed is preferable to a general warranty deed. T **F**·

19. The grantor in a deed may impose restrictions as to the use of real property. **T** F

20. Zoning restrictions, once established, cannot be changed. T **F**

21. Community clubhouses, parks, and public buildings are "community property" in the real estate sense of the term. T **F**

22. The house number and the name of the street is one of the best legal descriptions there is. T **F**

23. Land with the improvements thereon, is described as "real property." **T** F

24. Fee simple estate is the greatest estate in real estate. **T** F

25. Real property may be held in joint tenancy only by husband and wife. T **F**

26. The passing of title to real estate or an interest therein from one person to another is called a conveyance. **T** F

27. A deed without a date is void. T **F**

28. A deed dated on a Sunday but delivered on Monday is invalid. T **F**

29. An oral deed is void. **T** F

30. A deed should recite the marital status of the grantor. **T** F

31. A deed to real estate does not pass title until it is recorded. T **F**

32. An oral deed is valid if the grantee takes possession.. T **F**

33. It is lawful to deed real estate to a minor. **T** F
34. A deed has no legal effect until it is delivered to the grantee. **T** F
35. The consideration for a deed must always be money. T **F**
36. Better title is conveyed by a warranty deed than by a quit claim deed. **T** F
37. Good title to real estate and a good title of record are the same. T **F**
38. Real property must be free and clear of all encumbrances to be declared as a "homestead." T **F**
39. The recording of a deed is the obligation of the grantor. T **F**
40. A deed recites a consideration of $1.00; the actual price is $100,000. The deed is void because of fraud on the public in misrepresenting the selling price. T **F**
41. In joint ownership, if one of the parties dies, his interest goes to the surviving parties and not to the decedent's heirs. **T** F
42. Failure to attach the proper amount of State Revenue stamps renders the deed void. T **F**
43. A person under 21 years of age cannot hold title to real estate. **T** **F**
44. A valid deed must contain a granting clause. **T** F
45. A quit claim makes no warranty of title. **T** F
46. The legal description in a deed can be enlarged by oral testimony in court. T **F**
47. Escrow is another name for a wife's interest in her husband's property. T **F**
48. A deed takes effect only upon delivery. **T** F
49. A forged deed is void and does not convey good title under any circumstances. **T** F
50. In describing lands by metes and bounds, a course described as being "North 45 degrees east" runs in a northeasterly direction. **T** F
51. Title to real estate is passed by delivery of the abstract of title. T **F**
52. The term "tenants in common" refers to several persons who lease and occupy the same property. T **F**
53. Any person may be given power of attorney. **T** F
54. A person unable to write could not own real estate since he would be unable to sign a deed. T **F**
55. A deed to real estate cannot be assigned. **T** F
56. After a deed has been recorded, the grantee will lose the property if he loses the deed to it. T **F**
57. A "set-back" ordinance regulates the minimum distance allowable between street line and front of new buildings. **T** F
58. In the sale of real property, the seller is known as the grantee. T **F**
59. In describing lands by metes and bounds, a course may be described by trees, rocks and woods. **T** F

60. In order to create a joint tenancy, there must be present the four unities of time, title, interest and possession.   **T**   F
61. Clouds on title to real estate are removed by obtaining title insurance.   T   **F**
62. The most common form of land measurement in eastern rural areas is by metes and bounds.   **T**   F
63. A gift deed must always have a monetary consideration.   T   **F**
64. A quit claim deed warrants and guarantees nothing.   **T**   F
65. Title to real property without improvements may be conveyed by the issuance of a Bill of Sale.   T   **F**
66. A township is one mile square.   T   **F**
67. Property may be held in joint tenancy only by husband and wife.   T   F
68. A tenancy in common carries with it the right of survivorship.   T   **F**
69. A deed is of no effect until it has been signed, sealed, and delivered.   **T**   F
70. A single person and a married person may hold title to real estate as joint tenants.   **T**   F
71. A deed is recorded to give notice to the public that the party named in the deed has a vested right or interest in the property described.   **T**   F
72. One instrument often used to remove a cloud on a title to real estate is an escheat.   T   **F**
73. Real estate may be defined as any property not considered personal.   **T**   F
74. The buyer should pay for an attorney's examination of the title.   **T**   F
75. In the escrow of a deed, it is desirable for the broker to act as the escrow holder.   T   **F**
76. Assessments on real estate for tax purposes are made every even year.   T   **F**
77. A public utility company always has an easement in any property by act of the legislature.   T   **F**
78. An action to quiet title is used to remove a cloud on the title.   **T**   F
79. A married woman who acquired title before marriage should sign a deed only in her maiden name.   T   **F**
80. It is proper to give a quit claim deed even though your interest in the property is negligible or questionable.   **T**   F
81. An abstract of title guarantees a clear title.   T   **F**
82. When one owns real estate, his warranty deed gives no better protection than his quit claim deed would give.   T   **F**
83. A deed may sometimes be recorded without being acknowledged.   T   **F**
84. One who receives the deed is called the grantee.   **T**   F
85. An escrow agent is the agent for *both* buyer and seller.   **T**   F
86. A deed by a minor is voidable at his option.   **T**   F
87. A deed takes effect only from the date it is recorded.   T   **F**

88. Chain of title is the succession of conveyances from some accepted starting point whereby the present holder of real property derives his title. **T** F
89. A grantee receives no better title than his grantor had. **T** F
90. The owner of real property becomes the grantor when he sells the property. **T** F
91. An easement is an encumbrance on real estate. **T** F
92. An estate in severalty is an estate owned by one person alone. **T** F
93. It is necessary to itemize in the deed all improvements affixed to the real estate being conveyed if they are to be sold with the real property. T **F**
94. Ownership in "fee simple" is where one owns the property to hold to him and his heirs forever. **T** F
95. A Bill of Sale is the instrument by which the title to real estate passes. T **F**
96. Upon the death of one of two tenants in common to real estate, the interest and title in the land of the deceased owner descends to his heirs and not to the surviving party. **T** F
97. The term "tide lands" and "shore lands" apply to the same land. **T** F
98. Tenancy in common refers to ownership rather than occupancy. **T** F
99. When a grantor faultily executes a deed, he can be compelled to sign a corrected deed. **T** F
100. A trustee's deed is generally a warranty deed rather than a special warranty deed. T **F**
101. A chain of title refers to a unit of land measurement. T **F**
102. A good title and a marketable title generally mean the same thing. **T** F
103. Real estate and real property generally mean the same thing. **T** F
104. A community apartment house is considered a subdivision. **T** F
105. Where one is negligent in asserting his legal rights, he is guilty of estoppel. T **F**
106. Metes and bounds is a system of land description by measure and direction. **T** F
107. A beneficiary under a trust must always join in the deed by the trustee. T **F**
108. A deed by the officers of a corporation must be made in pursuance of a resolution of the board of directors authorizing the particular sale. **T** F
109. A deed to farm property will include the sale of all machinery and farm implements. T **F**
110. If a deed has been recorded and the consideration price has not been paid in full, the deed is void. T **F**
111. Title insurance offers protection against loss by fire. T **F**
112. An unpaid tax lien is an encumbrance on title. **T** F
113. A sheriff's deed is a general warranty deed. T **F**

114. No personal property can ever become real property. T **F**
115. A good and a valuable consideration are legally the same. **T** F
116. A declaration of homestead is of no effect until recorded. **T** F
117. Two brokers can own community property. T **F**
118. Real property in name of wife is presumed to be her separate property. T F
119. On death of father, children inherit one half of community property. T **F**
120. A quit claim deed generally conveys fee simple title. T **F**
121. An abstract of title is a summary or digest of all instruments affecting the title. **T** F
122. A deed to husband and wife creates an estate by the entireties. **T** F
123. Property may be owned by more than two joint tenants. **T** F
124. Recording a deed is the obligation of the grantor. T **F**
125. A grantor of a deed may impose restrictions as to the use of real property. **T** F
126. Building restrictions which run perpetually are invalid. **T** F
127. Zoning restrictions and building restrictions are the same. T **F**
128. A minor cannot avoid a real estate transaction if he misrepresented his age. T **F**
129. To be valid, a deed must always be signed by both the grantor and the grantee. T **F**
130. A habendum clause is essential in a deed in order to pass a valid title. T **F**
131. The date in the beginning of the deed should not be subsequent to the date in the acknowledgment. **T** F
132. The clause in the deed which indicates who is to give the property and who is to receive the property is called the covenant of seizin. T **F**
133. Attestation means witnessing the deed. **T** F
134. A deed may be acknowledged by a justice of the peace or a notary public. **T** F
135. In the conveyance of real estate, all permanent buildings must be described in the warranty deed. T **F**
136. A quit claim deed does not convey fee simple title. **T** F
137. A deed need not be in writing if grantor and grantee appear before the County Recorder of Deeds and swear that the transfer is voluntary and for consideration. T **F**
138. The actual selling price of real property must be shown in the deed. T **F**
139. A property owner may use his property as surety for another person's obligation. **T** F
140. Joint tenants with right of survivorship means literally that the building is being operated as a "joint" with police protection. T **F**
141. An unrecorded deed is good and valid as between the parties to the instrument. **T** F

142. A "deed" takes effect during the grantor's lifetime and a "will" at the testator's death. **T** F
143. The actual selling price of real property is never shown in the deed. T **F**
144. In the conveyance of real estate, all auxiliary buildings are described in the warranty deed. T **F**
145. Fractional sections of farm land are always caused by errors in survey. T **F**
146. A person who has real estate devised to him, is said to acquire title by adverse possession. T **F**
147. "Metes and bounds" has reference to the topography of the land. T **F**
148. Zoning ordinances are enacted primarily to define "no-parking" zones. T **F**
149. Real property may be defined as any property not considered as personalty. **T** F
150. An interest in ownership of personal property is usually termed an estate in fee simple. T **F**
151. A City Zoning Ordinance has reference to the local postal zones. T **F**
152. The recording of a deed to real property is the obligation of the grantee. **T** F
153. The full consideration in any real estate transaction must always be in legal tender. T **F**
154. The execution of a deed means that it was properly signed and acknowledged by the grantee. T **F**
155. A grantor impliedly warrants that he has fee simple title to the property. **T** F
156. The sole purpose of an acknowledgment to a deed is to promote the security of the title. T **F**
157. A purchaser at a foreclosure sale usually receives a bargain and sale deed. T **F**
158. The "Chain of Title" is found in the "Abstract of Title." **T** F
159. Real property includes everything that is not personalty. **T** F
160. One who dies holding tenancy in common may will his interest to his next of kin. **T** F
161. A septic tank system is a private sewage disposal system for individual homes. **T** F
162. A Sheriff's Deed and a Tax Deed are usually considered to be the same thing. **T** F
163. Title to property may pass to another by adverse possession. **T** F
164. A suit for specific performance is an action to quiet title. **T** **F**
165. In directions in a deed, east is always to the right of north. **T** F
166. Real estate may include more than just land. **T** F
167. Real Estate Commissioners are authorized by the license law to take acknowledgments. T **F**
168. A section of land contains 360 acres. T **F**
169. A $1.00 consideration is sufficient for an option. **T** F

170. One who has taken an option on certain real estate must complete the purchase of the property.   T **F**
171. The consideration in an option is always applied to the purchase price, if the option is exercised.   T **F**
172. Zoning regulations limit the use of real estate.   **T** F
173. Failure to record documents has no effect on their validity.   **T** F
174. It is usually false economy to fail to secure a title search when purchasing property.   **T** F
175. If you include your piano and television set in the sale of your home, they become a part of the real estate.   T **F**
176. A property may be transferred by deed when the consideration is only love and affection.   **T** F
177. The term "fee simple" means that it is the usual commission for the sale of real estate.   T **F**
178. An easement means making the payment easier on a mortgage.   T **F**
179. A warranty deed is used to convey title to chattels.   T **F**
180. A power of attorney can be given only to duly qualified attorneys at law.   T **F**
181. A deed to partnership property sold by the partners need not have the joinder of the wives of the partners.   **T** F
182. Two or more persons who take title to property by a single deed hold it as partners.   T **F**
183. It is not necessary to require a title search when conveying vacant property worth less than $1,000.00.   T **F**
184. It is legal to describe property by lot, block, and tract number if sold from a recorded plan.   **T** F
185. Laws passed by a governing body whereby certain described sections are set aside for certain purposes are known as zoning laws. **T** F
186. The deed which is executed in a foreclosure action is an Executor's Deed.   T **F**
187. The terms "real estate," "realty," and "real property" mean practically the same thing.   **T** F
188. An agreement under which an instrument or money is deposited with a third person to be delivered upon the performance of a condition is called a power of attorney.   T **F**
189. The ownership of real estate by two or more persons, each of whom has an undivided interest, without the "right of survivorship" is called a Tenancy in Common.   **T** F
190. It is not necessary to require a title search when conveying vacant lots.   T **F**
191. "Beneficiary," "Trustor," and "Trustee" are the legal designations of the parties to a trust deed.   **T** F
192. Upon the death of the father and mother, the children inherit one half of the community property.   T **F**
193. A "conditional sales contract" on real property can be recorded only if it has been acknowledged by the buyer.   T **F**

194. A final decree of divorce has the effect of an abandonment of a declaration of homestead. T **F**

195. Dating a deed is necessary to make it valid. T **F**

196. If a husband alone signs a listing on community property, the broker cannot collect a commission if the wife refuses to sell. T **F**

197. In a standard township, section 31 is located in the southwest corner. **T** F

198. Fee simple title is all the bundle of rights in real estate. **T** **F**

199. A standard township contains 23,040 acres of land. **T** F

200. A "Power of Attorney" is a title examiner who closes real estate transactions. T **F**

201. A ground rent is real estate. **T** F

202. Title by adverse possession is just as valid as title by a written instrument. **T** F

203. An easement is real estate. **T** F

204. A deed must be recorded in the county where the property is located. **T** F

205. A deed, once recorded, if lost, has no effect on the title. **T** F

206. The major objective of the Homestead Law is to protect against execution to satisfy debts. **T** F

207. A grantor who has improperly executed a deed, which has been recorded, cannot be required to execute a new deed. T **F**

208. Restrictions in a deed are desirable in order to maintain value of the property. **T** F

209. A restriction and an easement mean the same thing. T **F**

210. A grantee who delays in recording a deed is subject to a penalty. T **F**

211. Courts do not inquire into the sufficiency of the consideration price. **T** F

212. A recital of title is essential to the validity of a deed. T **F**

213. It is the obligation of the grantee to see that the deed is properly indexed. **T** F

214. A deed executed in a foreign country should be acknowledged before a minister or consul of this country. **T** F

215. Where a judgment note has been given in payment of the consideration and the note is not paid at maturity, the deed is void. T **F**

216. Either parent, by operation of law, is duly authorized to execute a deed for a minor child. T **F**

217. The sale of land includes all appurtenances thereto. **T** F

218. Building restrictions, as specified in the deed, are not encumbrances against the property. T **F**

219. The only essential unity in a tenancy in common is the equal right of possession. T **F**

220. A list of furniture included in a sale of property should be stated in the deed. T **F**

221. A deed by a partnership should be executed in the partnership name only. **T** **F**

222. A corporation deed should always recite the resolution of the board of directors, authorizing the conveyance. **T** F

223. Where property is sold within one year, it is not necessary to have the title examined. T **F**

224. A road through a private property used by another with permission of the owner is an appurtenance. T **F**

225. It is possible to exchange properties even though both are subject to existing mortgages. **T** F

226. Interest on delinquent real estate taxes always accrues at the rate of 1%. T **F**

227. In a standard township, section 30 is in the southwest corner. T **F**

228. A sheriff's deed and a tax deed are the same as far as warranties. **T** F

229. A deed to "John Saxman or Andrew Erbel" is valid. T **F**

230. A merchantable title is one free from clouds or defects. **T** F

231. A covenant of seizin is the grantor's guarantee that he is the owner of the property and has the power to convey title thereto. **T** F

232. There are no covenants to be found in a quit claim deed. **T** F

233. Signing a deed does not transfer title. **T** F

234. Failure to record a deed or a mortgage has no effect on its validity. **T** F

235. Alluvium and Avulsion are synonymous terms. T **F**

236. An executed deed transfers title to real estate. T **F**

237. An encumbrance is anything which affects the title to real estate. **T** F

238. Every fixture is a chattel. T **F**

239. In a rectangular survey a check is sixteen townships. **T** F

240. A title insurance policy excepts conditions shown by actual survey. **T** F

241. A quit claim deed of a husband need not be signed by his wife. T **F**

242. Condemnation of private property for public use is called acquisition. T **F**

243. A co-operative apartment ownership generally is more advantageous than in a condominium. T **F**

244. Tenancy in common refers to ownership. **T** F

245. A restrictive easement is one which runs with the land. **T** F

246. "Spot" zoning is permissible in hardship cases. **T** F

247. The total land area of a homestead is limited by statute. **T** F

248. A person having a freehold interest in land to be held during the life of another is a leasehold estate. T **F**

249. A tract (of land) and a check can be used interchangeably in measurement terms. **T** F

250. The warranty clause and the testimonium clause in a deed are similar and can be used interchangeably. **T** **F**
251. An irrigation ditch on a ranch is personal property. **T** **F**
252. A and B may own a ⅕ and ⅘ interest, respectively, as tenants in common. **T** F
253. A single man and a husband and wife may own property as joint tenants. **T** F
254. A husband and wife may own real estate only as community property. T **F**
255. Personal property is never held by Tenants in Common. T **F**
256. Title to real estate may pass without consent of the owner. **T** F
257. When the tide water is a boundary in the deed, title to the ordinary high water mark is conveyed. **T** F
258. A freehold interest is ownership of a fee simple or life estate. **T** F
259. Tenancy in common may be created by destruction of a joint tenancy. **T** F
260. As between the parties, a deed is invalid without subscribing witnesses or acknowledgment. T **F**
261. A minor can void his deed if he misrepresented his agent. T **F**
262. The recording of a deed guarantees its validity. T **F**
263. Alluvial land is generally unproductive land on which the return over cost of production is practically nil. T **F**
264. Horizontal rows of townships are called tiers. **T** F
265. Chain is a unit of measurement—16½ feet. T **F**
266. The United States Internal Revenue Tax was repealed on January 1, 1966. T **F**
267. Condominium ownership is a stabilizing factor in maintaining urban population. **T** F
268. Condominium ownership has greater safeguards to the individual owner than that of a co-op apartment. **T** F
269. Condominium ownership is less than 20 years old in this country. **T** F
270. An owner of a condominium must obtain approval of his fellow owners as to type of flooring and decor, in order to maintain uniformity. T **F**
271. Owner of a condominium unit is unable to obtain F.H.A. financing. T **F**
272. Condominium ownership is the result of a state enabling statute. **T** F
273. An estate is the interest one has in property. **T** F
274. A system of land registration by which the state guarantees the title is known as the Torrens system. **T** F
275. Rights which are incidental to the land and "go with the land" are encroachments. T **F**
276. A reconveyance deed is used in connection with a trust deed. **T** F
277. There are 20 acres included in the S½ of the NW ¼ of the SE ¼ of a section of land. **T** F

278. Title to a vacant tract of land may be conveyed by a bill of sale   T   **F**
279. A devise is the reversion of real estate to the State when the testator dies intestate.   T   **F**
280. An appropriation of land by an owner for some public use and acceptance for such use is called a dedication.   **T**   F
281. Reformation is an action to correct an error in a deed.   **T**   F
282. A devise of real estate may be changed by the maker of the will at any time before death.   **T**   F
283. An oral gift of real estate to take effect after death, made in the presence of two distinterested witnesses, is valid.   T   **F**
284. A fence existing for more than six years will be regarded as the true boundary line between two farms.   T   **F**

Multiple Choice

1. A man devised his residence to his widow and upon her death, it was to go to two of his three children. The widow received a
   (x) life estate.
   ( ) partial estate.
   ( ) remainder estate.
   ( ) leasehold.
2. Tenancy in common refers to
   ( ) occupancy.
   ( ) survivorship.
   (x) ownership.
   ( ) a lease that has restrictive covenants to tenants.
3. Real estate occupied as a home, by an owner, who enjoys special rights and privileges is
   ( ) a freehold.
   (x) a homestead.
   ( ) a joint tenancy.
   ( ) unjust enrichment.
4. Timber on land becomes personal property by
   ( ) sale of the land.
   ( ) written declaration of owner.
   (x) severance.
   ( ) eminent domain.
5. The water table is the
   ( ) measure of water flow.
   ( ) rate for cost of water.
   (x) depth where water is found.
   ( ) average rainfall per month.
6. An estate at will is a
   ( ) form of co-ownership.
   (x) tenancy of uncertain duration.

( ) inheritance of property by will.
( ) life estate.

7. Andrew Erbel, a single man, and William Rushton, a single man, wish to take the title to real property so that each will own a one-half interest, and if either of them dies, the other will own the entire property. The Grantee clause should read:
   ( ) Andrew Erbel, a single man, and William Rushton, a single man, each an undivided one-half interest as tenants in common.
   (x) Andrew Erbel and William Rushton, single men, as joint tenants.
   ( ) Andrew Erbel, a single man, and William Rushton, a single man, jointly and severally.
   ( ) Andrew Erbel and William Rushton, single men, as co-owners.
   ( ) none of the above is correct.

8. In order to record a deed, it must be in writing and
   ( ) signed by grantee.
   ( ) recite the actual purchase price.
   (x) acknowledged.
   ( ) be free of all liens.

9. The most comprehensive ownership of land at law is known as
   ( ) estate for years.
   ( ) life estate.
   (x) fee simple.
   ( ) defeasible title.

10. James Steele and Mary Steele, his daughter, buy a tract of ground for all cash and the property is deeded to them "with right of survivorship." James and Mary are:
    (x) joint tenants.
    ( ) tenants by the entireties.
    ( ) tenants in common.
    ( ) none of the above.

11. A wall erected on the line between two adjoining properties belonging to different persons which serves as an outside wall of both buildings is a
    (x) party wall.
    ( ) community wall.
    ( ) line wall.
    ( ) share wall.

12. The largest estate or ownership in real property is
    ( ) 640 acres.
    (x) a fee simple estate.
    ( ) a homestead.
    ( ) a littoral right.

13. A land description reading: The N ½ of the S ½ of the SW ¼ of the NW ¼ contains
    ( ) 15 acres.
    (x) 10 acres.

( ) 7 acres.
( ) 20 acres.

14. From the standpoint of the grantor in a deed conveying real estate which of the following types of deed creates the least liability?
( ) Special warranty.
( ) General warranty.
( ) Bargain and sale.
(x) Quit claim.

15. Land acquired by husband or wife by their labor after marriage in Arizona, Arkansas, California, Florida or Texas, is
( ) separate property.
( ) real property.
(x) community property.

16. A deed passes title when it is
(x) signed by the grantors.
(x) acknowledged.
(x) delivered to the grantees.
( ) recorded.

17. Community property is owned by
( ) the church.
( ) father and son.
( ) the city or community.
( ) a housing authority.
(x) husband and wife.

18. The instrument which conditionally conveys title to real estate is a
( ) conditional bailment lease.
( ) chattel mortgage.
(x) mortgage.
( ) land purchase contract.

19. A means of acquiring title where the occupant has been in actual, open, notorious, exclusive and continuous occupation of property under a claim of right is called
( ) reversion.
(x) adverse possession.
( ) fee simple.
( ) fee absolute.

20. The recording of a warranty deed
( ) passes the title.
( ) insures the title.
( ) guarantees the title.
(x) gives constructive notice of ownership.

21. The four unities required for joint tenancy are
(x) possession.
(x) time.
( ) husband and wife.
(x) title.
( ) location.
(x) interest.

22. The clause in a deed which sets forth the extent of the interests in the title being conveyed is
    ( ) the demising clause.
    ( ) the testimony clause.
    (x) the habendum clause.
    ( ) the indenture clause.
23. A person who has real property willed to him by a relative is said to acquire title by
    ( ) reversion.
    ( ) release.
    (x) inheritance.
    ( ) adverse possession.
24. A deed to be valid need not necessarily be
    ( ) signed.
    ( ) written.
    (x) sealed.
    ( ) delivered.
25. Describing land boundaries, setting forth the lines together with terminal points and angles, is termed description by
    ( ) acreage.
    (x) metes and bounds.
    ( ) perimeter.
    ( ) lot and block number.
26. A document which transfers possession of real property, but does not transfer ownership is
    ( ) a deed.
    ( ) a mortgage.
    (x) a lease.
    ( ) a deposition.
27. When a deed which is delivered but not recorded is lost or destroyed, the legal title to the property described therein
    (x) remains in the grantee named in the last deed.
    ( ) reverts to the last former owner of record.
    ( ) escheats to the state.
28. The party to whom a deed conveys real estate is called the
    (x) grantee.
    ( ) grantor.
    ( ) beneficiary.
    ( ) recipient.
29. The word "escrow" refers to
    ( ) a young crow.
    (x) deposit of legal documents with a third person to be delivered upon the fulfillment of certain conditions.
    ( ) deposits of money in a bank, subject to withdrawal by depositor.
    ( ) safe deposit box where deed is placed.
30. A quit claim deed conveys the interest of the
    ( ) grantee.

( ) mortgagee.
(x) grantor.
( ) lessee.

31. When real estate under lease is sold the lease
( ) expires.
(x) remains binding upon new owner.
( ) must be renewed.
( ) is broken.

32. An acquired legal privilege or right of use or enjoyment falling short of ownership which one may have in the land of another is known as
( ) a devise.
( ) an abstract.
(x) an easement.
( ) a riparian right.

33. Property held in joint tenancy, upon the death of one of the tenants, passes to the
( ) landlord.
( ) state.
( ) heirs of the deceased.
(x) surviving owner.

34. A conveyance of title with the condition that the land shall not be used for the sale of intoxicating beverages or liquors creates
( ) a nuisance estate.
(x) an estate on condition subsequent.
( ) an estate on condition precedent.
( ) a reservation.

35. Which of the following is *not* necessary to the validity of the deed?
( ) Signing.
( ) Acknowledgment.
(x) Recording.
( ) Delivery.

36. An encumbrance is anything which affects the
( ) grant deed.
( ) transfer of ownership.
( ) loan value.
(x) title.

37. If you contracted to sell the southwest quarter of the southwest quarter of the northwest quarter of a section of land, how many acres would pass by the deed?
( ) 15 acres.
(x) 10 acres.
( ) 40 acres.
( ) 160 acres.

38. Deeds are recorded in the
(x) County Courthouse.
( ) City Hall.

( ) State Capitol building.
( ) office of the title company.
39. If title to real property remains in the seller's name after it is sold on a monthly payment plan, the buyer would have purchased it under
( ) an F.H.A. mortgage.
( ) a conventional mortgage.
(x) a real estate contract.
( ) a V.A. approved mortgage.
40. A deed must
( ) contain the street address identification.
( ) state nature of the improvement on the land (dwelling).
(x) contain adequate description to identify the sold lot.
( ) state total area in the tract.
41. At the closing of a deal, which item is generally charged to the seller?
( ) Recording fee for deed
( ) Fire insurance
(x) Revenue stamps
( ) Attorney's examination
42. Title to real property passes by voluntary alienation by
( ) quit claim deed.
(x) grant deed.
( ) court decree.
( ) trustee in bankruptcy.
43. North and south boundaries of townships are created by
( ) state surveyor.
( ) metes and bounds descriptions.
( ) court decree.
(x) base lines.
44. A riparian owner is one who owns land bordering on
( ) a wild orchard.
( ) sub-marginal land.
( ) existing subdivision.
(x) a river or lake.
45. The person who cannot take an acknowledgment is
( ) an alderman.
( ) a Justice of the Peace.
(x) an interested party.
( ) a judge.
46. A government official who evaluates property for tax purposes is an
( ) assayer.
(x) assessor.
( ) administrator.
( ) surveyor.
47. Fraud is to truth as concealment is to
( ) statute of frauds.

( ) misrepresentation.
(x) disclosure.
( ) duress.

48. The overhang of a porch or balcony beyond the established line of a parcel of land is known as
( ) an easement.
(x) an encroachment.
( ) right of way.
( ) freeway.

49. The instrument which conveys title to a trustee is
( ) a mortgage.
( ) trustee's guaranty.
( ) an indenture.
(x) trust deed.

50. Clauses in a deed are dictated by
(x) agreement of sale
( ) the mortgagee
( ) the F.H.A.
( ) Real Estate Commission

51. What is the maximum number of grantees that can be named in a deed?
( ) Two.
(x) Any number.
( ) Four.
( ) Ten.

52. Property is identified in a conveyance instrument by the
( ) habendum.
( ) consideration.
(x) description.
( ) equity.

53. A proper escrow, once established, should be
( ) held by a licensed broker.
( ) voidable at the seller's option.
( ) voidable at option of either buyer or seller.
(x) beyond the control of any one interested party.

54. First grant or patent in chain of title is issued by
(x) a sovereign power.
( ) U. S. Government Patent Office.
( ) the recorder of deeds.
( ) the grantee of a fee simple deed.

54. A widow who is willed the use of the family home for the rest of her natural life, with provision that it shall go to the children upon her death, holds
( ) no interest in the property.
( ) a fee simple estate.
( ) a leasehold.
(x) a life estate.

56. Chain of title means

( ) a measurement used by a surveyor.
(x) a listing of all recorded instruments affecting the subject title.
( ) certificate of title.
( ) heirs named in a will to inherit property after death of testator.

57. The right of a water company to lay and maintain water mains along a designated line in the rear of a lot would be called
( ) an encroachment right.
(x) an easement.
( ) adverse possession.
( ) an appurtenance.

58. A title insurance policy, standard form, insures
( ) that there are no judgment liens against the property.
( ) that the property is free and clear of all encumbrances.
(x) the title only as it appears of record, subject to printed exceptions.

59. Property of a person who dies intestate, leaving no heirs, passes to the state by
(x) escheat.
( ) eminent domain.
( ) adverse possession.
( ) condemnation.

60. A section of land is
( ) 360 acres.
( ) 6 miles square.
( ) 6 square miles.
(x) 1 square mile.

61. The party appointed by a court to settle a deceased person's estate is
( ) a trustor.
( ) a trustee.
( ) a guardian.
(x) an administrator.

62. A description reading: the S $\frac{1}{2}$ of the SE $\frac{1}{4}$ of the NW $\frac{1}{4}$ of the NE $\frac{1}{4}$ of a section of land contains
( ) 15 acres.
( ) 12$\frac{1}{2}$ acres.
( ) 10 acres.
(x) 5 acres.

63. A valid declaration of homestead may be filed on a home by
( ) the lessee.
( ) trustee.
( ) mortgagee.
(x) head of family.

64. The number of square feet in an acre of ground is
( ) 5,280.
( ) 25,120.
(x) 43,560.
( ) 50,560.

65. In the West a township is
    - ( ) an incorporated city.
    - ( ) a 640-acre plot of land.
    - ( ) six square miles.
    - (x) six miles square.

66. Which of the following are incompetent to execute a deed?
    - (x) Minor.
    - ( ) Widow.
    - (x) Intoxicated person.
    - ( ) Single woman.
    - (x) Insane person.
    - ( ) Man over 80 years of age.

67. Deeds are acknowledged
    - ( ) to make them legal.
    - (x) to enable them to be recorded.
    - ( ) because of ancient custom.

68. A "quit claim" deed is used to
    - ( ) correct a defect in description.
    - (x) remove a valid or fancied right.
    - ( ) pass an absolute fee simple estate.

69. Which of the following forms of deeds have one or more guarantees of title?
    - ( ) Quit claim deed.
    - (x) Warranty deed.
    - ( ) Executor's deed.

70. Which of the following are essentials to a deed of real estate?
    - (x) Covenant of seizin.
    - (x) Description.
    - ( ) "Habendum" clause.
    - (x) Signature of seller.
    - ( ) Signature of buyer.

71. A deed which carries with it the implied rights of survivorship is called a
    - ( ) warranty deed.
    - ( ) grant deed.
    - (x) joint tenancy deed.
    - ( ) power of attorney.

72. Title to real estate passes to the grantee at the time the deed is
    - ( ) written.
    - (x) delivered.
    - ( ) notarized.
    - ( ) signed.

73. Real property owned by husband or his wife prior to their marriage is presumed to be
    - ( ) community property.
    - (x) separate property.
    - ( ) personal property.
    - ( ) tenancy in common.

74. A quit claim deed conveys only the interest of the
    ( ) grantee.
    ( ) property.
    ( ) claimant.
    (x) grantor.
75. A declaration of homestead is an instrument recorded in the Recorder's office for the purpose of
    ( ) acquiring title to property.
    ( ) conveying property to another.
    (x) exempting property from execution.
    ( ) satisfying a debt.
76. An authorization to a person to act for and in behalf of another in his absence is called
    ( ) an option.
    ( ) an easement.
    (x) a power of attorney.
    ( ) a release.
77. Which of the following are real estate and pass under a common warranty deed?
    (x) Chandeliers in a house.
    ( ) Awnings.
    (x) Furnace.
    (x) The fence surrounding the property.
    ( ) A portable gas stove.
    (x) The rock garden.
78. The right to cross over property owned by another is called
    ( ) adverse possession.
    (x) an easement.
    ( ) a homestead.
    ( ) a lien.
79. Unpaid taxes on real estate become
    (x) a lien.
    ( ) an easement.
    ( ) a judgment.
80. If the city wishes to take property for public improvements, it may acquire title by action based on
    ( ) attachment proceedings.
    (x) right of eminent domain.
    ( ) suit to quiet title.
    ( ) adverse possession rights.
81. Taking of property for public use is
    ( ) zoning.
    (x) condemnation.
    ( ) escheat.
    ( ) reversion.
82. An instrument which requires recordation to be legally effective is a
    (x) mechanic's lien.

( ) agreement to sell real estate.
( ) will.
( ) deed.

83. An easement is *not* extinguished by which one of the following:
    (x) decision of the property owner.
    ( ) when necessity no longer exists.
    ( ) release.
    ( ) abandonment.

84. Which one of the following applies to ownership of land
    (x) tenancy in common.
    ( ) tenancy at will.
    ( ) tenancy for years.
    ( ) tenancy of sufferance.

85. John L. Davis, Jr. and Marie E., his wife, own property jointly. In deeding it, the wife should sign

    ( ) Mrs. John L. Davis Jr.
    ( ) Marie E. Davis Jr.
    (x) Marie E. Davis.
    ( ) in her maiden name, now Mrs. John L. Davis Jr.

86. A charge levied against real estate for municipal functions is
    ( ) an assessment.
    (x) a tax.
    ( ) a lien.
    ( ) a judgment.

87. In order for a buyer to be certain that the property he is purchasing has no encroachment, he should obtain.
    ( ) purchaser's policy of title insurance.
    (x) survey.
    ( ) certificate of no defense.
    ( ) warranty deed.

88. The grantor's guarantee that he is the owner of the property and has the power to convey title is called the covenant of
    ( ) further assurance.
    ( ) seizin.
    ( ) quiet enjoyment.
    (x) warranty.

89. Eminent domain is
    ( ) a public park.
    ( ) a country home.
    (x) power to take property for public use.

90. A person who has real estate devised to him by a relative is said to have acquired title by
    ( ) adverse possession.
    (x) inheritance.
    ( ) reversion.
    ( ) release.

91. Condemnation of private property for public use is called the right of

(x) eminent domain.
( ) municipalities.
( ) acquisition.
( ) acquirement.

92. The rights to the water thereon of a person owning land containing or bordering upon a stream are called
( ) water rights.
(x) riparian rights.
( ) eminent domain.
( ) a reservation.

93. A clear title to real estate may be assured by securing
( ) a warranty deed.
( ) an abstract of title.
(x) a policy of title insurance.
( ) a guarantee of title.

94. Brown purchases property from Adams. Adams later gives another deed to Clark. Notice of Brown's interest may exist because of
( ) possession of abstract of title.
(x) possession of property by Brown.
( ) possession of adjoining property by Brown.
( ) possession of deed by Brown.
( ) Adams's not paying taxes.

95. A quit claim deed is of as much practical value to the grantee as a warranty deed would be
( ) if the grantee is insolvent.
( ) if the grantee is not given an abstract.
(x) if the title is not good and merchantable.
( ) if the grantor is not financially able to back up his warranty.
( ) if the grantee loses his deed.

96. A policy of title insurance "purchaser's form" insures the record title in the name of
( ) the mortgagee.
( ) a broker.
(x) the grantor.
( ) the grantee.

97. One who acquires property under a deed is
( ) an optionee.
( ) a vendee.
(x) a grantee.
( ) a trustee.

98. Severalty ownership is ownership
( ) by several persons.
( ) by title passing to the survivors upon death of one.
( ) of an undivided interest in property.
(x) by one person only.

99. A homestead right is surrendered by recording
( ) a satisfaction.
(x) an abandonment.

( ) a release.
( ) a reconveyance.

100. Owner of an undivided interest in land with no right of survivorship owns it by
( ) joint tenancy.
( ) severalty.
( ) absolute ownership.
(x) tenancy in common.

101. Title to fixtures, shelves, counters, and merchandise is transferred or conveyed by
( ) deed.
(x) bill of sale.
( ) chattel mortgage.
( ) escrow.

102. The tax on a given piece of real estate is determined by multiplying the tax rate (millage) by
( ) the selling price.
( ) appraised value of the property.
( ) insured value.
(x) assessed valuation.
( ) market value, less depreciation.

103. The legal rights which a wife has in her husband's property at his death are known as
( ) curtesy.
(x) dower.
( ) share by entirety.
( ) share by survivorship.

104. The title to land held in absolute ownership is called
( ) estate for years.
( ) a leasehold.
(x) fee simple.
( ) a base fee.

105. In order to accurately determine the boundaries of real property, one should obtain
( ) a title policy.
(x) a survey.
( ) an abstract.
( ) a decree of court.

106. The state of ownership in real property by which the husband and wife hold title to real estate and in which the right of survivorship cannot be destroyed by either party is known as
( ) estate in joint tenancy.
(x) estate by entirety.
( ) estate in common.
( ) estate by dower right.

107. The law which requires certain contracts to be in writing in order to be enforceable is called the

( ) written instrument law.
( ) parol evidence law.
( ) statute of limitations.
(x) statute of frauds.
108. From the standpoint of the grantor in a deed, which form of deed creates the least liability?
( ) Special warranty deed.
( ) General warranty deed.
( ) Bargain and sale.
(x) Quit claim deed.
109. An absolute conveyance of real property would be by a
( ) mortgage deed.
(x) general warranty deed.
( ) quit claim deed.
( ) gift deed.
110. When a notary public or other qualified official attests to the signature on a deed or mortgage, it is called an
( ) authorization.
(x) acknowledgment.
( ) execution.
( ) authentication.
111. At the closing of a deal, which item is generally chargeable to the seller?
( ) Recording deed.
( ) Title insurance.
(x) State Deed Transfer stamps (if required).
( ) Survey.
112. Mrs. Sims, wife of Alfred D. Sims, should sign a deed to real estate in which manner?
(x) Elsie M. Sims.
( ) Mrs. Alfred D. Sims.
( ) Mrs. Elsie M. Sims.
113. When speaking of "improvements" regarding real estate, it means
( ) fences, wells, drains, roadways, etc.
(x) everything except the land.
( ) additions made to the original house.
114. Creating an easement means
( ) restricting the style or cost of a house which can be built in a subdivision of lots.
( ) placing a dwelling over your property line onto another's property.
(x) giving someone the right, advantage, or privilege to use your land.
115. That part of a conveyance or other instrument affecting the title which identifies property is the
( ) habendum.
( ) consideration.

(x) description.

( ) equity.

116. In order for a would-be buyer of real estate to be certain of the validity of the title, he should order

( ) a survey.

(x) a search.

( ) an estoppel certificate.

117. If Jane White and James White, her husband, are living together on property legally described; a deed conveying the property to a purchaser, signed only by the wife, Jane, may be valid when

( ) it is recorded.

(x) property was acquired by wife before marriage (in community property states).

( ) the husband is out of the state.

( ) all liens are paid.

118. Which of the following is not necessary to the validity of a deed?

( ) Signing.

( ) Sealing.

(x) Recording.

( ) Delivery.

119. An encumbrance on real estate may be

( ) unpaid broker's commission.

( ) live stock.

(x) easement granting another a right of way over land.

( ) a building.

120. If you wish to have a driveway over your neighbor's yard, which instrument would you use?

( ) A quit claim deed.

(x) Easement.

( ) Assignment of contract.

( ) Estoppel certificate.

121. For which reason or reasons is a deed recorded?

( ) Insures certain title.

(x) Gives notice to the world.

( ) Required by the state.

( ) Save title insurance cost.

122. Ownership of property is transferred

( ) when grantor signs the deed.

( ) when the grantor's signature has been notarized.

(x) when delivery of the deed is made.

( ) when the correct documentary stamps are put on deed and cancelled.

123. The deed to a purchaser must include

(x) legal description of property.

( ) survey.

( ) title report.

124. A valid deed must contain

( ) the grantee's signature.
( ) an acknowledgment.
( ) evidence of recordation.
(x) a granting clause.
125. A notice of abandonment is recorded to release a
( ) mortgage.
( ) chattel real.
(x) declaration of homestead.
( ) listing.
126. A person buying property from an owner who claims it by adverse possession should insist upon
( ) a deed of release from the adverse occupant.
(x) a court decree.
( ) a deed of release from the title owner.
( ) a deed of indemnification.
127. Chain of title means
( ) a measurement used by a surveyor.
( ) the last deed of record.
(x) a part of the history of all instruments affecting the particular tract of ground.
( ) a secured policy of title insurance.
128. A charge levied by a local government to finance street paving is
( ) an ad valorem tax.
( ) a zoning charge.
( ) an equalizer.
(x) an assessment.
129. The sovereign power in determining title to land is
( ) the municipality.
(x) the State.
( ) the Attorney General.
( ) the Real Estate Commission.
130. In an escrow which document would not properly belong?
( ) contract of sale.
( ) warranty deed.
(x) trust deed note.
( ) insurance binder.
131. Deed is to property as will is to
( ) heir.
( ) probate.
(x) estate.
( ) court.
132. Under a deed to William Crow, Jr., and William Crow and Mary Crow, his wife, William Crow, Jr. would have
( ) a one-third interest.
(x) a one-half interest.
( ) void because of ambiguity.

( ) quittee.

133. A perch or rod is a unit of land measuring
  (x) 16½ feet.
  ( ) 66 feet.
  ( ) 12 feet.
  ( ) 21½ feet.

134. Et Ux is an abbreviation for "et uxor" meaning
  ( ) and husband.
  ( ) and father.
  (x) and wife.
  ( ) parties of the second part.

135. A quarter section of land is
  ( ) 240 acres.
  (x) 160 acres.
  ( ) 440 acres.
  ( ) 250 acres.

136. That covenant which is construed to mean that the grantor covenants that he has the exact interest in the property that the deed purports is a
  ( ) covenant of further assurance.
  ( ) covenant of warranty.
  ( ) covenant of the right to convey.
  (x) covenant of seizin.

137. The addition of one's land by the gradual deposit of soil through natural causes is
  ( ) annulation.
  ( ) avulsion.
  (x) accretion.
  ( ) ademption.

138. The voluntary parting with the ownership of real property is
  ( ) adverse possession.
  (x) alienation.
  ( ) forfeiture.
  ( ) eminent domain.

139. That which gives the appearance of title, but is not title in fact is
  ( ) community property.
  ( ) redemption.
  (x) color of title.
  ( ) subordination.

140. A grantor limits his liability to the grantee to anyone claiming, by, from, through or under him, with a
  (x) special warranty deed.
  ( ) a quit claim deed.
  ( ) a general warranty deed.

141. Devise is a
  ( ) sum of money for real estate.
  (x) gift of real estate by will.

( ) method to obtain title without deed, in a court action.

142. Any interest in, or right to, land by third persons, adversely affecting the value of the property is an
  (x) encumbrance.
  ( ) encroachment.
  ( ) appurtenance.
  ( ) escrow.

143. The most important element in a transfer of title is
  ( ) signing by owner.
  ( ) acknowledgment by owner.
  (x) delivery by owner.
  ( ) payment of the full consideration price.

144. Tender of deed is unnecessary where
  ( ) time is of the essence.
  ( ) date for performance has expired.
  ( ) comprehensive insurance policy has expired.
  (x) there is an anticipatory repudiation by buyer.

145. Limitations on the use and enjoyment of property are called
  ( ) remainders.
  ( ) hereditaments.
  ( ) tenements.
  ( ) reversions.
  (x) restrictions.

146. Which of the following would be held to be void and pass no title even in favor of an innocent purchaser?
  ( ) A quit claim deed.
  (x) A forged deed.
  ( ) A bargain and sale deed.
  ( ) A trustee's deed.

147. Under the early English common law, transfer of title to real property by delivery of possession was called
  (x) livery of seizin.
  ( ) adverse possession.
  ( ) chancery.
  ( ) laissez-faire.

148. Adams hands deed to Beal with the intent to pass title, but with an oral request not to record the deed until after Adams's death.
  ( ) Beal must comply or the deed will not be valid.
  (x) Valid delivery has occurred.
  ( ) Delivery will not occur until Adams's death.
  ( ) The deed is void.

149. Abstract of title is a
  ( ) contract for deed.
  (x) condensed history of the title.
  ( ) guarantee of title.
  ( ) rough painting of the property.

150. A quit claim deed may also be known as a
    ( ) special warranty deed.
    ( ) bargain and sale deed.
    ( ) reformation deed.
    (x) satisfaction claim deed.

151. The right to light and air accompanied by the transfer of title ownership to the land is called an
    ( ) alienable right.
    ( ) restriction.
    (x) appurtenance.
    ( ) easement.

152. It is the usual function of City Planning Commissions to pass upon
    ( ) new homes.
    ( ) new apartment buildings.
    ( ) new garages.
    (x) new subdivisions.

153. A zoning ordinance is a
    (x) restriction.
    ( ) easement.
    ( ) lien.
    ( ) appurtenance.

154. An area of land set off by local ordinance for a specific use is called
    ( ) a subdivision.
    (x) a zone.
    ( ) public improvement.
    ( ) cul de sac.

155. A freehold interest in land that is to end with the life of the grantee is known as
    ( ) an estate at will.
    ( ) an estate sufferance.
    (x) life estate.
    ( ) annuity.

156. Lines of meridian run
    ( ) east and west.
    ( ) any direction depending upon location of property.
    ( ) easterly or westerly from baselines.
    (x) north and south.

157. The column of townships running north and south is referred to as
    ( ) checks.
    (x) ranges.
    ( ) divisions.
    ( ) tracts.

158. A wall erected on a line between two adjoining properties belonging to two different persons is a
    ( ) share wall.
    (x) party wall.
    ( ) live wall.
    ( ) community wall.

159. Anything that is permanently fastened or attached to real estate is
( ) an attachment.
(x) real estate.
( ) personal property.
( ) a chattel.
160. A purchaser should obtain which one of the following to be sure there is no encroachment
( ) title insurance policy.
(x) survey.
( ) declaration of no set off certificate.
( ) each of the above.
161. An owner of land containing or bordering upon a stream, has rights to the water known as
( ) water rights.
(x) riparian rights.
( ) alluvion rights.
( ) allodial rights.
162. In a joint ownership, which one of the following unities is not present
( ) possession.
( ) time.
( ) title.
(x) location.
( ) interest.
163. A grantor limits his liability to the grantee of anyone claiming by, from, or through him, with a
(x) special warranty deed.
( ) general warranty deed.
( ) quit claim deed.
( ) unilateral deed.
164. In numbering a township, section 6 is always on the
( ) northeast corner.
( ) southeast corner.
(x) northwest corner.
( ) southwest corner.
165. If a municipality wishes to obtain title to property from an owner unwilling to sell, it can proceed by
(x) right of eminent domain.
( ) attachment proceedings.
( ) action to quiet title.
( ) adverse possession.
166. Words of conveyance are essential in the
( ) listing contract.
( ) agreement of sale.
(x) deed.
( ) bill of sale.
167. The S ½ of the SE ¼ of the NW ¼ of a section contains
(x) 20 acres.

( ) 40 acres.
( ) 80 acres.
( ) 160 acres.

168. When speaking of "improvements" regarding real estate, we mean
( ) fences, wells, monuments, drains, etc.
( ) additions to the original house.
(x) everything except the land.

169. Partners usually own real property as
( ) tenants by the entireties.
( ) joint tenants.
(x) tenants in common.
( ) tenants in severalty.

170. Owner of an undivided interest in land with no right of survivorship owns it as
(x) tenant in common.
( ) joint tenant.
( ) tenant in futuro.
( ) none of these.

171. Zone R-1 is restricted to
( ) refrigeration plant or the like.
( ) rolling mill plant or the like.
(x) single family homes.
( ) hospital or school.

172. An example of involuntary alienation is where title to real estate passes by
( ) quit claim deed.
( ) trustee deed.
( ) grant deed.
(x) sheriff's deed.

173. Which of these may not be considered an appurtenance
(x) bar.
( ) garage.
( ) orchard.
( ) Revolutionary chestnut tree.

174. A light company lays and maintains concealed electric along an agreed-upon line with owner. It does so by right of
( ) eminent domain.
( ) condemnation.
(x) an easement.
( ) a sub-surface appurtenance.

175. The greatest ownership of land in law is
(x) fee simple estate.
( ) reversionary estate.
( ) life estate.
( ) base fee.

176. Which of the following is usually paid by the buyer
(x) recording the deed.

( ) acknowledgment to the deed.
( ) cost for preparing deed.
177. Ownership by an individual is ownership in
(x) severalty.
( ) joint tenancy.
( ) inchoate.
( ) severance.
178. The summary of the most important parts of all instruments comprising the record title of the seller, arranged in chronological order is known as
( ) indenture.
(x) abstract of title.
( ) certificate of title.
( ) history of title.
179. Where property is acquired by Marie Davis, a single woman, and later conveys it after her marriage to John Saxman, she should sign the deed
( ) Mrs. John Saxman.
(x) Marie Davis Saxman.
( ) Marie Saxman, nee Marie Davis.
( ) Marie Davis.
180. Where a conveyance is to Patti Sims, unmarried, and Alfred Sims and Elsie Sims, his wife, Patti will own
( ) one-third of the property as a tenant in common.
(x) one-half of the property as a tenant in common.
( ) the property as a joint tenant with Alfred and Elsie.
181. Personal properties such as furniture or appliances are called
(x) chattels.
( ) incorporeal hereditaments.
( ) fixtures.
( ) realties.
182. Words of conveyance is an essential element in a (an)
( ) bill of sale.
(x) deed.
( ) contract of sale.
( ) exclusive listing contract.
183. The party responsible for payment of the title closing costs is determined by
(x) agreement of the parties.
( ) broker.
( ) title officer.
( ) local Real Estate Board.
184. A law which prohibits certain legal actions from taking place during a period of emergency is called
( ) statute of limitations.
( ) bill of rights.
( ) declaration relief.

(x) moratorium.
185. Trust deeds are used to
    ( ) transfer stock certificates to a seller.
    ( ) protect sub-contractors.
    (x) borrow money.
    ( ) transfer property from one co-owner to another co-owner.
186. Delinquent taxes are considered to be
    ( ) easements.
    ( ) personalty.
    (x) liens.
    ( ) attachments.
187. The dominant tenement is the property
    ( ) upon which the burden is imposed.
    (x) in whose favor the burden is created.
    ( ) the top story in an apartment building.
    ( ) owned by a person having the largest interest.

Chapter 4

THE FINANCING OF REAL ESTATE

The term "money market" is sometimes used in referring to those institutions whose function it is to make available money and credit to borrowers. The whole business structure of the United States is based upon the assumption that credit will be available to those who need it and can show the ability and willingness to repay.

The money market

At any one time various segments of our economy are competing for the investor's dollar. The investors on the other hand are competing with each other to obtain the best investments at the most favorable rates.

The investor gives up the privilege of spending his money when he lends it to another. In return for giving up the money and privilege of spending it, he exacts a promise from the borrower to repay it at a future time. He also requires that the borrower pay a certain amount for the use of the money. This is called interest. It is really rent for the use of the money.

The rate of interest which investors ask and get is determined by many complex economic factors. One of the most important of these factors is the availability of lendable funds, and the current demand for and supply of "mortgage money." Another is the risk involved in making the loan. A third is the business outlook for the future. These are only a few of the economic forces which determine the rate of interest in general and in a specific locality.

The supply of money through our banking system is controlled to a great extent by the Federal Reserve System and the local banks. The funds available for investment in real estate, however, are made up principally from the savings of firms and individuals.

Banks, for instance, cannot use funds deposited by their customers in their checking accounts to make long-term loans on real estate. Only funds deposited in savings accounts are available for such use. Savings and loan institutions and insurance companies also lend funds which are really the savings of individuals. Since these institutions are lending the money of others, the Federal and state

government have required of them a high degree of responsibility
for the funds placed in their care.

What investments compete for these savings?

One of the basic principles of investment is that a person should
never put all of his savings in one type of investment. By diversify-
ing his investments, he is able to minimize the over-all risk of loss.
At any time an investor can put his money into government bonds,
corporate bonds, savings accounts, mortgages, land contracts, real
estate, savings and loan institutions, or into the preferred or common
stocks of several hundred corporations. The investor, therefore, has
before him at all times a wide range of investment media from which
to pick and choose according to his likes and dislikes.

Mortgages

Almost since the beginning of written history we have records of
a debtor pledging some property as security for a loan. If the debt
were not paid, the property pledged was taken over or sold to satisfy
the debt.

In real estate financing the borrower gives a note in which he
unconditionally promises to pay a certain amount of money. This is
the debt instrument that sets up the obligation of the debt. The borrower also gives to the creditor a mortgage which pledges certain
property as security for the loan. It is sometimes called a "dead
pledge" because as long as the debtor carries out his promises and
obligations the mortgage has no effect. However, if the borrower
defaults on any of his promises, the pledge "comes to life" and gives
the creditor the right to have the property seized and sold to satisfy
the debt. The mortgage, however, does not prevent the sale of the
real estate.

People often say they are "paying on a mortgage" but this is misleading because actually they are paying on the note.

Banks as money lenders

Banks have been a traditional source of loans on real estate. National Banks are restricted by law as to the amount which they may
lend on real estate, and as to the time limit of such loans. If the installment payments are sufficient to amortize the entire principal of
the loan within the period ending on the date of its maturity, banks
may lend up to 80% of the appraised value of the real estate at the
time the loan is made. The maximum term for a National Bank
mortgage is 25 years except in cases of F.H.A. or G.I. loans. The

total loans that the bank may hold on real estate may not exceed at the time of making the loan the unimpaired capital plus the unimpaired surplus of the bank or 70% of its time and savings deposits, whichever is greater. The large increase in time and savings deposits have made banks much more active in the field of real estate financing.

Savings and loan associations

The savings and loan associations originated as a cooperative attempt to help members of the organization finance their own homes. Members could subscribe to shares in the organization and make payments on these shares. When they had paid in a sufficient amount, they were allowed to borrow from the association. Dividends were paid on the funds invested in the organization. However, these dividends depended upon profits and were subject to wide fluctuations.

Over the years savings and loan associations have changed in character so that today they are thrift organizations catering to the small and medium sized investor. Although they specialize in home loans, there has been a trend to invest a portion of the assets in apartment house loans to secure a greater yield. Federal Savings and Loans can make commercial and apartment loans up to 36 per cent of their total loans. Not more than 18 per cent can be commercial loans. Groups of savings and loans are taking participations in larger loans. They no longer accept only the members' savings, nor do they now loan exclusively to members.

They were pioneers in the use of amortizing loans on homes. Years before other lending institutions used the amortizing loan, the savings and loan associations were advertising the advantages of such loans to both the borrower and the lender.

Savings and loans have grown to be the largest factor in single family home financing on a conventional basis. They account for almost 50 per cent of this type of financing. According to the Federal Home Loan Bank Board it was estimated 98.9 per cent of the total savings in these institutions were invested in mortgages as of April, 1968. The same source estimated savings and loans' outstanding commitments at the same time were approximately four billion dollars.

Life insurance companies

Life insurance companies are one of the largest sources of funds for real estate loans. Because of our increased population, longer life expectancy, group insurance as a fringe benefit in labor contracts, the life insurance companies have found themselves in possession of increasing amounts of funds and for longer periods of time.

The increase in assets of life insurance companies in this country have been nothing short of phenomenal. In 1920 total assets were less than $8 billion; in 1961 the assets were in excess of $141 billion. In recent years their assets have been increasing at a rate of about $8 billion per year.

An examination of the assets of these companies reveals that real estate mortgages make up their second largest investment. At the end of 1963 their mortgage portfolio was $50.5 billion or over 35% of their total investment. The only other larger investment was that in bonds which accounted for about 47% of total assets.

Almost all the loans on real estate by these firms are of the amortizing type. This means the borrower starts to pay back the loan at the end of the first month. The typical conventional loan at the present time is for 15 to 25 years depending on the age of the property. In some exceptional cases it may go to 30 years. Most of these companies will lend up to 75% of appraised valuation and in some cases, depending upon the laws of the state in which the company is chartered, may lend up to 80% of valuation.

In spite of the longer mortgage terms, mortgage loans actually have a life of 12 or 13 years. This means that yearly pay in and payoff of outstanding loans will be in excess of $3 billion; this amount must be reinvested each year. Insurance companies are faced with the problem of finding secure, and at the same time, profitable yielding investments. In the past ten years the percentage increase in investment in real estate mortgages has been greater than the gain for any other type investment in their portfolio.

The trend of life insurance company investments has been to favor the bond and direct placement type of loans in the past two or three years. Rate of return on these has been greater than that of mortgages.

Some of the major insurance companies have been taking an equity position in some of the larger loans they place on income producing type properties. Others are requiring a percentage of the rents over a specified minimum (overage). This is being done to give a greater over all yield. It also provides a hedge against inflation on a fixed rate, long term investment.

Mutual savings banks

Most mutual savings banks are in the eastern part of the United States. They were set up in many cases to promote thrift by encouraging people to invest. Originally they invested in mortgages in their own immediate geographic area. With the advent of FHA and VA loans they started to invest nation-wide.

Mutuals are fairly restricted to the type of investment they can make. However, according to the National Association of Mutual Savings Banks, approximately 84 per cent of the investments held by the mutuals in 1967 were in mortgages. There is a trend to limit out of state conventional mortgages to larger loans on income producing type properties where a better yield can be obtained.

The mutual savings banks are the smallest group of lending institutions. Their loans on real estate are less than those of the commercial banks but in some areas *they are quite active in the loan field*.

They are not true banks because they do not offer checking facilities. They take the savings of individuals and invest them for the depositors. The profits obtained on these investments are then returned in the form of dividends.

Pension funds

Various pension funds, public and private, are showing real interest in mortgages as investment. This was particularly true in the insured or guaranteed loan field. Recently some have taken larger loans on hotels, apartments and shopping centers. At the end of 1945, pension funds had assets of a little over $2 billion. By the end of 1964 these assets had increased to approximately $44 billion and it is estimated to be almost double that today.

Some pension funds have shown interest in equity positions.

Private lenders

Many people with funds to invest are willing to loan on real estate. They feel that real estate is more desirable than other investments because it is possible to see the property which is pledged as security for the loan. To others land seems more secure because it will not depreciate or be destroyed by many common hazards.

Individuals will often loan on real estate on which institutional lenders will not or cannot legally lend. Thus private money sometimes fills a need for loans which would not otherwise be made. Many such loans entail more than average risk and therefore carry a higher interest rate than those made by institutional lenders. Individuals may also be willing to make short-term loans which ordinary lenders would not consider because of the cost of placing the loan.

Loans made by individuals, however, comprise only a small segment of all loans. But they help to round out the loan market and fill in gaps left by the organized lenders. Vital as this is, they do not actively compete with the institutional lenders.

Responsibility of institutional lenders

Institutional lenders are actually lending other people's savings. Because of this, laws controlling such institutions require of them a high degree of responsibility and business judgment. They also have certain responsibilities to the borrower and to the public.

In their fiduciary capacity they must see that the loans they make are economically sound and that there is adequate security in the property covered by the mortgage. From the standpoint of the borrower they must see that he is obtaining property which fills his needs and that the schedule of payments is such that he will be able to make them without undue hardship. If there is a default the borrower may lose all of the equity he has built up in the property. In medium and low income classes the home usually constitutes the only savings a family has other than Social Security. Therefore, a lending institution has a double responsibility to see that the loans which are made are economically sound for both the lender and the borrower.

G.I. loans

Loans which are guaranteed by the Veterans Administration under the Servicemen's Readjustment Act of 1944 are usually called G.I. Loans. Under this act each honorably discharged veteran of World War II and the Korean War is entitled to receive a guaranteed loan if he can qualify.

Under the amended act of May, 1968, each eligible veteran has an aggregate entitlement of $12,500.00 for loan purposes. Once this entitlement is used, he is not eligible for further benefits.

The loans under this act are made by regular institutional lenders and the veteran must apply to such a lender for a loan. The government does not furnish funds for the loan. Nor does the government guarantee all of the loan—only 60 per cent with a maximum of $12,500 of the loss on home loans. In cases of default where the property is sold but does not yield the unpaid balance of the loan, the Veterans Administration will pay in cash the guaranteed percentage of the loss to the lending institution. It may elect to take title to the property and pay off the lender in full. However, the Veterans Administration can hold the veteran for the amount of loss incurred.

G.I. loans originally had a statutory interest rate ceiling of 6 per cent. The amended act of 1968 removed this ceiling and authorized the Secretary of HUD in consultation with the Administrator of Veterans Affairs to establish a rate "to meet the mortgage market." This authority expires October 1, 1969. A "Commission to Study Mortgage Credit and Interest Rates" was established. This commission is to report by April 1, 1969. This will allow Congress and the President to consider what action is needed prior to October 1, 1969 when the authorization for the increased interest rate for both VA and FHA loans will expire.

The Commission is to report and make recommendations on three basic questions:

1. Necessity for statutory or legislative controls on guaranteed or insured loan interest rates.
2. The levels of such interest rates.
3. Ways to assure availability of mortgage credit.

The VA and FHA regulations were amended and the interest rate for both types of loans was increased to 6¾ per cent effective May 7, 1968.

Under the original law the selling price of a property for purchase through a G.I. loan could not exceed the appraised value as established by the VA. The provision in the law was inserted to protect the veteran buying a property that was not worth the selling price. In practice this meant that at times the veteran could not buy the house of his choice because of a difference in sales price and the "Reasonable Value" as set by the VA appraiser.

Public Law 90-301, effective May 7, 1968, changed this. The change applies only to property to be occupied by the veteran as his home. It does not change the value requirement for business or farm real estate (non-residence) transactions.

The VA will now guarantee loans even if the purchase price exceeds the reasonable value determination, provided:

a. The amount of the loan does not exceed the reasonable value.
b. The veteran must pay in cash the difference between purchase price and reasonable value plus the closing costs properly chargeable to, and to be paid by, the borrower.
c. The veteran must sign a certification acknowledging that he understands the purchase price is higher than the determined value and that he will pay excess in cash out of his own resources.

In some areas private lenders are unwilling to make loans under the VA loan program. In such cases the Veterans Administration is authorized to make direct loans for a limited time and under certain fund limitations: that is, the veteran must not have used up any of his entitlement, the loan must not exceed $17,500 and the loan must be for a dwelling to be used as a home or for the construction or improvement of a farm house. Of course, the veteran must qualify in other ways such as being a good credit risk.

The fact that a veteran has a G.I. loan on his property does not restrict the sale of the property to another any more than would a conventional mortgage. However, the sale of the property does not relieve the veteran of his responsibility on the note. He is responsible on the note until it is eventually paid off. If the non-veteran buyer takes the property "subject to the mortgage," the buyer recognizes the mortgage but he is not liable for the payment. If it is foreclosed, he will lose his equity in the property but is not liable on the note. If the buyer "assumes" the mortgage, then he takes the responsibility of paying the note. If he defaults, the veteran is also liable on the note. In a case where the veteran is forced to pay the balance of the debt, he has the right to sue the buyer for the amount he had to pay on the note.

A World War II veteran's entitlement will expire ten years from the date of discharge plus an additional period equal to one year for each three months of active duty performed by the veteran in World War II except that the entitlement shall not continue in any case after July 25, 1970.

The same formula is in effect for Korean conflict veterans except that entitlement shall not continue in any case after January 31, 1975.

The Home Owners' Loan Corporation

In 1933, the Home Owners' Loan Corporation was authorized to help in refinancing loans which were in default. At this time, many of the loans on homes were in default. In the year 1933, the typical home owner who had a mortgage on the property was two years delinquent on mortgage payments and three years delinquent on taxes. Home foreclosures were filed at a rate of almost 1,000 per day.

The Home Owners' Loan Corporation was set up to "bail out" both the home owners and the lending institutions who had made the loans. However, the H.O.L.C. did not insure the loans for lending institutions.

The Federal Housing Administration loans

In 1934, the Federal Housing Administration was formed with the idea of insuring the loans of lenders so that they would be more willing to lend to home owners. There are several parts or titles to the original act but the section of most interest to real estate people is Title II which makes provisions for insuring loans on one- to four-family dwellings, and Title I loans which are for improvement and repairs. The F.H.A. sets up the requirements which the borrower and the property must meet before the loan will be insured.

In general the standards of F.H.A. are rather high. They have devised a pattern of rating risks that attempts to evaluate all the factors that affect the property, including the qualifications and credit of the buyer. They have also been leaders in the attempt to standardize appraising procedures.

A lending institution, in order to qualify for making insured loans, must be a corporation with total assets in excess of $100,000. It must also file an application and be accepted by the F.H.A. as a qualified lender. The fact that a lending institution has qualified for making insured loans does not mean that all the loans it makes are insured. It can make insured loans or conventional loans as it sees fit. The advantage to the lender of making insured loans is that the risk involved decreases; but because the interest rate decreases with the lesser risk, the lender will receive a lower rate of interest.

The same regulations that permitted an increase in V.A. loans applies to F.H.A. loans. Effective May 7, 1968, the interest rate for F.H.A. insured Title II home loans was set at 6¾ per cent. The borrower must also pay for the insurance of the loan at a rate of ½ per cent per year on the unpaid balance of the loan. Since the loan is also a budget loan, he must pay each month an amount equal to one-twelfth of the taxes, fire insurance, assessments and other charges which there may be accruing against the property.

The Housing Act of 1965 entitles all veterans with 90 days' service, including peacetime service to qualify for an F.H.A. loan up to $15,000 with no down payment. However, the veteran will have to pay $200 which can be applied to initial payment for taxes, hazard insurance, and F.H.A. mortgage insurance premium. The act also provides for lower down payments to veterans on higher priced homes. The top mortgage is $30,000. Veterans who have received home loan benefits under the G.I. bill do not qualify for this special F.H.A. loan.

Qualifying for an F.H.A. loan

A home buyer may choose any approved lending institution in applying for a loan, and file his application on the approved F.H.A. forms. On these forms he gives a description of the property. He also outlines his financial status and gives a short personal history and an employment record unless he is self-employed.

The lending institution will then examine the application to see whether to submit it to the F.H.A. for approval. The lending institution, having made many such loans, can judge quite accurately the chances the potential borrower has of having his loan approved. If the lender feels that the loan will be approved, the application is forwarded to the regional F.H.A. office. The F.H.A. will then examine the application, appraise the property, and apply the mortgage pattern for the area. If the application meets the requirements for insurance, a Commitment for Insurance is issued. When this is received by the lending institution, the loan is made.

Some lending firms do not originate F.H.A. loans but prefer to purchase mortgages which have been made by other institutions. This buying of mortgages by a firm which did not originate them is known as the secondary mortgage market. If there is an active demand for loans, the originating firm can liquidate some of its loans and in this way have available funds for further lending. Without the secondary mortgage market, lending firms would have to wait to make further loans until collections or additional investments were made when they had loaned out the total of available funds.

In many cases, the originating firm in selling its mortgages to another firm continues to collect the payments on the mortgage and is paid a small fee for this service. This is an advantage to both because the originating firm has the history of the borrower and often knows local conditions better than the secondary firm. It relieves the buying firm of the detail work of collection. The secondary firm can also buy large blocks of mortgages without the cost of originating the loans.

During the period it has been in operation, the F.H.A. has foreclosed on only about 1 per cent of the real estate on which insured mortgages were placed. The loss to the insuring corporation has been only a small fraction of 1 per cent. This indicates that the lending practices outlined by the F.H.A. are sound.

It is generally felt that the F.H.A. has stabilized the lending market. By its standardization of procedure and consideration of the credit of the buyer as well as the security offered by the property, it has strengthened the whole mortgage market. The higher loan ratio under this program has reduced junior financing a great deal. The overall effect has also been to reduce interest rates and to make the amortizing mortgage a standard lending instrument.

Conventional loans

A conventional loan is one that is neither guaranteed nor insured. Several years ago such loans would have been non-amortizing and would have had maturities from three to five years. Today, due to the changes brought about by F.H.A. and V.A. practices, the typical conventional loan is also an amortizing loan. For the most part, conventional loans carry a slightly higher interest rate and the maturities are shorter than the F.H.A. and G.I. loans.

Conventional loans are made by lending institutions and by individuals as well. The interest rates charged are determined by local market conditions and by the risk involved. As indicated earlier in this chapter, individuals often make real estate loans on property which lending institutions cannot or will not make. In some cases the loan is really a form of credit loan because the property pledged does not have a ready market. Such loans often carry a relatively high interest rate due to the extra risk involved. On the other hand, loans made on new construction may be competitive with insured and guaranteed loans.

Private mortgage insurance corporations

The laws of most states permit lending institutions to lend above the statutory ratio of loan to value if the excess is insured by an acceptable insuring agency. The amount of this excess is usually 10 per cent to 15 per cent of the loan. The main purpose of this insurance is to supply additional security to financial institutions seeking higher yields from investments through mortgage loans of maximum loan-to-value ratios.

First in this private field was Mortgage Guaranty Insurance Corporation, known as MGIC. Others have since entered the field.

Other financial instruments

The Land Sales Contract. One of the problems involved in selling real estate is to obtain a satisfactory down payment from a purchaser. The seller often wants to "cash out" his equity and the buyer does not have that amount of money. If the seller does not need the money, he may be willing to sell the property on a land sales contract, often called a land contract.

Under a land sales contract the seller retains title but gives up possession to the buyer. The purchaser continues to hold the property as long as he keeps up his payments on the contract. If he defaults, the seller may dispossess him because the title is still in the hands of the seller, and the purchaser has only an equitable interest in the property. This is really the purchase of real property on the installment plan. If the seller wishes to have additional funds, he can sell the land sales contract just as he could sell a mortgage. Since he is actually financing the deal himself he can "cash out," if he wishes to do so, by selling the instrument.

Land sales contract deals are often placed in escrow. The seller makes out the deed in the name of the buyer and gives it to the escrow agent. The agent will collect for the seller and when the final payment is made, will deliver the deed to the buyer. If the purchaser should default, the escrow agent will return the deed to the seller and he can evict the buyer.

The land sales contract is also used as a junior financing instrument. For example, a man has an existing mortgage on a house that he wishes to sell. The lending institution will not allow a second mortgage to be placed on the property and the prospective buyer cannot buy out the equity of the owner with his down payment. To illustrate, the sales price is $15,000 and the existing mortgage is $9,000 leaving $6,000 to finance. The prospective buyer has only $2,000 to pay down. Under the circumstances, the seller may be willing to take back a land sales contract for the remaining $4,000. This does not constitute a second mortgage on the property. The buyer then pays on the mortgage to the lending institution and to the seller on the land sales contract. In this way the sale can be made without violation of the first mortgage.

The Purchase Money Mortgage. Another way in which a seller may finance the sale of property is by means of a purchase money mortgage. The seller agrees to sell to a buyer for a stated price. The purchaser agrees to pay a certain amount down on the purchase price. The seller then agrees to take back a purchase money mortgage for the remainder of the sale price. For example, the selling price of a house was $12,000 but the buyer had only $5,000 to pay down. The seller agreed to take a purchase money mortgage for the difference of $7,000. This mortgage is the same as any real estate mortgage except that it was given in lieu of cash when the deal was closed. If there is no existing mortgage on the property, it is a first mortgage. In some states a holder of a purchase money mortgage will not be allowed to obtain a deficiency judgment in a foreclosure if the property does not bring enough at the foreclosure sale to cover the unpaid balance of the debt. In other states he has the same rights as any other mortgagee.

The importance of real estate financing

The old adage that "You cannot sell if you cannot finance" is very true in the field of real estate. Since the homes of individuals make up a very sizable portion of the total wealth of the United States, it is very important that sound lending practices be used by the lending institutions, and that the government through its controls over the money market sees to it that the mortgage market is kept flexible enough to serve the needs of the people in a rapidly changing economy. At the same time, controls and good judgment must be used to prevent excesses and a collapse of the mortgage market similar to that which occurred during the depression of the 1930's.

Pledges

In recent years the plan of using pledges with savings and loan associations to increase the loan amount over and above the amount of a permitted real estate mortgage has been used. Under this plan the lending institution combines two lending privileges.

First: The amount of mortgage it can lend based on its statutory regulation of ratio of loan to value.

Second: A loan on a savings account. The pledge is against this savings account.

In a typical case the seller will open a savings account. This account will be pledged against a loan to the buyer which is over and above the mortgage. The seller does receive dividends on his savings account. He cannot withdraw the full amount until the original mortgage is reduced to a certain amount.

There are many plans for pledged accounts. Two basic plans are:

1. Mortgage $8,000, pledged account $1,000, total borrowing $9,000. The total amount is paid off at a level monthly payment rate. Under this plan, $100 will be released from the pledged account for each $200 paid off on the mortgage.

2. A plan for accelerated pay-off of the pledged account. In the case of an $8,000 mortgage and $1,000 pledge the mortgage will be amortized by a level monthly payment over a period of 20 or 25 years. The $1,000 will be paid off in 3 years or 5 years. The pledged account may be withdrawn after the three- or five-year period and the monthly payments of the borrower would be reduced accordingly.

Most lending institutions agree to notify the pledgee if there is a default on the mortgage so he can step in to protect his interest.

Discounts

V.A. and F.H.A. mortgage loan interest is determined by government regulation. In a case where interest is fixed, the yield is often not attractive enough to secure a ready market for funds. A good example of this is government bonds with interest rates below that which can be obtained from an insured savings account in either a bank or savings and loan association. These bonds do not have a ready market because of the fixed yields unless they are sold at a discount.

A rule of thumb used to determine yield on mortgages with an estimated life of 12 years is this: a four point or four per cent discount increases the yield of the mortgage approximately ½ of 1 per cent. Although most mortgages are for a longer term than 12 years, the average life of a loan is approximately 12 years. If you used a Prepayment Mortgage Yield Table based on a monthly payment mortgage for a term of 25 years and 6¾ per cent, you would get the following yields:

Price	Prepaid in			To Maturity
	8 yrs.	10 yrs.	12 yrs.	
95 (5% discount)	7.65	7.53	7.45	7.32
96 (4% discount)	7.46	7.37	7.31	7.20
97 (3% discount)	7.28	7.21	7.17	7.09
98 (2% discount)	7.10	7.05	7.03	6.97

Money is a commodity the same as anything else. When other commodities or investments, because of demand, command a higher price, discounts become prevalent to make the yields on mortgages competitive with other investment opportunities or securities.

Questions on the Financing of Real Estate

1. An authorized agent appointed by a lending institution to handle and process loans is usually described as
   ( ) a loan investigator.
   (x) mortgage correspondent.
   ( ) a loan correspondent.
2. A requirement of a borrower under a F.H.A. insured loan is that he
   (x) have cash for the down payment and closing costs.
   ( ) if married, have his wife sign as co-borrower.
   ( ) certify that he will occupy the premises.
3. Q. Does the appraisal by the VA determine the purchase price the veteran can pay for a house?
   A. No. An amendment effective May 7, 1968, changed the former law. The veteran must pay the difference in cash if the sales price exceeds the reasonable value.
4. Q. What procedure should you pursue if the appraisal value is less than contract price?
   A. Try to adjust the sales price to the VA value or pay difference in cash.
5. Q. Explain the term "Secondary Mortgage Market"—"Secondary Financing."
   A. Secondary mortgage market refers to the resale market of existing loans. This has no connection with the meaning of the term "Secondary financing" which refers to junior loans such as are made on second deeds of trust (mortgages) and the priority of such security on the loan is second to that of the senior first deed of trust (first mortgage).
6. Q. A real estate broker prepares an earnest money receipt wherein it is shown that cash has been received by the seller, when in fact, the said payment is represented by a note. The deal is to be F.H.A. financed. Does the broker have any liability in this connection?
   A. Yes; subject to a Federal criminal prosecution, with a penalty of $5,000 fine, up to 2 years imprisonment, or both.
7. Q. Does the F.H.A. permit secondary financing?
   A. No; at the closing the mortgagor certifies on the back of the F.H.A. commitment, that he will not have outstanding any other unpaid obligations contracted in connection with the mortgage transaction. An untruth constitutes a violation of the U.S. Criminal Code.
8. Q. In its relation to real property, what is the meaning of the term "amortization"?

A. The liquidation of a financial obligation on real property by payments at regular stated intervals, or on an instalment basis.

9. Q. What is the pre-payment penalty percentage rate governing F.H.A. guaranteed mortgages?
A. 1% of original mortgage.

10. Q. A broker accepts a deposit on a property and arranges for original F.H.A. financing. The appraisal does not come up to the prescribed amount. What should the broker do with the deposit money?
A. ( ) retain the deposit.
( ) deliver deposit to seller.
(x) return the deposit to buyer, if buyer demands it.
( ) reappraise the property at a higher value.
( ) substitute a new buyer.

11. Q. What does the term "money market" mean?
A. The money market is made up of those institutions whose function it is to supply money and credit to borrowers.

12. Q. To what extent is business dependent on the availability of loanable funds?
A. Our whole business structure is built upon the assumption that funds will be available to those who can show ability and willingness to repay their loans.

13. Q. How do investors and the lending institutions compete in the money market?
A. At any time the different parts of our economy that need loans are competing with each other for the available funds. On the other hand, the investors are competing with each other for the best investment and the most favorable rate of return.

14. Q. How are interest rates determined for different kinds of loans?
A. The interest rate at any time is the result of the different forces which are competing for the investor's money. Supply and demand have a great effect on the rate. The risk involved is also a determining factor. The final rate is the result of supply in relation to demand, the risk involved, the business outlook, and many more economic forces.

15. Q. How do the banks make loans on real estate?
A. Banks may loan out a certain percentage of the deposits which they have in the savings accounts of their customers. They cannot make real estate loans out of their checking deposits.

16. Q. Do banks create the credit with which to make real estate loans?
A. No. It is impossible for a bank or savings institution to create the credit. The funds loaned are the savings or investment of individuals or firms.

17. Q. How does an investor attempt to minimize the risks of investment?
A. By spreading his investments over different types of investments, he is able to decrease the overall risk of investment.

18. Q. What is a mortgage?
   A. A mortgage is an instrument by which the owner of certain property pledges it as security for a loan.
19. Q. Is a mortgage a debt instrument?
   A. No. It is only the instrument that pledges the property as security for the loan. The debt instrument is the note or bond signed by the borrower. Although both the note and the mortgage could be combined in one instrument, they are usually separate.
20. Q. Explain what is meant when the mortgage is called a "dead pledge."
   A. As long as the borrower makes his payments and fulfills all that he agreed to do in the mortgage, the instrument has no effect; it is inoperative. Only when the borrower fails to keep his promises or make proper payments does the mortgage "come alive" and make it possible for the creditor to seize the property.
21. Q. What do people mean when they say they are "paying on a mortgage"?
   A. They mean that they are paying on a note or bond which is secured by a mortgage on their property.
22. Q. Does a mortgage on a piece of real estate prevent the owner from selling it?
   A. No. The owner may sell the property whenever he wishes but he would still be responsible for the unpaid balance of the note he has signed. The buyer of the property would also have the mortgage as a lien against the property and in case of a foreclosure, he might lose his equity.
23. Q. What restrictions are placed on national banks as to their lending on real estate?
   A. National banks may lend only up to 80 per cent of the appraised value of real estate. They also may not make loans for a longer period than 25 years. These limitations do not apply to F.H.A. or G.I. loans but only to conventional loans.
24. Q. What percentage of total assets of a national bank could be loaned on real estate?
   A. A national bank may not hold loans on real estate in excess of 70 per cent of its time or savings deposits.
25. Q. How do savings and loan associations differ from banks?
   A. Savings and loan associations are unlike banks in that the funds deposited with them are not subject to check. They merely take the deposits of customers and loan them out. Although funds deposited with a savings and loan association can be withdrawn, the funds are not withdrawn by check as are bank funds.
26. Q. How have savings and loan associations helped to encourage the use of amortizing loans?
   A. The savings and loan associations were pioneers in the use of the amortizing loan. They were the first to point out the advantages of such loans to both borrower and lender.

27. Q. Why have savings and loan associations had such a growth in recent years?

A. The savings of the average family in the United States have increased a great deal in recent years and the savings and loan associations have catered to the small investor. They have encouraged thrift by taking very small deposits. As a result, many families have chosen these institutions in which to invest their savings.

28. Q. Why are life insurance companies one of the leading sources of mortgage loan money?

A. In recent years more and more life insurance has been purchased by the typical family. The life span of the average person has also been materially extended in the past twenty years. As a result of these two factors, the insurance companies have had an ever-increasing amount of funds to invest and real estate loans constitute their second largest investment—about 35% of the total investment.

29. Q. What type of real estate loans do the insurance companies make?

A. Insurance companies make practically all types of real estate loans to individuals. They make the three most common types: F.H.A., G.I., and conventional loans. Almost all of these loans call for the complete amortization of the loan over the loan period.

30. Q. Why is it said that insurance companies have a kind of "revolving fund" out of which to make loans?

A. Most of the loans made are amortizing and as a result the borrowers start to repay the loan at the end of the first month and make payments each month until the debt is repaid. This creates a stream of repayments flowing back to the company and these funds must be reinvested.

31. Q. How are mutual savings banks unlike commercial banks?

A. Mutual savings banks are savings institutions and do not offer checking facilities as do commercial banks.

32. Q. Are mutual savings banks one of the principal sources of real estate loans?

A. Mutual savings banks are becoming more active in mortgage lending. If there is one in your area, it is probably quite active in real estate financing.

33. Q. Why are private individuals often willing to make loans on real estate?

A. Many people feel that real estate loans are more secure than are other similar investments. They also can see the property which is mortgaged as security for the loan and make their own decisions as to the quality and value of it. Land will not wear out or be destroyed by many common hazards.

34. Q. Explain why private loans on real estate often carry higher interest rates than loans made by institutional lenders.

A. Private lenders are often willing to accept loans which institutional lenders will not make. However, such loans are more risky and the lenders ask for and get a higher interest to pay them for the extra risk.

35. Q. What are some of the responsibilities of institutional lenders?
   A. Institutional lenders have greater responsibility than private lenders because they are lending the savings of others. Therefore, they are responsible for seeing that the loans are sound investments for the borrower as well as the lender. They also have a responsibility to the public to be sure that the loans they make are economically sound. They must require that adequate security is maintained throughout the life of the loan.

36. Q. What responsibility does the lending institution have toward the borrower?
   A. The lender should make sure that the loan meets the individual's needs, but at the same time is not so large that the payments are a burden on his available income.

37. Q. What are some of the responsibilities of an appraiser for a lending institution?
   A. The appraiser for a lending institution has a great deal of responsibility to both the lender and the borrower. His duty is to make a sound estimate of the loan value of the property under appraisal. Assigning too high or too low a value is not fair to either party involved. Therefore, an appraiser should use all the skills and techniques available as well as good sound judgment in arriving at a loan value of a property.

38. Q. What is meant by the statement that a G.I. loan is guaranteed?
   A. A lending institution makes a loan to a qualified veteran. In the event the loan is not paid off the Veterans Administration will guarantee a certain amount of the loan.

39. Q. For what purposes may a veteran get a loan?
   A. To buy or build a home. To buy a farm and equipment or to purchase a business.

40. Q. Can a commission fee be charged a veteran for obtaining a G.I. loan?
   A. No commission may be charged the veteran although the lender may charge the borrower reasonable closing costs. The lender may also charge a reasonable flat charge for originating the loan.

41. Q. Who may have a loan guaranteed under the G.I. act?
   A. Any veteran who served at any time between September 16, 1940 and July 25, 1947, and was honorably discharged after at least 90 days' active service, or if he had a service-incurred disability in less than 90 days. Under an Act of Congress dated July 16, 1952, similar benefits were extended to veterans who derived entitlement from active service on or after June 27, 1950, and may be used until February 1, 1965.

42. Q. What is meant by an entitlement?

    A. The rights of a veteran to mortgage loan benefits.

43. Q. Would a widow of a veteran be eligible for a loan?
    A. An unmarried widow of a veteran who was eligible but who did not use his entitlement would be eligible for a loan.

44. Q. Are children of a deceased veteran eligible?
    A. No, only the unmarried widows.

45. Q. In a case where both man and wife are eligible, may they buy property together and in this way increase the amount which may be guaranteed?
    A. Guarantee may not exceed 60% with a maximum of $12,500 on a home loan or 50% with a maximum of $2,000 on a non-real estate loan.

46. Q. May a veteran join with a non-veteran in obtaining a loan?
    A. Yes, but the guaranteed part only applies to that share of the loan belonging to the veteran and does not guarantee any part of the non-veteran's loan.

47. Q. How much can a veteran borrow and still have the loan guaranteed?
    A. There is no limit of how much of a loan may be made by a lending institution to a veteran. However, real estate loans for home purposes are guaranteed only up to a maximum of $12,500. Real estate loans for farms or business purposes may be guaranteed only to a maximum of $4,000.

48. Q. For how long a period of time may a G.I. home loan be made and still be guaranteed?
    A. For any period up to 30 years.

49. Q. Can a G.I. get a longer term of years on a farm loan than a home loan?
    A. Yes, he may get a farm loan for any period up to 40 years.

50. Q. For how long can a G.I. get a guaranteed loan to go into business?
    A. Such loans can be made up to ten years unless real estate is involved.

51. Q. Can a G.I. use his full entitlement for each of the three types of loans?
    A. No, he can use his entitlement only once.

52. Q. May a veteran obtain a loan in one state to buy real estate in another state?
    A. Yes. However, most lenders will not make a loan if the funds are to be used in another state.

53. Q. Could a veteran obtain a G.I. loan to be used in a foreign country?
    A. No. The property which is security for the loan must be located in the United States, its territories, or possessions.

54. Q. May a veteran qualify for a loan while attending school and receiving educational benefits?
    A. Yes, if he can qualify with the lending institution.

55. Q. Could a veteran obtain a loan to buy a farm or business which he intends to operate on a part-time basis?

   A. Yes, if the lending institution is willing to make the loan.

56. Q. What circumstances gave rise to the formation of the Home Owners' Loan Corporation?

   A. The Home Owners' Loan Corporation was formed to refinance real estate loans which were in distress during the depression. The government felt that the refinancing of these loans would not only aid the home owners but also the lending institutions who held the mortgages.

57. Q. How widespread were defaults on home mortgages during the depression?

   A. It has been estimated that as much as 80 per cent of the home loans were in trouble at some time during the depression.

58. Q. In what way was the Home Owners' Loan Corporation related to the Federal Housing Administration?

   A. The Home Owners' Loan Corporation was set up to refinance existing loans on real estate. The function of the F.H.A. was to encourage the lending of money to home owners by insuring the loans made by the lending institutions.

59. Q. What parts of the F.H.A. Act are of the most interest to home owners or those who are interested in home ownership?

   A. Title I of the law makes provision for insuring loans to home owners for the improvement or repair of existing buildings. Title II is concerned with the insuring of loans made by qualified lenders on one- to four-family dwellings.

60. Q. How high are the standards set by the F.H.A. for insuring loans?

   A. In general the standards set by the F.H.A. are quite high. Not only must the property qualify but also the credit rating of the borrower is investigated and approved before the loan is accepted for insurance.

61. Q. Name some of the accomplishments of the Federal Housing Administration.

   A. The F.H.A. has made the amortizing loan the standard procedure on home loans. It has standardized appraising processes. It has also been instrumental in raising the construction standards, and in better planning and land utilization. The second mortgage has almost disappeared due to the high loan-to-value ratio made possible by insured loans. The mortgage market has also been extended and stabilized by the F.H.A.

62. Q. How does a lending institution become approved for making F.H.A. insured loans?

   A. The lending institution must apply to the F.H.A. for approval and answer certain questions about the firm and its practices. It must also be a corporation with assets in excess of $100,000.

63. Q. Must all loans made by an approved lending institution be F.H.A. insured loans?

A. An approved lending institution has merely qualified to make insured loans but it may make as many conventional or G.I. loans
as it wishes.

64. Q. How does the insuring of loans benefit the lending institution?
    A. The insuring of loans reduces the risk of the lending firm. This
    makes it possible for the lenders to make a higher percentage
    loan and to make longer maturity loans than would otherwise be
    possible.

65. Q. Does the government pay the cost of the insurance on F.H.A.
    loans?
    A. No. The borrower pays for the cost of the insurance at a rate of
    $\frac{1}{2}$ per cent of the unpaid balance of the loan.

66. Q. What is meant by a budget loan?
    A. A budget loan is one in which the monthly payments made by
    the borrower not only cover interest and a payment on the prin-
    cipal, but also one-twelfth of such expenses as taxes, insurance,
    assessments and other charges against the property. The lend-
    ing firm keeps these payments in a reserve account and pays the
    charges as they become due.

67. Q. If an F.H.A. insured loan is defaulted does the lending institu-
    tion receive cash for the unpaid balance of the loan?
    A. No. The lender is paid in debenture bonds of the insuring com-
    pany. These bonds carry an interest rate that is changed from
    time to time depending upon the date of the loan and the money
    market. On January 1, 1968, the debenture rate was raised from
    $4\frac{3}{4}$ per cent to $5\frac{3}{8}$ per cent. It has been much lower at times.

68. Q. How does a prospective home buyer choose a lending institution
    from which to obtain a loan?
    A. The buyer may choose any local institution which is qualified to
    make F.H.A. loans. This is just a matter of personal choice.

69. Q. What is the procedure for applying for an F.H.A. loan?
    A. The borrower chooses an approved lender and fills out the F.H.A.
    forms, and indicates the location of the property to be purchased.
    He also gives information as to his financial condition and a short
    history of his employment.

70. Q. What is the procedure after the application for an F.H.A. loan is
    filed?
    A. The lending institution will look over the application to see if it
    is complete and also to appraise the possibility of having the
    loan approved. If it is satisfactory it will be sent to a regional
    F.H.A. office.

71. Q. Could an approved lender purchase F.H.A. mortgages from other
    firms rather than originate the loans?
    A. Yes. A firm could purchase insured mortgages rather than make
    the loans if it prefers to do so.

72. Q. What is the secondary mortgage market?

A. The secondary mortgage market is made up of those firms who buy mortgages from the firms who originate them.

73. Q. How does the government participate in this secondary mortgage market?

A. The Federal National Mortgage Association was authorized by Congress in 1938. It was formed to provide a secondary market for insured mortgages. It is known as "Fanny May" and has the power to buy insured mortgages from lenders who need additional funds to make further loans.

74. Q. What is a conventional loan?

A. A conventional loan is any loan which is not insured or guaranteed by a governmental agency.

75. Q. How do conventional loans compare with insured and guaranteed loans as to interest rates and length of maturity?

A. Conventional loans usually have about ½ per cent to 1 per cent higher interest rates and shorter maturities than comparable insured and guaranteed loans.

76. Q. Can a lending institution refuse to make F.H.A. loans if it has funds available for loans?

A. Yes. A lending institution may refuse to make F.H.A. loans if it wishes to do so.

77. Q. What is a land sales contract, also known as a land contract?

A. The prospective purchaser of a piece of property enters into a contract with the owner of the property, whereby he agrees to purchase the property at a stated price and the owner agrees to sell. The owner gives up possession to the buyer but does not give him the title until the final payment is made. Upon the final payment being made the owner gives the buyer a deed which completes the transfer.

78. Q. What rights would a seller under a land sales contract have in case the buyer defaulted on his payments?

A. He may dispossess the buyer and recover possession of the property. The contract usually has a clause that states that in case the owner repossesses the property all of the payments made by the buyer shall be considered rent for the period of time he was in possession.

79. Q. To what extent is the owner financing the deal under a land sales contract?

A. The owner is actually financing all of the deal except for the down payment which the purchaser makes when he first takes possession of the property.

80. Q. Could a land sales contract be used to finance a deal where the buyer is assuming a mortgage but does not have enough cash to buy out the owner's equity?

A. Land sales contracts are often used where the buyer is assuming a mortgage which states that a second lien cannot be placed on the property, yet the purchaser does not have enough cash to buy

the equity of the owner. The seller takes back a land sales contract for the difference between the selling price and the down
payment and the mortgage is assumed by the buyer. If the owner
wishes to "cash out," he can sell the land sales contract.

81. Q. Under what circumstances is a purchase money mortgage given?
    A. A purchase money mortgage is used where the seller of the prop-
       erty is willing to finance the deal for the buyer. The seller takes
       the down payment of the buyer in cash and takes a note and a
       purchase money mortgage for the remainder of the selling price.
       It is necessary for the purchaser to record the deed before the
       seller records the purchase money mortgage or it will appear on
       the records as if the buyer were mortgaging property which is
       recorded in the seller's name.

82. Q. Are the rights of a mortgagee under a purchase money mortgage
       the same as under other mortgages?
    A. In many states the rights of the mortgagee of a purchase money
       mortgage are the same as any other. However, it would consti-
       tute a second lien if there were an existing mortgage on the
       property at the time of the sale. In other states the rights of the
       mortgagee are limited. The most common limitation is that in
       case of foreclosure where the property did not sell for enough
       to cover the unpaid balance of the purchase money mortgage,
       the holder of the mortgage could not get a deficiency judgment
       on the remainder.

83. Q. Do purchase money mortgages carry about the same interest
       rates as other mortgages?
    A. The interest rates on all mortgages vary with the risk involved;
       this also applies to purchase money mortgages. Since such mort-
       gages are often used to finance deals which would not be ac-
       cepted by institutional lenders the rates may be somewhat
       higher.

84. Q. Why do lending agencies usually prefer a conventional mort-
       gage over a V.A. mortgage?
    A. Because the interest returns are higher.

85. Q. Can a purchaser from a veteran assume the existing mortgage?
    A. Yes.

86. Q. What is the difference between a conventional loan, an F.H.A.
       loan and a G.I. loan?
    A. In a conventional loan, the mortgagee deals on its own and is not
       protected in any way by any government agency. In an F.H.A.,
       the lending institution, the government (F.H.A.), reduces the
       risk of the lending firm. In a G.I. loan, if the loan is not paid, the
       V.A. will guarantee a certain amount of the loan. The money in
       each case is loaned by the lending institution.

87. Q. What are the two basic reasons for discount points?
    A. 1. To allow the lender to compensate for different risks.
       2. Attract money that would not otherwise be available at a
          fixed rate of interest.

True and False

1. The interest in or value of real estate in excess of mortgage indebtedness is called an equity.   **T** F
2. A V.A. loan is insured by the Federal Housing Administration.   T **F**
3. A borrower must make application to the local F.H.A. director for an F.H.A. loan.   T **F**
4. A private lender is prohibited from lending more than 80 per cent of the market value of the property.   T **F**
5. Building and loan associations generally lend only on conventional loans.   **T** F
6. The building and loan associations were the first to amortize mortgage loans.   **T** F
7. The mortgagee pays the costs of financing the loan.   T **F**
8. Loans made by building and loan associations may be paid off at any time without a penalty.   **T** F
9. The "money market" is made up only of banks who lend on real estate mortgages.   T **F**
10. The whole business structure of the country is based upon the assumption that responsible persons who have the ability and willingness to repay can borrow money.   **T** F
11. In normal times there is not much competition for the investor's dollar.   T **F**
12. At any time investors are competing with each other to obtain the best investment at the most favorable rates.   **T** F
13. Interest paid for the use of money could be thought of as rent for the use of the money.   **T** F
14. The interest rate which a lender can charge is usually fixed by the Federal Government.   T **F**
15. The rate of interest on mortgage money at any time is determined by many complex economic factors.   **T** F
16. The risk involved and the future business outlook does not materially affect the interest rate on mortgages.   T **F**
17. At any time the amount of money available in our banking system is controlled to a considerable extent by the Federal Reserve System.   **T** F
18. The funds which commercial banks use to lend on real estate come from the checking accounts of their depositors.   T **F**
19. Banks are allowed to make loans on real estate from the savings of individuals, which are deposited in the savings accounts.   **T** F
20. The funds which savings and loan associations use for real estate loans are the savings of individuals.   **T** F
21. Investors tend to put their savings into the same type of investment regardless of business conditions.   T **F**

22. Lending institutions that lend out the savings of individuals are held to a high degree of responsibility and business judgment. **T** F

23. One of the principles followed by investors is to diversify their investments by putting their savings into several types of investments in order to reduce the risk. **T** F

24. The making of loans to individuals backed by a mortgage on real estate as security has been in common use for only about 50 years. T **F**

25. A mortgage is a pledge instrument that gives the mortgagee the right to seize and sell the property in case of default. **T** F

26. A mortgage is a debt instrument. **T** **F**

27. A mortgage and a note might be incorporated into one instrument. **T** F

28. A mortgage gives the mortgagee certain rights in the real property of the mortgagor. **T** F

29. A mortgage could be called a dead pledge for it is inoperative as long as the owner of the property makes the payments and does not violate the covenants of the mortgage. **T** F

30. An owner of property who has a mortgage on it could not sell the property without paying off the debt. T **F**

31. If a buyer takes a piece of property "subject to" an existing mortgage, he would be liable for the debt as well as the original mortgagor. T **F**

32. A purchaser of a piece of property "assumed" an existing mortgage. He could be held responsible for the unpaid balance by the mortgagee. **T** F

33. When a piece of real estate is sold and the buyer assumes the mortgage, both the seller and the purchaser are liable on the unpaid balance of the mortgage. **T** F

34. National banks are allowed to lend up to 80% of the appraised value of a piece of real estate on a conventional loan. **T** F

35. National banks can make loans for only ten years or less on conventional loans. T **F**

36. Due to the legal restrictions placed upon national banks, they are quite conservative in their loan policies. **T** F

37. Savings and loan associations are much like banks because they offer checking services for their depositors. T **F**

38. The early savings and loan associations were conceived as a cooperative attempt to help members finance their homes. **T** F

39. Savings and loan associations still hold to the policy of making loans only to their own members. T **F**

40. The savings and loan associations were pioneers in the use of the monthly payment amortizing loan. **T** F

41. Savings and loan associations no longer encourage the small investor to deposit his savings with the firm because the cost of keeping the accounts is too great. T **F**

42. Savings and loan associations would be considered thrift organizations rather than banking institutions.   **T**   F

43. Most lending institutions feel that amortizing loans are beneficial to both lender and borrower.   **T**   F

44. Life insurance companies make only a small percentage of the real estate loans.   T   **F**

45. The assets of life insurance companies are increasing at an annual rate of about $8 billion per year.   **T**   F

46. Total assets of savings and loan associations are greater than those of life insurance companies.   T   **F**

47. Real estate mortgages make up the largest single type of investment held by insurance companies.   T   **F**

48. Most insured and guaranteed loans made by life insurance companies are for 25 years or longer.   **T**   F

49. Most insurance companies make both insured and conventional loans.   **T**   F

50. The present-day amortizing loans make it necessary for insurance companies to continually make loans in order to keep their funds earning interest.   **T**   F

51. In recent years insurance companies have not increased their investments in mortgages as much percentagewise as some of their other investments.   T   **F**

52. Mutual savings banks are the smallest group of lending institutions that make loans on real estate.   **T**   F

53. The mutual savings banks pioneered the use of the long-term amortizing loan.   T   **F**

54. The mutual savings banks are true banks because they accept checking deposits as well as savings used for loans.   T   **F**

55. People who have funds to loan are often more willing to lend it on real estate because they feel it is more secure than on many other investments.   **T**   F

56. Private lenders will seldom accept loans on real estate if institutional lenders have turned down the loan.   T   **F**

57. Loans made by private individuals are often at higher rates of interest than those made by institutions due to the extra risk involved.   **T**   F

58. Institutional lenders are held to a higher degree of responsibility than individuals because they are lending the savings of others.   **T**   F

59. Firms which make loans on real estate have little responsibility to the public because they represent only the investor.   T   **F**

60. Veterans of both World War I and II are eligible for G.I. loans.   T   **F**

61. Each eligible veteran has a total entitlement of $7,500 for home loan purposes.   T   **F**

62. G.I. loans are made by the Federal Government directly to the individual.   T   **F**

63. The government guarantees only 60% of a loan on a home.   **T**   F

64. G.I. loans cannot carry more than a 5¼% interest rate.   T **F**

65. The purchase price of a property on which a G.I. loan is
granted can be slightly higher than the appraised value of
the property.   **T** F

66. If a veteran defaults on a loan and the government must pay
some of the loss, he is indebted to the Veterans Administra-
tion for the amount of the loss.   **T** F

67. A non-veteran cannot purchase a property from a veteran
and assume the G.I. loan.   T **F**

68. In case of default and foreclosure on a G.I. loan, the Veterans Administration will pay in cash the guaranteed per-
centage of the loss to the lender.   **T** F

69. The unmarried widow of an eligible veteran who had not
used his entitlement would be eligible for a G.I. loan.   **T** F

70. A lender cannot charge a veteran closing costs on a loan even
though the costs appear to be reasonable.   T **F**

71. A veteran could obtain a G.I. loan to buy either a home or a
farm.   **T** F

72. A lending institution cannot refuse to give a veteran a loan
if the veteran has a certified entitlement.   T **F**

73. A veteran could get a G.I. loan to buy a duplex if he were
going to live in part of it.   **T** F

74. Only one entitlement is allowed even though both husband
and wife are veterans.   T **F**

75. The government is a lending agency.   T **F**

76. A lending institution may make G.I. loans for any period up
to 30 years.   **T** F

77. A veteran could not be receiving education benefits and obtain a G.I. loan at the same time.   T **F**

78. Veterans' loans are the budget type where each monthly payment includes payment on such things as insurance, taxes,
etc.   **T** F

79. A lending institution cannot require a down payment if the
veteran is buying a new house.   T **F**

80. The Home Owners' Loan Corporation was set up during the
depression to insure loans of individuals who wanted to build
or buy a home.   T **F**

81. The F.H.A. makes loans directly to home owners.   T **F**

82. Most home loans which are insured by the F.H.A. are made
under Title II of the Act.   **T** F

83. Title I provides for unsecured home improvement and re-
pair loans.   **T** F

84. The F.H.A. believes that the principal security for a loan is
in the property itself.   T **F**

85. The government pays the cost of insuring F.H.A. loans.   T **F**

86. F.H.A. loans are budget type loans in which each monthly
payment includes part payment of taxes, insurance, and other
such expenses.   **T** F

87. A borrower may choose any approved lending institution from which to obtain an F.H.A. loan. **T** F
88. Lending institutions cannot refuse to accept an application for an F.H.A. loan if they have available funds to loan. T **F**
89. The "Fanny May" organization was set up by the government to create a secondary mortgage market to which lending institutions could sell insured mortgages when they needed funds for additional loans. **T** F
90. The F.H.A. has been forced to foreclose on only about 1% of the real estate on which it has insured loans. **T** F
91. Individuals can make F.H.A. insured loans if they can prove they were competent lenders. T **F**
92. Conventional loans are made by both individuals and lending institutions. **T** F
93. A conventional loan could not be an amortizing loan. T **F**
94. The F.H.A. considers the credit rating of the individual as well as the security of the property when approving a loan to be insured. **T** F
95. Conventional loans usually carry a higher interest rate because they are not insured or guaranteed. **T** F
96. A conventional loan could not be a budget mortgage. T **F**
97. A land sales contract is just another type of mortgage. T **F**
98. Title to property financed by a land sales contract remains in the seller or in the hands of the escrow agent until the final payment is made. **T** F
99. The interest rate on land sales contracts is usually higher than on most mortgages. **T** F
100. The seller of a piece of property under a land sales contract could not sell the contract because the buyer of the property might object. T **F**
101. Land sales contracts are sometimes used to finance deals where the lender on the existing mortgage will not allow a second mortgage. **T** F
102. If a deal using a land sales contract is closed through escrow, the seller would give a deed to the escrow agent made out in the name of the buyer. **T** F
103. When a mortgage has been paid off, the mortgagor should have the mortgagee sign a satisfaction of the mortgage and record this in order to clear the title of the lien. **T** F
104. Most firms who make construction loans do it in order to obtain a "permanent" loan on the property when the building is completed. **T** F
105. A construction loan requires little supervision by the lender because the builder has agreed to build according to plans and specifications. T **F**
106. The ability of a broker to find adequate financing for his prospects is one of the most important factors in making sales. **T** F

107. The government by using its controls over the mortgage market should attempt to promote an orderly market and to prevent too much or too little available mortgage money.   **T**   F

108. If a note given in a mortgage transaction is later outlawed by the Statute of Limitations, it would also extinguish the mortgage.   **T**   F

109. Profit on the sale of real property which has been held six months or longer may be classified as a capital gain and maximum Federal Tax would be about 25 per cent.   **T**   F

110. Congress regulates the interest to be charged upon F.H.A. loans.   **T**   F

111. An F.H.A. mortgage gives the purchaser greater security as to construction than does a conventional mortgage.   **T**   F

112. Endowment funds may not be loaned out on individual mortgages.   T   **F**

113. A single mortgage can be part conventional and part F.H.A.   T   **F**

114. A mortgage is similar to a land purchase contract in that it permits the purchase of a property through periodic payments.   **T**   F

115. It is possible to procure a G.I. Loan to purchase livestock and equipment for a farm.   **T**   F

116. A residence subject to a lien resulting from a G.I. guaranteed loan may not be sold except to another qualified veteran.   T   **F**

117. The agency of the Federal Government which insures a V.A. loan is the Veterans Loan Association.   T   **F**

118. Under all circumstances an F.H.A. insured loan may be paid in full before maturity without the payment of a "bonus" charge.   T   **F**

119. The agency which insures an F.H.A. loan is the Home Owners' Loan Corporation.   T   **F**

Multiple Choice

1. The form of mortgage often used in mortgage financing is
   ( ) the blanket mortgage.
   (x) open-end mortgage.
   ( ) fixed term mortgage.
   ( ) acceleration mortgage.
2. The best way for the home owner to liquidate a mortgage debt is by
   ( ) employer's withholding part of salary.
   ( ) bank credit.
   (x) amortization.
   ( ) savings bank account set off.
3. Construction loans for apartment buildings are paid off
   ( ) monthly.

( ) semi-monthly.
( ) quarterly.
(x) at maturity of debt.

4. Indicate which one of the following does not apply to personal risk in mortgages
( ) Character.
( ) Capacity.
(x) Call loan.
( ) Capital.

5. In lending money, the mortgagee must guard particularly against
(x) the obsolescence of the subject property.
( ) change in political form of government.
( ) new zoning restrictions.
( ) increase in taxes.

6. Conventional loans are made from
( ) mutual funds.
(x) private sources.
( ) "Fannie Mae."
( ) Home Owners' Loan Corporation.

7. The greatest risk to a lender is found in
(x) construction loans.
( ) F.H.A. loans.
( ) V.A. loans.
( ) conventional loans.

8. Amortization of loans was first developed by
( ) insurance companies.
(x) building and loan associations.
( ) F.H.A.
( ) commercial banks.

9. Forces which determine the rate of interest are
( ) political.
( ) local.
(x) economic.
( ) banks.

10. Banks can lend money for long term mortgages from
( ) money on checking accounts.
(x) money on savings accounts.
( ) stocks held as collateral.
( ) percentage of bank owned office building.

11. Federal Savings and Loan Associations can make commercial and apartment loans up to what percentage of their total loans?
( ) 66⅔ per cent.
( ) 80 per cent.
(x) 36 per cent.
( ) 75 per cent.

12. The largest sources in single-family home financing on a conventional basis are
( ) the national banks.

( ) the insurance companies.
( ) pension funds.
(x) savings and loan associations.

13. Generally, insurance companies will lend up to what percentage of the appraised property value?
( ) 60 per cent.
( ) 66⅔ per cent.
(x) 70 per cent.
( ) 90 per cent.

14. "Overage" in insurance company mortgage loans refers to
( ) borrowers over 65 years of age.
(x) requiring a percentage of the rents over a specified minimum.
( ) property over 45 years of age.
( ) requiring an acceleration of payments after five years.

15. Nationwide, which group of lending institutions is lowest in the mortgage lenders' field?
( ) Commercial banks
(x) Mutual savings banks.
( ) Insurance companies.
( ) National banks.

16. Mortgage loans entailing more than average risk are usually made by
( ) savings and loan associations.
(x) private lenders.
( ) mutual funds.
( ) pension funds.

17. Under the amended Servicemen's Readjustment Act of 1968, each eligible veteran has an entitlement for loan purposes in the aggregate amount of
( ) $7,500.
( ) $10,000.
(x) $12,500.
( ) $15,000.

18. Of this amount, the government guarantees
( ) 100 per cent.
(x) 60 per cent.
( ) 50 per cent.
( ) 80 per cent.

19. The statutory interest rate on G.I. loans, under the 1968 Act, is
( ) 6 per cent.
( ) 6¾ per cent.
( ) 7 per cent.
(x) a rate "to meet the mortgage market."

20. Effective May 7, 1968, V.A. and F.H.A. interest rates were established at
( ) 6 per cent.
( ) 7 per cent.
( ) 6½ per cent.

(x) 6¾ per cent.
21. Regardless of the term stated in the residence mortgage contract, the mortgage is usually paid off in
    ( ) 5–6 years.
    ( ) at maturity.
    (x) 12–13 years.
    ( ) 20–22 years.
22. If a non-veteran purchases a property subject to a G.I. loan
    ( ) the loan must be paid off.
    ( ) the veteran is released from liability.
    (x) the buyer must continue mortgage payments.
    ( ) the transaction is void.
23. Entitlement to a G.I. loan for veterans of World War II expires
    ( ) July 15, 1969.
    ( ) January 1, 1970.
    (x) July 25, 1970.
    ( ) January 1, 1971.
24. For a Korean veteran, the expiration date is
    ( ) January 1, 1972.
    ( ) July 15, 1973.
    ( ) January 1, 1974.
    (x) January 31, 1975.
25. In addition to 6¾ per cent interest on an F.H.A. loan, the borrower must pay an annual insurance charge of
    (x) ½ per cent.
    ( ) ¾ per cent.
    ( ) 1 per cent.
    ( ) none.
26. Many states permit lending institutions to lend above the statutory ratio of loan to value if the excess is insured by an acceptable insuring agency. The amount of this excess is usually
    (x) 10 to 15 per cent of the loan.
    ( ) 15 to 25 per cent of the loan.
    ( ) 20 to 25 per cent of the loan.
    ( ) 25 to 30 per cent of the loan.
27. A land sales, or instalment purchase contract can sometimes be used as a
    (x) junior financing instrument.
    ( ) vendor's lien.
    ( ) an equity of redemption.
    ( ) collateral for stock purchase.
28. Discounts or "points" on mortgages are
    ( ) a return in excess of interest paid by the mortgagee to a purchaser of his mortgage.
    ( ) a charge to the buyer in obtaining a mortgage in a competitive market.
    (x) a charge to the seller by the lender to increase the yield on

money invested.
( ) none of these.
29. "Points" are determined by
( ) F.H.A.
( ) American Bankers Association.
(x) condition of the money market.
( ) Federal Reserve Board.
30. In order to qualify as a lending institution under F.H.A., a corporation must have total assets in excess of
( ) $1,000,000.
( ) $50,000.
( ) $250,000.
(x) $100,000.

Chapter 5

MORTGAGES

MORTGAGES CONSTITUTE a very important phase in the development and growth of home ownership. They represent an extension of long-term credit, and the function of mortgage-lending may be said to be to promote the economic, social, and financial welfare of the community. Mortgages are also recognized as a dominant factor in the development of city and rural communities through promotion of home, farm, commercial, industrial, and investment ownership.

Definition and history

A mortgage is a pledge of real estate as collateral security for the repayment of money or the performance of some other act. Since early days the practice of pledging property for repayment of a debt has been prevalent. The mortgage grew out of the pledges of land for debt by the Anglo-Saxons. The early encumbrances operated in a very summary manner. If the debtor failed to meet his debt upon the exact day due, the pledged land became the absolute property of the creditor. A wide difference between the value of the land and the amount of the debt was of no consequence. This resulted at times in such injustice and hardship that the courts began to interfere. The legal principle, Equity of Redemption, was then developed which permitted the debtor, within a statutory period, to repay the debt together with a penalty in the form of interest and to reclaim his property. The pendulum of justice now swung to the other extreme, and a creditor taking property for nonpayment of a debt found it difficult to dispose of the same because a purchaser was reluctant to buy or improve since the debtor might turn up and demand the return of his property. The courts again stepped in and allowed the creditor to file a bill to foreclose the debtor's equity of redemption, and a day was fixed on or before which the debtor was required to pay up or suffer his property to be lost. This modification was the forerunner of the present-day mortgage. The term mortgage comes from the old French *mort* (dead) and *gage* (pledge).

In some states a mortgage is really a *transfer* of real estate upon condition as security for the payment of a debt. Between the original parties it is a conveyance of real estate; to third parties it is a lien. In other states a mortgage is considered and treated only as a lien. A lien is a hold or claim which one person has upon the property of another as a security for some debt or charge. A lien is an encumbrance and a person purchasing real estate encumbered by a mortgage takes the property subject to the lien. In California, Colorado, Illinois, Missouri, New Mexico, Tennessee, Virginia, West Virginia, and the District of Columbia, a Deed of Trust is used in a mortgage transaction. There the owner-borrower conveys the property to a third person, in trust for the holder of the note that represents the debt, rather than to the lender direct. The practical difference between a trust deed and a mortgage lies in the method of foreclosure after default.

In some estates, as in Alabama and Florida, a seller has a vendor's lien for the balance of the unpaid purchase price. A vendor's lien is the right of the seller to subject the land as security for the unpaid purchase price. The lien may be enforced by a bill in equity to sell the property for the amount due. It is not as good against subsequent creditors or purchasers, unless they have actual notice of it, or reference to the lien is contained in the recorded deed from seller to buyer.

Parties

There are essentially two parties in a mortgage transaction: the *mortgagor*, who is the borrower and the owner of the property and who executes a mortgage upon the property as security for payment of his debt; and the *mortgagee*, who is the lender of the money and the creditor and who receives the mortgage. In some states, when the mortgage is executed by the mortgagor, he also executes a personal obligation bond for double the amount of the mortgage debt. Thus, if an owner is borrowing $5,000 he executes a mortgage in that amount, and he also signs a personal obligation bond for $10,000, or in some states a judgment note. The bond is made for a double amount in order to take care of any delinquent interest, taxes, or other charges and assessments that might be added to the original debt. The bond contains a warrant of confession which permits the holder to confess judgment for the real debt due upon default. A mortgagee is not bound to release any part of the mortgaged premises without the payment of the entire principal. Giving a release is a matter of accommodation by the mortgagee. The bond or note is the evidence of the debt; the mortgage is the pledge of specific property as security. In the bond the debtor is referred to as the obligor and the creditor as the obligee. The bond creates no lien until it is entered on record as a judgment, at which time it becomes a lien against all of the debtor's real estate from the date of entry. However, as to the mortgaged premises alone, the lien dates back to the date of the mortgage and has priority from the mortgage date ahead of other judgments entered subsequently. If the mortgagor dies, judgment cannot be entered upon the bond or note because the warrant of attorney authorizing any attorney to enter judgment against the debtor is automatically revoked by death. Proceedings would have to be instituted under the mortgage instrument instead. While a mortgage deals with realty, it is, nevertheless, personalty and upon the death of the mortgagee would be distributed as personalty rather than as realty.

A mortgage is a contract and the law of contracts is generally applicable. The same care urged in the preparation of a deed should also be exercised in the case of a mortgage. The mortgage instrument is comprised of two parts, the conveyance of the property and the defeasance. The latter clause provides that if the debt is repaid and the other covenants are performed by the mortgagor, then the conveyance to the mortgagee shall be null and void.

The existence of a mortgage does not prevent the property from being sold by the debtor-owner; he does not have to obtain the consent of the mortagee-creditor. The mortgagee can look to the property as security for the debt no matter who owns it; so long as the debt remains unpaid. The purchaser of land encumbered by a mortgage is called the terre tenant.

Liability of purchaser of land

What liability does the purchaser of the mortgaged premises assume? Liability depends upon the type of clause used in the deed to refer to the mortgage. The clause used is a "short" or "long" form and liability differs accordingly.

Short- and long-form mortgage clause

As stated previously, the short-form clause is usually as follows: "Under and subject, nevertheless, to a certain mortgage in the present unpaid amount of $5,000.00, given by John Steele, the grantor herein, to the City National Bank, dated June 16, 1969 and of record in the Recorder's Office of Piedmont County in Mortgage Book Vol. 2117, Page 316." The long-form mortgage clause reads exactly the same, with this addition: "which mortgage, the grantee expressly assumes and agrees to pay as part of the consideration herein." Now, it must be remembered that the property is always liable for the debt. But it frequently happens, particularly in times of depressed real estate values, that the property value at a foreclosure sale is less than the mortgage indebtedness.

Deficiency judgment

During the depression years, 1931–1938, the mortgagee was entitled to a deficiency judgment for the difference between the sale price at the foreclosure sale and the mortgage debt. Very often the property was sold to the plaintiff mortgagee at a nominal price (costs and taxes) as there were no other bidders and the deficiency judgment was considerable.

The legislatures and courts, motivated by a social consciousness, recognizing the unfairness of this situation that permitted a mortgagee to acquire the property and to obtain a judgment for practically the entire debt as well, decreed that a debtor should have credit for the fair value of the property at the date of the foreclosure sale as an offset to the debt. Thus, today, if the property is sold to the plaintiff mortgagee for a nominal bid, the debtor would be liable only if the amount of the debt were in excess of the fair value of the property. But the possibility of a deficiency judgment, in *some* amount, is still very real. The mortgagee can look to the original owner for this deficiency, no matter through how many hands the property may have passed, because the original owner (mortgagor) is liable upon his contract obligation to repay the debt. Under the short-form clause the mortgagee has no right of action against the purchaser of the mortgaged premises, as there is no privity of contract, i.e., relationship, between the mortgagee and the purchaser of the property. The only way the original mortgagor could be relieved of all personal liability would be for him to insist that his purchaser do his own financing and have the original mortgage paid off and satisfied and the accompanying bond or note returned and cancelled. If the original mortgagor actually pays the judgment entered against him by the mortgagee, he would have the right of *indemnification* against his purchaser, but not otherwise. Under the long-form clause, the mortgagee is considered a third party or creditor beneficiary under the deed contract between the owner and purchaser and would have a right to sue the purchaser of the mortgaged premises for the deficiency, proceed against the original debtor, or both. The principle of law has been stated to be: "where the contract is purely one of indemnity, the indemnitee [seller] cannot recover until he has suffered actual loss or damage; the mere incurring of liability gives him no such right; but where the contract is to protect against liability, the indemnitee may recover as soon as his liability has become fixed and established even though he has sustained no actual loss or damage at the time he seeks to recover."[1] Where the buyer takes over an existing mortgage, the protection of the seller requires the use of the long-form clause in the deed. Since the deed is the formal consummation of an agreement of sale previously entered into, it behooves the broker or attorney preparing the agreement of sale to exercise adequate care in drawing the mortgage clause in the sales agreement.

Industrial property mortgage

In the case of industrial property the mortgage covers not only the real estate but the fixtures and equipment contained therein. It will also cover under its lien such machinery—fixtures and equipment added subsequent to the execution of the mortgage—as is necessary to the functioning of the complete plant. The fact that the additional equipment is installed long after the mortgage was given will not prevent its becoming additional security for the benefit of the mortgagee.

Blanket mortgage

Where a mortgage is given to include more than one parcel of real estate, the mortgagee cannot be required to release any one parcel from his *blanket* mortgage upon the payment of a pro-rata share of the mortgage debt. The contention that the remaining property is ample security is unavailing. The mortgagee is entitled to payment of the mortgage in full and to have all the properties as security until that time.

Release and postponement distinguished

Where a property is released from the lien of a mortgage, the rights of the creditor are forever barred insofar as the tract of land which he has released is concerned. It may be advisable in many instances for a creditor to postpone the lien of his judgment or mortgage instead of releasing it outright. Suppose that a creditor has a judgment of record against a debtor who owns several pieces of property. The debtor desires to improve one property and it is necessary for him to obtain a mortgage to finance the cost. The

---

[1] *American and English Encyclopedia of Law*, 2nd Edition, p. 178.

mortgagee will be reluctant to give a mortgage since the judgment creditor has a prior lien. If the judgment creditor releases the property upon which the mortgage is to be placed, the lien against that property is gone, but if he merely agrees to postpone his lien in favor of the new mortgage, his lien is continued as against the property to be improved. Thus, if that property is sold at a later date, the judgment creditor would have to be satisfied, or if the property were foreclosed at a later date, the judgment creditor would participate in the funds of distribution. A mortgage is susceptible to discharge by a sale for future taxes and municipal claims.

Closed and open mortgages

Nor can a mortgagee be required, in the absence of a condition to the contrary, to accept payment of the indebtedness before the maturity date. Thus, a "closed" mortgage is one which cannot be paid off before maturity (e.g. "payable at the expiration of five years from the date hereof"). The mortgagee can accept payment before maturity only if he is so inclined. Some lending institutions will accept prepayment upon payment of a premium. Mortgagees, insured under the Federal Housing Act, require one per cent of the original mortgage debt as a premium if the purchaser pays off the mortgage debt with borrowed funds. An open mortgage is one which is payable "within" a certain time (within five years from the date hereof) and can be paid off at any time. Building and Loan Associations will usually permit payment of the debt at any time.

Rights of mortgagor

The rights of the mortgagor and mortgagee depend, in the main, upon the provisions of the mortgage contract. Even under the conveyance theory of mortgages, the mortgagor is regarded as the real owner of the premises. As such, he has certain fundamental rights in the property. The most important right is that of possession and the accompanying right to sell the property subject to the mortgage. He may lease the premises and is entitled to the rents, profit, and revenue arising from the property. He may dispose of the property by will, subject to the mortgage. Where the mortgagee has taken possession, the mortgagor is entitled to an accounting during his stewardship.

Rights of mortgagee

Usually the mortgagee is not entitled to possession so that his rights in the property are few. He is entitled to payment of interest and installments of principal as they become due.

Mortgagee in possession

Where the property is income-producing, the creditor may, upon default, exercise his right of *mortgagee in possession*. This is accomplished simply by notifying the tenants in possession that the mortgage is in default and demanding payment of future rents to the mortgagee. A tenant will be protected against any claim of his lessor-owner by payment to the mortgagee. If the lease antedates the mortgage, the mortgagee, in those states subscribing to the conveyance theory of a mortgage, can compel the tenant to pay future rents to the mortgagee and upon the tenant's refusal can issue a landlord's levy to collect the rent. Upon subsequent foreclosure of the property the purchaser at the sale takes the property subject to the prior lease. If the mortgage antedates the lease, the tenant cannot be compelled to pay rent to the mortgagee, but if he does so (attorns), he must continue to pay rent during the mortgagee's tenure in possession. Should the tenant refuse the mortgagee's demand for rent, the latter's only recourse would be to foreclose the property and thereby terminate the lease. Even if the lessee attorns to the mortgagee, the plaintiff mortgagee, upon foreclosure at a later date, could nevertheless void the lease. His status as a mortgagee in possession is separate and independent from his status as owner as a result of the foreclosure proceedings.

A mortgagee in possession may also become liable for damages to a person injured on or about the mortgaged premises. If the mortgagee takes over such control and dominion of the property as to supplant the owner, then he also assumes tort liability to third persons. Mere receipt of rentals is insufficient, but actual control and possession are necessary to make a mortgagee liable. Courts in Kentucky, New York, and Pennsylvania have so held. "Actual control and possession" means collecting rents, negotiating leases, paying taxes, and authorizing necessary repairs. In short, it is necessary to establish that the mortgagee exercised those acts of dominion over the property which any owner of a similar property would do under the circumstances.

Assignment of mortgage

Just as the mortgagor-owner can sell the premises subject to the mortgage, so the mortgagee can sell the mortgage. This is effected by assignment. The purchaser of the mortgage, the *assignee*, acquires the same title and interest in the mortgage which his *assignor* had, but no better title. An assignee is said to stand in the shoes of his assignor. Any claim, demand, or setoff which the mortgagor had against the mortgagee he can set up with equal facility against the mortgagee's assignee. Thus, if the mortgagor had paid the mortgagee $1,000 upon a $5,000 mortgage debt, which mortgage the mortgagee had sold to his assignee for $5,000, the mortgage purchaser could recover only $4,000 from the debtor.

Certificate of no defense, declaration of no setoff, estoppel certificate

In order to protect himself against this possibility the purchaser should obtain a statement from the mortgagor acknowledging the full indebtedness. This is known as a Certificate of No Defense, an Estoppel Certificate, or a Declaration of No Setoff by which the mortgagor admits that he owes the debt and must pay it in full at maturity. The Certificate or Declaration also serves notice, and acknowledgment of notice upon the debtor of the transfer of the mortgage. Otherwise, he would be protected in continuing payments to the original creditor. The assignee of a mortgage should also require the mortgagee to turn over to him the mortgage instrument, the accompanying bond or notes, fire insurance policy, and any other papers relating to the mortgage transaction. The mortgagee should acknowledge upon the margin of the recorded mortgage the transfer to the purchaser or execute and record an assignment. The original mortgagor can compel the mortgagee to assign the mortgage to him upon tender to the creditor of the mortgage debt. It may be expeditious to make such a tender in order to avoid the possibility of a judgment deficiency in the future. For example, Simpson, a contractor, built two houses in 1945 and gave the bank a mortgage on each house for $6,500 as well as an accompanying bond in double that amount. He then sold each house and executed a deed containing the long-form mortgage clause. In 1959, he was very much surprised and alarmed to find that Clark, purchaser of one of the houses, owed the bank $7,700. In the 1959 market, the particular house could be sold for about $8,000. In case of a depression, the house would probably bring about $5,500. The potential danger to Simpson is very real. By tendering the bank $7,700, he can compel an assignment of the delinquent mortgage, foreclose the property, realize the amount of his investment and effectively terminate any possible liability on his part.

Voluntary deed

It frequently happens that a mortgagor, in order to avoid foreclosure and the possibility of a deficiency judgment against him, will agree to convey the property voluntarily to the mortgagee in settlement and satisfaction of the mortgage. It is important that the deed recite that the conveyance is *intended* as a satisfaction of the debt, as the deed, per se (by itself) will not have that effect. The debtor should insist that the mortgagee satisfy the mortgage of record and return the mortgage and any other evidence of the debt to him. The mortgagee, in accepting a voluntary deed for the property, should have the records examined to make sure that he is acquiring the property free and clear of any judgments or liens. Under a voluntary conveyance, the mortgagee would acquire no better title than the mortgagor had, whereas through foreclosure proceedings, he could divest liens and judgments entered of record subsequent to his mortgage.

Sheriff's foreclosure

Upon default in any of the mortgage terms the creditor is entitled to institute foreclosure proceedings against the mortgaged property. At the public sale the property is sold by the sheriff to the highest bidder. The deed is executed by the sheriff and gives no assurance or guarantee as to the validity of the title. The equity of the debtor is effectively wiped out. If the property brings an amount in excess of the debt, and there are no other liens to be paid, the mortgagor is entitled to the excess fund. Where a Deed of Trust is used, the instrument prescribes the procedure for sale of the mortgaged property.

Payment and satisfaction

A mortgage is usually terminated by payment and satisfaction. Where the debtor tenders payment of the debt, he is entitled to have the mortgage marked "Satisfied in full" of record and the mortgage papers returned to him. The mortgagee can personally satisfy the mortgage of record or he may do so by executing a *Satisfaction Piece*, which is a separate instrument, and duly recording it to show that the debt has been paid. After 20 years a mortgage is *presumed* to be paid and the burden of proving otherwise is upon the mortgagee. Where an old mortgage is of record and no payment or demand for payment has been made for more than 20 years, a party in interest can petition the court for an order satisfying the mortgage of record.

Chattel mortgages

A movement is under way for a single mortgage, or "package mortgage," which will include not only the real estate but also the refrigerator, laundry equipment, furniture, and even the family car. Most states provide for mortgaging of personal property by a chattel mortgage, which is generally used to finance the purchase price of furniture, household appliances, and commercial equipment. The chattel mortgage is recorded. Title is transferred to the purchaser, and he in turn can convey title to the article in question to a new buyer, but the title is subject to the balance due under the chattel mortgage. In an examination of the title of real estate, search should also be made for chattel mortgages. A chattel mortgage differs from a conditional sale in that, while possession passes in both cases to the buyer, title, in a conditional sale, remains in the seller until the last installment is made.

Questions on Mortgages

1. Q. Why does a borrower execute a note or personal obligation bond when he executes a mortgage?
   A. The note or bond is evidence of the debt and expedites the entry of judgment (by confession) in case of default.
2. Q. Is the consent of the mortgagee necessary in order for the debtor-owner to sell his property?
   A. Usually not; the mortgage instrument, however, may make such consent necessary.
3. Q. What two theories are there in regard to mortgages?
   A. In some states, a mortgage is a conveyance of real estate; in other states, it is considered merely a lien, similar to a judgment.
4. Q. Do all commercial banks belong to an association, which promulgates rules for lending money on mortgages?
   A. No.
5. Q. Why does a broker render a disservice to his owner when he stresses to the buyer that there is a mortgage on the property so that the buyer will not have to do any financing?
   A. Because the owner will continue potentially liable on the mortgage as long as it is unpaid.
6. Q. What is the difference between a first and second mortgage?
   A. A first mortgage is the one which is first recorded and has priority in distribution of funds at a foreclosure sale. A second mortgage is subordinate to a first mortgage.
7. Q. What is the difference between an open mortgage and a closed mortgage?
   A. An open mortgage can be paid off at any time before the maturity date while a closed mortgage cannot be paid off before the expiration date unless the mortgagee is willing to accept payment.
8. Q. Who are the parties to a mortgage?
   A. The mortgagor, who owns the property and borrows money upon the security of the property, and the mortgagee, who lends the money. The mortgage is executed by the mortgagor in favor of the mortgagee.
9. Q. What economic functions do mortgages serve?
   A. Mortgage credit has made possible the wider distribution of home ownership and the promotion of the economic, social, and financial welfare of the community.
10. Q. Name six sources of mortgage funds.
    A. Individuals, banks, insurance companies, savings and loan associations, endowment funds, Federal farm loan system.

11. Q. What is a junior mortgage?
    A. A mortgage in which the lender's claims against the owner's rights are subordinate to the claim of the first mortgage holder or to other liens.

12. Q. What additional security does a borrower give in addition to the mortgage proper?
    A. A bond or note undertaking to repay the debt as specified and a warrant of attorney authorizing an attorney at law to appear for and confess judgment against the debtor in event of default.

13. Q. Can a minor mortgage real estate owned by him?
    A. Yes, but the mortgage could be disaffirmed by the infant during his minority or within a reasonable time after attaining his majority. The creditor should deal only with the legally appointed guardian of the minor. A minor's warrant of attorney to confess judgment is absolutely void.

14. Q. What is a deed of trust?
    A. A written instrument, signed, sealed and acknowledged wherein a property owner pledges his property as security for a debt by conveying title to one or more trustees for the purpose named in the deed of trust.

15. Q. What are two functions of trustees named in a deed of trust?
    A. To foreclose in case of default under any of the terms of the deed of trust and to release the property upon payment or satisfaction of the debt.

16. Q. How many trustees are required to be named in a deed of trust?
    A. One or more. Sometimes a corporation is used as a single trustee. When individuals are used as trustees, generally two are named.

17. Q. How could a property be foreclosed or released under the terms of a deed of trust in which two trustees are named:
    (a) in the event of the death of one of the trustees?
    (b) in the event of the death of both trustees?
    (c) in the event of refusal of one or both trustees to act?
    A. (a) The surviving trustee could act.
    (b) Petition the court for the appointment of a substitute trustee or trustees.
    (c) Same as (b).

18. Q. What is meant by "first deed of trust" and "second deed of trust"?
    A. The distinction is merely the order in which they have been recorded. The one recorded first is the first deed of trust, and the one recorded next is the second deed of trust, and the priority of lien is thus established.

19. Q. What is a "deferred purchase money" deed of trust?
    A. A deed of trust pledging real estate as security for the payment of that part of the purchase price which has been deferred.

20. Q. Can a corporation execute a mortgage?
    A. Yes, if in the ordinary course of its business, but not for the purpose of increasing its indebtedness.

21. Q. Does a married woman have power to execute a mortgage on real estate owned by her?
    A. Generally a married woman can. In some states, she cannot unless she has been declared a feme sole trader.

22. Q. What is meant by the debtor's "equity of redemption"?
    A. A period of grace, *after default*, in which the debtor may redeem his property, provided it has not been foreclosed. Equity of redemption should not be confused with right of redemption which is the right the debtor has to redeem property after it has been sold for taxes.

23. Q. What indicia determine that an instrument is a mortgage rather than a conditional sale?
    A. 1. The fact that the transaction originated in an application for a loan of money.
       2. The fact that the grantor retained possession.
       3. The fact that grantor continued to pay taxes and made repairs and improvements.
       4. Gross inadequacy of price.

24. Q. Johnson has a mortgage on three contiguous tracts of equal value owned by Lee. The mortgage is for $9,000. Lee desires to sell one tract for $5,000 and asks Johnson to release the tract upon payment of $3,000. Johnson refuses. Can Lee compel Johnson to release the tract in question?
    A. No. Johnson has a "blanket mortgage" upon the three parcels and is entitled to the full security until the debt is paid. If he doesn't choose to accept a partial payment and release the tract, he cannot be compelled to do so.

25. Q. What rights does the mortgagor have?
    A. 1. The right of possession.
       2. The right to lease, deed, or will the property subject to the mortgage.
       3. The right to an accounting if the mortgagee is in possession.

26. Q. What are the rights of the mortgagee?
    A. 1. Right to interest and principal as due.
       2. Right to prevent the mortgagor from committing waste so as to lessen the mortgagee's security.
       3. Right to possession in case of a default.

27. Q. What is meant by amortization of a mortgage?
    A. Liquidation of the debt through regular periodic payments.

28. Q. What is the purpose of the Federal Farm Loan Act and how does it operate?
    A. It provides capital for agricultural development. First mortgage loans only are made. Amount of loan limited to 50% of land appraised and 20% of improvement appraisal; proceeds must be used to pay off an existing indebtedness or in farm production; debt is payable in annual or semiannual installments of principal and interest; mortgage term is from 5 to 40 years; rate of interest can-

not exceed 6 per cent. Loan amount varies from $100 to $10,000.

29. Q. Saunders owned certain premises subject to a mortgage to Thurston for $8,000. Saunders leased the premises to Stevens for 10 years. Later Saunders desired to obtain possession of the premises. He purchased the mortgage from Thurston in the name of Smith and foreclosed the property. Smith then notified Stevens to vacate. Who will win?

A. The tenant, Stevens, will win. Since Saunders is the lessor, he cannot commit any act to interfere with the tenant's quiet and peaceful enjoyment of the premises.

30. Q. What is an F.H.A. mortgage as the term is commonly used?

A. A loan that is guaranteed to the mortgagee-lending institution by the Federal Housing Administration.

31. Q. What is meant by an acceleration clause in either a mortgage or contract?

A. A clause giving the mortgagor or vendee the right to pay more than the regular payments or to pay the mortgage or contract in full at any time. It is also used to indicate that a mortgagee or lessor can accelerate the balance due under a mortgage or lease immediately after any default.

32. Q. What is a chattel mortgage?

A. A mortgage upon personal property such as livestock, equipment, or fixtures. It must be recorded.

33. Q. What is the difference between a bond or note and a mortgage?

A. A bond or note is the evidence of indebtedness and the promise to repay; a mortgage is a pledge of specific realty as security.

34. Q. If there is a discrepancy between the bond and mortgage as to the amount of the debt or the time of its repayment, which will prevail?

A. The bond.

35. Q. Does the purchaser assume personal liability for the mortgage debt?

A. It depends upon the mortgage clause in the deed. If the purchaser buys the property "under and subject to the mortgage," he assumes no personal liability. If he buys "under and subject to the mortgage, which he assumes and agrees to pay," he is personally liable for the payment of the mortgage debt.

36. Q. Ross executes a deed to Bonfield, "under and subject to the payment of a certain mortgage for $5,000 in favor of the First National Bank, dated January 3, 1958 and of record in the Recorder of Deeds' Office of Harkins County in Mortgage Book Vol. 2117, page 360." On June 1, 1968, the bank forecloses and the property is sold at the sheriff's sale for $4,100. What are the respective liabilities of Ross and Bonfield to the bank?

A. Ross is liable for any deficiency judgment to the bank. Bonfield is not liable to the bank, because he did not assume and agree to pay the debt. If Ross is required to pay the judgment to the bank, he, in turn, would be entitled to indemnification from Bonfield.

37. Q. Given the preceding facts, if Bonfield signed an extension agreement with the bank extending the term beyond the maturity date and agreeing to make the payments, what liability would ensue?

A. The bank could hold Ross or Bonfield for the deficiency because there is now privity of contract between Bonfield and the bank. Ross remains liable so long as the debt is unpaid.

38. Q. Who pays the premium on an insurance policy with a mortgage clause?

A. The mortgagor, to protect the mortgagee, to the extent of his interest, in case the mortgaged premises are destroyed or damaged by fire, or other casualty.

39. Q. Why is it important that a deed of release be promptly recorded after the debt has been paid or satisfied?

A. To guard against carelessness or accident which might result in loss of the cancelled note or notes, which loss would cause serious consequences.

40. Q. Adams purchased a tract of land from Baker. The property is encumbered by a past due mortgage, which Baker gave Conway when Baker purchased the property from Conway. Conway is willing and does extend the mortgage for another period of five years.

1. Should the extension of mortgage be entered into between Adams, the new owner, and Conway, the mortgagee, or should the extension agreement be signed by Baker and Conway?

2. After the extension of mortgage is signed by Conway, is Baker relieved of his obligation as the maker of the original mortgage?

3. What liability, if any, does Adams, the new purchaser, now have in connection with the mortgage?

A. 1. Adams and Conway, since Adams is now the owner of record of the property.

2. No. Baker is still responsible for conditions of the mortgage as of the date of the extension.

3. Adams, the new owner, is responsible for any new condition which may arise after the extension of the mortgage.

41. Q. What is the function of the Federal Housing Administration in the mortgage loan field?

A. It insures loans that are made by F.H.A. approved lending agencies.

42. Q. What is a reduction certificate?

A. A certificate showing the balance due on a mortgage at the time of closing a sale.

43. Q. Ogden, a real estate broker, is employed by Whitney, a mortgagee, to collect interest on a mortgage due him from Crane, the

mortgagor. Ogden collects the interest payments for three years and remits to Whitney, deducting a commission for his services. In 1969, Crane pays the mortgage debt of $4,000 to Ogden, who uses the money for his own purposes. Ogden dies two months later and his estate is hopelessly insolvent. In a contest between Whitney and Crane, who will suffer the loss?

A. The loss falls upon the mortgagor, Crane, for Ogden had no authority to collect the principal, and the responsibility was upon Crane to ascertain the extent of the agent's authority.

44. Q. Where a mortgagor makes extensive improvements to the property, can he set off the cost against the mortgage debt in case of a foreclosure?

A. No. All improvements become part of the freehold and go to increase the mortgagee's security for the debt.

45. Q. Is a mortgage assignable?

A. Yes, but the purchaser gets no better title or claim than the mortgagee had.

46. Q. What steps should the purchaser take or require in purchasing a mortgage?

A. 1. Transfer of mortgage and other papers to him.
2. Note the assignment upon the record.
3. Obtain a declaration of no setoff, estoppel certificate, or certificate of no defense from the mortgagor.

47. Q. Green executed a mortgage to Brown in 1958. Green leased the property to White for 5 years from May 1, 1959. Green failed to pay taxes or interest on the mortgage in 1960, and Brown notified White to pay the rents to him. White did so, and Green instituted an action for the rent against White. Will Green win?

A. No. White is protected in paying the rent to Brown, who, upon Green's default, can exercise his right of mortgagee in possession. White may attorn to Brown; that is, recognize Brown as his lessor.

48. Q. Given the same facts, suppose White refused to honor Brown's request for rent but continued his rent payments to Green. What redress does Brown have?

A. Brown cannot compel White to pay the rent; he would have to foreclose the property and obtain title, in which case he could then terminate White's lease.

49. Q. Suppose, given the preceding facts, that White paid the rent to Brown for a period of seven months and then Brown foreclosed the property and obtained title to it. Brown now notifies White that his lease is terminated. Can Brown do so?

A. Yes. Although Brown recognized the lease previously by accepting rent payments from White, he is not estopped from cancelling the lease after he becomes owner of the property. Brown's status as a mortgagee in possession is entirely different and apart from his rights as owner after foreclosure. This is true where the mortgage antedated the lease, as here.

50. Q. Is a valid oral lease assignable?

  A. Yes.

51. Q. Mitchell exercises his rights as a mortgagee in possession under a mortgage from Adler. Mitchell collects the rents from the six tenants, pays the taxes, makes necessary repairs, and generally exercises dominion over the property. A pedestrian is injured due to a defective sidewalk and sues Adler, who brings in Mitchell as an additional defendant. Is Mitchell liable?

  A. Yes. The mortgagee in possession assumes the status of an owner when he exercises control, direction, and dominion over the property.

52. Q. What is the purpose of a "mortgagee clause" attached to a fire insurance policy?

  A. To protect the mortgagee against destruction of the mortgaged premises, as the mortgagee's interest may appear. The insurance policy is kept by the mortgagee and a policy certificate is furnished the owner. The mortgagor pays the insurance premiums.

53. Q. Can a mortgagee accept a voluntary deed from mortgagor in lieu of foreclosure?

  A. Yes, but the mortgagee should make certain that there are no liens or encumbrances entered subsequent to his mortgage as he will take the property subject to them.

54. Q. When a mortgagee has made two assignments of the mortgage, which assignment will take effect?

  A. The first assignment will prevail. However, in the assignment of a specialty such as a mortgage, transfer of the instrument itself is the controlling factor in determining ownership of the mortgage.

55. Q. What should be done when the mortgage is paid off?

  A. The mortgagee should acknowledge payment and satisfaction upon the record or execute a satisfaction piece and record it. The mortgagor should require the return of all the mortgage papers executed by him and the fire insurance policy.

56. Q. What is a mortgagee's remedy for the failure of the mortgagor to pay interest upon the principal of the mortgage debt as agreed?

  A. If the property is revenue-producing, he can step in as mortgagee in possession and require the tenants to pay him the rent; or he can foreclose the property and sell it for his debt.

57. Q. A property on which there is a first mortgage of $4,000, a second mortgage of $4,000 and a third mortgage of $2,000, is sold under foreclosure, bringing a price of $5,000. What sum of money would each mortgagee receive if sold by first mortgagee?

  A. The first mortgagee would receive $4,000; the second mortgagee, $1,000; and the third mortgagee, nothing. The purchaser at the foreclosure sale would receive the property clear of the three mortgages.

58. Q. What is the name of the clause inserted in a contract when it is desired by the purchaser of real property to place a mortgage at a later date on the property to take precedence over a purchase money mortgage given at the time of purchase?

A. A subordination clause.

59. Q. Who executes a "Certificate of No Defense" or an "Estoppel Certificate" relating to a mortgage? For what purpose is it asked?

A. By the mortgagor. It is asked when the mortgagee sells or assigns the mortgage so that the purchaser will have the mortgagor's assurance that the debt is owing and unpaid.

60. Q. Who executes the deed to real property when it is sold by the court in an action to foreclose a mortgage?

A. The sheriff.

61. Q. Archer executes a mortgage to Hood for $5,000. Later Hood purchases merchandise from Archer for $750 and agrees to permit Archer to set the amount off against the mortgage debt. Subsequently Hood sells the mortgage to Cox. At maturity Archer refuses to pay more than $4,250 on the principal. How much can Cox collect?

A. Only $4,250 as Cox received no better title to the mortgage than Hood had. Cox should have obtained an Estoppel Certificate or Certificate of No Defense from Archer when he purchased the mortgage.

62. Q. Ash obtained a mortgage from the Peerless Mortgage Co. for $6,000. On the same day, the Peerless Mortgage Co. assigns the mortgage to the Traders' Bank, and Ash executes an Estoppel Certificate (same as a Certificate of No Defense or a Declaration of No Setoff). Later the Traders' Bank assigns the mortgage to the Rex Tile Co. for value. At maturity Ash refuses to pay more than $5,250, claiming that he has made payments of $750 to the Traders' Bank. If Ash can establish this fact, how much can the Rex Tile Co. collect?

A. Only $5,250. The tile company should have obtained a *new* estoppel certificate when it purchased the mortgage from the bank.

63. Q. A mortgage with amortization provisions and in the original sum of $10,000 is offered for sale two years after its inception. Name two legal documents to be used in effecting a proper transfer of the mortgage to the purchaser.

A. 1. An assignment of the mortgage by the mortgagee.
   2. An Estoppel Certificate by the mortgagor.

64. Q. An owner of five parcels of real estate is seeking a mortgage loan and offers all of the five parcels as security for the loan. The owner wishes to reserve the right to repay portions of the money borrowed at stated intervals before the due date of the mortgage and upon each payment to eliminate from the mortgage one of the five parcels covered by the mortgage. What is the name of the mortgage the owner will be required to execute, and what is the name of the document the owner will require from the mortgagee to free one of the parcels upon making a payment as stated above?

A. The mortgage is a *blanket* mortgage. The mortgagee will be required to execute a *release*.

65. Q. What is the difference between a *purchase money* mortgage and a *blanket* mortgage?

A. A purchase money mortgage is one given by the buyer to the seller in part payment of the consideration price. A blanket mortgage is one mortgage covering a number of properties.

66. Q. If you borrow and give an F.H.A. mortgage, is the loan made by the Federal Government?

A. No. The loan is made by a bank or other lending institution and guaranteed by the Federal Government.

67. Q. An F.H.A. mortgage is referred to as an insured mortgage. Whom does the insurance protect, the mortgagor or mortgagee?

A. The mortgagee.

68. Q. Is it necessary to record a mortgage in order to have a valid mortgage?

A. No, as between the two original parties, mortgagor and mortgagee. The mortgagee must record the mortgage in order for it to be a valid lien against the property ahead of a subsequent creditor, or in case of sale of the property by the mortgagor.

69. Q. In case of the death of the mortgagor, does the mortgage become immediately due?

A. No, the mortgage continues in accordance with its terms, if it is not delinquent and the property continues as security, no matter who inherits it.

70. Q. Does the death of the mortgagee have any effect upon the mortgage?

A. No; it passes as personal property in the estate.

71. Q. What is an "open end" mortgage?

A. The mortgagor has the right, after he has paid off part of the debt, to borrow additional funds from the mortgagee up to the original amount, at any time during the mortgage term.

72. Q. Abbott owes the Greenbacks Mortgage Co. $14,000 on a mortgage on his home. In 1966, he sells the home to Cabot for $17,000, and Cabot assumes and agrees to pay the mortgage. In 1967, Cabot sells the same residence to Lodge for the same price, "under and subject to the mortgage." In December 1968, Lodge sells the property to his brother-in-law, Stoner, at $16,000 and Stoner assumes and agrees to pay the mortgage in the then amount of $12,890. Stoner defaults, and the mortgage company realizes only $11,200 at a foreclosure sale. Can it collect from (a) Abbott (b) Cabot (c) Lodge (d) Stoner the deficiency?

A. (a) The mortgage company can collect from Abbott upon his original obligation (note or bond). (b) It can collect from Cabot because he assumed and agreed to pay the debt. (c) It cannot collect from Lodge, because he did not assume the debt. (d) It cannot collect from Stoner because Stoner's promise to assume and pay the debt was made to Lodge, who was not liable to the mortgage company.

73. Q. What is the main reason for a lender to require a provision in the mortgage that failure to pay the taxes when due constitutes a default of the mortgage?
   A. The lien created by unpaid taxes has priority over a mortgage on the property.

74. Q. What is the difference between "recording a mortgage" and "releasing a mortgage"?
   A. Recording a mortgage benefits the mortgagee in that it is public notice of the existence of the mortgage; releasing a mortgage benefits the mortgagor, because the mortgage is no longer a lien against the particular property which is released.

75. Q. What are the essentials of a mortgagee upon real property?
   A. (1) In writing (2) Competent parties (3) Purpose must be stated (4) A mortgaging clause (5) Description (6) Mortgagor's covenants (7) Signed by the mortgagor (8) Acknowledged by the mortgagor (9) Delivered to the mortgagee.

76. Q. What is the main difference between a mortgage and a deed of trust?
   A. A mortgage has a one year redemption period after foreclosure. A deed of trust can be foreclosed in 120 days, unless reduced by agreement.

77. Q. What instrument does the grantor receive when the beneficiary has been satisfied?
   A. Deed of reconveyance.

True and False

1. The date when the mortgage was executed determines its priority.	T	**F**
2. The mortgagor pays the title insurance fee on a mortgage.	**T**	F
3. A mortgagee, is protected by the recording acts.	**T**	F
4. A mortgagee is bound to accept payment of the mortgage at any time offered.	T	**F**
5. A mortgage must be recorded to become a lien on property.	T	**F**
6. The date of recording determines the priority of a mortgage.	**T**	F
7. A lending institution cannot refuse to give a veteran a loan if the veteran has a certified entitlement.	T	**F**
8. A seller must obtain a court order to sell mortgage property.	T	**F**
9. A minor cannot affirm his purchase of a property and disaffirm his purchase money mortgage.	**T**	F
10. A mortgagee is concerned more with the financial responsibility of the debtor than the security of the property.	T	**F**
11. A deed of trust is usually conveyed to a Public Trustee.	**T**	F
12. An escrow account must be forfeited by the seller when the purchaser assumes his mortgage.	T	**F**

13. Taxes have priority over recorded mortgages. **T** F
14. A blanket mortgage is one upon a dwelling which has two or more bedrooms. T **F**
15. The mortgagee should have possession of the Abstract of Title and fire insurance policies. **T** F
16. In a joint estate, either party can execute a valid mortgage. T **F**
17. There are no covenants to be found in a mortgage. T **F**
18. In the sale of real property, it is more advisable to sell the property with a clause that buyer assumes the mortgage than merely "under and subject to mortgage." **T** F
19. An acknowledgment is necessary on the bond or note accompanying the mortgage. T **F**
20. A veteran purchaser is not allowed to pay the V.A. appraisal fee. T **F**
21. A mortgage is released from the records by filing a deed of "reconveyance." T **F**
22. It is lawful for a purchaser to give a second lien to the owner and assume the outstanding balance of an F.H.A. note. **T** F
23. The evidence of a personal obligation which is secured by real estate is called a mortgage. T **F**
24. A deficiency judgment may be taken against the mortgagor in the foreclosure of a purchase money mortgage. **T** F
25. A chattel mortgage is used to borrow money on farm lands. T **F**
26. When a mortgage is overdue, and it is the desire of the owner to negotiate the continuance of the mortgage to a later date, he negotiates an extension agreement. **T** F
27. A mortgagor is the party who has loaned money on real property. T **F**
28. The word "amortization" as applied to a mortgage or deed of trust means a reduction of the debt which they may secure by the payment of regular installments. **T** F
29. An F.H.A. loan on real estate means that the Government of the United States has made a direct advance of money to the owner and has taken a mortgage or deed of trust as security. T **F**
30. A mortgage is a lien on specific real estate. **T** F
31. There is no difference between a purchase money mortgage and one given to secure a loan. T **F**
32. A mortgage is personal property. **T** F
33. Usury means charging more than the legal rate of interest. **T** F
34. A mortgage on personal property is called a chattel mortgage. **T** F
35. F.H.A. loans are never made for more than 60% of the appraised valuation of the property. T **F**
36. An open mortgage is one upon vacant land. T **F**
37. A mortgage terminates an existing lease on the property. T **F**
38. A construction mortgage is one for a limited period of time. **T** F
39. A low interest rate deters the flow of mortgage money. **T** F

40. In an estate by the entireties, either husband or wife can execute a valid mortgage. T **F**

41. When a loan is made under the G.I. Bill of Rights, the money loaned does not come from the United States Government. **T** F

42. It is possible to procure a G.I. loan to purchase livestock and equipment for a farm. **T** F

43. When a G.I. loan is obtained, it is lawful for the borrower to give a second mortgage, where there is an F.H.A. first mortgage. T **F**

44. It is lawful for the borrower upon an F.H.A. mortgage to give a second mortgage on the same property covered by the F.H.A. mortgage. T **F**

45. At the present time an F.H.A. loan may be paid off in full without penalty if it is paid from the borrower's own funds. T **F**

46. It is unlawful to sue on a bond or note secured by a mortgage on real estate without first starting to foreclose the mortgage. T **F**

47. There is a substantial difference between buying property subject to a mortgage and buying the property and assuming a mortgage thereon. **T** F

48. A purchaser of property at a foreclosure sale on a mortgage receives a general warranty deed. T **F**

49. Where an applicant for a mortgage loan is an excellent moral risk, a higher appraised value of the real estate is permitted than if the applicant is a poor risk. T **F**

50. A mortgagor cannot, at foreclosure, set off against the debt the value of improvements made by him during the mortgage term. **T** F

51. A mortgagee is bound to accept a voluntary deed from the mortgagor in lieu of foreclosure. T **F**

52. In the purchase of real property, it is more advisable to buy the property subject to an existing mortgage than to assume payment of it. **T** F

53. A "junior mortgage" will take precedence over the first mortgage or trust deed, if no interest is paid on the first mortgage for the period of the calendar year. T **F**

54. The operation of paying off a mortgage by periodic payments is called the prepayment of the mortgage. T **F**

55. A mortgagor is bound to obtain the consent of the mortgagee before he can sell the mortgaged premises. T **F**

56. A mortgagee in possession must account to the mortgagor for all revenue received by him from the property. **T** F

57. The so-called "blanket mortgage" is one that includes attached fixtures and appliances, as well as the real estate. T **F**

58. A mortgage clause which permits the mortgagee to advance the maturity date of the principal is called an acceleration clause. **T** F

59. A chattel mortgage is used to borrow money on a right of way. T **F**

60. A mortgage can be transferred from one person to another. **T** F
61. Where a mortgagee takes over control of the mortgaged premises, he, and not the owner, is liable for injuries on the premises. **T** F
62. An "estoppel certificate" is the same as a "certificate of no defense." **T** F
63. A mortgage for more than 20 years is void. T **F**
64. A mortgage must be paid off before the property can be sold. T **F**
65. Even though a mortgaged property is sold more than 3 times, the original mortgagor continues liable under his bond or note. **T** F
66. Where the mortgagee enters into an extension agreement with the new purchaser of the mortgaged premises, the original mortgagor is discharged from liability. T **F**
67. Where a purchaser of mortgaged premises "assumes and agrees to pay" the debt, he is liable to the mortgagee for full payment. **T** F
68. Where a purchaser of mortgaged premises "assumes and agrees to pay" the debt, the original mortgagor is no longer liable for the debt. T **F**
69. An agent appointed to collect interest on a mortgage has authority to collect the principal. T **F**
70. An administrator of an estate has no authority to execute a mortgage upon real estate belonging to the decedent. **T** F
71. A person inheriting real estate subject to a mortgage must pay off the mortgage immediately. T **F**
72. A sound conventional loan should be for not more than two-thirds of the property value. **T** F
73. The Home Owners Loan Corporation gave its assistance to distressed property owners during the depression. **T** F
74. The mortgagor pays the fee for recording the mortgage. **T** F
75. A first mortgage is always a first lien. T **F**
76. Subordinating or postponing the lien of a mortgage is always more advantageous to the mortgagee than releasing the lien. **T** F
77. A minor is not permitted to own a mortgage. T **F**
78. The mortgagee should have possession of the fire insurance policy. **T** F
79. The mortgagor is required to pay the fire insurance premiums. **T** F
80. A "satisfaction piece" means that the mortgage has been partially paid off. T **F**
81. The mortgagor's "equity of redemption" is a period of grace for payment of the debt. **T** F
82. Any excess of funds realized at a foreclosure sale belong to the mortgagor. **T** F
83. A mortgage represents a liquid asset of the mortgagee. T **F**
84. Payment to the borrower of the money loaned under a con-

struction loan is made when the construction of the improvements on real estate is completed. **T** **F**

85. There is no difference between a mortgage release and a mortgage satisfaction. **T** **F**

86. The obtaining, by a lender, directly or indirectly of more than the statutory rate of interest is called an assessment. **T** **F**

87. The person who lends money and to whom the property is mortgaged, is called the mortgagee. **T** F

88. Paying off a mortgage by regular periodic payments is called the prepayment of a mortgage. **T** **F**

89. It is to the seller's advantage to have a buyer obtain a new mortgage rather than to assume and agree to pay the existing mortgage. **T** F

90. When a mortgage is overdue and it is the desire of the owner to negotiate the continuance of the mortgage to a later date, he negotiates an Estoppel Certificate. **T** **F**

91. A blanket mortgage is a single mortgage on two or more parcels as security for a single loan. **T** F

92. A debtor who gives five properties of equal value to a lender as security for a mortgage loan can require the lender to release any one parcel upon payment of one-fifth of the mortgage debt. **T** **F**

93. Where a mortgagor makes an addition to a dwelling after the mortgage has been placed, he can receive credit for the cost of such addition in event of a mortgage foreclosure sale of the dwelling. **T** **F**

94. Certain real estate was sold in a foreclosure sale brought by the first mortgagee for $5,400. There was a first mortgage of $6,000 and a second mortgage of $2,400. The second mortgagee will receive $1,800. **T** **F**

95. In the preceding case, the second mortgagee will receive nothing. **T** **F**

96. The debtor is protected in making mortgage payments to the original mortgagee, even though there is an assignment of the mortgage to a new person duly recorded. **T** F

97. Where a mortgage has been assigned, the law requires the debtor to give the assignee a Declaration of No Setoff, or a Certificate of No Defense. **T** **F**

98. If the mortgage is past due, it cannot be assigned. **T** **F**

99. The monthly payments on an amortized loan include the interest. **T** F

100. When a mortgage debt is past due, is unpaid, and the holder of the mortgage wishes to force the sale of the property to satisfy the debt, he starts an action for Specific Performance. **T** **F**

101. A Certificate of No Defense is obtained from the mortgagee by the purchaser of a mortgage. **T** **F**

102. Property on which there is an F.H.A. mortgage can be further encumbered. **T** F

103. In all cases, the redemption period of the mortgagor is six months after foreclosure sale. **T** **F**
104. The holder of a mortgage may sell or transfer the mortgage to a third party; the new holder obtains no greater interest than that which the original holder had at the time of transfer. **T** F
105. A mortgage which is taken back as part of the selling price is called a Blanket Mortgage. T **F**
106. A borrower, under a mortgage, is allowed one year in which to redeem the encumbered property after mortgage foreclosure sale. T **F**
107. A mortgage may be satisfied by full payment or foreclosure. **T** F
108. A mortgage note is personal property. **T** F
109. A trust deed does not take priority over a previously recorded mortgage. **T** F
110. A mortgage is executed by the mortgagee in favor of the mortgagor. T **F**
111. An instrument which transfers possession of property but does not transfer ownership, is a mortgage. T **F**
112. A majority of a commercial bank's investments are in mortgages. T **F**
113. A mortgagee in possession may be liable for sidewalk injuries to a pedestrian. **T** F
114. A mortgage on an industrial plant covers the machinery and equipment necessary to operate the plant. **T** F
115. Where the mortgage is in default, it is more advantageous to the mortgagor to give a voluntary deed than to suffer foreclosure by mortgagee. **T** F
116. As real estate activity increases, mortgage foreclosures increase. T **F**
117. Interest rates on mortgages in comparison with yields from other investment, determines the supply of available mortgage funds. **T** F
118. A purchase money mortgage is one taken by the seller in part payment of the purchase price. **T** F
119. Where a mortgage calls for "not less than $66.00 per week," it can be paid off at any time. **T** F
120. It is now customary to place the mortgage on record, before it releases the funds to the mortgagor. T **F**
121. The closing statement to the seller should reflect all of the mortgage costs to the buyer. T **F**
122. It is the obligation of the seller to pay for the cost of preparing the mortgage papers. T **F**
123. Title insurance for the amount of the mortgage affords the owner no protection after the loan is paid off. **T** F
124. An owner's title insurance policy, in a mortgage case, can be obtained at a small additional expense. **T** F

125. The "pay off" figure on an amortized mortgage changes from month to month. **T** F

126. The proceedings to discharge an old mortgage, upon which no payments have been made for more than 20 years, is an action to quiet title. **T** F

127. Assignment of a mortgage is the same as negotiability of a promissory note. T **F**

128. A mortgagee can enjoin the removal of a building from the mortgaged premises. **T** F

129. Waste is an action by the mortgagee which lessens the value of the property. T **F**

130. Of the parties to a trust deed, the trustor is the "lendor." T **F**

131. A trust deed may be satisfied of record by marginal release. **T** F

132. Defeasance clause in a mortgage nullifies the conveyance. **T** F

133. A document which transfers possession of real property, but does not convey ownership, is a mortgage. T **F**

134. The evidence of a personal debt which is secured by a lien on real estate is called a mortgage. T **F**

135. A mortgage is considered satisfied when an offset certificate has been filed. T **F**

136. If a person "assumes" a mortgage, the most he can lose, in the event of foreclosure, is the amount of his equity in the property. T **F**

137. A Certificate of Reduction of Mortgage is generally required when the mortgage is sold. T **F**

138. A recorded mortgage binds all and any real property subsequently acquired by the mortgagor. T **F**

139. In order that a note or bond be legally enforceable it must be properly acknowledged. T **F**

140. A chattel mortgage is used to borrow money on farm acreage. T **F**

141. If a buyer assumes a mortgage, the original mortgagor is released from liability. T **F**

142. The clause which permits the placing of a mortgage at a later date which will take priority over an existing mortgage is the subordination clause. **T** F

143. Payment and satisfaction of a mortgage is the same thing. T **F**

144. A mortgage should be properly acknowledged and recorded. **T** F

145. Redemption is the right which a mortgagor has to redeem his property after the expiration date. T **F**

146. A chattel trust is never recorded as it is not secured by real estate. T **F**

147. An acceleration clause in a mortgage speeds up mortgage payments. T **F**

148. An interest rate of 10 per cent is considered usurious. **T** F

149. The legal compensation received from the use of real estate is called equity. T **F**

150. The recording of a "Satisfaction Piece" is the only way a mortgage record can be released. T **F**

151. Most interests in real property can be mortgaged. **T** F
152. A property subject to a G.I. guaranteed mortgage cannot be sold except to another qualified veteran. T **F**
153. A mortgage covering two or more lots in a recorded subdivision is a blanket mortgage. **T** F
154. It is possible to transfer one mortgaged property for another mortgaged property even though the mortgage amounts are unequal. **T** F
155. A title mortgage title insurance policy insures the mortgagor as well as the mortgagee. T **F**
156. The amount of a construction loan mortgage must be in the same amount as the permanent mortgage. T **F**
157. An Extension Certificate and an Estoppel Certificate mean the same thing. T **F**
158. The monthly interest on a mortgage is usually paid at the end of the month and not at the beginning. **T** F
159. Every mortgage is a Purchase Money mortgage. T **F**

Multiple Choice

1. The instrument which conditionally conveys title to real estate is a
   ( ) chattel mortgage.
   ( ) conditional bailment lease.
   ( ) escrow deed.
   (x) mortgage.
2. The instrument used to remove the lien of a deed of trust from the record is called a
   ( ) redemption of equity.
   ( ) satisfaction.
   ( ) certificate of no defense.
   (x) deed of reconveyance.
3. The interest or value which an owner has in the property over and above the mortgage debt is known as
   ( ) an escrow.
   ( ) an equality.
   (x) an equity.
   ( ) a surplus.
4. A purchase money mortgage is
   (x) a mortgage given to the seller or third person by the purchaser as part of the purchase price.
   ( ) a partial release of the first mortgage.
   ( ) a mortgage on personal property purchased.
   ( ) used in a land contract transaction.
5. The Trustor in connection with a trust deed is the party who
   ( ) lends the money.
   ( ) receives the payments on the note.

(x) signs the note.

( ) holds the property in trust.

6. A clause in a deed of trust or mortgage or accompanying note or bond, which permits the creditor to declare the entire unpaid sum due upon certain default of the debtor, is

(x) an acceleration clause.

( ) an elevator clause.

( ) a forfeiture clause.

( ) an excelerator clause.

7. A deed of trust is usually conveyed to the

( ) grantor.

( ) broker.

(x) public trustee.

( ) mortgagor.

8. A mortgage is released by

( ) reversion.

( ) reconveyance.

( ) quit claim deed.

(x) satisfaction.

9. The money for making F.H.A. loans is provided by

(x) qualified lending institutions.

( ) any governmental agency.

( ) the Federal Housing Administration.

( ) the Federal Deposit Insurance Corporation.

10. Which of the following pays the one per cent handling charge on an F.H.A. mortgage?

( ) The lending institution.

(x) The borrower.

( ) The seller.

11. A chattel mortgage is given to secure

( ) an eviction.

( ) chattels.

( ) a lease.

( ) money borrowed on real property.

(x) a loan on personalty.

12. A reduction certificate is required when

( ) the mortgage is assigned.

(x) the property is sold.

( ) a new mortgage is placed.

( ) the mortgage is being extended.

13. A Veterans Administration loan is guaranteed by the

( ) mortgage company.

( ) F.H.A.

(x) Veterans Administration.

14. The owner of five parcels of real property desires a mortgage loan and offers all five parcels as security. The mortgage he will be required to execute will be

( ) a purchase money mortgage.

( ) an amortizing mortgage.
(x) a blanket mortgage.
( ) a building and loan mortgage.
15. A mortgage is usually released of record by recording
    ( ) quit claim deed.
    (x) satisfaction piece.
    ( ) reconveyance.
    ( ) estoppel certificate.
16. In the event that a penalty is being charged in the prepayment of an F.H.A. loan it is
    ( ) $50.00.
    ( ) $75.00.
    (x) 1 per cent of the face of the mortgage.
    ( ) 2 per cent of the face of the mortgage.
17. A loan insured by the F.H.A. is usually borrowed from the
    ( ) government.
    (x) bank.
    ( ) seller.
    ( ) county.
    ( ) Federal Housing Administration.
18. A blanket mortgage covers
    ( ) farm property.
    (x) more than one parcel of real estate.
    ( ) personal property.
    ( ) a coal or gas furnace.
19. In the sale of a mortgaged property, it is necessary
    ( ) to obtain the consent of the mortgagee.
    ( ) to pay off the mortgage.
    (x) for the grantor to deliver a deed.
    ( ) to obtain a court order.
20. An F.H.A. mortgage is one which is
    ( ) so known because the principal is reduced monthly.
    ( ) financed by F.H.A. money.
    (x) insured by a Federal Government agency.
21. An agreement to waive prior rights in favor of another is called
    ( ) redemption.
    ( ) subjugation.
    (x) subordination.
    ( ) estoppel.
22. When a mortgage is given as part of the consideration price a mortgage clause will be written in the
    (x) insurance policy.
    ( ) equity of redemption.
    ( ) deed.
    ( ) mortgage.
23. Amortization is the process of
    (x) liquidation of a debt.
    ( ) depreciation.

( ) winding up a business.

24. Where a purchaser assumes and agrees to pay an insured mortgage debt, it is most advantageous to the
( ) mortgagee.
( ) purchaser.
(x) mortgagor.
( ) F.H.A.

25. Where a lease antedates a mortgage, the mortgagee in possession has a right to
( ) evict the tenant.
(x) collect the rent.
( ) foreclose the property and terminate the lease.

26. The existing mortgage which is taken back as part of the selling price is called
( ) a blanket mortgage.
(x) an assumed mortgage.
( ) a subordinated mortgage.
( ) an extension of mortgage.

27. An estoppel certificate is required when
(x) the mortgage is assigned.
( ) the property is sold.
( ) a new mortgage is placed.
( ) the property is being foreclosed.

28. In the absence of an agreement to the contrary, the mortgage normally having priority will be
( ) the one for the highest amount.
( ) the one which is a first mortgage.
(x) the one that was recorded first.
( ) the one that is a construction loan mortgage.

29. The mortgage that includes items such as refrigerators, ranges, and electric washers is referred to as a
( ) blanket mortgage.
(x) package mortgage.
( ) participation mortgage.
( ) private mortgage.

30. The mortgage covenant which permits the mortgagee to advance the due date of the principal of the mortgage is called
( ) prepayment clause.
( ) foreclosure clause.
(x) acceleration clause.
( ) demising clause.

31. The owner of a property places a bank mortgage on it. He later sells the property with the buyer assuming and agreeing to pay the existing mortgage. In the event the bank later forecloses and sells the property at an amount less than the balance of the mortgage, which statement is correct?
( ) Only the original owner is liable for the deficiency.
( ) Only the buyer is liable for the deficiency.

( ) Neither is liable. The bank can only collect what it realized on the sale of the property.

(x) The bank could look to the buyer or seller, or both for payment of the deficiency.

32. A chattel mortgage is usually given in connection with
( ) real property.
( ) farm lands.
( ) a trust deed.
(x) personal property.
( ) commercial property.

33. The instrument which may conditionally convey title is
( ) an option.
( ) a patent.
(x) a mortgage.
( ) a quit claim deed.

34. Trust Deeds are used to
( ) finance purchase of stocks.
( ) secure a judgment.
(x) borrow money.
( ) to bond an administrator of an estate.

35. A "satisfaction piece" is a writing that
( ) records payment of a deed of trust indebtedness.
(x) records and acknowledges a paid-off deed of trust.
( ) pays a landlord for damages to his property.
( ) renders satisfaction to a lessor for personal damages.

36. A "balloon" payment on a deed of trust refers to the
( ) first payment.
(x) final payment.
( ) middle payment.
( ) second payment.

37. An owner who desires a deed of trust loan and offers three properties as security will be required to execute which type of deed of trust
(x) blanket.
( ) F.H.A.
( ) conventional.
( ) building and loan.

38. A mortgage which is past due and subject to foreclosure at any time is called
(x) an open mortgage.
( ) a senior mortgage.
( ) a primary mortgage.
( ) a closed mortgage.

39. Money realized at a foreclosure sale on a mortgage in excess of the mortgage indebtedness belongs to
( ) purchaser at sheriff's sale.
( ) sheriff.
( ) mortgagee.

(x) mortgagor.
40. The usual term of a mortgage in the $20,000 price for dwellings is
   ( ) 12 years.
   ( ) 35 years.
   (x) 20 years.
   ( ) 10 years.
41. The borrower under a Trust Deed is the
   (x) grantor.
   ( ) grantee.
   ( ) cestuique trust.
   ( ) none of these.
42. A clause releasing one lot in a mortgaged subdivision is
   (x) release.
   ( ) an exoneration.
   ( ) prepayment clause.
   ( ) an equity.
43. When a mortgage is foreclosed, any lease made after the date of the mortgage is
   (x) terminated.
   ( ) binding upon tenant, but not the mortgagee.
   ( ) not affected in any way.
   ( ) binding upon purchaser at the foreclosure sale, but not upon tenant.
44. The mortgagor's right to reestablish ownership, after delinquency, is known as
   ( ) a statute of allowances.
   ( ) unjust enrichment.
   (x) equity of redemption.
   ( ) acceleration.
45. The Federal National Mortgage Association purchases
   ( ) chattel mortgages.
   ( ) F.H.A. mortgages.
   ( ) government-insured mortgages.
   (x) conventional mortgages.
46. Which one of the following statements is false
   (x) The Federal Government supplies the funds to the lending agency.
   ( ) The Federal Government insures the lending agency against losses.
   ( ) F.H.A. may insure either apartment house project or a residence mortgage.
   ( ) V.A. is limited to G.I. mortgages.

Chapter 6

JUDGMENTS

FROM EARLY times (1688) lands of debtors have been subject to liens as security for debts. Although almost every person is interested in judgments from viewpoints of creditor and debtor, very few people are sufficiently conversant with the legal principles that apply. In the first place, what is a judgment? In legal parlance, it may be defined as a decree of a court of competent jurisdiction declaring that one individual (the debtor) is indebted to another (the creditor), and fixing the amount of such indebtedness. A verdict obtained in every court is not necessarily a judgment. Some further step may be necessary to reduce the verdict to judgment; hence the qualification in the definition, "of a court of competent jurisdiction."

In personam and in rem

Judgments fall into two main classes, judgments *in personam* (against the person) and judgments *in rem* (against the thing or particular property). A judgment *in personam* may be termed a general lien; a judgment *in rem* may be called a specific lien. Most judgments are against the person, and as such, bind *all* his real estate. Adams sues Burns on a contract (in assumpsit) and obtains a judgment; or Jones sues Smith for damages due to an automobile accident (in trespass) and obtains a judgment. Both are *in personam.* A tax lien, an assessment for a street improvement, and a mechanic's lien are judgments *in rem.* That is, the judgment binds only the particular piece of real estate for which the tax was due, or benefited by the street improvement, or upon which the work was performed and for which materials were furnished by the mechanic or material supply dealer. It is a judgment against the particular person by reason of his being the owner of that particular piece of real estate. The effect of a judgment (in personan) is that a lien immediately attaches against the debtor's real estate upon the entry of the judgment. It automatically binds all the real estate located in the county where the judgment is entered. That is what is meant by the *lien* of the judgment. A lien may be defined, in technical language, as a hold or claim which one person has upon the property of another as a security for some debt or charge. It is the right which the creditor has under the law to have the debt satisfied out of the debtor's property. If the creditor merely has a claim, not reduced to judgment, the debtor can sell or mortgage his property, free and clear of such unsecured claim. If the creditor has reduced his claim to a judgment, a lien is thereby created against the real estate. A purchaser would then take the property subject to the lien and stand in the place of the debtor.

A judgment, other than a judgment *in rem*, binds every freehold interest in the land. A judgment entered against a life tenant will bind his interest in the property, which may be sold to satisfy the judgment. The purchaser would take the property for or during the lifetime of the debtor, as a tenant *pour autre vie* (for the life of another).

Lien on personal property

Judgments are not liens on the personal property of the debtor as they are on his real estate. A debtor may convey good title to a bona fide purchaser of his automobile or other personal property even though there is a judgment of record against him. Personal property may, however, be seized in satisfaction of a judgment debt. This is done by levy or attachment upon directions to the sheriff, the executive officer of the court, to seize and sell the described property. A mortgage, while it deals with real estate, is personalty, but the court can direct the sheriff to levy on a mortgage belonging to the debtor and sell it. The same is true of a leasehold. In other words, a creditor is entitled to proceed against any property of his debtor to recover his debt. In a sense, a debtor is a trustee for his creditors.

Release of judgment—postponement

It is always important to remember that a judgment attaches and adversely affects real estate of a debtor, as a lien, just as soon as it is entered of record. The judgment is a lien against all of the real estate owned by the debtor at the time the judgment is entered. The owner cannot give a purchaser good title to any part of the real estate owned by him. No prudent buyer would accept title thus encumbered, nor could the creditor be compelled to release any part of the debtor's real estate upon payment of any sum short of the full debt. A release is a matter of indulgence by the creditor. The real estate released should be noted on the margin of the recorded judgment. Where a judgment exists against a debtor's real estate and the debtor desires to place a mortgage upon the property, he may ask the judgment creditor to release the judgment for a part payment. If the debtor owns other real estate, the creditor may be receptive to the request. However, if no substantial payment is to be made upon the judgment and the creditor is willing to accommodate his debtor in placing a mortgage which shall be a first lien, it is preferable that he defer the lien of his judgment to the proposed mortgage instead of releasing the property from the judgment lien outright. By subordinating or postponing his lien, the particular property still affords some security to the creditor. When the debtor pays the judgment, he is entitled to have the judgment marked "satisfied" of record.

Lien period

The lien of a judgment does not last forever. As between the original debtor-owner and judgment creditor, execution may be had against the debtor's property at any time, so long as the debtor continues to own it and rights of mortgagees or other judgment creditors have not intervened. The lien of the judgment lasts for a limited period of time, and, if the judgment is not revived within the prescribed period of time, the lien against a subsequent purchaser, mortgagee, or judgment creditor is lost. In Pennsylvania, the lien of the judgment lasts five years. If the judgment is for longer than the statutory period and no action taken to revive it, a purchaser from the debtor takes the property free from the judgment. In other jurisdictions, the judgment is a lien for ten years.

Judgments arise in several ways, among which are court decision, default, and confession. Since litigation is always prevalent, a great many judgments arise through court action. Where the litigation takes place in a minor judiciary court such as a Justice of the Peace, a transcript of the verdict or judgment can be filed in the proper County Court so as to be a lien. A judgment by default arises where the law requires a person to take some sufficient legal step and he fails to do so. For example, Thompson sues Bryan and serves him with a copy of his statement of claim. Bryan is then required to file an answer within a certain period of time, say 20 days, and he fails to do so. Thompson can enter judgment against Bryan because of Bryan's default. The great majority of judgments probably arise through confession, authorized in a note, bond, or lease. They are known as judgments DSB, which stands for *debitum sine brevi* and means "debt without a writ or declaration."

By confession

A judgment by confession is as conclusive as a judgment on the verdict of a jury. The main distinction between a promissory note and a judgment note is that upon a default in payment of a promissory note, the holder must sue the maker before he can obtain a judgment, which in a judgment note, the holder may enter up judgment upon a default without any suit. This is so by reason of the language of the instrument which authorizes and empowers

. . . any Attorney of any Court of Record within the United States or elsewhere to appear for (me), and with or without declarations filed, confess judgment against (me) and in favor of said payee, his executors, administrators, or assigns, as of any term for the above sum with costs of suit, etc.

In fact, the holder of the note may confess judgment at any time, even before default or maturity, but no execution can issue until default. If the obligor is deceased, judgment may not be confessed against him as death revokes the agent's power to confess. Where one joint obligor dies, the note can be entered as a judgment against the survivor; it is irregular to enter the note against all of the obligors including the decedent. Judgment by confession operates in a very summary manner, and very often the debtor is unaware that a judgment has been entered against him until he tries to sell his property or place a mortgage upon it. If the debtor claims that the entry of the judgment is unjust, he may petition the court to open up the judgment; and if the court, in the exercise of its sound judicial discretion, believes that the debtor should be permitted to make a defense, it will open up the judgment and then the case is heard *de novo* (anew) to determine whether the plaintiff is entitled to his judgment. If the judgment appears erroneous upon its face, the proper proceeding is to strike it off by motion. The court will examine the record to ascertain the form of the judgment but will not go into the merits of the debtor's claim as in a petition to open up the judgment. A great volume of judgments on notes or bonds accompanying mortgages are confessed. Judgment, of course, can only be collected for the real debt due. Deficiency judgments have been discussed in connection with mortgage foreclosures. Although the majority of an infant's contracts are voidable at the infant's election, nevertheless a warrant of attorney by a minor to confess judgment against him is absolutely void. A judgment so confessed will be vacated upon a motion to strike it off. Since the confession is void, a minor is deemed incapable of ratifying it. A minor gives a judgment note in payment for a horse. Upon reaching his majority, he retains the horse, and the holder of the note confesses judgment on it, claiming a ratification. The judgment is stricken off. Where a minor, with others, gives a judgment note in payment of land, the minor would not be permitted to retain the land and refuse to pay for its value.

Decedent's debts

In most states debts of a decedent constitute a lien against his real estate. Property of a decedent is subject to a state inheritance tax, which remains a lien until paid. The estate, when in excess of $60,000, is also subject to a Federal estate tax which, under the law (1940), remains a lien for 10 years after the death. State taxes favor lineal heirs. The rate is usually much higher for a relative of the decedent or a stranger (collateral heirs) than it is for the surviving spouse, child, or parent. Where letters of administration have been taken out in an estate and the heirs desire to sell real estate, a petition may be presented to the court for leave to sell the real estate free from any debts, if there are satisfactory averments that all of the debts of the decedent have already been paid.

It has been previously stated that a judgment is a lien against all of the real estate which the debtor owns at the time the judgment is entered against him. It does not bind property he acquires by purchase or by will after the date of entry of the judgment. Such after-acquired property can be brought under the lien of the creditor's judgment by reviving the lien of the judgment. This can be done at any time. After-acquired property, sold by the debtor before revival of the judgment, would pass clear title to a purchaser without notice.

A judgment creditor may take the necessary legal action to foreclose the property in order to obtain satisfaction of the debt and the costs of the sale. Frequently, however, the creditor may do nothing since foreclosure proceedings necessitate an advance of costs and payment of any delinquent taxes against the property. The creditor may feel, rather, that in time the debtor will desire to sell or mortgage the property and will then have to make peace with the creditor and pay him off. This often happens. The creditor should be ever alert, however, that the lien of his judgment is not lost through passage of time. The creditor instituting foreclosure proceedings must be circumspect in complying with all legal requirements as to notice and advertisement of the property for sale. The property is put up at competitive public sale and sold to the highest bidder. Any excess funds realized at the sale, over and above the debts of record and costs, belong to the debtor-owner. Where there is more than one creditor, the funds are distributed in the order of priority of liens. The creditor who initiates the sheriff's sale obtains no preference on that account, but takes his place in distribution of funds according to the date when his judgment was entered. Where there is a first mortgage against the property, which is a first lien, and the property is sold on a later judgment lien, the first mortgage is not divested. The purchaser at sheriff's sale takes the property subject to the first mortgage. If the property is sold on the first mortgage, all liens would be divested, and the purchaser would obtain clear title. Where there are two or more mortgages of record, without any prior or intervening judgments, sale on a subsequent judgment would not divest any of the mortgages. The sheriff makes no warranty or guaranty of title. The risk and responsibility are entirely upon the purchaser.

Fraud on creditors

A property sold, mortgaged, or liened in an effort to hinder, delay, or defraud a creditor may be set aside by a creditor's petition to court for relief. A judgment entered the same day as a conveyance or mortgage of the property would constitute a prior lien against the property. In practice, a mortgagee may record his mortgage one day and disburse the funds the next day so as to have sufficient time to examine the records and ascertain that no judgment, mortgage, or adverse conveyance has been entered.

Mechanic's lien

A mechanic's lien is given to contractors, laborers, and material men, by statute, for work performed or materials furnished. It is really special class legislation, but has nevertheless been sustained by the courts. There must be strict compliance with the legal requirements as to serving the notice of intention to file the lien. A distinction as to time for filing a mechanic's lien is made as between new construction and repairs and as between a contractor and subcontractor. The contractor may enter into a "No Lien Contract" with the owner, and, as the name implies, no mechanic's liens can be filed for work or materials furnished on the job for the owner. If the "No Lien Contract" is recorded, sub-contractors are bound by its terms, even though they had failed to take the precaution of examining the records. This does not give the owner, however, "letter perfect" protection. If, after the "No Lien Contract" is filed, the terms of the contract are materially changed between owner and contractor, the "No Lien Contract" filed would be inoperative.

If there is no "No Lien Contract" filed, a sub-contractor, in Pennsylvania and other states, would have the right to file a mechanic's lien for his labor, even though the owner has made his required payments to the contractor. An irresponsible contractor often visits an unjust hardship upon the owner in this connection. Since the mechanic's lien protects the sub-contractor, the cost of a dwelling often is considerably higher than the actual contract price. A licensing law for contractors has been agitated in a number of states in order to make a contractor responsible to an owner under a building contract. In some states, a sub-contractor can recover only the balance due and owing by the owner to the general contractor under the building contract. The owner after receiving notice from a sub-contractor as to the value of his services is privileged to hold out such amount from the contract price and pay it directly to the sub-contractor. Notice from the sub-contractor is imperative. This is known as the "New York system."

In most states a mechanic's lien dates back to the beginning of the construction job. Thus mortgagees are apprehensive lest the mortgage not be consummated and recorded before ground is broken. The sub-contractor has priority over a mortgage if the mortgage was recorded after the work started, even though the sub-contractor—a plumber, for example—did not render any service until after the building was well advanced. The time for serving notice of intention to file a mechanic's lien dates from the time when all the work is completed. An owner can protect himself by requiring the general contractor to post a performance bond or by reserving to the owner the privilege of paying sub-contractors' claims upon certification of the architect that the work has been satisfactorily performed.

Many a purchaser from a contractor relies upon a release of liens, which must be executed by every sub-contractor and material man who did work or furnished materials on the job. Unfortunately, in too many cases all of the material men or sub-contractors have not executed the release. They may file a claim at a later date, which the purchaser must pay even though full payment of the purchase price has already been made to the builder. Also, the purchaser may be deceived by an unscrupulous builder who furnishes a release, for example, signed by a lumber company that furnished only a small portion of the lumber used. The buyer may mistakenly believe that all claims for lumber have been paid, whereas the lumber company that furnished the bulk of the lumber has not signed a release nor has been requested to do so. In purchasing a new building, it is recommended that title insurance be purchased insuring against mechanic's liens as well as against defects in title.

Marshalling

Where a creditor has two or more funds out of which to satisfy his debt, he cannot so elect as to deprive another creditor of his security who has but one fund. This is known as marshalling. For example, Benson entered judgment against Archer for $1,700 on June 16, 1958. Archer owns three parcels of improved real estate. On January 3, 1960, Chance places a mortgage on one tract for $1,500. Then, on March 20, 1961, Benson issues execution against the mortgaged tract. Chance can compel Benson to proceed first against the other two properties owned by Archer. Of course, if, upon the sale of the other two tracts, Benson does not receive the amount of his judgment in full, he may then proceed against the parcel upon which Chance holds his mortgage.

Indexing judgment

In concluding judgments, attention is directed to the necessity of identifying the debtor accurately in the judgment index. Omission of the middle initial of the debtor's name may prove fatal. The question is whether the debtor's name in the index is such as to put the searcher upon inquiry. Where property was held in the name of Daniel J. Murphy and judgment entered against Daniel Murphy, held judgment was not a lien. Where land was owned by W. A. Black and judgment was entered against W. G. Black, held no lien. However, a judgment entered against Rosie Reustle was held a good lien against property owned by Rosie C. Reustle. Rosie Reustle and Rosie C. Reustle were one and the same person, and the only person by that name in the county. A judgment against Caroline Kerl was a binding lien against real estate owned by Caroline C. Kerl. Each case necessarily depends upon its concomitant circumstances. The Pennsylvania Supreme Court,[1] in determining what constituted sufficient constructive notice, said:

It is not necessary that the name of the judgment debtor as docketed and indexed should be letter-perfect, nor do the cases hold that the omission of the middle initial in the entry of a judgment automatically and inevitably vitiates the entry and subordinates it to subsequent judgments more accurately docketed. Each case must depend upon concomitant circumstances.

Omission of a middle name may be misleading or harmful in cases where the surname is a relatively common one. The first or Christian name must be correct in the judgment. Title in name of Kathryn Steele, judgment entered against Catharine Steele held invalid.

---

[1] *Coral Gables, Inc. vs. Kerl,* 334 Pa. 441, 6 A. 2d, 275 (1939).

Questions on Judgments

1. Q. What is the effect of a recorded judgment on the real property of the judgment debtor?
   A. It is a lien upon all real property of the debtor in the county it is recorded.
2. Q. What is a deficiency judgment?
   A. A judgment entered for the difference between the amount of the debt owed and the amount realized from the sale of the debtor's real property at foreclosure sale.
3. Q. In searching for liens on real estate what would you look for?
   A. Mortgages, judgments, mechanic's liens, delinquent taxes, liens for certain city improvements, and delinquent vendor's liens.
4. Q. Does compliance with the Bulk Sales Law, in selling a business, relieve purchaser of all liability for outstanding indebtedness?
   A. No. It does not protect the purchaser against back sales tax which may be due and owing by the seller and which constitutes a prior lien against the assets of any business.
5. Q. Define a judgment.
   A. A judgment is a decree of a court of competent jurisdiction determining that one individual is indebted to another and fixing the amount of such indebtedness.
6. Q. What kinds of judgment are there?
   A. Judgments are of two kinds, *in personam* and *in rem*. Judgments which bind the person against whom they are rendered and all of his real estate are judgments *in personam*, and judgments which bind a particular piece of real estate only and are against a particular person because he is the owner of that property are judgments *in rem*.
7. Q. Do judgments bind personal property?
   A. Not in the sense that the judgment is a lien on the personal property of the debtor. Personal property, however, may be sold in satisfaction of a judgment.
8. Q. Is a judgment a lien on a mortgage?
   A. No. A mortgage is personal property and not realty.
9. Q. Jones obtains a judgment for $500 against Brown. The debtor, Brown, owns an automobile which he sells to Cox. Does Cox get good title to the automobile?
   A. Yes. The automobile is personal property.
10. Q. Suppose Adams obtains a judgment for $900 against Brant who owns tracts 1, 2, and 3. Can Brant sell tract 3 to Chalmers so that Chalmers will get a free unencumbered title to the property?
    A. No. Adams' judgment is a lien against *all* of Brant's real property.

11. Q. In the preceding case, suppose Brant offers to pay Adams $300 on account of the judgment and demands that Adams release tract 3 from the judgment so that Chalmers can obtain clear title. Must Adams release the lot?

A. No. Execution of a release is a matter of accommodation by the creditor. He cannot be compelled to execute a release even though partial payment of the judgment is tendered.

12. Q. Is a judgment a lien on property acquired by a debtor after entry of judgment?

A. No. Such after-acquired property can be brought under the lien of the judgment only by reviving the judgment.

13. Q. In what ways may judgment be entered?

A. By verdict, default, or confession.

14. Q. Ash sells a tract of ground to Boone on November 25, 1968, and on November 27, 1968, Crane secures a judgment against Ash. Boone records his deed December 6, 1968. Will Crane's judgment be a lien against the property?

A. Yes. The records showed Ash was the owner of the property when the judgment was entered.

15. Q. Suppose, in the preceding case, that Ash conveys the property to his wife on November 25, 1968. Could the deed be set aside?

A. Yes. The conveyance is a clear fraud upon creditors.

16. Q. How long does a judgment remain a lien?

A. Five years in some states, ten years in other states. (Indiana for example, the lien period is ten years.)

17. Q. Atkins secures a judgment against Burke for $600 on June 16, 1960. Can Atkins on March 21, 1969, sell the property on his judgment?

A. Yes. Although the lien period has expired, Atkins can still sell the property so long as a new purchaser's rights, or those of a creditor, have not intervened.

18. Q. White enters into an agreement of sale for the purchase of certain real estate on October 2, 1968. Black enters a judgment against White on October 4, 1968. The property is conveyed to White on November 25, 1968. Is Black's judgment a lien against this real estate?

A. Yes. White's equitable title or interest in the real estate can be bound by the lien of a judgment.

19. Q. Is a lease of years subject to lien of a judgment?

A. No. A lease of years is personalty. However, if there is an option to purchase, the leasehold can be sold in execution.

20. Q. Suppose the following liens and encumbrances exist against Martin's property:

(a) Fielding's mortgage for $4,000 entered on June 16, 1961.
(b) Pope's judgment for $2,250 entered on December 16, 1962.
(c) Swift's mortgage for $1,000 entered on February 2, 1963.
(d) Gray's judgment for $750 on February 1, 1964.

The property is sold on Gray's judgment on July 1, 1967. The costs and taxes amount to $710. The property is sold for $3,650 to Williams. How will this fund be distributed, and subject to what liens, if any, will Williams, the purchaser, take the property?

A. The costs and taxes of $710 will be paid first, leaving $2,940 for distribution. Pope will be paid in full. Swift will receive the balance of $690. Gray will get nothing. Williams will take the property subject to Fielding's mortgage. Where the first mortgage is a first lien and the sale takes place upon a subsequent lien, the mortgage is not divested.

21. Q. Suppose the following liens and encumbrances exist against Jones' property:
Benson's mortgage for $25,000 entered on October 2, 1959.
Conover's mortgage for $5,000 entered November 25, 1960.
Dodd's mortgage for $1,000 entered April 25, 1965.
Evans' judgment for $7,500 entered April 26, 1965.
Franklin's judgment for $1,200 entered January 3, 1966.
The property is sold on Evans' judgment and brings $9,750. The cost and taxes amount to $850. How will the $9,750 be distributed and subject to what liens, if any, will the purchaser, Johnson, take the property?

A. Costs and taxes will be paid first, leaving $8,900 for distribution. Evans will receive $7,500, Franklin will receive $1,200, and the balance of $200 will go to Jones, the owner. Johnson will take the property subject to the three mortgages of Benson, Conover, and Dodd. Where there are two or more mortgages against a property and no prior or intervening judgment, and a sale takes place upon a subsequent lien, none of the mortgages is divested.

22. Q. In the event that Grafton had a judgment of $150 entered on October 1, 1959, show how the fund in the preceding case would be distributed and subject to what liens, if any, Johnson would take the property.

A. After payment of costs and taxes, Grafton would receive $150 and the balance of $8,750 would be paid to Benson, Conover, Dodd, Evans, and Franklin would receive nothing. The purchaser would take the property free and clear of all liens. The judgment, being the first lien, divests all the mortgages and judgments.

23. Q. How could Benson and the other creditors have protected themselves?

A. By appearing at the foreclosure sale and bidding the property up to cover their liens.

24. Q. A mortgage entered against Roberts' property on March 21, 1948 is foreclosed on October 2, 1956. A judgment is entered against Roberts in favor of the United States Government on December 6, 1954. The mortgagee, Barnes, has failed to notify the Government prior to the sheriff sale of his intention to foreclose the

property. At the sale, the property is sold to Clark. Is the Federal lien divested by the sheriff sale?

A. No. Under the Federal law, the lien is not divested because of Barnes' failure to notify the Government of his intention to foreclose, thus giving the Government an opportunity to bid upon the property at the sheriff sale. Clark will take the property subject to the Government lien.

25. Q. Is title acquired by purchase at a treasurer's sale for unpaid municipal taxes good and marketable?

A. Ordinarily, a title insurance company will not insure a tax sale title. The title is, thus, not good and merchantable. Besides, the owner of the property usually has one year's time within which to redeem the property.

26. Q. What is the best way for the purchaser of a new home from a contractor to protect himself from the filing of mechanic's liens against the property?

A. Title insurance is the best protection. He could require a surety bond for performance or completion; a release of liens from all sub-contractors and material men; have the general contractor file a "no-lien" contract; pay out the money as the work progresses.

27. Q. Special tax assessments (or liens) are levied against City Property. Name four things for which special assessments may be levied.

A. Street paving, curb, sidewalk, sewer.

28. Q. A lien filed against real property by the contractor for labor or material is called a

A. ( ) labor lien.
   ( ) completion notice lien.
   (x) mechanic's lien.
   ( ) builder's lien.

29. Q. A property is sold in a foreclosure sale at $5,000. There was a first mortgage against the property for $4,600 and a second mortgage lien of $1,000. Unpaid taxes amounted to $400. Show the distribution of the $5,000 sale upon first mortgage.

A. Taxes will be paid first in amount of $400. First mortgagee will get $4,600. Second mortgagee will get nothing.

True and False

1. A judgment must be recorded to become a lien against real estate.   **T**   F
2. A lien is always an encumbrance.   **T**   F
3. In a "joint and several" obligation, suit must be entered against all of the obligors.   T   **F**

4. The duty is upon the creditor to see that his judgment is properly indexed. **T** F
5. An unsecured creditor can reduce his claim to a judgment by filing his claim in the clerk or prothonotary's office. T **F**
6. A prothonotary is the chief clerk of the county or district court. **T** F
7. The lien of a judgment binds real estate only. **T** F
8. A mechanic's lien is a general lien. T **F**
9. Personal property may be sold upon a judgment. **T** F
10. Postponing a lien is preferable to releasing a lien. **T** F
11. A judgment is not a lien on a mortgage. **T** F
12. A first mortgage is always a first lien. T **F**
13. Where a debtor owns two properties of equal value, a judgment creditor can be compelled to accept one half of the debt and release one property. T **F**
14. A DSB judgment is one entered by confession. **T** F
15. Where there are a number of judgment creditors, the one who institutes foreclosure is paid first out of the proceeds. T **F**
16. Where one joint obligor dies, the note can be entered as a judgment against the survivor. **T** F
17. Death of the obligor prevents a judgment being confessed against the decedent. T F
18. Execution may not be issued upon a judgment against a municipality. **T** F
19. A property can never be sold where there is a judgment against it. T **F**
20. A judgment entered by confession against a minor is void. **T** F
21. A leasehold is subject to the lien of a judgment. T **F**
22. A judgment against a husband will operate as a lien against property owned by husband and wife. T **F**
23. A judgment is protected by the recording acts. **T** F
24. A judgment is void after the lien period has expired. T **F**
25. A judgment is non-assignable. T **F**
26. Previous payment to the creditor is a good defense to suit by the assignee of the judgment. **T** F
27. Any excess of funds realized at a foreclosure sale belongs to the owner. **T** F
28. After a "notice of completion" is properly filed, no one can record a valid mechanic's lien. T **F**
29. A chattel is a mortgage on personal property. T **F**
30. A right to or interest in real estate that diminishes its value is called an encumbrance. **T** F
31. Tax liens have priority over a previously recorded trust deed or mortgage. **T** F
32. A recorded easement is considered an encumbrance but not a lien. **T** F
33. The obligee is the creditor. **T** F
34. Negotiability is the same as assignability. T **F**

35. Property conveyed to a close relative in contemplation of a judgment, but before the judgment is actually entered, can be set aside.   **T** F

36. A judgment entered against the seller of real estate, but before the deed to the purchaser is recorded, will be a lien against the real estate.   **T** F

37. Judgments are only entered in the courts of the county.   T **F**

38. A verdict before an alderman or Justice of the Peace constitutes a judgment.   T **F**

39. Judgments entered on a note or bond accompanying a mortgage date from the date when the mortgage was executed. **T** F

40. The effect of a mortgage is to create a lien.   **T** F

41. An *in rem* judgment is a specific lien against one property only.   **T** F

42. The lien of a judgment is six years.   T **F**

43. When a suit for damages is filed, the plaintiff has a cautionary judgment against the defendant.   T **F**

44. A suit in equity for real estate operates as a cloud against the real estate when the suit is filed.   **T** F

45. Judgments bear interest at five per cent until paid.   T **F**

46. Upon payment of a judgment, the creditor is required to satisfy the records.   **T** F

47. Where the judgment has been assigned of record, the debtor must pay the assignee and not the original creditor, even if he has not been notified of the assignment.   T **F**

48. Liens against real estate are satisfied in the order in which they are executed.   T **F**

49. A property, against which a judgment has been entered, must be sold within ten years or the judgment will be void.   T **F**

50. Property sold on a first mortgage which is a first lien will discharge all judgments against the same property.   **T** F

51. A judgment has priority over all other liens.   T **F**

52. An "encumbrance" is always a "lien."   T **F**

53. The lien of a trust deed is released by the recording of a properly executed deed of reconveyance.   **T** F

54. Judgment entered against Catherine Lynn is a good lien against property owned by Katherine Lynn.   T **F**

55. The lien of a judgment does not have priority over all other liens.   **T** F

56. A real estate broker may file a lien for his commission against the property sold, if he is not paid.   T **F**

57. Lis Pendens is a form of public notice filed against a named property that a suit is about to be filed.   **T** F

58. A contractor, who is not paid, may file an injunction against the subject property.   T **F**

59. A judgment is always an encumbrance against all the property the defendant owns.   T **F**

60. A property can be sold even if there are judgments against it. **T** F

61. Current unpaid real estate taxes constitute a lien against the real estate. **T** F
62. In Wisconsin, homestead is exempt from execution to the extent of $5,000. **T** F
63. A judgment entered by a Justice of the Peace in favor of a plaintiff constitutes a lien. T **F**
64. A defendant's automobile may be sold to satisfy a judgment. **T** F
65. A firm, furnishing paint to an owner in the repair of his home may file a mechanic's lien, to protect his claim. **T** F
66. When a deed of trust note is secured by a deed of trust, the latter but not the former should be recorded. T **F**

Multiple Choice

1. Judgments are entered by
   ( ) an Alderman.
   (x) court of competent jurisdiction.
   ( ) real estate Commission.
   ( ) a Justice of the Peace.
2. The majority of judgments are entered by
   ( ) court decisions.
   ( ) default.
   (x) confession.
   ( ) insurance companies.
3. A judgment entered of record, is a lien on the debtor's
   ( ) automobile.
   (x) residence.
   ( ) bank account.
   ( ) wages.
4. A judgment takes effect from the time
   ( ) the debt is incurred.
   ( ) suit is decided.
   ( ) verdict of a jury is given.
   (x) it is entered of record.
5. If a debtor owns three pieces of real estate and a judgment is entered against him, it will be a lien against
   ( ) the property first acquired by him.
   ( ) the property last acquired by him.
   (x) all three properties.
   ( ) homestead property only.
6. The period of lien of the judgment is determined by
   (x) statute of state.
   ( ) law of Congress.
   ( ) plaintiff.
   ( ) court.

7. The type of property of a debtor which can be sold on execution of a judgment is
   ( ) real property only.
   (x) real or personal.
   ( ) incorporeal real estate.
   ( ) personal property only.

8. Holder of a cognovit or judgment note can confess judgment
   ( ) after default only.
   (x) after execution and delivery of the note.
   ( ) after 30 days default.
   ( ) degree of court.

9. Judgment notes can be confessed for a debtor by
   ( ) an attorney-in-fact.
   ( ) an agent.
   ( ) a justice of the peace.
   (x) an attorney at law.

10. A mechanic's lien can be filed against an owner by
    ( ) a salesman against a broker.
    (x) a lumber company furnishing materials.
    ( ) an abstracter.
    ( ) the building superintendent after completion of building.

11. A judgment entered against a person who owns property would not be good against which one of the following
    ( ) a life estate.
    ( ) tenancy in common.
    ( ) joint tenancy.
    (x) estate by the entireties.

12. A judgment was entered against John Stone on May 3, 1969. The judgment would *not* be a lien against which one of the following:
    ( ) property purchased on April 25, 1950.
    ( ) property acquired by devise on November 25, 1968.
    (x) property purchased on June 14, 1969.
    ( ) property acquired by gift on March 17, 1969.

13. Property acquired by a debtor after judgment has been entered against him will be liened by the issuance of
    ( ) an action to quiet title.
    (x) *scire facias* proceedings.
    ( ) filing a civil suit in assumpsit.
    ( ) suit to annul a debtor's exemption.

14. Postponing a judgment, instead of releasing a judgment benefits
    ( ) the debtor.
    ( ) no one, since they are the same.
    (x) the creditor.
    ( ) a third party.

15. A judgment may be satisfied by sale of personal property through
    (x) levy and attachment proceedings.
    ( ) filing a creditor's bill.
    ( ) bill of interpleader.

( ) sequestration proceedings.
16. A judgment *in rem* binds only debtor's
( ) personal property.
(x) real property.
( ) household effects and furniture.
( ) automobile.
17. Judgments prevent the debtor's property from being
( ) sold.
( ) leased.
( ) mortgaged.
(x) none of these.
18. Adams has a judgment against Austin dated March 21, 1969. Austin owns two properties, designated Tracts 1 and 2. Clark holds a mortgage against Tract 1, dated April 24, 1969. Adams, in order to satisfy his judgment must proceed
( ) against Tract 1.
(x) against Tract 2.
( ) must wait until Austin sells Tract 1.
( ) must wait until mortgage is paid or foreclosed.
19. Alberts deeds property to Forster on January 3, 1968. The deed is recorded on January 13, 1969. Boone enters judgment against Alberts on January 10, 1969. Which of the following is true
( ) the judgment is now a lien against Forster.
(x) the judgment is a lien against the subject property.
( ) the deed is invalid.
( ) Forster can have the sale rescinded.
20. With a judgment entered on December 6, 1968, a first mortgage entered on January 21, 1969, a second mortgage entered on February 14, 1969, and a second judgment entered on March 4, 1969, in a foreclosure action brought by the second judgment creditor, the first judgment creditor would be paid
(x) first.
( ) second.
( ) third.
( ) fourth.

Chapter 7

LANDLORD AND TENANT

T HE LEASE contract, voluntarily entered into by the parties, largely determines the law by which the parties are governed. The lease contract may be verbal or in writing. The verbal lease is just as binding and of great legal efficacy as the written contract, providing that the term of the lease is not in excess of the period prescribed by the Statute of Frauds. The Statute of Frauds requires certain contracts to be in writing, particularly those relating to real estate. Contracts which cannot be performed within one year, as a rule, must be in writing. Thus, a lease for more than one year, in most states, as in Oklahoma, must be in writing in order to be enforceable. The period runs from the date when the contract is entered into, rather than from the date the lease term commences. In Pennsylvania, a lease in excess of three years must be in writing. For obvious reasons, a written lease is preferable to a verbal one. The tenure of human life is uncertain, and one or both of the parties to the contract may die during its term. In case of controversy or litigation, the surviving party would not be permitted to testify as he is a party in interest, and the other party is deceased. The essence of a lease is the payment of rent. A lease may be defined as a contract, oral or written, for the possession of lands and tenements, on the one hand, in return for a recompense of rent or other income, on the other hand. Suppose, for example, Arnold arranges with Burns that if Burns would take care of Arnold's property during his absence, he would allow Burns to occupy it free of cost and use coal and other supplies which might be on the premises with the understanding that Burns would vacate at any time Arnold might desire to reoccupy the property. Such an agreement is a mere license and vests no enforceable rights in Burns. A license is a personal privilege. It is not an estate in land, and it is not assignable. It may be termed a tenancy at will, which can be terminated at any time. A tenancy at sufferance is defined by Blackstone to be where one comes into possession of land by lawful title but keeps it afterwards without any title at all. The tenant is not a trespasser until the landlord elects to treat him as such.

Term

A tenancy for years is one for a fixed period of time, whether it is a month, year, or longer. A tenancy from year to year or month to month is one that continues for an indefinite number of definite terms. The estate continues indefinitely until one of the parties elects to terminate it by giving proper notice. Usually the lease is for a specified term, one month or one year.

Holding over

An implied renewal of a tenancy by the holding over of the tenant after the expiration of the lease, is presumed in case nothing is said in the lease to the contrary. All the terms and conditions in the former lease, therefore, will continue in force. Where the lease is for one year, from May 1, 1969 to April 30, 1970, it expires at 12:01 A.M. on May 1, 1970. Where the tenant holds over and continues to occupy the premises during all of the day of May 2, 1970, he will be liable for the whole rent for the second year. It would be no defense to claim that he occupied the premises during May 2nd under a mistake of law as to the time the lease expired. This would be the case even though the lessee previously had given written notice of his intention to quit the premises. Of course, a lessee cannot stay over after the expiration of the lease term for an additional few days and then claim he is entitled to possession for an additional year. The holding over must be *lawful,* i.e., with the consent of the lessor. Where the lease is for five years and the tenant remains in possession after the expiration of that term with the consent of the lessor, he cannot claim a new term for *five* years. The lease would be extended only for an additional *one* year, and so on from year to year until terminated by either party. The lease may be for one year, with a clause in the contract that if the tenant holds over lawfully, it shall be in force for another *month* and so on from month to month. The lease provision determines the rights of the parties.

The lease may be automatically continued in force in the absence of written notice of termination required under the lease, as follows:

From and after the expiration of the term hereby created, this lease and all its terms, provisions, covenants, confessions, and remedies shall be deemed to be renewed and in force for another year, and so on from year to year unless either party shall have given to the other written notice to terminate said tenancy sixty (60) days prior to the expiration of the current term.

Parties

There are essentially two parties to a lease, the lessor (owner) and the lessee (tenant). The parties are often referred to as landlord and tenant. Strictly speaking a landlord is an assignee of the owner, or the lessor to a sub-lessee, whereas a tenant is any person in possession under a lease. The lessee is the original party to a lease. The landlord's interest is called a "reversion." The interest of the tenant is usually an "estate for years" or a "term." The names of the parties are inserted in the lease for the purpose of identification. A mistake or omission in setting forth the parties, if it is not material or does not cast doubt upon the parties intended, will have no effect upon the validity of the contract. Generally speaking, anyone who is capable of making a contract is capable of making a lease. A lease may be executed by the owner of the property himself or by a properly authorized agent acting in his behalf. If the lease must be in writing under the Statute of Frauds, then the agent's *authority* to execute the lease must be *in writing*. A lease signed and sealed by an agent in his *own name alone* would be open to attack by lessor or lessee. The execution of a lease by an agent must be carefully made. An agent may execute a lease, *as agent,* for an undisclosed principal, in which case the agent is considered as the lessor. It would be signed "John Steele, agent." The best execution, from the standpoint of the agent, is to include the name of the lessor, as

> Adam Taylor
> by John Steele, agent

An agent who is appointed merely to collect rents has no authority to negotiate a lease for the owner.

If a *minor* leases land, the same rules apply as in the case of any other contract executed under a similar condition. Such a lease, in other words, is not void but only voidable by the minor, and may be disaffirmed by him during his minority or within a reasonable time after attaining his majority. A *guardian* of a minor stands, however, in exactly the same position that he would had he himself owned the property, so far as his power to lease is concerned. He has been appointed for the purpose of administering the affairs of the minor, and consequently possesses all the power which may be necessary for executing the lease. In the same way, a *trustee* may grant leases which are unimpeachable so long as the trustee has remained within the powers granted to him by the deed of trust. The trust instrument should be examined to ascertain the extent of the trustee's authority. An *administrator* cannot lease. He has been appointed for the purpose of winding up the state and has nothing to do with the renting of real estate. An *executor*, for the same reason, unless he has been made a trustee of the real estate, cannot lease any of the estate property. A *married woman* has full capacity to execute a lease for property owned by her. Where the property is owned by the entireties, in the name of husband and wife, either spouse can execute a valid lease upon the property owned by both. An *owner in common* has no authority to bind his co-owners by a lease. In order to bind all, the lease must be executed by all the owners.

Description

In making a lease it is not necessary to insert a minute description of the premises which is the subject of the property. The lease should provide that the premises are leased "as is"; that is, in their present condition. If the premises are in good repair, a statement to that effect should also be included. In case of commercial or industrial property, a full description should be used. In renting a furnished house, it is important to have a list of the furniture or other articles which are to pass with the house, attached to the lease. A clause should also be inserted giving the lessor the right to make an examination of the articles in order to ascertain the condition of the furniture, which the tenant is bound to preserve in good order.

Warranties

Upon execution of a lease, there is an implied warranty that the condition of the premises described in the lease shall remain the same between the time of the execution of the lease and the beginning of the term. If a material change has taken place in the character of the premises, the tenant is not bound to take possession, for the premises tendered are not those described in the lease. Where a landlord rented a city property, and, before the tenant took possession at the commencement of the term, allowed a third party to dump earth on the premises without the consent of the tenant and thereby changed the character of the leasehold, the landlord could not recover in an action for rent.

A tenant should require the lessor to covenant that the tenant will obtain possession of the premises at the commencement of the term, for otherwise the tenant can recover only damages for the delay in obtaining possession. Frequently, a tenant cannot obtain possession because of the unlawful holding over of the previous tenant. In a commercial establishment, this may result in considerable damage to the new tenant. Whether the new tenant can consider the breach sufficient to terminate the lease depends upon the circumstances. Adams' lease of dairy store premises from Brown had a 90-day sales clause. Brown sold the property to Clement, who immediately leased the premises to Denton for a dairy store at a considerably higher rental. The lease term was for five years, beginning February 15, 1969. Adams leased other premises about a half block distant but could not get possession until May 1, 1969. On April 1, 1969, Denton notified Clement that he would not honor the lease because of Clement's inability to give him possession. Denton claimed that he suffered irreparable harm since he could not take possession until after Adams was able to enter in active competition with him. Denton expected to obtain a considerable portion of Adams' present trade, which *induced* him to sign the lease, and was, in a sense, a condition precedent. Here, possession on February 15th was distinctly understood as a material element in the contract and Clement could not hold Denton to the lease. Clement could have protected himself from this situation by a provision that:

> Lessor or his agent shall not be liable in damages, or otherwise, for failure to deliver possession of the demised premises to the lessee at the commencement of the term, where such failure is due to the unlawful holding over by a prior tenant or occupant; this lease shall, nevertheless, remain in full force and effect, with an abatement of rent to the lessee until the date possession is made available to him.

Rent

One of the characteristics which distinguishes a lease from a license is the payment of rent. Rent may be payable not only in money but in provisions, chattels, or labor. When no time is fixed for the payment of rent in a lease for a term, such as a year, the rent is not payable until the end of the term. If a specified time is provided, the rent is due and payable at that date.

In most cases, the lease contains a clause stipulating that the rent shall be paid monthly in advance. It is considered good practice to insert an express covenant in the lease by which the tenant binds himself to pay the amount agreed upon. This is valuable because of the fact that while an implied agreement can be presumed in all cases for the tenant to pay the agreed rental, yet if there is an express covenant and the tenant should subsequently assign the lease, even with the lessor's consent, the first tenant would still be liable for the rent. The only way in which he can be relieved from this responsibility is by the formal release by the landlord of the tenant. This practically amounts to the cancellation of the first lease and the creation of a second agreement with the new tenant. If the tenant is of questionable financial responsibility, a landlord can protect himself by insisting that the tenant provide a satisfactory surety to guarantee the terms of the lease; or the landlord may require that the tenant put up a substantial sum of money as evidence of good faith, which shall be applied to the *rent for the last several months of the lease term*.

Sub-letting and assignment

One of the most important covenants frequently found in leases is one forbidding the tenant to sub-let. All covenants against sub-letting in a lease are strictly construed. A covenant against *assignment* will not be construed to include *sub-letting*. In exactly the same way, should the lease contain a proviso that the premises should not be sub-let, the tenant will not be prevented from assigning his lease to anyone to whom he sees fit. To prohibit sub-letting entirely, it is important to provide "or any part thereof." Since the lessor usually prepares the lease, any ambiguity will be construed against him, in accordance with the legal principle that an instrument, if ambiguous, is most strongly construed against the person who prepared it. A tenant, in sub-letting a portion of the leased premises, should see to it that the sub-tenant's rights do not rise higher than his own. In fact, a special clause should be inserted to the effect that the lease is made subject to the terms and conditions of the landlord's lease from the owner. In renting out a portion of a business or commercial floor, it is advisable to insert a clause that the sub-tenant shall observe the same hours of opening and closing his business as the landlord follows. Also that the sub-tenant, his employees, customers, and invitees will refrain from committing any act or conduct which may be construed as a nuisance.

Repairs

It is imperative that a tenant when leasing property should satisfy himself that it is not only fit, suitable, and satisfactory for his purposes, but also that it is likely to remain so during the lease term. This is so because the rule of "caveat emptor" (let the purchaser beware) holds good here with the same rigidity as is found in the case of all other relations between the landlord and tenant. In the absence of an express covenant, no agreement can be implied by which the landlord obligates himself to repair the premises. He is not bound to do so, and even should he voluntarily make some repairs, it cannot be presumed from this fact that he has assumed the obligation of doing so during the remainder of the lease.

The tenant is bound to make tenantable repairs, but he cannot be forced to make lasting and general repairs to the structure, which would put the property in a better condition than it was when he took possession. Generally, a tenant cannot be bound to make good such deterioration as arises from necessary wear and tear incidental to the proper and ordinary use of the property. Where a tenant agrees to make "all necessary repairs," it includes such as are necessary to protect the dwelling from waste and ruin.

Ordinarily, there is no obligation upon the landlord to make repairs. If, due to an existing defect, the tenant, a member of his family, or an invitee is injured, does the injured party have a right of action against the owner? The general rule of law is that a landlord who is entirely out of possession and control is not liable for an injury sustained by the tenant or by one visiting the tenant if the defect responsible for the accident was a patent one. The principle of law is fairly well established that, where the tenant rents the entire premises, the owner is not liable for any injury to the tenant or his invitees by reason of any dangerous condition existing at the time the tenant took possession. "The lessee's eyes are his bargain" and he takes the property "as is" with all existing faults.

Liability of lessor for repairs

A landlord is responsible where he conceals or fails to disclose a dangerous condition of which he had knowledge and one which a tenant was not likely to discover upon examination. A hidden, or latent, defect does impose a liability upon the landlord. He is also liable when he leases premises in a dangerous condition for a public use and has reason to believe the tenant will not first correct the defect. The lease of a theatre or a stadium is in this classification. In other words, where an owner leases public premises which constitute a nuisance, then, whether he is in or out of possession is immaterial insofar as relieving himself of liability is concerned. A department store or a public garage would not fall in the described category. Although a landlord may not be required to make repairs, nevertheless, if he undertakes repairs voluntarily, he becomes responsible for any accident occasioned by the negligent manner in which the work is performed. Where a landlord has covenanted to make repairs and fails to do so, and someone is injured as a result of such failure, the agreement to repair does not operate as a resumption of control by the landlord and he is not liable for the injury. Of course, in an action of assumpsit on the contract, the landlord would be liable for damage suffered by the tenant. He would not be liable in a tort action for negligence. Where a landlord has promised to make repairs as an inducement to the execution of a lease, the tenant should insist that the repairs be written into the lease contract. If verbal only, and if the landlord later refuses to perform, the tenant would run into difficulty in compelling performance under the parol evidence rule.

The contention that the promised repairs were a condition precedent which induced the contract might circumvent the parol evidence rule, but litigation can be avoided by including the repairs in the written lease. Repairs promised *after* the lease is executed would give a tenant no basis for performance if the landlord refused to keep his promise. Necessary legal consideration for the promise is lacking.

Sidewalk injuries

What has been stated relative to liability relates to accidents upon the premises. Another important question arises in connection with sidewalk injury cases. Here, again, an owner out of control and possession is not liable. An owner who rents out a portion of the premises or who rents out separate parts to different tenants is held to remain in possession and control of the sidewalk, stairways, and corridors and is, therefore, responsible. Where the municipality notifies the owner to repair a sidewalk and an injury results before the repair is made, the owner would be liable. A mortgagee in possession who exercises control and dominion over the leased premises is held to occupy the same role as the owner. In order to recover damages the injured party must establish the existence of a dangerous condition and that the owner had notice of it. The claimant must also be free of any contributory negligence. Dangerous conditions include an accumulation of snow or ice, a missing brick, an elevation or depression causing an uneven surface, an accumulation of debris concealing an uneven pavement or gutter, an accumulation of oil causing a slippery surface, a hole in the sidewalk, and faulty position of basement outlets or doors to the pavement.

Notice

Where an owner is sued for injuries, the owner must have had notice of the defective conditions. Notice to the owner may be *actual* or *constructive*. Actual notice is knowledge of the owner through observation or proximity. Constructive notice is where the defect has existed for such a long time that it will be presumed that the owner saw it or could have seen it with a reasonably frequent inspection. Since the municipality owes a duty of protective safety to its citizenry, the person injured will usually sue the city in the first instance. The city will then bring in the property owner as an additional defendant. The owner, in turn, may bring in the tenant as an additional defendant if the responsibility lies with the tenant. Suppose a tenant had employed a plumber to make a water connection which required digging up the pavement. Due to the plumber's failure to provide a proper barricade, Ash is injured. Following through on a suit by Ash against the city, the tenant, in turn, could bring in the plumber as an additional defendant.

Legal liability and contractual liability

While on the subject of repairs and liability, mention should be made of the distinction between legal liability and contractual liability. Apthorp leases a store to Barnes. The lease provides that the tenant, Barnes, is to keep and save Apthorp harmless for any injury or damage to any person upon the premises or sidewalk from any cause whatsoever. Barnes takes out public liability insurance in the Merchant's Mutual Co. Cox is injured on the step to the store and sues Apthorp. He recovers a verdict. Apthorp can seek reimbursement from Barnes under the clause cited. Barnes would not be protected under his insurance contract in the absence of a premium paid to cover the contractual liability. On the other hand, if Cox sued Barnes directly and obtained a judgment, the insurance policy would protect Barnes, for the claim is brought upon Barnes' legal liability as a primary party liable for the injury.

Additions, alterations, improvements

An important covenant contained in leases of business property is that which provides that all alterations, additions, and improvements made by the lessee upon the property shall remain until the end of the lease, at the option of the lessor. It is frequently further provided that the lessor shall have the option of requiring the tenant to restore the premises to their original condition. The meaning of these three words, "alterations, additions, and improvements," has been the source of much friction, and it is practically impossible to lay down a general rule which would be applicable in all cases. The conflicts usually arise between the parties over machinery and other fixtures annexed to the freehold. The tenant claims that such equipment is trade fixtures, and as such, personal property, which may be removed by him at the expiration of the lease. The landlord on the other hand contends that such property is included within the phrase "alterations, additions, and improvements." For example, if a tenant leased a store and installed shelving at considerable expense, which shelving enhanced the value of the building for renting purposes, the landlord would be within his rights in maintaining that such shelving constituted additions, alterations, and improvements, and in requiring that it be left upon the premises at the expiration of the lease. On the other hand, if the shelving installed were of little value and would cost more to remove than it was worth, the landlord could insist that the tenant remove such fixtures and restore the premises to their original condition in accordance with the terms of the covenant in the lease.

Surrender of premises

Whether a tenant is liable for damage caused by fire, the elements, "an act of God," or an inevitable casualty depends upon the language of the lease. If he agrees to return the premises at the expiration of the lease, reasonable wear and tear alone excepted, he must restore the premises if damaged by fire or other accident. If fire is excepted, the tenant would still be responsible for damage caused by flood, tornado, or other "act of God" or by an inevitable accident. Act of God and inevitable accident are not synonymous. Even if the clause is sufficiently comprehensive so as to exclude a liability for rebuilding, the tenant would still be liable for the payment of *rent,* unless there was a clause abating the rent. This is the common law rule, but it has been modified by statute in some states to the effect that the rent ceases until the property is repaired by the lessor. However, if the premises are only partially destroyed by fire and the tenant remains in possession, the rent does not abate. It is not uncommon in a commercial lease, to include a provision for the abatement of rent due to destruction of the leased premises, as follows:

It is understood and agreed by and between the parties hereto, that if during the term of this lease and any renewal hereof, the building is damaged or injured by fire, Act of God, or other casualty so that the demised premises are rendered unfit for occupancy to the extent that said premises cannot be repaired within ninety (90) days from the happening of such injury, then this lease shall cease and determine from the date of such injury. In such case, the Tenant shall pay the rent apportioned to the time of injury, and shall immediately surrender the leased premises to the Lessor, who may enter upon and repossess the same. If any such injury can be repaired within ninety (90) days thereafter, Lessor shall enter and repair, and this lease shall not be affected except that the rent shall be apportioned and suspended while such repairs are being made; but if said premises shall be so slightly injured by fire, Act of God, or other casualty, so as not to render same unfit for occupancy, then the Lessor agrees that the same shall be repaired with reasonable promptitude, and in that case the rent accrued or accruing shall not cease or determine.

Where the lessee has made extensive repairs at his own expense preparatory to taking possession, his investment should be protected by adequate fire insurance and a clause relative thereto, incorporated in the lease. The lease provision should read: "The proceeds of any fire insurance carried in both the Lessor's and Lessee's names and paid for by the Lessee, shall inure to the sole benefit of the Lessee."

Termination

There are various ways by which a lease may be terminated—by performance, agreement, or breach. The usual method is, of course, by performance; that is, the lease normally terminates at the expiration date.

Surrender of lease

The parties may mutually agree to terminate the lease before the expiration date. This is called a surrender. It is not necessary that such an agreement be in writing or in any particular form, and no consideration need be included in order to make the contract binding upon the parties, the presumption being that the advantage accruing to both parties is sufficient to give it full force and effect. In order, however, to make a surrender complete, it is necessary that it be specifically accepted by the landlord. Proof of acceptance must be clear and explicit. A lease may be terminated by breach of condition. Where one of the parties violates some important covenant in the lease, the other party may plead such act as grounds for the termination of the contract.

Eviction

Where the landlord is guilty of a violation of the lease, such breach is termed an eviction. It is a violent assertion of a right by the landlord as opposed to the rights which the tenant possesses. In other words, it is an unwarrantable ousting of the tenant by the landlord. The distinction between an eviction and an ejectment rests primarily upon this point. An eviction is a wrongful dispossession of the tenant. The action of ejectment is used to test, or establish, the title to real estate. An eviction has a somewhat different meaning from that generally attributed to it by the layman. It need not necessarily be a forcible ousting or removal of the tenant by the landlord from possession of the premises. As used here in connection with the law of landlord and tenant, it means the violation of any material covenant by the landlord which interferes with the tenant's quiet and peaceful enjoyment of the premises. Suppose, for example, a landlord should go upon the premises for the purpose of making repairs, there being no provision in the lease giving the landlord such right; the tenant could plead such action as sufficient grounds for cancelling the lease agreement. It is immaterial that the repairs to be made would benefit the tenant. So long as the work would be detrimental to the tenant's quiet and ennjoyment of the premises or would seriously interrupt his use of the property, he could plead it as grounds for terminating the lease. Such action on the part of the landlord constitutes a question of fact which would have to be determined by a jury in an action at law. The same thing would be true were the landlord to secure an injunction restraining the tenant from using a portion of the premises or preventing him from subletting to another, nothing being stipulated in the contract to warrant such an action by the landlord.

It must be remembered that the act complained of must be committed by the *landlord or an agent* representing the landlord or acting for him. The only ground upon which a tenant can plead eviction by a third party is in case the one whose act he complains of was exercising a right which he secured under a *paramount title to that of the landlord.* For example, if Jackson leased to Finch and afterward it turned out that the title was vested not in Jackson but in Chase and Chase should proceed to dispossess Finch, the action of Chase would amount to an eviction. If, however, the party whose acts were complained of proceeded under a questionable or defective title, the tenant could not plead immunity on the grounds that an eviction occurred. An overt act committed by a third party is not an eviction in contemplation of law. Anderson, the owner of a building, had leased the upper wall of the building to Brown for a term of three years for advertising purposes. Brown had erected an advertising sign upon the wall which could be seen by people passing in the vicinity. At the expiration of one year, Chambers, the owner of the adjoining property, a one-story building, erected an addition on the building in such a way that the view of Brown's wall was completely hidden from the eyes of passers-by and its value for advertising purposes destroyed. Consequently, Brown refused to pay rent on the grounds that an eviction had occurred, but the court disallowed the claim on the grounds that the injury had been inflicted neither by the owner nor by one having paramount title to the wall upon which the advertising was displayed, but by a third person, over whose action Anderson had no control. Entry by the city, or repairs ordered by the municipality, would not constitute an eviction. Eviction by the State, under its power of eminent domain, would not sustain a cause of action against the landlord. Fisk leased certain premises to Martin. They were part of a double house. Crum, the owner of the other half of the dwelling, had the party wall torn down after complying with the legal requirements. Martin claimed an eviction and refused to pay rent since he only had three walls on the leased premises. The tenant was held liable for rent. In another case, Appleby owned certain premises subject to a mortgage in favor of Eastman. Appleby then leased the premises to Crane for five years. Regretting his bargain, and seeking to get rid of Crane, Appleby purchased the mortgage from Eastman and took an assignment in the name of a "straw" party. The assignee then foreclosed and sought to eject Crane from possession. Appleby lost sight of the fact that under his lease to Eastman the covenant for quiet possession protected the tenant not only from direct acts of the lessor and his agent, but also from those of persons holding a paramount title. Thus, the lessor is liable in damages to the tenant if the mortgagee asserts his rights to put the tenant out of possession. If the lessor becomes the holder of the mortgage, his exercise of the right of possession would at the same time subject him to a liability for so doing. The same result would follow if he brings action in the name of another (a "straw" party).

A mortgagee in possession must be cognizant of the fact that the mortgagor might pay off the debt during the term of a lease given by the mortgagee to a tenant, terminate the lease, and thereby subject the mortgagee to a cause of action for eviction damages by the tenant. In order to avoid this possibility, a mortgagee in possession, when leasing property owned by the mortgagor, should include a provision in the lease as follows:

The lessee herein understands and agrees that the lessor is executing this lease under rights as mortgagee in possession of said premises and does not in any way or manner, covenant, agree, promise, or guarantee to the lessee, his heirs, or assigns, possession, quiet enjoyment or otherwise as against any person having a paramount title or interest to the within leased premises, anything contained in the written lease to the contrary notwithstanding.

On the other hand, if the lessee entertains any doubts or suspicions as to the lessor's legal right to lease the premises, he should insist upon a provision that:

The lessor hereby certifies and represents that he has full right and authority to make and execute this lease and further certifies and represents that the demised premises are at the time of entering into this lease, free and clear from any mortgage, lien, or other encumbrance, which, if proceeded upon, might or could divest this lease.

Tenant's remedy

If an actual or constructive eviction occurs and the tenant chooses to terminate the agreement, all of the rent which is past due and payable becomes an obligation which must be settled by the tenant upon demand. This action on the part of tenant terminates any right which the landlord has to demand rent after the date of the eviction. It is important to note that if the landlord should evict a tenant from a portion of the property, the tenant could, on this ground, evade the duty of paying rent on the portion which still remains to him. An eviction by landlord from part of the premises is, in the eyes of the law, an eviction from all of the property.

An important modification of this rule, however, exists in the case where a tenant is evicted from part of the premises by a paramount title invoked by a third party. In this case, the rent would be apportioned so that he would have to pay rent for that portion of the premises which still remained to him. If, however, the lessee takes the property with knowledge of the defective title of the lessor, it is then impossible for him to plead eviction as a defense against the payment of rent. After an eviction has occurred and the tenant remains in possession of the premises and takes no action which would indicate that he intends to hold the landlord responsible for the overt act, his continued occupation would constitute a waiver of the injury. When an eviction occurs, the tenant should promptly assert his rights in the matter. There are two courses which he may pursue: first, he may terminate the contractual relation between himself and the landlord by moving out and bringing suit for damages which he has sustained; or secondly, he may remain in possession of the premises and, after promptly notifying the landlord of the injury suffered and stating that he will hold the landlord responsible for the damage, he may bring suit for the amount he claims to have lost. In this event, however, it is necessary for him to continue to pay rent in exactly the same manner as though no breach had occurred.

Forfeiture

Corresponding to the tenant's right to terminate the lease by reason of breach of covenant by the landlord, is the landlord's right to terminate the lease where the tenant is guilty of a violation of a material covenant. This is known as a forfeiture. Under the common law, if a tenant should disclaim, disaffirm, or impugn the landlord's title by some positive act, he thereby forfeits all rights under the contract. The reason for this is obvious. If the landlord could not terminate the contractual relation, it might be possible for the tenant to work great harm to the property, not only by violating the spirit and letter of the agreement but also by going so far as to claim title to the property by adverse possession after continuous occupation for the statutory period. The law, therefore, provides that the landlord has the option of declaring the lease forfeited upon the breach of any material covenant by the tenant. The landlord then has the right to enter and take possession of the property unless it can be shown that he has by some act waived the breach which has occurred. Suppose, for example, that a landlord should accept rent from a tenant for a period subsequent to the commission of the acts in controversy; in this case, he would have waived his right to declare the contract forfeited by permitting the tenant to continue in possession. The most usual breach by the tenant is non-payment of rent.

Landlord's levy

It is important to note in this connection that distraint instituted for rent in default constitutes a technical waiver of the forfeiture which has occurred and permits the tenant successfully to maintain his right to possession under the terms of the lease. A landlord's levy is one of statutory enactment entirely. Under the common law, the landlord had no lien on the chattels of the tenant on leasing the premises or to the crops raised thereon. They were the absolute property of the tenant. It is in statutory law that the landlord has a method by which he can secure a lien upon the chattels and goods of the tenant. The right to distrain, however, exists in favor of the landlord only upon a claim for rent due and accrued.

Distraint defined

Distraint may therefore be defined as the right of a landlord to levy upon a tenant's goods and chattels for rent *in arrears*. The right does not reside in the landlord until there has been a default in rent, but he can bring this action the day after the rent is due.

Rent in arrears

If the rent is due on the first day of the month, as is generally true, and is not paid on that date, distraint proceedings may be instituted against the tenant on the second day of the month. In practice, however, the situation is often complicated by having conflicting due dates for the rent, the lease providing that the rent of $110 per month, for instance, shall be due and payable on the first day of the month, but if paid by the tenth of the month, there shall be a discount or rebate of $10 per month, or a net rental of $100.

Discount clause

Some leases provide that the rent shall be $100 per month, due and payable on the first day of the month, and if not paid by the tenth of the month, then the rent, in that case, shall be $110 per month. Since the rent is not in arrears until after the due date, the important practical question arises as to when the rent is in default; is it on the second day of the month or must the landlord wait until the eleventh day before instituting his right to distrain, or is the rent not in arrears until the first day of the following month? It would appear that even though the lease provides for the payment of rent on the first day of the month, the effect of the second due date is to avoid the responsibility of payment on the first day, and the tenant is, therefore, within his rights in tendering the correct amount of rent at any time during the month. No lawful levy can be made until after the month has elapsed. It would make no difference whether a discount or penalty clause is used. The question becomes particularly vexatious during the last month of the lease, as the landlord may be fearful that the tenant may remove without payment of the rent; yet he is powerless to act.

A landlord may estop himself from insisting upon the punctual payment of rent where he has indulged a tenant and accepted rent after the due date. Suppose the lease from Adams to Brown provides for the payment of rent on the first day of each month during the lease term from May 1, 1968 to April 30, 1969. Brown pays the May rent on the first day, but after that he makes his rent payments anywhere from the 15th to the 25th of the month. In October 1968, Adams could not distrain for the month's rent on October 2, because of his previous conduct in accepting the rent late. The doctrine of estoppel could be invoked against him. In order to reassert his right to punctual payment of rent, it would be necessary for Adams to notify Brown of his intention to hold him to punctual payment of the rent in the future.

The lessee need not tender payment in money when he has on previous occasions tendered a check which was accepted as payment of rent. If the landlord desires to insist upon payment in cash, the lessee is entitled to notice. Where rent is delinquent and the tenant makes a partial payment, the payment generally will be applied to the rent which first accrued. Rent paid "on account" will not give rise to the presumption that it was paid for the current period. The lessor may apply it to the most delinquent rent. This rule, of course, may be modified by agreement between the parties.

Goods subject to levy

All goods found upon the premises, irrespective of ownership, unless specifically exempted by statute, are subject to a landlord's levy. Goods upon the premises by reason of the tenant's trade or business, goods in the custody of the law, tools and implements of trade, and certain leased furniture, equipment, and apparatus are exempted from a landlord's levy by statute. In addition, the law usually allows a tenant a debtor's exemption of goods in a certain amount. (In Pennsylvania the exemption is $300.) However, a tenant may waive his debtor's exemption in the lease. Without such waiver, distraint very often would be futile as the tenant's goods and chattels are not worth more than the exemption. Courts will uphold the waiver of the exemption by the tenant. In an oral lease, it is impossible to prove such waiver by the tenant.

The general rule is that the landlord is given considerable latitude in levying upon all goods found upon the premises, irrespective of ownership. Where the goods of a stranger are upon the premises, in the possession of the tenant, not as a necessity of the latter's business or trade, but as a matter of favor, they are subject to distraint. For example, Jones, a neighbor of Smith, requested permission from Smith to store a valuable grand piano with Smith, temporarily. Jones was to pay no charge for this service, and Smith was to have the use of the piano during the time that it was in his possession. Smith defaulted in the payment of rent to Clark, his landlord, and Clark levied upon Jones's piano as well as upon other goods belonging to Smith. The levy was legal and it was therefore necessary for Jones, the owner of the piano, to pay Smith's rent in order to release the piano from the levy. In another case, Ash consigned a machine to Burke, a tenant of Crane, for trial, with a view to subsequent purchase. Burke sold his business to Dawson and stored the machine with Epp, who occupied another floor in the same building. Epp was not a warehouseman, but permitted the machine to be placed on his premises as an accommodation to Burke. Crane distrained upon the machine in Epp's custody for rent due from Dawson. Since Epp was merely a sub-tenant, all of his goods were liable for the rent. Ash brought replevin action for the machine, claiming that the machine was exempt from distraint as property delivered to Burke in the necessary way of trade, or, in all events, as property deposited with Epp on storage merely. Ash lost as the machine was liable for the rent under the general rule of law. However, if Ash should store his furniture in Burke's warehouse, Burke being a tenant of Crane, the furniture of Ash could not be sold under a distraint by Crane for rent due by Burke, since the goods are upon the premises by reason of the tenant's trade or business. The same would be true in case of an automobile, watch, or shoes left for repair in leased premises.

A lessor may prefer to oust a delinquent tenant rather than struggle with him periodically to recover the rent. Under a "tight" form lease, which contains a confession of judgment clause for possession, a non-paying tenant can be evicted promptly. Likewise, a tenant who holds over unlawfully (without the consent of the lessor) after the expiration of the lease, may be dispossessed in the same manner.

Effect of mortgage

Where a lease antedates a mortgage, the mortgagee takes the property subject to the lease if the mortgage is foreclosed at a later date. The lease cannot be terminated. In order for the mortgage to have precedence, it would be necessary to stipulate in the lease that it is subject and subordinate to any mortgage of record or which may at any time be placed upon the property. The tenant should have the right to pay any delinquency on the mortgage and apply such payments to the rent obligation. Ordinarily, a mortgage, placed upon the premises, before the execution of a lease, would have priority. The lease could be terminated by the mortgagee, upon his acquisition of the property through foreclosure. This is true even though the mortgagee accepted rents from the tenant during a period prior to foreclosure when the former was a mortgagee in possession. In other words, his rights as *owner* are separate and independent from his rights as *mortgagee in possession*.

Judgment clause

In the "tight" form lease, there is a provision that the lessor may confess judgment against the lessee for rent, where the tenant defaults or breaches any of the lease provisions. The rent is accelerated for the remainder of the term and judgment entered thereon. Or, the lease may provide for confessing judgment for possession. The lessor will avail himself of this remedy if he is more interested in regaining possession of the premises than in obtaining a money judgment. Where a lease contains a confession of judgment clause, it provides an owner with an effective method of reacquiring possession of the premises. It is not necessary, ordinarily, to obtain court approval. The lessor files a declaration or statement alleging default or breach by the lessee and directs the issuance of a writ for possession, which is served by the sheriff. If it is necessary "to throw the tenant out," the sheriff will require a deposit by the lessor, depending upon the number of rooms in the dwelling. It should be remembered that the lessor cannot institute a distraint proceedings for back rent and at the same time take other legal action to oust the tenant from possession.

Leased housing program

The "Leased Housing Program" is a program of Federal assistance to provide habitable living quarters for large low-income families in dwellings leased from private owners and real estate companies. It is designed to provide "instant" dwellings for these low-income groups more rapidly than through new housing; to make better use and rehabilitate present structures and thereby upgrade neighborhoods. The prime object is to encourage private interests to undertake this civic program by governmental guaranty of the income to such developers. This is accomplished by having the owner lease the structure to the Housing Authority of a city for a rent return and the Authority then sublets the unit to the individual tenants. The relationship between the owner and the Authority is upon the usual and ordinary relationship of Lessor and Lessee. Necessary mortgage financing is facilitated upon the strength of a "letter of intent to lease" from the Housing Authority to the owner. Rent is guaranteed by the Housing Authority to the owner even if the property is unoccupied—payable monthly. Since the program is intended to provide housing for large families, the dwellings or apartments should have a minimum of three bedrooms. The Housing Authority will adopt a rental scale according to the tenant's income and if less than the rent in the prime lease, the difference is paid by the Housing Authority. The lease may vary from one to five years. Since the Authority is the principal tenant, it is responsible to return the premises at the expiration of the lease term in the same condition as at the commencement of the term, reasonable wear or tear or accident by fire, excepted. Public liability is controlled pretty much by the law applicable to the usual relationship of landlord and tenant.

Questions on Landlord and Tenant

1. Q. What is the tenancy called where the lessee holds the land at the will of the lessor?
   A. Tenancy at sufferance; in some states, a tenancy at will.
2. Q. What is the obligation of the renting agent to the owner?
   A. To obtain the owner the greatest income, for the longest period of time, with the least expense on the property managed, keeping in mind the well-being of the tenant.
3. Q. Can a lease be enforced when the consideration is expressed in terms of farm products instead of money?
   A. Yes.
4. Q. In computing the income from an apartment house, there are several major items taken from the gross income in order to arrive at the net income. Name at least six (6).
   A. (1) taxes (2) insurance (3) repairs (4) depreciation on building (5) depreciation on furniture (6) collection of losses (7) management expenses (8) reserve for replacements (9) utilities (10) license fees.
5. Q. In a long term lease, what provision should be included relative to taxes?
   A. In a lease for 5 or 10 years, there should be a clause that the tenant agrees to pay any increase in taxes during the term of the lease.
6. Q. In the management of property, name four duties which an agent owes to his owner.
   A. (1) collect rents (2) keep proper records (3) remit net proceeds promptly (4) maintain and repair property.
7. Q. When a leased property is sold, and the lease does not expire for seven months after the sale takes place, at what time can the purchaser take physical possession of the property?
   A. Upon expiration of lease (7 months).
8. Q. What do you understand by a sub-lease?
   A. A lease granted to another person by the lessee.
9. Q. Distinguish between an assignment of a lease and the sub-letting of a lease.
   A. In a sub-lease or sub-letting of a lease, the lessee becomes the lessor and the sub-lessee becomes the tenant. Calls for a new lease. An assignment of a lease is a transfer by the lessee of his rights for the term of the lease.
10. Q. Name the essentials of a valid written lease.
    A. Parties, description, rental, term, demising, (leasing) signatures and delivery.

11. Q. In regard to lease terminology, what is the difference between an option and a first refusal?
    A. An option gives a definite right to buy the leased property at a designated price and within a specified time. A first refusal gives the tenant the first right to purchase the property at a price offered by at third party.
12. Q. In the investigation of a prospective tenant to determine his desirability, what information should be ascertained?
    A. Size of family, occupation, approximate income, previous address and former rental agent. A credit report is also recommended.
13. Q. What information should a rent receipt contain?
    A. Date paid, amount, address of property, rental period covered by payment, signature on receipt.
14. Q. Write an ordinary receipt for rent.
    A.

Des Moines, Iowa,
January 3, 1966.

Received of Henry Thompson _____ Sum of Seventy-five_____
_____ ($75.00) Dollars, for rent for month of January, 1961, for property at 1334 Capitol Street, Des Moines, Iowa.

Des Moines Realty Corporation,
Agent for James Black, Lessor.
By C. E. Prentice, Secretary.

15. Q. Where the tenant defaults in the payment of rent, can the landlord terminate the lease and evict a sub-tenant as well as the tenant?
    A. Yes, the sub-tenant's rights rise no higher than those of the tenant.
16. Q. Arthur verbally leases certain premises to James on February 1, 1968, for a one-year term from May 1, 1968, to April 30, 1969, with an option of two additional years at an increased rental. On April 1, 1969, Arthur notifies James that the property has been leased to Black. Does James have any cause of action against Arthur?
    A. No. Under the Statute of Frauds, the lease from Arthur to James had to be in writing in order to be enforceable. In most states, the period is one year from the making of the lease, or from February 1, 1968. In Pennsylvania, the period is three years.
17. Q. A lease is made by the Rapid Realty Co., agent, to John J. Flynn for a term of five years. The lease is approved by the owners. Prior to the expiration of the five-year term, the Realty Co. executes a new lease for an additional five-year period. Three months before the expiration of the original term, the owners notify Flynn to vacate the premises at the end of that term. The tenant insists he has a lease for another five-year term. Is he correct?
    A. No. The agent's authority to execute a lease beyond the period

fixed by the Statute of Frauds must be in writing, and it does not appear that the agent had such written authority.

18. Q. An agent executed a lease to Jenks, as John Steele, agent. Upon the tenant's default in rent, judgment is confessed against Jenks in the name of the owner, Adam Taylor. Jenks petitions the court to have the judgment stricken off. Will Jenks succeed?

A. Yes. The judgment was improperly entered as the owner was not a party to the lease.

19. Q. If, in the preceding case, the lease bore a notation "Approved by Adam Taylor," would Jenks succeed?

A. Yes. The notation does not establish Taylor as the owner and a party in interest. To all intents and purposes, he is a stranger to the instrument.

20. Q. Rogers leases premises to Pike for a one-year term. The lease provides that if Pike lawfully holds over after the expiration of the term, he would be a tenant "from year to year" and so on from year to year. The original lease term ends on April 30, 1966. On April 20, 1969, Rogers notifies Pike to vacate the premises at the end of the current term, April 30, 1969. Pike refuses. Can Pike claim possession for another year?

A. Yes. Rogers should have given Pike statutory notice (30-90 days, depending upon state).

21. Q. Andrews leases premises to Brown for five years. At the expiration of the period, Brown remains in possession. Brown claims the lease is automatically renewed for another five years. Andrews claims Brown has a lease only for one additional year. Who wins?

A. Andrews. The lease is not renewed for five years but from year to year.

22. Q. Jones leases premises to Brown for one year. The lease provides that if Brown remains over he shall be a tenant from month to month. After 14 months' occupancy, Jones gives Brown 30 days' notice to vacate. Brown claims he has a lease for an additional 10 months. Is Brown correct?

A. No. The lease contract determines Brown's rights. It specifically provides that upon Brown's holding over, the tenancy shall be upon a monthly basis and this provision will be enforced.

23. Q. A store lease provides that in event of sale, the lessee "agrees to vacate the said premises at any time upon receiving—O—days' notice in writing so to do, in case of sale of said property." Archer sells the property to Connor, who notifies the tenant, Benson, to vacate the premises in 30 days. Benson claims that he has a right to remain in possession until the expiration of the lease term, a period of 20 months. Who will win?

A. Benson will win. It is a matter of intention of the parties, and it is inconceivable that the lease could be terminated in advance of the expiration date without any previous notice at all.

24. Q. Lloyd leased certain premises to Barnes in February 1969, effective May 1, 1969. Before Barnes took possession, Lloyd permitted Cox to dump earth on the premises so that Barnes later refused to take possession. Can Lloyd collect rent from Barnes?

A. No. Upon execution of a lease, there is an implied warranty that the condition of the premises described in the lease shall remain the same between the time of the execution of the lease and the beginning of the term.

25. Q. Adams leased certain premises to Thomas and executed a release in favor of Clark, relinquishing his right to distrain upon certain articles owned by Clark and stored upon the premises. Later Adams sold the property to Dwight, who distrains for delinquent rent due him, upon Clark's property. Clark claims his property is exempt from levy because of Adams' release. Decide.

A. Dwight can sell Clark's property, because Adams' release is personal in its nature and not binding upon Dwight. A new release should have been obtained from Dwight.

26. Q. Can a tenant for life make a valid lease?

A. Yes, if it does not extend beyond the term of his own life. Since the life tenancy is uncertain, the joinder of the remainderman or reversioner should be had.

27. Q. A bank is a mortgagee in possession. It executes a lease to Casey for a two year term. During the lease term the mortgage debt is paid by Boone, the mortgagor, who ousts Casey from possession. Does Casey have a cause of action against the bank?

A. Yes. The landlord guaranteed the tenant quiet and peaceful enjoyment of the premises which was broken by Boone asserting a paramount title.

28. Q. How could the bank have protected itself?

A. By inserting a proper clause in the lease such as: "The lessee herein understands and agrees that the lessor is executing this lease under rights as mortgagee in possession of said premises and does not in any way or manner covenant, agree, promise, or guarantee to the lessee, his heirs, or assigns, possession, quiet enjoyment, or otherwise as against any person having a paramount title or interest to the within leased premises, anything contained in the within lease to the contrary notwithstanding."

29. Q. What are the interests of the landlord and tenant in a lease called?

A. Landlord's interest is called a "reversion." The interest of the tenant in the leasehold is usually an "estate for years."

30. Q. Ashley leases certain premises to Bridger for a motion-picture theatre for 10 years, with the right of assignment. Bridger expressly covenants to pay rent. Later Bridger forms a corporation and assigns the lease to the corporation. Upon the subsequent insolvency of the corporation, Ashley seeks to hold Bridger personally liable. Will he succeed?

A. Yes. By virtue of Bridger's express covenant to pay rent, he continues liable during the term of the lease. Assignment of the lease does not toll Bridger's liability. He would be relieved of liability only if his lease were cancelled and a new lease made to the corporation.

31. Q. A banking corporation leased certain premises to an oil company. Later the oil company refused to pay rent claiming that the banking corporation's lease was *ultra vires* (beyond the powers of the corporation). Will it succeed?

A. No. The contract is executed so the *ultra vires* doctrine would not apply. In addition, it is a long-established rule of law that a lessee cannot impeach the title of his lessor for any cause except fraud.

32. Q. What is the difference between a tenancy at will and at sufferance?

A. There is no real difference. A tenancy at will is where a party is in possession of property under a mere license while a tenancy at sufferance is where one comes into possession of land by lawful title but keeps it afterward without any title at all. A tenant in possession under a lease from the mortgagee in possession would be a tenant at sufferance, after the property is foreclosed insofar as the new owner is concerned.

33. Q. Allen leased certain premises to Beck for a period of one year beginning on March 2, 1968. The lessee remained in possession through March 2, 1969. Is Beck liable for another year's rent?

A. Yes. The lease expired at midnight on March 1, 1969. Where the lessee holds over and continues to occupy the premises during all of the day of March 2 of the following year, he will be liable for the whole rent for the second year.

34. Q. Ash leases certain premises to Blake for a three year term at $200 monthly. At the expiration of three months, a flood damages the premises to such an extent that the premises are uninhabitable for five months. What, if any, is Blake's liability?

A. He is liable for rent for the five-month period. If the lease has no Act of God clause, Blake would also be liable for the cost of repairing the premises, unless exempted by statute.

35. Q. Appel owns certain premises leased to Brent. There is also a mortgage against the property, which is in default, and Cooper, the mortgagee, as well as Appel, demands rent from the tenant. To whom should Brent pay the rent?

A. To Cooper. The mortgagee in possession, where the mortgage is in default, is entitled to the rent.

36. Q. A guest fell upon a landing in front of an apartment, due to a hole in the flooring. Is the lessor or tenant liable?

A. The lessor. In an apartment building, the lessor is bound to make necessary repairs to stairways, landings, and the like.

37. Q. Archer leased certain premises to Barnes. There is no provision in the lease requiring Archer to make repairs. The city orders the owner, Archer, to make extensive repairs. Can Barnes plead Archer's entry as unlawful?

A. No. It would not constitute an eviction even if the action of the city was unconstitutional. The act complained of was not due to any voluntary conduct on the part of the lessor.

38. Q. In the following list of terms, which four pertain to leasing?

A. *Covenant,* equity, prospectus, *assignment, distraint,* eminent domain, easement, lien, foreclosure, *eviction.* (The terms applying to leases are italicized.)

39. Q. What is the compensation or income received for the use of real property called?

A. Rent.

40. Q. What type of property, as a general rule, may be distrained on the rented premises in order to collect delinquent rent?

A. All property upon the premises irrespective of ownership unless specifically exempted by statute or previously released by the lessor.

41. Q. Jones leased certain store premises to Bogg, who purchased equipment under a conditional sales contract, duly recorded. Can Jones distrain upon such equipment for delinquent rent?

A. Yes. The owner of the equipment should have obtained a release from Jones before making the sale to Bogg; or unless specifically exempted by statute.

42. Q. When a tenant becomes in arrears in his rent, what action can be taken to protect the landlord's interest?

A. A distraint proceedings may be instituted to collect the rent, and, if there is a "tight" form written lease, confession of judgment for possession may be entered.

43. Q. What is meant by a "percentage" lease?

A. A lease which provides that the rental shall be a percentage of the gross volume of business done upon the leased premises, for example, 3 per cent. The lease usually provides for a guaranteed minimum monthly rental.

44. Q. What is meant by a "surrender" of the lease?

A. A mutual agreement to cancel the lease before the expiration date; it must be specifically accepted by the landlord.

45. Q. Where Anders leases property to Brown, a person of dubious financial responsibility, for a term of five years, what steps can Anders take to protect his interest?

A. 1. Require a surety on the lease.
   2. Require Brown to pay 6 months' rent in advance to be applied to the last 6 months of the lease term.

46. Q. Axton leased the roof of a building to Barnes for three years

for the purpose of erecting advertising signs. At the end of one year, Colfax, who owned adjoining property, erected an addition upon his property which obstructed the view of Barnes' signs. Barnes refused to pay further rent. Can Axton collect?

A. Yes. The lessor was in no way responsible for the interference. It is a "bad bargain" on Barnes' part.

47. Q. If a tenant refuses, at the expiration of the lease term, to sign a new lease upon different terms, can the landlord oust him from possesion?

A. Yes.

48. Q. If a member of the tenant's family is seriously ill or the premises are quarantined at the expiration date of the lease, what redress does the lessor have?

A. None, until the condition abates.

49. Q. If a property is leased at the time it is being sold, why should some mention be made of it in the agreement of sale?

A. Because a lease is an encumbrance within the meaning of the term.

50. Q. An owner of real estate, which is mortgaged, leases it to a tenant. The mortgagee forecloses and obtains title to the property. He then ousts the tenant from possession. Does the tenant have a right of action against the owner under such circumstances?

A. Yes. The owner has violated the lease covenant of quiet and peaceful enjoyment to the tenant.

51. Q. Where a leased property is sold, who assigns the lease to the purchaser—the lessor or lessee?

A. The lessor.

52. Q. Who is ordinarily liable for the payment of the utilities for leased premises?

A. The lessee.

53. Q. In commercial leases what important clauses should be included for the lessor's protection?

A. 1. Tenant to pay any increased insurance premiums due to lessee's use or occupancy of premises.
2. Tenant to pay any increased taxes during term of lease.
3. Subordination clause so that lessor may place a first lien mortgage upon the premises.
4. Tenant to carry plate glass insurance.

54. Q. A lease is drawn between P. Kelly and Kay Semel, beautician, for certain premises. Her father, Joseph Semel, has signed the lease as surety. Miss Semel, with the consent of her landlord, sub-leases the entire premises to Dorothy Adams. Is Miss Semel relieved from liability for the rent?

A. No. As the original lessee, she continues liable for rent during the term of the lease as she expressly covenanted to pay rent under the lease executed by her.

55. Q. In what ways may a lease be terminated?

A. 1. By performance; automatically terminates at expiration of term.
   2. By surrender; mutual cancellation of lease before expiration of term.
   3. By breach; act of lessor is known as an eviction; act of lessee is known as forfeiture.

56. Q. Under the terms of a valid lease, must the landlord keep his tenant safe from trespassing of others upon the leased premises?
A. No; it is the duty of the tenant to enjoin such trespass.

57. Q. A property was held in the name of James Patz alone. He leased it to a tenant with an option to purchase. The wife of Patz did not sign the lease. The tenant exercised the option, but before consummation, Patz died. The wife refuses to execute a deed. What are her status and rights?
A. Since the wife did not sign the lease containing the option, she could not be compelled to execute a deed. The tenant, accepting a deed from the executor, would take it subject to the widow's dower right. Of course, he can refuse to take such a deed, subject to the encumbrances of dower, and either sue the estate for damages or recover any money paid on the sales contract.
Moral to Tenant:—Have lessor's wife join in a lease containing an option to purchase clause.

58. Q. Can a tenant after leasing property for 25 years claim ownership by adverse possession against the heirs of the original lessor?
A. No; occupancy was permissive throughout and not hostile or adverse.

59. Q. What articles belonging to others are exempt from a landlord's levy for delinquent rent?
A. Leased articles, such as furniture, soda water apparatus, ice cream cabinets, shoe repair machinery, cigarette vending machines, beauty and barber shop equipment, certain electrical apparatus and pianos, are exempt in some states, provided that notice of the leased article is given to the lessor.

60. Q. Whose liability is protection of plate glass windows?
A. Usually that of the lessee.

61. Q. Joseph Gray leases a neighborhood store to the Craft Cleaning Company. Due to a labor dispute, violence occurs and the premises are damaged. Who is liable for the repairs?
A. The tenant.

62. Q. Albert leases certain premises to Bold for a cigar store. In six months the place is raided five times as a "numbers joint." Court action is taken to padlock the premises. What is the status of rent for the unexpired period of the lease?
A. The tenant would be liable for the rent. If the landlord had

guilty knowledge that the premises was to be used illegally, the courts would not enforce the lease.

63. Q. Make up a rent receipt in which the Paul N. Smith Agency is the broker-agent and Helen Gardner is the tenant at 1223 Maple Lane, Salt Lake City, Utah. The rent is $90 per month, with a $5 discount if paid by the 10th of the month. The rent is payable on the first of the month and the March 1969 rent is being paid March 6, 1969.

A.
Salt Lake City, Utah
March 6, 1969

Received of Helen Gardner. . . . .

Sum of . . . . . Eighty-five . . . . ($85) . . . . . . Dollars,

for rent for month of March 1969 . . . .

for premises located at 1223 Maple Lane, Salt Lake City, Utah.
Paul N. Smith Agency, Inc.
by Adele Trumper, Secretary

True and False

1. A valid oral lease is assignable.   **T** F
2. A lease given by a lessee to a third party is a release.   T **F**
3. Leases may include fixtures along with the real estate.   **T** F
4. A tenancy from month to month may be terminated at any time without notice.   T **F**
5. An estate for years and a tenancy from year to year mean the same thing.   T **F**
6. Every lease must be signed by the tenant.   T **F**
7. The terms "tenant" and "lessee" are generally used in the same sense.   **T** F
8. A "tenant by sufferance" is one who is unable to remove from the premises at the end of the term because of serious illness.   T **F**
9. Where a tenant has been transferred to another city by his employer, he may terminate his lease.   T **F**
10. A sales clause in a lease means that the lease can be terminated in event of sale of the property.   **T** F
11. Where a sales clause has been exercised, the tenant is entitled to moving expenses.   T **F**
12. An oral lease favors the tenant.   **T** F
13. "First right of refusal" is the same as an option to purchase the property under a lease.   T **F**
14. All leases over three years must be recorded.   T **F**
15. A tenant of a fourth floor apartment finds that the elevator service is permanently discontinued. The tenant may move on that account.   **T** F
16. If the tenant fails to pay his rent when due, such action immediately terminates the lease.   T **F**

17. Joint tenancy means ownership of real estate, not the leasing of it. **T** F
18. There are no covenants to be found in a lease. T **F**
19. If the monthly rental is to remain the same, a long-term lease on real property need not be in writing to be enforceable. T **F**
20. A lease stated that the rent was to be paid monthly, but did not specify that the rent should be paid in advance. In that case, the rent was due and payable on the last day of the month. **T** F
21. A sub-tenant has no greater rights than his tenant. **T** F
22. When a lease of a store does not provide who shall make necessary repairs to the premises, the cost of such repairs falls upon the lessor. T **F**
23. A lease is a contract. **T** F
24. A lease for five years, signed and sealed only by an agent, does not bind the owner. **T** F
25. An oral lease for one year is valid. **T** F
26. Sale of a property terminates an existing lease. T **F**
27. Lease of a property in disrepair constitutes a violation of law. T **F**
28. A lessee is the tenant. **T** F
29. An agent's authority to execute a lease for more than three years must be in writing. **T** F
30. A lease usually favors the tenant. T **F**
31. A married woman has authority to execute a lease to property owned by herself and her husband. **T** F
32. A lease must be for a money rental. T **F**
33. An administrator of an estate cannot execute a lease. **T** F
34. The beneficiary of a trust estate must always join in the lease by the trustee. T **F**
35. A lease for three years automatically renews itself for three more years if the tenant remains on the premises. T **F**
36. A lease is assignable if there is no clause in the lease to the contrary. **T** F
37. Sub-letting and assignment are the same. T **F**
38. In an assignment the original lessee continues liable for the rent payments. **T** F
39. A tenant is liable for ordinary repairs. **T** F
40. The landlord is liable for repair of frozen water lines. T **F**
41. A tenant can refuse to pay rent where the owner has failed to make repairs agreed upon. T **F**
42. A lessor is liable for injuries where he leases premises in a defective condition. T **F**
43. A lessor is not liable for damages where he voluntarily makes repairs and does so negligently. T **F**
44. A tenant of a dwelling is liable for rent if the property is destroyed by fire. **T** F

45. A lease for five years need not be in writing if the tenant pays a substantial amount of rent in advance.   T **F**

46. The lease of a tenant in a store building expires if there is a change of ownership of the property.   T F

47. Death of the lessor terminates the lease.   T **F**

48. A lease on a property being sold constitutes an encumbrance on that property.   **T** F

49. A percentage lease is one based upon a percentage of the assessed valuation.   T **F**

50. All leases must be recorded.   T **F**

51. On a percentage lease the monthly rental is always the same and does not vary.   T **F**

52. If a tenant does not pay his rent when due, the landlord may immediately treble the rent.   T **F**

53. A lease for less than one year need not be in writing to be enforceable.   **T** F

54. When a lessee rents to another a part of the property which he holds under lease, he is "sub-letting."   **T** F

55. City property may be leased for any period from one to ninety-nine years.   **T** F

56. In condemnation proceedings, the tenant is entitled to compensation for loss of his lease.   **T** F

57. A 22-year lease on farm land is valid.   **T** F

58. A lease is a bilateral contract which conveys the right of possession to real property.   **T** F

59. A release clause is used when a tenant has secured an option to renew the lease for an additional term.   T **F**

60. Where leased property is condemned by the municipality, the lessee has a right of action against the lessor for damages.   T **F**

61. A landlord must keep his tenant safe from trespassing of others upon the leased premises.   T **F**

62. A tenant in an apartment building must pay rent if the building is destroyed by fire.   T **F**

63. A tenant in possession of the entire building is liable for injuries suffered upon the leased premises.   **T** F

64. A lessor has no right to go upon the leased premises to show prospective purchasers the property unless the right is reserved in the lease.   **T** F

65. A tenant is always entitled to the first right to purchase the leased property if it is for sale.   T **F**

66. Where the landlord violates the lease, it is termed an eviction.   **T** F

67. An estate for years is for some determinate period.   **T** F

68. Where the leased property is taken under eminent domain, the tenant can recover for the value of his lease from:
    (a) the lessor.   T **F**
    (b) the body or corporation condemning the property.   **T** F

69. Rent is in default the day after it is due.   **T** F
70. Where a lessor accepts delinquent rent for five months, he
    cannot refuse to accept rent for the next month because it
    is after the due date.   **T** F
71. Rent controls apply to all leased properties.   **T** **F**
72. A sales clause in a lease refers to the period of time a tenant
    must be given in order to terminate the lease.   T **F**
73. Any dwelling lease can be terminated before its term if the
    property is purchased by a veteran.   T **F**
74. Treble damages could be assessed against a landlord for
    charging rents above the maximum rental under O.P.A.   **T** F
75. A tenant for one year who holds over after the term would
    be a tenant for an additional year.   **T** F
76. A verbal lease for one year with an option to renew for three
    years must be in writing.   **T** F
77. A mortgagee in possession of leased premises cannot collect
    the rent unless he has written assignment from the owner.   T **F**
78. A lessor may levy for rent upon a stranger's goods found
    upon the premises.   **T** F
79. A tenancy at will can only be terminated by the tenant.   T **F**
80. In case of ambiguity in a lease, it is construed most strongly
    against the person who prepared it.   **T** F
81. Where the premises are destroyed by an act of God, the
    tenant is relieved from paying rent.   T **F**
82. On levying for delinquent rent, the lessor, or his agent, may
    break open an outer door in the tenant's absence.   T **F**
83. Rent controversies are determined in a special "people's
    court."   T **F**
84. A landlord is not liable for injuries suffered by the tenant
    due to a hidden defective condition of the premises.   T **F**
85. A landlord is liable for injuries to a guest suffered in the col-
    lapse of a public building such as a grandstand.   **T** F
86. Where the tenant defaults in the payment of rent, the land-
    lord can terminate the lease and evict a sub-tenant as well
    as the tenant.   **T** F
87. Where a landlord distrains for rent, he cannot, at the same
    time, terminate the lease.   **T** F
88. The first floor tenant of an apartment house is liable for snow
    removal.   T **F**
89. The law requires all leases to be in writing.   T **F**
90. A leasehold is considered an estate for years.   **T** F
91. Sale of a property for cash automatically cancels a month to
    month lease.   T **F**
92. The term "tenants in common" refers to several persons who
    lease and occupy the same property.   T **F**
93. A tenant who continues to occupy the premises after the ex-
    piration of the lease is called a Hold-Over.   **T** F
94. A landlord may send mechanics into leased premises to make

alterations even though the lease contains no specific authority
to do so.   T **F**

95. Goods exempt from a landlord's distraint arise from statute.   **T** F
96. A mortgagee in possession cannot lease the mortgaged premises.   T **F**
97. A lease by a mortgagee in possession can be terminated by the owner if he pays off the mortgage debt.   **T** F
98. A lessor has a reversionary interest in the leased premises.   **T** F
99. Act of God and accident by fire are the same.   T **F**
100. A tenant is required to repair frozen water pipes.   **T** F
101. The rule of "caveat emptor" applies to the tenant in leasing a property in a state of disrepair.   **T** F
102. A straight monthly rental, by tenant, is preferable to a percentage lease with a minimum monthly rental.   T **F**
103. Where a lease contains a "first right of refusal" clause the tenant is certain as to what he will have to pay for the property if he elects to purchase it.   T **F**
104. There is an implied warranty that the lessee will enjoy quiet and peaceful possession during the term of the lease.   **T** F
105. All goods found upon the leased premises are subject to a landlord's levy for delinquent rent.   T **F**
106. A mortgagee in possession of leased premises has the same rights to distrain as an owner.   **T** F
107. A mortgagee in possession must account to the owner for all rents received.   **T** F
108. Tenancy at will refers to ownership rather than occupancy.   T **F**
109. A freehold is an estate in real estate held under a lease.   T **F**
110. A broker has the right to assign a lease for the owner to the purchaser, if the property is sold.   T **F**
111. A broker's right to commission for rents ceases under a lease prepared by the broker containing a sales clause, when the property is sold.   **T** F
112. An owner would be liable for injuries to a pedestrian injured due to a fall over a raised sidewalk or trap door.   T **F**
113. In order to recover damages for injuries, the claimant must be free of contributory negligence.   **T** F
114. Broken windows in a leased property are the tenant's responsibility.   **T** F
115. A mortgagee of leased premises is more interested generally in the term of the lease than in the rental.   T **F**
116. Before leasing premises to an unknown applicant, the broker should check with the applicant's previous lessor or agent.   **T** F
117. A lessor is better protected by accepting a lease from a new tenant of presently leased premises than by permitting the present tenant to assign the existing lease.   T **F**
118. The terms "leasing" and "listing" are used interchangeably.   T **F**
119. A writing which transfers possession of real estate, but does not transfer ownership is a lease.   **T** F

120. An option to purchase clause in a lease is generally preferable to a first right of refusal clause, from the lessor's standpoint.   T **F**

121. A tenant who installs a fancy chandelier in a rented property and destroys the old one, is permitted to remove it at the expiration of lease term.   T **F**

122. A deposit accepted by a broker on a vacant apartment obligates the owner to lease it to the party making the deposit.   T **F**

123. An eviction corresponds to a forfeiture as to breach of a lease.   **T** F

124. A tenant who continues to occupy the premises after the expiration of the lease is called a squatter.   T **F**

125. A release clause is commonly used in a lease.   **T** **F**

126. Failure by a tenant to pay his rent when due does not constitute a termination of his lease.   **T** F

127. The terms of a written lease cannot be changed by oral agreement.   **T** F

128. In order that a landlord have the right to send mechanics into leased premises the lease must contain this authority.   **T** F

129. A lease given by a lessee is called a re-lease.   T **F**

130. "Tenancy at sufferance" is leasing by one tenant to another.   **T** F

131. Dispossession of a tenant by a landlord is known as an eviction.   **T** F

132. Eviction is the violation of a material lease provision by the lessor.   **T** F

133. A landlord may send a carpenter into leased premises to make repairs even though the lease contains no specific authority to do so.   T **F**

134. A tenant who assigns a lease to a third party is still liable for rent, even though lease permits the assignment.   **T** F

135. A fourth floor tenant is notified that the elevator service will shortly be discontinued permanently. The lease is silent about furnishing elevator service. The tenant may move.   **T** F

136. A lease of property which requires the lessor to pay all property charges through ownership is called a net lease.   T **F**

137. No lease is assignable unless it expressly grants this right to lessee.   T **F**

138. Ground rent is rent paid by an *owner* and not by the *tenant*.   **T** F

139. In community owned property, a husband can not alone execute a valid lease for more than one year.   **T** F

140. A "demising" clause may be found only in leasing contracts.   T **F**

141. "Graduated" lease can provide for a change in the rent to be paid, either lowering or raising the rent.   T **F**

142. A three day notice to vacate is all that is necessary to evict a tenant who fails to pay his rent.   T **F**

143. A lease cannot be recorded unless it is acknowledged by lessor.   **T** F

144. A tenant at will can assign his lease.   T **F**

145. A tenant at sufferance can assign his lease.   T **F**

146. A lessee is one who gives a mortgage upon his property in return for a loan. T **F**
147. "Tenancy at sufferance" is one in possession of property at the discretion of a court. T **F**
148. Accident by fire and inevitable casualty do not mean the same thing. **T** F
149. A fixture under a lease and a fixture in the sale of a residence mean the same thing. T **F**
150. Tenancy in common does not refer to a lease occupancy. **T** F
151. The legal return received from the use of property is called rent. **T** F
152. An owner can compel a tenant to remove store shelving at the end of the lease term. **T** F
153. The gross money expectancy from any income property is the gross income less the operating expenses. T **F**
154. A writ of restitution must be obtained to evict a tenant for non-payment of rent. T **F**
155. A lease given by an owner to a tenant is considered personal property. **T** F
156. Where a lessee assigns his lease to a new party, with the consent of the lessor, he is not liable for the rent for the remainder of the term. T **F**
157. Parol testimony can always be introduced to explain the terms of a written lease. T **F**
158. Under a net lease, the lessor is liable for property taxes. **T** F
159. The manager of an apartment building is entitled to keep rebates on supplies purchased. T **F**
160. If a tenant fails to surrender possession at the expiration of a lease term, he is always considered a tenant by sufferance. T **F**
161. A "first right of refusal" clause favors the lessor more than an "Option" clause in a lease. **T** F

Multiple Choice

1. Which one of the following will not terminate a lease?
   ( ) Performance.
   ( ) Breach.
   ( ) Surrender.
   (x) Vacancy.
2. Which one of the following types of tenancies does not apply to a lessor-lessee relationship?
   ( ) Tenancy at will.
   (x) Tenancy in common.
   ( ) Tenancy for years.
   ( ) Leasehold.
3. When a leased property is sold, the sale has the following effect upon the tenant:

( ) Tenant must record lease in recorder's office.
( ) Tenant must obtain assignment from purchase.
(x) No effect.
( ) Tenant must move out after 30 days' notice.
4. An estate at will is a
( ) form of partnership.
(x) tenancy of uncertain duration.
( ) inheritance of property by will.
( ) life tenancy.
5. The legal compensation or income received from the use of real property is called
( ) ground rent.
( ) interest.
(x) rent.
( ) owner's equity.
6. The owner of real estate who leases it to another is called
( ) vendor.
( ) lessee.
(x) lessor.
( ) optionee.
7. A lease cannot be recorded unless it is acknowledged by the
( ) lessee.
(x) lessor.
( ) vendor.
( ) seller.
8. A landlord rents a store to a men's clothier on a "percentage lease." On which of the following is the percentage usually based?
( ) Market value.
( ) Assessed value.
(x) Tenant's gross sales.
( ) Tenant's net income.
9. When real estate under lease is sold, the lease
( ) expires.
( ) is broken.
( ) must be renewed.
(x) remains binding upon new owner.
10. When a lease antedates a mortgage, and the mortgagee becomes the mortgagee in possession, the tenant must pay the rent to
(x) mortgagee.
( ) landlord.
( ) court.
( ) himself and hold until foreclosure sale.
11. When a tenant is delinquent in his rent under a written lease, the owner may have him evicted by
( ) notifying the real estate commission.
( ) having the Office Housing Expeditor take legal action.
( ) giving tenant 30 days' notice.
(x) bringing court action.

12. Where a guest is injured on a leased dwelling, he may bring action (in most states) against
    ( ) lessor.
    (x) lessee.
    ( ) city.
13. A lease should be in writing
    ( ) to make the agreement binding.
    (x) to avoid misunderstandings.
    ( ) to benefit the tenant or landlord.
14. Under a lease for 3 years, if the tenant remains in possession after the expiration of the term, the lease is
    ( ) cancelled.
    ( ) renewed for 3 years.
    (x) renewed for 1 year.
15. Where a leased property is destroyed by fire
    (x) the tenant must continue to pay rent.
    ( ) the lease is terminated.
    ( ) the lessor must provide other accommodations.
16. A lease to be binding must be signed by the
    ( ) broker.
    ( ) beneficiary.
    (x) lessor and lessee.
    ( ) lessee and broker.
17. Distraint is a proceedings to
    ( ) prevent a tenant from removing.
    (x) collect delinquent rent by lessor.
    ( ) impeach the lessor's title.
18. A lease may be terminated
    (x) if the lessor interferes with tenant's quiet enjoyment.
    ( ) if property is sold by lessor.
    ( ) if lessor becomes delinquent in his mortgage payments.
19. A lease by an infant lessor is
    ( ) void.
    ( ) voidable by lessor or lessee.
    (x) voidable by lessor.
    ( ) not renewable.
20. A pedestrian injured due to the negligent accumulation of snow and ice in front of an apartment building can recover damages from
    ( ) the municipality.
    ( ) the real estate broker who negotiated the lease.
    ( ) the first floor tenant.
    (x) the lessor.
21. In a distraint for rent, leased counter equipment can be
    ( ) claimed by owner of equipment.
    (x) sold by lessor.
    ( ) claimed by tenant as his debtor's exemption.
22. Pedestrian traffic counts are usually taken to determine
    ( ) urban population.

( ) size of shopping area.
(x) rental value of a location.
( ) average age group.

23. "Spot zoning" is usually determined by
( ) lease contract.
( ) owner of property.
( ) city law department.
(x) Board of Adjustment.

24. Gregg orally leases a store to Morris for one year. The lease is
( ) invalid.
(x) valid.
( ) a month to month lease.
( ) a tenancy at will.

25. A sub-lease is for
( ) basement premises.
( ) a new tenant of the entire premises.
(x) a portion of the leased premises.

26. The right to distrain is
(x) statutory.
( ) by agreement of the parties.
( ) by the code of ethics.
( ) a court decree.

27. Where a tenant's furniture is damaged by water due to the negligence of an upstairs tenant, she can
( ) refuse to pay rent until made whole.
( ) move out if this has happened before.
( ) complain to the city officials.
(x) bring a civil action against the upstairs tenant.

28. Where a tenant is delinquent in rent for many months, it is preferable for the lessor to
( ) confess judgment for amount of rent.
( ) institute a landlord's levy.
(x) confess judgment for possession of premises.
( ) notify local credit association.

29. Where a 4 room apartment is leased to a young couple and later the parents of the couple move in, the landlord can
(x) do nothing.
( ) terminate the lease.
( ) increase the rent proportionally.
( ) require tenant to post bond against any damage.

30. Where a husband owner of real estate leases property for five years and dies shortly afterwards, the
( ) lease is terminated.
( ) lease is carried out by Probate or Surrogate's Court.
(x) lease is taken over by devisee of leased property.
( ) court appoints licensed broker to administer lease.

31. A lease which requires the tenant to pay all expenses of the property in addition to his rent is called

( ) a gross lease.
( ) an assigned lease.
( ) a percentage lease.
(x) a net lease.

32. Net income is arrived at by deducting all expenses and safety factors from the
( ) sales price.
( ) net price.
(x) gross annual income.
( ) market price.

33. Where a lease requires an initial deposit for four months rent, the deposit usually applies to
( ) first four months of the term.
( ) held to protect lessor against breakage.
(x) last four months of term.
( ) any four months during term, selected by lessor.

34. When a commercial property is being offered for sale, and a tenant wishes to renew a long term lease, the managing broker should renew the lease with
( ) a percentage clause.
(x) a cancellation clause.
( ) a distraining clause.
( ) an elevator clause.

35. According to the Statute of Frauds, a verbal lease for five years is
( ) enforceable.
(x) not enforceable.
( ) assignable.
( ) renewable.

36. When a lease of a store does not provide who shall make necessary repairs to the premises, the cost of such repairs are borne by
(x) the lessee.
( ) the lessor.
( ) the legatee.
( ) the grantor.

37. Under a "net" rental agreement, the tenant generally meets all but one of the following charges
( ) taxes.
(x) mortgage interest.
( ) assessment.
( ) liability insurance.

38. A percentage lease is a lease
( ) which provides for a percentage of rents to be paid to the broker as a commission.
( ) covers only a certain percentage of property, where there are two or more persons sharing the premises.
(x) where rent is based on percentage of tenant's receipts.
( ) covers the lending of money and interest charged thereon.

39. A lease for less than one year
(x) may be oral.

( ) must be in writing.
( ) may be oral, but must be reduced to writing within one year.
40. A tenancy at will is
( ) tenancy for a specified duration.
( ) possession of property under a will.
( ) life estate.
(x) none of the above.
41. A chain store firm in determining value of a site is motivated by
( ) spot zoning.
(x) pedestrian count.
( ) traffic count during and between 8:00 A.M. and 8:00 P.M.
( ) latest census figures.
42. Where a lessee holds farm property at the will of the lessor, he has a
(x) tenancy at sufferance.
( ) freehold estate.
( ) common of pasturage.
( ) holdover tenancy.
43. Taking property into custody, or seizure of goods by due legal process is called
( ) an eviction.
( ) a forfeiture.
(x) an attachment.
( ) an action in trespass.
( ) none of these.
44. Cancellation of a lease by mutual consent of lessor and lessee is called
( ) Action of Rescission.
( ) Action of Revocation.
(x) Surrender and Acceptance.
( ) Lis Pendens action.
45. A real estate broker usually represents
(x) the lessor.
( ) an adverse party.
( ) lessor and lessee.
( ) lessee.
46. A document which transfers possession for recompense, but not ownership is
( ) a special warranty deed.
( ) option.
( ) easement.
(x) lease.
47. An oral lease for five years is unenforceable under
(x) the statute of frauds.
( ) statute of limitations.
( ) under an Act of Congress.
( ) the common law.
48. The Statute of Frauds is a law
(x) requiring certain contracts to be in writing.
( ) requiring a license to operate as a broker or salesman.

( ) regulating escrow accounts.
( ) regulating estates owning real estate.

49. An owner may evict a tenant, who is delinquent in his rent, by
( ) giving 30 days' notice to vacate.
( ) notifying the Real Estate Commission.
( ) notifying the Department of Human Relations.
(x) bringing court action.

50. A tenant spends $10,000 in improving the landlord's property. Annual taxes are then increased $240. The tenant
( ) is liable for the tax increase.
( ) is liable for one-half of the tax increase.
(x) is not liable for any taxes.
( ) the lease is terminated.

51. The owner of real estate who leases it to another is a(n)
(x) lessor.
( ) optionee.
( ) vendee.
( ) lessee.
( ) feoffee.

52. A lease which provides for a step-by-step increase in rentals at regular intervals is called
( ) an instalment lease.
( ) a percentage lease.
( ) an open lease.
(x) a graduated lease.

53. Net return on investment property is computed by deducting all expenses from
(x) gross annual income.
( ) gross annual income less depreciation.
( ) appraised value.
( ) market price.

54. Fixtures under the ordinary lease, at the expiration of the lease will be the property of
(x) lessor.
( ) lessee.
( ) mortgage.
( ) ground rent owner.

55. Accepting rebates on purchases of materials for an office building is unlawful for which one of the following:
( ) owner.
( ) tenants.
( ) seller.
(x) building manager.

56. A lease of part of the premises by a tenant to another party is
( ) assignment of lease.
( ) a release.
(x) subletting.
( ) an eviction.

Chapter 8

VALUATION AND APPRAISAL[1]

Basic Valuation Concepts

Property valuation may be considered as the heart of all real estate activity. Only a practical understanding of real estate valuation will enable real estate brokers and salesmen to carry out their functions in a useful and dependable manner in serving their clients and in meeting their obligations to the general public.

Even though they may not qualify as expert appraisers, brokers and salesmen should be familiar with the theoretical concepts of value, the forces which influence values and the methods by which such values may best be estimated. Such a knowledge is essential in arriving at a logical solution as to the highest and best, and hence the most profitable use of property.

It is a daily occurrence for the real estate broker to be asked by clients as to the worth, a fair price, a fair rental, a fair basis for trade, or a proper insurance coverage for property. He needs to know how to answer such questions intelligently. To be successful in business, he must determine whether he can profitably spend his time in trying to sell a property at a listing price which the owner is willing to set. In this regard he must keep in mind that in accepting a listing he obligates himself to put forth his best efforts to find a buyer for the property.

Value designations

There are many different designations or definitions of value. They may be divided into the following two main classifications: (1) *Utility value*—or the value in use or warranted use to an owner-user. This frequently is termed *subjective* value, and it includes a valuation of amenities which attach to a property. (2) *Market value*—or value in exchange. This is the price at which property can be sold

---

[1] The text material on Valuation and Appraisal has been taken from the 1960 State of California Reference Book and Guide (pp. 491-507, incl.) with permission of the California Real Estate Commissioner, Hon. Burton E. Smith.

or exchanged at a given time or place as a result of market balancing. It may be based on a "willing-buyer" and "willing-seller" concept. This is frequently termed the *objective* value.

Value of property most generally means the market value. Market value is said to be the price in terms of money for which a property would sell in the open market, seller not being obliged to sell, the buyer not being obliged to buy, with a reasonable length of time to effect the sale. This also supposes that both seller and prospective buyer are fully informed of all uses to which the property is adapted and for which it is capable of being used. Value is what the property is worth. Price is what one can get for the sale of the property in terms of money.

Among the various types of value that have been designated from time to time are book value, tax value, market value, cash value, capital value, speculative value, par value, true value, exchange value, reproduction or physical value, replacement value, insurance value, investment value, rental value, and cost value.

Value can be distinguished from "cost" as well as from "price." The principal differences may be explained as follows:

(a) Value has to do with the combined factors of present and future anticipated enjoyment, or profit. The value sought in the appraisal of property may be said to be the discounted worth of all desirable things (benefits) which may accrue from a skillful use of it. A conclusion in regard to these things will clearly be a matter of opinion—an intelligent estimate based on a thorough analysis of all available influencing factors and on reasonable and more or less warranted assumptions.

(b) Cost represents a measure of past expenditures in labor, material, or sacrifices of some nature. While cost may be, and frequently is, a factor upon which value is partially based, it need not be, as it does not control present and future value. An example of this fact is the value of an oil well, which in one case may prove to be a big producer and of great value, while in another case may prove to be a dry hole and of no value, although both may have cost the same to develop and drill.

(c) Price is what one pays for a commodity. Usually it is considered to be the amount of money involved in a transaction. Whether we receive in value more or less than what we pay for will depend on the soundness of judgment in appraisal of value, or upon fortuitous future developments. Under an efficient market structure, prices will usually tend to equal values, varying only as buyers and sellers have unequal knowledge or economic strength.

Purposes and characteristics of value

The purpose of an evaluation or an appraisal is usually indicated in the value concept employed, for example: assessed value, condemnation value, liquidation value, cash value, mortgage loan value, fire insurance value, etc. The purpose of an appraisal frequently dictates the valuation method employed and influences the resulting estimate of value.

There are only four elements of value, all of which are essential. These are utility, scarcity, demand, and transferability. None alone will create value. For example, a thing may be scarce but, if it has no utility, there is no demand for it. Other things, like air, may have great utility and may be in great demand, but are so abundant as to have no commercial value. Likewise, the commodity must be transferable as to use or title to be marketable. Generally speaking, a commodity will have commercial or marketable value in proportion to its utility and relative scarcity. Utility creates demand, but demand, to be effective, must be implemented by purchasing power.

Fundamental to the concept of value is the idea of the "highest and best use." This can be defined as follows; the highest and best use is that use which is most likely to produce the greatest net return over a given period. Sometimes "net return" takes the form of amenities, but more usually it is thought of in terms of money. The "given period" may be dependent on the purpose for which the property is desired. For example, the "given period" to be analyzed would be shorter for a speculative venture than for a long-term investment.

Location is also a factor. For example, a site in a downtown district of a city which could most profitably be used for a time as a parking lot without improvements might later become more desirable as a location for a new commercial structure. In addition, any analysis to reach a decision as to the "highest and best use" must include consideration as to the future supply and demand for such use within the area and a possible oversupply with attendant decrease of market value.

Special Forces Influencing Value

The value of real estate is created, maintained, modified and destroyed by the interplay of the following three great forces:

(a) Social ideals and standards. Examples of social forces include: population growth and decline, marriage, birth, divorce and death rates, attitudes toward education, recreation, and other instincts and yearnings of mankind.

(b) Economic adjustments. Examples of economic forces include: natural resources—including location, quantity and quality, industrial and commercial trends, employment trends, wage levels, availability of money and credit, interest rates, price levels, tax loads, etc.

(c) Political or governmental regulations. Examples of political forces include: building codes, zoning laws, public health measures, fire regulations, government guaranteed loans, government housing, credit controls, etc. Each and every one of these many social, economic and political factors affects cost, price, and value to some degree. The three of them interweave and each one is in a constant state of change.

Factors influencing value

Directional Growth. In any estimate of value, attention should be paid to "the city directional growth." The city directional growth refers to the manner and direction in which the city tends to grow. Properties in the direction of growth in different sections of the city tend to increase in value, especially if the growth is steady and rapid.

Location. This includes access. This factor of valuation is often measured by traffic counts, which, in turn, have to be interpreted in purchasing power as well as volume of traffic. A property must have access by street, right-of-way, easement, alley or other means, to have value.

Utility. This includes capacity to produce. This important factor involves judgment as to the best use to which a given property may be put. Building restrictions and zoning ordinances affect utility.

Size. The width and depth often determine the possibilities and character of use.

Shape. Parcels of land of irregular shape cannot usually be developed so advantageously as rectangular lots.

Thoroughfare Conditions. The width of streets, traffic congestion, condition of pavement all affect the value of those properties fronting any given street.

Action of the Sun. The south and west sides of business streets are usually preferred by merchants, because the pedestrian traffic seeks the shady side of the street in warm weather, and merchandise displayed in the windows is not damaged by the sun.

Character of Business Done. The larger cities develop retail, financial, wholesale, and commission-house districts, and women's and men's shopping sections, for the cheap, medium and high-grade trade.

Social Atmosphere in Residential Districts.

Plottage.   Which is the added value of several parcels of land when brought under one ownership making possible a higher utility than could be found for the parcels considered separately.

Proportion of Length to Front.   This is important in determining the best uses to which a given property may be put. A lot must be of usable width and depth to have value.

Character of the Soil.   A factor in residential and some classes of manufacturing properties.

Conspicuousness.   Largely a factor of publicity value, and becomes of great importance to businesses depending upon advertising.

Grades.   These vary from level land to hillside properties.

Obsolescence.   Caused by changes in types and methods of construction, style of architecture, interior arrangements for specific purposes which render a particular building out of date. Changes in the uses of neighboring property may also contribute to the obsolescence of a building.

Appreciation.   A sustained trend of rising costs in labor and materials has caused appreciation in nearly all cases to be more rapid than physical and economic (obsolescence) depreciation combined.

Building Restrictions and Zoning.   These sometimes operate to depress values and at other times to increase values. For example, there may be a vacant lot on a residence street which will sell for only $50 a front foot for residence use, but would sell for $300 per front foot as an apartment site. Or a vacant lot in a zoned area may sell for more per foot as a business site because of the supply of business sites being restricted by zoning. Many other examples might be given.

Residential property

In making a rough estimate of the value of residential property, it is usual to evaluate the lot and the present value of the building as a limit, allowing for depreciation, checking the values of properties in the neighborhood, the assessed valuation and recent sales made in the neighborhood. Ordinarily, in California, the estimate of the cost of replacing buildings is made by the square foot method. The square foot method is merely the multiplication of the length by the breadth of the house, and the sum obtained thereby is multiplied by approximate construction costs per square foot, depending upon the type of construction involved. The sum, after having depreciation subtracted therefrom and the value of the land added, represents, roughly, the value of the property. However, special attention should be paid to the condition of the building, the interior fixtures, plans and workmanship, interior decoration, plumbing, heating, and electric fixtures, type of roof, the lawn and shrubbery, with particular attention to the foundation and the underpinnings of the house in connection with possible termite infestation.

Industrial property

Industrial lands are usually valued upon an area basis; that is, either by the square foot, or by the acre. Frequently this is expressed at so much an acre up to a value of $4,500 an acre, which is approximately 10 cents a square foot, and above that amount, in terms of square feet. The reason for valuing in terms of area is that the lands are seldom sold in regular shapes. Thus it is customary that such lands are bought and sold upon an area basis, and therefore are appraised in that manner.

Topography. The topography of undeveloped land is of importance, and consideration should be given to the cost of grading, if required.

Subsoil. The character of the subsoil is frequently overlooked, and yet may be vital. Quicksand, rock, or other characteristics may make a certain site impossible for a given industry. Drainage also may be a vital factor.

Plottage Value. There is an added or plottage value from assembling lots into a reasonable-sized industrial site, but on the other hand, it is generally recognized that an area of unusual size has a lesser unit value, in the same way that the value per square foot of a commercial lot decreases, according to any of the published tables, with increased depth.

Track Layouts. In the study and valuation of unimproved, but potentially valuable, industrial lands, the assistance of a competent engineer, familiar with plant and track layouts, is frequently a decided advantage.

Agricultural or farm lands

In estimating the value of agricultural land, the nature and long-term trend of prices for the crop which is grown or intended to be grown is probably the chief determining factor. If the property is to be used for a dairy farm, then the character of the soil, whether suitable for hay and grain, water supply for the cattle and crops, proximity to markets, climatic conditions, labor conditions in the district, breed of cattle and their general conditions are extremely important. If the land is to be used for fruit growing, then it is essential to ascertain if the water supply is ample, if the land is suitable for the type of crops to be grown, if the cost of water is not excessive, a full knowledge of climatic conditions, with special reference to frosts and protection against frost, age and condition of the trees, their past production, market conditions, labor conditions, and the price of produce in past years.

If the land is to be used for vineyard or root crops such as truck gardens, then consideration must be given to suitability of the soil, water supply, the cost of water, proximity to markets, labor supply and climatic conditions.

In agricultural land evaluation, it is also well to remember that all fruit and nut trees under four years of age from time of planting in orchard form, and all grape vines under three years old from time of planting in orchard form, and all growing crops are exempt from taxation.

Farm land valuation is highly specialized and requires the assistance often of soil and crop experts.

Appraisal Techniques

Definition of appraisal

To appraise means to arrive at an estimate and opinion of the value of a property. An appraisal is usually a statement of the market value, or value for loan purposes, or value as defined by the appraiser, of a parcel of property as of a specified date. It is a conclusion which results from the analysis of facts.

Real estate appraising is being definitely standardized by virtue of the experience and practice of men in organizations in all parts of the country who encounter the same class of valuation problems, and who, by various methods and processes, succeed in solving them in a scientific way. It is natural that differences of opinion exist as to the value of real estate and the means of determining its value in specific cases.

Methods of appraising properties

It is generally accepted that there are three ways to approach a value estimate. These methods or types of approach are:

1. *Comparison.* A comparison is made as to price, value, utility and location in relation to other vacant or improved land situated in the same neighborhood.
2. *Reproduction Cost.* This approach computes costs of reproducing the improvements with an added assigned value for

the land, secured by comparison with other lands. Deductions for depreciation are made as applicable.

3. *Capitalization* (for Income Property). Using this process, value is established by consideration of the present and prospective future income of the property. Conclusions from this approach are always checked by the óther two methods.

Frequently, the skilled appraiser will use all three methods in appraising a given property. No single method of approach by itself can always be depended upon to produce reliable estimates. Each appraisal must be solved after analyzing the special problem which is being presented.

Not only does every piece of real estate differ in some respects from all other properties, but there are many different purposes for which an appraisal may be made. These, in turn, could result in a considerable, yet logical, variation of estimated valuation, based on the specific type of value being sought. For example, the nature of the property, whether non-investment, investment or service; the purpose of the purchase, whether for use, investment, or speculation; and the purpose of the appraisal, such as sale, loan, taxation, insurance and the like, all constitute matters which will influence the proper methods of appraisal approach and the final figure reached by the appraisal.

Consequently, the first step in any appraisal procedure is to have a clear understanding of the reasons for making the appraisal and the objective to be sought. The adequacy and reliability of available data also are determining factors in the selection of the specific approach method or methods to be employed. A lack of certain pertinent or up-to-date information may well eliminate an otherwise possible approach method.

In other instances, proper procedures may only call for an appropriate discounting of conclusions drawn from such data. Thus, based on its adaptability to the specific problem, one method is usually given greater weight than the other approach methods.

In most appraisals, all three approach methods will ordinarily have something to contribute. Each approach method is used independently to reach an estimated value. Then as a final step, by applying to each separate value a weight proportionate to its merits in that particular instance, conclusions are reached as to one appropriate value. This procedure is known as correlation.

For the real estate broker or salesman dealing primarily in single family residences, a good understanding of the advantages and disadvantages as well as the limitations of the market data (comparison) approach is especially desirable. However, there will be situations where this approach cannot be relied upon exclusively for reaching a reasonable estimate of value. Consequently a reasonable understanding of the proper procedures and application of all three approaches is necessary for the well-qualified real estate broker.

We will now proceed to elaborate on and examine more closely the three approaches to value.

Market Comparison (Comparable Sales)

This approach is most generally adaptable for use by real estate brokers and salesmen. It lends itself well to the appraisal of land, buildings, and residences which exhibit a high degree of similarity, and for which a ready market exists. It is also particularly applicable as a check against the other methods of appraising all types of properties where the market value is the end result being sought.

The mechanics of the process involves the use of market data of all kinds in order to compare closely the property being appraised with other similar properties. The sources used for determining a market value include actual sales prices, listings, offers, rents and leases, and an analysis of social and economic factors affecting marketability.

Some of these prices are obtainable from the appraiser's own records, financial news services, classified advertisements, abstract companies, and Federal revenue stamps. In the latter case, while a price may be calculated from the value of the revenue stamps, this figure must be accepted with caution. It may not represent the actual price because no maximum limit is set as to the number of stamps which may be purchased. Thus, to create the impression of high prices, more stamps may have been used than are actually required. On the other hand, the price paid may be much more than is indicated by the stamps used as these need represent only the equity consideration involved. The tax is not applicable to existing mortgages or trust deeds which are assumed. Again, in cases of property exchanges, it may be to the mutual advantage of the interested parties to understate or overstate the transaction price for tax or other purposes, the federal tax on deeds was repealed January 1, 1968.

Listing prices may often indicate the probable top market value, while bid prices may normally indicate the lowest probable value. Both are subject to variation based on motivation, but a reasonable number of such figures will provide a bracket within which a current fair value will be found. Offers are likely to approach market values more closely than are listings which frequently are made to test the market. However, an offer to purchase is not usually a matter of common knowledge.

The procedure used in the market data (comparison) approach

method is to assemble data concerning sales and other market data of comparable properties. The greater the number of good comparisons used, the better should be the conclusions which may be drawn therefrom. The approach is based on the assumption that property is worth what it will sell for in the absence of undue stress, if reasonable time is given to find a buyer. For this reason, the appraiser should look behind sales and transfers to ascertain what influences may have affected sales prices—particularly if only a few comparisons are available.

Proper comparisons between properties should be based on an actual and thorough inspection of such properties. For nearly comparable properties, penalties should be assessed for poor repair, freakish design, existing nuisances, etc. Conversely, additional values should be allowed for attractive design, view, special features, better condition, higher quality of materials, landscaping, and the like. Unless the sales being compared are of recent date, consideration must also be given to adjusting values in keeping with the general economic worth of the dollar as of such dates. The average of the adjusted prices for all selected comparable sales usually provides a measure of value for the property being appraised.

Some of the advantages of using this approach method are as follows:

1. It is the simplest of the various methods to learn and to use. The factor of economic obsolescence of the neighborhood presumably is included in the values as set by the market price.

2. It is particularly applicable for appraisal purposes involving the sale, exchange and loan transactions of single family residences. These make up the great bulk of real estate transactions. It is valuable as a check against the values determined by the other approach methods.

Some of the disadvantages of the comparison approach method are as follows:

1. Its reliability is greatly reduced by the lack of suitable comparisons. These must be adequate in number, reliable as to source, and sufficiently recent to justify reasonable conclusions to be drawn from them.

2. Being based primarily on current or short-term values, it is influenced by temporary market fluctuations, and may not satisfactorily forecast long-range values.

3. Scattered comparison may exaggerate or disregard special influences that have affected sales prices.

4. Individuals using this approach frequently neglect to make enough inspections to get a true comparison of values between the properties being used for this purpose.

Cost Approach (Reproduction or Replacement)

When cost is applied as a measure of appraising value, it is normally assumed to be the cost new of *replacing* the subject property with property having exactly the same utility and amenities. Strictly speaking, *reproduction* cost new is generally accepted as meaning the cost that would be incurred if the property were to be reproduced as an exact replica. To do this might well involve materials and construction practices long since outmoded, and thus it would be impracticable to estimate such costs. Consequently, this approach is more appropriately designated as the "replacement cost method," or simply as the "cost-approach method." There are some appraisals, however, which are based on reproduction costs, such as those made to determine insurance values.

The cost approach is an estimate of the investment which would be required to duplicate the property in its present condition. Since people ordinarily will not pay more for a property than it would cost to replace the property at the time, or to obtain an equally satisfactory substitute property, the cost approach tends to set the upper limit of value.

The progressive steps in the cost approach are as follows:

(a) An independent estimate is made as to the value of the land. This is always the current market value of the land, considered as vacant and available for improvement to its highest and best use. This value is not determined by the historic cost of the land.

(b) An estimate is made as to the replacement cost new of all improvements on the property. Accuracy requires the application of principles of building cost estimating.

Replacement cost implies the taking of an inventory of the materials and manufactured equipment making up the property and then applying to this inventory the current prices of similar materials, equipment, labor costs and all overhead costs which would be necessary to construct a suitable replacement of the property as of the appraisal date. The methods used in such estimates vary from the very technical and detailed procedures used by contractors and mortgage loan companies, to the simpler shortcut methods such as the square-foot and cubic-foot methods, which are used by most appraisers.

To use the simpler methods, an estimate of total cost is made by comparison with other similar buildings whose costs are known and have been reduced to units per square foot of floor area of living space or per cubic foot of the building content. Applying these costs to the actual area of the property under appraisal will give an approximate valuation, provided the data as to costs are accurate and the buildings and improvements are similar as to quality and design. Corrections must be made for such differences as well as for changes in cost levels which may have taken place between the date of basic costs and the date of the new estimate. In California it is customary to use the square-foot method for residences, warehouses, loft buildings and structures of like character.

Cost figures are also obtainable from local contractors or from numerous services which publish building costs. Actually, building costs will vary considerably, based on the efficiency of the builder and the amount of profit which is included in such costs. There is a great variation also in the quality and design of structures, so that unless the appraiser is experienced in such matters, his estimates of value may be inaccurate.

(c) The third step in the cost approach method is to determine the existing depreciation of the property. This amount must be deducted from the replacement cost new to determine the present value of all improvements. The difficulties of correctly estimating depreciation tend to increase with the age of the property and require skill, experience, and good judgment. A value determined by using the cost approach is no more reliable than is the estimate of depreciation. There is no justification in assuming that improvements necessarily depreciate at a rate corresponding to their age, although all too frequently this simple method is employed by the inexperienced appraiser.

(d) The final step in the cost approach method is to add the value of the land, as determined in (a) above, to the depreciated replacement cost new, (b) and (c) above.

The cost-approach method is frequently used to get a ceiling upon the value established by the other two approach methods. It is particularly appropriate for appraising newly-built properties where depreciation is incidental. It is also the most appropriate approach method for public service properties. These have no active market, and thus lack market data which can be used for a comparison approach, and there is no income on which to base an income or capitalization approach.

The cost approach requires a higher degree of training and ability than either of the other methods.

Capitalization (Income) Approach

The income approach is concerned with the present worth of future benefits of property. This method is particularly important in the valuation of income-producing property, although rarely can it be taken as the only pertinent approach. It is usually measured by the net income which a fully informed person is warranted in assuming the property will produce during its remaining useful life. An exception, where gross income may be used rather than net income, is found in the "appraisal" of one or two unit family residences by using a gross rent-multiplier. This would be the case of property which no longer has a ready market for home owners but has deteriorated into rental properties. Such property normally is not considered as income property, as this was not its original purpose or function.

The procedure used in the capitalization approach involves the following three main steps:

(a) A net annual income is derived, preferably over a period of years, by deducting total expenses from gross income. Unless such figures have remained fairly constant, it is important that trends in income and expenses be taken into account in forecasting future net income. The existence of current high profits should indicate the probability of early competition and the lessening of future profits.

(b) A selection is made of an appropriate capitalization rate, or "present worth" factor. This is the crux of the matter and is a most important step.

The rate is dependent upon the return which investors will actually demand before they will be attracted by such an investment. The greater the risk of recapturing the investment price, the higher will be the accompanying rate as determined in the market for such properties. By analyzing market prices, these rates can be approximated at any given time.

A variation of only 1 percent may make a substantial difference in the capitalized value of the income. For example, based on an annual income of $30,000, and a capitalization rate of 5 percent, the resultant capitalized property valuation would be $600,000. Capitalizing this same income at a rate of 6 percent would result in a value of only $500,000 in valuation due to a difference in the capitalization rate of only 1 percent.

(c) The final step after having determined the net income and the capitalization rate is to capitalize the income. This may be merely a mathematical calculation of dividing the income by the rate if the income is considered to be a perpetuity. For example, the valuation of property which has an assumed perpetual annual income of $30,000 and a capitalization rate of 5 percent is $600,000. The lower the rate, the greater the valuation, and the greater the assumed security of the investment. So-called annuity tables are used in capitalizing incomes for fixed periods of varying duration.

An important element in all capitalization rates is provision for a return of the investment on the improvements to the property during their remaining economic life. This may be called an amortization of such investments. It may be provided for by straight-line depreciation, which recovers a definite sum every year for the period of years estimated to be the economic life of the improvement, at the end of which time the cost of replacement will be accrued. It may also be provided for by other methods, such as establishing "sinking funds," or a declining balance depreciation. These are more technical procedures which are used by professional appraisers.

In the hands of those who are familiar with its use, the capitalization approach may be helpful in determining the value of vacant land. This is accomplished by calculating probable incomes that would result if the property were used for different purposes and permits a determination of the most profitable or highest and best use of the land.

The technique used is known as the "land residual process." It seeks the capitalized value remaining in property after deductions are made for a return *on* and a return *of* the investment in the improvements alone.

The capitalization approach is particularly advantageous where insufficient market data are available for proper use of the market data approach.

Income (capitalization) approach applied. In determining the value of an income-producing property, one method that the appraiser may use is:

1. Estimate the adjusted gross income of the land and buildings, making proper allowances for vacancies and collection losses;
2. Ascertain the correct amount of all taxes;
3. Ascertain the annual cost of adequate insurance;
4. Estimate the stabilized maintenance and management expense per annum;
5. Estimate an annual amount of reserve funds for necessary replacement of equipment or furnishings prior to the end of the estimated economic life of the building;
6. Compute the net income of the entire property before depreciation by deducting items 2, 3, 4, and 5 from item 1;
7. Capitalize the remainder at a reasonable rate according to the risk involved, which will result in a valuation of the property as a whole.

Example: 10-unit apartment house—4 years old. Each apartment presently leased at $100 per month.

10 × $100 = $1,000 per month or $12,000 per year

Proven vacancy factor—10 percent

10 percent × $12,000 = $1,200 per year

$12,000
− 1,200
———————
$10,800   Gross income (adjusted for vacancy factor)

Expenses (annual) —Management $1,200
                    Taxes   960
                    Insurance   240
                    Utilities   600
                    Reserve for Replacements   +   400
                                                ————————
                                                  $3,400

$10,800 Gross Income
− 3,400 Expenses
——————
$ 7,400 Net Income

Capitalization Rate—8 percent $\dfrac{\$7,400}{.08} = \$92,500$ Valuation

If it is desired, a valuation for the land alone may be arrived at
through the following additional steps:

8. Compute the interest on the value of the improvements today,
   at a reasonable rate, according to the risk involved in the building investment only;
9. Deduct item 8 from item 6 above and capitalize the result at
   a rate justified by the risk involved in the land investment only,
   which will result in a value for the land alone.

In computing the net income from an apartment house there are
several major items for deduction from the gross income to indicate
the net income. Major items are:

(a) Taxes;
(b) Insurance;
(c) Repairs;
(d) Depreciation on furniture;
(e) Vacancies and collection losses;
(f) Management;
(g) Reserve for replacements.

Gross multipliers

Since much of the business in real estate has to do with the sale of
middle-aged and older residential property, the real estate broker

and salesman should understand the use of the "gross multiplier" or "gross monthly multiplier" to assist in appraising such properties on the basis of value in capitalization. This method is based upon the market relationship between rental value and the sale prices of such properties. For instance, a certain type of property might be generally sold at 100 times the monthly gross income. Prices determined by gross multipliers are usually considered as general indications of value only and not as a substitute for actual appraisal.

Assuming that care has been taken to use comparable properties and that multipliers have been developed from adequate factual evidence, estimates made on such a basis can be quite useful as a rule of thumb in approximating market valuations.

Summary

In summarizing it may be said that the market data (comparison) method is the most widely used of all valuation methods. Investment property is frequently appraised by the income capitalization method while the replacement cost (reproduction cost) method lends itself to special valuation problems. The methods are sometimes used independently and at other times concurrently as modifiers or checks.

The purpose of the appraisal will have a definite bearing in determining the method of valuation. For example, if the purpose is for sale, purchase, exchange or condemnation, the value concept sought is current market value. Valuation for property taxation, while theoretically based on market value, generally results in a lower valuation. Appraisals made for mortgage purposes give consideration to long-range income and are usually conservative. In this regard, mortgage loan appraisals by FHA or VA require appraisals made by approved appraisers and the appraisal procedure is fully prescribed by these agencies.

Depreciation

In connection with the appraisal of real property, depreciation is defined as "loss in value for any cause." It is customarily measured by estimating the difference between the current replacement cost new and the estimated value of a property as of the date of appraisal.

Depreciation includes all of the influences that reduce the value of a property below its replacement cost new. The principal influences are often grouped under three general headings and subdivided as follows:

1. Physical deterioration, resulting from:
   a. Wear and tear from use;
   b. Negligent care (sometimes termed "deferred mainte-
      nance");
   c. Damage by dry rot, termites, etc.
2. Functional obsolescence, resulting from:
   a. Poor architectural design and style;
   b. Lack of modern facilities;
   c. Out-of-date equipment;
   d. Capacity (in relation to site).
3. Economic and social obsolescence, resulting from:
   a. Misplacement of improvement;
   b. Zoning and/or legislative restrictions;
   c. Detrimental influence of supply and demand;
   d. Change of locational demand.

The first two groups are considered to be inherent within the
property itself. The third group of depreciating influences consists
of economic and social factors which are extraneous to the property
itself.

Depreciation is deducted from the current new replacement cost
of the building involved to arrive at the current value of improvements. The resulting figure is then added to the appraised value of
the land to obtain the total appraised value of the property. Accrued depreciation may be classified either as curable or incurable.
The latter classification includes those instances that would require
complete replacement or excessive repair costs and thus be too
costly to remove and replace, or to repair.

Three methods may be used to estimate "accrued depreciation."

The first is the observed-condition method. Under this method
the accrued depreciation is usually determined by establishing the
total cost of making all repairs to correct curable physical deterioration and functional obsolescence, plus the estimated loss in value
due to incurable physical deterioration and functional and economic
obsolescence.

The observed-condition method is the most widely used in actual
practice.

The second method is known as the age-life method. This is
based on depreciation tables which have been developed to reflect
age-life experience in the depreciation of structures of various types
and uses, assuming average care and maintenance. Some depreciation tables, such as contained in Bulletin F, published in 1942 by the
U. S. Treasury Department, Bureau of Internal Revenue, under the
title "Income Tax Depreciation and Obsolescence Estimated Useful

Lives and Depreciation Rates," reflect not only normal physical deterioration but also all economic and functional obsolescence as well.

The third method is a technical one used by appraisers as a by-product of the capitalization approach to value. It is known as the building-residual technique. Under this method the land is valued independently of the building and the fair annual net return on the land is deducted from the estimated net annual income of the property (land and building). The residual amount is said to be attributable to the depreciated building and is capitalized to indicate the building value. The depreciation figure is the difference between the residual value of the building as shown above and that of a new structure of similar type. It provides a good check on the cost approach appraisal.

Accrual for depreciation

Future depreciation is the loss in value which has not yet occurred but will come in the future and is of significance in the capitalization of income method. In the income approach to valuation, it is based on the remaining economic or useful life during which time provision is made for the recapture of the value of improvements. It is the return "of" the investment—as differentiated from the return (interest and profits) "on" the invested capital. Under the income approach this depreciation may be measured by one of two different methods. These are:

Straight-line depreciation, a definite sum deducted from the income each year during the total estimated economic life of the building to replace the capital investment.

Sinking-fund method, which also includes a fixed annual depreciation deduction from income, but with yearly reserves set up from such funds which at compounding interest will offset the depreciation. Accruals for future depreciation to replace the capital investment are in addition to and essentially different from both maintenance charges and reserves for periodic replacement of curable depreciation. Should there be any estimated salvage value to the property at the end of its economic life, this amount need not be returned through the annual depreciation charge under either the straight-line or the sinking-fund method.

Depreciation usually is recognized as a proper charge against income. It is an authorized expense for investment property or property used in trade or business, where the property is subject to fair wear and tear. Under income tax regulations depreciation is not an authorized expense for residential property unless such property is used for rental income. The rate of depreciation, for income tax purposes, may be determined by several different methods.

Book depreciation

It should be understood that differences exist between a book depreciation and estimated loss in value determined by a professional appraisal. The former is a theoretical figure adopted for accounting purposes. The latter is based on observed conditions and engineering and economic analysis as of the date of appraisal.

In accruals for future depreciation where both estimates are based on theory, since the accountant and the appraiser select rates of depreciation for different purposes, they may vary considerably. While both estimators may use the same period as to the remaining economic life of the property and may also use the same method, additional considerations may affect the resultant rate. Whereas the accountant may be restricted because of accounting conventions, the appraiser is under no such restrictions. The real estate agent who is determining values should understand the necessity for following proper appraisal procedures and should not rely on book values either to estimate accrued depreciation or for future depreciation accruals.

Contrasting with depreciation is *appreciation* of values which result from inflation or from special supply and demand forces relating to the specific property. Appreciation may reduce or offset entirely a normal anticipated decrease of value due to depreciation.

In concluding this chapter on concepts, valuation and appraisal techniques, let us wave three warning flags. It is to be noted that there is no real difference between the words *valuation* and *appraising*. The first is broader, tends to be economic in origin and emphasizes theory; whereas the latter refers more to practice, methods and techniques. Next, anybody can make an appraisal, even a layman, but the *worth* of an appraisal report is determined by the experience, compensation qualifications, and motives of the man behind it. And, finally, let us not be deceived by any broad statement that appraising is an exact science. It is a science as is any of the other social sciences, but people and property cannot be appraised with the exactness and accuracy reached by the mathematical and physical sciences.

Questions on Appraisals

1. Q. What is an appraisal?
   A. An expression of opinion of the value of a property as of a given date and under certain limiting conditions. It is an estimate of the present worth of future benefits.
2. Q. Explain why cost differs from price and value.
   A. Cost is the amount of expenditure necessary for, or incurred in, the creation of a thing whereas price is the amount it will sell for at the moment. Value is the power to command other commodities in exchange.
3. Q. Into what four general classifications may data be divided concerning a property to be appraised?
   A. 1. Title data.
      2. Cost estimate.
      3. Market price.
      4. Income and capitalization.
4. Q. Distinguish between value and market value.
   A. Value is the present worth of future benefits arising from ownership. Market value is "the highest price estimated in terms of money which the property will bring if exposed for sale in the open market with a reasonable time allowed to find a purchaser buying with full knowledge of all the uses and purposes to which it is adapted and for which it is capable of being used."
5. Q. In analyzing a parcel of land to estimate its value, what is the first thing necessary to determine?
   A. Highest and best use.
6. Q. Is there a definite relationship between an improper development and depreciation?
   A. Yes. If it is an improper improvement, it is functionally deficient and does not produce the highest amount of return of which the land is capable.
7. Q. Enumerate three generally accepted approaches to a real estate value estimate.
   A. 1. Comparison with known sales of other properties.
      2. Reproduction cost less depreciation.
      3. Capitalization of the estimated net income.
8. Q. What two kinds of value may property have?
   A. Property may have a use value or value in exchange.
9. Q. Explain the difference between real property and real estate.
   A. Real estate is the land and those things which are permanently fastened to it. Real property is all the rights and benefits to be derived from the ownership of real estate.

10. Q. What are "amenities" as the term applies to real estate?
    A. Amenities are the satisfactions of enjoyable living to be derived from a home or profits from income property.
11. Q. What are the rights which are represented by the ownership of real estate?
    A. (a) Possession.
       (b) Enjoyment.
       (c) Control.
       (d) Disposition.
12. Q. Why is appraising more a study of people's activities than an exact science?
    A. It is the people's actions in the market which determines the price at which property may be sold. Therefore, an appraiser must evaluate the thinking as well as the actions of people. If people think that real estate is worth a certain amount, that will be its selling price.
13. Q. Explain "highest and best use" as it applies to real estate.
    A. The use which will produce the greatest amount of amenities or profit is the highest and best use.
14. Q. How is the idea of highest and best use applied in appraising?
    A. In evaluating property it is necessary to determine its highest and best use because this is the starting point for the appraisal.
15. Q. If a property cannot be sold, does it have no value?
    A. It would not have any exchange value at that time, but its use value would not be affected by current market conditions. It is just as capable of producing the amenities of living as ever.
16. Q. Why does usefulness plus scarcity create maximum value?
    A. People desire those things which are useful to them. However, if the things desired were available to all in unlimited quantity, they would have no value for they could be had for the taking. Only when the useful items become scarce are people willing to give other things in exchange for them. The more scarce they become, the higher the price is bid up.
17. Q. In what ways have governmental agencies affected the value of real estate?
    A. The government through the F.H.A. and G.I. loan programs have determined to a certain extent where and what type of buildings should be built. By their rules under which buyers were qualified for loans, they have also affected the price of real estate.
18. Q. How have the F.H.A. and G.I. loan program affected appraisal procedure?
    A. The rules and regulations issued by these government organizations have tended to standardize the appraisal approach of lenders. These agencies have attempted to standardize not only procedure but also terminology and minimum construction practices.

19. Q. What is the definition of value used by the Federal Housing Administration?
   A. The price which typical buyers would be warranted in paying for the property for long-term use or investment, if they were well-informed and acted voluntarily and without necessity.

20. Q. How does the definition of value used by the Veterans Administration differ from that used by the F.H.A.?
   A. The Federal Housing Administration's definition stresses that it is what a buyer is warranted in paying, while the Veterans Administration states that it is a price that a qualified appraiser would recommend to a purchaser as being a proper price under prevailing conditions.

21. Q. How does the American Institute of Appraisers define market value?
   A. "The highest price estimated in terms of money which a property will bring if exposed for sale in the open market, allowing a reasonable time to find a purchaser who buys with knowledge of all the uses to which it is adapted and for which it is capable of being used." [1]

22. Q. Name three kinds of depreciation which might affect the value of a property.
   A. (a) Physical depreciation—wear and tear or action of weather.
      (b) Functional depreciation or obsolescence—such as a poor floor plan or inadequate space.
      (c) Economic depreciation—run-down neighborhood, poor police protection, and other forces outside of the property itself.

23. Q. What are some of the indicators of the activity of the real estate market?
   A. (a) Mortgage foreclosures.
      (b) Number of deeds recorded.

24. Q. Under what conditions and to what kind of property would each approach be given the most consideration?
   A. 1. Comparison in midlife residential properties.
      2. Reproduction cost in new residential and service properties.
      3. Capitalization in investment properties.

25. Q. Is it necessary to know the purpose of the appraisal?
   A. Yes. In order to stress certain types of information necessary in forming an opinion. For example, in assessment cases, comparison with other assessments; in sale or purchase, comparison with sales as of certain periods of time.

26. Q. Name at least five general purposes for which appraisals of single family homes are made.
   A. 1. Sale.   4. Taxation.   7. Partition.
      2. Purchases.   5. Inheritance tax.   8. Insurance.
      3. Mortgages.   6. Condemnation.   9. Liquidation.

---

[1] May, Arthur A.

27. Q. List the following in the order of importance in residential analysis: age of building; suitability of residence to site; physical condition of building.
  A. 1. Suitability of residence to site.
       2. Physical condition of building.
       3. Age of building.

28. Q. Name four types of city data to be assembled.
  A. 1. Economic background.
       2. Population.
       3. Cultural facilities.
       4. Transportation pattern.

29. Q. Name four types of neighborhood data to be assembled.
  A. 1. Physical or structural.
       2. Shopping facilities.
       3. Transportation facilities.
       4. Nuisances or economic influences.

30. Q. Does the wholesale price of textiles in New York City have any bearing upon local real estate?
  A. Yes. It is an indication of the economic conditions prevailing as compared with other economic periods. Real estate follows the general pattern of all commodity markets.

31. Q. Is an appraisal (a) absolute value? (b) a guess? (c) an estimate?
  A. (c) An estimate of the public's opinion of the value.

32. Q. What qualities in an appraiser will convert a guess into an estimate?
  A. Training in fundamentals of land economics, knowledge of real estate in general, experience in operating and managing real estate.

33. Q. What is a summation appraisal?
  A. The addition of the estimated land value to the reproduction cost of the improvements.

34. Q. Do three approaches to value indicate more than one value?
  A. No. Three approaches to value merely limit the range within which the value will be and give credence to the judgment of the appraiser.

35. Q. In an active real estate market, do single-family houses usually sell upon the basis of their cost or income?
  A. Their cost.

36. Q. Under what conditions may a house be worth less than its cost?
  A. When it is an over-improvement.

37. Q. (a) What is an over-improvement?
       (b) What is an under-improvement?
  A. (a) That improvement which does not produce an adequate return for the amount invested in a building.
       (b) That improvement which does not sufficiently improve the

land to produce the highest return of which the land is capable.

38. Q. What charges would you make against gross income from a rented property?
    A. Vacancy and collection losses, management, maintenance, taxes, and insurance.

39. Q. Would the capitalization rate be high or low for the following properties?
    (a) Business property in 100% suburban location.
    (b) Apartment building in a blighted area.
    (c) A new single-family residence in an old neighborhood.
    A. (a) Low. (b) High. (c) High.

40. Q. What is meant by "unearned increment"?
    A. Value added to land by increased population and demand for which owner is in no way responsible.

41. Q. What additional factor should be considered in the valuation of a business other than those of goods and fixtures?
    A. Good will of the business.

42. Q. What is the difference between assessed valuation and market value?
    A. Assessed valuation is the valuation fixed for purposes of taxation; market value is the amount for which the property may be sold in the open market.

43. Q. (a) What is functional obsolescence?
    (b) What is economic depreciation?
    (c) How does physical deterioration manifest itself?
    A. (a) Inadequate or improper design or outmoded equipment.
    (b) Influences external to the property which influence its income or desirability because of their undesirability, or nuisances.
    (c) In wear and tear, action of the elements, fungus growth, insects.

44. Q. What effect does purchasing power of the population in a district have upon real estate values?
    A. It limits the value to the ability to pay.

45. Q. How do you estimate the cubical contents of a building?
    A. By measuring the building and multiplying the width by the depth by the height of the various sections of the structure.

46. Q. What is straight-line depreciation?
    A. A fixed amount deducted annually from the income indefinitely.

47. Q. What is meant by the economic life of a building?
    A. The period of time during which it will earn an adequate income to justify its existence.

48. Q. Outline the principal steps in the appraisal process.
    A. 1. Definition of the problem.
       2. Preliminary survey:
          a. Cost less depreciation.

   b. Market approach.

   c. Income approach.

  3. Process of correlation.

  4. The value estimate.

  5. The appraisal report.

49. Q. Name several important value factors to be considered in appraising a city residence.

  A. The purchasing power of the neighborhood population, availability of transportation, educational and cultural facilities, the physical characteristics of the house, and the ratio of land to building value.

50. Q. Name several important value factors to be considered in appraising an improved farm.

  A. Distributional facilities for the produce of the farm, the probable productivity of the soil, climatic conditions, adequacy of the buildings, physical characteristics of the building, and water supply.

51. Q. Briefly explain the three residual methods of capitalizing income into value.

  A. 1. *Land residual process.* Capitalize the amount remaining from the income after a proper allowance has been made for the earnings of the building. Process to be used when a building is new and its cost is known.

  2. *Building residual process.* Capitalize the amount remaining from the income after a proper allowance has been made for the earnings of the land. Process to be used when a building is old and the cost or value of the land can be closely estimated.

  3. *Property residual process.* Capitalize the entire amount to the property, and, when the building is fully depreciated, calculate the reversionary value of the land. Process to be used when the building is a proper improvement and a long level income may be expected.

52. Q. What characteristics of property should be compared in interpreting market price data?

  A. 1. Size of structure, construction, replacement cost, special features.

  2. Rental value, gross and net income.

  3. Site and other improvements.

  4. Age, condition, obsolescence, functional utility.

  5. Neighborhood.

53. Q. Is a new house in a failing neighborhood worth its reproduction cost?

  A. It is if the cost is within the limits of the purchasing power of the neighborhood population.

54. Q. In appraising for market value are you concerned with mortgages upon the property?

A. No. The usual procedure is to appraise as if free of encumbrances.

55. Q. Why may a business be worth more than the value of the fixtures and merchandise?

A. The location and clientele may be already established—"good will."

56. Q. In computing the net income from a furnished apartment house, there are several major cost items to be deducted from the gross income to arrive at the net income. Name eight such distinct items.

A. (1) Taxes.
    (2) Insurance.
    (3) Repairs.
    (4) Depreciation on furniture.
    (5) Depreciation on building.
    (6) Vacancies and collection losses.
    (7) Management.
    (8) Reserve for replacements.

57. Q. Will economic changes affect market price and market value to the same extent?

A. No. Some changes will affect both while other changes will affect one more than the other.

58. Q. What would be an all-inclusive definition of depreciation as it applies to real estate?

A. All of those things which decrease the value of a property. Another definition might be the decrease in value of a property due to any cause.

59. Q. What is accrued depreciation?

A. It is the difference between the remaining life of the subject building and the normal life for such buildings. This difference is the amount of depreciation which has actually occurred.

60. Q. What is the difference between accrued depreciation and deferred maintenance?

A. Accrued depreciation is the amount of depreciation of all kinds which has accrued to a building; deferred maintenance is that part of physical depreciation which can be restored by repairs and maintenance.

61. Q. Why is location so important in the evaluation of real property?

A. Location is important because the area near a property tends to fix the amount which can be obtained for the property. The surroundings are the source of so-called area or economic depreciation which destroys more value than any other cause.

62. Q. What are some of the things to look for in appraising a location?

A. Who lives there? What is their income? What are their interests? What per cent of the area is built up? How old are the houses? What are the restrictions and zoning? Are there non-

harmonious groups in the area? Do the houses conform struc-
turally and architecturally? This is only a partial list.

63. Q. Why should an appraiser use more than one of the three accepted approaches in evaluating a property?
A. More than one approach should be used to check the results obtained from the other approaches. A person should use as many
of the approaches as will apply to the property under appraisal.

64. Q. On what type of property would the cost approach tend to be
most accurate?
A. On newly improved property in a good neighborhood and an
active real estate market.

65. Q. On what kind of property would the income approach be most
widely used?
A. On commercial and investment property which was rented to
tenants.

66. Q. Under what circumstances would an appraiser use the market
approach?
A. The market approach should be used in all cases where it is
possible to find comparable sales. It can also be used to evaluate
unimproved land where the other two approaches are difficult
to apply.

67. Q. What is a capitalization rate?
A. A capitalization rate is the percentage figure used to evaluate an
income flow and to convert it into a capital amount. It is different from an interest rate in that it does not reflect the return-on-
debt instrument as an interest rate does, but reflects what investors demand for their investment in equity ownership. At
any specific time it can be found in the market by dividing the
average net profit of a property by the price at which the property is sold. By computing this percentage for comparable sales
a valid capitalization rate can be obtained.

68. Q. When can it be said that sales of other property are comparable
to a subject property?
A. Other properties are comparable if they have similar neighborhood influences, architecture, floor plans, sized lots, and are
capable of producing the same volume of benefits.

69. Q. What type of sales should be excluded as comparable in appraising?
A. Several types of sales should be excluded. The following is not
a complete list:
    a. where grantee is any governmental agency or a public utility.
    b. where grantee is a bank, insurance company, building and
       loan association or a mortgage loan company.
    c. where grantee is a charitable, religious or educational or-
       ganization.
    d. where grantee and grantor are relatives or corporation affili-
       ates.

e. where property is a subject of an undivided interest.

70. Q. How is the land evaluated when using the reproduction approach?

A. The land will be evaluated by using the market approach on comparable sales.

71. Q. What is the difference between reproduction and replacement costs?

A. Reproduction cost means the cost of reproducing a building exactly as it was built with the same or similar materials at present costs for labor and materials. Replacement cost means the cost of purchasing a property which would serve the same purpose as the subject property.

72. Q. Give three methods used in estimating the cost of buildings.

A. a. The quantity-survey method.
b. The square-foot method.
c. The cubic-foot method.

73. Q. Why is it sometimes difficult to determine the net income of rental properties?

A. Because of inadequate bookkeeping on the part of the owner and because of the lack of maintenance and the writing off of adequate depreciation.

74. Q. To what extent is the judgment of the appraiser involved in an appraisal?

A. Good judgment is an all-important factor in a good appraisal. Only by weighing the data gathered in the scale of good judgment can a satisfactory appraisal be made.

75. Q. Do houses ever sell above their cost?

A. Yes. When housing is short, homes may sell well above their reproduction cost.

76. Q. In what way does the income of the people in a neighborhood affect the value of real estate?

A. The income of people in the area limits the price of property because people seldom spend more than 30% of their income for housing.

77. Q. Could most sales of property be used as comparables in using the market approach?

A. No. Many sales must be excluded because the sales used must meet the requirements of informed persons who are not under outside pressures. Sales to government agencies or as a result of condemnation under eminent domain should also be excluded.

78. Q. What is the difference between market price and market value?

A. Market value is what a prudent, informed buyer free from outside pressures is justified in paying for a piece of property for long-term use or investment, while market price is what he would have to pay under current market conditions.

79. Q. Does the fact that three approaches are used to determine the appraisal value mean that there are three values?

A. No. The three approaches are used to arrive at a reasonable estimate of value. They are tools to be used in gathering information upon which the final estimate is based.

80. Q. Could it be said that inflation might make it necessary to consider depreciation in appraising a property?

A. No. Depreciation actually occurs, so it must be considered even though it has been hidden by the increase in value due to inflation.

81. Q. How is the real estate market unlike other markets?

A. There is no open market where buyers and sellers may gather. The market is made for the most part by real estate brokers. The chances of contacting more than a small per cent of all prospective buyers is very remote.

82. Q. Select three terms from the following which pertain to the appraisal of real estate.

covenant	comparison
capitalization	default
encroachment	foreclosure
consideration	option
eviction	summation

A. (1) capitalization. (2) comparison. (3) summation.

83. Q. In relation to real property, state the difference between "assessed valuation" and "assessment."

A. "Assessed valuation" is the amount for which real property is evaluated by a unit of government for taxation purposes. "Assessment" is a pro-rata charge or tax levied against a property for a special improvement such as a sewer, pavement, or street. Also, it may mean the actual tax to be paid on real property arrived at by multiplying the assessed valuation of the property by the assessment rate (millage), for tax purposes.

84. Q. Explain the principal steps in the "reproduction cost" approach to an appraisal of property.

A. This approach is comprised of three principal steps. First, compute the cost of reproducing or replacing the improvements with a suitable equivalent; second, add thereto an estimate value for the land, secured by comparison with other similar land; and, third, make deductions for an estimated depreciation of the value of the improvements. An example would be a newly built property, on one just used for public service.

True and False

1. Loss to a building from any cause is called deterioration.   T **F**
2. The value of land is more dependent upon its utility than its size.   **T** F

3. Market value usually determines the true value of real estate. **T** F
4. There are usually three approaches to a value estimate. **T** F
5. "Improved to the highest and best use" means the largest amount the property will produce in money or amenities. **T** F
6. Purchasing power of the population tends to limit the value of real estate in a neighborhood. **T** F
7. A house is never worth less than its cost. T **F**
8. The economic life of a building is the time during which its income justifies its existence. **T** F
9. Zoning regulations limit the use of real estate. **T** F
10. Market value and market price are synonymous. T **F**
11. An under-improvement is any improvement underground. T **F**
12. Two adjacent lots on a main business street, having the same area and the same topography but one having a frontage of 40 feet and the other a front of 35 feet, have the same value. T **F**
13. All sales prices are conclusive evidence of value. T **F**
14. There are three kinds of depreciation which affect the value of property. **T** F
15. Reproduction cost tends to set the upper limit of value. **T** F
16. Interest is the rental charge of money for its use. **T** F
17. A summation value is the sum of the land value and the building value. **T** F
18. Economic obsolescence is caused by undesirable neighbors. **T** F
19. There is only one type of value for a given property. T **F**
20. Functional obsolescence may be caused by poor planning. **T** F
21. The word appraisal means a process or method by which an opinion of the value of a property is derived. **T** F
22. Depreciation is a loss in value from any cause. **T** F
23. When making an appraisal, the purpose of the appraisal should be known and so stated. **T** F
24. In appraising residential property the possible income is given the greatest consideration. T **F**
25. The rate of capitalization of the net income is that rate demanded by the public and which reflects the risk involved as compared with other investments. **T** F
26. Straight-line depreciation is a fixed annual sum deducted from the value of a building which will return its cost during its economic life. **T** F
27. Building restrictions and zoning regulations always increase the value of property. T **F**
28. The value of land is dependent upon its utility and not upon its size. **T** F
29. The term "assessed valuation" always means market price. T **F**
30. The term "appraised value" means the present market value. **T** F
31. It could be said that no appraiser has ever recorded all of the pertinent information which affects the value of a piece of property. **T** F

32. The valuation of residential property makes up only about one-half of all appraisals in the United States.   T **F**

33. An appraisal for a mortgage loan is usually very close to selling price.   T **F**

34. An appraiser is usually asked to find the market value of the property involved.   **T** F

35. The risks of investment in real estate lie principally in the factors surrounding the property rather than in the physical property itself.   **T** F

36. In the final analysis a mortgage loan valuation is an evaluation of the risks involved.   **T** F

37. The valuation for a part of a lot taken by condemnation to widen a street would be close to the market price for that part of the lot.   T **F**

38. The term "value" is a mathematical concept.   T **F**

39. Economists tend to favor the idea that the value of a material thing is its value in exchange.   T **F**

40. Most people who buy homes could be said to be "well informed" as to the uses of the property.   T **F**

41. The courts have contributed a great deal to the definition of value.   **T** F

42. The typical real estate sale fits quite closely the definition for determining value.   T **F**

43. The terms of sale could affect the "value" of a piece of property.   T **F**

44. If a piece of property cannot be sold on the existing market then the appraiser would have to say that it has no exchange value.   **T** F

45. There is often more demand for expert appraisals during a depression than during a boom period.   **T** F

46. It would be correct to say that cost and value are almost always the same.   T **F**

47. For the most part it is not very difficult to gather adequate data on the costs of construction or the life span of neighborhoods.   T **F**

48. "Judgment" as far as appraising is concerned could be said to be made up largely of the ability to discriminate between relevant and the irrelevant.   **T** F

49. Information concerning the attitude of lending-institutions should be gathered by the appraiser.   **T** F

50. The general information gathered for appraisal purposes may be used over and over again for different appraisals if it is kept up to date.   **T** F

51. Court decisions seldom affect real estate values for they are only enforcing the laws that are already on the statute books.   T **F**

52. The population growth around a city has little effect on real estate values within the city itself.   T **F**

53. There has been an increased use of the right of eminent domain by governmental bodies in recent years.   **T**   F

54. Cost will always fix the upper limit of value even in war times when materials are scarce.   T   **F**

55. Cities are usually built on poor land in order to preserve the good land for agricultural purposes.   T   **F**

56. The population trend in the United States is probably of more importance to an appraiser than the trend within the city itself.   T   **F**

57. In the past, population growth within an area was a good indicator of the trend in real estate values.   **T**   F

58. Those who are interested in real estate have been able to quite easily analyze those factors which cause city growth and determine values.   T   **F**

59. A more thorough knowledge of the economics of cities might have prevented many millions of dollars in losses.   **T**   F

60. Real estate values in a city that has both commerce and manufacturing as a source of payrolls would be more stable than if only manufacturing were present.   **T**   F

61. A city of many small factories would tend to have more stable real estate values than one in which there are just a few very large factories.   **T**   F

62. Minority groups usually pay a higher cost per room for their housing than do native whites for comparable shelter.   **T**   F

63. The overflow movement of minority groups from one district to another is usually dictated by economic compulsion rather than a desire by the group to move into a new district.   **T**   F

64. If a city is left to follow its natural growth lines, it will follow the path of least resistance.   **T**   F

65. Real estate carries a heavier tax load proportionately than other types of wealth.   **T**   F

66. In the ordinary city there is a great deal of information available on the changing status of neighborhoods.   T   **F**

67. One will find a greater contentment in living if the people of a neighborhood have about the same income, culture, and education.   **T**   F

68. Values in a neighborhood will not be affected by rentals as long as the percentage of such rentals is less than 50% of the houses.   T   **F**

69. Designs of buildings tend to "wear out" with the passing of time as well as with the physical depreciation of the building.   **T**   F

70. A neighborhood could have thousands of houses as long as there was a high degree of conformity of buildings and people.   **T**   F

71. A large neighborhood will tend to resist deteriorating influences more than a smaller one.   **T**   F

72. Local codes and ordinances have little effect on values for
    they apply to all buildings in the area.   T **F**
73. School enrollment data is a good source of information in
    real estate trends.   **T** F
74. The peak point of desirability in a neighborhood is prob-
    ably reached just before the original owners begin to sell
    and move out.   **T** F
75. The appraiser need not be concerned with the status of the
    title of a property because he is not expected to render legal
    decisions.   T **F**
76. The majority of property which is appraised is held in fee
    simple by the owners.   **T** F
77. Value is determined by the sum total of the bricks, lumber,
    mortar, and other materials that go into a building.   T **F**
78. Land economics could be described as a study of the uses
    that grew out of land when viewed as property.   **T** F
79. Optimum value will be achieved when a property offers the
    most utility to the greatest possible number of people.   **T** F
80. To get the maximum utility out of land all houses on a street
    should be set back the same distance.   T **F**
81. Only one bathroom in a home of five bedrooms would be
    classified as functional obsolescence.   **T** F
82. Depreciation is not allowed on land.   **T** F
83. Urban renewal is a process whereby government funds are
    used to facilitate private investment in improving city land
    use.   **T** F
84. As a general rule the quality of materials and labor in a
    building designed by an architect will be of satisfactory
    quality.   **T** F
85. In an older house the appraiser will probably have to judge
    the quality of construction by actual inspection.   **T** F
86. The shape of the lot is not important as long as it is large
    enough to accommodate the house.   T **F**
87. Economic obsolescence could be computed even if a "good"
    neighborhood could not be found for comparison purposes.   T **F**
88. Functional obsolescence would be reflected by a decrease
    in rental value in the market place.   **T** F
89. The cost and value of a property would be synonymous only
    if the property were improved to its highest and best use.   **T** F
90. In computing the reproduction cost of an old building one
    should also include the broker's commission as a cost.   T **F**
91. The cubic foot is often used as the unit in computing repro-
    duction costs.   **T** F
92. Once the reproduction cost of a building has been found,
    this amount is reduced by straight-line depreciation for the
    number of years that the facility has been built; the result
    thus obtained is depreciated reproduction cost of the im-
    provement.   T **F**

93. The cost approach calls for more skill and training than either of the other approaches. **T** F

94. An appraiser need not inquire into the motives of a buyer or seller of a property which he uses for a bench mark if it seems to be a normal transaction in other ways. T **F**

95. Listing prices tend to fix the ceiling of value. **T** F

96. If two houses are in the same block, they can be assumed to be comparable for appraisal purposes. T **F**

97. If the real estate market were unstable, one would need more current data than if the market were fairly stable. **T** F

98. In the final analysis the comparative approach is a comparison of prices rather than a comparison of properties. T **F**

99. In most appraisals a person would need data on more than two bench mark properties. **T** F

100. The capitalization of income to arrive at value was first used on commercial properties. **T** F

101. Value could be said to be the present worth of all the rights to future benefits arising from the ownership of the property. **T** F

102. In appraising single-family houses one can often use a gross income-multiplier instead of capitalizing the net income. **T** F

103. The rate for capitalization increases as a neighborhood grows older. **T** F

104. A residential lot with a frontage of 25 feet would be worth one-half as much as one with a 50-foot frontage. T **F**

105. A safe rule-of-thumb is to allow $5 for each shrub used in landscaping. T **F**

106. An appraiser need not be concerned with restrictions on a property he is appraising because the most of them are not enforced. T **F**

107. The appraisal of a residential property involves all of the techniques used in the evaluation of real estate. **T** F

108. The loan to property value ratio is lower today than twenty years ago. T **F**

109. There has been no increase in the use of eminent domain by governmental bodies since the war. T **F**

110. If a building has excessive wear or damage which can be cured, the "cost to cure" would be a deduction in arriving at an estimate of value by the reproduction-cost method. **T** F

111. An increase in state income taxes will not materially influence the price of real estate because the moneys received from the tax will be spent within the state. T **F**

112. In the past the population growth within an area has not been a good indicator of the trend in real estate values. T **F**

113. Real estate values in a city where most employees are government workers would be less stable than in a manufacturing city. T **F**

114. Because there is a trend toward a greater variety in the

styles and construction of homes, a house which is conserva-
tively designed tends to decrease in value more rapidly than
the contemporary homes.   T **F**

115. The appraiser need not concern himself with the balance of
the elements in planning as long as they do not seriously
restrict the use of the house.   T **F**

116. When using the unit-in-place method, it is assumed that all
of the cost of building is included in the unit cost.   T **F**

117. When using unit prices, an appraiser can usually disregard
such things as extra corners and extra partitions because
their cost is incorporated in the unit price.   T **F**

118. Such items as architect's fees and interest on the loan during the construction period would be included in unit costing. **T** F

119. If records have been kept on a building, the total of accrued
depreciation would be the amount recorded in the reserve
for depreciation.   T **F**

120. The use of average age-life tables for computing depreciation is probably more accurate in a specific case than in
observing the condition of the building.   T **F**

121. The economic obsolescence of homes in America is prob-
ably greater than in any other country.   **T** F

122. The courts have tended to uphold recorded depreciation as
a base for accrued depreciation rather than observed con-
dition because the former can be more easily proved.   T **F**

123. By "reproduction cost new" we mean the cost of exact
duplication in today's market with the same or closely re-
lated materials.   **T** F

124. In appraising an old house a person is interested in the
original cost in order to find the amount of accrued depreci-
ation.   T **F**

125. The quantity survey method is the same as the unit-in-place
method.   T **F**

126. When one is using the unit-in-place method any differences
in such things as heating systems are added to or subtracted
from the other costs.   **T** F

127. Bench mark buildings for the cubic-foot method should have
just average construction quality and utility.   **T** F

128. In arriving at the cubic feet in a house a person would take
the inside rather than the outside measurements.   T **F**

129. The reconditioning of a building is really an attempt to
overcome the deferred maintenance of the building.   **T** F

130. A home built with a poor floor plan would have loss of value
due to functional depreciation as soon as it was built.   **T** F

131. Deferred maintenance tends to accelerate depreciation of a
property.   **T** F

132. Functional obsolescence is accelerated by the invention of
new equipment.   **T** F

133. Functional inadequacy may be ignored in an appraisal if the people of the neighborhood accept it.   T   **F**

134. An over-improvement on land would create economic obsolescence.   **T**   F

135. If the property under appraisal is under-improved, no reduction in value is necessary because you are appraising the property "as is."   T   **F**

136. Economic depreciation probably causes more loss in value than any of the other forms of depreciation.   **T**   F

137. Straight-line depreciation is the process most often used by appraisers in computing the amount of depreciation accrued on a building.   T   **F**

138. The taking of depreciation on a building is actually a process of amortizing the investment in the building.   **T**   F

139. Economic depreciation will be reflected in the loss of rental value.   **T**   F

140. Economic obsolescence does not affect the value of land because land is not subject to depreciation.   T   **F**

141. Real estate is assessed every odd year.   T   **F**

142. Accepting employment or compensation for appraisal of real property contingent upon reporting a predetermined value, is a ground for revocation of license.   **T**   F

143. Issuing an appraisal report on any real property in which the licensee has an interest unless his interest is clearly stated in the report is a ground for revocation of license.   **T**   F

144. Marginal land is that on which the cost of operation approximates the gross income.   **T**   F

145. Net income after depreciation is the principal guide to the appraiser's determination of value on an improved retail business property.   **T**   F

146. Single-family dwellings are usually appraised by capitalization.   T   **F**

147. Appraisal is an estimate of quantity, quality and value.   **T**   F

148. The gross money expectancy from any income property is the gross income less the operating expenses.   T   **F**

149. In appraising income-producing property, allowance should be made for vacancies even though the property is completely rented.   **T**   F

150. The value of a residential lot is generally figured on a front foot basis.   **T**   F

151. Obsolescence and deterioration are the same.   T   **F**

152. A linear foot and a square foot are the same.   T   **F**

153. The market value or sales price is never more than the appraised value.   T   **F**

154. Market value is usually determined by the price a willing seller will take and a willing buyer will pay.   **T**   F

155. Net income after depreciation is the prime factor in arriving at a true appraisal of a retail business property.   **T**   F

Multiple Choice

1. A "rule of thumb" method for determining the price a wage earner can afford to pay for a home is by multiplying his annual income by
   ( ) One and a half.
   (x) Two and a half.
   ( ) Four.
   ( ) Six.
2. No depreciation is allowed for federal tax purposes on
   ( ) A 15 year old improvement.
   (x) Land.
   ( ) Auxiliary warehouses.
   ( ) Life tenant's interest as lessor in a lease.
3. Net income is determined by deducting all expenses from the
   ( ) Net rental.
   ( ) Figuring eight per cent on assessed value.
   ( ) Sales Price.
   (x) Gross income.
4. The tax on a given piece of real estate is determined by multiplying the tax rate (millage) by
   ( ) the selling price.
   ( ) appraised value of property.
   (x) assessed valuation.
   ( ) market value, less depreciation.
5. A report setting forth the estimate and conclusion of value is
   ( ) an abstract.
   ( ) a critique.
   ( ) closing statement.
   (x) an appraisal.
6. The period over which a property may be profitably utilized is called its
   (x) economic life
   ( ) amortized life.
   ( ) income life.
   ( ) net life.
7. Amortization means
   ( ) appreciation.
   (x) liquidation.
   ( ) depreciation.
   ( ) adolescence.
8. Two of the three main types of depreciation are physical deterioration and functional obsolescence. The third is
   ( ) dry rot.
   (x) economic obsolescence.
   ( ) adverse possession.
   ( ) determination of net income.

9. Physical deterioration results from
   ( ) tax liens.
   ( ) overcrowded occupancy.
   (x) deferred maintenance.
   ( ) poor basement drains.
10. The three main approaches to residential appraising are replacement cost approach, the capitalization approach and
   ( ) net income approach.
   ( ) highest and best use determination.
   (x) market data approach.
   ( ) building-residual technique.
11. Marginal real estate is
   ( ) border strip between two lots.
   ( ) yielding farm land.
   (x) land which barely repays cost of operation.
   ( ) waste land due to erosion, swamps, etc.
12. Which of the following creates the greatest value in retail income property?
   ( ) Type of construction.
   ( ) Parking facilities.
   (x) Pedestrian traffic.
   ( ) Vehicular traffic.
13. An appraiser in his work
   ( ) finds value.
   ( ) determines value.
   ( ) computes value.
   (x) estimates value.
14. Market price is
   ( ) the true market value.
   ( ) best price at public sale.
   ( ) price asked for the property on an open market.
   (x) the amount, in terms of money, paid for the property.
15. By far, the largest volume of work of real estate appraisers is the appraisal of
   (x) single-family dwellings.
   ( ) multiple-family dwellings.
   ( ) commercial income property.
   ( ) industrial acreage.
16. In computing the square footage of a home, you would use the
   ( ) inside measurements.
   (x) outside measurements.
   ( ) both the inside and outside measurements.
   ( ) neither the inside nor outside measurements.
17. The lessening in value or estimated worth because of outmoded function is called
   ( ) lessened use.
   (x) obsolescence.
   ( ) depreciation.

( ) wear and tear.
18. Highest and best use is defined as
    ( ) industrial property rezoned for single family use.
    (x) that use which will yield the highest return on investment.
    ( ) exclusive residential hilltop or "view" lots.
    ( ) property purchased for owner use and occupancy.
19. Income approach for an appraisal would be most widely used
    ( ) on a newly opened subdivision.
    (x) on commercial and investment property rented to tenants.
    ( ) on property heavily mortgaged.
    ( ) on property heavily insured.
20. Capitalization would be lowest upon the following property:
    (x) business property in 100% suburban location.
    ( ) apartment building in a blighted area.
    ( ) a new single-family home in an old neighborhood.
21. Land suitable for citrus growth must be
    ( ) nearly level.
    ( ) free from fog.
    ( ) available to good drainage.
    (x) relatively free from frost.
22. The selling price of real estate is usually based on its
    ( ) intrinsic value.
    ( ) speculative value.
    ( ) exchange value.
    (x) market value.
23. Capitalization is a process used to
    (x) convert income into value.
    ( ) determine cost.
    ( ) establish depreciation.
    ( ) determine potential future value.
24. An allowance in an income tax return for periodic decreases in value
    of income property, is called
    ( ) obsolescence.
    (x) depreciation.
    ( ) deterioration.
    ( ) fringe benefit.
25. Gross income and effective gross income, in appraisal terminology,
    are not the same. In determining *effective* gross income, which one
    of the following would be deducted?
    ( ) insurance and taxes.
    ( ) repairs.
    ( ) depreciation on appliances and furniture furnished tenants.
    (x) vacancy and credit losses.
26. In "directional growth," which center is involved?
    ( ) manufacturing.
    (x) residential.
    ( ) industrial.
    ( ) commercial.

27. The selling price of homes is usually determined by
( ) a minute inspection.
( ) opinion of a builder.
(x) comparison with similar properties.
( ) cost to construct.

28. In computing the square footage of a home for purposes of an appraisal, you would use
(x) the outside measurements.
( ) the inside measurements.
( ) both inside and outside measurements.
( ) none of these.

29. Estimating the value of real property is called
( ) assessment.
(x) appraising.
( ) surveying.
( ) tabulating.

30. The jurisdiction of a Planning Commission is to pass on
( ) new dwelling houses.
( ) new commercial structures.
( ) apartment buildings and town houses.
(x) new subdivisions.

31. The appraised value of a new structure is similar to its
( ) assessed value.
(x) replacement value.
( ) cost.
( ) none of these.

32. In appraising older structures, consideration must be given to
(x) depreciation.
( ) rental potential.
( ) number of occupants.
( ) none of these.

33. Loss of value due to a building being unsuitably located is
( ) functional obsolescence.
(x) economic obsolescence.
( ) economic depreciation.

34. Which one of the following is not one of the main approaches to appraising
( ) capitalization.
( ) comparison.
(x) survey.
( ) summation.

35. Which of the following is the main type of depreciation?
( ) capitalization obsolescence.
( ) exterior obsolescence.
(x) economic obsolescence.
( ) gross obsolescence.

36. In order to estimate market value of an improvement, it is important to

( ) obtain the amount of income.
( ) consider the tax millage.
(x) estimate depreciation.
( ) ascertain amount of a mortgage commitment.
37. Local government assessments are levied on the basis of
( ) the Russell System.
(x) front foot of the property.
( ) square foot area.
( ) two-thirds of last selling price.
38. A person must own real estate for how long in order to take advantage of the short term capital gain tax?
(x) Six months.
( ) One year.
( ) Eighteen months.
( ) Two years.
39. To obtain a gross rent multiplier, the appraiser must obtain from comparable properties
( ) the cost and annual income.
(x) the monthly rent and selling price.
( ) the net income and selling price.
( ) the net income and rate of capitalization.
40. After the economic life of a multiple unit building has been exhausted, the owner has left, in economic terms
( ) the unearned increment.
( ) the assessed value.
( ) his profit.
(x) the residual value.

Chapter 9

LICENSE LAWS

Constitutionality

A BROKER clearly has a needed and useful function. But the abuses which have been practiced by some members of the real estate group show, too, that the justification of the broker exists only when the service which he renders is efficient, intelligent, and honest. Because his relation to the economic mechanism is so delicate and important, and because the social consequences of incompetent or dishonest action on his part are so grave, communities learn, sooner or later, that they must demand that the broker have certain qualifications of education and character. This need has translated itself into regulation by law. One by one, our states have adopted statutes aimed at regulating the business of real estate brokerage, until, at present, regulatory laws are in force in all fifty states, the District of Columbia, and five provinces in Canada.

In every one of the fifty states where regulatory laws are in effect, the technique used to accomplish the regulation is a system of

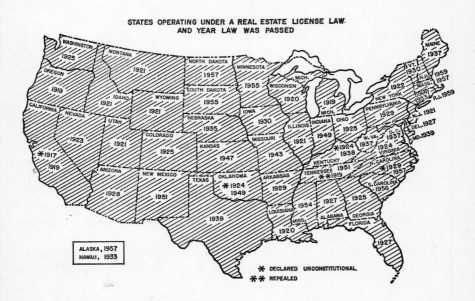

STATES OPERATING UNDER A REAL ESTATE LICENSE LAW.
AND YEAR LAW WAS PASSED

licensing. Under these systems, persons must obtain a license in order to engage lawfully in the real estate brokerage business, and only those applicants who possess certain required qualifications are eligible for licensure. Moreover, the continued privilege to engage in the business is conditioned upon the licensee abiding by certain prescribed standards of conduct in the operation of his business.

Are license laws constitutional?

Now, the very purpose and function of licensure acts obviously operate to deprive countless individuals of the privilege of engaging in the kind of a vocation which they feel they have a natural and inalienable right to pursue. Because these laws are restrictive of the free right to engage in the brokerage business, they have been challenged time and again in the courts of the various jurisdictions. The attack on their constitutionality has been on every conceivable front; hardly a legal weapon has been left untried; yet, in the main, these laws have withstood every challenge, and in their broad basic concepts they have been established almost universally as valid and constitutional.

Qualifications of character and competence

The most important question touching the constitutionality of these license laws is, of course, whether the state has the right to demand at all that only persons with certain qualifications of education, knowledge, or character be permitted to engage in the real estate brokerage business. This kind of regulation, say the opponents of licensing laws, violates the "due process" clause of the Fourteenth Amendment of the Federal Constitution. The "due process" clause provides:

. . . nor shall any State deprive any person of life, liberty, or property without due process of law; . . .

It is argued that under this, the "due process" clause, or under similar provisions of state constitutions, every person is protected in his right to pursue a gainful occupation, and if one chooses to engage in the real estate brokerage business, the state cannot rightfully prohibit him from doing so, regardless of whether he be well- or ill-equipped and regardless of the social consequences of his engaging therein.

True it is that the due process clause does prohibit many forms of purported business regulation by the state. There can be no prohibition of the right to pursue a lawful and useful occupation under the guise of regulation. But where the object of legislation is needed regulation of a business and not the destruction of it, the power to the state to enact the legislation cannot be denied. The due process clause has never been held to render the state powerless to protect her citizens by throwing reasonable safeguards around the exercise of any right an individual possesses. There is a broad reservoir of power which inheres in every sovereign state, to protect the health, safety, and property of her citizens. This is what is known in the law as "police power." And under this, the "police power," the courts of the various states have sustained the power of the state to restrict the right of engaging in the real estate brokerage business to those who possess certain educational and character qualifications. Thus, in an early and important case, *Riley v. Chambers,* 185 P. 855 (1919), the argument was made before the Supreme Court of California, that it is an arbitrary invasion of private rights and liberties to prevent a person from engaging in a lawful and innocuous business or occupation because of his moral character or reputation. The Court said:

This [the contention of counsel, as above stated] may be true of some businesses and vocations. It is certainly not true of all. Where the occupation is one of which it can be fairly said that those pursuing it should have certain particular qualifications, it is within the power of the Legislature to exact reasonable assurances of those pursuing the occupation that they do possess these qualifications. The most familiar illustrations of this are the qualifications of preliminary training and learning required of professional men such as lawyers, physicians, dentists, pharmacists, and architects. Where the occupation is one wherein those following it act as agents and representatives of others and in a more or less confidential and fiduciary capacity, it certainly can be fairly said that those pursuing it should have in a particular degree the qualifications of "honesty, truthfulness and good reputation." The occupation of a real estate agent is of just this sort. He acts for others and in a more or less confidential and fiduciary capacity. As a result there is particularly required of him for the proper discharge of his duties honesty and truthfulness, and the Legislature has the right to require some assurance of their possession by everyone following the occupation. One strong assurance of their possession is a good reputation.

The Court upheld the statute as valid, basing its decision on the theory that the licensing principle of the California Act achieved a kind of regulation within the police power of the state.

The California Court, in reaching its decision, relied on the leading decision of the United States Supreme Court in the case of *Hall v. Geiger-Jones Company,* 242 U. S. 539, 37 Sup. Ct. 217, 61 L. Ed.

380, Ann. Cas. 1917 C, 643 (1917), where the right of the State of Ohio to license dealers in securities was upheld.

In 1922, the Supreme Court of the United States had under consideration the constitutionality of Section Eight of the Tennessee Real Estate Brokerage License Act of 1921.[1] This Section provided that:

The Commission is hereby authorized to require and procure any and all satisfactory proof as shall be deemed desirable in reference to the honesty, truthfulness, reputation, and competency of any applicant for a real estate broker's . . . license . . . prior to the issuance of any such license.

The Court said:

In conclusion, we may say, that if the word "procure" is more than a tautological repetition of the word "require," it was only to confer the power of affirmative direction upon the Commission, necessarily to be exercised in supplement to the action of the applicant and with the same publicity and opportunity of the applicant to meet adverse evidence. And the Act, construed as we construe it, will take no power from the Commission necessary to the performance of its duties, and will leave no power with it that it can exercise to the detriment of any right assured to an applicant for a license by the Constitution of the United States.

Several years after the decision of *Bratton v. Chandler*, the Supreme Court of Louisiana was called upon to decide the constitutionality of the Louisiana Act of 1920.[2] In upholding the validity of the law, the Court said:

The object and purpose of the act under consideration was to regulate the business of real estate brokers, and in order to protect the general public interest and welfare, to permit no one to engage in such a business except those who may be found after due and proper investigation to be honest, truthful, and of good reputation. No unfair or improper discrimination is made, and every person, whether a resident or non-resident of the State, who may possess the qualifications required, and who complies with the terms of the act, is permitted to engage in the business.

That the statute comes within the legitimate exercise of the police power of the State, we entertain no doubt.

As early as 1924, in upholding the provisions of the New York Licensing Law of 1922, the New York Supreme Court held:

---

[1] Bratton v. Chandler, 260 U. S. 110, 67 L. Ed. 157 (1922), per McKenna, J.
[2] Zerlin v. Louisiana Real Estate Board, 158 La. 111, 103 So. 528 (1925).

What makes for the general welfare is a matter of legislative judgment, and judicial review is limited to power and excludes policy. . . . I hold that the business of real estate broker or salesman . . . is a proper subject of legislative regulation.[3]

And two years later (1926), the Court of Appeals of New York, the highest court of that state, reached the same result as the Supreme Court. In *Roman v. Lobe*, 243 N. Y. 51 (1926), 152 N. E. 461, the Court considered not only the validity of the law as affected by the character qualification for licensure, but the educational qualification as well. Cardozo, J., points with vigor and clarity in the Lobe case to the peril of incompetence over and above the danger of untrustworthiness. If the state can require that an applicant for licensure have certain educational and competence qualifications—and it is generally recognized that the state has such power—then the state should have power also to compel an applicant to submit to examination to prove his fitness. The state does have such power. Cardozo, J. said:

The Legislature has a wide discretion in determining whether a business or occupation shall be barred to the dishonest or incompetent (citing cases). Callings, it is said, there are, so inveterate and basic, so elementary and innocent, that they must be left open to all alike, whether virtuous or vicious. If this be assumed, that of broker is not one of them. The intrinsic nature of the business combines with practice and tradition to attest the need of regulation. The real estate broker is brought by his calling into a relation of trust and confidence. Constant are the opportunities by concealment and collusion to extract illicit gains. We know from our judicial records that the opportunities have not been lost. With temptation so aggressive, the dishonest or untrustworthy may not reasonably complain if they are told to stand aside. Less obtrusive, but not negligible, are the perils of incompetence. . . . The broker should know his duty. To that end, he should have "a general and fair understanding of the obligations between principal and agent." . . . Disloyalty may have its origin in ignorance as well as fraud. He should know, as the Legislature has said . . . What is meant by a deed or a lease or a mortgage . . .
. . . We hold that the Legislature acts within its lawful powers when it establishes a system of licenses for real estate brokers with annual renewals.

Further quotations are unnecessary to demonstrate how completely the courts of this country have accepted the regulation of the real estate brokerage business through a system of licensing as constitutional. Suffice it to indicate other decisions on the question.

In 1924, the Wisconsin Act of 1923 was upheld by the Supreme

---

[3] Groetzinger v. Forest Hills Terrace Corporation, 205 N. Y. S. 125, 127 (1924).

Court of Wisconsin in the case of *Payne v. Volkman,* 183 Wis. 412; 198 N. W. 438 (1924).

In 1925, the Criminal Court of Appeals of Oklahoma held the Real Estate Commission Act (Chapter 129, Session Laws of Oklahoma, 1925), to be within the proper exercise of the police power, but held the Act unconstitutional on the ground that no valid appropriation had been made, and that it would be against public policy to operate the department not supported by public funds. *Ex Parte Pope,* 242 P. 290 (1925). A new license law was passed in 1950.

In 1929, the Supreme Court of Florida upheld the constitutionality of the Florida Act of 1927 in the case of *State v. Rose,* 122 So. 225.

In 1932, the Supreme Court of Arkansas upheld the License Law of that state (Act No. 148 of Acts of 1929 (page 742), amended by Act No. 142 of Acts of 1931 (page 380)). *State v. Hurlock,* 49 S. W. (2d) 611.

Appellate courts of Pennsylvania have tacitly accepted the validity of the Licensing Act of that state. *Young v. Department of Public Instruction,* 105 Pa. Super. 153 (1932).

In the case of *Verona v. Schenley Farms Co.,* 312 Pa. 57 (1933), the Supreme Court, in passing upon the suit of a Pittsburgh Alderman for $150,000 claimed to be due him for services in a real estate transaction, discussed the Pennsylvania license law. The particular question before the Court was whether the plaintiff acted as a real estate broker and if so, whether an alderman was exempt from the provisions of the Act. The act exempts Justices of the Peace; no mention is made of Aldermen, although the jurisdiction of the two offices is substantially the same. The Court held, in effect, that the absence of a real estate broker's license was fatal to his cause. In discussing the Act, the Supreme Court said:

The obvious purpose of the Act of 1929 is to prevent fraud and public wrong by correcting well-recognized mischief theretofore existing . . . The Legislature concluded that the time had arrived when the subject must be dealt with. . . . Although the Act has been in force only a few years, this provision has been frequently applied.[4]

---

[4] Among the complaints on which the department has acted, and which indicate the variety of fraud and wrong to be prevented or redressed by the statute, are the following, appearing in reports of proceedings before the department, collected by Semenow (*Pennsylvania Law of Real Estate Brokerage,* New York: Prentice-Hall, Inc., 1931, page 132 et seq.): Collecting rents without accounting for them; embezzlement of down money; deceiving principal as to identity of buyer; acting as agent of both buyer and seller; misrepresentation by salesman as to rental of property; receiving funds by misrepresentation as to identity of principal; false representations in advertising circulars concerning lots; false statements by broker; false representations made in obtaining money; misrepresentations of condition of title.

The Act of 1939 now exempts Aldermen, as well as Justices of the Peace.

The Court of Appeals of Kentucky at first upheld the Kentucky Act, in the case of *Hoblitzel v. Jenkins*, 204 Ky. 122, 263, S. W. 764 (1924), but later held the Act unconstitutional insofar as it made the obtaining and retention of a licence depend on the moral fitness of the applicant or licensee; *Rawles v. Jenkins*, 212 Ky. 287, 279 S. W. 350 (1925).

At the 1938 regular session of the Kentucky legislature, a new real estate license law was passed, which is now in effective operation. The constitutionality of the Kentucky license law was upheld in the case of *Sims v. Reeves*, 261 S.W. 2d 812 (1953). The law was later amended to make it statewide in its operation and in 1960, a qualification of a high school education, or its equivalent, was inserted.

The Supreme Court of North Carolina, in the case of *State v. W. J. Dixon*, 1 S. E. (2) 521 (1939), held the North Carolina licensing act unconstitutional and therefore invalid, as affronting Article II section 29 of the North Carolina Constitution. This section provides:

The General Assembly shall not pass any *local, private, or special act or resolution . . . regulating* labor, *trade*, mining or manufacturing. . . .

The North Carolina statute was not statewide in its application. Brokers in only thirty-six counties of the state's 100 counties were affected by its provisions, with the result that the Court held it to be local, private, or special, and therefore contravened the state constitution. A new license law was enacted by North Carolina in 1957 and its validity was sustained by the Supreme Court in the case of *State v. Warren*, 114 S.E. 2d 660 (1960). The Court cited at length, *State v. Rose, supra* and *Roman v. Lobe, supra*. It is significant that the Court observed:

We are not bound by the decisions of the Courts of the other states, but should this Court hold the Act unconstitutional, North Carolina would be the only State to maintain this position. Such overwhelming authority is highly persuasive.

The New Mexico license law of 1951 was declared valid by the Supreme Court in the case of *State v. Spears*, 75 N.M. 400 (1953). The Connecticut Act of 1953 was similarly upheld in the case of *Cyphers v. Allen*, 142 Conn. 699 (1955).

Thus, every jurisdiction where the issue has been raised has consistently recognized the validity of such regulation. Nor is this result in any way surprising. Despite the recency of modern licensing laws in this field, it is significant that for almost a century, real estate brokers in many states, though not subjected to a test of character and competence, have been prohibited from doing business without a license. The validity of this requirement has been uniformly upheld. The United States Supreme Court upheld such a requirement in the case of *Bradley v. City of Richmond*, 227 U. S. 477, 480 (1913); in Illinois, *Brawn v. City of Chicago*, 110 Ill. 186 (1884); in Pennsylvania, *Luce v. Cook*, 227 Pa. 224 (1910); in Minnesota, *Buckley v. Humason*, 50 Minn. 195 (1892); and in Arkansas, *City of Little Rock v. Barton*, 33 Ark. 436 (1878). Although these older acts were in no wise as drastic as the modern licensing laws, these decisions, as Cardozo, J. points out in the case of *Roman v. Lobe*, 243 N. Y. 51 (1956), page 56:

. . . have significance, none the less, in marking off the business of the broker as distinct from occupations which by general acquiescence are pursued of common right without regulation or restriction.

Moreover, the United States Supreme Court has upheld laws regulating brokers of other kinds in so many instances, that the particular laws relative to real estate brokers must also have been valid. Thus, dealers in securities, *Hall v. Geiger-Jones Company*, 242 U. S. 539 (1917); *Merrick v. Halsey & Company*, 252 U. S. 568 (1917); insurance brokers *La Tourette v. McMasters*, 248 U. S. 465, 468 (1919); and brokers dealing in farm produce, *Payne v. Kansas*, 248 U. S. 112 (1918).

License fee requirement

The payment of a fee is universally made a condition prerequisite to the issuance of a real estate brokerage license. Such a requirement is valid. The purpose of the fee is usually not considered to be an exercise of the taxing power to raise revenue; it is imposed for the purpose of regulation, as an exercise of the police power. Under this theory, the fee is a charge for services rendered—it defrays the cost of regulation of the licensing system.[5] In a Tennessee case,[6] it was urged that a fee of $25 exacted as a condition of the license was out of proportion to the expense incident to issuing the license, and that the charge of such a fee, therefore, could not be justified as a police measure. The Court answered, however:

We do not think that the fee charged is at all disproportionate or excessive. Officers of the State, whose time belongs to the State, and who

---

[5] Cook Co. v. Fairbanks, 222 Ill. 578, 78 N. E. 895 (1906); Dalrymple v. City of Milwaukee, 53 Wis. 178, 10 N. W. 141 (1881); State v. Case, 39 Wash. 177, 81 P. 554 (1905).
[6] Davis v. Hailey, 143 Tenn. 247, 227 S. W. 1021 (1921).

are otherwise compensated by the State, are required by this statute to investigate and pass on the solvency of the bond of every applicant for license, to examine his recommendations, and to do other things in connection with the issuance of the license. A fee of $25.00 or of $20.00 is not so excessive, if it indeed be excessive at all, as to render the requirement invalid as a police measure. It makes no difference that revenue results incidentally.

Whether the sum of money sought to be collected is a tax or a fee is important in many connections. The distinction often determines the following important considerations:

The power to levy assessment

Thus, the Supreme Court of Arkansas held invalid an ordinance of a municipal corporation which prohibited anyone from engaging

in selling or buying real estate or (collecting) rent or rents on property . . . without first having obtained and paid for a license therefor. . . .

This bald provision that a license be taken out and paid for, without provisions as to regulation, inspection, or supervision, was obviously passed, not for the purpose of regulating that business, but to raise revenue.

And since, at that time, the particular class of municipal corporation did not have power to impose a tax on occupations, the ordinance was held invalid.[7]

The amount of the assessment

The purpose of the assessment being to provide a fund for defraying the cost of regulation, the validity of license fees is generally held to be conditioned upon their having reasonable relation to amount needed for regulation and administration. In the case of *Texarkana v. Hudgins Products Company*, 112 Ark. 17, 164 S. W. 736, the Court said:

. . . we think the test of the reasonableness of an ordinance imposing a license for the purpose of regulation may be said to be that, if it is such a sum as is so manifestly excessive and out of proportion to the regulation which will probably be required to make the ordinance effective, so that it is certain the city will derive a profit from the enactment of the ordinance, then in all such cases it may be said that the purpose of the ordinance is to raise revenue, and such ordinances are void, when no statute authorizes their enactment for the purpose of raising revenue.

---

[7] City of North Little Rock v. Kirk, 292 S. W. 993 (1927).

Generally, the license law is not intended as a revenue producer for the state. Fees paid by licensees are intended merely to cover the necessary costs incurred in the administration and enforcement of the license law. Any profits accruing to the state treasury are incidental and not primary. In many states, prior to the enactment of license law legislation, brokers were required to pay license fees to the state under the general revenue laws. Such fees, in payment of a mercantile license, were applicable to all forms of trade and business. Real estate brokers were then subject to the payment of both fees and the question has been raised whether the payment of two fees constitutes double taxation in violation of constitutional provisions.

The state of West Virginia required an annual license fee of $50, payable to the State Tax Commissioner, and charged solely for state revenue purposes. Under the provisions of the West Virginia license law, an additional annual fee of $50 was required to be paid to the West Virginia Real Estate Commission. It is obvious that an annual tax of $100 on every real estate broker is onerous. The question of double taxation was raised in the case of *State of W. Va. v. Charles F. Jackson,* 120 W. Va., 521 (1938). The question presented in that case was whether the Act of 1937 establishing the Real Estate Commission repealed the tax fee (Code 1931, 11-12-1 (h), 40). The state contended that the earlier act was not repealed by the Act of 1937.

The Supreme Court held that the payment of only one license fee was required. The Court said:

Here, however, we find inserted in the repealer clause (1937) the words, "including licensing acts." Insertion of these words in the repealer clause indicates that existing licensing acts insofar as they apply to the persons engaged in the business of buying and selling real estate, are inconsistent with the new act. In other words, the language used evinces a legislative intention to require but one license to engage in such business, a license issued by the West Virginia Real Estate Commission. Any other interpretation would render the words "including licensing acts" of no effect whatever. It is a cardinal rule of statutory construction that significance and effect shall, if possible, be accorded to every section, clause, word or part of the act. 25 R.C.L., 1004, sec. 246. See *Long Flame Coal Co. v. State Compensation Commissioner,* 111 W. Va. 409, 414, 163 S. E. 16; *State v. Hall,* 86 W. Va. 1, 7, 102 S. E. 694; *Building & Loan Association v. Sohn,* 54 W. Va., 101, 112, 46 S. E. 222.

Method of administering license laws

Laws are not constitutional simply because their purpose or aim is constitutional, or because the principle used to accomplish their aim is valid. It is also necessary that the manner of achieving the aim be consonant with constitutional principles and not violative of constitutional guarantees. Let us see, therefore, how the method and manner of administering the various real estate brokerage license laws meet the tests of constitutionality. As we shall see later in our discussion, a typical pattern is followed by licensing acts in force: an administrative body is created, appointed by the executive, sometimes called a "Board," sometimes a "Commission," whose duty it is to administer and enforce the provisions of the Act. The Board grants or withholds licenses, according to whether or not an applicant satisfies the prerequisites; it revokes or suspends the license of violators of the provisions of the Act, and for certain violations institutes criminal proceedings against them.

The main arguments challenging the validity of the administrative body arrangement are twofold:

1. It is contended that the power of such a body to grant or to withhold the granting of licenses, or to revoke licenses, is arbitrary and may be exercised capriciously. Whether or not the Board acts favorably or unfavorably in a given case, it is said, depends at best upon subjective criteria which conform to no fixed standards.

2. It is argued that the function of such administrative bodies violates the fundamental American governmental principle of separation of powers. By granting the Board authority to adopt rules and regulations for the conduct of licensees or applicants therefor, the legislature delegates its legislative power, it is contended; and by giving the Board authority to hear and to decide whether a licensee should or should not retain his licence, the judicial power is encroached upon.

Neither of these contentions has prevailed. The first argument— that the power of the Board is arbitrary, and hence violates the due process clause of the Federal Constitution, or some analogous provision of a state constitution—was clearly answered by the most eminent authority in the land, the United States Supreme Court, in considering the constitutionality of the Commissioner's office under the Securities Law of the State of Ohio, whose function is analogous to that of administrative bodies under Real Estate Brokerage License Laws.

. . . It is contended that the discretion thus vested in the commissioner leaves "room for the play and action of purely personal and arbitrary power."

We are a little surprised that it should be implied that there is anything recondite in a business reputation or its existence as a fact which should require much investigation. If in special cases there may be controversy, those cases the statute takes care of; an adverse judgment by the commissioner is reviewable by the courts. . . .

Besides, it is certainly apparent that if the conditions are within the power of the State to impose, they can only be ascertained by an executive officer. Reputation and character are quite tangible attributes, but there can be no legislative definition of them that can automatically attach to or identify individuals possessing them, and necessarily the aid of some executive agency must be invoked. The contention of appellees would take from government one of its most essential instrumentalities, of which the various national and state commissions are instances. . . .[8]

The contention that the Board's power is arbitrary was likewise disposed of in a case involving a real estate brokerage law, where the California Supreme Court said:

Another and cognate objection is that the Act is invalid because it gives the commissioner arbitrary power to determine who may have a license, and therefore who may lawfully engage in the real estate business. If such arbitrary power were in fact conferred by the Act, it may well be that the objection would be good. But such power is not conferred either in granting of licenses or in their revocation. An applicant for a license is entitled to it if he presents the required recommendation and certificate, unless the commissioner is not satisfied that he has in fact the qualifications of honesty, truthfulness, and a good reputation; in other words, the commissioner has no discretion unless he doubts the possession by the applicant of those applications which it was the purpose of the Act to assure.

But it may be said that the power of the commissioner to refuse a license if he is not satisfied as to the character of the applicant, practically gives him arbitrary power, as he alone can determine whether he is satisfied or not. This, however, is not true. While the commissioner has the power to refuse a license if he is not satisfied as to the character of the applicant, his discretion is not arbitrary. There must exist facts which reasonably justify his conclusion that the applicant is not of good character and reputation. If such facts do not exist, it is his duty to issue the license, and this duty can be enforced by the courts.[9]

It is important to observe that the possibility of arbitrary or tyrannical action on the part of the Board is precluded by the right to apply to the courts for redress. Most license laws make ample provision, by appeal or otherwise, for judicial supervision of the exercise by licensing Boards of their power to revoke licenses granted by them. But even if such provision is not made,[10] the right to have wrongful action of the Board reviewed in some form of procedure

---

[8] Hall v. Geiger-Jones Company, 242 U. S. 539 (1917), at page 553, per McKenna, J. Also reported in: 61 L. Ed. 480, Ann. Cas. 1917 C., 643.

[9] Riley v. Chambers, 185 Pac. 855, 8 A. L. R. 418 (1919).

[10] So far as the United States Constitution is concerned, statutes need not provide for appeal. Administrative action with regard to either granting or revoking a license may be made final: Reetz v. Michigan, 188 U. S. 505 (1903).

nevertheless exists, and this right, it has been held, cannot be denied a debarred person.[11] Thus, in the case of *State v. Whitman,* 156 So. 705, 95 A. L. R. 1416 (1934), the Supreme Court of Florida decided:

> To the extent, therefore, that an administrative statutory tribunal or agency is vested with statutory power to make decisions having a judicial character or attribute, as distinguished from mere exercise of delegated legislative or executive functions under the law, resort may be had to the courts of the land for the purpose of review, whether any special method of appeal be provided or not, and in such case, the courts of general jurisdiction to whom complaint is addressed against an alleged improvident, erroneous, or unjustified administrative decision shown to divest or impair some legal right, . . . will grant an aggrieved party relief against quasi-judicial decisions of such administrative agencies, by means of those available common law processes adapted and designed to be used by the courts to restrain excessive or unauthorized exercise of power on the part of subordinate jurisdiction or quasi-judicial tribunals.

In addition, there are certain other constitutional requirements which must be satisfied by administrative board action and which safeguard the individual against arbitrary treatment. Notice and hearing are generally required before revocation, or refusal to grant a license. Statutes which impose no restrictions as to the causes for which a license may be revoked have been held invalid as permitting arbitrary administrative action. The requirement of a hearing implies the right to introduce evidence of having a decision rendered on the basis of such evidence. It has often been decided that administrative board decisions must be supported by evidence.

The second argument challenging the validity of the typical system of administration—that such a system violates the doctrine of separation of powers—has met with as little success in overthrowing the acts as has the first contention. The separation of powers is, as we know, basic in the structure of our governments, both Federal and state. This doctrine demands that the three departments of government—legislative, executive, and judicial—be kept separate and apart. Each branch must operate within its own sphere, exercise the powers assigned to it, and none can delegate its functions or duties to the other. The power to make, change, or repeal laws, legislative power, resides exclusively in the legislature; the power to enforce laws, the executive power, resides exclusively in the executive department; and the power to interpret and apply the laws, the judicial power, is exclusively in the judiciary. By this

---

[11] Cofman v. Ousterhous, 40 N. D. 390, 168 N. W. 826, 18 A. L. R. 219 (1918); People ex rel. Lodes v. Health Department, 189 N. Y. 187, 82 N. E. 187, 17 R. C. L. 556.

distribution of powers, a dangerous concentration of power is avoided.

The question, then, is this: when a board or commission—part of the executive branch of government—sets up rules and regulations which must be complied with by licensees, is it "legislating" in the sense that the separation of powers is violated? Or, when it sits in judgment of licensees, to determine whether or not a license shall be revoked or suspended, is it acting in a judicial capacity in contravention of the doctrine? The courts have answered both these questions in the negative. In the oft-cited case of *Breechen v. Riley,* 187 Cal. 121 (1921), the Supreme Court of California upheld the power of the Real Estate Commission to revoke licenses, under the authority granted to it by the statute. The Court quoted from the case of *Suckow v. Anderson,* 182 Cal. 247, as follows:

It is now well established in this State that tribunals such as the board of medical examiners or other boards empowered to revoke licenses which they have previously granted, for cause defined by law, are not courts in the strict sense; they are not exercising "the judicial power of the State" as that phrase is used in the Constitution conferring judicial power upon courts, and that statutes creating such boards and conferring upon them such powers are constitutional.[12]

Likewise, the Supreme Court of Florida held that the revocation of a real estate broker's license is not essentially a judicial function, and that such a function could be exercised by administrative or executive officers.[13] And the same Court, in a later case, sustained the power of the board to ascertain facts constituting the qualifications of applicants for licenses, against the contention that such power violated the separation of powers doctrine.

The ascertainment of the facts constituting the qualifications of applicants for registration necessarily had to be delegated to a legislative agency in this Act, called a commission. There is nothing violative of constitutional principles, or even uncommon in our experience and practice, in this.[14]

Undue distinctions and discriminations

One of the most important constitutional guarantees which we possess is contained in section one of the Fourteenth Amendment to the United States Constitution:

---

[12] Breechen v. Riley, 187 Cal. 121.
[13] Prettyman v. Florida Real Estate Commission, 92 Fla. 515, 109 So. 442 (1926).
[14] State v. Rose, 97 Fla. 710, 122 So. 225, 237.

Nor shall any State . . . deny to any person within its jurisdiction the equal protection of the laws.[15]

This guaranty was aimed at the danger of undue favor and the granting by state legislatures of individual or class privilege, on the one hand, and at hostile discrimination or the oppression of inequality, on the other.[16] As Justice Matthews said in the case of *Yick Wo v. Hopkins*, 118 U. S. 356, 369:

. . . The equal protection of the laws is a pledge of the protection of equal laws.

Real estate brokerage license laws have been said to violate this fundamental guaranty on many scores. Why, to begin with, single out the real estate brokerage business to be licensed? Is it not a denial of equal protection of the laws to impose regulation on one kind of broker without imposing it on brokers of all kinds? The answer is in the negative, and the reason therefor is found in the admirable statement of law uttered by the eminent jurist Justice Holmes in the case of *Patsone v. Pennsylvania*, 232 U. S. 138, 58 L. Ed. 539 (1914):

. . . we start with the general consideration that a State may classify with reference to the evil to be prevented, and that if the class discriminated against is or reasonably might be considered to define those from whom the evil is mainly to be feared, it properly may be picked out. A lack of abstract symmetry does not matter. The question is a practical one dependent upon experience. . . . It is not enough to invalidate the law that others may do the same thing and go unpunished, if as a matter of fact, it is found that the danger is characteristic of the class named. . . . The State "may direct its law against what it deems the evil as it actually exists without covering the whole field of possible abuses. . . ."

Exemptions

The class of cases that most closely touches the equality clause is that involving the validity of exemptions granted by the licensing laws. Every existing real estate brokerage license law contains a provision exempting certain enumerated classes of persons from the operation of the Act. In other words, certain persons who do acts of the kind contemplated by the statute, are, nevertheless, not required to obtain a license in order to lawfully do such acts. This

---

[15] A similar provision is found in most state constitutions, construed similarly and really not necessary in view of this.

[16] Truax v. Corrigan, 257 U. S. 312, 66 L. Ed. 254 (1921), per Taft, C. J.

does appear to be patently discriminatory. Yet, analyzed more closely, the typical exemptions found in the statutes are found to have some reasonable basis in fact for their existence. And that is all that the law requires to sustain them.

While reasonable classification is permitted, without doing violence to the equal protection of the laws, such classification must be based upon some real and substantial distinction, bearing a reasonable and just relation to the things in respect to which such classification is imposed.[17]

The history of licensing laws is not without examples of arbitrary exemptions. Thus, the very first modern real estate brokerage licensing law passed in this country was stricken down because it attempted to grant an unreasonable exemption. The California Act of 1917 exempted from its provisions:

corporations, associations, co-partnerships, companies, firms, and individuals, after they have secured from the insurance commissioner or the bureau of building and loan supervision a certificate of authority or license to do business within the State.[18]

The Supreme Court of California, in holding the exemption to be unconstitutional, pointed out that the laws relative to the procuring of a license to engage in the insurance business or the building and loan business were much more simple and far less burdensome than those prescribed by the Act in question. The former made no effort to insure that applicants for licensure have character qualifications; there was no requirement for bond, as there was in the Real Estate Brokerage Act, nor did the former require that licensees maintain offices, as did the latter.

Another exemption in the later California Law came dangerously close to rendering that Act unconstitutional. Only beneficent judicial construction saved it. The Act exempted from its provisions:

persons holding a duly executed power of attorney from the owner.

The Supreme Court upheld this exemption by construing it to mean power of attorney to act for and in place of the principal in consummating the transaction as distinguished from merely negotiating it.

These examples of unconstitutional exemptions illustrate the exception and not the rule. The kinds of exemptions provided for in the Acts are fairly well standardized. And of the standard classes of exemption, those which have been challenged in the courts have withstood the attack. Let us examine these.

---

[17] Southern Ry. Co. v. Greene, 216 U. S. 400, 417, 54 L. Ed. 536.
[18] Cal. Laws 1917.

FIRST. *Attorneys-at-law.* Attorneys are exempted from the operation of almost all of the license laws now in effect. This exemption was challenged in the case of *Young v. Department of Public Instruction*, 105 Pa. Sup. 153 (1932), but the Court upheld it as a constitutional discrimination:

The contention is that a classification of real estate brokers which excludes attorneys-at-law and Justices of the Peace from the statutory regulation and control to be exercised over other persons engaged in that business is arbitrary and capricious and not grounded upon substantial distinctions of the subjects classified. In view of the purpose of, and the necessity for, the Act of 1929, our opinion is that the classification made by it is founded on real and substantial distinctions. Attorneys-at-law are not in the class at which the statute was aimed, because they had not been the source of mischief sought to be remedied. Real estate transactions have been carried on by members of the bar for years as a part of their professional duties performed for their clients, and they are responsible to the courts for their fidelity to their clients in such circumstances. They are admitted to the bar only after they have established that they possess good moral character and have established their qualifications to practice law. The distinction between real estate brokers and lawyers is well recognized and was sufficient reason for exempting the former from the provisions of the Act.[19]

SECOND. *Trustees selling under a deed of trust.* This exemption appears in almost all of the license laws. The California Court upheld this exemption as valid:

The fourth point is that trustees selling under a deed of trust are excepted, and no exception is made of trustees doing anything else than selling, such as leasing, or renting, or collecting rents. The reply is that trustees, whether selling or doing something else, do not come within the purview of the Act. The express exception of trustees selling under a deed of trust adds nothing, and the Act would be the same if it made no mention of trustees.[20]

THIRD. *Persons holding power of attorney from owner to consummate transaction.* Legislators have been careful, since the California case of *Riley v. Chambers*, 185 Pac. 855, (1919), to define expressly that the power of attorney be a power to consummate the transaction, and not simply a power of attorney, and so stated, the exception is no doubt valid, as the California Court held.

An unusual attack was made against the California Act for bringing within its purview a class of persons who, in the earlier history of license law legislation, were not considered properly to be within

---

[19] This case also held valid an exemption of Justices of the Peace.
[20] Riley v. Chambers, supra.

the purview of such acts—persons who engaged in a single or isolated act of brokerage without engaging in a course of business. It was contended in an important case, which ultimately reached the United States Supreme Court, that insofar as the statute sought to prohibit one individual from employing another to handle a single transaction of the kind contemplated by the statute, it was unconstitutional as depriving persons of freedom of contract. The Supreme Court of California, in answering this contention, said:

No particular or convincing reason can be urged why the participants in a single negotiation of the sort defined in said Act should not be subjected to the same supervision as those engaging in a series of similar transactions, since at the last analysis every transaction of the kind coming within the purview of the statute is an isolated transaction, whether conducted singly or as a series of transactions carried on in the course of a business or vocation, and since the lawmakers have seen fit to embrace the participants in each single transaction within the purview, requirements, and inhibitions of the act in question, we can see no adequate reason for holding that in so doing they have violated the constitutional right of freedom to contract any more than they would have done by confining the scope of the statute to those carrying on such transactions in the course of a business or vocation.[21]

Alleged discriminations other than exemptions

Discriminations have been charged against provisions of the acts other than the exemption provisions. The California Act was challenged for the reason that a different penalty is prescribed for violation by an individual than that prescribed for violations by corporations. It was also attacked because it prescribes penalties for individual and corporate transgressors, whereas partnerships, as such, were left immune. Both these objections were overruled by the Court.[22]

The California Act was also challenged on the ground that it discriminates against collectors of rent by including them within the provisions of the law, while collectors of other obligations are not included. The Supreme Court of that state, in answer to the contention, said:

The remaining objections are . . . that the Act makes a difference between collectors of rents and collectors of other obligations. Those en-

[21] Haas v. Greenwald, 196 Cal. 236, 237 P. 38 (1925), affirmed, without opinion, on the basis of Bratton v. Chandler, supra, in United States Supreme Court: 72 L. Ed. 415.
[22] People v. Schomig 239 P. 413 (1925). Decided by District Court of Appeal. Hearing denied by Supreme Court.

gaged in collecting rents and not otherwise engaged in the real estate business might well have been omitted from the operation of the Act. But the business of collecting rents is so closely connected with the real estate business generally, and it is so usual for the first to be carried on as part of a general real estate business, that we cannot say the legislature was not justified in classifying them together and thereby making a distinction between collectors of rent and other collectors.[23]

The same case held, too, that it was not unreasonable to distinguish between brokers and salesmen, in charging the former a license fee of $10.00 per year and the latter a license fee of $2.00 per year, or in requiring the former to submit certificates of character by two landowners, and the latter, certificates by their employers only.

In *Maury v. State*, 93 So. 802 (1922), a statute was considered which imposed a license tax upon "each person, firm, or corporation engaged in buying, selling, or renting real estate on commission," with a provision that if such person, etc., "also engages in the business of loaning money as an incident merely to the real estate business, they shall also pay an additional license fee of fifty dollars." A majority of the Court upheld the law.

Discriminations against non-residents

The application of provisions of the license laws to out-of-state brokers brings into play still another important provision of the United States Constitution—the comity clause. Article IV, section 2 of the Constitution provides:

The citizens of each State shall be entitled to all privileges and immunities of citizens in the several States.

The principal object of this clause of the Constitution was that stated in its original form in the Articles of Confederation—

the better to secure and perpetuate mutual friendship and intercourse among the people of the different States in this Union.[24]

It secures to the citizens of every state all the rights and advantages in every other state that pertain to citizenship, in such state. What these rights and advantages are cannot be found in the Constitution, for they are not enumerated. It is for the Courts to say what they are. One such very important privilege is the right to engage in business in the state. Thus, no state could say that the citizens

---

23 Riley v. Chambers, 185 P. 855, 858.
24 *Articles of Confederation,* fourth article.

of all other states, save her own, were ineligible for licensure to engage in the real estate brokerage business. The State of Florida attempted to do this very thing in its 1927 Act. But the Supreme Court of the state held the provision invalid insofar as it applied to natural persons. The Court said:

That clause [requiring every applicant to be a resident of the State of Florida] is violative of Article IV, section 2, and Fourteenth Amendment, Constitution of the United States, and section 1, Declaration of Rights, Florida Constitution, insofar as it applies to natural citizens. It denies to citizens of each State all the privileges and immunities of citizens of this State.

In *Land Co. v. Fetty*, 15 Fed. (2d) 942 (1926), it was held that a Georgia lumberman employed for a single transaction of finding a purchaser for a tract of standing timber in Florida, but not licensed there, was not a broker within the statute defining a real estate broker. (Florida Laws, 1923, Chap. 9177.) The Court, stating that the Act was highly penal, construed the provision making one transaction the doing of business within the phrase "as a whole or partial vocation," as meaning that the Act was intended to apply to persons holding themselves out to the public as real estate brokers, and not to require every person specially employed for a specific transaction to take out a license.[25] In *Aronson v. Carobine*, 129 Misc. 800, 222 N.Y.S. 721 (1927), it was held that where a real estate broker licensed in New York is engaged in New York to sell property located in New Jersey and the broker finds a purchaser in New York, the broker is entitled to his commission, although he has not complied with the New Jersey law requiring broker to be licensed. *Lex loci contractus* (law of the place of the contract) will govern. To the same effect is *Tillman v. Gibson*, 44 Ga. App. 440, 161 S. E. 630 (1931).

In *Moore v. Burdine*, 174 So. 279 (1937), (La.), a broker conducted business in Louisiana for the sale of Mississippi Gulf Coast properties to prospects in Louisiana. Although the contract of employment was executed in Mississippi, it was held that the contract was to be performed in Louisiana; that the law of the place of *performance* determined whether contract could be legally executed. Since the plaintiff broker had not taken out a license in Louisiana, the contract was illegal and the courts of Louisiana would not enforce it. The Court relied on S. 360 of Conflicts of Law Restatement:

---

[25] 86 A. L. R. 640.

If the performance of a contract is illegal by the law of the place of performance at the time of performance, there is no obligation to perform so long as the illegality continues.

This rule, said the Court, is a well-recognized exception to the general rule that *lex loci contractus* governs.

An Illinois broker, licensed in that state, went to New York and there negotiated a contract for the sale of land in Illinois. The plaintiff broker sued for commission in Illinois. The defendant contended that the brokerage contract was illegal because the plaintiff was not a licensed broker in New York. The New York statute forbids a person, partnership, or corporation from holding itself out or temporarily acting as real estate broker or salesman without first procuring a license; the statute forbids such person to sue for services rendered without alleging and proving he had a license; it makes violation a misdemeanor and one act constitutes a violation. The Court held that the contract was void under New York law where it was made and therefore it will not be enforced by the courts of Illinois. The rule is well settled that validity, construction, and obligation of a contract must be determined by the law of the place where it is made or is to be performed, but the remedy is governed by the law of the forum. The rule is that when a statute declares that it shall be unlawful to perform an act, and imposes a penalty for its violation, contracts for such acts are void and incapable of enforcement. The object of the statute is public welfare and protection of vendor and purchaser.[26]

A number of states, where the license requirements are comparable, have entered into reciprocity agreements.

---

[26] Frankel v. Allied Mills, 369 Ill. 578, 17 N. E. (2) 570 (1938).

Questions on License Law

1. Q. Does the license law require a broker to have an employee licensed who does only stenographic or other clerical work in the broker's office?
   A. No; however, if the employee gives information regarding listed properties or those for rent, the safer practice is to have the employee licensed as a salesman.

2. Q. Can the widow of a deceased licensed broker operate as a broker under the decedent's license until the expiration of her husband's license?
   A. No; a license is personal to the person to whom issued and does not survive him.

3. Q. Can a person lawfully act as a broker or as a salesman in a single isolated transaction without having a license?
   A. In most states no.

4. Q. What must a broker do with his license when he receives it?
   A. Post it in a conspicuous place in his office (not in California).

5. Q. Does a person who merely lists property, but never shows property come under the provisions of the license law?
   A. Yes.

6. Q. What must a builder do if he wishes to employ salesmen to sell houses built by himself?
   A. He must secure a broker's license. A salesman can be employed only by a *licensed broker*. Or, the salesman would have to qualify for a broker's license.

7. Q. Can a salesman lawfully accept a commission from a purchaser or seller in addition to the compensation paid him by his employing broker, even though his broker approves?
   A. No; he can accept compensation only from his employer-broker.

8. Q. May a licensed real estate salesman work for two licensed real estate brokers at the same time?
   A. No; he can only work for the broker with whom he is registered.

9. Q. Is the term "valuable consideration" as used in the license law definition of a real estate broker limited to a money consideration?
   A. No; a valuable consideration may consist of property, the rendition of services, or anything which has a monetary value.

10. Q. A licensed broker tells his milkman to keep his eyes open in meeting his customers and "If you get me any leads that result in a sale, I'll pay you $50 for each sale I make." Two sales are made. Can the broker pay him $100?

A. No; payment of a fee to an unlicensed person is grounds for revocation of license. A person accepting such payment would be subject to criminal prosecution for operating as a broker without a license.

11. Q. What must a broker do with the license of his salesman:
    (a) while in his employ?
    (b) upon severance of employment?
    A. (a) Post license in his office.
    (b) Return salesman's license to Real Estate Commission.

12. Q. List four classes of persons who are not required to be licensed to sell real estate.
    A. 1. Owner.
       2. Person operating under power of attorney.
       3. Attorney-at-law in the performance of duties as such.
       4. Executor, receiver or trustee.

13. Q. Name five grounds for suspension or revocation of license.
    A. See license law in your state.

14. Q. Name five activities included in the definition of a real estate broker in your state.
    A. See license law in your state.

15. Q. Name five requirements for a broker's license in your state.
    A. See license law in your state.

16. Q. Enumerate the penalties for operating as a broker in your state without a license.
    A. See license law in your state.

17. Q. Enumerate the various fees for licenses in your state.
    A. See license law in your state.

18. Q. The Metropolitan Realty Corporation is duly licensed, with Mr. Smith, the secretary, holding the original broker's license, and Mr. Thomas, the treasurer, the additional broker's license. Mr. Price, the president, has not had adequate experience to apply for a broker's license. Can he be issued a salesman's license?
    A. No. In most states, an *officer* of a corporation must be licensed as a broker, if he actively engages in the real estate business.

19. Q. In the event that an officer of a real estate brokerage corporation, who is unlicensed to represent it, negotiates a sale of real estate, which is listed with the corporation, is the corporation or the officer entitled to the usual commission for making the sale?
    A. No. Licensure is a prerequisite to a claim for commission. The officer must be licensed in order to predicate a claim for commission by the corporation he represents. The corporation, being an artificial person, can only operate through its officers and representatives.

20. Q. John Adams, a small town real estate broker, is duly licensed and has built up a substantial brokerage business. He has one licensed salesman in his employ. John dies, survived by his widow, Mary.

1. Can Mary Adams operate the business, as John Adams' widow and sole heir?
2. Can Mary Adams operate the business through the licensed salesman?

A. 1. No. A broker's license is personal and is not transferable.
2. No. A salesman must be employed at all times by a licensed broker.

21. Q. Higgins, a licensed broker in New York, but not in Florida, contacts Wiggins, a Florida licensed broker, and together, they contact Pickens at West Palm Beach, Florida, regarding the purchase of the Sea Breeze Hotel listed with Wiggins for sale. Higgins and Wiggins have agreed to split 50-50 the commission received by Wiggins if Pickens buys. The sale is made and Wiggins pays Higgins one-half of the commission as agreed. Has Wiggins violated the license law?

A. Yes. Higgins is not licensed and since he carried on active negotiations in Florida, he required a Florida license. It was illegal for Wiggins to pay a commission to an unlicensed person.

22. Q. Do real estate appraisers, mortgage brokers, rent collectors require a license in your state?

A. See license law in your state.

23. Q. Is the doctrine of "caveat emptor" (buyer beware) an adequate defense for the acts of a broker or salesman in his treatment of a purchaser in a transaction where the commission is paid by the seller?

A. No. If the statement he made was likely to influence, persuade or induce, his license can be suspended or revoked.

24. Q. Distinguish between the work of the broker and that of a salesman.

A. A broker represents the owner or purchaser. The salesman operates under the supervision and direction of his employing broker.

25. Q. A broker employs a person to go from place to place contacting members of the public, recommending to them the desirability of property on the New Jersey Shore being marketed by the broker and suggesting to them that they see the broker, if interested. The broker pays such an emissary a monthly salary and expenses. Does such person require a license as a real estate salesman?

A. Yes; his activities constitute real estate dealings.

26. Q. In a partnership one member has asked that he be licensed as a broker and the other as a salesman. Can licenses be issued in accordance with these applications?

A. No; in every partnership every active partner must be licensed as a broker.

27. Q. How much time must a broker devote to the real estate business in order to renew his license?

A. There is no provision in any license law to date which requires a broker to devote all or the major part of his time to the real estate business. Once a broker obtains a license, it may be renewed so long as there is no violation of the license law on his part.

28. Q. How many real estate transactions must a salesman complete in order to be eligible for a broker's license?

A. Here again, the license law is silent in regard to the actual time and effort that a salesman must devote to the real estate business. (But see Rules and Regulations for your state.)

29. Q. Adams files a complaint against Brown, a real estate broker, alleging serious fraudulent misrepresentations made by Brown to Adams in connection with a real estate transaction. At the hearing scheduled on the complaint, Brown offers to surrender his license voluntarily and requests that the hearing be called off. The Real Estate Commission refuses to accept the surrender of Brown's license and proceeds with the hearing. Brown files an appeal from the Commission's revocation of license. Was Brown within his rights in offering to surrender his license in lieu of a hearing?

A. No. Brown could not waive hearing on the charges. The hearing was proper. The Commission had the duty, as well as the right, to proceed with the hearing upon the complaint, to determine whether the broker was a fit person to hold a real estate license at a later date. There is an important difference between surrender of a license voluntarily and revocation of license for cause.

30. Q. During 1967, three separate complaints are filed against Bates, a real estate broker. Each time that a hearing is scheduled, the complainant, upon receiving restitution, withdraws the complaint and refuses to prosecute. In April 1969, Ames files a complaint against Bates claiming substantial misrepresentations in a real estate transaction. A hearing is scheduled, again Bates makes restitution, and the complainant fails to appear at the hearing, sending a letter that he is withdrawing the complaint. Can the Real Estate Commission take any action?

A. Yes. The Commission has authority, upon its own motion, to *initiate* a complaint. However, in this case, it could subpoena the complainant and his witnesses to appear at the hearing and testify as to the averments in the sworn complaint.

31. Q. Alden is president and the sole stockholder of a real estate corporation. He employs six real estate salesmen. A number of complaints are filed against the firm on account of misrepresentations made by the salesmen. Each time, Alden denies personal knowledge of the misrepresentations made. Whenever a complaint is filed, the salesman is discharged and his license surrendered for cancellation. The corporation has a reputation as

a "high pressure" outfit. Is the corporation subject to any disciplinary action?

A. Yes. License laws generally provide that a broker's license may be suspended or revoked where he is deemed guilty "of a continued or flagrant course of misrepresentation or making of false promises through agents or salesmen." A broker cannot close his eyes to the continued flagrant misrepresentations of his salesmen and escape personal responsibility.

32. Q. Adams listed his residence for rent at $250 per month with Bates, a broker. The property, of substantial value, is vacant at the time. A stranger calls at the broker's office and inquires about the property. Bates tells him that he can inspect the property, but he will have to make a deposit of $10 to insure the return of the key. The supposed prospect goes to the premises and "strips" it of valuable chandeliers, plumbing, and fixtures. He then returns the key to Bates and receives his $10 deposit. Adams files a complaint against Bates, alleging that the broker was negligent and incompetent. Bates defends on the grounds that it is customary to permit a prospect to inspect premises and to entrust a key to the prospect for that purpose, and that he took the precaution of requiring a money deposit for the return of the key. Is the broker amenable to disciplinary action?

A. Yes; not only is Bates guilty of gross carelessness, but incompetency as well. Since the prospect was a total stranger to Bates, the broker's fiduciary obligations to his owner required that he protect his client's property by accompanying the prospect to the property.

33. Q. May a licensed broker or salesman lawfully offer, give, or pay to a third person who is not a licensed broker or salesman a share of his commission on a deal for services performed by such unlicensed person?

A. No; such offer or payment is unlawful under the express provisions of the Act.

34. Q. May a real estate salesman be lawfully employed by or accept compensation from any broker other than the broker under whom he is licensed at the time?

A. No.

35. Q. Where a real estate salesman employed by one broker is assisted in a deal by a real estate salesman employed by another broker, under an arrangement whereby both salesmen are to have a part of the commission, is it lawful for the first salesman to pay directly to the second salesman the latter's share of the commission?

A. No; payment to the second salesman must be made through the employing broker.

36. Q. Assume that a real estate salesman changes his employer and fails to notify the Commission; what is the effect?

    A. The failure to notify the Commission automatically cancels the salesman's license.

37. Q. What is the effect, upon the licenses of salesmen, of a revocation or suspension of the license of the broker by whom said salesmen are employed?

    A. Immediate and automatic suspension; however, should any of said salesmen enter the employ of another broker during the same year, a new license will be issued to the salesman upon the surrender of his original license and pocket card.

38. Q. What is the real estate broker's duty with reference to the licenses of his salesmen?

    A. He is required to display the same prominently in his place of business.

39. Q. What is the difference between a "Realtor" and a real estate broker?

    A. A "Realtor" is a real estate broker who is an active member of a local board having membership in the National Association of Real Estate Boards.

40. Q. Adams, a real estate broker, sells his real estate business to Brady, a licensed real estate broker, and agrees not to engage in the real estate business within a distance of two miles for a period of 5 years. Shortly after the sale, Adams opens a real estate office within two blocks from Brady. The latter filed a complaint against Adams with the Real Estate Commission, claiming that Adams was guilty of untrustworthiness. May the commission revoke Adams' license?

    A. Yes; so held in *O'Hare vs. Gilchrist*, 210 N. Y. App. Div. 518.

41. Q. A license law statute provides that a broker "shall be guilty of a misdemeanor for having any salesman in his employ who has not secured the required license." The Ideal Realty Corporation, holder of a broker's license and at the same time engaged in the sale of its own property, employs Jones, who does not obtain a license. Is the corporation guilty of a violation of the above statutory provisions?

    A. Yes, even though corporation is also engaged in selling its own real estate.

42. Q. Roberts sued Clark for a real estate commission. He failed to set forth in his statement of claim or to prove that he was a licensed broker. May he recover?

    A. No; omission is fatal to broker's cause.

43. Q. Ash sells Beale certain property for $15,000 and says he thinks it will be worth $25,000 in two years. At the end of two years, Beale can sell the property for only $12,500. Is Ash guilty of misrepresentation?

    A. No; Ash has expressed an opinion. His statement constitutes mere "puffing" of goods.

44. Q. Stone, a broker, tells Crow, "Buy this property, I have seen the

city's plans for an airport and it includes this property." Stone has not seen the plans. Crow relies upon Stone's statement and purchases the tract. The city did not build the airport. Crow files a complaint. Decide.

A. Stone's license should be suspended or revoked as he is guilty of fraud. The broker made a misrepresentation of a material fact which induced the contract.

45. Q. What does the license law require as to maintaining a place of business as a broker?

A. Each broker shall maintain a place of business and display a real estate sign; his license must be conspicuously displayed inside said place of business.

46. Q. Who is a real estate salesman under the license law?

A. One who is employed by a licensed real estate broker to perform any of the activities included in the definition of a real estate broker.

47. Q. Can a salesman enter the employ of a person who has taken his broker's examination but not yet received his broker's license?

A. No; a salesman must be employed by a *licensed* broker at all times.

48. Q. A property has been listed with a broker for sale at $6,500. The broker obtains a buyer at $7,000 and seeks to retain the extra $500 and collect a commission of $325, representing five per cent of $6,500. The owner files a complaint. To what amount is the broker entitled?

A. $350, representing five per cent of the consideration price of $7,000. The broker is duty-bound to obtain as high a price as he possibly can for his principal, the owner.

49. Q. Fike, a salesman, is employed by Jordan, a licensed broker. Thomas, another licensed broker, asks Fike to sell a property listed with him for sale. Fike succeeds. Can he collect from Thomas?

A. No; a salesman can operate only through the broker by whom he is employed. If Thomas desires to share the commission, payment should be made to Fike's employer, Jordan.

50. Q. If you desire to use the word "Realtor" in your advertisement, what must you do to obtain that privilege?

A. Join a local real estate board, which is affiliated with the National Association of Real Estate Boards.

51. Q. Discuss the purpose of the real estate license law.

A. To protect the public from dishonest and incompetent brokers and salesmen; to protect licensed brokers and salesmen from unfair and improper competition; and generally to raise the standards of the business or profession and prescribe standards and qualifications for licensing brokers and salesmen.

52. Q. Is it ethical for a broker to sell his own property to a customer? If so, under what conditions?

    A. Yes, providing the broker makes the position clear that he is the owner of the property.

53. Q. State in detail what procedure a salesman or broker must follow as soon as a prospective purchaser signs the preliminary agreement or offer to purchase.
    A. A broker or salesman shall promptly tender written offer to purchase to the seller and upon obtaining a proper acceptance of offer to purchase, shall promptly deliver true executed copy of same, signed by the seller to both purchaser and seller.

54. Q. What is the responsibility of a broker in taking a check or promissory note and receipting for the amount as cash paid?
    A. A check is not cash until it is paid. The broker is obliged to disclose to owner the kind of deposit received. Broker's license suspended in a California case where a non-negotiable note had been received as a deposit, the implied representation made to the principal being that the deposit was cash.

55. Q. Does the Real Estate Commission have the power to make rules and regulations?
    A. Yes. The Commission may do all things necessary and convenient for carrying into effect the provisions of the Act and may from time to time promulgate necessary rules and regulations not inconsistent with it.

56. Q. Is a license or pocket card transferable to another person?
    A. No. The license shall show the name and address of the licensee to whom it is used.

57. Q. Does the Real Estate Brokers' License Act permit the issuing of a real estate license to a partnership as such?
    A. No. No license shall be issued to a partnership, association, or corporation as such, except in Illinois and Maine.

58. Q. Does the Commission have authority, on its own motion, to investigate any action of a broker or salesman and call the matter to a hearing?
    A. Yes.

59. Q. Can a salesman renew his license before the license of the employing broker is renewed?
    A. No.

60. Q. What constitutes misrepresentation?
    A. Misstatement of a material fact which induces the contract. It may be innocent or wilful. If wilful, it may constitute fraud.

61. Q. What duty rests upon a buyer in verifying representations made to him by the broker?
    A. Representations made that can be verified by a casual inspection, if the opportunity to inspect is available, would not be grounds for holding a broker responsible for misrepresentation.

62. Q. Check the representations which, if found to be untrue, would, in your opinion, constitute grounds for avoiding a contract of sale and for instituting disciplinary action against the broker.

A. (x) 1. The heating plant, plumbing, and electrical wiring are in good condition.
   (x) 2. The cellar is dry and in good condition.
   (x) 3. Action could be brought to have an adjoining dilapidated house condemned by the municipal authorities.
   (x) 4. Sixty feet frontage could be sold from the lot for $2,000.
   (x) 5. The taxes amount to $320 a year (in some states).
   (x) 6. The zoning ordinance permits alteration of the premises into apartment units.

63. Q. The Ajax Realty Co. advertises that it will give a 21-inch television set free to every purchaser of a dwelling through its office. Is this permissible?
    A. No. Since the broker is giving something of value to an unlicensed person, it constitutes a violation of the Act.

64. Q. May a real estate salesman's license be issued to a person not employed by a broker?
    A. No; a salesman must be employed by a licensed broker.

65. Q. Broker Ash had an exclusive listing on a property at $13,500. His salesman Bowen persuaded the owner to reduce the price to $12,500. The property was then sold to Crooks, another salesman of Ash, who then sold it immediately to a buyer, with whom both Bowen and Crooks had been negotiating previously, at a price of $14,000. Broker Ash received one-half of the commission on the sale price of $12,500. Salesmen Bowen and Crooks split their profit. Broker Ash was aware of all aspects of the transaction, but refused to share in the proceeds beyond his share of the commission. The seller was unaware of Crooks' connection with the firm. Did the licensees violate the license law?
    A. Yes, the broker violated his fiduciary responsibility of loyalty, by permitting his salesmen to profit at the expense of his principal. The salesmen were guilty of a scheme to make a secret profit, which constitutes downright dishonesty. Vital information was withheld and the owner was induced to take a lower price.

66. Q. What recourse does an applicant have in case the Commission declines arbitrarily to license an applicant?
    A. Institute a mandamus action in court against the Commission.

67. Q. Does the licensing law apply to part-time brokers or salesmen?
    A. Yes.

68. Q. The "Square Inch—Square Deal Co." advertises for persons to sell square-inch tracts of land, owned by the company, on Pike's Peak. The purchaser pays $1.00 and receives a deed, signed by the President, Chief Running Deer. The persons hired are to receive 50 cents for each sale made. Must the latter persons be licensed?

    A. Yes; even though minute in size, the subject matter of the sale is real estate.

69. Q. In what ways can a broker improve the efficacy of license laws?
    A. 1. By adhering scrupulously to a high standard of ethics.
      2. By exercising personal supervision over and training salesmen.
      3. By membership in realty organizations, attending real courses, institutes, etc., in order to improve competency.
      4. By reporting violations to the State Commission.

70. Q. What legal papers may a licensed broker prepare?
    A. Only those concomitant with and which grow out of his employment,—listing contract, agreement of sale, earnest money receipt, leases, simple deeds; and where no charge is made. The Texas Law specifically prohibits a licensee from preparing "a deed, note, deed of trust, or will."

71. Q. Is a licensed broker responsible for all illegal acts of his salesmen?
    A. No; unless he has full knowledge of such illegal acts.

72. Q. A broker is convicted of violation of the Federal income tax laws. Would this constitute grounds for revocation of license?
    A. Probably not, unless a real estate transaction was involved.

73. Q. In endorsing the application of a prospective salesman, what statements does the broker make?
    A. Certification that applicant is honest, truthful, of good repute and that he will be employed by said broker.

74. Q. Name 2 requirements which a broker must meet which are generally not required of a salesman.
    A. Apprenticeship; property owner recommenders.

75. Q. Upon hearing held upon a complaint, if the decision is in favor of the licensee, can the complainant appeal to court?
    A. No.

76. Q. Does the Real Estate Commission have jurisdiction in commission disputes between (a) seller and broker (b) broker and salesman?
    A. (a) No.
      (b) Most states, no. In New Jersey, yes.

77. Q. The license law is said to be a valid exercise of the police power of the state. Why?
    A. In order to protect the public in its real estate dealings.

78. Q. When and where was the first license law passed?
    A. California, 1917, which was declared unconstitutional. Oregon, Michigan and California passed license laws in 1919, which were held valid.

79. Q. What are the most important qualifications for a real estate license?
    A. Character and competency.

80. Q. In how many states are there license laws at the present time?
    A. In all 50 states.

81. Q. Is conviction of an F.H.A. provision a "like offense" under the license law as grounds for disciplinary action?

A. Yes, where law specifies conviction of certain named crimes.

True and False

1. The Executive Secretary of the Commission is a member of the Real Estate Commission. **T F**
2. All full time brokers are Realtors. **T F**
3. Local realty boards are affiliated with the Real Estate Commission. **T F**
4. The splitting of commissions under any circumstances is illegal. **T F**
5. Once a broker licensed in New York negotiates a single real estate deal in Florida, he requires a Florida license. **T F**
6. A salesman and a broker may actively engage in the real estate business as a partnership. **T F**
7. A salesman who fails his first examination may obtain a probationary license. **T F**
8. The license law is a police measure. **T F**
9. A supersedeas stays the effect of a revocation of license ordered by the Commission. **T F**
10. "Door bell" solicitation of listings is grounds for suspension of license. **T F**
11. The Code of Ethics is a part of the Real Estate License Law. **T F**
12. No refund of the license fee or any part thereof can be made after the license is issued. **T F**
13. A salesman must renew his own license. **T F**
14. Reciprocity is not compulsory upon any state in granting a license to a licensed non-resident applicant. **T F**
15. The Governor is an ex-officio member of the Real Estate Commission. **T F**
16. Each real estate office must carry the names of its salesmen on the door or window of the office. **T F**
17. A single separate account only is needed for the deposit of earnest monies. **T F**
18. A salesman who conceals the existence of termites in selling a home is guilty of fraud. **T F**
19. In most states, a licensed real estate broker may not lawfully sell business opportunity properties. **T F**
20. The amount of bond required is determined by the volume of the broker's business in the preceding year. **T F**
21. The committing of one real estate deal is prima facie evidence of brokerage. **T F**
22. In Georgia, an applicant for a broker's license must have at least a high school education or equivalent. **T F**

23. A broker must immediately notify the Commission when he changes his business address. **T** F

24. It is satisfactory to use a dormitory room as an office so long as the broker's license is displayed there. T **F**

25. The real estate license law prohibits a salesman from working in real estate more than 48 hours a week. T **F**

26. A contractor who employs salesmen must be licensed as a broker. **T** F

27. A broker's license cannot be converted to a salesman's license and vice versa. **T** F

28. A broker must immediately notify the Commission when he changes his residence address. T **F**

29. The license law requires every broker to maintain a definite place of business. **T** F

30. A real estate broker can be disciplined for the misconduct of his salesman. **T** F

31. A person engaged solely in the rental of real estate must be licensed. **T** F

32. A licensed salesman may go to work for another broker without requesting the Commission for transfer of license. T **F**

33. A broker is required to report cessation of employment of his salesman to the Real Estate Commission. **T** F

34. A broker may not employ another broker in the capacity of salesman. T **F**

35. A broker's license and a salesman's license are identical and mean the same thing. T **F**

36. Obtaining registration as a broker by fraudulent means constitutes a misdemeanor. **T** F

37. The broker must obey all lawful instructions made known to him by his principal. **T** F

38. A broker may not act for anyone whose interests in the transaction are adverse to those of his principal. **T** F

39. A broker need not let it be known that he is actually the owner when dealing with a prospective purchaser. T **F**

40. A person who works as a real estate broker only on Sundays is not required to have registration. T **F**

41. Two brokers registered individually may occupy the same office space and need not have individual signs. T **F**

42. A broker is not permitted under the license law to use unregistered persons merely to show properties. **T** F

43. A salesman is unable to renew his certificate until that of the employing broker is renewed. **T** F

44. A broker's right to collect commission is not impaired on a deal made after the expiration of his certificate and before renewal of same. T **F**

45. If two brokers share office space but conduct their business separately, it would be permissible, under the license law, to use the same letterheads. T **F**

46. The void certificate of an officer or member of a corporation or partnership does not affect the certificate of a corporation or partnership.   T **F**

47. The Commission may deny the renewal of a license to a broker who has refused to stop selling by a method which is dishonest or untruthful.   **T** F

48. A person who has been convicted of certain felonies may be denied a license even though he presents recommendations from several friends and brokers.   **T** F

49. A broker's license may be suspended but not permanently revoked for representing both buyer and seller and receiving commissions from both without their knowledge and consent.   T **F**

50. Any licensee is entitled to a hearing before having his license revoked.   **T** F

51. A broker who collects rents for clients and co-mingles the money with his own so that he cannot make proper accounting may have his license revoked.   **T** F

52. The fee for a branch office license is $15.00.   T **F**

53. A real estate license should be kept in a safe deposit box for safe keeping.   T **F**

54. It is a violation of law for a broker to pay commissions directly to a salesman employed by another broker.   **T** F

55. A clerk in a real estate office who prepares real estate listings and sales agreements need not be licensed as a salesman.   **T** F

56. The Real Estate Commission has jurisdiction over contractors and builders who build and sell their own properties.   T **F**

57. A salesman is responsible to his broker for collections that he may make.   **T** F

58. All real estate licenses must be renewed in May.   T **F**

59. A real estate salesman can be jailed for operating without a real estate license.   **T** F

60. A veteran of foreign wars can obtain a salesman's license by oral examination.   T **F**

61. A collector of rent must be licensed if paid for that service. **T** F

62. Negotiating leases comes within the licensing act.   **T** F

63. A broker must display the licenses of his salesmen in the broker's office.   **T** F

64. Brokers employing salesmen are relieved of all responsibility for the acts of the salesmen if the salesmen are bonded.   T **F**

65. Realtors are members of the National Association of Real Estate Boards.   **T** F

66. A real estate salesman who desires to transfer to another broker merely picks up his license from the first broker and places it upon display in the office of the second broker.   T **F**

67. The Commission may revoke the license of a broker who fails to remit commissions he owes to another broker.   T **F**

68. The Commission may waive the qualification examination for license if the applicant has had several years of real estate experience.   T   **F**

69. All real estate licenses expire three full years from date of issue.   T   **F**

70. An alien may be licensed as a real estate salesman in Illinois if he has received his first papers.   **T** F

71. A licensed salesman may go to work for another broker immediately upon the filing of an application for transfer.   T   **F**

72. The committing of one act prohibited by the license law constitutes a violation.   **T** F

73. A salesman may advertise listings in his own name without mentioning his broker.   T   **F**

74. A broker should consent to the transfer of a salesman's license even though the salesman owes him money which the broker loaned him.   **T** F

75. The Commission is empowered to subpoena persons to produce books and papers at a formal hearing for the revocation of a license.   **T** F

76. A real estate broker's or salesman's license can, under no circumstances, be suspended without a formal hearing first being granted to the offender.   **T** F

77. A real estate broker can be disciplined for the misconduct of his salesman, provided he had actual knowledge of such fact.   **T** F

78. A real estate salesman's license can be issued to the vice-president of the XYZ Realty Corporation.   T   **F**

79. All persons who, on behalf of another, sell, purchase, or lease or who offer to sell, purchase, or lease real property for a fee or commission must hold real estate brokers' or salesmen's licenses.   **T** F

80. After the revocation or suspension of a broker's or salesman's license, he is permitted to operate pending determination of his appeal to court.   **T** F

81. A real estate brokerage business may be conducted by a salesman at his residence, without the necessity of obtaining a branch office license.   T   **F**

82. A real estate broker's license can be issued only to a person who maintains a definite place of business in the state.   **T** F

83. The Commission may hold a hearing on its own motion if it does not have a verified written complaint from the complainant.   **T** F

84. A salesman must carry his license with him at all times for identification.   T   **F**

85. Usually a salesman cannot transfer his license to the employ of another broker unless he obtains the consent of his former broker.   **T** F

86. Controversy over the division of earned commissions should be brought before the Commission for settlement. T **F**

87. A real estate broker may employ only one salesman for each year he has been licensed as a broker. T **F**

88. A salesman's license must be displayed in a conspicuous place in his home. T **F**

89. A person who sells property under a court order is not required by law to have a license. **T** F

90. All licenses issued by the Commission are good for a period of one year from the date on which they are issued. T **F**

91. It requires a majority vote of a Real Estate Commission to suspend or revoke a license. **T** F

92. It is not necessary to be licensed to sell cemetery lots. T **F**

93. The broker should at all times be in possession of and display the license of his salesman. **T** F

94. A person may not engage in the real estate business until he has received his license. **T** F

95. A person engaged solely in the rental of real property other than his own for compensation must be licensed. **T** F

96. The license law provides a schedule of commissions which may be charged by licensed brokers for making various real estate transactions. T **F**

97. A broker's license should be prominently displayed in his place of business. **T** F

98. A salesman who has passed his examination can begin work immediately even though he has not received his license. T **F**

99. A broker is liable for misconduct in a real estate matter even if he is a bonded real estate board member. **T** F

100. Placing a For Sale sign on vacant property without the consent of the owner may jeopardize a broker's license. **T** F

101. Principals of schools are exempt from the license law in selling real estate. T **F**

102. Subpoena means compelling a person to appear before the Commission at a hearing. **T** F

103. All sales of real estate must be handled through a licensed real estate broker or licensed salesman. T **F**

104. A municipality has no part in regulation of real estate brokers under the licensing act. **T** F

105. The licensing act is not an act designed for revenue. **T** F

106. A broker can employ any number of licensed salesmen. **T** F

107. A person who sells real estate must have a license in order to enforce the collection of a commission. **T** F

108. "Interim License" may be issued after an applicant has failed one examination, if he applies for the succeeding examination. T **F**

109. The license law has eliminated "curb stone" brokers. **T** F

110. A licensee paying a commission to an unlicensed person may lose his license on that account. **T** F

111. The license law has eliminated the "opportunist" broker who "horned in" on a deal because he was a friend of the buyer. **T** F
112. The license law is the greatest single factor in elevating the real estate business to professional status. **T** F
113. A licensed salesman may supervise a branch office. T **F**
114. A high school education as a requirement for a broker's license would add to the professional status of the real estate business. **T** F
115. No refund of fee can be made after a license is issued. **T** F
116. Where a salesman makes misrepresentations without the knowledge or authority of his broker, the Real Estate Commission will not hold the broker responsible for the salesman's fraud. T F
117. The failure of a real estate salesman to notify the Real Estate Commission of his change of employer within 10 days automatically cancels his license. T F
118. A broker desiring to operate under a firm name or a fictitious name must be so licensed. T F
119. If a salesman ceases to be employed by his registered employer, his certificate remains in force. T **F**
120. A salesman can renew his certificate before that of his employing broker is renewed. T **F**
121. A salesman cannot legally continue to operate after expiration of his certificate and before renewal. **T** F
122. A widow of a deceased broker may operate for the remainder of the license year under the decedent's license. T **F**
123. A broker licensed in Michigan may act as a broker in any other state of the United States. T **F**
124. A decision of a Real Estate Commission, upon a complaint, in favor of the licensee is final. **T** F
125. No real estate broker may serve as a member of the Real Estate Commission. T **F**
126. A member of the Real Estate Commission cannot operate as a broker during his tenure as Commissioner. T **F**
127. A builder cannot employ a salesman to sell houses for him, for commission, unless the builder is licensed as a broker. **T** F
128. An attorney-at-law may employ a salesman to sell real estate listed with the attorney for sale. T **F**
129. An unlicensed person making a real estate transaction is guilty of a misdemeanor (or a felony, in some states). **T** F
130. A person over 75 years of age cannot obtain a broker's license. T **F**
131. When deposit money is received by a real estate salesman, he is permitted by law to make use of such money for his personal account up to the amount of his rightful sales commission before the deal is closed. T **F**
132. A licensed real estate salesman must be ready at all times, upon request, to show his license card. **T** F

133. Real estate listings may be taken in the name of the salesman so long as any deal is closed in the name of the employing broker.   T **F**

134. A real estate office may be placed in charge of a licensed real estate salesman, in event of the broker's absence or illness, if the Real Estate Commission is so informed in writing.   T **F**

135. The act of a real estate salesman, within the scope of his authority, is considered to be the act of his employing broker. **T** F

136. A salesman binds his broker for acts beyond the *actual* scope of his authority, if within the *apparent* scope of his authority. **T** F

137. A broker who has authority to accept interest payments on a mortgage, also has authority to accept payment of the mortgage principal.   T **F**

138. It is a violation of the license law for a broker to engage in the real estate business on Sunday.   T **F**

139. A person who is not licensed may sell real estate for a friend if he does not charge any compensation.   **T** F

140. The Realtor's Code of Ethics and the Real Estate License Law are the same.   T **F**

141. A broker who receives a license from the state is privileged to use the term "Realtor."   T **F**

142. A licensee may renew his license at any time before the expiration of the following year.   T **F**

143. A salesman may not sue anyone except his broker for the collection of a real estate commission.   **T** F

144. In most states, an auctioneer of real estate requires a broker's license.   **T** F

145. The real estate license act was passed to eliminate competition.   T **F**

146. The license law is a regulatory measure and not a revenue measure.   **T** F

147. The Real Estate Commission can regulate the type and size of sign that a broker must have on the outside of his place of business.   **T** F

148. A salesman may not copy the listings of his broker for use after he leaves his employment.   **T** F

149. A broker may sign an agreement of sale for his principal where he has an exclusive listing contract of employment.   T **F**

150. A rule or regulation of the Real Estate Commission requiring a broker to give the owner a copy of the listing is valid.   **T** F

151. When moving his office to a new address, a broker must return his old license to the Commission and receive a new one issued for the new address.   **T** F

152. A broker, licensed in another state, may obtain a license in this state promptly upon payment of the regular fee.   T **F**

153. If a salesman severs his connections with a broker, the broker may transfer such salesman's license to a new salesman employee.   T **F**

154. The word "Realtor" may always be used in lieu of "Real Estate" in advertising a real estate brokerage business.   T **F**

155. If a real estate salesman works on a straight salary basis and does not participate in the commissions, he nevertheless requires a license.   **T** F

156. The license of a broker was revoked. The salesman may continue to operate under his present license.   T **F**

157. The Nebraska Real Estate Association and the Nebraska Real Estate Commission are the same.   T **F**

158. An employing broker is responsible for the action of his salesmen.   **T** F

159. Objectionable features which materially reduce the value of property should be called to the prospect's attention, before taking a deposit.   **T** F

160. The main requirement for licensure is success in a previous business.   T **F**

161. A broker is not required to have a branch office license unless the branch office maintained by him is located in another town or city.   T **F**

162. A person must be a property owner in order to be licensed as a broker.   T **F**

163. The Real Estate Commission may suspend the license of a broker found to be dishonest, without the formality of holding a hearing.   T **F**

164. A salesman may split a commission with any other licensed salesman or broker.   T **F**

165. A broker is not required to give the Commission notice if he moves his office to another location in the same community.   T **F**

166. A salesman may leave the employ of one broker and go to work for another broker without notifying the Commission provided he applies for his license the following year under the new broker.   T **F**

167. There should be a written contract between a broker and a salesman covering the terms of the salesman's employment.   **T** F

168. A broker may maintain an office in a grocery store provided he has adequate office equipment.   T **F**

169. A Justice of the Peace who sells real estate and employs a single salesman must be licensed.   **T** F

170. The real estate broker's licensing act requires
  (a) Active officers of a real estate corporation to have a broker's license.   **T** F
  (b) Salesmen who work only on Sundays to be licensed.   **T** F
  (c) Renewal of all licenses during May of each year.   T **F**
  (d) Owner's consent or exclusive agency to place a For Sale sign on property listed.   **T** F
  (e) A written examination for real estate brokers.   **T** F
  (f) The licensing of real estate rental brokers.   **T** F

    (g) The honesty and good repute of all applicants to be
vouched for.   **T**   F

171. A broker is required to keep his office open to the public at
least 40 hours a week.   T   **F**

172. All real estate closings should be handled by the broker and
not by his salesmen.   **T**   F

173. An indictment of a real estate broker upon a charge of obtaining money under false pretense is *prima facie* grounds
for suspension of license.   T   **F**

174. All Real Estate Commissioners are bonded for that office.   T   **F**

175. A real estate salesman cannot maintain a branch office in
his home during evening hours.   **T**   F

176. It is the duty of the broker to notify the Commission when a
salesman leaves his employ.   **T**   F

177. Rules and Regulations for licensees must be approved by the
legislature before they are valid.   T   **F**

178. A fee is charged for a transfer of license or change of business address.   **T**   F

179. A licensee may be represented by counsel in a hearing before the Commission.   **T**   F

180. A Commission is a quasi-judicial body, not bound by strict
rules of evidence.   **T**   F

181. License laws promote professionalization of the real estate
business.   **T**   F

182. The Code of Ethics supersedes the Rules and Regulations of
the Commission.   T   **F**

183. Charging less than the usual rate of commission is grounds
for suspension of license.   T   **F**

184. The Real Estate Commission acts as a collection agency for
recovery of earnest money by a disappointed buyer.   T   **F**

185. A broker should keep records of each real estate transaction
for at least three years.   **T**   F

186. A licensed real estate broker should be in charge of *each*
branch office.   **T**   F

187. There is no *economic* justification for the real estate broker. T   **F**

188. A broker may change a signed agreement of sale, if it is a
minor change.   T   **F**

189. The members of the National Association of Real Estate
Boards were largely responsible for the passage of every
license law.   **T**   F

190. Rhode Island was the 50th state to pass a license law.   **T**   F

191. The National Association of Real Estate License Law Officials
is a "clearing house" for license law information.   **T**   F

192. A person who makes loans on real estate from his own money
must be licensed under the real estate law.   T   **F**

193. An unlicensed broker may assign his claim for commission
to his attorney who requires no license under the law.   T   **F**

194. When an unlicensed officer of a real estate brokerage cor-

poration negotiates a deal, neither the corporation nor the
officer is entitled to a commission.   **T**   F

195. If a broker is delinquent in renewing his license and negotiates a sale, he cannot recover his commission.   **T**   F

196. If a broker fails to give an owner a copy of the listing contract
signed by the owner, he cannot recover a commission.   T   **F**

197. It is good business practice for a broker managing an apartment building, to receive secret rebates, provided he does not
charge the owner more than the prevailing prices.   T   **F**

198. A broker is duty bound to investigate a salesman's reputation
for honesty, truthfulness and integrity before employing him.   **T**   F

199. At a hearing, the broker or salesman is usually referred to as
"the complainant."   T   **F**

200. Every state now requires an examination as a prerequisite to
a broker's license.   **T**   F

201. California was the first state to pass a valid license law.   **T**   F

202. A salesman's identification license card should be displayed in
his broker's office.   T   **F**

203. Concealment or omission of material facts may constitute
misrepresentation.   **T**   F

204. A real estate broker's license may be suspended temporarily
before a hearing where a serious complaint has been filed.   T   **F**

205. A broker is bound to turn over his books of record to a Commission investigator.   **T**   F

206. The penalty for operating without a license upon a second
conviction is the same as for a first offense.   T   **F**

207. An owner may lawfully pay a commission to an unlicensed
neighbor by giving him a power of attorney.   **T**   F

208. A corporation may obtain a salesman's license in the employ
of a licensed broker corporation.   T   **F**

209. Where brokers are appointed to a Real Estate Commission,
they are usually Realtors.   **T**   F

210. The case of an individual charged with operating without a
license is first heard by the Real Estate Commission.   T   **F**

211. A broker may revoke the license of his salesman, where he
finds the salesman misrepresenting on a large scale.   T   **F**

212. If liquidated damages are construed to be a forfeiture, they
will not be enforced.   **T**   F

213. A forfeiture and liquidated damages mean the same thing.   T   **F**

214. An auctioneer who is employed by a licensed broker does not
need a license to sell real estate at public auction.   T   **F**

215. A licensed broker and a licensed salesman may operate a
partnership if the partnership papers are first filed with the
Commission.   T   **F**

216. It is unlawful for a broker to rebate commissions to a buyer.   **T**   F

217. The order of the Real Estate Commission suspending, but not
revoking a license, is final.   T   **F**

218. Mailing real estate brochures by a licensed broker in Pennsyl-

vania to prospects in Kentucky requires him to be licensed
. in Kentucky.   T **F**
219. Violation of a state Fair Housing Act by a broker may be
grounds for revocation of license.   **T** F

Multiple Choice

1. Where an unlicensed salesman negotiated his first sale of real estate,
   the commission would be payable to the
   ( ) salesman's broker only.
   (x) no one.
   ( ) buyer.
   ( ) salesman.
2. Which group is exempt from the licensing law?
   (x) Referee in bankruptcy.
   ( ) Person handling leases only.
   ( ) Salesman employed by a builder.
   ( ) Person employed to sell subdivision lots.
3. A salesman applicant can solicit listings and talk to prospects when
   (x) he obtains his license.
   ( ) he has filed application for license.
   ( ) he takes examination.
   ( ) he passes examination.
4. A salesman, upon receiving his license, may operate from
   ( ) the broker's principal office.
   ( ) any branch office in the county.
   (x) address on the license.
   ( ) any office broker designates.
5. The Real Estate Commission shall at all times perform its official
   duties in such manner as to protect and safeguard the interests of
   ( ) the State legislature.
   ( ) all real estate licensees.
   (x) the general public.
   ( ) persons filing complaints against licensees.
6. The Commission has the power after due hearing to
   (x) suspend or revoke any license issued by it.
   ( ) assess a penal fine of $1,000.
   ( ) suspend a license and impose a fine.
   ( ) issue an order of mandamus.
7. When a broker is licensed for the first time, he must
   ( ) advertise that fact once in a newspaper of general circulation.
   (x) have a sign on the outside of his place of business.
   ( ) sign a written lease for office for at least one year.
8. If a license is issued on October 1, it will expire
   ( ) one year from date of issue.
   ( ) six months from date of issue.

(x) end of license year fixed by license law.
9. Since violations of the license law are detrimental to the public and licensees generally, it is your duty to
( ) keep quiet about them.
( ) inform the newspapers so they may be exposed.
(x) notify the Real Estate Commission.
( ) notify the local real estate board.
10. A salesman employed by another broker wishes to join your firm: what ethical procedure should you follow?
( ) Employ him immediately.
( ) Write to the Real Estate Commission.
( ) Notify the other broker in writing.
(x) Call the other broker and have an understanding with him.
11. Appointments to the Real Estate Commission in states requiring an examination are made by the
( ) Superintendent of Public Instructions.
( ) Insurance Commissioner.
( ) Secretary of State.
(x) Governor.
12. For a broker to act for more than one party in a real estate transaction without the knowledge and consent of all parties is
( ) ethical.
(x) grounds for disciplinary action.
( ) contrary to the Administrative Code.
( ) all right if no party suffers monetary damage.
13. When a license is issued to a corporation, who of the following is entitled to act as a real estate broker?
( ) All members of the corporation.
(x) One officer of the corporation.
( ) All officers of the corporation.
14. Which of the following acts, if performed by a person on behalf of a third person for a promised commission, will constitute him a real estate broker and necessitate his procuring a license?
(x) Collecting rent on real estate.
( ) Offering to sell machinery necessary to farm real estate.
(x) Offering to collect rents for a mortgagee in possession.
( ) Offering to build buildings on real estate as a contractor.
15. A salesman's license must always be
( ) carried by the salesman on his person.
( ) kept in salesman's kit.
(x) displayed in broker's office.
( ) held by the Real Estate Commission.
16. Persons found guilty of operating in the real estate business without a license may be fined by
( ) the District Attorney.
(x) a court of law.
( ) the Real Estate Commission.

( ) the Attorney General.

17. When a real estate broker discharges a salesman in his employ for dishonesty or any other reason, he must notify the Real Estate Commission
   (x) within ten days (usually).
   ( ) immediately.
   ( ) within 30 days.
   ( ) any old time.

18. Any person who collects a real estate commission and is not licensed is guilty of
   ( ) duress.
   ( ) a felony.
   (x) a misdemeanor.
   ( ) negligence.

19. What is the origin of the statement, "No sign should ever be placed on any property without the consent of the owner"?
   (x) State law.
   ( ) Regulations of the Real Estate Commission.
   ( ) Code of Ethics of the National Assn. of Real Estate Boards.

20. When a real estate broker engaged in business as a corporation violates the real estate law, the officer subject to the prescribed penalties is
   ( ) its president.
   ( ) its secretary.
   ( ) its general manager.
   (x) the officer who participates in such violation.

21. The Real Estate Commission may revoke the license of a broker who is found guilty of
   ( ) slandering his competitors.
   ( ) intemperance.
   (x) misrepresentation.
   ( ) violation of the motor vehicle code.

22. The license law requires a broker to
   ( ) spend all his time in the real estate business.
   ( ) spend more than one-half of his time in the real estate business.
   (x) makes no provision as to time a broker must spend in real estate business.
   ( ) make the real estate business his major activity.

23. The Commission is empowered to require every real estate broker to have a license before transacting any such business by virtue of
   (x) the Real Estate Brokers License Act.
   ( ) rules and regulations of the Real Estate Commission.
   ( ) the Code of Ethics.

24. For his acts in connection with business, a real estate salesman is usually responsible to the
   ( ) seller.
   ( ) mortgagee.

( ) buyer.

(x) employing broker.

25. The Real Estate License Law was passed
   ( ) to raise revenue.
   (x) to protect the public.
   ( ) for political reasons.
   ( ) to keep brokers from cheating each other.

26. There are three elements necessary to constitute fraud in a mis-representation. Two of these are that the misrepresentation concerns a material fact and that the party to whom the statement is made has a right to rely upon it. The third element necessary is that:
   ( ) the property will re-sell for a particular amount.
   ( ) the statement is funny.
   ( ) the broker knows the truth.
   (x) the party to whom the statement is made acts on it to his damage.
   ( ) the prospect did not employ the broker.

27. A prospect, or person with whom the broker is dealing "at arm's length," when he is in the locality and able to inspect the property for himself, ordinarily has a right to rely on the broker's representations as to
   ( ) everything the broker says.
   ( ) nothing the broker says.
   ( ) future prospects of the property.
   ( ) patent defects in construction of the building.
   (x) concealed details of construction of the building.

28. The criminal provisions of the license law may be invoked where a broker is guilty of
   ( ) double commissions.
   ( ) adverse interest.
   ( ) embezzlement.
   (x) operating without registration.
   ( ) fraud.

29. A builder who desires to employ a salesman for commission to sell houses built by him must
   ( ) have the salesman obtain a salesman's license.
   ( ) notify the Commission of the contract between the builder and the salesman.
   (x) obtain a broker's license.
   ( ) pay the salesman less than half of the usual commission.

30. Which of the following is not grounds for revocation of a broker's license?
   ( ) Misrepresentation.
   (x) Closing a real estate transaction.
   ( ) The crime of extortion.

31. Deposit money received by a salesman must be turned over to

( ) owner.
( ) Real Estate Commission.
(x) broker for deposit in his trustee account.
( ) an attorney.

32. A real estate salesman who changes his employer must
( ) notify his local real estate board.
( ) notify the abstract or recorder of deeds.
( ) notify the local member of the Real Estate Commission.
(x) notify, in writing, the office of the Real Estate Commission.

33. No real estate should be advertised except in the name of the
( ) seller.
( ) salesman who obtains the listing.
(x) principal-licensed broker.
( ) real estate salesman on the premises.

34. A Realtor is a member in good standing of the
( ) Real Estate Commission.
( ) National Association of License Law Officials.
(x) local real estate board, affiliated with the National Association
of Real Estate Boards.
( ) local Chamber of Commerce.

35. A real estate salesman's license may be revoked for
( ) slandering his competitor.
( ) failure to spend forty hours per week as a real estate salesman.
( ) violation of NAREB's code of ethics.
(x) misrepresentation in a real estate transaction.
( ) violation of a local zoning ordinance.

36. A broker's license may be suspended or revoked for which of the
following causes?
( ) Over-charge of a sales commission in a real estate transaction.
( ) Conviction of drunkenness.
( ) Failure to pay a money judgment.
(x) Failure to account or remit funds belonging to others.

37. A prospect with whom the broker is dealing "at arm's length" when
he is upon the property and may easily investigate for himself,
ordinarily has a right to rely upon the broker's representations as to
( ) title.
( ) future prospects.
( ) all statements the broker makes concerning the physical structure.
(x) past rentals of property.

38. A builder who desires to employ a salesman on commission to sell
houses built by him should
( ) notify the Real Estate Commission of the contract between the
builder and the salesman.
( ) record the contract between the builder and salesman.
(x) obtain a broker's license.

( ) pay the salesman not more than one half of the customary commission.

39. It is whose duty to prosecute persons engaged in the real estate business without a license?
 (x) District Attorney.
 ( ) Attorney General.
 ( ) Real Estate Commission.
 ( ) Tax Collector.

40. A salesman and broker desire to engage in the real estate business as a partnership. They may
 ( ) register the partnership with the broker as the active broker, and the salesman as an employee.
 (x) not do so.
 ( ) not be registered as a partnership, but may be registered as a corporation.
 ( ) be registered as a joint venture.

41. A broker licensed in California who wishes to sell property in an adjoining state
 ( ) since he is licensed in California can also operate in all other states automatically.
 (x) should immediately contact the proper agency in the adjoining state to obtain a license there.
 ( ) must contact a broker in the adjoining state and work through him only.

42. A real estate salesman may lawfully accept a bonus commission for the completion of a difficult sale,
 ( ) if the seller wishes to give him one.
 ( ) if he pays the tax on it.
 (x) only from his employing broker.
 ( ) if he receives it from the buyer.

43. Broker "A" has two good salesmen, "B" and "C," who have been in his employ for two years, and salesman "D" who has been licensed for only three months. However, "D" has proven himself to be a very good salesman. "A," "B," "C," and "D" desire to form a partnership to engage in the real estate business. "A" is to have a 40% interest in the partnership. Which statement is correct?
 ( ) They can form the partnership as desired.
 ( ) They cannot form the partnership as each must have an equal interest.
 (x) They cannot form the partnership until each partner is licensed as a broker and "B," "C," and "D" are not licensed as brokers.
 ( ) They can form the partnership since all of the parties are licensed as salesmen or brokers.

44. A broker has a written promise of a $500 commission if he can secure certain acreage. The owner agrees to sell if he can keep one-fourth of the mineral rights and will pay the broker $500 commission. The

transaction was closed. The seller knew of the broker's commission arrangement with the buyer. Which of the following is true?
( ) Broker made a clever deal and was entitled to the extra earnings.
(x) Broker is subject to disciplinary action by Commission.
( ) Since the seller knew of the fee paid by buyer, it was ethical.
( ) Broker violated the Statute of Frauds.

45. An unlicensed broker cannot collect a real estate commission in court because
( ) Statute of Frauds prohibits it.
( ) it violates the rules of the Real Estate Commission.
(x) it violates a state law.
( ) it violates an Act of Congress.

46. A property should not be advertised for sale except in the name of the
( ) owner.
( ) salesman, to whom property is assigned.
(x) broker.
( ) tenant in possession.

47. In transferring from one broker "A" to broker "B" a salesman should
( ) notify Broker "A" that he is leaving.
( ) start working immediately for "B" and notify "A" within 10 days.
(x) first notify Real Estate Commission of change and request transfer of license.
( ) post his license in "B's" office.

48. Broker "A" has a listing on a property. Broker "B" has a prospect. "B" should
( ) obtain prospect's signature to an offer to purchase.
( ) obtain listing from owner.
(x) contact "A" and obtain his permission to act as co-broker.
( ) do nothing.

49. For a broker to act for buyer and seller without their knowledge is
( ) grounds for seller to declare the sale void.
( ) grounds for the buyer to declare the sale void.
(x) grounds for disciplinary action by Commission.
( ) subject to a penalty of a fine.

50. Where a violation of the license law occurs in a corporation, who is subject to disciplinary action?
( ) the general manager.
( ) all officers, but no stockholders.
(x) the officer responsible for violation.
( ) the president.

51. A salesman may operate a branch office for his broker
( ) if his salesman's license is displayed.
( ) if his broker's license is displayed.
( ) if the office is his home.
(x) under no circumstances.

52. A real estate broker's license which has been revoked may be reinstated by
( ) paying a penalty fine.
(x) by qualifying as an original applicant.
( ) by making application for a writ of mandamus.
( ) by making written application to Commission for reinstatement.
53. Members are appointed to the Real Estate Commission by
(x) the Governor.
( ) Secretary of State.
( ) the State Real Estate Association.
( ) the House Judiciary Committee.
54. A broker's license may be revoked for
(x) failure to account for or to remit funds belonging to others.
( ) failure to charge any commission.
( ) making sales on Sunday.
( ) failure to make a sale within one year.
55. Which persons are specifically exempt from the Real Estate Licensing Act?
( ) Receivers.
(x) Executors.
( ) Part time salesmen.
( ) Listers of real estate.
56. The term "Realtor" is a copyrighted word and can be used only by
( ) any licensed broker.
( ) brokers who are full time.
(x) a member of the National Association of Real Estate Boards.
( ) none of the foregoing.
57. When a broker discharges a salesman, he should
( ) give the salesman his license.
(x) return the license to the Real Estate Commission.
( ) remove license from wall and keep it in file until all of salesman's deals have been closed out.
( ) instruct salesman to return license to Real Estate Commission.
58. An appeal from a decision of the Commission may be taken to
( ) Attorney General of the State.
( ) directly to the Supreme Court.
(x) Circuit or District Court.
( ) referee in bankruptcy.
59. A license may be revoked upon proof of
( ) charging more than the usual rate of commission.
( ) dispute between broker and salesman as to a commission.
(x) violation of F.H.A. law.
( ) refusal to accept a listing.
60. A license issued on May 15 is valid until
( ) May 15 of the following year.
(x) end of current license year.
( ) January 15 of the following year.
( ) 60 days.

61. A salesman, in transferring to a new broker employer, should make application
    ( ) at next renewal period.
    ( ) within 60 days.
    ( ) within 30 days.
    (x) immediately.
62. A broker's license is revoked for one year. His two salesmen
    ( ) must remain on inactive status the balance of the license year.
    ( ) would lose their licenses for one year.
    (x) may, upon proper application, transfer to another broker.
    ( ) may continue to operate the broker's business.
63. A licensed broker selling a property on which he holds an option must notify the buyer that he is the
    (x) optionee.
    ( ) optionor.
    ( ) tenant.
    ( ) lessee
    ( ) escrow holder.
64. A member of the National Association of Real Estate License Law Officials is a
    ( ) Realtor.
    ( ) licensed broker.
    (x) license law state.
    ( ) Secretary of State.
65. A salesman may operate a branch office for his broker
    ( ) if he is the sales manager.
    ( ) if his license is displayed there.
    ( ) if he resides in the same building.
    (x) under no circumstances.
66. The Real Estate Commission sets the maximum commission to be charged as
    ( ) 5 per cent.
    ( ) 6 per cent.
    ( ) 7 per cent.
    (x) no maximum.
67. A licensed broker may share a commission with
    ( ) the person who introduced the buyer to the broker.
    ( ) salesman of another broker, who assisted in the sale.
    (x) a licensed broker who assisted in sale.
    ( ) an attorney at law, who is a friend of the seller.
68. John Sloan is a licensed salesman who desires to transfer his license to Samuel Simon, trading as Eureka Realty Co. His license should be transferred as a salesman in employ of
    (x) Samuel Simon.
    ( ) Eureka Realty Co.
    ( ) Kept in name of former employer.
    ( ) Do nothing.
69. When a licensed broker dies, his business may be operated by

( ) his widow.
( ) his chief salesman.
( ) person who inherited the business.
(x) none of these.
70. In participating in a "dual contract" situation, which ones of the following participants would be subject to criminal prosecution?
(x) Buyer.
(x) Seller.
(x) Broker.
(x) Lending institution representative.

Chapter 10

FILL-IN, MATCHING, AND KEY-WORD QUESTIONS

1. The gradual increase in the value of real property is called *appreciation*.
2. A Chattel Mortgage is security for a *debt or note*.
3. P.I.T.I. means principal, interest, taxes and *insurance*.
4. Property held under a lease is called *a leasehold*.
5. Where a licensee violates a rule or regulation of the Real Estate Commission, he will be charged with *improper conduct, bad faith, or untrustworthiness*.
6. In the preparation of a closing statement, a mortgage assumed by the buyer would be listed as a *credit* to the buyer and as a *debit* to the seller.
7. The amount of earnest money to be paid is determined by *agreement of parties*.
8. A purchaser at a foreclosure sale upon a mortgage receives a *sheriff's deed*.
9. Real estate taxes are usually computed on the basis of the *calendar* year.
10. Where a material misrepresentation has been made to a buyer, he is entitled to relief in court in an action for *recission*.
11. Community property may only be acquired by *husband and wife*.
12. Unproductive land on which the cost of production approximates the gross return is *marginal* land.
13. A contract for purchase of real estate upon an installment basis wherein the deed is delivered to the purchaser upon payment of the last installment, is called a *land contract*.
14. A plan or map of a certain piece or pieces of land is a *plat*.
15. A real estate license may be revoked for making any substantial *misrepresentation*.
16. A real estate broker's license must at all times be conspicuously displayed at *office*.
17. Unpaid taxes on real property become a *lien*.
18. When a real estate salesman is discharged for dishonesty, the broker must immediately notify the *Real Estate Commission*.

19. Mechanic's Liens are usually filed against real property for payment of _labor or materials._

20. An unlicensed salesman negotiated the sale of a parcel of real estate. Both broker and salesman claimed the commission. It is payable to _neither._

21. Before suspending or revoking any license, the Real Estate Commission must grant the licensee a _hearing._

22. An estimate of value of real estate by a qualified expert is called an _appraisal._

23. The loan secured by a mortgage is evidenced by a _note._ (Bond)

24. A salesman in the employ of a real estate broker put through a deal. In order to collect his commission, an action may be brought against the seller by the _broker._

25. A real estate salesman must lead a prospect through the following five steps before the prospect buys—(1) desire, (2) action, (3) belief, (4) attention, (5) interest. Rearranged in proper sequence they would be—_attention, interest, belief, desire, action._

26. When specific properties are benefited by public improvements, the charges (or taxes levied) to pay for such improvements are called _assessments._

27. A deed without warranties is a _quit claim deed._

28. The two types of property are called _real_ and _personal._

29. The spouse of a married titleholder of a home should sign a sales contract and deed to relinquish or release _dower_ and _curtesy_ rights.

30. A contract secured through fraud or misrepresentation would not be _valid._

31. The amount of commission to be charged in a real estate transaction is determined by the _listing contract._

32. The process of paying off a loan by installment is called _amortization._

33. The overhang or projection of a foundation wall, a porch, or a balcony beyond the established line of a parcel of land is known as an _encroachment._

34. To make a binding contract there must be at least _two parties._

35. An acquired privilege or right of use or enjoyment falling short of ownership which one may have in the land of another is known as an _easement._

36. If a person owns a part interest in a home he is buying on time, such interest is called an _equity._

37. A salesman's half of a 5 per cent commission on a $6,250 sale would be _$156.25._

38. A right of the state by which the state can obtain possession of any property which is needed for a public purpose is _eminent domain._

39. If the annual 5 per cent interest payment amounts to $350.00, the principal or total sum due would be *$7,000.*

40. Mud tubes or shelter channels on walls or joists or cellar window sills apparently rotted indicate the presence of *termites.*

41. Title to chattels is usually transferred by a *bill of sale.*

42. The compiled ordinances or laws regulating the construction of buildings within the jurisdiction of a municipality is called the *zoning and building code.*

43. The branch of the state government that is responsible for the enforcement of the real estate broker's license law is the *Real Estate Commission.*

44. If a witness is served with a summons to appear before the Real Estate Commission, such summons is called a *subpoena.*

45. If we multiply the floor area of a building by its height, we arrive at a figure designated as its *cubage.*

46. A mortgage given for a part of the purchase price of a home is called a *purchase money mortgage.*

47. A note is negotiated by the signature of the holder on its "reverse side." This is called *an endorsement.*

48. The name of the instrument by which personal property is ordinarily mortgaged is a *chattel mortgage.*

49. The instrument which is used to convey title to real property is called *a deed.*

50. The instrument which is used to convey title to personal property is called a *bill of sale.*

51. The fixing of value of real estate for purposes of taxation is called *assessing.*

52. The right to cross over property belonging to another is called *an easement.*

53. A commission agreement between licensed brokers or salesmen need not be *written.*

54. The moral duty and the principles of right action and fair dealing set forth for the guidance of professional conduct are known as *canons of ethics* or *code of ethics.*

55. A careful measurement made by a qualified person from established data to determine the boundaries of a tract of land is known as *surveying.*

56. The board skirting the walls of a room on the floor line is called *baseboard, quarter round.*

57. The lowest floor level in a building is the *basement* floor.

58. *Foundation* is the walls of a building below the first or ground floor.

59. One who assigns or transfers property is called *an assignor.*

60. In a deed there must be good or valuable *consideration.*

61. An authorization given by one person to act for him on his behalf is called *a power of attorney*.

62. The rights which a wife has upon her husband's death in lands owned by him in fee simple is called *dower*.

63. The element of depreciation usually found in older type buildings and which affects the appraised value is known as *obsolescence*.

64. Applications for a real estate license are made to the *Real Estate Commission* (or Commissioner).

65. A marginal release or a satisfaction is often used to release a *mortgage*.

66. The cestuique trust under a trust instrument is the *beneficiary*.

67. A note or bond is usually given to secure the payment of a *mortgage*.

68. Where a broker holds a written listing protecting him against a sale by the owner or another broker during a limited period of time he is said to hold *an exclusive-right-to-sell contract*.

69. Deeds are usually acknowledged before a *notary public*.

70. Where a mortgagee cannot personally be present to satisfy a mortgage, the writing which may be filed for that purpose is called *a satisfaction piece*.

71. An agreement between two or more parties to do or not to do a certain thing is called *a contract*.

72. The instrument which the purchaser of a mortgage should obtain from the mortgagor is known as an *estoppel certificate* (also known as a certificate of no defense or a declaration of no setoff).

73. The clause in a deed which permits the buyer to proceed against the seller for damages due to a defect in title is the *warranty clause*.

74. The parties to a lease are known as *lessor* and *lessee*.

75. A real estate salesman must be in the employ of a broker who is properly *licensed*.

76. A common unit other than the square foot which is used in determining the value of developed land is the *front foot*.

77. A summary of the most important part of all instruments comprising the recorded title of the seller, arranged in chronological order is *an abstract of title*.

78. The system of recording used to eliminate tedious and expensive searches of titles is the *Torrens system*.

79. If a man's income is $195.00 per month and his home cost $2\frac{1}{2}$ times his annual income, the home would cost him $5,850.00.

80. The rule of law in leasing or selling property where the parties deal "at arm's length" is called *caveat emptor* (let the purchaser beware).

81. A lease is transferred by the lessor to a purchaser of the leased property by *assignment*.

82. The public regulation of the character and intensity of use of real property through the employment of police power is known as *zoning*.

83. Real estate license laws are constitutional because they represent a valid exercise of the state's *police power*.

84. A decree of court determining that one individual is indebted to another and fixing the amount of the indebtedness is called a *judgment*.

85. Title to property occupied in defiance of the real owner for a long period of time may pass to the occupier through *adverse possession*.

86. In order to prevent the proposed violation of a building restriction covenant an action should be brought for an *injunction*.

87. A person who belongs to a local real estate board affiliated with the National Association of Real Estate Boards is a *Realtor*.

88. The compensation or income received for the use of real property is known as *rent*.

89. A limitation upon the use or occupancy of real estate placed by public legislative action is known as *zoning*.

90. Where one is negligent in asserting his legal rights, his claim may be barred by a *statute of limitations*.

91. One who institutes a suit at law is *the plaintiff*.

92. The interest or value of an estate remaining to the mortgagor over and above the encumbrance is known as *his equity*.

93. An agreement between two persons which creates a legal obligation is called a *contract*.

94. The conveyance of an estate in land by way of a pledge for the security of a debt, to become void upon payment of the debt, is called a *mortgage*.

95. A deed which purports merely to convey whatever interest in the particular land the grantor may have, excluding any implication that the grantor has a good title or any title, is known as a *quit claim deed*.

96. A person who receives real estate under a will is known as the *devisee*.

97. The person appointed to administer the estate of a decedent who did not leave a will is called an *administrator*.

98. The person named in a will to administer the estate is the *executor*.

99. *Percolation test* is a soil test to determine if the soil will take sufficient water seepage for use of septic tanks.

100. A private sewage disposal facility for individual homes is a *septic* (cess pool) system.

101. The person to whom real estate is conveyed by deed is the *grantee*.
102. The person to whom personal property is sold is the *vendee*.
103. Where a deed is delivered to a third person pending the performance of some condition, it is a delivery *in escrow*.
104. The owner's right to buy back property sold for delinquent taxes is called the right of *redemption*.
105. Joint tenancy implies the right of *survivorship*.
106. A chattel mortgage is given to obtain a *loan*.
107. The trade name of a business sold usually includes the *good will*.
108. A broker occupies a *fiduciary* relationship to his principal.
109. A person who holds an option for the purchase of real estate is the *optionee*.
110. The transfer of interest in a bond, mortgage, lease or other instrument is called *assignment*.
111. Dispossession of a tenant by a landlord from a leased property is known as *eviction*.
112. A forged deed is always *void*.
113. A sub-lessee who, in turn, sub-lets to another is said to hold a *sandwich lease*.
114. Generally speaking, a person can afford to pay $2\frac{1}{2}$ times his annual income for a home.
115. In the absence of a specific agreement as to commission, the amount to be paid is determined by *custom*.
116. Where one holds property absolutely to himself and his heirs forever, he is said to own the property in *fee simple*.
117. An absolute conveyance of property would be by *fee simple deed*.
118. Title to real estate passes to the grantee at the time the deed is *delivered*.
119. A conveyance which releases all right, title and interest of the grantor is called a *quit claim deed*.
120. A freehold that is limited to end with the life of the person to whom it is granted is a *life estate*.
121. A written instrument legally sufficient to transfer an estate of freehold from one person to another is a *deed*.
122. Real estate given to a person by will is known as a *devise*.
123. Stamps due on a deed are paid by the *seller*.
124. The statute which requires certain contracts relating to real estate to be in writing is the *Statute of Frauds*.
125. Where a mortgagee requires a tenant of leased premises to pay the rent to him because the mortgage is in default, he is said to be a *mortgagee in possession*.
126. An initial payment made by a possible purchaser of real estate to

bind him to the terms of his offer to purchase is called *earnest money* (also known as a down payment; hand money).

127. An agent's authority to execute a binding agreement of sale for an owner must be *written*.

128. An agreement granting the exclusive right to purchase real estate for a limited period of time is known as an *option*.

129. A contract between two or more parties for the use of property for consideration is known as a *lease*.

130. The main characteristic which distinguishes a lease from a license is *rent*.

131. The action of a landlord in levying upon a tenant's goods for rent in arrears is known as *distraint*.

132. A salesman must be recommended by a *broker*.

133. Funds held by a broker, belonging to others, must be kept in a *trust account*.

134. Charging more than the legal rate of interest is *usury*.

135. A written instrument which transfers possession of property, but does not transfer ownership is a *lease*.

136. A salesman in the employ of a broker put through a sale. The seller refused to pay the commission due. In order to collect, suit may be brought against the seller by the *broker*.

137. A person who acts as a real estate broker without a license is guilty of a *misdemeanor*.

138. In the event a tenant defaults in rent payments, the landlord may start an action for *distraint*.

139. If the buyer insisted that title should close upon the exact date agreed upon, the clause which should be inserted in the agreement is that time is of *the essence*.

140. The action to compel the seller to execute a deed in pursuance of a written agreement is an action for *specific performance*.

141. A person who fails to act promptly under the circumstances is guilty of *laches*.

142. A single mortgage which covers more than one property is a *blanket mortgage*.

143. The transfer of all of a tenant's rights and interest under a lease to another is known as an *assignment*.

144. When a commercial property is being offered for sale, and a tenant wishes to renew a long-term lease, the managing broker should renew the lease with a *first right of refusal*.

145. The amount of commission to be paid a broker in a real estate deal is fixed by *agreement of parties*.

146. A lien given by the statute to those who perform work or furnish

materials in the improvement of real estate is called a *mechanic's lien.*

147. The general term in appraising covering loss from any cause is called *depreciation.*

148. A measure of land consisting of 43,560 square feet is called an *acre.*

149. If we multiply the width of a building by its length, we arrive at a figure called its *area.*

150. A warranty deed is used in connection with the sale of *real estate.*

151. The delivery of a warranty deed usually passes *title.*

152. A broker should not act as such in selling real estate in which he has an undisclosed *interest.*

153. The section of land located in the extreme southeast corner of a township is number *36.*

154. In some states a mortgage is known as a *deed of trust.*

155. A loan not guaranteed by some governmental agency is called a *conventional* loan.

156. One who seeks to obtain leads and tips on listings and sales is known in the trade as a *"bird dog."*

157. The license law is the greatest single factor in elevating the real estate business to a *profession.*

158. A clause in a mortgage which gives the mortgagor the privilege of paying the mortgage indebtedness before it becomes due is called *pre-payment mortgage.*

159. The covenant which makes it mandatory that the seller execute any additional instruments necessary to perfect the title at any future date is called the covenant of *further assurance.*

160. A lease which requires the tenant to pay all expenses of the property in addition to his rent is called *net lease.*

161. A real estate broker drew a lease providing that the rent was to be paid *monthly,* but did not specify therein that rent should be paid in advance. In such a case, the rent is due and payable on *the last day of the month.*

162. An authorization is made in New York State for the sale of land located in New Jersey; such authorization is enforceable in accordance with the laws of *New York.*

163. In the absence of an agreement between a real estate broker and his client as to commission, the commission is determined by *the prevailing rate.*

164. A mortgage is in default for non-payment of *interest* or *principal.*

165. In order to protect his rights, the mortgagee should institute *foreclosure* proceedings.

166. An automatic water pump used in basements to raise water to the sewer level is called a *sump* pump.

167. The Director of the license law is usually appointed by the *Real Estate Commission*.
168. A mortgage may be satisfied by payment for *foreclosure*.
169. The mortgage covenant which permits the mortgagee to advance the due date of the principal of the mortgage is called the *acceleration clause*.
170. Paying off a mortgage loan by regular monthly payments over an extended period of time is known as *amortization*.
171. A salesman's license pocket card should be carried with him as an *identification* to prospects.
172. A chattel mortgage is given to secure a loan on *personal property*.
173. A person who is the beneficiary under a trust of a decedent is the *cestui que trust*.
174. An individual who gives an option on a property is the *optionor*.
175. Where the mortgagor is in default, the mortgagee may *foreclose*.
176. The legal compensation for the use of money is *interest*.
177. One who executes a will is called the *testator*.
178. Until the death of the testator, the will is *revocable*.
179. Commission disputes between a broker and a salesman should be determined *in court*.
180. That part of the real estate instrument which identifies the subject property is called the *description*.
181. A legal document, filed in the office of the county clerk, giving notice that a court action is pending, affecting the property, is called *lis pendens*.
182. An individual who holds an option on a property is called *an optionee*.
183. A note is negotiated by *an endorsement*.
184. A freehold that is limited to end with the life of the person to whom it is granted is called a *life estate*.
185. A certificate of no defense is generally required upon a transfer of the mortgage, from the *mortgagor*.
186. In improved real estate, loss from any cause is termed *depreciation*.
187. Almost all members of the various state Real Estate Commissions are *Realtors*.
188. One who receives title under a deed is called the *grantee*.
189. The Canons by which a Realtor is governed is called the *Code of Ethics*.
190. An oral contract for the conveyance of land is unenforceable under the *Statute of Frauds*.
191. An authorization to sell real estate must be signed by the *owner*.
192. A wife's rights in her husband's property until his death are *inchoate*.

193. A roof with sloping sides and ends is called a *hip roof*.
194. A protruding gable on a neighbor's land is an *encroachment*.
195. An article may be changed from real estate to personalty by *detachment* or severance.
196. Generally, when looking at a map, the direction on your left will be the *west*.
197. The Federal Agency which insures a V.A. loan is the *Veterans Administration*.
198. An escrow or trust account required by law is for the protection of the *public*.
199. An important asset of a business, which is carried on the owner's books at a nominal value, is *good will*.
200. Bringing down an abstract to date is usually charged to the *seller*.
201. An increase in the value of property due to economic or related causes is known as *appreciation*.
202. A buyer should seek advice as to the meaning of terms in a contract from *an attorney*.
203. Under the law of agency, a broker is considered a *fiduciary*.
204. The person who becomes the owner of real estate upon the death of the present owner is called the *remainderman*.
205. Where a person inherits property from an adverse claimant, his adverse possession is connected through *tacking*.
206. Where one purchases property from a party who has adversely occupied it for seven years, there is *privity of contract*.
207. In the transfer of real estate, the signature of *the grantee* is not necessary on the deed.
208. The Housing Act prohibiting discrimination in the sale and rental of real estate was passed in *1968*.

Key word—Questions—True and False

(If false, give correct answer)

1. A listing contract which authorizes a broker to sign a contract of sale for his owner *is unusual*.
   A. True
2. A *straight fee* may be paid by a broker to an unlicensed person who only submits listings.
   A. Nothing
3. The *Home Owners Loan Corporation* is the Federal Agency most in demand in financing home purchases.
   A. Federal Housing Administration

4. A mortgage is considered satisfied when an *offset certificate* has been filed.
   A. Satisfaction Piece
5. To be enforceable, a written listing contract must be signed by *seller* and *buyer*.
   A. Broker and Seller
6. The rule of "*caveat emptor*" applies to a tenant who leases a property in disrepair.
   A. True
7. The largest ownership in real estate is called a *remainder estate*.
   A. Fee simple
8. Permitting a later mortgage to take precedence over an earlier mortgage is termed *Right of First Refusal*.
   A. Subordination
9. A broker should prepare an agreement of sale in *duplicate*.
   A. Quadruplicate
10. A listing is terminated by the death of the *salesman* who obtained it.
    A. Broker or owner
11. A person who answers the broker's ad and looks at the property is the broker's *client*.
    A. Customer
12. Placing "*For Sale*" signs on property is one of the best ways of securing new listings.
    A. "Sold"
13. A non-exclusive listing and *a net* listing are the same.
    A. An open
14. Violation of a material covenant in a lease by the tenant is an *eviction*.
    A. Forfeiture
15. The words, "by, from, through or under" the grantor indicate the deed from the grantor is a *general warranty deed*.
    A. Special warranty deed
16. When an agreement of sale is executed by seller and buyer, the latter acquires *equitable title*.
    A. True
17. An absolute conveyance of real property would be by a *warranty deed*.
    A. True
18. In computing the square footage of a home you would use the *outside* measurements.
    A. True
19. A suit in equity by a buyer to compel a seller to carry out the terms of an executed agreement of sale is known as *Equity of Redemption*.
    A. Specific Performance
20. *Mandamus* is a form of public notice filed against a property that a suit is about to be filed.
    A. Lis Pendens

21. If a tenant remains in possession after expiration of a lease for a three year term, he is again a tenant for *three years*.
    A. Tenant from year to year
22. Paying off a mortgage loan by regular monthly payments over an extended period of time is known as *prepayment*.
    A. Amortization
23. When requested a six months rent payment upon signing a lease, the lessor should apply such rent to the *first* six months of the lease term.
    A. The *last* six months
24. The *beneficiary* is the party who executes a deed.
    A. Grantor
25. A net listing is usually to the *owner's* advantage.
    A. *Broker's* advantage
26. A deed to Louis Stone or Henry Sloan is *void*.
    A. True
27. The government official who evaluates property for tax purposes is an *escrowee*.
    A. Assessor
28. If the owner must pay the broker a commission, if the owner sells the property during the specified period, the broker has an *exclusive* agency.
    A. Exclusive right to sell
29. Listings obtained by a salesman are considered to be the *salesman's* personal property.
    A. Broker's
30. Whether the broker is the efficient cause of the sale is a question of *law*.
    A. Fact
31. In the Atlanta Board multi-list association, a member must be a *licensed broker*.
    A. Realtor
32. A sales agreement must be *witnessed* in order to be recorded.
    A. Acknowledged
33. Fence posts are *personal* property.
    A. Real
34. A heavy tractor used to till farm land *is not* real estate.
    A. True
35. The *buyer* should pay for the continuation of an abstract of title.
    A. Seller
36. The *seller* should pay for an attorney's examination of the title.
    A. Buyer
37. An oral contract to sell real estate is *void*.
    A. Unenforceable
38. Rescission of a real estate contract is addressed to the *law* side of the court.
    A. Equity

39. In an appeal to a higher court, the defendant in the appellate court is the *appellant*.
    A. Appellee

40. In an action before the Commission, the licensee is termed *the respondent*.
    A. True

41. Where a broker receives earnest money on a deal, he should deposit same in his *insurance account*, insured under the F.D.I.C.
    A. Escrow or Trust Account

42. Where a person operates as a real estate broker without a license he is guilty of a *felony*.
    A. Misdemeanor

43. A report setting forth the estimate of quantity, quality and value of real estate as of a certain date is known as a *summation*.
    A. Appraisal

44. All active officers in a corporation, other than the President, must hold licenses as *salesmen*.
    A. Brokers

45. The most frequent ground for which a licensee is disciplined is *misrepresentation*.
    A. True

46. A Real Estate Commission may issue a *mandamus* to compel a witness to appear before it at a hearing.
    A. Subpoena

47. License laws promote *security* to a real estate broker.
    A. Professionalization

48. *Chattel* and *personal* property mean the same.
    A. True

49. A seller generally pays for the *examination* of the abstract.
    A. Continuation

50. An incumbrance is anything which affects the *loan value*.
    A. Title

51. *Hand money* is money given to an unofficial stakeholder on a real estate deal.
    A. It is deposit or earnest money.

52. The primary purpose of an acknowledgment is for *attestation*.
    A. Recording

53. Unpaid taxes on real estate constitute a *judgment*.
    A. Lien

54. Title to real estate passes to the grantee at the time the deed is *signed*.
    A. Delivered

55. Increase in land on shore or bank due to change in flow of a stream is known as *avulsion*.
    A. Alluvion

56. The interest which a wife of a partner acquires in partnership property is *dower*.
    A. Nothing

57. Two brokers can own property as *joint tenants.*
    A. True
58. A "Chain of Title" is a term often used by *surveyors.*
    A. Abstracters
59. A deed to real estate *can* be assigned.
    A. Cannot
60. A percentage lease is based on the *net profits* of the business.
    A. Gross volume
61. Taxes *have* priority over recorded mortgages.
    A. True
62. The Commission frowns on the use of *exclusive* listings.
    A. Net
63. The case of an individual charged with operating without a license is first heard by the *Real Estate Commission.*
    A. Court
64. An individual who holds an option on a property is called *an obtainer.*
    A. An optionee
65. A freehold that is limited to end with the life of the person to whom it is granted is called an *annuity.*
    A. Life estate
66. A buyer's first right of refusal clause in a lease benefits the *seller.*
    A. True
67. A building contractor, to protect himself, when the owner refuses to pay him for work done, files a *deficiency judgment.*
    A. Mechanic's lien
68. The commission to be charged by a real estate broker is fixed by the *legislature.*
    A. Parties
69. Generally, when looking at a map, *South* will be at your right.
    A. East
70. A listing of the same property which is held by several different brokers is called a *multiple* listing.
    A. Open
71. *Devise* is the reversion of property to the state due to the lack of heirs.
    A. Escheat
72. An acre of land contains *43,630* square feet.
    A. 43,560
73. The *"Chain of Title"* is found in the Abstract of Title.
    A. True
74. Pro-ration of taxes between seller and buyer is *apportionment.*
    A. True
75. A broker may lawfully receive a commission from a *co-broker.*
    A. True

76. Commission disputes between broker and salesman should be brought before the *Real Estate Commission.*
    A. In court
77. The person ordinarily liable for the payment of utilities for a leased property is the *lessee.*
    A. True
78. A certificate of no defense is the same as an *estoppel certificate.*
    A. True
79. Where a buyer refuses to go through with a deal, the seller should make *specific performance.*
    A. Tender of deed and demand of purchase price
80. Any licensed broker who is a bona fide member of a service club is a *Realtor.*
    A. Not true
81. The *lessee* generally pays the taxes on leased property.
    A. Lessor
82. A contract with a minor is *void.*
    A. Voidable by the minor
83. In numbering a township section, number 6 is always in the *northwest* corner.
    A. True
84. The amount of earnest money to be paid is determined by a *minimum of 5 per cent of the purchase price.*
    A. Agreement of the parties
85. As a general rule the *optionee* has the right to collect rents on the optioned property during the life of the option.
    A. Optionor
86. A unit of measure 5,280 feet long is a *chain.*
    A. Mile
87. A dividing wall between two buildings, owned separately, which is used by both properties, is a *brick* wall.
    A. Party
88. An individual appointed by a court to settle a deceased person's estate is called a *guardian.*
    A. Administrator
89. If the owner refuses to pay an earned commission, the broker should file *a lien.*
    A. A suit in court
90. Title to vacant land may be conveyed by executing *a bill of sale.*
    A. A deed
91. If a broker is delinquent in paying his annual renewal fee, his license is *considered to be in force for only the thirty day grace period.*
    A. Cancelled
92. A *binder* is a decree of court declaring one individual is indebted to another and fixing the amount of such indebtedness.
    A. Judgment

93. *The beneficiary* is the one who gives a mortgage on his property in return for a loan.
    A. The mortgagor
94. *Title I* of the FHA Act provides for unsecured home improvement and repair loans.
    A. True
95. The *"Fanny Mae" organization* was set up by the Federal Government to create a secondary mortgage market.
    A. True
96. A mortgage represents a *liquid* asset of the mortgagee.
    A. Frozen
97. Farm property cannot be leased for more than *twenty years*.
    A. Any period
98. Broken windows in a leased premises are the responsibility of *the tenant*.
    A. True
99. The legal compensation for the use of money is called *rent*.
    A. Interest
100. A purchaser at a foreclosure sale usually receives a *Bargain and Sale deed*.
    A. Sheriff's deed, tax deed
101. A lease cannot be recorded unless it is acknowledged by the *notary public*.
    A. Lessor
102. There are *36* feet in a rod.
    A. 16½
103. There are *36* sections in a township.
    A. True
104. Title to real estate passes when the deed is *signed, sealed and recorded*.
    A. Signed, sealed and delivered.
105. An *escrowee* is a government official who evaluates property for tax purposes.
    A. Assessor
106. A good title and a *marketable* title are generally considered to mean the same thing.
    A. True
107. There are *360* acres in a section.
    A. 640
108. There are *forty* acres in the SE ¼ of the NW ¼ of the NE ¼ of a section of land.
    A. Ten
109. When a grantor faultily signs a deed, he can be compelled to execute a *reformation* deed.
    A. True
110. Witnessing a deed is *attestation* of the deed.
    A. True

111. A quit claim deed is used to remove an *out-dated mortgage.*
    A. Cloud on title
112. A main objective of the Homestead Law is to protect against *executions* to satisfy debts.
    A. True
113. A deed acknowledged in a foreign country should be before a *notary public of that country.*
    A. Minister or Consul of this country
114. Owner of a condominium unit is able to obtain *F.H.A.* financing.
    A. True
115. Condominium ownership is the result of a *federal* enabling act.
    A. State
116. *Alluvial land* is generally unproductive land on which the cost of production approximates the gross return.
    A. Marginal
117. The process of paying off a loan by instalments is known as *acceleration.*
    A. Amortization
118. A decision of the Real Estate Commission may be appealed to the *Attorney General.*
    A. Court
119. *Tenancy at Sufferance* is the leasing by a tenant to another.
    A. Subletting
120. A *zoning ordinance* is an ordinance of a city limiting the character and use of property.
    A. True
121. A suit to quiet title is used to remove an *out-dated mortgage.*
    A. True

Chapter 11

SIMPLE ARITHMETIC, LAND DESCRIPTION PROBLEMS, AND CLOSING STATEMENTS

(For detailed working of arithmetic problems, see end of chapter.)

1. Q. If the annual 5 per cent interest payment on a mortgage amounts to $350, what is the amount of principal?
   A. $7,000
2. Q. A lot 80 feet by 120 feet deep cost $75 per front foot. What is the cost of the lot?
   A. $6,000
3. Q. A man built a house which was rectangular in shape. The dimensions were 24 feet by 36 feet. What is the total number of square feet in this house?
   A. 864 sq. ft.
4. Q. A loan made April 17 is repaid June 26. For how many days should the interest be calculated?
   A. 69 days
5. Q. How many board feet are there in 48 pieces of 2″ x 4″ lumber, each of which is 12 feet long?
   A. 384 board feet
6. Q. January 1 to March 15 is what fraction of a year?
   A. $\frac{5}{24}$ of a year
7. Q. Three and one-half months is what fraction of a year?
   A. $\frac{7}{24}$ of a year
8. Q. The decimal .375 is equal to what fraction?
   A. $\frac{3}{8}$
9. Q. The decimal .38⅓ is equal to what fraction?
   A. $\frac{23}{60}$
10. Q. The fraction ⅛ is what per cent?
    A. 12½%
11. Q. The fraction ⅙ is what per cent?
    A. 16⅔%
12. Q. What is the sum of ½ and ¾ and ⅛?
    A. 1⅜
13. Q. What is the difference between 1¼ and ⅜?
    A. ⅞
14. Q. One-half acre and five-eighths acre and three-sixteenths acre equals how many acres?
    A. 1$\frac{5}{16}$ acres
15. Q. If a farmer sells one-half of 20 acres and plans to divide one-

507

fourth of the balance into lots, how many acres are left?

A. 7½ acres

16. Q. What is one-half of one-fourth?

A. ⅛

17. Q. What is one-half divided by one-fourth?

A. 2

18. Q. Twenty-five days is what part of a year?

A. ⁵⁄₇₃

19. Q. Twenty-one days is what part of a month?

A. ⁷⁄₁₀ or .7

20. Q. Three-fifths is equivalent to what per cent?

A. 60%

21. Q. Eighty-seven and one-half per cent is equivalent to what fraction?

A. ⅞

22. Q. Six months is what part of three years?

A. ⅙

23. Q. How much is ⅔ multiplied by ½?

A. ⅓

24. Q. How much is ⅔ divided by ½?

A. ⁴⁄₃ or 1⅓

25. Q. How much is ½ divided by ⅔?

A. ¾

26. Q. Two-thirds of a year is how many months?

A. 8 months

27. Q. One-fifth of a year is how many days?

A. 73 days

28. Q. One-sixth of an acre is how many square feet?

A. 7,260 sq. ft.

29. Q. What part of an acre is 5,445 square feet?

A. ⅛ acre

30. Q. A farmer wants to sell part of his land but one-fourth he is giving to his son; ³⁄₁₆ to his daughter. What part of the land is left to sell?

A. ⁹⁄₁₆

31. Q. Add: 26½ + 19¾ + 8⅚ + 44⅔

A. 99¾

32. Q. Divide: 18½ ÷ 4⅙

A. 4¹¹⁄₂₅

33. Q. $223.65 is 5¼% of what amount?

A. $4,260.00

34. Q. Multiply: .75 × .83⅓   (express your answer in lowest fraction)

A. ⅝

35. Q. The value of a frame home at the end of 7 years was estimated to be $8,085. What was the original cost if the yearly depreciation was 2½%?

A. $9,800.00

36. Q. A property sells for $19,750.
You as listing salesman are to receive 12½% of the total 6% commission collected on the sale.
What amount will you receive?
A. $148.13

37. Q. What is the interest rate on a $13,800 loan when the monthly interest payments are $71.30 on the full amount?
A. 6.2 or 6⅕%

38. Q. An owner lists property for sale with a broker to net him $9,000, after paying the broker a 7 per cent commission. At what price would the broker have to sell the property?
A. $9,677.42

39. Q. A farm fronts on two roads running at right angles to each other. The frontage on one road is 5,280 feet, and on the other 2,640 feet. A third boundary line runs parallel to the shorter of the two road frontages, alongside the farm for a distance of 5,280 feet. How many acres is the farm?
A. 480 acres

40. Q. The mortgage loan on a house is $9,500. The monthly interest and amortization of principal require $9.50 per $1,000 of loan. The annual taxes are $291. The fire and extended coverage insurance rate is 98¢ per $100 on a three year policy on the amount of the original loan.
a. What is the monthly payment on interest and principal?
b. What is the monthly tax payment?
c. What is the monthly insurance payment?
d. What is the total monthly payment to be made on interest, principal, taxes and insurance?
A. a. $90.25
   b. $24.25
   c. $2.59
   d. $117.09

41. Q. A tract of land is bisected by a stream, leaving two triangular plots. One lot has a street frontage of 500 feet and a depth of 760 feet. How many acres does it (the one lot) contain?
A. 4.36 acres

42. Q. A farm earns $3,600 net after allowing $24 a month for all expenses. A buyer wants 6 per cent return on his money. What would he have to pay for the farm so as to gross 6 per cent?
A. $64,800

43. Q. One "rule of thumb" says that a person can afford to buy a home costing 2½ times his annual income.
What would be the minimum weekly salary of a factory worker to buy an $18,915 home using this rule?
A. $145.50

44. Q. A subdivider purchased a parcel of land 1320′ by 1980′.

How many ⅓ acre sites can he obtain in this parcel allowing 16⅔% of the total for streets and a school site?

A. 150

45. Q. An owner of a home had it listed for sale at a price which exceeded the F.H.A. appraisal by 15 per cent. He lowered the asking price to the appraisal figure, which was $9,265. What was the original listing price?

A. $10,654.75

46. Q. A lot 75′ wide and 115′ deep is assessed at $24 per front foot. The house is assessed at 4.8 times that of the lot. The tax rate is 68 mills. What are the annual taxes?

A. $709.92

47. Q. The owner of a farm said that ¼ was not usable, ⅗ was under cultivation, the remaining 60 acres was a grass meadow. How many acres is the whole farm?

A. 400

48. Q. A house is 27 feet long, 18 feet wide, and 9 feet high. Contractor "A" bids 29¢ per cubic foot, not including attic. Contractor "B" bids $1.95 per square foot of floor area, plus $17.50 per cubic yard of concrete used for a 6″ concrete floor. Contractor "C" bids $1,195.

(a) Q. What was contractor "A's" bid?

A. $1,268.46

(b) Q. What was contractor "B's" bid?

A. $1,105.20

(c) Q. Which contractor bid the lowest?

A. B

(d) Q. What is the dollar difference between the high and low bid?

A. $163.26

49. Q. A broker sold a lot 125 feet wide and 160 feet deep for 17 cents per square foot, but the purchaser assumed a paving lien of $2.25 per front foot. What total amount would the purchaser have to ask for the property if he expected to make a profit of $295 and give a clear title to the property?

A. $3,976.25

50. Q. If a man has a $325 weekly gross income from his property and a monthly expense of $845 on it, what is the annual per cent of interest return on his investment of $84,500?

A. 8 per cent

51. Q. What is the interest on $4,000 for 3 years, 5 months, and 20 days at 6½ per cent per annum?

A. $902.80

52. Q. A salesman has an agreement with his broker that all commissions collected on sales are to be divided as follows: 10% to the licensee who obtains the listing and the balance to be divided equally between the broker and the licensee who makes the sale. Salesman closes a $23,000 sale and the office collects a

5% commission of the gross sales price. What is the amount of commission earned by a salesman who made the sale but did not obtain the listing?

A. $517.50

53. Q. A sale was closed on a 190 acre farm on March 1, 1969. The sale price was $175.50 per acre. The buyers paid $5,000 in cash at the time of making the offer and agreed to assume a mortgage of $18,300, plus interest of $183, and signed a contract of sale in the amount of $3,972.07. How much additional cash did the buyer need at closing?

A. $5,889.93

54. Q. Jones built a house which was 26 feet by 38 feet and the average height was 14 feet. What is the number of cubic feet in this house?

A. 13,832 cu. ft.

55. Q. James Brown built a home which was 28 feet by 40 feet. It was a single-story ranch type. The cost of building averaged $11.25 per square foot. What was the total cost of the home?

A. $12,600

56. Q. Cole is asked to appraise an open lot with no improvements on it. The neighborhood is about 75 per cent built up. Most lots in the area are from 55 to 65 feet wide. The lot under appraisal is 60 feet. Comparable sales are found which indicate that lots are selling from $60 to $75 per front foot. What is a good estimate of price range for this lot?

A. $4,050

57. Q. An owner insists upon receiving $8,250 net for his property and will pay the broker 5% commission. What sales price must be asked to accomplish this?

A. $8,684.21

58. Q. What is the annual interest rate on a $5,000 loan when the quarterly interest payments are $93.75?

A. 7½%

59. Q. What will the taxes be for six months on property valued at $8,000 if the tax rate is $2.27 per $100 valuation per year?

A. $90.80

60. Q. An acre of land contains 43,560 sq. ft. What is the cost of a lot 132 ft. by 330 ft. at $800.00 per acre?

A. $800.00

61. Q. How much additional cash must a buyer furnish in addition to his $500 deposit if the lending institution grants 60% of an $8,000 home?

A. $2,700.00

62. Q. A man purchased a building for $120,000. His gross income was $23,000 per year. His expenses amounted to $11,000. What rate of return did he earn on his investment?

A. 10%

63. Q. An apartment house owner receives $4,800 per year net income from his investment of $60,000. What percentage does he receive on his money?

A. 8%

64. Q. $57.50 is 5% of what sum?

A. $1,150.00

65. Q. A lot 75 feet wide and 110 feet deep sold for $8,750.
What was the price per front foot?
What was the price per square foot?

A. $116.66 per front foot
$1.06 per square foot

66. Q. A broker sold a lot of 75 feet frontage by a depth of 120 feet at a price of 20¢ per square foot but the purchaser was to assume sewer and paving bills at the rate of $5.50 per front foot.
The buyer stated that he would list the property but would expect a profit of 10% plus the broker's commission of $590.00.
What would the new price be?

A. $3,023.75

67. Q. A two-story house cost $8,568 to build.
If the house had a frontage of 34 feet, a depth of 28 feet and was 30 feet high including the basement, what was the cost of the house per cubic foot?

A. $.30 per cubic foot

68. Q. If you bought two lots for $4,000 each, then made three lots out of this parcel and sold the lots for $3,000 each, how much did you make?
What per cent of profit was this on your investment?

A. $1,000.00
12½%

69. Q. A property has a net income of $8,500 a year.
If you want to earn 8% on your investment, how much would you pay for the property to realize this rate of return?

A. $106,250.00

70. Q. Compute the cost of excavation for a cellar 25 feet wide, 30 feet long and 5 feet deep at $2.90 per cubic yard.

A. $402.78

71. Q. You represent a seller offering a tract of land 495 feet wide and 1,320 feet deep. The selling price is at the rate of $200.00 per acre. What is the total price?

A. $3,000.00

72. Q. A man bought two lots for $3,000 each, divided them into three lots and sold the three lots for $2,400 each.
What was his percentage of gross profit?

A. 20%

73. Q. Bell wishes to build a flat-roofed building 130 feet long, 30 feet wide and 24 feet high.
Dusch offers to build such a structure for $8.90 per square foot.

Sherwin offers to build the building for $.37½ per cubic foot. How much will Bell save by giving the building contract to Dusch?

A. $390.00

74. Q. In a contract for sale of real estate, the sales price is fixed at $6,000 and of this amount $1,200 is paid down at the time of the sale and the balance is payable in monthly installments of $50.00 plus and in addition to which the buyer pays interest. The contract is dated January 1, 1965 and the 1st payment is due February 1, 1965.

Assuming that all payments are made regularly and not more than $50.00 is paid on the principal on any installment date, state when contract will be paid in full.

A. January 1, 1973

75. Q. Jones is working on a 50-50 split commission with your firm. He sells the S ½ of the NE ¼ of Sec. 27, T-8-N, R-14-E of 6th P.M. for $207.50 per acre.

The commission schedule for your agency calls for 5% on the first $20,000; 3% on the next $15,000; and 1½% on the balance of the selling price.

Jones must pay 7½% of his share of the commission to Lawrence, the salesman who listed the property.

What is the net amount Jones will receive for this sale?

A. $383.87

76. Q. There is a balance of $9,000 due on a real estate contract that requires monthly payments of $80.00 plus interest at 6% per annum payable monthly.

What would be the total monthly payments for:

(a) the first month   (b) the third month   (c) the fifth month?

A. (a) $125.00
   (b) $124.20
   (c) $123.40

77. Q. A broker has a problem of subdividing a ten acre tract into 50 × 100 foot lots; after allowing 85,600 square feet for the necessary streets, how many lots will the broker realize from this subdivision?

A. 70

78. Q. A certain commercial property was a two story structure. It measured 46 feet by 80 feet. The height of the first story was 16 feet and the second was 14 feet. The estimated unit cost of reproduction is 80¢ per cubic foot for the first story and 60¢ per cubic foot for the second story. What is the estimated reproduction cost of this building?

A. $78,016.00

79. Q. A man bought two lots, one for $3,000 which was 60% the cost of the other. What was the cost of the other lot?

A. $5,000

80. Q. There is an F.H.A. conditional commitment on a duplex which is not going to be occupied by owners, for $24,750. On closing the loan the mortgage banker collected a 4% discount. The F.H.A. insured value rates were as follows:
    97% of the first $15,000
    90% of the next $5,000
    75% of the balance, not to exceed $27,500
    Because the owner is not going to live in the property, he can borrow only 85% of the amount which he could borrow if he did occupy the property. How much discount will the borrower have to pay (in dollars and cents)?
    A. $768.83
81. Q. Lawrence leased a storeroom to Davis on a percentage basis. The lease calls for a minimum monthly rental of $400 plus 5% of the gross yearly business over $80,000. How much rent would Lawrence receive yearly from Davis, if Davis did a gross business of $120,000?
    A. $6,800.00
82. Q. A 6,400 square foot hillside lot is to be subdivided and sold. One-fourth of the lot is too steep to be useful and $3/16$ of the lot is taken up by a small stream. The remaining area is flat. If $1/8$ of the usable area is reserved for roads, how many square feet of usable area is left?
    A. 3,150 sq. ft.
83. Q. A lot measuring 100 feet wide and 330 feet deep, would be approximately what fraction of an acre?
    A. $3/4$ acre
84. Q. There is a close relationship between the monthly rent obtainable for a property and the price the property will bring on the market. In an area that was beginning to run down, properties on the average were selling for 92 times their monthly rent. In a newer district they were selling for 112 times the rent. If a property had a monthly rental of $95 per month, what would it be worth in each of the areas?
    A. $8,740 in older district; $10,640 in newer district
85. Q. A man purchased a lot for $2,000. He built a house on the lot which cost $14,500. During the construction period, he had several offers to rent the property for $125 per month. Six months after he moved in, the city condemned 15 feet of the front of the lot for widening the street to speed up traffic. In attempting to rent the house, he found that the best offer was $110 per month. By investigation we find that the current capitalization rate is 6%.
    a. What type of depreciation has this property suffered?
    b. By capitalizing the loss of income, what is the amount of loss in value?
    A. a. Economic depreciation
       b. $3,000

86. Q. Assuming that Mr. Davis has $13,500 invested in his property, what will be the net return on his investment (in percentage) per year if he rents his property for $150 per month and if the yearly cost for taxes is $396; for insurance $66; and for miscellaneous expense $123?

A. 9%

87. Q. An office building has a total income of $53,200 per year. The yearly expenses are: Taxes, $8,925.25; Insurance, $1,510.60; Heating and Air-conditioning, $4,920.05; and Miscellaneous Expense, $3,644.10. If the owner values the building at $360,000, what will be his net return?

A. $34,200

88. Q. Cooper sold two vacant lots for a total of $11,385, which was 15 per cent more than he paid for them three years ago. During the time he owned the lots, he paid taxes each year at the rate of 48 mills on the assessed valuation of 45 per cent of his purchase price. If he figures a yearly interest loss of 3½ per cent on his original investment, what was his profit or loss?

A. $199.53 loss

89. Q. A lot is 50 feet front by 180 feet. The owner, John Davis, had only $5,000 cash. The lot cost $63 per front foot, and the house cost was $9,216. He secured a mortgage for the balance. If his interest was 5½ per cent per annum, payable semi-annually, what was the amount of his first semi-annual interest payment?

A. $202.57

90. Q. The above owner, Davis, decided to build a fence around his original lot. The cost of the fence was 80¢ per linear foot excluding gates at the front and rear of the lot. These gates are 3½ feet wide and cost $16.75 each. What is the total cost of the fence including the gates?

A. $395.90

91. Q. Davis next decides to construct a driveway. Concrete costs $13.50 per cubic yard and labor costs are 20¢ per square foot. What will be the total cost of the driveway which is 36 feet long, 8 feet wide and 3 inches thick?

A. $93.59

92. Q. A loan made April 17 is repaid June 26. For how many days should the interest be calculated?

A. 69 days

93. Q. Jim Underwood and John Davis traded properties. Underwood's property was valued at $14,250. Davis' property was valued at $17,350. The difference in equities was $2,015.07. Underwood's equity was $4,901.25. His equity is greater than Davis' equity. What was the total amount of encumbrance against each property?

A. Underwood $9,348.75
Davis $14,463.82

94. Q. How many cubic yards of gravel would be needed to fill a trench 36 feet long, 9 feet wide and 18 inches deep?
    A. 18 cubic yards

95. Q. J. R. Brady pays $125 a month rent. He could buy the property for $9,800. He has $2,000 in his savings account earning 2% per year, compounded semi-annually; fire insurance premium is $22.50 per annum; taxes are $146.40 annually; upkeep is 1½% of property cost; and depreciation is 2% of the property cost. He could borrow the remainder of the purchase price at 4½% interest per year.
    (a) What would be the total cost of owning the house the first year?
    (b) What would he save by owning instead of renting?
    A. (a) $903.10
       (b) $596.90

96. Q. Charles Walker has purchased a lot for $9,000. It has a frontage of 100 feet and contains one-half acre of land. Ascertain what the lot cost. (a) per front foot. (b) per square foot. (c) what it would cost per acre. (d) what is the depth of the lot?
    A. (a) $90. (b) 41 cents. (c) $18,000 (d) 217.8 feet.

97. Q. If building costs are $12.50 per sq. ft. and you build a house 33' wide × 48' long, with an offset for a game room of an additional 6' × 20', how much would it cost to build the house?
    A. $21,300

98. Q. If 5¼% is the annual rate of interest and the monthly interest payment is $58.45, what is the amount of the original loan?
    A. $13,360

99. Q. A broker is sub-dividing a 4½ acre tract into 50' × 100' lots. After allowing 71,020 square feet for the necessary streets, in how many lots can the tract be divided?
    A. 25 lots

100. Q. There is a balance of $7,500 due on a land purchase contract that requires monthly payments of $60.00 plus interest at 6% per annum, payable monthly. What would be the total payment for the 1st, 3rd and 5th months?
    A. $97.50; $96.90; $96.30

101. Q. What would be the F.H.A. insurable loan on a dwelling if the F.H.A. insured 97% of the first $13,500 of valuation and 85% of the remainder and the F.H.A. valuation is $18,500?
    A. $17,345

102. Q. Montgomery owns a property which gives him a gross income of $1,600 per month. His annual expenses are 45%. What is his net income per year on the property?
    A. $10,560

103. Q. Bennett has a principal balance of $6,000 on his mortgage. His interest rate is 5% per annum. His taxes and insurance total $108 per year. His monthly payment is $60, covering interest,

taxes, insurance, and the balance applied to principal. What is his principal balance after making the first payment?

    A. $5,974

104. Q. A building has been leased to a supermart with the rent based on 1½% of the gross sales, with a minimum rental of $10,000 annually.

    (a) If its first year sales were $600,000, how much rent was paid?

    (b) If its fourth year sales were $1,000,000, how much rent was paid?

    A. (a) $10,000

        (b) $15,000

105. Q. A property is worth $16,000 and the furniture and household effects are worth $5,600. The owner insures them at 72% of their value. The annual rate on the dwelling is $3.10 per $1,000 and $3.65 on the personal property. If the premium for a 3-year policy is 2½ times the premium for one year, how much can the owner save by taking out a 3-year policy?

    A. $25.21

106. Q. What is the annual interest rate on a $6,000 loan when the interest payments are $105 semi-annually on the full amount?

    A. 3½%

107. Q. $25 is 5% of what amount?

    A. $500

108. Q. The loan on a property is 65% of its appraised valuation. If the interest rate is 5% and the first semi-annual interest payment is $167.50, what is the appraised value of the property?

    A. $10,307.69

109. Q. John Kane, salesman, is working on a 50-50 split commission with his employing broker, L. Fairchild. Kane sells a 280-acre farm at $105 per acre. The commission schedule calls for 5% on the first $15,000; 3½% on the next $10,000 and 2% on the balance. Kane must pay another salesman, Paul Stark, who listed the property, 10% of his share of the commission. What is the net amount Kane will receive?

    A. $534.60

110. Q. There is a balance of $12,000 due on a real estate contract that requires monthly payments of $120, plus interest, at 5% per annum, payable monthly. What would be the total monthly payments for the first month, third month, fifth month?

    A. First month—$170   Third Month—$169   Fifth Month—$168

111. Q. A salesman brings in a listing on a $5,000 home and is to receive 10% of the total 5% commission when the property is sold. If a second salesman sells the house and the 10% is deducted from his half of the commission, the second salesman would receive how much?

    A. $100

112. Q. The assessed value of all property in the city of Uranium is $12,000,000. The city budget is $600,000. Your property is assessed at $40,000. What taxes would you pay?
   A. $2,000

113. Q. A broker receives half the first month's rent for leasing an apartment and 5% of each month's rent thereafter for collecting the rent of $85 per month. What would be his total commission after 18 months?
   A. $114.75

114. Q. A salesman brings in a listing on a $5,000 home and is to receive 15% of the total of 5% commission when the property is sold. If another salesman sells the house and the 15% is deducted from his half of the commission, he would receive how much?
   A. $87.50

115. Q. The taxes on a house were $126. The taxes were due January 1st and were paid by the owner. What refund would he get from a purchaser if he sold the house and the taxes were prorated as of September 15th?
   A. $36.75

116. Q. The schedule of commissions for negotiating a 20-year lease was 5% for the first year, 2% for each of the next four years, 1½% for each of the next 10 years, and 1% for each year thereafter. What was the total commission earned if the yearly rent was $6,500?
   A. $2,145

117. Q. A man has an opportunity to buy a lot for $1,000 and a guarantee of resale value one year later of $1,200. He also has an opportunity to lend $1,000 to an individual with repayment within a year at 10% interest. Which is the better investment and by what amount?
   A. The lot by $100

118. Q. A man borrows $1,000 for 9 months at 5% per year. What amount does he have to repay?
   A. $1,037.50

119. Q. A man borrows money for 6 months at 6% payable in advance. How much must he borrow in order to have $1,000 cash immediately?
   A. $1,030.93

120. Q. A lending institution advertises that it has no hidden charges or costs—that the charge on loans is simply 3% on the unpaid balance each month. If a man borrows $120.00 and pays $10.00 plus interest each month, what is the actual rate of interest paid for the year?
   A. 19½%

121. Q. If a man receives $525.00 at the end of 6 months on money invested at 6% per year, how much has he invested?
   A. $17,500

122. Q. A real estate salesman receives 5% commission for selling a house for $16,800. How much did the salesman receive? How much did the owner receive?

A. $840, salesman received $15,960, owner received.

123. Q. If property is assessed at $14,000 and the tax rate is $21 per $1,000 of assessed valuation, how much will the tax be?

A. $294.00

124. Q. A man borrowed $1,500 which he agreed to repay at 5½% interest a year. He paid $27.50 interest; how long did he keep the money?

A. 4 months

125. Q. A construction company developing a new shopping center borrowed $2,000,000 repayable in 5 years. If $550,000 interest was paid, what was the rate of interest?

A. 5½%

126. Q. A man bought a farm for $8,800 and sold it for $10,000. His selling expenses were $100.00. His profit was what per cent of the cost?

A. 12½%

127. Q. If Mr. Jones had a furnished patio at the rear of his home, he could sell his property for $15,000. Without this addition he can get only $14,500. If a 12′ by 18′ pavement 4″ thick costs $18.00 a cubic yard and labor $1.80 per cubic yard, barbecue pit $35.00, and furniture $212.00, how much profit would Mr. Jones make by adding and furnishing a patio?

A. $200.20

128. Q. How many acres are there in the following diagram?

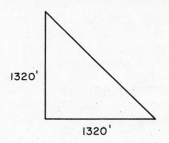

1320′

1320′

A. 20 acres

129. Q. A house and lot sold for $22,500. The transaction closed on May 15, 1969. A first trust deed and note with a balance of $15,200 at time of closing, bearing interest at 6¼ per cent per annum and payments of $100 per month, including interest, on the first day of each month, is assumed by the purchaser. Payments are current. What interest is due on the loan at the time of closing?

A. $39.58

130. Q. A small acreage sold for $3,600. A cash payment of $1,200 was made and the balance is to be paid in four equal annual principal instalments plus interest. The interest rate on all deferred payments is 6 per cent. What amount will be paid in interest?

A. $360

131. Q. At the end of a six month period, a borrower paid $600 of the principal, plus the interest due, on a loan of $2,400 at 6% interest. He made regular payments annually of $600 plus interest due until the loan was repaid. What was his total interest cost?

A. $288

132. Q. Adams owns nine acres of downtown property which he listed for sale with Brown for $78,300. Crowe would like to purchase a part of the listed property. He requires 100 feet × 145.2 feet. Based on the listed price, what will he have to pay for this portion?

A. $2,900

133. Q. Ray Upton inherited $6,500, which was $2\frac{1}{6}$ times as much as his sister Ann received. How much did Ann inherit?

A. $3,000

134. Q. A building burned 16 bulbs at 25 watts each, 24 hours a day, and 2 bulbs (25 watts each) burned 12 hours daily. All bulbs are used every day. What is the June electric bill if the cost is based on $3\frac{1}{2}$¢ per kilowatt-hour?

A. $10.71

135. Q. The perimeter of a rectangular lot is 108 yards. The length is 6 yards greater than twice the width. What are the length and width of the lot?

A. 16 yards × 38 yards

136. Q. Mr. Brown bought a home for $25,000, built a swimming pool costing $1,500 and spent $625 on filtering and cleaning equipment. The following month he received an unexpected promotion and had to relocate in another state. If he listed his property at $30,000, how much profit could he expect to make? What per cent would the profit be over his investment?

A. $2,875   10.6%

137. Q. Mr. Gray has a $5,000 mortgage on his summer home. He makes quarterly payments of $300.00 plus 6% annual interest on the balance. How much did he pay the first year including interest?

A. $1,473

138. Q. A man has an option of buying a house for $21,000 cash or for $1,000 down and three annual payments of $7,000. If his money realizes 5% compounded annually, which is the better plan and by how much?

A. The payment plan by $85.00

139. Q. A man can buy a house for $12,500 cash or for $4,000 down and $9,000 at the end of the year. If his money is invested at 5% compounded semi-annually, which plan should he follow? Why?

A. Pay $12,500 cash because his money cannot earn the $500 difference in one year.

140. Q. (a) Add: (b) Subtract: (c) Multiply:

$756.32		
827.56		
432.47		
761.33	$981,876.03	$41,986
532.45	897,439.98	499

     A. $3,310.13 $ 84,436.05 $20,951,014

141. Q. A salesman sells a property for $5,800. His contract with the broker is 60% to the broker and 40% to salesman. The sales commission with the owner is 5%. What is the broker's share of the commissions?

     A. $174

142. Q. You are employed as a salesman by Henry Bowen and Co. It is agreed that all commissions collected by the office on sales made by you are to be divided as follows: 10% to the sales manager and the balance to be divided equally between your employer and yourself. You close a deal on which the sales price is $8,500 and the office collects a 5% commission on the sales price. What amount of commission is due you?

     A. $191.25

143. Q. A note is dated April 15, 1968, the amount of the note is $1,700; the interest rate is 5%; interest is payable quarterly; none of the interest is paid. How much interest will be due on January 15, 1969?

     A. $63.75

144. Q. The value of a frame house at the end of 6 years was estimated to be $7,650. What was the original cost of the house if the yearly rate of depreciation was $2\frac{1}{2}$%?

     A. $9,000

145. Q. The commission rate for selling an apartment house was 5% of the first $10,000 and $2\frac{1}{2}$% for all over that amount. The broker received a commission of $730. What did the property sell for?

     A. $19,200

146. Q. In a contract for the sale of real estate, the sales price is fixed at $5,800. Of this amount $1,600 is paid down at the time of sale, and the balance is payable in monthly installments of not less than $30 each, in addition to which the buyer pays the accrued interest. The contract is dated January 2, 1961; the first principal payment is due February 1, 1961. Assuming that all payments are made regularly and not more than $30 is paid on principal on any installment date, state when the contract will be paid out in full.

     A. September 2, 1972

147. Q. The real value of a certain property is $6,000. It is assessed at 60% of its real value. It is taxed at the rate of 55 mills on the assessed value. What are the taxes?

     A. $198

148. Q. A broker sold a lot 60 ft. by 120 ft. at the price of 10 cents per square foot, but the purchaser assumed a paving lien of $2.50 per front foot. What price would the purchaser have to ask for the lot if he wanted to sell at a profit of $150 and give clear title to the lot?
     A. $1,020

149. Q. Assume that a buyer of real estate, as part of the purchase price, gives back to the seller a mortgage for $20,000, bearing interest at the rate of 4% per annum. The principal of the mortgage is to be repaid in installments of not less than $500 each, plus the interest accrued at the time of payment of each installment. The mortgage is dated December 1, 1968 and the first install-ment is due March 1, 1969. What sum will be due on the mort-gage on March 1, 1969?
     A. $700

150. Q. On September 1, 1968, you gave your note bearing said date to a mortgage company in which you promised to pay $2,000 in monthly installments of not less than $35 each inclusive of in-terest at 6% per annum on the monthly balances of the note. Each payment as made is applied (1) to accrued interest and (2) to reduction of the principal of the note. You make only the following payments:
     October 1, 1968 $35
     November 1, 1968 $60
     December 1, 1968 $45
     On January 1, 1969 (a) how much have you paid as interest? (b) what is the unpaid balance of the note?
     A. (a) $29.49   (b) $1,889.49

151. Q. Taxes on a parcel of property are $1,325.28 for the current year. The first one-half of the taxes were paid by the seller. The deal will be closed as of December 15. In prorating the taxes, how much should be charged the seller for his share?
     A. $607.42

152. Q. A man has property which gives him a gross income of $325 per month, his monthly expenses average $155 per month, what is his net income per year on the property?
     A. $2,040

153. Q. Figure the cost of a tract of land 250 ft. frontage by 750 ft. in depth, at a cost of $950 per acre.
     A. $4,088.80

154. Q. The selling price of a certain property is $13,000. The sale can be financed if the buyer can pay 18% down, plus a loan com-mission of 1.5% of the loan. How much money must the buyer have to pay the down payment and loan cost?
     A. $2,499.90

155. Q. A tract of land, 65 ft. wide and 150 ft. deep sold for $1.25 per sq.

ft., plus $10 for each front foot. What was the price of the land?

A. $12,837.50

156. Q. A piece of property 326.7 feet long and 200 feet wide is for sale. The owner wants $5,000 an acre. What is the selling price?

A. $7,500

157. Q. If building costs in your area are $12.50 per sq. ft. and you wanted to build a dwelling house 33 ft. wide and 48 ft. long, with an offset for the family room of an additional 6 ft. by 20 ft., how much would it cost to construct this dwelling house?

A. $21,300

158. Q. The length of the South side of the NE ¼ of the NE ¼ of a section is how many feet?

A. 1,320 feet (40 acres)

159. Q. What would be the cost to build a driveway 36 feet long, 9 feet wide, and 4 inches thick if concrete costs $15 per cubic yard and labor costs are twenty cents per square foot?

A. $124.80

160. Q. An investor paid $36,000 for a four-unit apartment house. Each apartment rents for $85 per month. It is estimated that by good management a profit of 45% of gross rentals could be made. What rate of return should this man make on his investment?

A. 5.1%

161. Q. How many acres are there in the W ½ of the SW ¼ of the SW ¼ of a section?

A. 20 acres

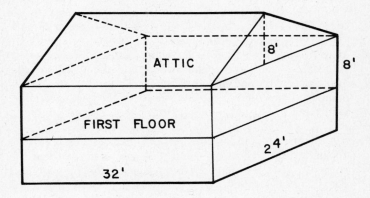

ATTIC

FIRST FLOOR

8'

8'

32'

24'

PEAR STREET   LOT SIZE

50' wide
180' deep

The house shown in the diagram was built by Mr. Brown on a lot 50 feet by 180 feet. This is a one-story house, with basement and expansion attic.

The house faces south and fronts on Pear Street.

The following 15 questions are based, at least partially, on the diagram.

162. Q. What is the total cubic content of the house, including attic and basement?

  A. 15,360 cubic feet

163. Q. What is the building cost of the house per square foot of main floor space if the cost of the house, exclusive of the lot, was $10,828.80?

  A. $14.10

164. Q. The assessed valuation of the 50 foot lot was $44 per front foot. The house was assessed at $6,500. The tax rate is 48 mills. What are the yearly taxes?

  A. $417.60

165. Q. Mr. Brown had only $6,500 cash. The lot cost $65 per front foot, and the house cost was $10,828.80. He secured a mortgage for the balance. If his interest was 5% per annum, payable semi-annually, what was the amount of his first semi-annual interest payment?

  A. $189.47

166. Q. Mr. Brown received two bids for the construction of the house. The bid from "A" was for 77½¢ per cubic foot for the main floor, basement and attic. The second bid, from "B" was for $4.70 per square foot of floor area for the main floor, basement and attic. Which was the lower bid? How much lower?

  A. "B" $1,075.20 lower

167. Q. If the house cost $10,828.80 to build, and depreciated an average of 2% each year, what would be the value of the entire property at the end of ten years, if, in the meantime, the lot had increased in value 22% above its original cost of $65 per front foot?

  A. $12,628.04

168. Q. Mr. Brown paid $65 per front foot for his lot. He paid $10,828.80 to the building contractor and paid the architect 5% of the building cost. He then placed a mortgage on the property for three-fourths of the total cost. What was his equity in the property, after he placed the mortgage?

  A. $3,655.06

169. Q. Mr. Brown decided to build a fence around his original lot. The cost of the fence was 85¢ per linear foot excluding gates at the front and rear of the lot. These 4-foot gates cost $21.75 each. What is the total cost of the fence including the gates?

  A. $427.70

170. Q. Concrete costs $14.25 per cubic yard and labor costs are 27¢

per square foot. What will be the total cost of Mr. Brown's driveway which is 36 feet long, 6 feet wide and 4 inches thick?

A. $96.32

171. Q. Assuming that Mr. Brown has $14,000 invested in his property what will be the net return on his investment (in percentage) per year if he rents his property for $155 per month and if the yearly cost for taxes is $402; for insurance $78; and for miscellaneous expense $260?

A. 8%

172. Q. The monthly payments on the mortgage referred to in Question 168 above are $75 including interest at 6% per annum on the unpaid balance. All payments are due and payable on the 10th day of each month. If the first monthly payment was made on May 10th of this year and if all subsequent payments have been made when due, what would be the principal balance after making the June payment this year?

A. $10,924.74

173. Q. Mr. Brown paid $65 per front foot for his original lot. He later decided to enlarge the original lot and can buy adjoining land to the east at a price of $1.50 per square foot. He wants to limit his total investment in land to $7,300. How many square feet will there be in his entire lot after he buys the additional land?

A. 11,700 sq. ft.

174. Q. Mr. Brown owned a lot immediately to the west of his original lot. He sold this extra lot for $4,250 net after paying the commission. He had owned the lot for 5 years and during that time he had paid taxes on it at the rate of $42.25 per year per $1,000 of assessed valuation which was 55% of the original purchase price of $3,100. If you figure an annual 4% interest loss on his original investment, did Mr. Brown make a profit or take a loss on this transaction?

A. Profit, $169.82

175. Q. Mr. Brown has purchased a 1½ acre hillside lot at the rear of his original lot which he intends to sell for building purposes. One-fourth of the lot is too steep to be useful and one-third of the lot is taken up by a small stream. The remaining area is flat. If one-sixth of the usable area is reserved for roads, how many square feet will be left for building purposes?

A. 22,687.5 sq. ft.

176. Q. Don Duncan, a salesman, is working on a 50-50 split commission basis with your firm. He sells Mr. Brown's property for 15% less than the listed price of $17,000. The commission schedule of your firm calls for 6% on the full selling price. Duncan must pay another salesman, Roy Rayer, 20% of his share of the commission. What is the net amount Duncan will receive for the sale?

A. $346.80

177. Q. What is the annual interest rate on an $8,000 loan when the in-

terest payments are $100 per quarter on the full amount?

A. 5%

178. Q. A property sold for $50,000 with a down payment of 15%. The first mortgage (Deed of Trust) for the balance is payable at $7.50 per thousand per month, including interest at 5½% per annum. What will be the monthly payments?

A. $318.75

179. Q. An investment property has averaged a net income of $3,000 per year over the past five years. The owner has charged off adequate depreciation during the period. Assuming that 5% is a fair profit on this property, what is a reasonable estimate of the capitalized value of the property?

A. $60,000

180. Q. A lot 69 feet wide and 142 feet long sold for $2,645.46. How much would the owner receive per square foot?

A. Twenty-seven cents.

181. Q. A broker sells a 50′ × 100′ lot for 75¢ a square foot. If the sales commission is 5%, how much does the seller receive?

A. $3,562.50

182. Q. What is the annual rate of interest on a $4,200 loan when the quarterly interest payments are $57.55?

A. 5½%

183. Q. A farm of 60 acres, listed for sale at $150 per acre, was finally sold for $7,650 on condition that the purchaser pay the 10% commission of the sale price. How much did the buyer save below the list price?

A. $585

184. Q. A seller paid his 1968 taxes in the amount of $300. He sells the property on March 15, 1968. He should receive a tax refund from the buyer in what amount?

A. $237.50

185. Q. Brown leases a storeroom to Smith on a percentage basis. The lease calls for a minimum monthly rental of $300 and 5% on the gross yearly business over $80,000. How much rent would Brown receive yearly from Smith if Smith did a gross business of $120,000?

A. $5,600

186. Q. A lot 86 feet wide and 110 feet deep sold for $7,095. What was the price per front foot? Per square foot?

A. $82.50 per front foot
$.75 per square foot

187. Q. You have determined that there are 1,600 square feet in a house, and the garage is 20′ × 30′. The cost of the building of the house is $11 per square foot and $4 per square foot for the garage. The 50 foot lot on which the house is located costs $15 per front foot. What is the total cost of the house, garage, and lot?

A. $20,750

188. Q. C. D. Sloan built a house 33′ 6″ × 45′ 6″, which had an offset for
the family room of an additional 5′ × 15′. If construction costs
were $12.85 per square foot, how much would it cost to build
the house?
   A. $20,550.36
189. Q. A lot near Manor Creek has been appraised as follows: 3,250
square feet hillside area at $0.14 a square foot; 2,000 square feet
of stream area at $0.08½ a square foot and 7,250 square feet
of flat area at $1.00 a square foot. If the tract is to be sold as a
whole, what must the price be per square foot?
   A. $0.63 per square foot
190. Q. A property was sold on the basis of 5 per cent commission on
the first $10,000 of the sale and 2½ per cent on the excess
amount over $10,000. The total commission was $730. What was
the selling price of the property?
   A. $19,200
191. Q. John Ford is building two patios. One is in the shape of a
square, with 30 feet on each side. The other is in the form of a
circle, with a diameter of 27 feet. Which is the larger and by
how much?
   A. a. Square
      b. 327.735 square feet larger
192. Q. A room in an office building is 40 feet long, 24 feet wide and
15 feet high. How many workers should occupy the room, if 200
cubic feet of air space is allocated to each person?
   A. 72 persons
193. Q. A basement is 20 feet long, 15 feet wide. How many cubic yards
of earth were removed, if the basement was dug to a depth of
9 feet? It cost the owner $3.40 per cubic yard of earth removed.
What was the total cost?
   A. a. 100 cubic yards
      b. $340
194. Q. Smith is building a house with dimensions of 45 feet by 25 feet
and 8 feet deep. If he engages trucks capable of carrying 4
cubic yards each, how many truck-loads will be required in the
excavation operation?
   A. 84 truck-loads
195. Q. Smith also employs a well digger, whose rate is $9.00 for the
first foot dug and an increase of $1.25 for each additional foot
dug. Before the well was fully completed, it was necessary to
dig 60 feet. What was the cost of the well?
   A. $2,752.50
196. Q. Stone has moved into a new office, measuring 15 feet by 24 feet.
He purchases wall-to-wall carpet at $14.95 per square yard;
what did the carpet cost him?
   A. $598
197. Q. Mrs. Stone has bought a new home and intends to make her

own window drapes. A helpful salesman tells her there are 8 windows to be draped and each requires 2 yards of material. She purchased the material at a sale at $3.90 per yard. What did the drapes cost her?

A. $62.40

198. Q. "A" is exchanging his house for a farm owned by "B." "A" agrees to allow "B," the owner of the 240 acre farm, $60 per acre to apply on "A's" house, which is valued at $23,500. How much cash difference will "B" owe "A"?

A. $9,100

199. Q. Louis Dubbs, Broker, has a property listed at $16,000. George Adams purchases it for $13,600 and sells it for $16,000. What percentage profit did he make?

A. 17.6%

200. Q. A man purchased a building for $120,000. His gross income was $23,000 per year and his expenses were $11,000. What rate of return would he receive on his investment?

A. 10%

201. Q. The 1968 taxes on a residence are $400; the millage rate for all taxes is 40 mills. The taxing authority has assessed property at 50% of the established market value. What is the market value?

A. $20,000

202. Q. If an apartment building costing $21,000 has an income of $140 per month, what percentage would it be returning annually on the investment?

A. 8%

203. Q. Mr. Stone has a principal balance of $6,000 on his mortgage. His interest rate is 5% per annum. His monthly payment is $60 cover-interest, and the balance applied against the principal. What is his principal balance after making his first payment?

A. $5,965

204. Q. The sales price of a property is $10,000. The land value is $1,500. What amount of fire insurance should be recommended that the buyer carry?

A. $8,500

205. Q. A section of land is exactly square and contains exactly 640 acres and all boundaries run exactly north and south, or east and west, as the case may be, and a person buys all land in the section lying southwesterly of a line which crosses the section and running north 45° west, at $1,250 per acre, cash on date of closing. What amount of United States Internal Revenue stamps are necessary to be placed on the deed?

A. No stamps are necessary. They have not been required since January 1968.

206. Q. Doe leases a storeroom to Roe on a percentage basis. The lease calls for a minimum monthly rent of $300 and 5% on the gross yearly business over $80,000. How much rent would Doe receive

yearly from Roe if Roe did a gross business of $140,000?
A. $6,600

207. Q. A farm of 60 acres listed for sale at $150 an acre, was finally sold for $7,650 on condition that the purchaser pay the 10% commission of sale price. How much did the buyer actually save on the transaction?
A. $585

208. Q. Assume that a $9,000 fire insurance policy is dated March 1, 1968. It was issued for three years at a premium of $158.40. What is the prorated value of the unused portion as of November 16, 1968?
A. $121

209. Q. A 100 by 100-foot lot was assessed at $15 per front foot and the house assessed at $3,200. What was the total yearly tax if the rate was 40 mills?
A. $188.00

210. Q. A small home can be rented for $50 a month or bought for $6,800 ($6,200 for the house; $600 for the lot). The annual cost of owning and living in a $6,800 home may be computed as follows:
Interest 3%. Painting and repairs of house 2½%. Taxes $24 per $1,000 on 75% value of house and lot. Insurance $4.50 per $1,000 on $6,200, the value of the house. 5% for care of lot; value of lot $600.
How much less would it be to buy the property and live in it than to rent it?
A. $5.05 per month. (Interest $17; Repairs $12.92; Taxes $10.20; Insurance $2.33; Lot upkeep $2.50. Total monthly expenses $44.95. Rent $50 less $44.95)

211. Q. The value of a house at the end of eight years was estimated to be $14,400. What was the value of the house when new if the yearly rate of depreciation was 2½%?
A. $18,000

212. Q. A property is assessed for $5,000. The tax rate is $3.50 per $100 with 5% discount for promptness and a 5% penalty for tardiness. What three possible amounts could be paid as taxes on this property?
A. $175 $166.25 $183.75

213. Q. What is three months' interest on $566.66 at 5% per annum?
A. $7.08

214. Q. The seller's equity in a real estate contract is $2,160, payable in monthly installments of exactly $45 per month, no more, no less. These installments do not include any interest. Assuming that the first payment is made October 1, 1976, that payments are due on the first day of each month thereafter, the last payment will become due on what date?
A. September 1, 1980

215. Q. $150 is 2½% of what amount?
    A. $6,000

216. Q. How many square feet are there in an acre?
    A. 43,560

217. Q. A real estate broker is given a contract to manage an apartment building, the eight units of which yield a monthly rent of $50 each. The maximum commission allowed is 5% of rents collected and one-half month's rent for each apartment rented, but the latter charge is not to exceed one leasing commission for each unit per year, and not more than one commission of either kind is to be levied against any one unit in any one month. What is the possible maximum yearly commission for the building?
    A. $420

218. Q. A fire insurance policy was taken out for three years dated June 1, 1967, and the premium for three years was $36. The property was sold January 1, 1969. How would you prorate the premium?
    A. Buyer would be charged $17

219. Q. $25 is 5% of what amount?
    A. $500

220. Q. A new house and lot cost Snyder $14,000. Of this total price it was estimated that the lot was worth $2,000. The owner held the property for six years. Assuming an annual depreciation of 2½% on the house and an annual increase in value of 8% on the lot; what was the total value of the property at the end of six years?
    A. $13,160

221. Q. What is the gross yearly income of a property that has six apartments, two apartments paying a monthly rental of $55 each, two apartments at $75 monthly each, and two apartments at $90 monthly each?
    A. $5,280

222. Q. At settlement on June 15, 1969 a purchaser assumes the existing mortgage of $4,500 on which the interest at 5% per annum has been paid up to December 15, 1968. Prorate the amount due at settlement and state whether this item is a debit or credit to purchaser?
    A. $112.50 which is a credit to the purchaser

223. Q. What is the annual interest rate on an $8,000 loan when the interest payments are $80 per quarter on the full amount?
    A. 4%

224. Q. The net amount received by Mr. Wheller for his property after his broker had deducted a sales commission of 4% and an allowance of $70 for advertising was $7,850. What was the selling price?
    A. $8,250

225. Q. A building was sold for $50,000. At the time of closing the deal, credit was given the purchaser for a $20,000 first mortgage and a $7,000 second mortgage. What amount of Federal documentary stamps was placed on the deed in 1967?

A. $25.30

226. Q. After making proper deductions for expense of operation there is left a net income of $1,800 a year. What percentage of income is this on a purchase price of $20,000?

A. 9%

227. Q. A lot of 55 feet frontage and 100 feet depth has been sold at $35 per front foot. Compute your commission at 5% of the selling price.

A. $96.25

228. Q. Alfred Sims bought a lot for $1,000. He sold it for $1,300 at the end of three years, having paid $25 taxes on it for each year. What is his profit counting lost interest of 2% on his investment each year as an expense?

A. $165

229. Q. A house valued at $10,000 was insured against fire for 80% of the value. The rate was $.60 per $100 for a three-year period. How much was the premium for one year?

A. $16

230. Q. A property is assessed at $5,800. The school tax rate is $1.55 per $100 of assessed valuation. What is the amount of the school tax on the property?

A. $89.90

231. Q. What would a business be worth which shows a profit of $275 a month and is earning 8% on the total investment?

A. $41,250

232. Q. What is the total income of a business for the month of October which does a gross average of $42.50 per day including Sundays?

A. $1,317.50

233. Q. You bought a piece of land 200 ft. square and are erecting a house thereon, 40 ft. square and an average height, including cellar, of 30 ft. Costs were as follows:
Land, $25 per front foot, and building $.35 per cu. ft. What is the total cost excluding any other charges?

A. $21,800

234. Q. In the Township of Fineview the tax rate is: Township 16 mills, school tax 22½ mills, County Tax 2¼ mills. How much are the taxes on the property worth $5,000, assessed at 70% of its value?

A. $142.62

235. Q. If the amount of a loan is $13,500, and the annual rate of interest is 5½%, what would be the amount of the semi-annual interest payment?

A. $371.25

236. Q. The taxes on a property were $126. The taxes were due January 1st and were paid by the owner. What refund would he get from

a purchaser if he sold the property and the taxes were prorated as of September 15th?

A. $36.75

237. Q. A purchaser has decided to insulate his dwelling by covering the attic floor, measuring 24 feet by 32 feet, with rock wool. Each bag of rock wool will cover 36 square feet. How many bags will be required?

A. 21⅓ (22 bags)

238. Q. A lot is 40 feet wide and 75 feet deep. The entire lot has a side-walk around it 6 feet wide and 3 inches deep. What is the total area of the walk?

A. 1,236 square feet

239. Q. What will be a person's investment of principal, if he intends to earn an income of 6 per cent, so that he will receive $1,800 in interest each year?

A. $30,000

240. Q. At the end of the calendar year, the Hope Realty Company finds it earned $30,000. Listing fees, commissions and over-riding expenses equaled 18 per cent of gross sales. What was the volume of sales for the year?

A. $36,585.37

241. Q. How many lots or portions of lots could you divide an acre into, if each lot is 60 feet by 120 feet, and a roadway is to be taken out, which is 30 feet wide and 200 feet long?

A. 5.2 or 5⅕ lots

242. Q. John Davis bought a lot, 50 feet by 125 feet, at $65 per front foot. He paid $10,828.80 to build a house, which depreciated an average of 2 per cent each year. What would be the value of the entire property at the end of ten years if, in the meantime, the lot had increased in value 22 per cent above its original cost of $65 per front foot?

A. $12,628.04

243. Q. Smith paid $65 per front foot for his lot (with a frontage of 50 feet). He paid $10,828.80 to build and he paid the architect 5 per cent of the building cost. He then placed a mortgage on the property for three-fourths of the total cost. What was his equity in the property, after he placed the mortgage?

A. $3,655.06

244. Q. There are 20 fence posts, each 6.85 feet apart. How many yards from the beginning of the first post to the end of the last post, if each post is 4¾ inches wide?

A. 46.023 yards

245. Q. A $46,500 investment shows annual earnings of 6½%. What is the monthly return?

A. $251.88

246. Q. Mrs. Stender owns a 27-room apartment house. Five tenants pay $17 per week; nine tenants pay $15 per week; eight tenants

pay $16 per week; and five pay $18 per week plus $3.75 per week for a garage. What is the gross yearly income?

A. $23,751

247. Q. Mrs. Seberry purchased a piece of real estate for $6,500. At a later date she offered it for sale through a broker's office at an increase of 30%. The property did not sell and she finally reduced the asking price by 25% and the property was sold. She paid a commission of 5% of the sale price to the broker. Did she gain or lose and by how much?

A. Loss—$479.38

248. Q. What is the interest on $874 for 2 years, 8 months, 15 days at 4½% per annum?

A. $106.50

249. Q. A mortgage company agrees to lend the owner of a property a sum equal to 66⅔% of its appraised valuation, at an interest rate of 5%. The first year's interest is $200. What is the appraised valuation?

A. $6,000

250. Q. A house sold for $7,500 at a profit of 20%. What did the house cost?

A. $6,250

251. Q. The owner of a block of 14 building lots, each with a frontage of 75 ft. desires to realize $33,750 from the sale thereof, withholding, however, two lots for himself. What must be the sales price for the lots sold per front foot?

A. $37.50

252. Q. If a tract of land comprising 108,900 square feet was sold for $1,250 per acre, what is the total amount realized from the sale?

A. $3,125

253. Q. A rectangular piece of land containing an acre is 5½ rods wide, what is the length?

A. 29 1/11 rods

254. Q. From 160 acres of land, 42¼ acres were sold to one man and ⅓ of the remainder to another. How many acres remain unsold?

A. 78½ acres

255. Q. A man paid $7,888.30 for a farm containing 89 acres 90 square rods of land. What was the price per acre?

A. $88.08 per acre.

256. Q. A farm of 100 acres is divided into house lots. The streets require ⅛ of the whole farm, and there are 140 lots. How many square rods are there in each lot?

A. 100 square rods

257. Q. Jim Moore receives his tax bill of $490.30. The tax rate is 42 mills per dollar. The property is assessed at 58.25% of its value. What was the actual value of the property?

A. $20,040.87

258. Q. A broker has 5¼ acres of land, which he is dividing into lots, 60

feet wide and 100 feet deep. Allowing 36,690 square feet for the necessary streets, into how many lots could the tract be divided?

A. 32 lots

259. Q. The owner of a piece of land 500 × 350 ft. laid a sidewalk and curb around the entire lot, placing the curb along the lot lines. Sidewalk cost $3,200 and curb $2.00 a lineal yard. What was the total cost?

A. $4,333.33

260. Q. If you bought a house for the listing price less 20% and sold it for the listing price, what per cent profit would you make?

A. 25%

261. Q. Compute the interest on $3,120.50 from November 1, 1965 to May 1, 1967, at 5½% per annum.

A. $257.44

262. Q. If 16 acres of land cost $720, what will 197 acres cost?

A. $8,865

263. Q. How many acres are there in a parcel of land 600 feet × 300 feet?

A. 4.13 plus

264. Q. The net amount received by a seller for his property, after the broker had deducted a sales commission of 5% and an allowance of $40 for advertising, was $9,080. What was the selling price?

A. $9,600

265. Q. McDevitt has a principal balance of $6,000 on his mortgage. The interest rate is 5½% and taxes and insurance payments total $108 per annum. His monthly payment is $60. What is his principal balance after making the first payment?

A. $5,976.50

266. Q. Compute the cost of excavation for a cellar 25 feet wide, 30 feet long and 5 feet deep at $2.90 per cubic yard.

A. $402.75

267. Q. What would the quarterly interest payment amount to on a $6,000 loan calling for simple annual interest at 5½%?

A. $82.50

268. Q. Ray Dolan bought a square piece of land comprising 10,000 square feet. He is building a house on it 45 feet square and of an average height including basement of 30 feet. His costs were $25 per front foot for the land and $.35 per cubic foot for the dwelling. What is the total cost?

A. $23,762.50

269. Q. A lot 75 feet wide and 165 feet deep sold for $193.50 per front foot. What was the selling price of the lot?

A. $14,512.50

270. Q. How many acres of land are there in a section?

A. 640 acres

271. Q. How many sections comprise a township?

A. 36 sections

272. Q. What is the area of a square-acre lot in terms of feet on each side?
     A. 208.7 feet on each side
273. Q. In a 12-unit apartment building, three units rented for $100 each per month, two units for $125 each per month, and one unit for $150 per month. The other six units rented for $65 each per month. What was the gross annual income?
     A. $13,080
274. Q. What would a property be worth if the net return is $950 per month, and the yearly earning is to be 8% on the investment?
     A. $142,500
275. Q. How many acres in the south half of the north half of the southwest quarter of Section 9 of Township 24, range 42 E.W.M., Spokane County, Washington?
     A. 40 acres
276. Q. A plot of ground is a rectangle with a frontage of 760 feet and a depth of 500 feet. How many acres does it contain?
     A. 8.72 acres
277. Q. A business property valued at $10,000, to earn 16% on the total investment annually, should return a monthly income in what amount?
     A. $133.33
278. Q. What factors are to be considered in determining the tax rate?
     A. Assessment and tax millage.
279. Q. On a section chart, how many acres would be in the following descriptions:
     (a) NE ¼ of NE ¼ of NW ¼?
     (b) NE ¼ of NW ¼ of NE ¼ of NW ¼?
     A. (a) 10 acres
        (b) 2½ acres
280. Q. A building is insured for $24,500. The annual rate is $.16 per $100 and the owner buys a three-year policy, the rate of which is 2½ times the annual rate.
     (a) What is the monthly cost?
     (b) What is the total premium?
     A. (a) $2.72
        (b) $98
281. Q. A percentage lease calls for a minimum rent of $300 per month and 4% of the gross business over $150,000. If the total rent paid at the end of the year was $4,800, how much business did the tenant do during the year?
     A. $180,000
282. Q. A real estate deal is closed as of April 15, 1961. The city taxes amount to $180. They have been paid. The school taxes in the amount of $240 are also paid. The county taxes amounting to $118 have not been paid. Compute apportionment of taxes between buyer and seller.

A. $263.09 buyer owes seller for taxes

283. Q. A broker has 1.87 acres of land listed with him for sale at 22½ cents per square foot. The total selling price is how much?
A. $18,327.87

284. Q. A property is assessed at $6,000. The school tax rate is $1.55 per $100 of assessed valuation. What is the amount of the school tax on the property?
A. $93

285. Q. A lot measuring 100 feet by 108.9 feet would be equivalent to what portion of an acre?
A. ¼ acre

286. Q. If an $8,000 home is assessed at 80% of its value and the combined tax rate is $4.20 per $100, what is the amount of the total annual tax?
A. $268.80

287. Q. What is the interest on $8,000 at 4½% per annum for nine months and fifteen days?
A. $285

288. Q. A man bought two 60-foot lots for $3,000 net each, and divided them into three lots of equal frontage, which he sold for a price of $2,400 each. What was his percentage of gross profit?
A. 20%

289. Q. The selling price of a home was $9,300. The broker's commission was 5% and other charges to the seller paid from escrow amounted to $95. How much money did the seller receive?
A. $8,740

290. Q. If a seller wishes to trade his residence at a price of $15,750 subject to a mortgage in the amount of $6,240 on an apartment house costing $62,350 subject to a mortgage in the amount of $36,675, what would be the amount of cash difference?
A. $16,165

291. Q. What would be the depth of a rectangular lot containing 1,080 square yards with a frontage of 90 feet?
A. 108 feet

292. Q. An apartment house has a gross income of $1,134 per month with annual expense of $2,500. What price would a buyer pay for the building to show a net return of 8% on his investment?
A. $138,850

293. Q. A broker sold a lot 125 feet wide and 160 feet deep for 17 cents per square foot, but the purchaser assumed a paving lien of $2.25 per front foot. What total amount would the purchaser have to ask for the property if he expected to make a profit of $295 and give a clear title to the property?
A. $3,976.25

294. Q. The commission rate for selling an apartment house was five per cent on the first $15,000; three per cent on the next $20,000; and 1½% on the balance. The broker received a commission of

$1,710. What was the selling price of the property?

A. $59,000

295. Q. A lot 65 feet wide and 150 feet deep sold for $7,670. What was the price per front foot?

A. $118

296. Q. Adams owns a property which gives him a gross income of $325 per month. His monthly expenses average $155 per month. What is his net income per year on the property?

A. $2,040

297. Q. What is the annual rate of interest on a $4,200 loan, when the quarterly interest payments are $57.75 per quarter?

A. 5½%

298. Q. The owner of a farm employs a licensed broker to sell his farm and agrees to pay a commission of 5%. There is a mortgage on the farm dated June 1, 1957, in the amount of $3,000, with interest at 5% per annum, which the purchaser is assuming. Two payments of $250 each have been made on the mortgage. The owner has paid the interest on the mortgage to June 1, 1960. The sales price is $8,750, and the date of closing is June 30, 1960.

(a) What is the amount of commission due the broker?

(b) What is the amount of mortgage interest owed by the seller to the buyer at the date of closing?

(c) Assuming that the seller had paid the annual taxes of $136 in full for the year ending December 31, 1960, what is the amount of tax adjustment due the seller by the buyer?

A. (a) $437.50   (b) $10.42   (c) $68.00

299. Q. A property is worth $12,000, and the furniture and household goods are worth $4,000. The owner insures them for 80% of their value. The annual rate on the dwelling is $2.80 per $1,000, and on the furniture and household goods, $3.30 per $1,000. If the premium for a three-year policy is 2½ times the premium for one year, what savings would be effected by taking out a three-year policy?

A. $18.72

300. Q. If Dan Clure purchased an apartment building for $40,000 and the total amount of rents received was $6,000 annually, and annual expenses totalled $2,000, what per cent does his investment pay?

A. 10%

301. Q. A sale of real estate is closed on September 12, 1969. The county taxes for 1968 are $875.24, which have not yet been paid, so they will be paid by the purchaser. In prorating these taxes for the calendar year, what is the amount of the apportionment and will this amount be a debit or credit to the purchaser at the closing?

A. $612.66 which will be credited to the purchaser.

302. Q. Lawrence leased a storeroom to Davis on a percentage basis.

The lease calls for a minimum monthly rental of $400 and 5% of the gross yearly business over $80,000. How much rent would Davis receive yearly from Lawrence, if Lawrence did a gross business of $120,000?

    A. $6,800

303. Q. A 40-acre grove sold for $2,200 per acre. The profit the seller made over the cost of the property to him was 10%. What did he pay for the grove?

    A. $80,000

304. Q. If an apartment house costing $42,000 has a net income of $280 per month, what per cent would it be returning on the investment?

    A. 8%

305. Q. What is the cost of a lot 264 feet wide by 660 feet deep at $800 per acre?

    A. $3,200

306. Q. A salesman's half of a 5% commission for the sale of a 320 acre ranch at $175 an acre would be how much?

    A. $1,400

307. Q. A farm earns $3,600 net after allowing for all expenses. A buyer wants 6% return on his money. What could he pay for the farm so as to net him 6% on his investment?

    A. $60,000

308. Q. In appraising a one-story house 32 × 40 feet at a replacement cost of $9.50 per square foot, and allowing 5% depreciation for one year, what would your appraisal be?

    A. $11,552

309. Q. An acre of land contains 43,560 square feet. How many lots or portions of lots could you divide an acre into if each lot is 60 × 120 feet and a roadway is to be taken out which is 30 feet wide and 200 feet long?

    A. 5.21+ lots

310. Q. If the net income from an apartment costing $12,000 is $100 monthly, what would the yearly percentage rate of earnings on the investment be?

    A. 10%

311. Q. A broker has a problem of sub-dividing a 10 acre tract into 50 × 100 foot lots; after allowing 85,000 square feet for the necessary streets, into how many lots could the tract be subdivided?

    A. 70.1 lots

312. Q. How many square feet of concrete would be needed to build a sidewalk 6 feet wide around the boundaries of a 60 × 100-foot corner lot?

    A. 996 sq. ft.

313. Q. How much would the above walk cost if you paid 23¢ per square foot?

    A. $229.08

314. Q. How many does the sum of 2,583 and 4,905 exceed the difference of 9,421 and 2,892?
  A. 959
315. Q. Shields purchased W ½ of NE ¼ of section 10, T-16, R 18 E for the sum of $250 per acre. He subdivided land into 100 lots. The cost of the development was $6,500. Lots were sold at $750 each. What profit did Shields make?
  A. $48,500
316. Q. A tract of ground 30 rods by 16 rods contains how many acres?
  A. 3 acres
317. Q. A person whose income is $325 per month should be able to purchase a home valued at 2½ times his annual income. What would be the value of his home?
  A. $9,750
318. Q. A developer purchased a parcel of land 2,640 feet by 9,900 feet. How many ½ acre sites can be obtained in this parcel allowing 10% of the total for streets and 10% for playgrounds and 20% for a factory?
  A. 720 one-half acre sites
319. Q. What is the cost of roofing a gable-type house (24' × 32') if the roof measures 15 feet from eaves to peak and 34 feet long, if shingles cost $.08 per square foot delivered and $.026 per square-foot labor to apply?
  A. $108.12
320. Q. A lot with 50-foot lake frontage and 150 feet deep sold for $7,500. What was the price per square foot? What was the price per front foot?
  A. $1.00 per sq. ft. $150 per front foot
321. Q. Of a certain farm, ⅙ is in pasture, ⅝ is under cultivation, and the remainder in woodland. If the woodland is 50 acres, how many acres are there in the whole farm?
  A. 240 acres
322. Q. Kilroy sold two vacant lots for a total of $9,430, which was 15% more than he paid for them four years ago. During the time that he owned the lots, he paid taxes each year at the rate of 45 mills on the assessed value of 60% of his purchase price. Figuring a 3% yearly interest loss on his original investment as an expense, did he gain or lose on the sale? In what amount?
  A. $639.60 Loss
323. Q. How many square rods in an acre?
  A. 160 sq. rd.
324. Q. A lot near Magic Springs has been appraised as follows: 3,250 square feet of hillside at 14¢ a square foot; 2,000 square feet of stream area at 8½¢ a square foot; and 7,250 square feet of flat area at $1.00 a square foot. If the lot is to be sold as a whole, what must the price be per square foot to realize the appraised value of the lot?
  A. $.63 per square foot

325. Q. A two story house cost $9,000 to build. If the house had a frontage of 30 feet, a depth of 30 feet and was 30 feet high, including basement, what was the cost per cubic foot?
   A. $.33⅓

326. Q. A man plans to put in a driveway 30 feet long and 6 feet wide. If concrete work and labor together cost $2.75 per square foot, what is the cost of the driveway?
   A. $495

327. Q. A perch or rod is a unit of land measuring how many feet?
   A. 16½ ft.

328. Q. How many feet in a chain?
   A. 66 ft.

329. Q. What would be the amount of interest a purchaser would have to pay for the first month on a contract balance of $7,200 payable at $40 per month, including interest at the rate of 6% per annum?
   A. $36

330. Q. An investor bought 20 acres of land. He plans to divide it into 50′ × 150′ homesite lots and leaving 5 acres for streets, playgrounds and parks. How many lots will he have to sell?
   A. 87+ lots

331. Q. A percentage lease calls for a minimum rent of $600 per month plus 5% of the gross business over $115,000 per month. If the total rent paid by the end of the year was $9,300, what was the tenant's gross volume of business for the year?
   A. $1,422,000.00

332. Q. The assessed valuation of a house is $10,000. If the tax rate is $19 per $1,000 assessed valuation, what are his taxes?
   A. $190 taxes

333. Q. Two houses are 30 yards apart. What would the distance be (expressed in feet) if the houses were three paces closer?
   A. 81 feet

334. Q. A patio is 20 yards long and 10 yards wide. There are stones all around it, each two feet long. How many stones are needed?
   A. 90 stones

335. Q. A ranch contains 3 square miles. How many acres does it contain?
   A. 1,920 acres

336. Q. A lot is 300 feet wide, 450 feet long. A building was erected on the lot 27 feet from the front and 18 feet from the rear. The building contained 12,825 square yards. How wide was the building?
   A. 285 feet

337. Q. A salesman's commission at the end of the first year was increased one-fifth, at the end of the second year it was increased one-fifth. If the third year's commission was $7,280, what was his commission the first year?
   A. $5,055.56

338. Q. Neely wishes to construct a store building on the corner of Main and Edgeworth Avenues. The building is to have 8,100 square feet of ground floor space. Phillips owns lots 1 to 5, inclusive, and will sell any or all of the lots but will not cut up any of them. Each lot is 50 feet wide and fronts on Edgeworth Avenue. Each lot is 100 feet deep, parallel to Main Street. There is a 20-foot setback on Main Street lots and a 15-foot setback on Edgeworth Avenue. If the selling price of lots fronting on Main Street is $112.50 per front foot and $87.25 per front foot for lots fronting on Edgeworth Avenue, what will be the total investment in land required by Neely if he purchases the lots needed for the proposed building?

A. $19,975.00

339. Q. In the above case, how many square feet can be used for building purposes of the corner lot?

A. 2,550 sq. ft.

340. Q. Dolan paid $75 per front foot for his lot which is 60 feet front and 100 feet deep. He later decides to enlarge his lot and can buy an adjoining tract at the price of 75 cents per square foot. He wants to limit his total investments in land to $7,500. How many square feet will he have altogether after he buys the additional tract?

A. 10,000 sq. ft.

341. Q. Thompson and Tyler agreed to trade properties—each to assume the encumbrances on the property taken in trade and the difference in equities to be paid the party with the greater equity by paying 20% cash and the balance to be carried on a second mortgage. Thompson's property was valued at $20,000 with a first mortgage encumbrance of $8,555.00 and a second mortgage encumbrance of $1,655.10. Tyler's property was valued at $18,450.00 with a mortgage encumbrance of $13,841.79. (a) What is Thompson's equity? (b) What is Tyler's equity? (c) Who is due the difference in equity? (d) How much of the difference will be paid in cash? (e) How much will be carried on a mortgage? (f) Against whose property will be the mortgage (after transfer of properties)?

A. (a) $9,789.90 (b) $4,608.21 (c) Thompson (d) $1,036.34
(e) $4,145.35 (f) Tyler's property

342. Q. A buyer lacks $250 to close a real estate deal. The seller agrees to accept a note due in one year from that date, with interest added to back of note at time of signing at 6% per annum. Eleven payments are to be made at the rate of $16.25 per month. What will be the amount of the last payment?

A. $86.25

343. Q. The taxes on a certain house were $126. The taxes were due on January 1, and were paid by the owner. What tax refund would the owner receive from the purchaser if the house were sold on March 15?

A. $99.75

344. Q. The assessment on a property is: $13,300 on the building, $1,050 on the lot. On re-assessment the assessment on the lot has been increased $350. If the tax rate is raised 4.25 mills, what will the increase in taxes be on this property?

A. $62.48

345. Q. A property is assessed at $12,500 and the tax rate is 32 mills. Taxes are due October 1. What refund would the owner of this property get from a purchaser if he sold the property and the taxes were prorated as of April 1?

A. $200.00

346. Q. A man's home is worth $6,000 and his household goods are worth $4,000. He insures each of them for 80% of their value. The annual rate on the dwelling is $2.80 per $1,000 and the rate on the contents $3.30 per $1,000. The premium for a three-year policy is 2½ times the premium for one year. What is the three-year premium on the complete policy?

A. $60.00

347. Q. A party purchased 150 acres of land for $15,000 thirty years ago. The tax rate has averaged 20 mills and an assessed valuation of $50 per acre. If the property were sold now for $300 per acre paying a 10% brokerage commission, what would the owner's net profit be?

A. $21,000

348. Q. Which would be the better of two offers for a lot 5 feet front and 150 feet deep, and how much better? "A" offers $40 per front foot and "B" offers 30¢ per square foot.

A. "B" 's offer by $25

349. Q. A broker leases a store measuring 30 feet wide by 100 feet deep for a period of five years at an annual rental of $2.50 per square foot. What would be the broker's total earnings if the rate of commission is 5% for each year?

A. $1,875

350. Q. A contractor tells you he can reproduce a building for 55 cents per cubic foot and you determine that the building has a ground floor area of 36 feet by 40 feet, and an average height of 14 feet. What would be its reproduction cost?

A. $11,088

351. Q. If an $8,000 home assessed at 60% of that amount has a combined tax rate of $4.21 per $100, what would be the amount of the total annual tax?

A. $202.08

352. Q. An agent collected rents monthly as follows: $25 for each of four flats; $40 for each of six flats; $50 for each of two flats. He paid out $18 for water and $6 for repairs. He was to receive 3% of the gross rentals as commission. What were the total collections and net to owner?

    A. $440, total collections $402.80, net to owner

353. Q. A rectangular lot 210 feet long and 200 feet wide was subdivided into 8 lots of 50′ × 90′ with a road running lengthwise through the middle of the lot. What per cent of the lot area was reserved for the road?

    A. 14.28 per cent

354. Q. Mr. Redman has property assessed at $54,500. Find the amount of his taxes if the tax rate is 20 mills per $1.00.

    A. $1,090 for taxes

355. Q. J. James paid $484 property tax. If his property was asssessed at $11,000, what was the tax rate in mills? Express this rate in dollars per $100.

    A. 44 mills $4.40 per $100

356. Q. A Realtor sells a 50′ × 100′ property at 75¢ a square foot. If his commission is 5%, how much does he give the owner?

    A. $3,562.50

357. Q. A lot was sold for $10,000. The buyer pays $4,000 down and the balance in equal installments in five years. (a) How much a month does he pay on the principal? (b) If he pays 5% interest per year on the balance, how much interest does he pay at the end of the first month?

    A. (a) $100   (b) $25

358. Q. The monthly rent for an office is $75. The size of the office is 12 feet by 20 feet. What is the annual rate per square foot?

    A. $3.75

359. Q. If a $10,000 home is assessed at 80% of its value and the combined tax rate is $3.80 per $100 assessed valuation, what is the amount of the total annual tax?

    A. $304 taxes

360. Q. Mr. Brown built a house 33 feet by 45 feet which had an offset for the family room of an additional 5 feet by 15 feet. If construction cost was $12.85 per square foot, how much did it cost to build the house?

    A. $20,046

361. Q. Taxes on a parcel of property are $1,325.28, for the current year. The first one-fourth of the taxes were paid by the seller. You sell the property and will close the deal and make the prorates as of December 15th. How much will you charge the seller for his share of the taxes?

    A. $938.74 seller owes.

362. Q. What would be the F.H.A. insurable loan on a dwelling if the F.H.A. valuation is $20,000 and the F.H.A. insured 97% of the first $15,000 valuation and 85% of the remainder?

    A. $18,800 total insurable loan

363. Q. On September 1, 1967, a house was insured against fire for 90% of its $24,000 value. The insurance rate paid was 54 cents per $100 for a three year period. The house was sold February 1,

1969. What was the unearned premium to be charged the buyer?

A. $61.56

364. Q. You as a broker sold two lots fronting on Elm Street. Each lot has a frontage of 63 feet. The corner lot sold for 23% more than the adjacent lot which sold for $115.00 per front foot. What was the combined total selling price of the two lots?

A. $16,156.35

365. Q. What would be the broker's net commission on the sale of a property for $9,350 with 6% commission out of which amount the broker's expenses are as follows:

10% listing fee off top of gross commission

50% of remainder for salesman's commission

12% of gross commission for advertising

7% of gross commission for office expense

A. $145.86

366. Q. A piece of land 990 feet by 660 feet is for sale. The owner is asking $3,000 an acre. What is the selling price?

A. $45,000

367. Q. A lot 60 feet wide and 150 feet deep sold for $150.00 per front foot. What was the selling price of the lot?

A. $9,000, selling price

368. Q. A bank gives interest twice a year. Find the difference between simple interest and compound interest on $1,090 for a year at 4%.

A. $.44 Difference

369. Q. On April 1, 1968, Anna James bought a house for $9,000. During the year she spent $190 for repairs, $1,200 for a garage, $295 in taxes and $50 for insurance. The following April she sold the house for $11,250. Find the total gain.

A. $515 gain

370. Q. The sales in a real estate company in 1967 amounted to one-fourth more than in 1966. They were one-fifth more in 1968 than in 1967. If sales in 1968 amounted to $300,000. What did the sales amount to in 1966 and 1967?

A. 1966: $200,000

1967: $250,000

371. Q. A man bought a house for $14,160. Due to health conditions, he was forced to sell for $8\frac{1}{3}$ per cent less than he paid. Find the selling price and the loss.

A. $1,180 loss $12,980 selling price.

372. Q. How much additional cash must a buyer furnish in addition to his $1,000 deposit if the lending institution grants $66\frac{2}{3}\%$ on a $12,000 home?

A. $3,000

373. Q. An insurance premium for three years is $72.00. The buyer is going to set up an insurance reserve with his loan to pay for the premium three years later. What will be the amount of the monthly reserve?

A. $2.00

374. Q. The rental income from a duplex is $240 per month. Find the cost of the house if the annual income is 9 per cent of the cost.
A. $32,000 cost of house

375. Q. J. Johnson paid $16,000 for his new home. The assessed value is 60% of the market value. The tax rate is $2.50 per $100 of assessed valuation. Find the assessed valuation and the tax.
A. $9,600 assessed valuation $240 taxes

376. Q. If 5¼% is the annual rate of interest and the monthly interest payment is $58.45, what is the amount of the original loan?
A. $13,360.00

377. Q. What is the annual interest rate on a $6,000.00 loan when the interest payments are $105.00 semi-annually on the full amount?
A. 3½%

378. Q. A salesman's half of a 5% commission for the sale of a 320 acre ranch at $175.00 an acre would be how much?
A. $1,400.00

379. Q. A lending institution requires that a buyer have a net monthly income 4½ times the monthly mortgage (total), and they use a flat 10% deduction of the gross income to compute the net income. What would be the minimum gross annual salary of a person to qualify for a $20,000 home with 25% down and the balance to be amortized over a 20 year period at 6% interest, with monthly mortgage payments of $138.00 (total)?
A. $8,280

380. Q. What would be the cost of excavating a basement 48 feet long, 30 feet wide, and 9 feet deep at 35¢ per cubic yard? (27 cubic feet = 1 cu. yd.)
A. $168.00

381. Q. Salesman "A" obtains an exclusive listing for $24,500 and is to receive 20% of the 6% commission received by the broker on the sale as a listing fee. Salesman "B" sells the property at a 4% reduction of the listed sales price, and is to receive 35% of the commission after Salesman "A" has been paid. 3% of the full commission is to be paid to the Multiple Listing Service. How much does Salesman "B" receive?
A. $383.28

382. Q. A small town has a proposed budget of $260,000 to be met by taxation. The assessed valuation of taxable property is $6,500,000. Will a tax rate of 30 mills provide sufficient funds to meet the budget?
A. No

383. Q. A chain-store company is interested in taking a 21-year lease on a store property in a certain location. You have located an ideal site for this store, which is for sale for $10,000 and is listed with you. You know a builder whose entire capital is $5,000 who would be willing to build. You also know an investor willing to buy the property after it has been constructed, and you

have assurance that the chain store company would lease the property. How would you arrange this deal to everybody's satisfaction, and how many commissions would you earn in this transaction?

A. Have the builder buy the land giving $5,000 cash and a purchase money mortgage with a subordination clause. Negotiate a construction loan mortgage. Sell property to investors. Lease property to chain-store. Four commissions (sale of land, construction loan mortgage, sale of property, and lease).

384. Q. Plot the following metes and bounds land description:
Starting at the NW corner of the NW ¼ of Section 9, draw a line to the SF corner of the SW ¼ of the NW ¼ of Section 9; thence, to the SE corner of the SW ¼ of the SE ¼ of Section 9; thence, to the SW corner of Section 9; thence, one mile due north to the point of beginning.
How many acres in this tract?

A. 200 acres

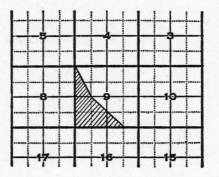

385. Q. Below is shown a portion of Tract 618, as per map recorded in Book 37, Page 19, Official Map Records of Maricopa County. A parcel consisting of the shaded areas was sold.
(a) Describe the conveyed portion by a fractional description.
(b) How many square feet in parcel conveyed?
(c) The portion of the parcel with 125 ft. depth was sold for $500 a front foot on 7th Street, and the portion on the rear of Lot 9 was sold for $2.20 per sq. ft. What was the total consideration?

A. (a) The south 15′ of Lot 7; all of Lot 8, and the east 50′ of Lot 9; all in Tract 618, as per map recorded in Book 37, Page 19, official cial maps of record of Maricopa County.
(b) 11,250 sq. ft.
(c) $38,000.00 total consideration.

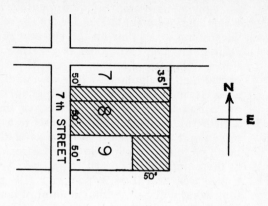

386. Q. There is a 15 foot building setback ordinance applying to all lots fronting on Main Street and a 20 foot setback applying to all lots fronting on Cross Street, as indicated by the dotted lines on the following diagram:

MAIN STREET

100 FEET	LOT 5	LOT 4	LOT 3	LOT 2	LOT 1	CROSS STREET
	50 FEET	50 FEET	50 FEET	50 FEET	50 FEET	

(a) Presuming no other setback or areaway requirements, how many square feet of Lot 1 can be used for building purposes?

(b) J. F. Jolly wishes to construct a store building on the corner of Main and Cross Streets. The building is to have 8,100 square feet of ground floor space. Mr. Jones owns Lots 1 to 5, inclusive, and will sell any or all of the lots, but will not cut up any one of them. What is the minimum number of lots Mr. Jolly will have to buy to allow construction of the building described?

(c) If Mr. Jolly buys all of the lots and pays $127.50 per front foot for lots 2, 3, 4, and 5 and $185.00 per front foot for the lot fronting on Cross Street, what would be his total cost for all of the lots?

A. (a) 2,550 sq. ft.

(b) Lots 1, 2, and 3.

(c) $44,000.00

387. Q. On the following diagram, you are to plot out the following legal description and insert the dimensions of the area described.

(a) "Beginning at a point on the easterly side of 24th Avenue at a point 150 feet north of the northerly side of "B" Street; thence east and parallel with "A" Street a distance of 200 feet to a point 100 feet west of the westerly side of 23rd Avenue; thence north 50 feet; thence east a distance of 25 feet to a point 75 feet west of the westerly side of 23rd Avenue; thence south 150 feet to a point; thence west to a point on the easterly side of 24th Avenue 50 feet north of the northerly side of "B" Street; thence north 100' to the point and place of beginning."

(b) If the area described in part (a) sells for 42¢ per square foot, what will be the total amount of commission collected by a broker if he works on a 5% straight commission?

A. (a) See drawing.

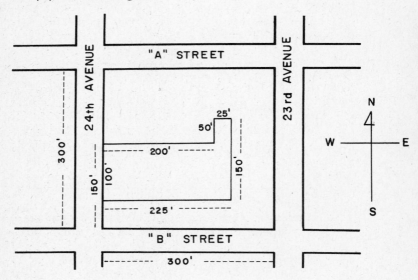

(b) $498.75

388. Q. The following diagram represents Section 14, Township 22 N, Range 17 E of the 6th Principal Meridian.

(a) You are to indicate the area and shade in the following:
S ½ of SW ¼ of the NE ¼
E ½ of SE ¼ of the NW ¼
N ½ of the SW ¼
W ½ and NE ¼ of NW ¼ of SE ¼
(a) See drawing.
(b) How many acres are contained in this tract?

A. 150 acres

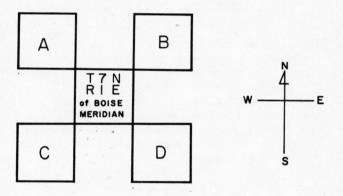

389. Q. The diagram below consists of five townships. The township in the center has been designated as Township 7 North, Range 1 East of the Boise Meridian.

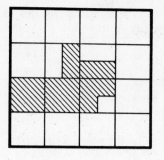

    (a) Give the township and Range numbers for Township A.
    (b) Give the township and Range numbers for Township D.
  A. (a) T8N—R1W
    (b) T6N—R2E

390. Q. The following diagram has been designated as Township 7 North, Range 1 East of the Boise Meridian.
    (a) Number these sections correctly.
    (b) Shade in the N ½ of Section 17; the W ½ of the W ½ of Section 25; the SW ¼ of Section 32; and the NE ¼ of the NW ¼ of Section 4.
    (c) How many acres in the Township have you shaded?
  A. (a) and (b)
    (c) 680 acres

6	5	4 ■	3	2	1
7	8	9	10	11	12
18	■ 17	16	15	14	13
19	20	21	22	23	24
30	29	28	27	26 ■	25
31	32 ■	33	34	35	36

391. Q. Draw a Township Plan on a scale of approximately one inch to the mile and number all sections correctly. Mark this plat showing directions and work out the following description:

(a) "Beginning at the NW corner of the NW ¼ of Section 10, thence southeasterly to the SW corner of the SW ¼ of Section 11, thence southwesterly to the NW corner of the SE ¼ of Section 21, thence northwesterly to the SW corner of the NE ¼ of Section 17, thence northeasterly to the point of beginning."

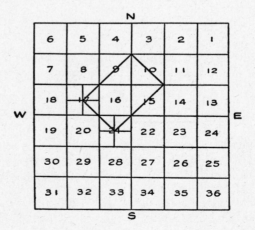

(b) How many acres in the above described tract?

(c) What is the name of this type of description?

A. (a) Drawing above (b) 1,920 acres (c) Metes and Bounds

392. Q. The following diagram represents five adjacent townships, the center one of which has been designated as Township 20 North; Range 1 East of the 6th P.M.

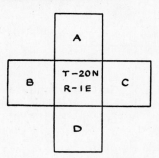

(a) Give township and range numbers for Township "A" in above diagram.

(b) Give township and range numbers for Township "B" in above diagram.

(c) Give township and range numbers for Township "C" in above diagram.

(d) Give township and range numbers for Township "D" in above diagram.

A. (a) T-21 N; R-1E

(b) T-20 N; R-1W

(c) T-20 N; R-2E

(d) T-19 N; R-1E

393. Q. The diagram below has been designated as Section 32; T-12-N; R-3-E of the 6th P.M.

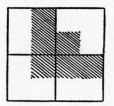

(a) On the above plat, how many acres are contained within the shaded area?

(b) What would be the cost per acre if the above tract sold for $23,340?

A. (a) 240 acres (b) $97.25

394. Q. (a) Draw a diagram of the NE ¼ of the SW ¼ of a section of land.

(b) How many acres are in the plot?

A. (a)

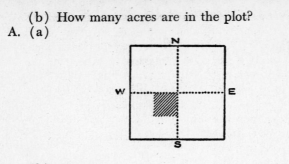

(b) 40 acres

395. Q. Below is a diagram of a section of land. Locate and shade in the following tracts, and show how many acres in each:
  (a) E ½ of SE ¼ of NW ¼
  (b) NE ¼ of SW ¼
  (c) NW ¼ of NW ¼ of SE ¼
  (d) N ½ of NW ¼
  (e) If the land described sells for $52.50 per acre, what was the selling price?
  (f) What would the sales commission be at 10%?

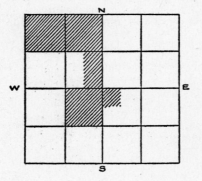

A. (a) 20 acres   (b) 40 acres   (c) 10 acres
   (d) 80 acres   (e) $7,875   (f) $787.50

396. Q. Draw a plat of a SQUARE block consisting of 10 identical lots 40′ by 100′.
  (a) The top of the plat will face north and the lots will face north and south. The lots will be numbered from 1 to 10, clockwise, beginning with the northwesterly lot. Show the dimensions.
  (b) Show the following described tract: "Beginning at the intersection point of the south and west boundaries of the number 10 lot, thence due north 100 feet, thence southeasterly to a point on the south boundary of lot 8 twenty feet west of the intersecting point of the south and east

boundaries of lot 8, thence due west to the place of beginning."

(c) How many square feet in the above described tract?

(d) How many square feet remain in just the lots affected by the above described tract?

(e) Excluding all of lots 8, 9, and 10, how many square feet remain in the balance of the entire tract?

A. (a) and (b)

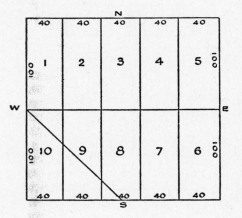

(c) 5,000   (d) 7,000   (e) 28,000

397. Q. The diagram below has been designated as Sec. 17, T-3-N, R-16, EBM.

(a) Shade the SW ¼ of NE ¼.

(b) How many acres in this shaded portion?

A. (a)

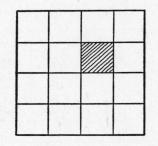

(b) 40 acres

398. Q. Give the correct description of the following parcel of land, marked with

(a) an "X", situated in Sec. 31, T-4-N, R-5-EMB.

(b) How many acres in this area marked with an "X"?

A. (a) NW ¼ NW ¼; SE ¼ Sec. 31; T4N, R 5 EMB.
    (b) 10 acres

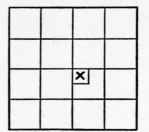

399. Q. (a) Draw a Township plat and number all sections in the
            proper order.
        (b) Work out the following description:
            "Beginning at the SE corner of section 4, thence south-
            easterly to the SE corner of section 10, thence southwesterly
            to the NW corner of the SE quarter of section 21, thence
            southeasterly to the NE corner of section 28, thence north-

N

6	5	4	3	2	1
7	8	9	10	11	12
18	17	16	15	14	13
19	20	21	22	23	24
30	29	28	27	26	25
31	32	33	34	35	36

W   E

S

easterly to the SE corner of the NW quarter of section 22, thence northwesterly to the SW corner of section 9, thence northeasterly to the point of beginning."

(c) How many acres in the tract described in Part (b)?

(d) How many acres of section 15 are included in the tract in Part (b)?

(e) What is the name of the type of description in Part (b)?

A. (a) and (b).

   (c) 1,600   (d) 320   (e) Metes and Bounds

400. Q. (a) How do you arrive at area in terms of square feet?

(b) How do you arrive at cubage?

A. (a) Multiply the frontage (or width) by the depth.

(b) Multiply frontage by depth by height.

401. Q. (Pennsylvania) Make up a settlement sheet from the following information:

Adam Steele, unmarried, is selling his property located at 613 Highland Avenue, Pittsburgh, Pa., to Henry Wagner at a consideration price of $3,500. The purchaser has paid $200 hand money. The deal is being closed as of May 15, 1969. The county taxes, amounting to $21.28 per year, have not yet been paid. The city and school taxes for 1969, amounting to $72.47 per year, have been paid by the seller. Fire insurance policy premium for policy expiring January 30, 1970, in the amount of $2,500, was $13.13. The rent is $32.50 per month.

A.   STATEMENT OF SETTLEMENT

                       Date: May 15, 1969

Seller: Adam Steele
Purchaser: Henry Wagner
Premises: 613 Highland Ave., Pittsburgh, Pa.

WITH PURCHASER

	Credit	Debit
Consideration		$3,500.00
Hand Money	$ 200.00	
4½ mos. County Tax (1969)	7.98	
7½ mos. City and School Tax (1969)		45.29
8½ mos. Fire Ins. Policy		9.30
½ mo. rent	16.25	
Due at settlement	3,330.36	
	$3,554.59	$3,554.59

WITH SELLER

Due at settlement	$3,330.36	
State Stamps		$ 35.00
City Stamps		35.00
Notary Fee		.50
Net Due seller		3,259.86
	$3,330.36	$3,330.36

402. Q. (Arizona) A broker listed a property for $21,500. He finally sold it for $20,500. The commission paid to broker was 5%. The property was assessed at 52% of the sale price and the tax rate is $4.828 per hundred. Taxes are paid in full for the fiscal year 1968-69. There is an $8,500 mortgage of record at 6% interest. The interest is payable semi-annually July 1st and January 1st of each year, and the interest is paid to July 1st, 1968. The improvements on the property are valued at $16,000. The fire insurance policy is for 85% of this value at the premium rate of 78¢ per hundred for three years. The paid-up policy runs to January 1, 1969. Policy of Title Insurance for $20,500 costing $72.50 is paid for by the seller. The escrow charges are $32.00 divided equally between seller and buyer. Revenue stamps and a charge of $1.50 for drawing the deed are paid for by the seller. Closing date on escrow is October 1, 1968.
How much money does the seller receive?

A.

Debit		Credit	
Existing Mtge.	$8,500.00	Selling price	$20,500.00
R. E. Comm.	1,025.00	Pro-rate Tax	386.00
Interest	127.50	Pro-rate Ins.	8.85
Title Ins.	72.50	Total Cr.	$20,894.85
Escrow Charge	16.00	Debit	9,742.50
Drawing Deed	1.50	Cash Due	$11,152.35
Total	$9,742.50		

403. Q. (Arkansas) Prepare a closing statement using only the facts furnished here. Assume that you negotiated the sale as a real estate broker. Be sure to fully itemize each receipt and disbursement so that each party to the transaction can determine the purpose for which his money was expended. It is imperative that you show exactly (1) the additional amount of cash which is paid by the buyer on the closing date, and (2) the net amount received by the seller, including earnest money, after all expenses are deducted. A prospect signs an offer with you to buy a small residence property for $8,000.00, agrees to assume an existing mortgage and deposits with you $300.00 earnest money. The owner accepts this offer. The mortgage is in the original sum of $4,000.00 and bears interest at 6% per annum; $800.00 has been paid on the principal; the interest on the balance has been paid through January 31, 1969. Seller agrees that buyer shall be given credit for accrued interest. The 1968 general taxes in the amount of $53.28 have been paid in full. No taxes of any kind are delinquent. Seller agrees that buyer shall be given credit for prorating of 1969 taxes to the closing date on the same basis as the amount of taxes paid for 1968. There is one year fire insurance policy on the improvement in the amount of $5,000.00 expiring July 1, 1970, on which a premium of $28.56 has been paid. It is agreed to charge the buyer with the unused premium on a pro-rata basis and leave the policy in force. Your commission is 5%. The cost of continuation of the abstract to date is $15.00. The closing date is August 1, 1969. The only money that you will end up with, as the broker, will be the commission, revenue stamp money and abstract fee.

A.   SETTLEMENT WITH BUYER

	Debit	Credit
Sale price	$8,000.00	
Insurance adjustment	26.18	
Mortgage		$3,200.00
Interest		96.00
Earnest money		300.00
Taxes		31.08
Amount to collect from buyer at closing		4,399.10
	$8,026.18	$8,026.18

SETTLEMENT WITH SELLER

	Debit	Credit
Sale price		$8,000.00
Insurance adjustment		26.18
Mortgage	$3,200.00	
Interest	96.00	
Taxes	31.08	
Commission	400.00	
Abstract	15.00	
Net due seller	4,284.10	
	$8,026.18	$8,026.18

404. Q. (California) A broker sold a single-family residence for $17,800.00. The escrow closed on December 20, 1968, and it was agreed that prorations were to be made as of the close of escrow. The second half of the current fiscal year property taxes had been paid. The taxes were $468.00 per annum. A paid-up three year fire insurance policy expiring December 31, 1969, costing $75.60 originally, was also to be prorated in escrow. A standard title insurance policy, costing $154.00 was to be paid for by the buyer. The escrow instructions provided that seller would pay a 2 per cent discount fee for obtaining a new first trust deed loan securing a note in the amount of $10,750.00 to refinance a first trust deed of like amount. The existing second deed of trust in the sum of $3,250.00 contained a subordination clause. The second trust deed was assumed by the buyer. The broker handled the escrow, but he did not charge a fee for this service. The broker's commission of 6 per cent of the sale due from seller was to come from the proceeds of the escrow. From the above facts prepare closing statements for seller and buyer. Show all charges and credits. Assume there are no other costs to either party than those indicated above.

SELLER'S CLOSING STATEMENT

Purchase Price		$17,800.00
Taxes ($468 for ⅓ month @ $39.00)		13.00
Insurance ($75.60 12⅓ months @ $2.10)		25.90
Commission ($17,800 × .06)	1,068.00	
Loan Charges ($10,750 × .02)	215.00	
Assumed Second Deed of Trust	3,250.00	
Refinanced First Deed of Trust	10,750.00	
Balance to Seller	2,555.90	
	$17,838.90	$17,838.90

BUYER'S CLOSING STATEMENT

Purchase Price	$17,800.00	
Taxes	13.00	
Insurance	25.90	
Assumed Second Deed of Trust		3,250.00
Proceeds of Loan		10,750.00
Title Insurance	154.00	
Received from Buyers		3,992.90
	$17,992.90	$17,992.90

405. Q. (Florida) Diane Smith has contracted to purchase a duplex owned by C. P. Murphy for $38,000. Mr. Robert Realtor, the broker, representing Mr. Murphy, has accepted a deposit from Miss Smith of $2,000. Miss Smith has agreed to assume the existing first mortgage for $26,500. Mr. Murphy has agreed to take back a second mortgage for $5,000 at 7 per cent payable monthly over a ten-year term. Closing will take place on June 30. All prorations are on a twelve equal months basis. The duplex was assessed by both the City and County for $34,000. The millage in the City is 13 mills and in the County, 17 mills. The property insurance was prepaid for two years as of January 1 of this year in the amount of $160. Both apartments in the duplex were rented January 1 of this year. Each unit rents for $180 a month. The first month's payment on the second mortgage of $58.06 is to be paid in advance at closing. The title company's bill for the abstract to seller was $65. The seller was to furnish deed ($10.00) and to provide state documentary and surtax stamps for the deed. The broker's commission is 6 per cent. Lawyer's fees of $25 for the mortgage and note, recording fees of $4.50 and documentary and intangible taxes based on the amount of the mortgage are payable by buyer. In addition, the buyer purchased title insurance costing $380. Recording the deed fee is $3.00. Based on the above information, prepare the following schedules: (1) Seller's Closing Statement; (2) Buyer's Closing Statement; (3) Broker's Reconciliation Statement.

A. (1) SELLER'S CLOSING STATEMENT

DATE OF CLOSING MONTH June DAY 6 YEAR 1969

	Debit	Credit
Purchase Price		$38,000.00
First Mortgage—Balance	$26,500.00	
Second Mortgage	5,000.00	
Prorations and Prepayments:		
Rent	360.00	
Prepayment: 2nd Mortgage		58.06
Insurance		120.00
Taxes: City	221.00	
County	289.00	
Expenses:		
Abstract Continuation	65.00	
Attorney's Fee	10.00	
Documentary Stamps:		
Florida Surtax	12.65	
State on Deed	114.00	
Brokerage	2,280.00	
Total Debits and Credits	34,851.65	38,178.06
Balance Due Seller	3,326.41	
GRAND TOTALS	$38,178.06	$38,178.06

(2) BUYER'S CLOSING STATEMENT

DATE OF CLOSING MONTH June DAY 6 YEAR 1969

	Debit	Credit
Purchase Price	$38,000.00	
First Mortgage—Balance		26,500.00
Second Mortgage		5,000.00
Binder Deposit		2,000.00
Prorations and Prepayments:		
Rent		360.00
Prepayment: 2nd Mortgage	58.06	
Insurance	120.00	
Taxes: City		221.00
County		289.00
Expenses:		
Attorney's fee	25.00	
Documentary Stamps:		
Mortgage—Note	7.50	
Intangible Tax—Mortgage	10.00	
Recording:		
Mortgage	4.50	
Deed	3.00	
Title Insurance	380.00	
Total Debits and Credits	38,608.06	34,370.00
Balance Due from Buyer		4,238.06
GRAND TOTALS	$38,608.06	$38,608.06

(3)   Cash Reconciliation Statement

(BROKER'S STATEMENT)

	Receipts	Disbursements
Deposit	$2,000.00	
Check from buyer at closing	4,238.06	
Brokerage fee		2,280.00
Check to seller at closing		3,326.41
Seller's expense (less brokerage)		201.65
Buyer's expense		430.00
TOTALS	$6,238.06	$6,238.06

406. Q. (New York) Adam Smith purchased a property from Bud Jones on July 1: price $7,900.00, deposit on contract $400.00, closing date to be August 15. The annual city taxes are $126.00, the annual county taxes $60.00, and the annual water charge $18.00. All of these items have been paid as of January 1, and the monthly rental is $66.00 which was paid to the end of the month. The purchaser is to assume a $3,000 mortgage at 5 per cent. Interest was paid on July 1. Insurance policy is obtained by buyer at date of closing; the premium is $48, for a three year period. The seller is to pay the broker 4 per cent commission. Prepare an itemized statement which will indicate how much the seller owes the purchaser on closing, how much the purchaser owes the seller and how much commission was earned.

A.

	Seller Owes	Purchaser Owes
Price		$7,900.00
Deposit		400.00
Balance		7,500.00
City Tax		47.25
County Tax		22.50
Water		6.75
Rent	33.00	
Interest	18.75	
	51.75	
Commission	316.00	
GRAND TOTALS	$367.75	$7,576.50

407. Q. (Wisconsin) John and Mary Hays, husband and wife, sell their home to Alfred and Elsie Sims, his wife, through the Sloan Agency, Inc. for $31,000. The commission is 6 per cent. The Hayses have a mortgage with the Spring Bank, with a present balance due of $27,452.00 at 6 per cent annual interest, principal and interest payable on June 8 and December 8 of each year. Principal to be paid in multiples of $100.00 with no less than $300.00 paid on the principal on each due date. The Hayses agree to take back a second mortgage in a principal sum not to exceed $2,500.00 for five years with interest at 7 per cent and balance in cash. The taxes for 1968 were $680.00. An earnest money payment of $500.00 is made and buyers agree to pay an additional $500.00. The Simses assume the existing mortgage of $27,452.00, maturity date of December 8, 1990. The sellers accept, as part of the purchase price, a lot valued at $1,500.00. The balance of purchase price is due in cash at the closing. The transaction is to be closed April 5, 1969. The interest, taxes and insurance are to be prorated on date of closing. The insurance policy on the premises is dated December 1, 1968, and expires on November 30, 1971. The total premium which was paid by the sellers was $196.00. The broker has advanced $37.50 for the abstract extension, $50.00 for Attorney's fees and $38.00 for a survey. Prepare closing statement from the above information and the broker's settlement with seller.

A.

STATEMENT FOR CLOSING
REAL ESTATE TRANSACTION

	Due Seller	Credit Buyer
Sale Price	$31,000.00	
Down Payment		1,000.00
Subject to First Mortgage:		
Principal $27,452.00		28,001.74
Interest $ 549.74		
Tax Adjustment 1969 prorated		
from January 1, 1969 to Apr. 5,		
1969 (1968 tax $680.)		179.42
Insurance Premiums prorated	173.42	
TOTAL	$31,173.42	$29,181.16
Less Credit to Buyer	29,181.16	
BALANCE DUE SELLER	$ 1,992.26	
Balance of $1,992.26 due		
Seller as follows:		
Lot	1,500.00	
Check or Cash to Balance	492.26	
TOTAL	$ 1,992.26	

BROKER'S SETTLEMENT WITH SELLER

	Charges	Due Seller
Cash Balance received from Buyer		$ 492.26
Down Payments		1,000.00
Charges Against Seller:		
Abstract Extension or Title Policy	37.50	
Attorney's Fees	50.00	
Commission	1,860.00	
Services (Itemize):		
Survey	38.00	
TOTAL	$1,985.50	$1,492.26
Less Charges Against Seller		1,985.50
Balance Due Broker From Seller		$(493.24)

Completed Solutions to Arithmetic Problems

1. $\$350 = 5\%$
   $\$350 \div 5 = \$70$
   $100 \times 70 = \$7{,}000$
2. $80 \times \$75 = \$6{,}000$
3. $24 \times 36 = 864$ square feet
4. 30 days (April) − 17 days = 13 days
   13 days + 31 days (May) + 25 days (June) = 69 days
5. 1 board foot = 12 square inches × 1 inch (thickness)
   $2'' \times 4'' = 8$ square inches $= \frac{2}{3}$ of 12 square inches
   $\frac{2}{3} \times 12' = 8$ board feet in one piece of lumber
   8 board feet × 48 = 384 board feet
6. January 1 to March 15 = $2\frac{1}{2}$ months
   $2\frac{1}{2} \div 12 = \frac{5}{2} \times \frac{1}{12} = \frac{5}{24}$
7. $3\frac{1}{2} \div 12 = \frac{7}{2} \times \frac{1}{12} = \frac{7}{24}$
8. $.375 = \frac{375}{1000} \qquad \frac{375 \div 25}{1000 \div 25} = \frac{15}{40} \qquad \frac{15 \div 5}{40 \div 5} = \frac{3}{8}$
9. $.38\frac{1}{3} = 38\frac{1}{3} \div 100 = \frac{115}{3} \times \frac{1}{100} = \frac{115}{300} = \frac{23}{60}$
10. $\frac{1}{8} = 1 \div 8 = .125 = 12\frac{1}{2}\%$
11. $\frac{1}{6} = 1 \div 6 = .16\frac{2}{3} = 16\frac{2}{3}\%$
12. $\frac{1}{2} + \frac{3}{4} + \frac{1}{8} = \frac{4}{8} + \frac{6}{8} + \frac{1}{8} = \frac{11}{8}$ or $1\frac{3}{8}$
13. $1\frac{1}{4} - \frac{3}{8} = \frac{10}{8} - \frac{3}{8} = \frac{7}{8}$
14. $\frac{1}{2} + \frac{5}{8} + \frac{3}{16} = \frac{8}{16} + \frac{10}{16} + \frac{3}{16} = \frac{21}{16}$ or $1\frac{5}{16}$
15. $\frac{1}{2}$ of 20 = 10 acres $\qquad \frac{1}{4}$ of 10 = $2\frac{1}{2}$ acres $\qquad 10 - 2\frac{1}{2} = 7\frac{1}{2}$ acres
16. $\frac{1}{2} \times \frac{1}{4} = \frac{1}{8}$
17. $\frac{1}{2} \div \frac{1}{4} = \frac{1}{2} \times \frac{4}{1} = \frac{4}{2} = 2$
18. $\frac{25}{365}$ Divide both numerator and denominator by 5 = $\frac{5}{73}$ of a year
19. $21 \div 30 = \frac{21}{30} = \frac{7}{10}$ or .7
20. $\frac{3}{5} = 3 \div 5 = .60$ or 60%
21. $87\frac{1}{2}\% = .87\frac{1}{2} = 87\frac{1}{2} \div 100 = \frac{175}{2} \times \frac{1}{100} = \frac{175}{200} = \frac{7}{8}$
22. 3 years = 36 months $\qquad \frac{6}{36} = \frac{1}{6}$ of 3 years
23. $\frac{2}{3} \times \frac{1}{2} = \frac{2}{6}$ or $\frac{1}{3}$
24. $\frac{2}{3} \div \frac{1}{2} = \frac{2}{3} \times \frac{2}{1} = \frac{4}{3}$
25. $\frac{1}{2} \div \frac{2}{3} = \frac{1}{2} \times \frac{3}{2} = \frac{3}{4}$
26. $\frac{2}{3} \times 12 = \frac{2 \times 12}{3} = \frac{24}{3} = 8$ months

27. $\frac{1}{5}$ of $365 = 365 \div 5 = 73$ days
28. $\frac{1}{6} \times 43,560 = 7,260$ sq. ft.
29. $5,445 \div 43,560 = .125$ or $\frac{1}{8}$ acre
30. $\frac{1}{4} + \frac{3}{16} = \frac{4}{16} + \frac{3}{16} = \frac{7}{16}$ amount for children
    $1 - \frac{7}{16} = \frac{16}{16} - \frac{7}{16} = \frac{9}{16}$ balance
31. $26\frac{6}{12} + 19\frac{9}{12} + 81\frac{10}{12} + 44\frac{8}{12} = 97\frac{33}{12} = 99\frac{9}{12} = 99\frac{3}{4}$
32. $18\frac{1}{2} = \frac{37}{2}$
    $4\frac{1}{6} = \frac{25}{6}$
    $\frac{37}{2} \div \frac{25}{6} = \frac{37}{2} \times \frac{6}{25} = \frac{111}{25} = 4\frac{11}{25}$
33. $5\frac{1}{4}\% = 5.25\%$
    $\$223.65 = 5.25\%$ of the amount
    $\$223.65 \div 5.25 = \$42.60 = 1\%$ of the amount
    The amount $= 100\%$
    $\$42.60 \times 100 = \$4,260$ the amount
34. $.83\frac{1}{3} = 83\frac{1}{3} \div 100 = \frac{250}{3} \div 100 = \frac{250}{3} \times \frac{1}{100} = \frac{250}{300} = \frac{5}{6}$
    $.75 = \frac{75}{100} = \frac{3}{4}$
    $\frac{3}{4} \times \frac{5}{6} = \frac{5}{8}$
35. $7 \times 2\frac{1}{2}\% = 17\frac{1}{2}\%$ depreciation
    $100\% - 17\frac{1}{2}\% = 82\frac{1}{2}\%$ present value $100\% =$ value
    $\$8,085 \div 82.5 = \$98 = 1\%$ of original value
    $\$98 \times 100 = \$9,800$ original value
36. $\$19,750 \times .06 = \$1,185$ total commission $12\frac{1}{2}\% = .125$
    $\$1,185 \times .125 = \$148.125$ or $\$148.13$
37. $\$13,800 \div 12 = \$1,150$ mo. loan
    $\$71.30 \div \$1,150 = .062$ or 6.2% or $6\frac{1}{5}\%$
38. $\$9,000 + 7\%$ commission $=$ selling price
    $\$9,000 = 93\%$ of selling price
    $\$9,000 \div 93 = \$96.7742$
    $\$96.7742 \times 100 = \$9,677.42$
39. $2640 \times 5280 = 13,939,200$ square feet
    $5280 - 2640 = 2640$ feet; $13,939,200 \div 2 = 6,969,600$
    $13,939,200 + 6,969,600 = 20,908,800$ square feet
    $20,908,800 \div 43,560 = 480$ acres
40. a. $\$9,500 \div 1,000 = 9.5$
       $9.5 \times \$9.50 = \$90.25$
    b. $\$291 \div 12 = \$24.25$
    c. $\$9,500 \div 100 = 95$
       $95 \times \$.98 = \$93.10$
       $\$93.10 \div 36 = \$2.59$
    d. $\$90.25 + \$24.25 + \$2.59 = \$117.09$
41. $500 \times 760 = 380,000$ square feet
    $380,000 \div 2 = 190,000$ square feet in lot
    $190,000 \div 43,560 = 4.36$ acres
42. $\$24 \times 12 = \$288$ expenses
    $\$3,600 + \$288 = \$3,888$ gross earning
    $\$3,888 = 6\%$ return
    $\$3,888 \div 6 = \$648$
    $\$648 \times 100 = \$64,800$

43. $18,915 ÷ 2.5 = $7,566 year's income
    $7,566 ÷ 52 = $145.50 week's income

44. 1320' × 1980' = 2,613,600 sq. ft. $16\frac{2}{3}\% = \frac{1}{6}$
    43,560 sq. ft. = 1 acre
    2,613,600 ÷ 43,560 = 60 acres
    $\frac{1}{6}$ of 60 = 10 acres
    60 − 10 = 50 acres
    50 × 3 = 150 $\frac{1}{3}$-acre lots

45. $9,265 = 100% of appraisal value
    115% of appraisal value = original listing price
    $9,265 × 115% = $10,654.75 − the original listing price

46. 75' × $24 = $1,800 assessment—front
    $1,800 × 4.8 = $8,640 assessment on house
                  $\overline{\$10,440}$ × $.068 = $709.92 annual taxes

47. $\frac{1}{4} + \frac{3}{5} = \frac{5}{20} + \frac{12}{20} = \frac{17}{20}$ not usable or under cultivation
    $1 - \frac{17}{20} = \frac{20}{20} - \frac{17}{20} = \frac{3}{20}$ = 60 acres meadow land
    60 ÷ 3 = 20 acres in $\frac{1}{20}$ of land
    20 × 20 = 400 acres total farm

48. Contractor A 18' × 27' × 9' = 4,374 cu. ft. in house
           (a) 4,374 × $.29 = $1,268.46, bid of contractor A
    Contractor B 18' × 27' = 486 sq. ft. floor area
                486 × $1.95 = $947.70
                18' × 27' × $\frac{1}{2}$ = 243 cu. ft. concrete floor
                27 cu. ft. = 1 cu. yd.
                243 ÷ 27 = 9 cu. yd. concrete needed
                9 × $17.50 = $157.50, cost of concrete floor
           (b) $947.70 + $157.50 = $1,105.20, bid of contractor B
           (c) Contractor B
           (d) $1,268.46 − $1,105.20 = $163.26

49. 125 × 160 = 20,000 sq. ft.
    20,000 × $.17 = $3,400 property cost
    $2.25 × 125 = $281.25 paving cost
    $3,400 + $281.25 + $295 = $3,976.25

50. $325 × 52 = $16,900 yearly gross income
    $845 × 12 = $10,140 yearly expense
    $16,900 − $10,140 = $6,760
    $6,760 ÷ $84,500 = .08 or 8%

51. $6\frac{1}{2}\%$ × $4,000 = $260
    3 × $260 = $780
    $260 ÷ 12 = $21.67
    5 × $21.67 = $108.35
    $\frac{20}{30}$ × $21.67 = $14.45
    $780 + $108.35 + $14.45 = $902.80

52. 5% × $23,000 = $1,150
    90% ÷ 2 = 45% of commission for salesman
    45% × $1,150 = $517.50

53. $190 \times \$175.50 = \$33,345$ sale price
$\$5,000 + \$18,300 + \$183 = \$23,483$
$\$33,345 - \$23,483 = \$9,862$ balance
$\$9,862 - \$3,972.07 = \$5,889.93$ cash needed

54. $26 \times 38 = 988$ square feet
$988 \times 14 = 13,832$ cubic feet

55. $40 \times 28 = 1,120$ square feet
$1,120 \times \$11.25 = \$12,600$

56. $\$75 + \$60 = \$135$
$\$135 \div 2 = \$67.50$
$60 \times \$67.50 = \$4,050$

57. $\$8250 = 95\%$ of selling price
$\$8250 \div 95 = \$86.8421 = 1\%$ of selling price
$\$86.8421 \times 100 = \$8,684.21$ selling price

58. $\$93.75 \times 4 = \$375$ paid each year
$\$375 \div 5000 = .075$ or $7\frac{1}{2}\%$

59. $\$8000 \div 100 = 80$ per $\$100$
$\$80 \times 2.27 = \$181.60$ per year
$\frac{1}{2}$ of $181.60 = \$90.80$ taxes for 6 months

60. $132' \times 330' = 43,560$ sq. ft. $= 1$ acre, $\$800$

61. $\$8000 \times \$.60 = \$4800$
$\$4800 + 500 = \$5300$
$\$8000 - \$5300 = \$2700$

62. $\$23,000 - 11,000 = \$12,000$ gain
$\$12,000 \div 120,000 = .10$ or 10%

63. $\$4800 \div \$60,000 = .08$ or 8%

64. $\$57.50 \div 5 = \$11.50$ or 1% of the sum
$\$11.50 \times 100 = \$1,150.00$

65. $\$8,750 \div 75 = \$116.66$ per front foot
$75' \times 110' = 8,250$ sq. ft.
$\$8,750 \div 8,250 = \$1.06$ per sq. ft.

66. $75' \times 120' = 9,000$ sq. ft.
$9,000 \times \$.20 = \$1,800$ property
$\$590$ broker's commission
$75'$ frontage $75' \times \$5.50 = \$412.50$ sewers and paving
$\$1,800 + \$412.50 = \$2,212.50$ total
$\$2,212.50 \times .10 = \$221.25$ expected profit
$\$2,212.50 + \$221.25 + \$590 = \$3,023.75$

67. $34' \times 28' \times 30' = 28,560$ cu. ft.
$\$8,568 \div 28,560 = \$.30$ cost per cu. ft.

68. 3 lots at $\$3,000$ each $= \$9,000$ $\$1,000 \div \$8,000 = \frac{1}{8}$ or $12\frac{1}{2}\%$
2 lots at $\$4,000$ each $= \underline{\ 8,000}$
            profit $\overline{\ \ \$1,000}$

69. $\$8,500 \div 8 = \$1,062.50 = 1\%$ of investment
$\$1,062.50 \times 100 = \$106,250$ investment

70. $25' \times 30' \times 5' = 3,750$ cu. ft. 27 cu. ft. $= 1$ cu. yd.
$3,750 \div 27 = 138.89$ cu. yd.
$138.89 \times \$2.90 = \$402.78$

71. $495' \times 1,320' = 653,400$ sq. ft.　　　$43,560$ sq. ft. $= 1$ acre
　　$653,400 \div 43,560 = 15$ acres
　　$15 \times \$200 = \$3,000$ total price

72. 3 lots @ $\$2,400 = \$7,200$　　　$\$1,200 \div \$6,000 = .20$ or 20%
　　2 lots @ $\$3,000 =$ _6,000_
　　　　　　profit $= \overline{\$1,200}$

73. $130' \times 30' = 3,900$ sq. ft.　　　$130' \times 30' \times 24' = 93,600$ cu. ft.
　　$3,900 \times \$8.90 = \$34,710$ cost by sq. ft.
　　$93,600 \times \$.37\frac{1}{2} = \$35,100$ cost by cu. ft.
　　$\$35,100 - \$34,710 = \$390$ saved by giving contract to Dusch

74. $\$6,000 - \$1,200 = \$4,800$, balance due
　　$12 \times \$50 = \$600$ paid each year
　　$\$4,800 \div \$600 = 8$ years
　　First payment February 1, 1965
　　Last payment January 1, 1973

75. S$\frac{1}{2}$ of NE $\frac{1}{4}$ of Sec. 27, T-8-N, R-14-E of 6th P.M. $= \frac{1}{8}$ of the Sec.
　　$\frac{1}{8}$ of 640 $= 80$ acres
　　$80 \times \$207.50 = \$16,600$
　　$\$16,600 \times .05 = \$830$ commission
　　$\frac{1}{2}$ of $\$830 = \$415$, Jones' half of the com.
　　$\$415 \times .075 = \$31.13$, Lawrence's commission
　　$\$415 - \$31.13 = \$383.87$ Net amount J. receives

76. $\$9,000 \times .06 \times \frac{1}{12} = \$45$ interest 1st month
　　　　_45.00_
　　$\overline{\$9,045.00}$ due
　　　　_125.00_ paid 1st month
　　$\overline{\$8,920.00}$ balance $\times .06 \times \frac{1}{12} = \$44.60$ interest 2nd month
　　　　_44.60_ interest
　　$\overline{\$8,964.60}$ due
　　　　_124.60_ 2nd month
　　$\overline{\$8,840.00}$ balance $\times .06 \times \frac{1}{12} = \$44.20$ interest 3rd month
　　　　_44.20_ interest
　　$\overline{\$8,884.20}$ due
　　　　_124.20_ paid 3rd month
　　$\overline{\$8,760.00}$ balance $\times .06 \times \frac{1}{12} = \$43.80$ interest 4th month
　　　　_43.80_ interest
　　$\overline{\$8,803.80}$ due
　　　　_123.80_ paid
　　$\overline{\$8,680.00}$ balance $\times .06 \times \frac{1}{12} = \$43.40$
　　$\$80.00 + \$43.40 = \$123.40$ fifth payment

77. $43,560' \times 10' = 435,600$ sq. ft. in 10 acres.
　　$435,600 - 85,600 = 350,000$ sq. ft. to be subdivided
　　$50' \times 100' = 5,000$ sq. ft. in each lot
　　$350,000 \div 5,000 = 70$ lots

78. $46' \times 80' \times 16' = 58,880$ cu. ft. first floor
　　$58,880 \times \$.80 = \$47,104$ cost of 1st floor

$46' \times 80' \times 14' = 51,520$ cu. ft. 2nd floor
$51,520 \times \$.60 = \$30,912$ cost of 2nd floor
$\$47,104 + \$30,912 = \$78,016$ total cost

79. $\$3,000 \div 60 = \$50$ or 1%
$100 \times \$50 = \$5,000$, cost of other lot

80. $\$15,000 \times .97 = \$14,550$ insured value on $\$15,000$
$\$5,000 \times .90 = \$4,500$ insured value on next $\$5,000$
$\$24,750 - \$20,000 = \$4,750$ to be insured at 75% of value
$\$4,750 \times .75 = \$3,562.50$ insured value on balance
$\$14,550 + \$4,500 + \$3,562.50 = \$22,612.50$, insurable if occupied
$\$22,612.50 \times .85 = \$19,220.63$, insurable if not occupied
$\$19,220.63 \times .04 = \$768.83$ discount collected on closing the loan

81. $12 \times \$400 = \$4,800$ rental
$\$120,000 - 80,000 = \$40,000$, balance @ 5%
$\$40,000 \times .05 = \$2,000$
$\$4,800 + \$2,000 = \$6,800$, rent for the year

82. $\frac{1}{4} + \frac{3}{16} = \frac{7}{16}$ unusable
$1 - \frac{7}{16} = \frac{9}{16}$ usable
$\frac{1}{8} \times \frac{9}{16} = \frac{9}{128}$ for roads
$\frac{9}{16} - \frac{9}{128} = \frac{63}{128}$ usable balance
$\frac{63}{128} \times 6,400 = 3,150$ sq. ft. usable

83. $330' \times 100' = 33,000$ sq. ft.   ($43,560$ sq. ft. $= 1$ acre)
$33,000 \div 43,560 = .75$ or $\frac{3}{4}$ acre

84. $92 \times \$95 = \$8,740$ in older district
$112 \times \$95 = \$10,640$ in newer district

85. b. $\$125 - \$110 = \$15$
$\$15 \times 12 = \$180$ yearly loss
$\$180 \div .06 = \$3,000$ loss in value

86. $\$150 \times 12 = \$1,800$ yearly income
$\$396 + \$66 + \$123 = \$585$ yearly expense
$\$1,800 - \$585 = \$1,215$ profit
$\$1,215 \div \$13,500 = .09$ or 9%

87. $\$8,925.25 + \$1,510.60 + \$4,920.05 + \$3,644.10 = \$19,000.00$ total
expense
$\$53,200 - \$19,000 = \$34,200$

88. $\$11,389 = 115\%$; $\$11,389 \div 115 = \$99.03$; $\$99.03 \times 100 = \$9,903$
original price
$\$9,903 \times .45 = \$4,456.35$; $\$4,456.35 \times .048 = \$213.90$ taxes;
$\$213.90 \times 3 = \$641.70$; $.035 \times \$9,903 = \$346.61$ yearly interest)ss;
$3 \times \$346.61 = \$1,039.83$; $\$11,389 - \$9,903 = \$1,486$
$\$1,039.83 + \$641.70 = \$1,681.53$; $\$1,681.53 - \$1,486 = \$195.53$ loss

89. $\$63 \times 50 = \$3,150$ lot price
$\$3,150 + \$9,216 = \$12,366$ total cost
$\$12,366 - \$5,000 = \$7,366$
$.055 \times \$7,366 = \$405.13$ annual interest payment
$\$405.13 \div 2 = \$202.56\frac{1}{2}$ round off to $\$202.57$

90. $100 + 360 = 460$ foot lot perimeter
$2 \times 3\frac{1}{2} = 7$ feet for gates

$460 - 7 = 453$ feet

$.80 \times 453 = \$362.40$

$2 \times \$16.75 = \$33.50; \$33.50 + \$362.40 = \$395.90$

91. $8 \times 36 = 288$ square feet

$.20 \times 288 = \$57.60$ labor cost

36 ft. $\times$ 8 ft. $\times$ ¼ ft. = 72 cu. ft.

72 cu. ft. $\div$ 27 = 2.666 cu. yds.

2.666 cu. yds. $\times$ $13.50 = \$35.99$

$\$35.99 + \$57.60 = \$93.59$

92. 30 days (April) $-$ 17 days = 13 days

13 days + 31 days (May) + 25 days (June) = 69 days

93. $\$4,901.25 - \$2,015.07 = \$2,886.18$, Davis' equity

$\$17,350 - \$2,886.18 = \$14,463.82$, Davis' encumbrance

$\$14,250 - \$4,901.25 = \$9,348.75$, Underwood's encumbrance

94. (3′ = 1 yd.)

36′ = 12 yd.   9′ = 3 yd.   18″ = 1½′ = ½ yd.

$12 \times 3 \times$ ½ = 18 cu. yd.

95. $351.00, interest on loan $12 \times \$125 = \$1,500$, year's rental

$\;$ 40.20, interest lost on $2,000 $\$1,500 - \$903.10 = \$596.90$, saved

$146.40, taxes   by owning

$\;$ 22.50, fire insurance

$147.00, upkeep

$196.00, depreciation

$\overline{}$

$903.10, cost first year

96. (a) $\frac{1}{100}$ of $9,000 = \$90$, front foot value.

(b) one acre contains 43,560 sq. ft.; ½ acre is 21,780 sq. ft.; $9,000 $\div$ 21,780 sq. ft. = 41 cents value per sq. ft.

(c) $9,000 = \$18,000$, value of one acre

(d) 21,780 sq. ft. $\div$ 100 ft. = 217.8 ft. depth

97. 33′ $\times$ 48′ = 1,584 sq. ft.

$\;$ 6′ $\times$ 20′ = $\;\;$ 120 sq. ft.

1,584 + 120 = 1,704 total sq. ft.

1,704 sq. ft. $\times$ $12.50 = \$21,300$, cost

98. $12 \times \$58.45 = \$701.40$, yearly payment   5¼% = .0525

$701.40 $\div$ .0525 = \$13,360$, amount of original loan

99. 4½ $\times$ 43,560 = 196,020 sq. ft.   196,020 $-$ 71,020 = 125,000 sq. ft.

50′ $\times$ 100′ = 5,000 sq. ft.   125,000 $\div$ 5,000 = 25 lots

100. Monthly interest = balance $\times$ .06 $\times$ $\frac{1}{12}$

$7,500.00, balance $7,320.00, balance

$\;\;\;\;$ 37.50, interest   36.60, interest

$\overline{}$ $\overline{}$

$7,537.50, total $7,356.60, total

$\;\;\;\;$ 97.50, 1st payment   96.60, 4th payment

$\overline{}$ $\overline{}$

$7,440.00, balance $7,260.00, balance

$\;\;\;\;$ 37.20, interest   36.30, interest

$\overline{}$ $\overline{}$

$7,477.20, total $7,296.30, total

   97.20, 2nd payment   96.30, 5th payment
$7,380.00, balance
   36.90, interest
$7,416.90, total
   96.90, 3rd payment
101. .97 × $13,500 = $13,095 $18,500 − $13,500 = $5,000
      .85 × $5,000 = $ 4,250
                    $17,345, insurable
102. 12 × $1,600 = $19,200, annual income
      $19,200 × .45 = $8,640, expense
      $19,200 − $8,640 = $10,560, net income
103. $6,000 × .05 = $300 annual interest $300 ÷ 12 = $25, monthly int.
      $108 ÷ 12 = $9, monthly taxes and ins. $25 + $9 = $34, mo. expenses
      $60 − $34 = $26, paid on principal
      $6,000 − $26 = $5,974, balance
104. .015 × $600,000 = $9,000, 1½% of gross sales
      Must pay minimum of $10,000, first year
      .015 × 1,000,000 = $15,000, rent the fourth year
105. $16,000 × .72 = $11,520, 72% of value
      $11,520 ÷ 1,000 = 11.52, $1,000 units to be insured
      11.52 × $3.10 = $35.71, cost of insurance on dwelling
      $5,600 × .72 = $4,032, 72% of value
      $4,032 ÷ 1,000 = $4.032, $1,000 units
      4.032 × $3.65 = $14.72, insurance on furnishings
      $35.71 + $14.72 = $50.43, insurance per year
      $50.43 × 3 = $151.29, three year premium if paid yearly
      $50.43 × 2½ = $126.08, if premium paid once every three years
      $151.29 − $126.08 = $25.21, saved
106. $6,000 × ½ = $3,000, half year
      $105 ÷ $3,000 = .035 or 3½%
107. 5% = $25 $25 ÷ 5 = $5 or 1% of amount   100% = amount
      100 × $5 = $500, the amount
108. .05 × ½ = .025, rate for ½ year
      $167.50 ÷ .025 = $6,700 or 65% of value
      $6,700 ÷ 65 = $103.0769 or 1% of value
      100 × $103.0769 = $10,307.69, appraised value of property
109. 280 × $105 = $29,400, selling price of farm
      $15,000 × .05 = $750, commission on first $15,000
      $29,400 − $15,000 = $14,400, balance
      $10,000 × .035 = $350, commission on next $10,000
      $14,400 − $10,000 = $4,400, balance
      $4,400 × .02 = $88, commission on balance
      $750 + $350 + $88 = $1,188, total commission
      $1,188 ÷ 2 = $594, 50-50 split commission
      $594 × .10 = $59.40, commission to be paid Stark
      $594 − $59.40 = $534.60, Kane receives

110. Interest = Balance $\times$ .05 $\times$ $\frac{1}{12}$

$12,000, Balance	$11,809.00, total
50, interest	169.00, paid 3rd mo.
$12,050, total	$11,640.00, balance
170, paid 1st mo.	48.50, interest
$11,880, balance	$11,688.50, total
49.50, int.	168.50, 4th payment
$11,929.50, total	$11,520.00, balance
169.50, paid 2nd mo.	48.00, interest
$11,760.00, balance	$11,568.00, total
49.00, interest	168.00, paid 5th mo.

111. $5,000 $\times$ .05 = $250, 5% commission
$250 $\times$ .10 = $25, 10% commission of 5% commission
$250 $\div$ 2 = $125, 50% commission
$125 − $25 = $100, second salesman received

112. $12,000,000 $\div$ $600,000 = 20, ratio of assessed value over taxes
$40,000 $\div$ 20 = $2,000, taxes

113. $\frac{1}{2}$ of $85 = $42.50, 1st mo.
17 $\times$ .05 $\times$ $85 = $72.25, next 17 mo.
$42.50 + $72.25 = $114.75, total commission

114. $5,000 $\times$ .05 = $250, 5% commission
$250 $\times$ .15 = $37.50, 15% commission
$\frac{1}{2}$ of $250 = $125, 50-50 split
$125 − $37.50 = $87.50, salesman receives

115. January 1 to September 15 = 8$\frac{1}{2}$ months, 12 − 8$\frac{1}{2}$ = 3$\frac{1}{2}$ mo. refund
$126 $\times$ $\frac{7}{24}$ = 36\frac{3}{4}$ or $36.75, refund   3$\frac{1}{2}$ $\div$ 12 = $\frac{7}{24}$ of a year

116. 1 $\times$ $6,500 $\times$ .05 = $325.00, commission first year
  4 $\times$ $6,500 $\times$ .02 = $520.00, commission next 4 yr.
10 $\times$ $6,500 $\times$ .015 = $975.00, commission next 10 yr.
  5 $\times$ $6,500 $\times$ .01 = $325.00, commission next 5 years
20 years commission $2,145.00

117. $1,200 − $1,000 = $200, profit on lot in one year
$1,000 $\times$ .10 = $100, profit on loan in one year
                $100, difference

118. $1,000 $\times$ $\frac{9}{12}$ $\times$ .05 = $37.50, interest for 9 months
$1,000 + $37.50 = $1,037.50, amount to be repaid

119. 6 months = $\frac{1}{2}$ year $\frac{1}{2}$ of 6% = 3% due in 6 months
100% − 3% = 97% or $1,000
$1,000 $\div$ 97 = $10.30926 or 1% of the money
$10.30926 $\times$ 100 = $1,030.93 or 100%, all the money needed to have
   $1,000 cash immediately

120. Bal. $120.00 $\times$ .03 = $3.60, int. $23.40 $\div$ $120 = .195 or 19$\frac{1}{2}$%
Bal. $110.00 $\times$ .03 = $3.30, int.
Bal. $100.00 $\times$ .03 = $3.00, int.
Bal. $ 90.00 $\times$ .03 = $2.70, int.
Bal. $ 80.00 $\times$ .03 = $2.40, int.

Bal. $ 70.00 × .03 = $2.10, int.
Bal. $ 60.00 × .03 = $1.80, int.
Bal. $ 50.00 × .03 = $1.50, int.
Bal. $ 40.00 × .03 = $1.20, int.
Bal. $ 30.00 × .03 = $0.90, int.
Bal. $ 20.00 × .03 = $0.60, int.
Bal. $ 10.00 × .03 = $0.30, int.
$23.40, total interest

121. 6 months = ½ year   ½ of 6% = 3% interest due in 6 months
$525 = 3% of the amount invested
$525 ÷ 3 = $175 or 1% of the amount
$175 × 100 = $17,500, or 100% or the total amount invested

122. $16,800 × .05 = $840, salesman $16,800 − $840 = $15,960, owner

123. $14,000 ÷ 1,000 = 14, units of $1,000   14 × $21 = $294, tax

124. $1,500 × .055 = $82.50, interest for one year
$27.50 ÷ $82.50 = .333 or ⅓ of a year   ⅓ of 12 = 4 months

125. $2,000,000 × 5 = $10,000,000
$550,000 ÷ $10,000,000 = .055 or 5½%

126. $10,000 − $8,800 = $1,200, gross profit
$1200 − $100 = $1,100, net profit
$1,100 ÷ $8,800 = .125 or 12½%, profit

127. 12′ × 18′ × ⅓ = 72 cu. ft.   (4″ = ⅓ ft.)
72 ÷ 27 = 2⅔ cu. yd.   (27 cu. ft. = 1 cu. yd.)
2⅔ × $18.00 = $48.00, paving costs
2⅔ × $1.80 =   4.80, labor costs
$35.00, barbecue pit
$212.00, furniture
$299.80, total costs
$500 − 299.80 = $200.20 profit

128. 1320 × 1320 = 1,742,400 square feet
1,742,400 ÷ 2 = 871,200
871,200 ÷ 43,560 = 20 acres

129. .0625 × $15,200 = $950 yearly interest
$950 ÷ 24 = $39.58

130. $3,600 − $1,200 = $2,400; .06 × $2,400 = $144
$2,400 − $600 = $1,800; .06 × $1,800 = $108
$1,800 − $600 = $1,200; .06 × $1,200 = $72
$1,200 − $600 = $600; .06 × $600 = $36
$144 + $108 + $72 + $36 = $360

131. $2,400 × .06 = $144 yearly; $144 ÷ 2 = $72 (first six months)
$2,400 − $600 = $1,800; $1,800 × .06 = $108
$1,800 − $600 = $1,200; $1,200 × .06 = $72
$1,200 − $600 = $600; $600 × .06 = $36; $72 + $108 + $72 +
$36 = $288

132. $78,300 ÷ 9 = $8,700 per acre
100 × 145.2 = 14,520 square feet
14,520 ÷ 43,560 = .33 or ⅓ acre
⅓ × $8,700 = $2,900

133. $2\frac{1}{6} = \frac{13}{6}$

$\$6,500 \div \frac{13}{6} = \$6,500 \times \frac{6}{13} = \$3,000$

134. 25 w. × 24 hours = 600 watt-hours

600 w-h × 16 = 9600 watt-hours

25 w × 12 hours = 300 watt-hours

300 w-h × 2 = 600 watt-hours

9600 w-h + 600 w-h = 10,200 watt-hours

10,200 w-h ÷ 1,000 w = 10.2 kilowatt-hours

10.2 (kw-h) × 3.5¢ = 35.7¢; 35.7¢ × 30 (days in June) = \$10.71

135. 108 yards − 12 yards = 96 yards

96 yards ÷ 6 = 16 yards, width

16 yards × 2 = 32 yards; 32 yards + 6 yards = 38 yards, length

136. \$25,000 + \$1,500 + \$625 = \$27,125, invested

\$30,000 − \$27,125 = \$2,875, expected profit

\$2,875 ÷ \$27,125 = .106 or 10.6% profit over investment

137. Bal. \$5,000 × .06 × $\frac{1}{4}$ = \$75.00, int. 1st quarter

Bal. \$4,700 × .06 × $\frac{1}{4}$ = \$70.50, int. 2nd quarter

Bal. \$4,400 × .06 × $\frac{1}{4}$ = \$66.00, int. 3rd quarter

Bal. \$4,100 × .06 × $\frac{1}{4}$ = \$61.50, int. 4th quarter

$\qquad\qquad\qquad\qquad$ \$273.00, total interest

$\qquad$ 4 × \$300.00 = $\quad$ \$1,200.00, total quarterly payments

$\qquad\qquad\qquad\qquad$ \$1,473.00, total payments 1st year

138. \$21,000 − \$1,000 = \$20,000, balance after down payment

\$20,000 × .05 = \$1,000, interest at end of 1st year

\$20,000 + \$1,000 − \$7,000 = \$14,000, balance after 1st payment

\$14,000 × .05 = \$700, interest at end of 2nd year

\$14,000 + \$700 − \$7,000 = \$7,700, balance after 2nd payment

\$7,700 × .05 = \$385, interest at the end of the 3rd year

\$7,700 + \$385 − \$7,000 = \$1,085, balance after last payment

\$1,085 − \$1,000 = \$85, balance after deducting \$1,000 extra payment
on payment plan

\$85.00 saved by using the payment plan

139. \$12,500 − \$4,000 = \$8,500, balance after down payment

\$8,500 × .05 × $\frac{1}{2}$ = \$212.50, interest after 6 months

\$8,500 + \$212.50 = \$8,712.50, balance with interest added

\$8,712.50 × .05 × $\frac{1}{2}$ = \$217.81, interest at end of year

\$8,712.50 + \$217.81 = \$8,930.31, balance with interest but not
enough to meet the \$9,000 payment

140. (a)　(b)　　　(c)　　　\$41,986

$\qquad\qquad\qquad\qquad\qquad\qquad$ 499

$\qquad\qquad\qquad\qquad\qquad$ $\overline{\qquad\qquad}$

$\qquad\qquad\qquad\qquad\qquad$ 377874

$\qquad\qquad\qquad\qquad\qquad$ 377874

$\qquad\qquad\qquad\qquad$ 167944

$\qquad\qquad\qquad\qquad$ $\overline{\qquad\qquad}$

$\qquad\qquad\qquad\qquad$ \$20951014

141. \$5,800 × .05 = \$290.　　\$290 × .60 = \$174, broker's share.

142. \$8,500 × .05 = \$425.00, 5% office commission

.10 × \$425　=　$\underline{\quad 42.50}$, 10% commission to sales manager

$\qquad\qquad$ \$382.50, balance

$382.50 ÷ 2 = $191.25, commission due salesman

143. 9 months from April 15, 1968 to January 15, 1969 = ¾ year
$1,700 × .05 × ¾ = $63.75, interest due

144. 6 × .025 = .15, depreciation in 6 years
100% − 15% = 85%, value then = $7,650
$7,650 ÷ 85 = $90, or 1% of value
100 × $90 = $9,000, original value of house

145. $10,000 × .05 = $500, 5% of first $10,000
$730 − $500 = $230, balance
$230 ÷ .025 = $9,200, value of over $10,000
$10,000 + $9,200 = $19,200, selling price of property

146. $5,800 − $1,600 = $4,200 $4,200 × .06 = $252, interest
$4,200 + $252 = $4,452 $30 on $4,200 + interest per mo.
$4,200 ÷ 30 = 140 mo. payments   140 ÷ 12 = 11 yr. 8 mo.
Feb. 1, 1961, first payment + 11 yr. 8 mo. = Sept. 1972

147. $6,000 × .60 = $3,600, assessed value   55 mills = $.055
$3,600 × .055 = $198, taxes

148. 60′ × 120′ = 7,200 sq. ft.   7,200 × $.10 = $720, property cost
60′ × $2.50 = $150, paving $150 = profit
$720 + $150 + $150 = $1,020, sales price

149. Dec. 1, 1968 to Mar. 1, 1969 = 3 mo. or ¼ yr.
$20,000 × .04 × ¼ = $200, interest
$500 + $200 = $700 due on mortgage March 1, 1969

150. Interest = balance × .06 × $\frac{1}{12}$

$2,000, balance		$1,924.87, balance
10, interest		9.62, interest
$2,010, total		$1,934.49, total
35, payment		45.00, payment
$1,975.00, balance		$1,889.49, balance
9.87, interest		9.45, interest (Dec.)
$1,984.87, total		$1,898.94, balance
60.00, payment		$10 + $9.87 + $9.62 = $29.49, int. pd.

151. $1,325.28 ÷ 2 = $662.64 paid
$662.64 ÷ 12 = $55.22, ½ month payment to be paid by buyer
$662.64 − $55.22 = $607.42, taxes charged seller

152. $325 − $155 = $170, net income per month
$170 × 12 = $2,040, net income per year

153. 250 ft. × 750 ft. = 187,500 sq. ft.
187,500 sq. ft. divided by 43,560 sq. ft. = 4.304 acres.
4.305 @ $950 = $4,088.80.

154. $13,000 × .18 = $2,340, down payment
$13,000 − $2,340 = $10,660, amount to borrow
$10,660 × .015 = $159.90, loan commission
$2,340 + $159.90 = $2,499.90, amount needed

155. 65 ft. × 150 ft. = 9,750 sq. ft.
9,750 × $1.25 = $12,187.50
65 ft. × $10 = $650; total price: $12,837.50

156. 43,560 sq. ft. = 1 acre
326.7′ × 200′ = 65,340 sq. ft.   65,340 ÷ 43,560 = 1½ acres
1½ × $5,000 = $7,500, selling price

157. 33′ × 48′ = 1,584 sq. ft.
6′ × 20′ = 120 sq. ft.
1,704 sq. ft. × $12.50 = $21,300.

158. 1 mile = 5,280′
¼ of 5,280 = 1,320′ on the south side of NE ¼ of NE ¼ of a section

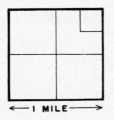

←— I MILE —→

159. 36′ × 9′ × $.20 = $64.80, labor cost per sq. ft.
4″ = ⅓ ft.   36′ × 9′ × ⅓ = 108 cu. ft.   27 cu. ft. = 1 cu. yd.
108 ÷ 27 = 4 cu. yd.   4 × $15 = $60, cost of concrete
$60 + $64.80 = $124.80, total cost

160. 4 × $85 = $340, rent income per month
.45 × $340 = $153, profit
$36,000 ÷ 12 = $3,000, investment per month
$153 ÷ $3,000 = .051 pr 5.1% return on investment

161. SW ¼ = 160 acres
SW ¼ of SW ¼ = 40 acres
W ½ of 40 acres = 20 acres

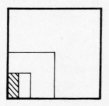

162. 32′ × 24′ × 20′ = 15,360 cu. ft.   (Because of gable use only ½ of 8′
height in attic: 8′ + 8′ + 4′ = 20′ total ht.)

163. 32′ × 24′ = 768 sq. ft.
$10,828.80 ÷ 768 = $14.10, cost per sq ft.

164. 50 × $44 = $2200, assessed value of lot
                $6500, assessed value of house
         ――――――
           $8700, total assessment
$8,700 × $.048 = $417.60, year's taxes

165. $50 \times \$65 = \$\ \ 3{,}250$, cost of lot

           $\underline{\$10{,}828.80}$, cost of house

           $\$14{,}078.80$, total cost

         $\underline{-\ \$\ \ 6{,}500.00}$, cash payment

           $\$\ \ 7{,}578.80$, balance

    $\$7{,}578.80 \times \frac{1}{2} \times .05 = \$189.47$, first semi-annual interest payment

166. $32' \times 24' \times 20' \times \$.775 = \$11{,}904$, bid A

      $32' \times 24' \times 3' \times \$4.70 = \ \ \underline{\$10{,}828.80}$, bid B

      Bid B cheaper by $\$\ \ 1{,}075.20$

167. $10 \times 2\% = 20\%$ depreciation in 10 years

      $\$10{,}828.80 \times .20 = \$2{,}165.76$, amount of depreciation

      $\$10{,}828.80 - \$2{,}165.76 = \$8{,}663.04$ value in 10 years

      $\$65 \times .22 = \$14.30$, increase in value per front ft.

      $\$65 + \$14.30 = \$79.30$, cost per front ft. 10 years

      $\$79.30 \times 50 = \$3{,}965$, cost of lot in 10 years

      $\$3{,}965 + \$8{,}663.04 = \$12{,}628.04$, total value of property in 10 years

168. $\$10{,}828.80 \times .05 = \$541.44$, architect's charge

      $50 \times \$65 = \$3{,}250$, cost of lot

      $\$10{,}828.80 + \$3{,}250.00 + \$541.44 = \$14{,}620.24$, total investment

      $1 - \frac{3}{4} = \frac{1}{4}$ equity $\frac{1}{4}$ of $\$14{,}620.24 = \$3{,}655.06$, equity

169. $\$21.75 \times 2 = \$43.50$, cost of gates

      $180' - 4' = 176'$ linear measurement excluding gate

      $176' + 50' + 176' + 50' = 452'$ total linear ft.

      $452 \times \$.85 = \$384.20$, cost of fencing

      $\$384.20 + \$43.50 = \$427.70$, total cost of fencing and gates

170. $36' \times 6' \times \$.27 = \$58.32$, labor costs $4'' = \frac{1}{3}$ ft.

      $36' \times 6' \times \frac{1}{3} = 72$ cu. ft. 27 cu. ft. $= 1$ cu. yd.

      $72 \div 27 = 2\frac{2}{3}$ cu. yd. $2\frac{2}{3} \times \$14.25 = \$38.00$, cost of concrete

      $\$58.32 + \$38.00 = \$96.32$, total cost of driveway

171. $12 \times \$155 = \$1{,}860$, income on property per year

      $\$402 + \$78 + \$260 = \$740$, yearly expenses

      $\$1{,}860 - \$740 = \$1{,}120$, profit per year

      $\$1{,}120 \div \$14{,}000 = .08$ or 8% net return on investment

172. From problem 168, $\frac{3}{4}$ of total cost $=$ mortgage

      $\frac{3}{4}$ of $\$14{,}620.24 = \$10{,}965.18$, mortgage

      $\$10{,}965.18 \times .06 \times \frac{1}{12} = \$54.83$, interest

        $\underline{+\ \ 54.83}$, interest

      $\$11{,}020.01$, balance plus interest

        $\underline{-\ \ 75.00}$, payment

      $\$10{,}945.01$, new balance $\$10{,}945.01 \times .06 \times \frac{1}{12} = \$54.73$

        $\underline{+\ \ 54.73}$, interest

      $\$10{,}999.74$, balance plus interest

        $\underline{-\ \ 75.00}$, payment

      $\$10{,}924.74$, balance after June payment

173. $50 \times \$65 = \$3{,}250$, cost of original lot

      $\$7{,}300 - \$3{,}250 = \$4{,}050$, balance to be invested in land

$4,050 ÷ $1.50 = 2,700 sq. ft. can be bought
2,700 ÷ 180 = 15' front ft. can be bought
15' + 50' = 65', frontage   180' × 65' = 11,700 sq. ft.

174. $3,100 × .55 = $1,705, taxable
$1,705 ÷ 1,000 = 1.705 units
1.705 × $42.25 × 5 = $360.18, taxes
$3,100 × .04 × 5 = $620, interest loss
$3,100 + $360.18 + $620.00 = $4,080.18, total transaction
$4,250.00 − $4,080.18 = $169.82, profit

175. 1 acre = 43,560 sq. ft.   1½ acre = 65,340 sq. ft.
¼ of 65,340 = 16,335 sq. ft. too steep
⅓ of 65,340 = 21,780 sq. ft. in stream
           38,115 sq. ft. not usable
65,340 − 38,115 = 27,225 sq. ft. usable
⅙ of 27,225 = 4,537.5 sq. ft. for roads
27,225 − 4,537.5 = 22,687.5 sq. ft. for building

176. 100% − 15% = 85%, selling price
$17,000 × .85 = $14,450, selling price
$14,450 × .06 = $867.00 commission
½ of $867 = $433.50, Mr. Duncan's 50% commission
$433.50 × .20 = $86.70, Mr. Rayer's commission
$433.50 − $86.70 = $346.80, net amount Mr. Duncan received on sale

177. 4 × 100 = $400 annual payment
$400 divided by $8,000 = .05 or 5%

178. $50,000 × .15 = $7,500 down payment
$50,000 − $7,500 = $42,500 balance
$42,500 ÷ $1,000 = 42.5 units of $1,000
42.5 × $7.50 = $318.75 monthly payments

179. $3,000 = 5% of value
$3,000 ÷ 5 = $600 or 1% of value
100 × $600 = $60,000 capitalized value of property

180. 69' × 142' = 9,798 sq. ft.
$2,645.46 ÷ 9,798 = $.27 per sq. ft.

181. 50' × 100' = 5,000 sq. ft.   5,000 × $.75 = $3,750, selling price
$3,750 × .05 = $187.50, sales commission
$3,750 − $187.50 = $3,562.50, seller receives

182. 4 × $57.55 = $230.20, annual interest payment
$230.20 ÷ $4,200 = .0548 or about 5½% interest rate

183. 60 × $150 = $9,000 list price $7,650 × .10 = $765 sales commission
$7,650 + $765 = $8,415, selling price
$9,000 − $8,415 = $585 buyer saved

184. ¹⁄₁₂ of $300 = $25, tax for one month
March 15, 1968 to December 31, 1968 = 9½ mos.
9½ × $25 = $237.50

185. 12 × $300 = $3,600 yearly rental
$120,000 − $80,000 = $40,000 amount over $80,000
$40,000 × .05 = $2,000, 5% over gross of $80,000
$3,600 + $2,000 = $5,600, Brown received yearly

186. $7,095 ÷ 86 = $82.50 per front ft.   86′ × 110′ = 9,460 sq. ft.
$7,095 ÷ 9,460 = $.75 per sq. ft.

187. 1,600 × $11 = $17,600, cost of house
20′ × 30′ = 600 sq. ft.   600 × $4 = $2,400, cost of garage
50′ × $15 = $750, cost of lot
$17,600 + $2,400 + $750 = $20,750, total cost

188. 33′ 6″ = 33½′   45′ 6″ = 45½′   33½′ × 45½′ = 1,524.25 sq. ft.
15′ × 5′ = 75 sq. ft. for family room
1,524.25 + 75 = 1,599.25 total sq. ft.
1,599.25 × $12.85 = $20,550.36, total cost of building house

189. 3,250 sq. ft. × $.14 = $455.00
2,000 sq. ft. × $.085 = $170.00
7,250 sq. ft. × $1 = $7,250.00
$455 + $170 + $7,250 = $7,875 total price
3,250 sq. ft. + 2,000 sq. ft. + 7,250 sq. ft. = 12,500 sq. ft. area
$7,875 ÷ 12,500 = $.63

190. .05 × $10,000 = $500 commission on the first $10,000
$730 − $500 = $230 = the 2½ percent commission on the excess
$230 ÷ 2.5 = $92
$92 × 100 = $9200 excess
$10,000 + $9200 = $19,200

191. 30′ × 30′ = 900 sq. ft. area of square
$3.14 × radius^2$ = area of circle
27′ ÷ 2 = 13.5′ radius
3.14 × 13.5′ × 13.5′ = 572.265 sq. ft. area of circle
900 sq. ft. − 572.265 sq. ft. = 327.735 sq. ft.

192. 40′ × 24′ × 15′ = 14,400 cu. ft.
14,400 ÷ 200 = 72 persons

193. a. 20′ × 15′ × 9′ = 2700 cu. ft.
27 cu. ft. = 1 cu. yd.
2700 cu. ft. ÷ 27 cu. ft. = 100 cu. yds.
b. 100 × $3.40 = $340

194. 45′ × 25′ × 8′ = 9,000 cu. ft.
27 cu. ft. = 1 cu. yd.
9,000 cu. ft. ÷ 27 cu. ft. = 333⅓ cu. yds.
333⅓ cu. yds. ÷ 4 cu. yds. = 83⅓ or 84 truck-loads

195. 60′ × $9.00 = $540
59 + 58 + 57 . . . + 4 + 3 + 2 + 1 = 1770
$1.25 × 1770 = $2,212.50
$540 + $2,212.50 = $2,752.50

196. 15′ × 24′ = 360 sq. ft.
9 sq. ft. = 1 sq. yd.
360 sq. ft. ÷ 9 sq. ft. = 40 sq. yds.
40 × $14.95 = $598

197. 8 × 2 yds. = 16 yds.
16 × $3.90 = $62.40

198. 240 × $60 = $14,400, B's allowance
$23,500 − $14,400 = $9,100 B owes A

199. $16,000 − $13,600 = $2,400, profit
$2,400 divided by $13,600 = 17.6%
200. $23,000 − $11,000 = $12,000, net income
$12,000 ÷ $120,000 = .10 or 10% return on investment
201. $400 divided by 40 mills = $10,000 assessed value
$10,000 : 50% :: (×) : 100%
$10,000 × 100 divided by 50 = $20,000
202. $140 × 12 = $1,680, annual income
$1,680 ÷ $21,000 = .08 or 8% return on investment
203. $6,000 × .05 × $\frac{1}{12}$ = $25.00, interest 1st month
$6,000 + $25.00 = $6,025
$6,025 − $60 = $5,965, balance (plus insurance and taxes)
204. $10,000 − $1,500 = $8,500, amount of fire insurance on house
205. No stamps are necessary.
206. $140,000 − $80,000 = $60,000, gross over $80,000
$60,000 × .05 = $3,000, 5% on gross over $80,000
12 × $300 = $3,600, minimum monthly rent
$3,600 + $3,000 = $6,600, Doe receives
207. 60 × $150 = $9,000, list price
$7,650 × .10 = $765, 10% on sales price
$7,650 + $765 = $8,415, buyer paid
$9,000 − $8,415 = $585, buyer saved
208. Mar. 1, 1968, to Nov. 16, 1968 = 8½ months   3 years = 36 months
8½ ÷ 36 = $\frac{17}{72}$ part of premium used
$\frac{17}{72}$ × $158.40 = $37.40, amount of premium used
$158.40 − $37.40 = $121.00, unused portion of premium
209. 100′ × $15 = $1,500, property assessment
$3,200, house assessment
$\overline{}$
$4,700, total assessment
$.040 × $4,700 = $188.00, total yearly tax
210. $6,800 × .03 × $\frac{1}{12}$ = $17.00, interest per month
$6,200 × .025 × $\frac{1}{12}$ = 12.92, painting and repairs
.75 × 6.8 × $24 × $\frac{1}{12}$ = 10.20, taxes
6.2 × $4.50 × $\frac{1}{12}$ =   2.33, insurance
$600 × .05 × $\frac{1}{12}$ =   2.50, upkeep
$\overline{}$
$44.95, expenses
$50.00 − $44.95 = $5.05, cheaper per month to buy
211. 8 × 2½% = 20%, dep. in 8 yrs.   100% × $180 = $18,000
$14,440 = 80%
$14,400 ÷ 80 = $180 or 1% of value
212. $5,000 × $3.50 × $\frac{1}{100}$ = $175
$175 × .05 = $8.75
$175 + $8.75 = $183.75, if tardy $175, if paid on time
$175 − $8.75 = $166.25, if prompt
213. $566.66 × 15 × $\frac{3}{12}$ = $7.08, interest
214. $2,160 ÷ $45 = 48 payments

$48 \div 12 = 4$ years

October 1, 1976 to September 1, 1980

215. $150 = 2\frac{1}{2}\%$ $150 \div 2\frac{1}{2} = \$60$, 1% $100 \times \$60 = \$6,000$ amount

216. 43,560 sq. ft. = 1 acre

217. $8 \times \$50 = \$400$ month

    $50 \times 12 \times \frac{1}{2} = \$300$, $\frac{1}{2}$ monthly rent for year on one apartment

    $12 \times \frac{1}{2} \times .05 \times \$400 = \$120$. 5% of rents collected for $\frac{1}{2}$ year

    $\$300 + \$120 = \$420$, maximum

218. June 1967 to June 1970 = 3 years = 36 months

    January 1969 − January 1967 = 1 year, 7 months = 19 months

    $36 - 19 = 17$ months not used

    $17 \times \$1.00 = \$17.00$

219. $25 = 5\%$ $25 \div 5 = \$5$, 1% $100 \times \$5 = \$500$, amount

220. $\$12,000 \times 0.25 \times 6 = \$1,800$ depreciation on house

    $\$2,000 \times .08 \times 6 = \$960$, increase in value on lot

    $\$14,000 + \$960 - \$1,800 = \$13,160$, total value of property after 6 yr.

221. $2 \times \$55 = \$110$, monthly rental $\$440 \times 12 = \$5,280$, gross

    $2 \times \$75 = \$150$, monthly rental   yearly income on the 6

    $2 \times \$90 = \$180$, monthly rental   apartments

    $\overline{\$440}$, total monthly rental

222. June 1 to December 1 = 6 months = $\frac{1}{2}$ year

    $\$4,500 \times \frac{1}{2} \times .05 = \$112.50$, credit to purchaser

223. $4 \times \$80 = \$320$, annual interest

    $\$320 \div \$8,000 = .04$ or 4%

224. $\$7,850 + \$70 = \$7,920$ $100\% - 4\% = 96\% = \$7,920$

    $\$7,920 \div 96 = \$82.50$, 1% of amount $100 \times \$82.50 = \$8,250$, amount

225. $\$20,000 + \$7,000 = \$27,000$ mortgaged

    $\$50,000 - \$27,000 = \$23,000$ taxable   Tax stamp = $1.10 per $1,000

    $\$23,000 \div \$1,000 = 23$ taxable units

    $23 \times \$1.10 = \$25.30$ in documentary stamps

226. $\$1,800 \div \$20,000 = .09 = 9\%$

227. $55 \times \$35 = \$1,925$ cost by front footage

    $\$1,925 \times .05 = \$96.25$, commission

228. $3 \times \$25 = \$75$, taxes for 3 years $\$75 + \$60 = \$135$, expenses

    $\$1,000 \times .02 \times 3 = \$60$, interest $\$300 - \$135 = \$165$, profit

229. $\$10,000 \times .80 = \$8,000$, 80% of value

    $\$8,000 \div 100 = 80$ insurable units $80 \times \$.60 = \$48$, 3 years' insurance

    $\$48 \div 3 = \$16$, one year's insurance

230. $\$1.55 \times \$5,800 \times \frac{1}{100} = \$89.90$, school tax

231. $12 \times \$275 = \$3,300$, profit per year $\$3,300 = 8\%$

    $\$3,300 \div 8 = \$412.50$, 1% of profit

    $100 \times \$412.50 = \$41,250$, total profit

232. 31 days in October

    $31 \times \$42.50 = \$1,317.50$, total income for month

233. $200 \times \$25 = \$5,000$, cost of land $40' \times 40' \times 30' = 48,000$ cu. ft.

    $48000 \times \$.35 = \$16,800$, cost of house

    $\$16,800 + \$5,000 = \$21,800$, total cost

234. $16 + 2\frac{1}{2} + 2\frac{1}{4} = 40\frac{3}{4}$ mills or \$.04075   \$5,000 × .70 = \$3,500
$.04075 × \$3,500 = \$142.62$

235. $\$13,500 × .055 × \frac{1}{2} = \$371.25$, semi-annual interest payment

236. January 1 to September 15 = $8\frac{1}{2}$ months used $12 - 8\frac{1}{2} = 3\frac{1}{2}$ mo.
$3\frac{1}{2} × \frac{1}{12} × \$126 = \$36.75$, refund

237. $24' × 32' = 768$ sq. ft. (22 bags)
768 sq. ft. ÷ 36 sq. ft. = $21\frac{1}{3}$

238. $80' × 6' = 480$ sq. ft.
$150' - 24' = 126'$
$126' × 6' = 756$ sq. ft.
756 sq. ft. + 480 sq. ft. = 1,236 sq. ft. The walk is inside the lot.

239. $1800 = 6%
$1800 ÷ 6 = $300
$300 × 100 = $30,000

240. $30,000 = 82% gross volume sales
$30,000 ÷ 82 = $365.85365
$365.85365 × 100 = $36,585.37

241. $60' × 120' = 7,200$ sq. ft.
$30' × 200' = 6,000$ sq. ft.
43,560 sq. ft. − 6,000 sq. ft. = 37,560 sq. ft.
37,560 sq. ft. ÷ 7,200 sq. ft. = 5.216 lots

242. $.02 × \$10,828.80 = \$216.576$ depreciation each year
$10 \text{ yrs.} × \$216.576 = \$2,165.70$
$\$10,828.80 - \$2,165.76 = \$8,663.04$ value of house
$50' × \$65 = \$3,250$ original cost of lot
$1\frac{2}{2} × \$3,250 = \$3,965$ lot value
$\$3,965 + \$8,663.04 = \$12,628.04$

243. $3,250 = lot cost; $10,828.80 building cost
$.05 × \$10,828.80 = \$541.44$ to architect
$\$3,250 + \$10,828.80 + \$541.44 = \$14,620.24 = total cost
total cost − $\frac{3}{4}$ total cost (mortgage) = $\frac{1}{4}$ total cost = equity
$14,620.24 ÷ 4 = $3,655.06

244. $20 × 4\frac{3}{4}" = 95"$
$95" ÷ 12 = 7.92'$
$19 × 6.85' = 130.15'$
$130.15' + 7.92' = 138.07'$; $138.07' ÷ 3$ (feet in one yard) = 46.023 yards

245. $\$46,500 × .065 × \frac{1}{12} = \$251.88$

246.
5 @	\$17	=	\$ 85
9 @	15	=	135
8 @	16	=	128
5 @	18	=	90
5 @	3.75	=	18.75, garages

$\overline{}$ \$456.75, week

52 weeks = 1 year
52 × \$456.75 = \$23,751, gross
income yearly

247. $6,500 × .30 = $1,950, increase
$6,500 + $1,950 = $8,450, asking price
$8,450 × .25 = $2,112.50, reduction
$8,450 − $2,112.50 = $6,337.50, selling price
$6,337.50 × .05 = $316.88, commission

$2,112.50 + $316.88 = $2,429.38, loss
$2,429.38 − $1,950 = $479.38, loss

248. $4\frac{1}{2}\%$ of $874 = $39.33, interest for one year
1 month = $\frac{1}{12}$ of $39.33 or $3.277
2 years, 8 months, 15 days = $32\frac{1}{2}$ months
$32\frac{1}{2} \times 3.277 = $106.50

249. $66\frac{2}{3}\% = \frac{2}{3}$　　　.05 = $\frac{5}{100}$　　　$\frac{2}{3} \times \frac{5}{100} = \frac{10}{300} = \frac{1}{30}$
$200 ÷ $\frac{1}{30}$ = $6,000, appraised valuation

250. $100 + 20 = 120\% = $7,500　　　　　$7,500 ÷ 120 = $62.50 or 1%
$100 \times $62.50 = $6,250, cost of house

251. $14 − 2 = 12$ lots for sale　　　　$75 \times 12 = 900$ front feet
$33,750 ÷ 900 = $37.50 per front foot

252. $108,900 ÷ 43,560 = $2\frac{1}{2}$ acres
$2\frac{1}{2} \times $1,250 = $3,125, amount realized from sale

253. 160 sq. rd. = 1 acre
$160 ÷ 5\frac{1}{2} = 29\frac{1}{11}$ rods

254. $160 − 42\frac{1}{4} = 117\frac{3}{4}$ acres　　　　$\frac{1}{3} \times 117\frac{3}{4} = 39\frac{1}{4}$ acres
$117\frac{3}{4} − 39\frac{1}{4} = 78\frac{1}{2}$ acres unsold

255. 160 sq. rd. = 1 acre　　　$90 ÷ 160 = \frac{9}{16}$ acre
$7,888.30 ÷ 89\frac{9}{16} = $88.08 per acre

256. $100 \times 160 = $ 16,000 sq. rd.
$\frac{1}{8} \times 16,000 = \underline{\ 2,000}$　　　　　$14,000 ÷ 140$ lots = 100 sq. rods
　　　　　　　　14,000 sq. rd.

257. $490.30 ÷ .042 = $11,673.81 or 58.25% of value
$11,673.81 ÷ 58.25 = $200.4087 or 1% of value
$100 \times $200.4087 = $20,040.87 value of property

258. 43,560 sq. ft. = 1 acre　　　$5\frac{1}{4} \times 43,560 = 228,690$ sq. ft.
$228,690 − 36,690 = 192,000$ sq. ft.　　　$60' \times 100' = 6,000$ sq. ft. in lot
$192,000 ÷ 6,000 = 32$ lots

259. $500' + 350' + 500' + 350' = 1,700'$　　　　$3' = 1$ yd.
$1,700 ÷ 3 = 566\frac{2}{3}$ yd.
$566\frac{2}{3} \times $2 = $1,133.33 cost of curb
　　　　　　　$3,200.00 cost of sidewalk
　　　　　　$\overline{\$4,333.33}$, total cost

260. $100\% − 20\% = 80\%$　　　$20 ÷ 80 = .25$ or 25%

261. $3,120.50 \times 1\frac{1}{2} \times .055 = $257.44, interest

262. $720 ÷ 16 = $45, cost of 1 acre
$197 \times $45 = $8,865, cost of 197 acres

263. $600' \times 300' = 180,000$ sq. ft.　　　$180,000 ÷ 43,560 = 4.13+$ acres

264. $9,080 + $40 = $9,120　　　$9,120 = 95% S. P. (less 5% com.)
$9,120 ÷ 95 = $96 or 1% value　　　$100 \times $96 = $9,600, S. Price

265. $6,000 \times .055 \times \frac{1}{12} = $27.50, interest first month
$108 ÷ 12 = $　　　　　　9.00, taxes and insurance
　　　　　　　　$\overline{\$36.50}$, total expenses
$60 − $36.50 = $23.50, paid on principal
$6,000 − $23.50 = $5,976.50, balance

266. $25' \times 30' \times 5' = 3,750$ cu. ft.　　　27 cu. ft. = 1 cu. yd.
$3,750 ÷ 27 = 138.88$ cu. yd.　　　$138.88 \times $2.90 = $402.75, cost

267. $6,000 × .055 × ¼ = $82.50, quarterly interest
268. 100 × $25 = $ 2,500, frontage   45' × 45' × 30' = 60,750 cu. ft.
     60,750 × $.35 = 21,262.50 by cu. ft.
                     ——————
                     $23,762.50, total cost
269. $193.50 × 75 = $14,512.50, selling price of lot
270. 640 acres = 1 section
271. 36 sections = 1 township (6 miles long and 6 miles wide) each section one square mile
272. Find square root: Or estimate divisor, divide
        2 0 8. 7   and average:
      √ 43560.00   43560 ÷ 200 = 217.8
        4   200 + 217.8 = 417.8
                                             417.8 ÷ 2   = 208.7

        408 | 3560
              3264
        4167 | 29600
               29619

273. 3 @ $100 = $300, per mo.   12 × $1,090 = $13,080, gross
     2 @ $125 = 150, per mo.   annual income
     1 @ $150 = 150, per mo.
     6 @ $ 65 = 390, per mo.
                ——————
                $1,090, total per mo.
274. 12 × $950   = $11,400 or 8% of investment
     $11,400 ÷ 8 = $1,425 or 1%   100 × $1,425 = $142,500 investment
275. Sec. 9 = 640 acres   ¼ of 640 = 160 acres   ¼ of 160 = 40 acres
276. 760' × 500' = 380,000 sq. ft.   380,000 ÷ 43,560 = 8.72 acres
277. .16 × $10,000 = $1,600 annual income
     $1,600 ÷ 12 = $133.33 mo. income
278. Assessment and tax millage
279. (a)   (b)

NE 1/4 = 10 ACRES
NE 1/4 = 40 ACRES
NW 1/4 = 160 ACRES

2 1/2 ACRES

280. 2½ × .16 × ¹⁄₁₀₀ × $24,500 = $98, total premium for 3 years
     $98 ÷ 36 = $2.72, monthly cost
281. 12 × $300 = $3,600, yr. rental $4,800 − $3,600 = $1,200 or 4%
     $1,200 ÷ 4 = $300 or 1%   100 × $300 = $30,000, amount over $150,000
     $150,000 + $30,000 = $180,000, total business
282. 8½ × ¹⁄₁₂ × 180 = $127.50, buyer owes seller
     8½ × ¹⁄₁₂ × $240 = 170.00, buyer owes seller
                        ——————
                        $297.50, buyer owes seller
     3½ × ¹⁄₁₂ × $118 =   34.41, seller owes buyer
                        ——————
                        $263.09, buyer owes seller

283. 43,560 sq. ft. = 1 acre $1.87 \times 43,560 = 81,457.2$ sq. ft.
     $81,457.2 \times .225 = \$18,327.87$, selling price
284. $\$6,000 \times \frac{1}{100} \times \$1.55 = \$93.00$, school tax
285. $100 \times 108.9 = 10,890$ sq. ft. $10,890 \div 43,560 = .25$ or $\frac{1}{4}$ acre
286. $\$8,000 \times .80 = \$6,400$ assessed value
     $\$6,400 \times \frac{1}{100} \times \$4.20 = \$268.80$, annual tax
287. $\$8,000 \times .045 \times \frac{19}{24} = \$285$ interest $(9\frac{1}{2} \times \frac{1}{12} = \frac{19}{24}$ yr$)$
288. $\$7,200 - \$6,000 = \$1,200$ gain $\$1,200 \div \$6,000 = .20$ or 20%
289. $\$9,300 \times .05 = \$465$, broker's commission
     $\$465 + \$95 = \$560$, expenses
     $\$9,300 - \$560 = \$8,740$, seller received
290. $\$62,350 - \$15,750 = \$46,600$ $\$46,600 - \$36,675 = \$9,925$
     $\$9,925 + \$6,240 = \$16,165$, cash difference
291. 9 sq. ft. = 1 sq. yd. $90 \div 9 = 10$ $1,080 \div 10 = 108$ feet
292. Valuation of property = assumed perpetual income $\div$ rate to be
     realized
     $\$1,134 \times 12 = \$13,608$, gross yr. income
     $\$13,608 - \$2,500 = \$11,108$ or 8% $\$11,108 \div .08 = \$138,850$, price
293. $125 \times \$2.25 = \$281.25$, paving $160' \times 125' \times \$.17 = \$3,400$
     $\$3,400 + \$281.25 = \$3,681.25$, cost
     $\underline{ 295.00}$, profit
     $\$3,976.25$, selling price
294. $\$15,000 \times .05 = \$1,710$
     $\underline{ 750}$, commission on first $\$15,000$
     $\$960$
     $\$20,000 \times .03 = 600$, commission on next $\$20,000$
     $\overline{ \$360} \div .015 = \$24,000$
     $\$15,000 + \$20,000 + \$24,000 = \$59,000$ Selling Price
295. $\$7,670 \div 65 = \$118$, price per front foot
296. $\$325 - \$155 = \$170$, monthly income
     $12 \times \$170 = \$2,040$, net income per year
297. $\$57.75 \times 4 = \$231$, year's interest payment
     $\$231 \div \$4,200 = .055$ or $5\frac{1}{2}\%$
298. $\$8,750 \times .05 = \$437.50$, broker's commission
     $\$3,000 - \$500 = \$2,500$, mortgage balance
     $\$2,500 \times .05 \times \frac{1}{12} = \$10.42$, interest due buyer
     Taxes paid for January 1 to December 31 = 12 months
     June 30 to December 31 = 6 months or $\frac{1}{2}$ year
     $\$136 \times \frac{1}{2} = \$68$ due seller
299. $\$12,000 \times .80 = \$9,600$, insured value of property
     $\$4,000 \times .80 = \$3,200$, insured value of furniture and goods
     $\$9,600 \times \frac{1}{1000} \times \$2.80 = \$26.88$, premium on property
     $\$3,200 \times \frac{1}{1000} \times \$5.30 = \$10.56$, premium on household goods
     $\overline{ \$37.44}$, yearly premium
     $3 \times \$37.44 = \$112.32$, three-year premium on a yearly basis
     $2\frac{1}{2} \times \$37.44 = 93.60$, premium on a three-year basis
     $\overline{\phantom{2\frac{1}{2} \times \$37} \$\ 18.72}$, saved on a three-year basis

300. $6,000 − $2,000 = $4,000, income
$4,000 ÷ $40,000 = .10 or 10%
301. 30 days in September $\frac{12}{30} = \frac{2}{5}$ of a month
From January 1 to September 12 = $8\frac{2}{5}$ months
$875.24 × $8\frac{2}{5}$ × $\frac{1}{12}$ = $612.66, credit to purchaser
302. 12 × $400 = $4,800, minimum monthly rental for a year
$120,000 − $80,000 = $40,000, gross yearly business over $80,000
$40,000 × .05 = $2,000, 5% of gross business
$4,800 + $2,000 = $6,800, rent
303. 40 × $2,200 = $88,000, selling price = 110%
$88,000 ÷ 110 = $800 or 1%
100 × $800 = $80,000, cost
304. 12 × $280 = $3,360 income
$3,360 ÷ $42,000 = .08 or 8%
305. 264′ × 660′ = 174,240 sq. ft.   43,560 sq. ft. = 1 acre
174,240 ÷ 43,560 = 4 acres
4 × $800 = $3,200 cost of lot
306. 320 × $\frac{1}{2}$ × .05 × $175 = $1400, commission
307. $3,600 ÷ .06 = $60,000 cost of farm
308. 32 × 40 × $9.50 = $12,160 cost $12,160 × .05 = $608, depreciation
$12,160 − $608 = $11,552, appraisal
309. 30′ × 200′ = 6,000 sq. ft.   43,560 − 6,000 = 37,560 sq. ft.
60′ × 120′ = 7,200 sq. ft. in lot   37,560 ÷ 7,200 = 5.21+ lots
310. 100 × 12 = $1,200 yearly income $1,200 ÷ $12,000 = .10 or 10%
311. 43,560 × 10 = 435,600 sq. ft.   435,600 − 85,000 = 350,600 sq. ft.
50′ × 100′ = 5,000 sq. ft., each lot   350,600 ÷ 5,000 = 70.1 lots
312.   106′ × 66′ = 6,996 sq. ft.
                                 100′ × 60′ = 6,000 sq. ft.
                                    996 sq. ft. for walk

```
              106'
        ┌─────────────────┐
        │  ┌───────────┐  │
   66'  │  │ 60'  100' │  │
        │  └───────────┘  │
        └─────────────────┘
```

313. 996 × $.23 = $229.08 cost of walk
314. 2,583   9,421   7,488
      4,905   2,892   6,529
      ‾‾‾‾‾   ‾‾‾‾‾   ‾‾‾‾‾
      7,488 sum   6,529 difference   959 excess
315. 80 × $250 = $20,000, cost   100 × $750 = $75,000, selling price
                6,500, dev. cost   26,500, total cost
                  ‾‾‾‾‾‾‾‾‾‾   ‾‾‾‾‾‾‾‾‾‾
             $26,500, total cost $48,500, net profit
316. 30 × 16 = 480 sq. rd.   160 sq. rd. = 1 acre
480 ÷ 160 = 3 acres
317. $325 × 12 × $2\frac{1}{2}$ = $9,750, value of the home
318. 2,640 × 9,900 = 26,136,000 sq. ft.
43,560 sq. ft. = 1 acre
26,136,000 ÷ 43,560 = 600 acres

10% + 10% + 20% = 40%

.40 × 600 = 240 acres for streets, playgrounds and factory

600 − 240 = 360 acres left for homesites

2 × 360 = 720 one-half acre sites

319. 15′ × 34′ = 510 sq. ft.　　　2 × 510 = 1,020, sq. ft. both sides

$.08 + $.026 = $.106 per sq. ft.　　　1,020 × $.106 = $108.12, cost

320. 50′ × 150′ = 7,500 sq. ft. area

$7,500 ÷ 7,500 = $1.00 cost per sq. ft.

$7,500 ÷ 50 = $150 per front foot

321. $\frac{1}{6}$ + $\frac{5}{8}$ = $\frac{19}{24}$ acre in use

1 − $\frac{19}{24}$ = $\frac{5}{24}$ in woodland

$\frac{5}{24}$ = 50 acres　　　50 ÷ 5 = 10 acres in one twenty-fourth

24 × 10 = 240 acres in whole farm

322. 115% = $9,430　　　$9,430 ÷ 115 = $82, or 1% of value

100 × $82 = $8,200, cost

$8,200 × .60 × .045 × 4 = $885.60, taxes

$8,200 × .03 × 4 = $984, interest lost

$9,430 − $8,200 = $1,230 gain

$984.00 + $885.60 = $1,869.60, loss

$1,869.60 − $1,230 = $639.60 loss

323. 160 sq. rd = 1 acre

324. 3,250 × $.14 =　　　$455, hillside

2,000 × $.085 =　　　170, stream

7,250 × $1 =　　　7,250, flat area

12,500 sq. ft. =　$7,875, total appraisal

$7,875 ÷ 12,500 = $.63 per sq. ft.

325. 30′ × 30′ × 30′ = 27,000 cubic feet

$9,000 ÷ 27,000 = $.33$\frac{1}{3}$ per cu. ft.

326. 30′ × 6′ = 180 sq. ft.

180 × $2.75 = $495.00, cost of driveway

327. 16$\frac{1}{2}$ feet = 1 rod or perch

328. 66 feet = 1 chain

329. $7,200 × .06 × $\frac{1}{12}$ = $36, first month's interest

330. 20 − 5 = 15 acres for homesites

50′ × 150′ = 7,500 sq. ft. in each lot

43,560 sq. ft. = 1 acre

15 × 43,560 = 653,400 sq. ft. for sub-division

653,400 ÷ 7,500 = 87+ lots

331. 12 × $600 = $7,200, yearly rent

12 × $115,000 = $1,380,000 gross business per year

$9,300 − $7,200 = $2,100 five per cent over gross of business

$2,100 ÷ .05 = $42,000, amount over gross minimum

$1,380,000 + $42,000 = $1,422,000, gross volume of year's business

332. $10,000 ÷ $1,000 = 10 taxable units

10 × $19 = $190, taxes

333. 1 pace = 3′

3 × 3′ = 9′

30 × 3′ = 90′

$90' - 9' = 81$ feet

334. $20 + 20 + 10 + 10 = 60$ yards
$60 \times 3' = 180'$
$180' \div 2' = 90$

335. $5,280' \times 5,280' = 27,878,400$ sq. ft.
$27,878,400 \div 43,560 = 640$ acres
3×640 acres $= 1920$ acres

336. $18' + 27' = 45$
$450' - 45' = 405'$ length of building
9 sq. ft. $= 1$ sq. yd.
$9 \times 12,825$ yards $= 115,425$ sq. ft. area
$115,425$ sq. ft. $\div 405' = 285'$

337. $100\% =$ first year commission
$120\% =$ second year commission
$144\% =$ third year commission
$\$7,280 \div 144 = \$5,055.56$

338. $85' \times 30' = 2,550$, lot 1
$85' \times 50' = 4,250$, lot 2
$85' \times 50' = 4,250$, lot 3
$\overline{11,050}$, 3 lots involved
in transaction
$100'$ on Main $\times \$112.50 = \$11,250$
$100'$ on Edgew. $\times \$87.25 = \$8,725$
$\overline{\$19,975}$

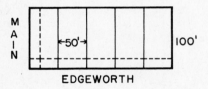

EDGEWORTH

339. $85' \times 30' = 2,550$, sq. ft. can be used for building

340. $60 \times \$75 = \$4,500$, cost by front footage
$\$7,500 =$ total amount to be invested $\quad \$7,500 - \$4,500 = \$3,000$
$\$3,000 \div \$.75 = 4,000$ sq. ft.
$60' \times 100' = 6,000$ sq. ft.
$\overline{10,000}$ sq. ft.

341. $\$20,000 - \$8,555 - \$1,655.10 = \$9,789.90$, Thompson's equity
$\$18,450 - \$13,841.79 = \$4,608.21$, Tyler's equity
$\$9,789.90 - \$4,608.21 = \$5,181.69$, difference in equity due
Thompson
$.20 \times \$5,181.69 = \$1,036.34$ cash
$\$5,181.69 - \$1,036.34 = \$4,145.35$, third mortgage against Tyler

342. $\$250 \times .06 \times 1 = \$15.00 \qquad \$250 + \$15 = \$265.00$, due
$\$16.25 \times 11 = \$178.75$ paid $\qquad \$265 - \$178.75 = \$86.25$ bal. due

343. $\$126 \times 2\frac{1}{2} \times \frac{1}{12} = \$26.25 \qquad \$126 - \$26.25 = \$99.75$, refund

344. $\$13,300 + \$1,050 + \$350 = \$14,700$

$14,700 × $.00425 = $62.48, increase in taxes

345. $12,500 × .032 × ½ = $200, refund

346. .80 × $6,000 = $4,800 $4,800 × ⅟₁₀₀₀ × $2.80 = $13.44

    .80 × $4,000 = 3,200 $3,200 × ⅟₁₀₀₀ × $3.30 = $10.56

    2½ × $24 = $60 premium $24.00

347. $50 × 150 = $7,500 assessment $.02 × $7,500 = $150

    $150 × 30 = $4,500 taxes for 30 years

    $15,000 + $4,500 = $19,500 invested

    150 × $300 = $45,000 selling price

    $45,000 − $4,500 = $40,500, selling price less broker's com.

    $40,500 − $19,500 = $21,000 profit

348. 5 × $40 = $200, "A" offer   5 × 150 × $.30 = $225, "B" offer

    $225 − $200 = $25, "B" offer better

349. 30 × 100 × .05 × 5 × $2.50 = $1,875, broker's earnings

350. 36 × 40 × 14 × $.55 = $11,088, reproduction cost

351. $8,000 × .60 × ⅟₁₀₀ × $4.21 = $202.08, total annual tax

352. 4 × $25   = $100 $13.20 + $18 + $6 = $37.20, expense

    6 × $40   = $240 $440 − $37.20 = $402.80, net to owner

    2 × $50   = $100

    total rent = $440

    $440 × .03 = $13.20, commission

353. 210' × 200' =   42,000 sq. ft.   6,000 ÷ 42,000 = ⅟₇ or

    50' × 90' × 8 =   36,000 sq. ft.   .1428 or 14.28%

    saved for roads =   6,000 sq. ft.

354. 20 mills = $.02

    $54,500 × $.02 = $1,090 taxes

355. $484 ÷ $11,000 = $.044 or 44 mills

    $0.44 × 100 = $4.40 tax per $100

356. 50' × 100' × $.75 = $3,750, selling price

    $3,750 × .05 = $187.50, commission

    $3,750 − $187.50 = $3,562.50, owner receives

357. $10,000 − $4,000 = $6,000 balance   5 × 12 = 60 mo. in 5 yr.

    $6,000 ÷ 60 = $100 per month

    $6,000 × .05 × ⅟₁₂ = $25, interest at the end of the first month

358. 12 × $75 = $900 annual rent   12' × 20' = 240 sq. ft. space

    $900 ÷ 240 = $3.75, annual rate per square foot

359. .80 × $10,000 = $8,000

    $8,000 ÷ $100 = 80 taxable units

    80 × $3.80 = $304 taxes

360. 33' × 45' = 1,485 sq. ft.   1,560 × $12.85 = $20,046.00

    5' × 15' =   75

    1,560 sq. ft.

361. ¼ × $1,325.28 = $331.32 pd. by seller

    $331.32 ÷ 3 = $110.44 tax per month

    $110.44 ÷ 2 = $55.22, tax exemption for ½ mo.

    $331.32 + $55.22 = $386.54 credit to seller

    $1,325.28 − $386.54 = $938.74 seller owes

362. $15,000 × .97 = $14,550 insurable

$20,000 − $15,000 = $5,000 remainder
$5,000 × .85 = $4,250 insurable
$14,550 + $4,250 = $18,800 total insurable

363. $24,000 × .90 = $21,600 insurable. $21,600 + 100 = 216 per $100
216 × $.54 = $116.64 premium for 3 yr.   Feb. 1, 1969—Sept. 1, 1967
3 yr. = 36 mo.   36 − 17 = 19 mo. to be returned
$116.64 ÷ 36 = $3.24 mo. prem. $3.24 × 19 = $61.56 charged buyer

364. 63 × $115 = $7,245, selling price adjacent lot
$115 × .23 = $26.45 more for corner lot
$115 + $26.45 = $141.45 selling price of corner lot
63 × $141.45 = $8,911.35
$7,245 + $8,911.35 = $16,156.35 total selling price

365. $9,350 × .06 = $561 commission. $561 × .10 = $56.10 listing fee.
$561 − 56.10 = $504.90   ½ of $504.90 = $252.45 Salesman's
$561 × .12 = $67.32 advertising.   commission.
$561 × .07 = $39.27 office expense.
$561 × .12 = $67.32 advertising.
$56.10 + $252.45 + $67.32 + $39.27 = $415.14 total expenses
$561.00 − $415.14 = $145.86 net commission

366. 990′ × 660′ = 653,400 sq. ft.
43,560 sq. ft. = 1 acre
653,400 ÷ 43,560 = 15 acres
15 × $3,000 = $45,000, selling price of land

367. 60 × $150 = $9,000, selling price

368. $1,090 × .04 × 1 = $43.60 simple interest for one year
$1,090 × .04 × ½ = $21.80, interest for ½ year
$1,090 + $21.80 = $1,111.80
$1,111.80 × .04 × ½ = $22.24 interest second half of year
$21.80 + $22.24 = $44.04 compound interest for 1 year
$44.04 − $43.60 = $.44 difference between simple and compound
    interest

369. $190 + $1,200 + $295 + $50 = $1,735, expenses
$9,000 + $1,735 = $10,735, invested in house
$11,250 − $10,735 = $515, gain

370. 1966 sales = 100%; 1967 sales = 125%;
1968 sales = 150%
$300,000 ÷ 150 = 2,000 × 100% = $200,000 1966 sales;
2,000 × 125% = $250,000 1967 sales

371. $8\frac{1}{3} = {}^{25}\!/_3 = {}^{100}\!/_{12}$
${}^{100}\!/_{12}\% = \frac{1}{12}$
$\frac{1}{12}$ of $14,160 = $1,180, loss
$14,160 − $1,180 = $12,980, selling price

372. ⅔ of $12,000 = $8,000—Amount of mortgage
                1,000—Deposit money
             $9,000—Available
$12,000 − $9,000 is $3,000—Amount needed

373. Three years is 36 months. $72.00 ÷ 36 = $2.00

374. $240 × 12 = $2,880 yearly rental
$2,880 = 9% of cost

$2,880 ÷ 9 = $320 or 1% of cost

100 × $320 = $32,000, cost of house

375. .60 × $16,000 = $9,600 assessed value

$9,600 ÷ $100 = 96 taxable units

96 × $2.50 = $240 taxes

376. $58.45 × 12 = $701.40, interest payment for year

5¼% = .0525

$701.40 ÷ .0525 = $13,360, amount of original loan

377. $105 × 2 = $210, annual interest payment

$210 ÷ $6,000 = .035 or 3½%, interest rate

378. 320 × $175 = $56,000, sale of ranch

$56,000 × .05 = $2,800, 5% commission

½ of $2,800 = $1,400, salesman's half of commission

379. 12 × $138 = $1,656, yearly mortgage payment

4½ × $1,656 = $7,452, 90% of income

$7,452 ÷ 90 = $82.80, 1% of income

100 × $82.80 = $8,280, minimum gross annual salary necessary

380. 48' × 30' × 9' = 12,960 cu. ft.

27 cu. ft. = 1 cu. yd.

12,960 ÷ 27 = 480 cu. yd.

480 × $.35 = $168, cost of excavation

381. $24,500 × .04 = $980, 4% reduction in sales price

$24,500 − $980 = $23,520, new selling price

$23,520 × .06 = $1,411.20, 6% broker's commission

3% of $1,411.20 = $42.34, due M.L.S.

$1,411.20 − $42.34 = $1,368.86, for commissions

20% of $1,368.86 = $273.77 "A's" commission

$1,368.86 − $273.77 = $1,095.09, balance of commission

35% of $1,095.09 = $383.28

382. $260,000 ÷ $6,500,000 = $.04 or 40 mills

A tax rate of 30 mills would not provide sufficient funds to meet the planned budget.

383. Answer with problem.

384. One full quarter = 160 acres

¼ of quarter = 40 acres

160 + 40 = 200 acres

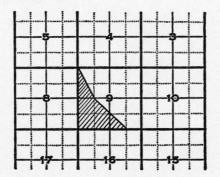

385. (a) The South 15′ of Lot 7; all of Lot 8 and the East 50′ of Lot 9; all in tract 618, as per map recorded in Book 37, page 19, official maps of record of Maricopa County.

(b) 125′ × 15′ = 1,875 sq. ft., Lot 7
125′ × 50′ = 6,250 sq. ft., Lot 8
62.50′ × 50′ = 3,125 sq. ft., Lot 9
        11,250 sq. ft. conveyed portion

(c) 15′ + 50′ = 65′ frontage
on 7th Street
65 × $500 = $32,500 front footage on 7th Street
Lot 9 = 2,500 sq. ft.
2,500 × $2.20 = $5,500
$32,500 + $5,500 = $38,000

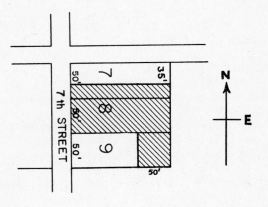

386. (a) Lot 1 for building
100′ − 15′ = 85′ with offset   50′ − 20′ = 30′ with offset
85′ × 30′ = 2,550 sq. ft. for building

(b) From part (a) lot 1 contains 2,550 sq. ft. for building
Lot 2 has 85′ × 50′ or 4,250 sq. ft.
4,250 + 2,550 = 6,800 sq. ft. in lots 1 and 2
Lot 3 also has 4,250 sq. ft.
Lots 1, 2 and 3 must be bought to have a building on the corner and containing 8,100 sq. ft.

(c) 4 × 50′ = 200′ frontage, lots 2, 3, 4, 5.
200′ × $127.50 = $25,500 cost for frontage
100′ × $185   = 18,500
                $44,000 total cost
100′ frontage on lot 1

387. (a) See drawing.

(b) 225′ × 100′ = 22,500 sq. ft.
    25′ × 50′   = 1,250 sq. ft.
                 23,750 sq. ft. Total area

$23,750 \times \$.42 = \$9,975$
$\$9,975 \times .05 = \$498.75$ commission

388. 1 section = 640 acres
$\frac{1}{16}$ of 640 = 40 acres in each square
$2 \times 40 = 80$ acres in two full squares
2 half squares = 1 full square = 40 acres
$\frac{3}{4}$ of 40 = 30 acres
$80 + 40 + 30 = 150$ acres, total

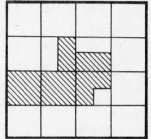

389. Answered with problem.
390. (a) See drawing.
    (b) N $\frac{1}{2}$ of Sec. 17 = 320 acres
        W $\frac{1}{2}$ of W $\frac{1}{2}$ of Sec. 25 = 160 acres
        SW $\frac{1}{4}$ of Sec. 32 = 160 acres
        NE $\frac{1}{4}$ of NW $\frac{1}{4}$ of Sec. 4 = 40 acres
    (c) $320 + 160 + 160 + 40 = 680$ acres
391. Description contains 3 full sections
    1 section = 640 acres
    $3 \times 640 = 1,920$ acres
392. Answer with problem.
393. (a) Shaded area = $\frac{6}{16}$ of section
        1 section = 640 acres
        $\frac{6}{16} \times 640 = 240$ acres
    (b) $\$23,340 \div 240 = \$97.25$ cost per acre.
394. $\frac{1}{16}$ of 640 = 40 acres.
395. (a.) $\frac{1}{2} \times \frac{1}{4} \times \frac{1}{4} = \frac{1}{32}$ $\frac{1}{32} \times 640 = 20$ acres
    (b.) $\frac{1}{4} \times \frac{1}{4} = \frac{1}{16}$ $\frac{1}{16} \times 640 = 40$ acres
    (c.) $\frac{1}{4} \times \frac{1}{4} \times \frac{1}{4} = \frac{1}{64}$ $\frac{1}{64} \times 640 = 10$ acres
    (d.) $\frac{1}{2} \times \frac{1}{4} = \frac{1}{8}$ $\frac{1}{8} \times 640 = \underline{80}$ acres
                                                        150 acres
    (e.) $150 \times \$52.50 = \$7,875$ S. P.
    (f.) $\$7,875 \times .10 = \$787.50$ Commission
396. (c.) $200 \times 200 = 40,000$ sq. ft. total.
        $\frac{1}{8}$ of 40,000 = 5,000 sq. ft. in described parcel.
    (d.) $20 \times 100 = 2,000$ sq. ft.
        $5,000 + 2,000 = 7,000$ sq. ft.
    (e.) $120 \times 100 = 12,000$ sq. ft. in lots 8, 9, and 10.
        $40,000 - 12,000 = 28,000$ sq. ft. in balance

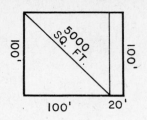

397. ⅟₁₆ of 640 = 40 acres.
398. ¼ of ⅟₁₆ = ⅟₆₄   ⅟₆₄ of 640 = 10 acres
399. (a & b) See drawing.
     640 acres in each section
     Sections 9, 10, 15, 16 each contain 320 acres
     Secs. 21, 22 each contain 160 acres
     4 × 320 = 1280 acres
     2 × 160 = 320 acres
               ‾‾‾‾‾‾‾‾‾‾‾
               1600 acres
400-403. Answers with problems.

Real Estate Forms

Forms

A REAL ESTATE broker should be competent to prepare instruments which are incidental to and a concomitant part of his real estate business. However, he should be ever circumspect, in this connection, not to encroach upon the province of the attorney. The forms, which he should have readily available for use, are thus necessarily limited to those directly related to his everyday practice. The forms which follow are designed to meet the broker's needs. In most instances, they have been filled in so as to prove more helpful.

A-1   No. 2106

AUTHORIZATION TO SELL CONTRACT
(Listing Contract)

Dated .... April 24, 1969 ....
at Glendale, Kentucky

Between .... *LOIS MAE GIRARD, single* ....
Owner

. . . .

AND

REALTY SALES COMPANY, 428 MARKET ST., GLENDALE, KY. for the sale of real estate at .... *1101 Riverview Ave., Glendale (3) Ky.* ....

In consideration of $1.00, receipt whereof is hereby acknowledged, and other valuable consideration, the undersigned Owner hereby employs .... REALTY SALES COMPANY ..... as the sole and exclusive agent irrevocably for a period of ... three (3) months.... from the date hereof, for the sale of premises described on the reverse of this contract, and which data constitutes a material part of the contract of employment, and agrees to pay said .... REALTY SALES COMPANY ..... a commission of .. seven(7) per cent ...... on the gross consideration price or at any other terms and price accepted by the Owner, upon the sale, exchange or transfer, or upon the exercise of an option to purchase clause in a lease, whether made by myself or by any other person during the above mentioned term of employment, or any extension or renewal thereof.

The authority of .... *REALTY SALES COMPANY* .... shall terminate at the expiration of the above term, unless renewed, without any further liability on the part of the owner unless the sale, transfer, lease or exchange of the above property is made or effected directly or indirectly by me, the undersigned owner, or through any agent, within a period of ... *six (6) months* ... from the expiration of this employment contract or any extension or renewal thereof, to any person or persons with whom ...... *REALTY SALES COMPANY* ...... has been negotiating or dealing for the

597

sale, transfer or exchange of said property, in which event, the owner agrees to pay ..... *REALTY SALES COMPANY* ..... the above commission, which shall become immediately due and payable.

I hereby authorize said ...... *REALTY SALES COMPANY* ..... to place a "For Sale" sign upon said property, which shall be the only such sign displayed thereon during the term of this contract or any extension or renewal thereof.

All earnest money deposits paid upon the purchase price shall be held by the agent in an escrow or trust account until consummation of the deal or termination thereof.

In event said deposit money or any part thereof is forfeited as liquidated damages, such sum or sums shall be divided equally between broker and owner. However, broker shall not receive any sum greater than the agreed upon commission.

I HEREBY ACKNOWLEDGE RECEIPT OF A COPY OF THIS AUTHORIZATION TO SELL CONTRACT.

...... Lois Mae Girard .... (SEAL)
Owner
REALTY SALES COMPANY
by...... Marie E Baier ......(SEAL)
Broker

This contract is hereby. renewed and extended upon the same exclusive right to sell terms and conditions for a period of .... from .... 196.... to .... 196......

.... (SEAL)
Owner
REALTY SALES COMPANY
by........................ (SEAL)
Broker

Dated . *April 1*, 1969

A-1(a)   SIMPLE LISTING CARD

LISTED   District....... *Edgewater*....... Date Listed....... *April 1 , 1968*.....
BY   Constr. & Design........ *Brick*..
Office   Rooms, 1st Floor......3...... 2nd......3...... 3rd...... *None*.......
         Bath.....*tile*....Shower....*yes*....Breakfast Room, Sun Room....*No*....
         Hardwood Floors....*yes*....Double....*yes*....Water Heater ...*Galv.*.....
         Insulated.....*yes*.....
         Heating System.....*Hot Air*.....Coal....Coal & Fruit Cellars....*yes*....
         Plumbing.....*Galv.*......
CLASS   Screens....*yes*.....Weather Stripped.....*yes*.....Concrete Porches......
....4   *yes*.....Roof.....*asb. slat Copper Gutters*.....Spouting.....*Galv.*......
....3   General Condition....*good*...when Built....*1950*.....Builder....*G. C.*
....2   *Carson*.....Garage.....*Integral*......
X..1   Lot Size .....*50 x 110*.....Level.....*Slopes rear*.....Alley.....*yes*.....
         Paved Street.....*yes*.....
         Assessment.....*$6500*.....Taxes: City.....*$90*.....School.....*$54*.....
         County.....*$36*.....Total.....*$180*.....
         Mortgage.....*$4000*.....Monthly Payment.....*$36*.....Interest Rate....
         5%.....Mortgagee.....*City Bank*.....
         Rental.....*Owner occupied*....Tenant.....Phone.....Sale Clause.....
         Place Sign.....*yes*.....
         Special Features.....*Possession June 16, 1969* ....
         ....
         Directions ....
         Price....*$10,800*....Address....*1101 Riverview Ave. near Nelson Ave.*.....
         Title in name of.....*Lois Mae Girard*..............................

As a duly appointed Agent for seller and in consideration of the appointment thereof by the seller, the undersigned Agent does hereby agree during the term hereof to make efforts to sell such property, and to process the listing through the North End Brokers Association, Inc., and to cause it to be delivered to all other participating members of said Organization. Said Agent further agrees to have a picture taken of the premises to be distributed to such members of the North End Brokers Association, Inc., who participate in the picture listing service.

PHONE _____Court 1-3722_____
_____ (FIRM NAME)
(MEMBER OF NORTH END BROKERS ASSOCIATION, INC.)
BY _____ (BROKER)

A-2   OFFER TO PURCHASE

Date....*April 25, 1969....*

....*Horace Webb....*
    Agent

We agree to purchase the property known as ....*No. 1917 States St., Little Rock, Ark., being a 2½ story brick dwelling containing 7 rooms and bath, with garage on lot 60 ft. by 150 ft., and more fully described in deed recorded in Deed Book, Volume 1189, page 14*.. ....
Consideration Price........*$12,000* ....
Terms:........*All cash upon delivery of Deed*..............................
. . . .
It is understood that a good and marketable title is to be furnished and deal is to be closed within 30 days from date of acceptance by owner.

Taxes, rents, insurance and interest........*to be pro-rated as of delivery of deed* ....Possession to be given:......*Subject to existing lease expiring June 1, 1966.*

We hereby deposit with........*Horace Webb*........the sum of........*Six Hundred ($600.00) Dollars*........as earnest money, receipt of which is hereby acknowledged, to apply on the purchasing price. Said earnest money shall be returned to us upon demand if this offer to purchase is not accepted by the owner within..... *five (5) days*......from the date hereof or upon acceptance by the owner, shall be forfeited as liquidated damages if we fail to comply with the above terms.

        ....*Andrew Maloney* ....(SEAL)
                        Buyer
       ....*Betty Jane Maloney* ......(SEAL)
                        Buyer

WITNESS:
......*Horace Webb*......

ACCEPTANCE

The foregoing offer is hereby accepted by us this......*26th*......day of....... *April*........*1969.*

        ....*Henry Jordon*...................
                   Owner
        ....*Eileen Jordan*...................
                   Owner

WITNESS:
....*Horace Webb*....

A-3

NORTH END BROKERS ASSOCIATION, INC.

EXCLUSIVE SALE AND LISTING AGREEMENT.

(In triplicate)

In consideration of the services to be performed by the undersigned broker, hereinafter called Agent, the undersigned Seller does hereby grant to said Agent for a term of three months from date hereof and effective immediately the sole and exclusive right to submit offers for the sale or contract to sell and to receipt for deposit in connection therewith, on the following described property situated in the City of _____, County of _____, Washington, to-wit: All of that property, belonging to me, commonly known and designated as _____, legally described as follows or as on the reverse side hereof.

The undersigned seller warrants that he has the legal right to sell the above described property at the terms and conditions set forth herein. The information given on the Listing Form below the signatures on this agreement, and any provisions set forth on the reverse side hereof are hereby made a part of this Agreement.

LOT _____ BLOCK _____ ADDITION _____

SELLING PRICE $_____ TERMS _____

POSSESSION _____

The owner authorizes the Agent to install a key-box on the premises, which box may be opened by a master key held by all members of the North End Brokers Association, Inc., and their salesmen, and in said box one key to the premises will be kept; and allow Agent or North End Brokers Association, Inc., members to show said property at any reasonable time.

Rents, insurance, taxes, interest, and reserves on assumed encumbrances are to be prorated from date of closing. Seller agrees to furnish purchaser's policy of title insurance, evidencing ability to convey good and sufficient title, and agrees to pay one half of any escrow cost.

When said Agent procures an offer to purchase on the terms set forth in this Agreement, or on other terms acceptable to the seller, or if seller removes said property from the market, of if seller directly or indirectly or through any other person or entity other than said Agent during the term hereof sells, contracts to sell, or exchange or lease with option to purchase, or if seller within two months after the expiration of this Agreement, should sell, contract to sell, or exchange or lease with option to purchase said property to any person who has during the term of this agreement been advised directly or indirectly through the offices of the Listing Broker or any member of the North End Brokers Association, Inc., that the property is for sale, then said Agent shall be conclusively presumed to be the procuring cause of such sale, contract of sale or exchange, or lease with option to purchase, and said seller agrees to pay said Agent a Commission of 5% of selling price of said property.

In the event this Real Estate is sold on contract, seller agrees that the terms and provisions of Puget Sound Title Insurance Co. Form No. 109, Washington Title Insurance Co. Form L. 37, and Lawyers Title Insurance Co. Form L. 19, Real Estate Contracts are satisfactory and that an Earnest Money Receipt and agreement specifying a contract submitted on any of said three forms meets the requirements of this agreement.

It is understood that said Agent is a member of the North End Brokers Association, Inc., and it is further agreed that said Agent shall refer this listing to said Association to be by it referred to all other participating members of said organization, and said other members shall have the same rights and privileges under this Agreement as though each of them had executed a separate Agreement containing the terms and provisions hereof except that in no event shall seller be obligated to pay to any member or members of said Association more than one commission.

Seller agrees that he will not accept any offer unless submitted by the undersigned Agent or unless said offer recites that the submitting broker is a member in good standing of the North End Brokers Association, Inc.

Seller hereby acknowledges receipt of copy of this Agreement, and approves all information contained on this form, both above and below the signatures hereon, however, seller hereby authorizes said agent to insert and amend legal description over all signatures but does not authorize said Agent to insert or change any of the financial details of the property over the signature.

_____, Washington _____

_____ SELLER

_____ SELLER

(Both husband and wife must sign if community property)

PHONE _____

600

As a duly appointed Agent for seller and in consideration of the appointment thereof by the seller, the undersigned Agent does hereby agree during the term hereof to make efforts to sell such property, and to process the listing through the North End Brokers Association, Inc., and to cause it to be delivered to all other participating members of said Organization. Said Agent further agrees to have a picture taken of the premises to be distributed to such members of the North End Brokers Association, Inc., who participate in the picture listing service.

PHONE _____ _____(FIRM NAME)

_____(MEMBER OF NORTH END BROKERS ASSOCIATION, INC.)

DATE _____ BY _____(SALESMAN)

Location _____ Price _____

	B	1	2	
Floor				
Brms				
Lvgrm				
Dngrm				
Brknk				
Baths				
Shower				
Toilet				
Recrm				
Frple				
Hdw Fl				

Occupied By _____ Phone _____

Owner _____ Phone _____

Address _____

Listing Office _____ Phone _____

Key _____ Taxes _____

Poss. Date _____ Listed _____ Exp. Date _____

Mtg. Bal. _____ @ _____ mo. @ _____ % FHA? _____

Contr. Bal. _____ @ _____ mo. @ _____ % GI? _____

Terms of Sale _____

Heat _____
Bsmt _____
Gar _____
Roof _____
Ext _____
Age _____
Lot _____
Sewer _____

Additional Information Below (Kitchen, Entry Hall,
Style, School, Bus, Streets, etc.)

_____

_____

_____

_____

MEMBERS AND EMPLOYEES OF THE N.E.B.A. USE THEIR BEST EFFORTS IN COMPILING AND TRANSMITTING THIS INFORMATION FROM OWNERS. HOWEVER, IT IS SUBJECT TO CORRECTIONS AND OMISSIONS AND THERE IS NO LIABILITY FOR NEGLIGENCE OF THE N.E.B.A. OR ANY OF ITS MEMBERS

NEBA File No. _____

Location _____

Date Rec'd	Rms	Brms	Bath	Gar	Heat	Age	Price

This Agreement,

Made the _____19th_____ day of _____January_____ one thousand nine hundred and ___69___

Between___ WILLIAM B. ANDERSON AND CLEO L. ANDERSON, his wife, of Youngstown, County ____
of Mahoning and State of Ohio, _____

_____ parties of the first part, and___ GEORGE C. BARTREM and_____
HARRY A. BARTREM, of the same place, _____ part ies of the second part.

Witnesseth, That said first party, heirs, executors or assigns, sells and agrees to convey, by good title in fee, to said second
party _____their_____ heirs or assigns. _____by deed of general warranty on or before March 1, 1969.
All _____

(Description follows.)

The said second party paying therefor the price or sum of____ Seven Hundred Fifty _____

_____ ($750.00) _____ Dollars, which is hereby agreed to be paid to said first party,
or legal representatives, as follows, to wit:___ Seventy-five ($75.00) Dollars upon the signing of
these agreements, and the balance of Six Hundred Seventy-five ($675.00) Dollars
at the rate of Twenty-five ($25.00) Dollars monthly beginning· March 1, 1969 , on
the first day of each and every month thereafter, until fully paid; said payments
shall first apply to interest at 6 per cent on the unpaid balance, and the remainder shall apply to principal.

Together with lawful interest from the date hereof, on the amount unpaid, payable to WILLIAM B. ANDERSON_____
and CLEO L. ANDERSON, his wife, their heirs and assigns. _____

And the said second party further agrees to pay all taxes and assessments falling due after this date, to keep the buildings
now or hereafter on said premises properly insured in a reasonable amount, the loss, if any, payable to said first party
as additional security. And it is also further agreed that prompt payment and time is part consideration, and of the
essence of this contract, and therefore, if default of payment is made of any one or more of said installments of the principal
after they fall due, the first party may, at his election, demand payment either of the second party in person, or by posting

on the premises; and if payment thereof is not made in _____thirty_____ days thereafter, all moneys theretofore
paid by the second party, shall thereby be and become forfeited and belong to the said first party; and the rights of the
second party under this agreement, and all right, title or interest of said second party, heirs or assigns, in said described
premises, shall become null and void, unless said forfeiture is afterwards waived in writing by said first party. It being
expressly understood, that no process of law shall be necessary to this effect; nor shall any collateral, supplementary,
or change of this agreement be alleged or set up by either party unless in writing and signed by the party to be affected.

The Deed to be made and delivered at any time, on payment of ___all of___ the purchase money and interest.

Possession to be given upon delivery of deed .

And for the true performance of the covenants and agreements aforesaid, each of said parties bindeth himself, his
heirs, executors and administrators, unto the other, his executors, administrators and assigns, firmly by these presents.

_____

_____

_____

Witness our hands and seals the day and year first above written.

Attest:
STELLA MALONEY

WILLIAM B. ANDERSON   (SEAL)
CLEO L. ANDERSON   (SEAL)
GEORGE C. BARTREM   SEAL
HARRY A. BARTREM   SEAL

Make Deed to (full name)   HARRY A. BARTHEM

        Address,   1601 Wells St., Youngstown, Ohio

From (full name)   WILLIAM B. ANDERSON

        Address,   6336 Baum Blvd. Youngstown, Ohio

Wife's name (in full)   CLEO L. ANDERSON

Attorney for Purchaser is   WILLIAM C. WRIGHT

        Address,   710-5 Security Savings Bldg., Youngstown, Ohio

For reference to title, see   Deed book Vol. 1134 Page 601

A-5   EARNEST MONEY RECEIPT

Detroit, Michigan . . . . *May 2, 1969* . . . .

Received of . . . . . *Edward G. Davis* . . . .
. . . . of . . . . . . *Detroit, Michigan* . . . .
hereinafter referred to as the Purchaser, the sum of . . . . . *Five Hundred ($500.00)*
. . . . . . Dollars as earnest money and in part payment for the purchase of the following real estate situated in the . . . . . . *City of Detroit* . . . . . . , County of . . . . . *Wayne*
. . . . . , State of . . . . . *Michigan* . . . . . . , being property of . . . . . *Thomas C. Halsey*
and Marie E. Halsey, his wife . . . . . situate at . . . . . *6775 Dade Boulevard lot 70 x*
175 2-story frame dwelling and garage (see Deed Book, Vol. 2554, page 316 for full
description) . . . .
. . . .
for the sum of . . . . *Nine Thousand Five Hundred ($9,500.00) Dollars to be paid*
as follows: the sum of $500.00 herein receipted for, the sum of $2500 upon delivery
of deed, and the balance of $6500 by the Purchaser assuming and agreeing to pay a
mortgage in that amount, dated June 9, 1966, in favor of the Barnsdale Federal
Savings and Loan Association . . . .

It is agreed that if the Owner does not approve this sale, or if the title to the said
premises is not marketable or cannot be made marketable and such as will be insured by a title abstract contract, within 30 days after notice to Owner, the said
earnest money shall be refunded. Otherwise, upon default by the Purchaser in the
performance of any of the conditions contained herein, then the earnest money shall,
at option of lessor, be forfeited as liquidated damages, and all rights of the respective
parties shall be at an end.

The property is to be conveyed by good and sufficient deed free and clear of all
liens and encumbrances, but subject to building restrictions, easements and zoning
ordinances of record. Taxes, rents, insurance and interest to be pro-rated as of date
of delivery of deed. Possession to be given at date of closing, by assignment of
lease, subject to existing laws and regulations.

I hereby agree to purchase the above property as set forth; title to be in the name
of . . . . *Edward G. Davis and Ella Davis, his wife.*

. . . . *B. A. Sands, Broker* . . . .
I acknowledge receipt of a copy of this earnest money receipt.

. . . . *Edward G. Davis* . . . . (SEAL)
WITNESS:
. . . . *Fred P. Smith* . . . .

APPROVAL AND ACCEPTANCE

Date . . . . *May 3, 1969* . . . .
We hereby approve and accept the sale of the above described property as above
set forth. We acknowledge a receipt of a copy of this earnest money receipt.

. . . . *Thomas C. Halsey* . . . . (SEAL)
Owner
. . . . *Marie E. Halsey* . . . . (SEAL)
Owner
WITNESS:
. . . . *Fred P. Smith* . . . .

A-6

AGREEMENT OF SALE

Date of this Agreement . . . . *April 4, 1969* . . . .
Name of Seller . . . . *KATHERINE J. SEMEL, unmarried, of the*
Borough of Zelienople, County of Butler, and State of Pennsylvania . . . .

Name of Buyer .... *RALPH T. PRENTICE, of the City of Cleveland, County of Cuyahoga, State of Ohio*..............

Name of Real Estate Agent .... *South Pittsburgh Realty Company*..........

WITNESSETH, that seller, for the consideration hereinafter mentioned, does covenant, promise, grant and agree, to and with the said buyer, by these presents, that seller shall and will, on or before .... *June 1, 1969*.............. at the proper costs and charges of the seller, by deed of .... *general*.......... warranty, well and sufficiently grant, convey and assure unto the said buyer, in fee simple, clear of encumbrances, excepting coal, gas, oil and other mineral rights heretofore sold, reserved or leased, and existing building or use restrictions, if any, of record, the following described property:

> *ALL that certain lot or piece of ground situate in the Borough of Mt. Oliver, County of Allegheny and State of Pennsylvania, being Lot No. 36 in the Crescent Hills Plan of Lots, of record in the Recorder's Office of Allegheny County in Plan Book Volume 29, pages 13 and 14, and being more particularly bounded and described by deed recorded in the Recorder's Office of Allegheny County in Deed Book Volume 2516, page 780.*
>
> *HAVING thereon erected a six (6) room, two (2) bath, brick and stone dwelling with integral garage, known as 3421 Hillmont Avenue.*

TOGETHER with all and singular the buildings, improvements, and other the premises hereby demised, with the appurtenances, it being understood that gas and electric light fixtures, heating and plumbing systems, and laundry tubs installed in said buildings are included in this sale.

In consideration whereof buyer doth covenant, promise and agree, to and with seller, by these presents, that buyer shall and will well and truly pay or cause to be paid unto the said seller the sum of .... *Twenty-One Thousand ($21,000.00) Dollars in manner following: One Thousand ($1,000.00) Dollars evidenced by cash ☐, personal check ☒, cashier's check ☐ .... as deposit on account of the purchase price, and the balance of Twenty Thousand ($20,000.00) Dollars, in cash, upon delivery of deed. It is understood and agreed that Buyer is to pay Pennsylvania Stamp Transfer Tax.*

Taxes, interest, and rents to be pro-rated as of .... *date*..............
of delivery of deed.

For title references see Deed Book Vol. ......*2516*......, page ......*780*......

Possession to be given ....upon delivery of deed........ The buyer, at his own expense, agrees to place adequate fire insurance on the premises covered by this agreement.

Should the buyer fail to make settlement, as herein provided, the sum or sums paid on account of the purchase price, at the option of the seller, may be retained by the seller, either on account of the purchase money, or as liquidated damages. In the latter case the contract shall become null and void. In the latter event, all monies paid on account shall be divided equally between the seller and the broker, but in no event shall the sum paid to the broker be in excess of the rate of commission due him.

The earnest money paid under this contract is to be held in escrow by the broker. It is understood between the parties hereto that the property herein sold has been inspected by the buyer, or his or their agent, and that the same is being purchased as a result of such inspection.

It is understood that .... *The South Pittsburgh Realty Company*.......... is acting as agent only in bringing the buyer and seller together and will in no case whatsoever be held liable to either party for the performance of any term or covenant of this agreement or for damages for non-performance thereof. Seller agrees to pay the said agent the rate of commission recommended by the .... Greater Pittsburgh Board of Realtors. This agreement shall extend to and be binding upon the heirs, executors, administrators, successors and assigns of the parties hereto. Whenever used in this agreement, the singular number shall include the plural, the plural the singular, and the use of any gender shall be applicable to all genders.

IN WITNESS WHEREOF, the said parties to this agreement have hereunto set their hands and seals, the day and year first above written.

SEALED AND DELIVERED IN THE
PRESENCE OF:

As to 1 ...... *Ben Serratore* ......
As to 2 ...... *James Campbell* ......

     1 ...... *Katherine J. Semel* ...... (SEAL)
     2 ...... *Ralph J. Prentice* ...... (SEAL)

B-2   QUIT CLAIM DEED
               (Usual Form)

THIS INDENTURE made the .....*twenty-first day of December*..... in the year of our Lord ....*one thousand nine hundred sixty-eight (1968)*.... BETWEEN ....*AL-FRED SIMS and ELSIE SIMS, his wife, both of Philadelphia, State of Pennsylvania*.... (hereinafter called the parties of the first part), and ......*DON FREU-DEN of the City of Philadelphia, State of Pennsylvania*...... (hereinafter called the party of the second part).

WITNESSETH, That the said parties of the first part, for and in consideration of the sum of ....*two thousand ($2,000.00) dollars,*.... lawful money of the United States of America, to them well and truly paid by the said party of the second part, at and before the sealing and delivery of these presents, the receipt whereby is hereby acknowledged, have ......*remised, released and quit claimed,*...... and by these presents do ....*remise, release and quit claim*.... unto the said party of the second part, and to ....*his heirs and assigns*.... forever, ...ALL THAT CERTAIN

[description and recital follow]

This conveyance being intended to buttress and confirm the title so conveyed to the said ......*DON FREUDEN, his heirs and assigns,*...... as to any right, title and interest that the said ......*Alfred Sims and Elsie Sims, his wife,*...... may have had or may now have in and to said premises, TOGETHER with all and singular, the tenements, hereditaments and appurtenances thereunto belonging, or in any wise appertaining, and the reversions, remainders, rents, issues and profits thereof: AND also, all the estate, right, title, interest, property, claim and demand whatsoever, as well in law as in equity, of the said parties of the first part, of, in, or to the above-described premises, and every part and parcel thereof, with the appurtenances. TO HAVE AND TO HOLD all and singular the above-mentioned and described premises, together with the appurtenances unto the said party of the second part, ...*his heirs and assigns*.... forever.

IN WITNESS WHEREOF, The said parties of the first part have hereunto set, their hands and seals the day and year first above written.

Sealed and delivered in
the presence of us,
......*JOHN DOLL*..........
......*JOEL ROBERTS*.......

     ......*ELSIE SIMS* .... (SEAL)
     ......*ALFRED SIMS* ...... (SEAL)

RECEIVED, the day of the date of above Indenture, of the above-named .. ...*DON FREUDEN,*...... the sum of ....*two thousand ($2,000.00) dollars*.... being the full consideration above mentioned.

(Acknowledgment)

     .... *ALFRED SIMS* ....
     ......*ELSIE SIMS* ....,.

OPTION

This Agreement,

Made and concluded this ___9th___ _____ day of ___March___, _____ A. D. 19 69

Between ___J. HOWARD LONG and STELLA J. LONG, his wife,___ _____
of St. Louis, Missouri, _____ part ies of the first part; and
SAMUEL D. RUTH, of the same place, _____
_____
_____ for themselves, _____ party of the second part:

Witnesseth, That the said parties of the first part, their heirs, executors, administrators and assigns, in consideration of the sum of ___one hundred ($100)___ Dollars to ___them___ in hand paid by said part y of the second part; the receipt of which is hereby acknowledged, as well as in consideration of the covenants and agreements hereinafter mentioned, hereby give and grant to the said party of the second part ___his___ heirs and assigns, the exclusive right or option, to purchase at any time within ___sixty (60) days___ from the date hereof, all that certain ___3 story brick___ ___store and apartment building, 1200 Antioch Ave.___ _____ situate in ___City of St. Louis___ _____ County of ___St. Louis___ and State of ___Missouri___ _____, as follows, viz:
_____
_____(Description follows)_____
_____
_____
_____
_____
_____
_____
_____

for the consideration of the sum of ___Twenty-two Thousand ($22,000.00)___ _____
Dollars payable as follows: ___Two Thousand ($2,000.00) upon signing of an agreement of sale___ ___in usual form, and the balance of Twenty Thousand ($20,000.00) Dollars upon___ _____ ___delivery of deed, within thirty (30) days thereafter___ _____

provided the said part y of the second part, ___his___ heirs and assigns, shall within ___sixty (60) days___ from the date hereof, notify the parties of the first part ___their___ heirs and assigns, in writing, that ___he___ will take, accept and purchase said ___real estate___ _____ at the price and terms aforesaid.

In case of notice of acceptance is given as aforesaid, the said parties of the first part ___their___ heirs and assigns agree to deliver within a reasonable time thereafter to the party of the second part ___his___ heirs and assigns a general warranty deed for said ___real estate in fee simple___ clear of all ___liens and___ ___encumbrances___, xxxxxxxxxxx xxxxxxxxxxxxxxxxxxxxx xxxxxxxxxxxxxxxxxxxxxxxxxxxxxxxxxxxxxxxxxxxxxxxxxxxxx ___Taxes, insurance and rents to be pro-rated as of date of delivery of deed.___

Time is of the essence of this option, and if the part y of the second part ___his___ heirs or assigns shall not notify the parties of the first part ___their___ heirs and assigns, that ___he___ elects to take, accept and purchase said _____ ___real estate___ at the price and terms aforesaid, at or before the expiration of ___sixty (60) days___ from the date hereof, then this agreement shall forthwith become null and void and of no affect.

For the true performance of the covenants and agreements aforesaid, each of said parties bindeth himself, his heirs, his executors and administrators, unto the other, his executors and administrators and assigns, firmly by these presents. Witness our hands and seals the day first above written.

Witness:

Robert L. Dolan

J. Howard Long (SEAL)
Stella J. Long (SEAL)
Samuel D. Ruth (SEAL)
(SEAL)

Offer to Purchase Real Estate

To _____, Realtor

_____, Indiana

The undersigned, hereinafter called purchaser, hereby agrees to purchase from the owner, hereinafter called the seller, through you as broker, the real estate known as No._____ St, in the City (or town)

of _____, County of _____, State of _____,

the legal description of which is:

_____

_____

_____

and to pay as the purchase price therefor the sum of

_____ DOLLARS ($_____)

payable as follows:

_____ DOLLARS ($_____)

as earnest money deposited with the broker herewith, which shall be applied on the purchase price at the closing of this transaction, and the balance of the purchase price shall be payable in accordance with Paragraph as hereinafter set forth:

PARAGRAPH 1 (SALE BY DEED) The balance of the purchase price shall be paid in cash upon delivery of warranty deed.

PARAGRAPH 2 (SALE BY DEED ASSUMPTION OF MORTGAGE) A down payment of

_____ DOLLARS ($_____),

of which the earnest money is a part, subject to a mortgage now of record in unpaid amount as of _____ 19___

of _____ DOLLARS ($_____),

interest at _____%, monthly payments of $_____, including principal and interest.

which the grantees agree to assume and pay.

PARAGRAPH 3 (SALE BY CONTRACT) The balance of the purchase price shall be paid as follows:

A down payment of _____ DOLLARS ($_____)

of which the earnest money deposit shall be a part, and the balance of

_____ DOLLARS ($_____

shall be paid under the terms of the approved Indiana Real Estate Association, Inc., form of LAND CONTRACT to be executed by the parties at the closing of the transaction, the interest rate therein to be _____% Monthly payments of $

PARAGRAPH 4 (SALE ON OTHER BASIS) If neither Paragraphs 1, 2, or 3 is applicable, then upon the following terms:

Purchaser shall have complete possession on

Failure by seller to surrender possession on date of delivery of deed or land contract shall not make the seller a tenant of purchaser, but in such event seller shall be obligated to pay purchaser $_____ per day as liquidated damages for each day seller holds over, and this provision shall not deprive purchaser of any other legal or equitable remedy available under the law.

Rents, if any, and interest on mortgage indebtedness, if any, shall be prorated as of date of closing.

Insurance shall be (prorated) (cancelled) as of date of closing.

Taxes shall be prorated as of the date of closing, that is to say, seller shall be charged with and pay taxes on said real estate payable in the current year and for that portion of taxes payable the following year calculated as of the date of closing, and purchaser shall pay all taxes subsequent thereto. Seller shall be charged with and shall pay all delinquent payments on assessments for public improvements, if any, and all payments on such assessments currently due. Purchaser shall pay all assessments for public improvements becoming payable and becoming a lien after date of closing.

Purchaser shall be furnished, at seller's expense, a complete and merchantable abstract of title continued to date as quickly as the same can be prepared, said abstract to show a merchantable or insurable title to said real estate in the name of the grantors who will execute and deliver a general warranty deed (or contract of sale if so specified herein) conveying said real estate (or in the case of a contract of sale, agreeing to convey) in the same condition as it now is, ordinary wear and tear excepted, free and clear of all liens and encumbrances except as stated herein and subject to easements or restrictions of record, if any. However, if sellers have Owners Title Insurance, in that event purchasers shall be furnished, at sellers' expense, an Owners policy of Title Insurance in the amount of $_____. Should additional time be required for making or continuing such abstract, or for correcting defects of title, reasonable extension of time shall be given.

This transaction is to be closed within _____ days after said abstract showing merchantable title or binder for title insurance is delivered.

This offer is void if not accepted in writing on or before 12:00 o'clock noon of _____ day of _____, 19____.

This purchase includes such lighting fixtures, window shades, venetian blinds, curtain rods, linoleum cemented to floors, storm sash, screens, awnings, fences, clothes poles, laundry tubs, shrubbery, traverse rods, drapery cranes, water heater, gas burner, oil burner, stoker, heat regulator, water pump, sump pump, pressure tank, water softener, towel racks and bars, door bells or chimes, lattices, television tower, antenna and rotor now installed or in use on the premises. Seller guarantees that all of the above accessories or appliances are fully paid for or will be fully paid for, at the final closing of this transaction, unless otherwise herein stated.

The risk of loss or damage to improvements on said real estate or a substantial portion thereof by fire or otherwise, until delivery of deed or contract, is assumed by seller, and if all or a substantial portion of said buildings are so destroyed or damaged prior to execution of said deed or contract of sale, this agreement at the election of the purchaser shall not be binding upon the purchaser, and in such event any earnest money deposited shall be returned to the purchaser.

(OVER.)

609

Purchaser agrees to complete purchase of said real estate in accordance with terms and conditions hereof, said earnest money deposit shall be retained by the broker under his listing contract with said seller and shall be applicable to the broker's and the seller's damages, but seller may also sue for specific performance or pursue any other legal remedy available to seller under the law.

It is expressly agreed that all terms and conditions of this contract are included herein, and no verbal agreements of any kind shall be binding upon the parties, and this contract shall be binding upon the parties hereto, their heirs, administrators, executors, successors and assigns.

FURTHER CONDITIONS: _____

_____

_____

_____

_____
Purchaser

_____   _____
Address   Tel. No.
(of Purchaser)

The broker hereby acknowledges receipt of said earnest

money deposit in the amount of $ _____

_____
Broker

By _____
(Broker) or (Salesman)

As the owner and seller of the property described herein _____ hereby accept the foregoing Offer to Purchase

this _____ day of _____, 19____, and agree to sell in accordance therewith and to pay to

_____
Realtor and

licensed broker, the sum of _____ Dollars ($ _____)

commission for his services rendered in this transaction.

_____
Seller

_____   _____
Address   Tel. No.
(of Seller)

This Indenture

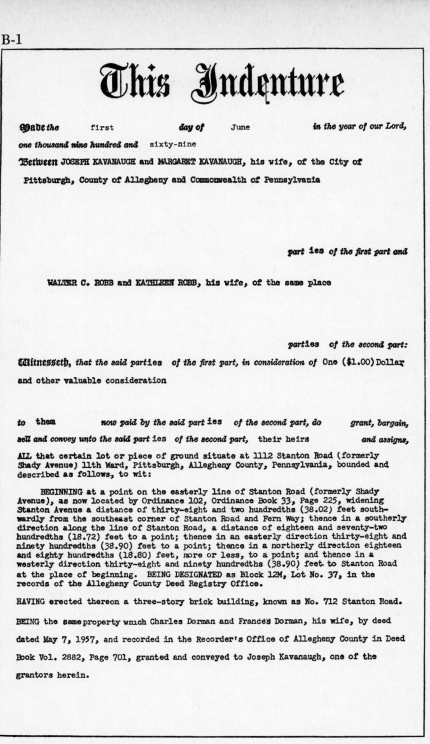

Made the first *day of* June *in the year of our Lord,* *one thousand nine hundred and* sixty-nine

Between JOSEPH KAVANAUGH and MARGARET KAVANAUGH, his wife, of the City of

Pittsburgh, County of Allegheny and Commonwealth of Pennsylvania

part ies *of the first part and*

WALTER C. ROBB and KATHLEEN ROBB, his wife, of the same place

parties of the second part:

Witnesseth, *that the said parties of the first part, in consideration of* One ($1.00) Dollar

and other valuable consideration

to them *now paid by the said part* ies *of the second part, do* *grant, bargain,* *sell and convey unto the said part* ies *of the second part,* their heirs *and assigns,*

ALL that certain lot or piece of ground situate at 1112 Stanton Road (formerly Shady Avenue) 11th Ward, Pittsburgh, Allegheny County, Pennsylvania, bounded and described as follows, to wit:

BEGINNING at a point on the easterly line of Stanton Road (formerly Shady Avenue), as now located by Ordinance 102, Ordinance Book 33, Page 225, widening Stanton Avenue a distance of thirty-eight and two hundredths (38.02) feet southwardly from the southeast corner of Stanton Road and Fern Way; thence in a southerly direction along the line of Stanton Road, a distance of eighteen and seventy-two hundredths (18.72) feet to a point; thence in an easterly direction thirty-eight and ninety hundredths (38.90) feet to a point; thence in a northerly direction eighteen and eighty hundredths (18.80) feet, more or less, to a point; and thence in a westerly direction thirty-eight and ninety hundredths (38.90) feet to Stanton Road at the place of beginning. BEING DESIGNATED as Block 12M, Lot No. 37, in the records of the Allegheny County Deed Registry Office.

HAVING erected thereon a three-story brick building, known as No. 712 Stanton Road.

BEING the same property which Charles Dorman and Frances Dorman, his wife, by deed

dated May 7, 1957, and recorded in the Recorder's Office of Allegheny County in Deed

Book Vol. 2882, Page 701, granted and conveyed to Joseph Kavanaugh, one of the

grantors herein.

with the appurtenances: **To Have and to Hold** the same unto and for the use of the said part of the second part   their heirs   and assigns forever,

And the said   Joseph Kavanaugh and Margaret Kavanaugh, his wife

for themselves,   their   heirs, executors and administrators covenant with the said part   of the second part   their heirs   and assigns against all lawful claimants

the same and every part thereof to Warrant and Defend.

Witness   hand s and seal s of the said part ies of the first part.

Attest:

DON D. REED

JOSEPH KAVANAUGH	(SEAL)
MARGARET KAVANAUGH	(SEAL)
	(SEAL)
	(SEAL)
	(SEAL)
	(SEAL)
	(SEAL)
	(SEAL)
	(SEAL)
	(SEAL)
	(SEAL)
	(SEAL)

$5.50 United States
Internal Revenue Stamps

Commonwealth of Pennsylvania,
County of Allegheny   } **ss:**

On this the   first   day of   June   , A. D. 19 69 ,
before me   a notary public,   the undersigned officer, personally appeared

JOSEPH KAVANAUGH and MARGARET KAVANAUGH, his wife,

satisfactorily proven to be the person s whose name s are   subscribed to the within instrument and acknowledged that they   executed the same for the purposes therein contained.

In Witness Whereof I hereunto set my hand and official seal.

DON D. REED

(SEAL)

Notary Public

My commission expires June 16, 1971

(Title of Officer.)

This Indenture

Made the   twenty-fourth   day of   January   *in the year of our Lord*
one thousand nine hundred and sixty-nine

Between GERALD T. THOMAS and FRANCES M. THOMAS, his wife, of the City of
Pittsburgh, County of Allegheny and State of Pennsylvania, MARIE E. FISHER
and EDWARD F. FISHER, her husband, of the Borough of Brentwood, County and
State aforesaid, MARY T. HARRISON and DONALD R. HARRISON, her husband, of the
Township of Mt. Lebanon, County and State aforesaid, being all the heirs and
next of kin of RONALD G. THOMAS, deceased

A
N
D

       THE DOUGHERTY STEEL COMPANY,

a corporation or body politic, created by and existing under the laws of the Commonwealth of
Pennsylvania, having its domicile in the   City of Pittsburgh

            County of Allegheny, Pennsylvania   *of the second part:*

Witnesseth, *That the said part* ies   *of the first part, for and in consideration of the sum of*

    Twenty-seven Thousand ($27,000.00)   *Dollars,*

lawful money of the United States of America, unto them   *well and truly paid by the said*

party of the second part, at or before the sealing and delivery of these presents, the receipt whereof

is hereby acknowledged have   *granted, bargained, sold, aliened, enfeoffed, released, con-*

veyed and confirmed, and by these presents do   *grant, bargain, sell, alien, enfeoff, release,*

convey and confirm unto the said party of the second part, its successors and assigns, forever.

All
       (Description follows.)

(Recital)
       BEING the same premises which WILLIAM PICKETT, unmarried, by his deed
dated June 9, 1959, and of record in the Recorder's Office of Allegheny County,
Pennsylvania in Deed Book Vol. 2210, Page 311, granted and conveyed to RONALD G.
THOMAS and EDNA THOMAS, his wife; the said EDNA THOMAS having died on March 21,
1960, absolute title in fee simple vested in the surviving spouse, RONALD G. THOMAS;
the said RONALD G. THOMAS, having died on September 5, 1961, unmarried, absolute
title in fee simple vested in his surviving issue, GERALD T. THOMAS, son; MARIE
E. FISHER, daughter, presently intermarried with EDWARD F. FISHER, and MARY T.
HARRISON, daughter, presently intermarried with DONALD R. HARRISON, the grantors
herein.

Together with all and singular, the buildings, improvements, ways, waters, water courses, rights, liberties, privileges, hereditaments and appurtenances whatsoever thereunto belonging, or in anywise appertaining, and the reversions and remainders, Rents, issues and profits thereof; and all the estate, right, title, interest, property, claim and demand whatsoever of the said parties of the first part, in law, equity or otherwise, howsoever, of, in and to the same and every part thereof.

To Have and to Hold the said buildings, improvements hereditaments and premises hereby granted, or mentioned, and intended so to be, with the appurtenances, unto the said party of the second part, its successors and assigns, to and for the only proper use and behoof of the said party of the second part, its successors and assigns, **Forever.**

And GERALD T. THOMAS and FRANCES M. THOMAS, his wife; MARIE E. FISHER and EDWARD F. FISHER, her husband, and MARY T. HARRISON and DONALD R. HARRISON, her husband

the said parties of the first part, for themselves, their heirs, executors and administrators, do by these presents covenant, promise and agree to and with the said party of the second part, its successors and assigns, that they , the said parties of the first part, their heirs, all and singular the hereditaments and premises hereinabove described and granted, or mentioned, and intended so to be, with the appurtenances, unto the said party of the second part, its successors and assigns, against them , the said parties of the first part, and their heirs, and against all and every other person or persons whomsoever, lawfully claiming or to claim the same or any part thereof,

shall and will Warrant and Forever Defend.

In Witness Whereof, the said parties of the first part have to these presents set their hands and seals . Dated the day and year first above written.

Sealed and Delivered
in the Presence of

ROBERT A. MacDOWELL

GERALD T. THOMAS	SEAL
FRANCES M. THOMAS	SEAL
MARIE E. FISHER	SEAL
EDWARD F. FISHER	SEAL
MARY T. HARRISON	SEAL
DONALD R. HARRISON	SEAL

(ACKNOWLEDGMENT)

Certificate of Residence.

I, do hereby certify that precise residence is

Witness my hand this day of 19

C-1   THIS MORTGAGE

MADE the ....*sixteenth*.... day of ....*January*.... in the year of our Lord, one thousand nine hundred and sixty-nine....

FROM ....*Edward J. George of Ohio Township, County of Erie and State of Pennsylvania*..*mortgagor, to*

....*John A. Mason, of the City of Erie, County and State aforesaid*..............

....

....*mortgagee,* Witnesseth:

WHEREAS, the said ....*Edward J. George, mortgagor*........................

by ....*his*.... bond of even date herewith, stand ....*s*.... bound unto said mortgagee in a certain penal sum, conditioned for the payment of ....*Twenty-Five Hundred ($2500.00) Dollars, payable as follows: The sum of Two Hundred Fifty ($250.00) Dollars on April 15, 1969 and a like and equal sum of Two Hundred Fifty ($250.00) Dollars quarterly thereafter until July 16, 1967 when the balance then remaining unpaid shall become due and payable*.... with interest thereon from the date hereof at ....*five*.... per cent per annum payable ....*quarterly*....; and all premiums and charges for such insurance on the mortgaged buildings, as shall from time to time be taken out by the mortgagee, ...*his heirs, executors, administrators*.... or assigns, to better secure the said debt and interest and all taxes and municipal claims against the mortgaged premises, as soon as payable, penalties and costs, which if paid by the mortgagee, ...*his heirs, executors, administrators*.... or assigns, may be added to said real debt and also, in case of default, all fees, costs and expenses of collection, including an attorney's commission of ....*five*.... per centum.

NOW THEREFORE the said mortgagor, in consideration of one dollar to ....*him*.... paid by the said mortgagee, and for securing payment and performance as aforesaid, do....*es*.... grant, bargain, and convey unto the said mortgagee, ...*his heirs*.... and assigns

....*All that certain lot or piece of ground situate in Ohio Township, County of Erie, Pennsylvania, being more particularly bounded and described as follows: Beginning at a point in the center line of Ocean Road, where the same is intersected by the South boundary line of property now or formerly of Erie County; thence from said point of beginning South 11° 10' East, along the center line of said Ocean Road, a distance of eighty-nine and sixty hundredths (89.60) feet to a point; thence continuing along said center line South 3° 31' East, eighty-two and forty hundredths (82.40) feet; thence still continuing along said center line South 7° 15' West, a distance of two hundred sixty-eight and fifty hundredths (268.50) feet to line of land now or formerly of John MacLachlan; thence South 60° 40' East, a distance of one hundred fifty-seven and fifty-one hundredths (157.51) feet along line of said property now or formerly of John MacLachlan, to an iron pin; thence North 29° 21' East, a distance of ninety (90) feet to an iron pin in the dividing line between the property herein described and property conveyed by Joseph S. Steen, et ux, to Robert Townsend, et ux, by Deed dated December 6, 1949, recorded December 6, 1949, in Deed Book Vol. 1970, page 221; thence along said land of Townsend, North 6° 28' 30" East, a distance of four hundred forty-five and seventy hundredths (445.70) feet to the southerly line of land of Erie County above mentioned; thence along said line of land of Erie County South 88° West, a distance of two hundred twenty and fourteen hundredths (220.14) feet, more or less, to the point in the center line of the said Ocean Road, at the place of beginning*.....

....BEING *the same premises which Joseph S. Steele and Mae E. Steele, his wife, by their deed dated of even date, and to be recorded, granted and conveyed unto Edward J. George, mortgagor herein*.....

TOGETHER with all and singular the buildings, ways, waters, water courses, rights, liberties, privileges, improvements, hereditaments and appurtenances whatsoever thereunto belong, or in anywise appertaining and the reversions and remainders, rents, issues and profits thereof.

TO HAVE AND TO HOLD the same unto, and for the use of the said mortgagee, ... *his heirs, executors, administrators*.... and assigns.

PROVIDED, however, that if the said mortgagor pay and perform, according to the condition of said bond, everything to be paid and performed as aforesaid, then the estate hereby conveyed and granted shall become and be void.

But in case of default of such payment or performance at any time or in any particular, for the space of ....*thirty*.... days, every sum to be paid as aforesaid shall then become and be payable forthwith, and an Action of Mortgage Foreclosure or other lawful writ or writs hereon may forthwith be issued, and prosecuted to judgment and execution, for the same, with interest and all damages for default and costs, and with an attorney's commission of ....*five*.... per cent for collection. And all stay of execution which is or shall be given by law, is waived.

WITNESS the hand and seal of the said mortgagor the day and year aforesaid.

....*Edward J. George*.... (SEAL)

ATTEST:
....*Martin H. Kohler*....

COMMONWEALTH OF PENNSYLVANIA }
COUNTY OF ....*Erie*....   } ss.

Before me, a ......*notary public*...... in and for ......*said County and State*...... on this ......*sixteenth*...... day of ......*January*...... A.D. 1969 ..... came the above named ......*Edward J. George, personally known to me*......and acknowledged this Mortgage to be......*his*......act and deed, to the end that it may be recorded as such.

WITNESS my hand and ....*notarial*.... seal.

....*Martin H. Kohler*....
....*My commission expires May 1, 1971*....

CERTIFICATE OF RESIDENCE

I, ...*Ralph W. Sims, Att'y*.... Do hereby certify that ....*mortgagee's*....precise ....*residence is 2117 Cherokee St., Erie, Pa.*.....

Witness my hand this ....*sixteenth*.... day of ....*January*.... 1969.....

....*Ralph W. Sims*....
Att'y

Know all Men by these Presents

That I, EDWARD J. GEORGE, of Ohio Township, County of Erie and State of

Pennsylvania

held and firmly bound unto   JOHN A. MASON, of the City of Erie, County and State

aforesaid,

in the sum of Five Thousand ($5,000.00)   *Dollars,*
to be paid to the said JOHN A. MASON,   his   *certain*
attorney, his heirs, executors, administrators   *or assigns; to which payment well and truly to be*
made I *do bind* myself,   *my   heirs, executors and administrators, and every of them, jointly and sev-*
erally by these presents. And I *do hereby empower any Attorney of any Court of Record within the United States or*
elsewhere, to appear for me   *and with or without declaration filed, confess judgment or judgments against* me
in favor of the said JOHN A. MASON, his heirs, executors, administrators   *and assigns,*
as of any term for the above penalty together with costs of suit, attorney's commission of five   *per cent.*
for collection, waiver of inquisition and condemnation of any property that may be levied upon by virtue of any execution,
which may issue forthwith on failure to comply with the conditions hereof; . I   *hereby waive all exemption laws*
now in force or hereafter passed and release all errors.

Witness my   hand *and seal* the   sixteenth   *day of* June
in the year of Our Lord one thousand nine hundred and sixty nine

The Condition of this Obligation is such, *That if the above bounden*

EDWARD A. GEORGE, his

heirs, executors and administrators shall and do well and truly pay, or cause to be paid, unto the said
JOHN A. MASON, his heirs, executors, administrators   *or assigns, the just sum of*
                                                                          Dollars,
TWO THOUSAND FIVE HUNDRED ($2,500.00)

as follows: - The sum of Two Hundred Fifty ($250.00) Dollars on September 16, 1969
and a like and equal sum of Two Hundred Fifty ($250.00) Dollars quarterly there-
after until Sept. 16, 1971, when the balance then remaining unpaid shall become
due and payable

with interest thereon from the date hereof at five *per cent. per annum payable* quarterly *annually until the*
whole of said principal debt or sum be fully paid; and all premiums and charges for such insurance on the buildings
upon the land described in the accompanying mortgage, as shall from time to time be taken out by the said obligee
his heirs, executors, administrators   *or assigns, to better secure the said*
debt and interest; and also all taxes and municipal claims against said land as soon as payable, penalties, and costs,
which if paid by the said obligee his heirs, executors, administrators,   *or assigns,*
may be added to said real debt, then this obligation to be void; otherwise to remain in full force and virtue.
    But in case of default for thirty   *days in payment of any of the moneys herein required to be paid*
the whole of said principal debt or sum as it then may be, and accrued interest thereon shall become due and payable
and execution may issue forthwith, for the same, together with all fees, costs and expenses of collection, including an
attorney's commission of five   *per cent.*

Attest: EDWARD J. GEORGE _____ (SEAL)

                                                   _____ (SEAL)

LEONARD STEWART   _____ (SEAL)

                                                   _____ (SEAL)

C-3   MORTGAGE
                           (California—Short Form)

THIS INDENTURE, made the ....3rd.... day of ...February.. , 19..69.., between ....Emil Engelhard.... party of the first part, and ....Allan Coe....,
party of the second part, Witnesseth:
That the said party of the first part, for and in consideration of the sum of
............One ($1.00)............ dollar lawful money of the United States of
America, to him in hand paid, does by these presents grant, bargain, sell, convey and
confirm unto the said party of the second part, and to his heirs and assigns, forever,
all that certain piece or parcel of land situate in ......Los Angeles......, county
of ......Los Angeles......, State of ......California......, bounded and described as follows, etc., Together with all and singular the tenements, hereditaments,
and appurtenances thereunto belonging, or in any wise appertaining. This conveyance is intended as a mortgage to secure the payment of .... One thousand
($1,000)...... dollars (specify time of payment, interest, etc., and whether evi-
denced by a note or bond), and these presents shall be void if such payment be
made (according to the terms of note or bond). But in case default be made in the
payment of the principal or interest as herein provided, then the said party of the
second part, his executors, administrators and assigns, are hereby empowered to sell
the said premises with all and every of the appurtenances, or any part thereof, in
the manner prescribed by law; and out of the money arising from such sale to retain the said principal and interest, together with costs and charges of such sale; and
5 per cent for attorney's fees; and the balance, if any there be, shall be paid by the
party making such sale, on demand, to the said party of the first part, his heirs or
assigns.
IN WITNESS, etc.

C-4   SATISFACTION OF MORTGAGE
                                (Satisfaction Piece)

From ...JACKSON BENNETT ....⎞
                   Mortgagor   ⎟   Mortgage Dated ..December 6, 1965..
.... ⎟   Mortgage Recorded ......December 6,
To MUTUAL BENEFIT MORTGAGE⎟   1965....
   CO.   Mortgagee ⎜   in Mortgage Book Vol. ...2774... Page
Assigned to ..JASON L. BENNETT..⎟ ....316.... in the Recorder's Office of
                   Assignee   ⎟   Allegheny County, Pennsylvania. Debt
.... ⎠ $....4,000.00....

                   KNOW ALL MEN BY THESE PRESENTS
That ....JASON L. BENNETT.... the ....assignee.... above named, acknowledged to have RECEIVED PAYMENT AND SATISFACTION in full of the above recited
mortgage upon property situate in ....Clairton.... Allegheny County, Pennsylvania ....
                           (Description follows)
....
....
....
....
....
....
....
....

. . . .
. . . .
and . . . .*I*. . . . do hereby direct the Recorder of Deeds to NOTE this satisfaction upon
the margin of the above recited mortgage.
IN WITNESS WHEREOF . . . . . *I* . . . . . have hereunto set . . . .*my*. . . . hand. . . .
and seal. . . . this . . . .*17th*. . . . day of . . . .*January*. . . . A.D. 19. . . .*69* . . . . .

Witnesses Present:
. . . .*PAUL W. LEFFLER*. . . . . } . . . .*JASON L. BENNETT*. . . . (Seal)
. . . . (Seal)
. . . . (Seal)
. . . . (Seal)
(Acknowledgment)

C-5   ASSIGNMENT OF MORTGAGE

From . . . . .*HIRAM T. MILLER*. . . . . Mortgagor . . . . To . . . . . .*FELIX CRAMPTON*. . . . . . . Mortgagee Assigned to . . . . Assignee	Mortgage Dated . . . .*May 11, 1966*. . . . Mortgage Recorded . . . .*May 11, 1966* . . . . in Mortgage Book Vol. . . . .*2206* . . . .Page . . . .*192*. . . . . . in the Record- er's Office of Allegheny County, Penn- sylvania. Debt $. . . . . . *10,000.00*. . . . . .

KNOW ALL MEN BY THESE PRESENTS

That . . . .*FELIX CRAMPTON*. . . . the . . . .*mortgagee*. . . . above named for and
in consideration of the sum of . . . .*Ten Thousand*. . . . Dollars ($. . . . . . .*10,000.00*),
lawful money of the United States of America to . . . .*him*. . . . in hand paid by
. . . . *JAMES P. ROE* . . . . at or before the sealing and delivery of these presents,
the receipt whereof is hereby acknowledged, has granted, bargained, sold, assigned,
transferred and set over, and by these presents does grant, bargain, sell, assign, transfer and set over unto the said . . . .*JAMES P. ROE*. . . . and assigns the above stated
Mortgage together with all the rights, remedies, incidents, and appurtenances thereunto belonging, or in anywise appertaining, and all the right, title, interest, estate,
property, claim and demand whatsoever of, in and to the same, and the premises
therein described; together with the bond or obligation in said Indenture of Mortgage mentioned, and thereby intended to be secured, and the warrant of attorney to
confess judgment thereto annexed, and all moneys due and to grow due therefrom.
TO HAVE AND TO HOLD the same unto the said . . . .*JAMES P. ROE, his executors,
administrators*. . . . and assigns, to . . . .*him*. . . . and . . . .*his*. . . . proper use and
behoof, subject to the provisions or condition of redemption in said Indenture of
Mortgage contained, and direct the Recorder of said County to NOTE upon the
margin of the record of said Mortgage, this Assignment thereof.
WITNESS . . . .*my*. . . . hand . . . .*and seal*. . . . this . . . .*12th*. . . . day of . . . .*November*. . . . A.D. 19. . . .*68*. . . .

Witnesses present:

. . . .*PAUL T. SNOWDEN*. . . . .*FELIX CRAMPTON*. . . . (SEAL)
. . . . (SEAL)
(Acknowledgment)

C-6

EXTENSION OF MORTGAGE

From ......*ALBERT C. GROSS and* ....*MARY L. GROSS, his wife* ...... Mortgagors... To .....*PAUL W. LANE*......... Mortgagee... Assigned to ..*EDWARD R. FISHER*.. Assignee...	Mortgage Dated ....*May 2, 1963*..... Mortgage Recorded ...*May 2, 1963*.. in Mortgage Book Vol.....*2680*..... Page ....*316*.... in the Recorder's Office of ....*Atlantic County, New Jersey* .... Debt $....*9,000.00*.....

And now .....*May 2, 1969*..... for value received the ......*assignee*......
above named do......*es*...... hereby extend the time for payment of the debt
secured by said mortgage and its accompanying bond for a period of ....*two*....
years from ..*July 2, 1969*.. subject to all other terms and conditions as set forth
in above recited mortgage, and the said ....*mortgagors*.......... hereby
agree...... to the above terms and conditions.

IN WITNESS WHEREOF, ...*EDWARD R. FISHER*...... part..*y*.. of the first
Mortgagee..or Assignee..
and ....*ALBERT C. GROSS and MARY L. GROSS, his wife*..........
Mortgagor..or Present Owner..
part..*ies*.. of the second part have hereunto set their hands and seals the day and
year first above written.

Witnesses:

.....*MARY G. HENDERSON*......

.....*FRANK W. SHOOK*..........

....*EDWARD R. FISHER*...(SEAL)

....*ALBERT C. GROSS*.....(SEAL)

....*MARY L. GROSS*......(SEAL)

.........................(SEAL)

STATE OF .....*NEW JERSEY*......⎱
COUNTY OF ......*ATLANTIC*......⎰ SS:

On the ..*2nd*.. day of ...*May*...
A.D. 19 .*69*.., before me a ..*Notary Public*.. in and for said County
and State came the above named .....*EDWARD R. FISHER*...... and acknowledged the foregoing Extension of Mortgage to be .....*his*...... act and
deed, and desired the same to be recorded as such.

WITNESS my hand and ......*notarial*...... seal, the day and year aforesaid.

.............*FRANK W. SHOOK*............

....*Notary Public*....

My commission expires ..*November 3, 1971*..

Bond and Mortgage

From

ROLAND T. BOWLES and

IRENE C. BOWLES, his wife,

to

CHESTER L. BROWN

Bond	$ 10,000.00
Real Debt	$ 5,000.00

Dated the 6th *day of* December   19 68
*secured by mortgage of same date, recorded in the
Recorder's Office of* Beaver   *County,
Pennsylvania, in Mortgage Book Vol.* 1174
Page 613   , *on certain Real Estate.*

To all Whom it may Concern:

ROLAND T. BOWLES and IRENE C. BOWLES, his wife,   *hereby certify and acknowledge that a mortgage made by* ROLAND T. BOWLES and IRENE C. BOWLES, his wife,

to   CHESTER L. BROWN

dated December 6,

A. D. 19 68 , *for* Five Thousand ($5,000.00) Dollars *payable* at the rate of Forty ($40.00) Dollars monthly, beginning January 1, 1969   *with interest*

at the rate of six (6) per cent

payable monthly   , *recorded as above set forth, together with the Bond of* Ten Thousand ($10,000) Dollars   *accompanying the same, is justly, fully and entirely owing and payable according to the terms and conditions thereof* in the sum of Four Thousand Five Hundred Sixty ($4,560.00) Dollars as of December 6, 1968

And we   *hereby also, further certify to any person or persons who may desire to purchase the same, that* we   *have no drawback, claim, set-off, or other defense of any kind whatsoever, to the payment of any part of said mortgage, either principal, interest or commissions,* in said sum of Four Thousand Five Hundred Sixty ($4,560.00) Dollars

when due and payable or collectible by the terms and conditions therein recited as aforesaid.

Witness *our* hands *and seal* s *this* 6th   *day of* December   *A. D.* 1968.

Attest:

CLYDE L. BUSH

ROLAND T. BOWLES   (SEAL)

IRENE C. BOWLES   (SEAL)

(SEAL)

(SEAL)

(SEAL)

Commonwealth of Pennsylvania,

County of Allegheny   } **ss:**   (ACKNOWLEDGMENT)

On this   6th   *day of* December   *A. D.* 19 68 , *before me*

in and for said County and State, came the above named

ROLAND T. BOWLES and IRENE C. BOWLES, his wife,

and acknowledged the foregoing Indenture to be their *act and deed and desired the same to be recorded as such.*

Witness *my hand and*   notarial   *seal, the day and year aforesaid.*

Diane Smith

My Commission Expires   October 14, 1972

C-8

MORTGAGE
(Florida)

THIS INDENTURE, made this ...... day of......, A.D., 19..., between ....,
called the Mortgagor, and ...., called the Mortgagee; witnesseth that the said
mortgagor, for and in consideration of the sum of ...... dollars, to .... in
hand paid by the said mortgagee, the receipt whereof is hereby acknowledged,
.... granted, bargained and sold to the said mortgag..., ... heirs and
assigns forever, the following described land, situate, lying and being in the County
of ...., State of .... to wit:

(Description)

And the said Mortgagor.. do.... hereby fully warrant the title to said land, and
will defend the same against the lawful claims of all persons whomsoever.

Provided always, that if said Mortgagor..., ... heirs, legal representatives
or assigns shall pay to the said Mortgagee..., ... legal representatives or assigns, a certain promissory note, a copy of which is on the reverse side hereof, and
shall perform and comply with each and every stipulation, agreement and covenant
of said note and of this mortgage and the estate hereby created shall be void, otherwise the same shall remain in full force and virtue. And the said mortgagor..
covenant.. to pay the interest and principal promptly when due; to pay the taxes and
assessments on said property; to carry insurance against fire on the building.. on
said land for not less than $......, approved by the mortgagee.., with standard
mortgage loss clause payable to mortgagee.., the policy to be held by the mortgagee..; to keep the building.. on said land in proper repair; and to waive the
homestead exemption.

Should any of the above covenants be broken, then said note and all moneys
secured hereby shall, without demand, if the mortgagee...., ... legal representatives or assigns so elect, at once become due and payable, and the mortgage be
foreclosed, and all costs and expenses of collection of said moneys by foreclosure or
otherwise, including solicitor's fees, shall be paid by mortgagor...., and the same
are hereby secured.

IN WITNESS WHEREOF, the said mortgagor.... hereunto set.... hand and seal....
the day and year first above written.

Signed, sealed and delivered in the presence of:

.......................(SEAL)

(Copy of note)

...... year.... after date, for value received, ... promise to pay to ......, or
order, ...dollars, with interest thereon at the rate of ......per cent per annum
from date until paid, said interest being payable ...., both principal and interest payable at .... This note secured by mortgage on real estate of even
date herewith, and is subject to all the terms and covenants therein contained.

Dated this ...... day of ......, 19....

....

(Signature)

C-10

VENDOR'S LIEN CLAUSE

KNOW ALL MEN BY THESE PRESENTS:

That we Charles A. Davis and Elizabeth C. Davis, his wife, of Pine Bluff, Arkansas,
for and in consideration of the sum of One Thousand Dollars ($1,000.00) paid and
to be paid by William Archer, grantee, as follows: Five Hundred Dollars ($500.00)
cash in hand paid, the receipt of which is hereby acknowledged and for the balance

of Five Hundred Dollars ($500.00) said grantee has executed his promissory note of even date herewith payable to Charles A. Davis, said note being due and payable as follows: One Hundred Dollars ($100.00) on or before January 2, 1969, and One Hundred Dollars ($100.00) on or before January 1st of each year thereafter until paid in full, together with 5% interest from date until maturity and 8% from maturity until paid. A vendor's lien on the property herein conveyed is retained to secure the purchase price. If default is made in the payment of any installment of principal or interest, the principal sum and accrued interest shall at once become due and payable without notice, at the option of the holder of said note.

......*CHARLES A. DAVIS*.........(SEAL)
......*ELIZABETH C. DAVIS*.......(SEAL)

November 26, 1968

C-9

DEED OF TRUST

THIS DEED, Made this 20th day of January, in the year of our Lord, One Thousand Nine Hundred and Sixty-Nine, between WILLIAM J. FIKE and ELIZABETH C. FIKE, his wife, of the City of Wheeling, County of Ohio and State of West Virginia, parties of the first part, and J. ROLAND BRADY, Trustee, of the same place, party of the second part.

WITNESSETH: That for and in consideration of the sum of Five Dollars, the receipt of which is hereby acknowledged, and of the trust hereinafter set forth, the said parties of the first part do grant unto the said party of the second part, with covenant of general warranty, the following described property, that is to say:

Lot Numbered Seventy-four (74) as designated on the Plat of lots, streets, and alleys known as "Longvue Acres," a plat of which is to be recorded in the Office of the Clerk of the County Court of Ohio County, West Virginia, in Plat Book No. 12, page number 33, and a copy of a part of said plat is attached to the Deed to said parties of the first part, from the Craft Realty and Builders, Inc.

This grant is subject, however, to the following restrictions and reservations, that is to say: It is a condition of this grant that no building or structure, except open porches, verandas or stoops shall be erected nearer to Longvue Avenue than the building line established on the plat hereinbefore referred to, that no buildings other than private garages or a private dwelling house shall be erected on the property hereby conveyed, and that not more than one such dwelling house shall be erected on such property, that no dwelling house erected on the property hereby conveyed shall face other than on Longvue Avenue; that no dwelling house erected on the property hereby conveyed shall cost less than Eight Thousand ($8,000.00) Dollars.

Being the same property which Craft Realty and Builders, Inc., a West Virginia corporation, by its deed dated the 19th day of January, 1969 and to be recorded in the County Clerk's Office of Ohio County, West Virginia, granted and conveyed to William J. Fike and Elizabeth C. Fike, his wife, the parties of the first part herein.

IN TRUST, however, to secure unto the holder and owner thereof, the prompt and punctual payment at maturity, of both principal and interest, of a certain negotiable promissory note, of which the following is a true copy:

$10,000.00   Wheeling, W. Va., January 20, 1969
......*Two years*......after date......*We*......promise to pay to the order
of.......................*Ourselves*....................*TEN THOUSAND*
..........................Dollars with interest from date at the rate of
6% per annum, payable Quarterly. Value received, negotiable and payable at

THE BANK OF WHEELING
Wheeling, West Virginia

Endorsed in blank
William J. Fike   (Signed)   *William J. Fike*
Elizabeth C. Fike   *Elizabeth C. Fike*

ALSO to secure the prompt payment of any note or notes which may hereafter be given in renewal or extension of the above described note, or of any part thereof, or for any interest thereof. Said first parties agree to keep the buildings, which are now or which may hereafter be erected upon the land hereby conveyed, insured against loss or damage by fire in the sum of not less than $10,000.00 as further security for the payment of said debt. The policies therefor shall be issued by underwriters satisfactory to the trustee herein, shall be made payable to said trustee as his interest may appear, and shall be delivered to the holder of said debt. Upon failure of the said first parties to so keep said property insured, or to pay the taxes upon said property when the same become due and payable, the said property may be so insured and said taxes paid by the trustee herein, or the holder and owner of said note or notes, or any renewal thereof, and all payments made by said trustee, or the holder and owner of said note or notes, or any renewal thereof, for such insurance and taxes, or either thereof, shall be secured by this Deed of Trust.

Any sale of property made by the trustee by virtue of this deed may be upon the following terms: Cash, or if the said trustee so elects, one-third of the purchase money, or so much more thereof as the purchaser may elect to pay cash in hand on the day of sale, and the residue in two equal installments, payable respectively in Six Months and Twelve Months from the day of sale, with interest, the purchaser giving his negotiable promissory notes for the deferred payments, the legal title being retained as further security until all of the purchase money shall have been paid.

Notice of any such sale shall be given by the said trustee by advertisement published at least once a week for four successive weeks, preceding the day of sale, in some newspaper published in Ohio County, West Virginia, and a sale may be adjourned from time to time without other notice than oral proclamation at the time and place appointed for selling from which the adjournment is made.

The trustee may act by agent or attorney in the execution of this trust.

WITNESS the following signatures and seals:

....../s/ *William J. Fike* ....(SEAL)
....../s/ *Elizabeth C. Fike* ....(SEAL)

STATE OF WEST VIRGINIA ⎱ SS.
COUNTY OF OHIO   ⎰

I, ...*L. J. Ferrell* ..., a Notary Public of Ohio County, do certify that William J. Fike and Elizabeth C. Fike, his wife, whose names are signed to the writing above, bearing date the 20th day of January, 1969, have this day acknowledged the same before me in my said county.

Given under my hand this *21st* day of *January, 1969.*

My Commission expires   ....L. J. Ferrell..........
March 24, 1971   Notary Public

D-1   LEASE OF DWELLING

THIS LEASE WITNESSETH, That .....*CONRAD T. WEIR*....., herein called
LESSOR, hereby leases to ....*RAY L. STITT*...., herein called LESSEE, for the
term of ....*one (1) year*.... commencing on the ....*first day of January, A.D.
1969* ....and ending on the *31st day of December, A.D. 1969* ... for the total rent
of ....*Eight Hundred Forty ($840.00)*.... Dollars, the following real estate, in its
present condition in the ....*City of Chicago, Cook County, Illinois*....:
    All that certain ....*dwelling, consisting of six rooms and bath at 633 Mohawk
Ave., Chicago, Illinois*..... In consideration Whereof, the Lessee covenants to pay
as rent in ..*monthly*.. installments, without demand in advance from the beginning of the term; that is to say, ...*the sum of Seventy ($70.00) Dollars on Janu-
ary 1, 1969 and the sum of Seventy ($70.00)*.... Dollars on ....*February 1,
1969*.... and a like and equal sum ....*monthly*.... in advance during the term
of this lease or any renewal thereof, following the day last aforesaid until the whole
of said rent is paid. And the said Lessee doth covenant with the Lessor:
    1. That he will, during the continuance of the term hereby granted, pay rent
hereinbefore reserved at the times at which the same is made payable;
    2. That he will also, from time to time during said term, pay all gas, electricity and
water rates which may be assessed upon the demised premises, or on the owner or
occupier, in respect thereof, and that he will not suffer nor commit any waste of the
premises;
    3. That he will, during the said term, keep the said premises in good and tenant-
able repair, externally and internally, reasonable wear and tear excepted;
    4. That he will make no alterations or additions to or upon said premises without
the consent of the said lessor being first obtained in writing;
    5. That he will not assign this lease nor underlet the said premises, or any part
thereof, without such previous consent in writing.
    6. That the lessor or his agents may, at reasonable times, enter upon said premises
to examine the condition of the same, to take or send persons on said property, seeking to rent or purchase, make repairs or improvement and post notices of To Let
or For Sale.
    7. That he will, at the termination of said tenancy, quietly yield up the said prem-
ises, with the fixtures which are now or at any time during said term shall be thereon,
in as good and tenantable condition, in all respects, reasonable wear and use and
damage by fire and other unavoidable casualties excepted, as the same now are.
    Provided, that in case said buildings and premises, or any part thereof, shall at
any time be destroyed or damaged by fire or other unavoidable casualty, so that the
same shall be unfit for occupation or use, then the rent hereby reserved, or a fair and
just proportion thereof, according to the nature and extent of the damage sustained,
shall be suspended and cease to be payable until said premises shall be rebuilt or
made fit for occupation and use by the said lessor, or these presents shall thereby be
determined and ended, at the election of the said Lessor.
    Provided also, and these presents are upon the condition, that if said rent, or any
part thereof, shall be at any time be in arrear or unpaid, or if the Lessee shall at any
time fail or neglect to perform or observe any of the covenants, conditions, or agreements herein contained and on his part to be performed and observed, or if the
Lessee shall become bankrupt or insolvent or shall compound with his creditors,
then and in any such case it shall be lawful for the Lessor or any person or persons
duly authorized by him in that behalf, without any formal notice or demand, to
enter into and upon said demised premises, or any part thereof, in the name of the
whole, and the said premises peaceably to hold and enjoy thenceforth as if these
presents had not been made, without prejudice to any right of action or remedy of
the Lessor in respect of any antecedent breach of any of the covenants by the Lessee
herein contained. Upon any such default, the entire rent for the balance of the term

shall at once become due and payable and for value received and forthwith on
every default of payment of rent by Lessee under this lease, or on any and every
breach of covenant or agreement by Lessee under the terms of this lease, the Lessee
does hereby empower any attorney of any court of record within the United States
or elsewhere, to appear for Lessee and with or without declaration filed, confess
judgment against the Lessee, and in favor of said Lessor, his heirs, devisees, and
executors, administrators, or assigns, as of any term, for the sum due by reason of
said default in the payment of rent, including unpaid rent for the balance of the
term if the same shall have become due and payable under the provisions herein,
and/or for the sum due by reason of any breach of covenant or agreement by Lessee
herein, with costs of suit and attorney's commission of ....$100.00.... for collec-
tion, and forthwith issue writ or writs of execution thereon, with release of all errors,
and without stay of execution and inquisition and extension upon any levy on real
estate is hereby expressly waived, and condemnation agreed to, and exemption of
any and all property from levy and sale by virtue of any exemption law now in
force or which may be hereafter passed is also expressly waived by Lessee, and in
case of violation of any of the covenants or agreements in this lease by Lessee, the
said Lessee further, at the option of said Lessor, authorizes and empowers any such
attorney, either in addition to or without such judgment for the amount due according to the terms of this lease, to appear for said Lessee and confess judgment forthwith against Lessee, and in favor of Lessor, in an amicable action of ejectment for
the premises above described, with all the conditions, fees, releases, waivers of stay
of execution and waiver of exemption to accompany said confession of judgment in
ejectment as are set forth herein for confession of judgment for said sum or sums
due.

If the premises at any time be deserted or closed, the Lessor may enter by force,
without liability to prosecution or action therefor, and may distrain for rent and also
re-let the premises as Agent of the Lessee for any unexpired portion of the term and
receive the rent therefor and apply it on this lease.

All rights and liabilities herein given to or imposed upon either of the parties
hereto, shall extend to their heirs, executors, administrators, successors and assigns
of such party. If the Lessee lawfully occupies the premises after the end of the term,
this lease and all its terms, provisions, conditions, covenants, confession or confessions
of judgment, waivers, remedies and any and all of Lessor's rights herein specially
given and agreed to, shall be in force for another ....month ... and so on from
..month.... to ....month.... as long as the relation of Lessor and Lessee continues.

IN WITNESS WHEREOF, the parties hereto set their hands and seals this ....3rd....
day of ....December...., A.D. ....1968.....

Sealed and Delivered in the presence of

.......BEN POPE.......   ......CONRAD T. WEIR.......(SEAL)
                                ......RAY L. STITT..........(SEAL)

This Lease Witnesseth, That   JOHN WEBER

as Lessor, by   McFADDEN REALTY CO., agent,   hereby Leases to

Frank Sherman and Elizabeth M. Sherman, his wife,   as Tenant, for the Term

of   one year   commencing on the   1st   day of   October   A.D. 19 68

and ending on the   thirtieth   day of   September   A.D. 19 69

for the total rent of   Seven Hundred Twenty ($720.00)   Dollars,

the following apartment in its present condition in   Pittsburgh,   Allegheny

All that certain first-floor four-room apartment, with sun porch, bath, and use of

basement, at 6018 Negley Ave., Pittsburgh, Pa.

In Consideration Whereof, The Tenant covenants to pay as rent in   monthly   installments, without demand in advance.

at   6018 Negley Ave., Pittsburgh, Pa.   from the beginning of the term: that is to say, the sum of

Sixty   ($ 60.00   ) Dollars on the signing of this Lease for   October

rent, 19 65 and the sum of   Sixty   ($ 60.00   ) Dollars on the first day

of each and every month thereafter, during the term, or any renewal thereof; to pay, as due, all   utilities, except water,   gases used thereon, and to make all necessary repairs thereto, and to keep the premises clean, free of rubbish, and in such condition as the Board of Health may require, during the term, and, if the Lessor pays for the same or any part thereof, Lessor shall enforce payment thereof in the same manner as rent in arrear, as hereafter provided, to remove no additions or improvements made by the Lessor or by the Tenant, nor alter the premises, nor sub-let the same, or any part thereof, nor to post bills, or erect bill boards, nor assign this Lease voluntarily, by judicial sale or otherwise, without the written consent of the Lessor, under penalty of instant forfeiture of this Lease and the terms hereof, and the payment of $ 60.00   as additional rent; to use the premises only for   dwelling to accommodate three persons   and to surrender the same at the end of the term in as good order as they now are, reasonable wear and tear alone excepted. The tenant waives to the Lessor the benefit of all laws now or hereafter in force in this State or elsewhere exempting property from liability for rent, or for debt, expressly waiving the Act of Assembly, entitled "An Act for the relief of the poor," approved the tenth day of April, A. D. 1829, and its several supplements; also Act No. 20, approved April 6, 1951, entitled "The Landlord and Tenant Act of 1951".

The Tenant further agrees to perform, fully obey and comply with all the ordinances, rules, regulations and laws of all public authorities, boards or officers, relating to said premises, or the improvements thereon, or to the use thereof, and further not to use or occupy, or permit any person or body to use or occupy, the said premises, or any part thereof, for any purpose or use in violation of any law, statute or ordinance, whether Federal, State or municipal, during the term of said lease.

As a security for the rent, the Tenant grants, bargains and sells to the Lessor all property of every kind, on or to be brought on the premises, and whenever rent, or anything reserved as rent, is unpaid, the Lessor may seize or distrain said property, on or off the premises, and sell the same on due legal notice for all rent or other payments due as rent, expenses, etc., and for all rent not due holding the same as security.

It is further agreed that if said Tenant shall default in the payment of any installment of rent, or of any other sum provided for under this lease as the same becomes due and payable, or shall remove or express or declare an intention to remove any of the goods and chattels from the premises, or should an execution issue against the Tenant, bankruptcy proceedings be begun by or against said Tenant, or an assignment be made by Tenant for the benefit of creditors, or a receiver appointed for Tenant, then and in such case the entire rent for the balance of the term shall at once become due and payable as if by the terms of this lease it were all payable in advance. In case of such assignment, bankruptcy proceedings, appointment of a receiver, or of a suit on legal process of Tenant from which Lessor shall have the right to demand and receive the rent for the balance of the term, which shall be first paid out of the proceeds of such assignment, bankruptcy or receiver's proceedings or sale on legal process, any law, usage or custom to the contrary notwithstanding.

For value received and forthwith on every default, of payment of rent by Tenant, or on any and every breach of covenant herein, the Tenant hereby empowers any Attorney of any Court of Record within the United States or elsewhere, to appear for Tenant and after one or more declarations filed, confess judgment against Tenant, and in favor of said Lessor, his heir executors, administrators or assigns, as of any term for the sum due by reason of said default or breach of covenant, with costs of suit and Attorney's commission of $ 50.00   for collection and issue Fieri Facias for said amount, with release of all errors and without stay of execution and inquisition and extension upon any levy on real estate is hereby waived, and condemnation agreed to; and in case of the violation of any of the covenants or agreements in this Lease by Tenant, the said Tenant further, at the option of the said Lessor, authorizes and empowers any such attorney, either in addition to or without such judgment for the amount due according to the terms of this Lease, to appear and confess judgment forthwith against Tenant and in favor of Lessor in an amicable action of ejectment for the premises above described, with all the conditions, fees, releases, waivers of stay of execution and exemption to accompany said confession of judgment in ejectment as are set forth in said confession of judgment for said sums due; and authorizes the entry of such amicable action, without leave of Court; and the immediate issuing of a writ of Habere Facias Possessionem, with clause of Fieri Facias for the amount of such judgment and costs, without leave of Court; and Lessor may without notice re-enter and expel the Tenant from the premises and also any person holding under him or them, and in each case, this Lease or a true copy thereof shall be a sufficient warrant of any person.

A determining of the term, or the receipt of rent after default, or after judgment, or after execution, shall not deprive the Lessor of other action against the Tenant for possession for rent, or for damages. The Lessor may use the remedies herein given or those prescribed by law, or both, and the Lessor or Agent may enter, at will, to inspect the premises, to take or send persons on said property, seeking to rent or purchase, make repairs and post notices of "To Let" and "For Sale."

If the premises at any time be deserted or closed, the Lessor may enter by force, without liability to prosecution or action therefor, and may distrain for rent and also re-let the premises, as Agent of the Tenant, for any unexpired portion of the term, and receive the rent therefor and apply it on this Lease.

The Lessor shall not be liable for any injury or damage to any person or to any property at any time on said premises or building from any cause whatever which may arise from the use or condition of said premises or building or from ice thereon, or from water, rain or snow which may leak into, issue or flow from any part of said building, or from the pipes or plumbing of the same, or from any other place or quarter, or from any other cause, during said term or any renewal thereof.

NOTE — The following conditions or any rules adopted for the premises are to be understood as part of the general Lease:

(1) There must be nothing taken in or out of the front entrance, such as trunks, boxes, barrels, furniture, goods or ware of any kind.

(2) The Tenant shall furnish garbage can, with tight cover, keep it in place designated, and must keep cover on same at all times, and must at all times place garbage in can; under no consideration will garbage be allowed to lay loose or can be left open.

(3) Each Tenant must have their own cans, boxes, paper and rubbish of every kind removed at their own expense, and at no time leave anything lying around in yard or cellar, or do or permit anything to be done which may increase the rate of fire insurance, and no carpet, rug, or other article shall be hung or shaken out of any window, or allowed to drop out of any openings, including doors and windows and Lessee shall not sweep or throw, or permit to be swept or thrown from the leased premises any dirt or other substances into any other part of said building.

(4) No animals or parrots shall be kept in or about the premises.

(5) Tenant shall not obstruct side-walk, hall nor stairway, nor use the same for any purpose other than ingress and egress, nor place any sign or notice on the building without the consent of the Lessor, nor permit children to loiter in main hall nor stairway.

(6) Tenants, their servants, or guests, shall not make or commit any improper noises or disturbances in or about the building, nor throw anything whatsoever out of the window, nor interfere in any way with other tenants or those having business with them. Violation of any one of the above rules shall be dealt with as any other violation of this Lease, and any damage caused by same, collected as rent.

Lessor to furnish light and heat for main halls and stairways and steam heat for all apartments; also sufficient hot water for ordinary requirements of apartment, but reserves the right to shut off same without any abatement of said rent in case of unnecessary waste.

The Tenant also expressly waives to the Lessor the benefit of the Act of Assembly, No. 20, approved April 6, 1951, entitled "The Landlord and Tenant Act of 1951" and for valuable consideration, covenants and agrees to vacate, remove from and deliver up possession of the said premises at any time upon receiving thirty days' notice so to do, in which case the Lessor or his assigns may re-enter and take possession thereof.

All rights and liabilities herein given to or imposed upon either of the parties hereto, shall extend to their heirs, executors, administrators, successors and assigns of such party. If the Tenant lawfully occupies the premises after the end of the term, this Lease and all its terms, provisions, conditions, covenants, confession or confessions of judgment, waivers, remedies and any and all of Lessor's rights herein specially given and agreed to, shall be in force for another

month   and so on from   month   to

month   as long as the relation of Landlord and Tenant continues.

In Witness Whereof, The parties hereto set their hands and seal this   1st   day of   October   .A.D. 19 68.

Sealed and Delivered in the Presence of

Anna Cole

John Weber (SEAL)

By McFadden Realty Co, agent (SEAL)

per H.T. McFadden, Pres. (SEAL)

Frank Sherman (SEAL)

Elizabeth M. Sherman (SEAL)

D-3

FARM LEASE

THIS AGREEMENT WITNESSETH, That Stanley Arbuckle, of Butler, Pa., doth hereby let and demise unto Wilson Brady for the term of two years from the first day of March, A.D., nineteen hundred and sixty-nine, at the rent of six hundred dollars per annum, to be paid quarterly in advance by the lessee at 601 High St., Butler, Pa., or at such place as the lessor or subsequent owner may require, all that certain (description of farm) the first quarterly payment of rent to be made on the first day of March, nineteen hundred sixty-nine, which said rent the said lessee doth hereby agree to pay to the said lessor on the days and times aforesaid, and that he shall not nor will assign this lease nor underlet said premises, or any part thereof, or use or occupy the same other than as a farm, without the written consent of the said lessor first had and obtained and endorsed hereon, and shall and will during the said term keep, and at the termination thereof deliver up, the said premises in as good order and repair as they are now in, reasonable wear and tear, fire, Act of God or inevitable accident only excepted.

Duties of Tenant

The Lessee agrees as follows, viz.: That he will use on the said premises all the hay, straw and fodder which shall be grown thereon; that he will not sell, assign, pledge, remove, or cause or suffer to be removed any of the dung, manure or compost made or which shall be on said premises, and that he will use and spread the same thereon at proper times and places for the nourishment thereof, and that upon the termination of this lease or any subsequent letting thereunder he will leave upon the said premises any remaining hay, straw, fodder or manure, which shall then become the property of the lessor: that he will not convert into tillage or garden ground any of the pasture or meadow ground; that he will not mow any of the meadow or pasture ground more than once in any one year; that he will not cut down or use any of the trees upon the said premises; that he will mow or keep down in the usual manner thistles, docks, and other seeding weeds; that he will keep the fences in good repair, the lessor furnishing such materials for the purpose as he may think necessary; that he will cultivate the said farm with respect to crops and in every respect according to the usual course and custom of good husbandry, sowing winter grain with a sufficient quantity of timothy and clover seed.

Penalty on Failure to Pay Rent

And if the rent shall remain unpaid on any day on which the same ought to be paid, then the lessor may enter the premises, and proceed by distress and sale of the goods there found, to levy the rent and all costs and officer's commissions. The said lessee further agrees that all goods on the said premises, and for thirty days after removal shall be liable to distress for rent and hereby waives the benefit of all exemption laws in relation thereto or to any execution.

Required Notice for Renewal

And it is hereby mutually agreed, that either party hereto may determine this lease at the end of the said term, by giving the other notice thereof, at least three months prior thereto, but in default of such notice, this lease shall continue upon the same terms and conditions as are herein contained, for a further period of two years and so on from year to year or until terminated by either hereto giving to the other three months' written notice for removal previous to the expiration of the second or any succeeding or extended term under this lease, express or implied.

Forfeiture upon Breach

And it is further agreed, that if the lessee shall die or if there shall be any involuntary assignment of this lease by law or otherwise, or if the said rent shall at any time be in arrear and unpaid, or if the said lessee shall underlet or otherwise use the said premises than as above expressed, or shall fail to comply with the conditions of this lease or shall not well and truly perform and fulfill all and every the covenants and agreements herein contained on the part of the lessee to be performed and kept then this lease shall, at the option of the said lessor, cease and absolutely determine, and any attorney may immediately thereafter, as attorney for the said lessee, at the sole request of the said lessor, sign an agreement for entering in any competent court, an amicable action and judgment in ejectment (without any stay of execution or appeal) against the said lessee and all persons claiming under said lessee for the recovery by the lessor of possession of the hereby demised premises, without any liability on the part of the said attorney, for which this shall be a sufficient warrant; and thereupon a writ of habere facias possessionem may issue forthwith without any prior writ or proceeding whatsoever, and the lessee hereby releases to the lessor all errors and defects whatsoever in entering such action or judgment, or causing such writ of habere facias possessionem to be issued, or in any proceeding thereon, or concerning the same; and hereby agree that no writ of error or objection or exception shall be made or taken thereto; and a copy of this lease verified by affidavit, being filed in said action, it shall not be necessary to file the original as a warrant of attorney, any law or rule of court to the contrary notwithstanding. No such determination of this lease, nor taking or recovering possession of the said premises, shall deprive the lessor of any other action against the lessee for possession for rent or for damages.

Taxes

Lessee further agrees to pay one-half of the annual taxes when they become due, as rent, and upon failure so to do, the lessor may collect the same in the same manner as herein provided for the collection of delinquent rent.

It is mutually agreed that this lease shall extend and apply to and bind the respective heirs, assignees, devisees, executors and administrators of the lessor and lessee and all covenants, agreements, conditions and provisions herein shall apply to and bind the owner of the lease or demised premises as if the same ran with the land or as if they were original parties and the lessee agrees that no objection shall be made to the said ejectment proceedings by reason of rent not having been demanded or collected when due or by any waiver.

IN WITNESS WHEREOF, the said parties have hereunto set their hands and seals this fourteenth day of February, one thousand nine hundred sixty-nine.

Sealed and delivered in the ⎫
    presence of   ⎬
.....*William Holmes*..... ⎭

     .... *Stanley Arbuckle* .....(SEAL)
     .....*Wilson Brady* ....(SEAL)

D-4

ASSIGNMENT OF LEASE

For value received, I, John Weber, the Lessor within named, do hereby sell, assign, transfer and set over to Mark L. King, his heirs, executors, administrators and assigns, all my right, title and interest in and to the within Lease, dated May 1, 1967, subject to the terms and conditions thereof.

WITNESS my hand and seal this 29th day of November, A.D. 1968.

......*JOHN WEBER*......(SEAL)

ATTEST:
......*H. T. McFADDEN*......

D-5

SURETY ON LEASE

FOR VALUE RECEIVED, I, George T. Baum, agree to be bail absolute to the lessor in the lease dated November 1, 1968, wherein Henry Pyle is the Lessor and Adam Myers is the tenant, as long as the liability of the Tenant continues under said Lease, or the renewals thereof, that the covenants of the Tenant will be properly kept, and that on any default therein as to payment of rent or otherwise, immediate recourse may be had to me, George T. Baum, by suit or otherwise. And I further agree to pay to the Lessor such sum or sums of money as will be sufficient to make up any deficiency, and fully satisfy the conditions of this agreement as well as said Lease, without requiring any notice of non-payment or proof of demand being made. All exemptions as to property are hereby waived.

WITNESS my hand and seal this 1st day of November, A.D. 1968.

ATTEST: ......*GEORGE T. BAUM*......(SEAL)
......*FRANK T. SNYDER*......

D-6

PERCENTAGE LEASE PROVISIONS

(1) Tenant covenants and agrees to pay for the within leased premises from April 1, 1969 to March 31, 1973, the sum of $500.00 on April 1, 1969 as minimum rental for the month of April, 1969 and the sum of $500.00 on May 1, 1969 as minimum rental for the month of May, 1969 and a like equal sum of $500.00 as minimum rental on the first day of each and every month thereafter up to and including March 1, 1973.

(2) Tenant covenants and agrees to pay to Lessors as additional rental during each lease year of the term hereof an amount equivalent to 3% of the gross sales made upon or from the demised premises in excess of $200,000.00 annually. Any such additional rental due and payable to the Lessors pursuant to the provisions hereof shall be paid to the Lessors by the Tenant within thirty (30) days after the expiration of each lease year during the term hereof.

(3) Tenant shall furnish to Lessors on the tenth day of each and every month during the term of this lease, commencing with May 10, 1969, a statement specifying the gross sales made upon or from the demised premises for each preceding calendar month.

(4) Tenant covenants and agrees to furnish to the Lessors within twenty (20) days after the end of each lease year during the term hereof a final verified statement specifying the total gross sales made upon or from the demised premises for the preceding lease year.

(5) Tenant agrees to install, keep and maintain on the demised premises a system of recording the gross sales of Tenant's business in said premises. The records of said gross sales shall be available for inspection by Lessors during regular business hours and at such times during the term of the lease as Lessors may deem advisable.

(6) Lessors shall have the right at any time to examine and audit Tenant's records of gross sales made upon or from the demised premises for the various periods

aforesaid. In the event that an independent audit by an auditor agreeable to both parties reveals that the verified statement from Tenant to Lessors proves to be incorrect by 5% or more, then Tenant shall be liable for the expenses incurred by Lessors in making such independent audit, otherwise Lessors shall pay for such audit, and Tenant, in any event, shall pay the correct additional rental, if any, as determined by such independent audit.

(7) The term "gross sales" as used in the term of this lease shall be interpreted to mean the aggregate of all sales by Tenant, whether on a cash, credit or installment basis from the sale of goods, wares, merchandise or services to the public made upon or from the demised premises, after deductions of all refunds, allowances and credits made to customers by Tenant in connection with merchandise sold by or returned to Tenant, but sales taxes collected from customers shall not be included in gross sales, but there shall not be deducted for the purpose of calculating gross sales the amount of any license or occupational tax or any other tax measured by the sales or receipts from sales made by Tenant. The return or transfer of merchandise from one of Tenant's stores to another shall not be construed as retail sales, nor shall any sum be paid to Lessors on such merchandise returned or transferred.

(8) Tenant covenants and agrees to keep his store on the demised premises open for business during regular business hours during each business day during the term hereof and to use for sales the area as occupied by Tenant, except when closed for the purpose of making renovations, repairs or by reason of strikes, labor disputes or other causes beyond the control of the Tenant.

(9) Tenant covenants and agrees that he will not during the term of this lease, or during any renewal period thereof, open or operate another store, similar to that conducted on the herein demised premises within a radius of 1500 feet from the herein demised premises.

D-7

SUB-LEASE AGREEMENT

Made between.....*James A. Herron*.....by his renting Agents, ...*Thorwood Corporation*.....Lessor and....*Walter A. Bunt* ...Lessee, now occupying..... *601-5*.....on the.....*sixth*....floor of the.....*Herron Building*.....under a lease dated.....*May 1, 1969*.....

Lessor hereby agrees and consents to the subletting of part of the above specified premises, to wit, ...*Rooms 601 and 602*....with the understanding that the Sub-tenant accepts the premises subject to all conditions as set forth in the said lease of May 1, 1969, and which he agrees to perform and fulfill as if he were the Lessee and that any breach of the lease made by the Sub-tenant shall constitute a breach as if made by the Lessee.

It is further understood and agreed that in granting this privilege to the Lessee, the Lessor does not waive any of his rights under the existing lease nor does he abrogate any of his rights for the recovery of the premises or for distress or otherwise, for rent, or for other charges which may become due.

Unless otherwise approved, the Lessee shall sublet part of the premises specifically to............*James L. O'Toole*............

WITNESS our hands and seals this.....*fourth*..... day of.....*January 1969*.....
..........*James A. Herron*..........

In presence of:
1. .....*R. McInerney as to*.....
2. .....*Wallace Judd as to*....

1. By.....*Thorwood Corporation*......
1. Per...*N. Theodore Flocos, Pres.* ...
2. .....*Walter A. Bunt* ....
Approved:
....*James A. Herron, Jan. 5, 1969*....
Accepted:
....*James L. O'Toole, Jan. 5, 1969*....
Sub-tenant

D-8

PERCENTAGE LEASE TABLE
Revised as of June, 1960*
(California)

Type of Business	Range in % of Sale	Type of Business	Range in % of Sale
Aircraft	3–4	Over $5,000,000	1–2
Antiques and used furniture	6–8	Draperies, curtains and	
Army and navy	7–8	upholstery	5–7
Art, curios, gifts, etc.	5–10	Dressmakers	6–8
Auto tires, batteries, tubes	4–5	Drive-in Restaurant	5–8
Auto supplies—chain	2–3	Drugs and toilet preparations	4–7
Auto agencies	2–3	Drugs: chain and cut rate	2–5
Auto: repairs and parts	2.5–4	Dry goods	4–5
Awnings, flags, tents	5–7		
		Eggs and poultry	4–5
Bakeries and bakery goods	5–7	Electric appliances	4–8
Bakeries in supermarkets	3–4		
Barber shops	10–15	Farm implements, and supplies	2–3
Barber supplies: wholesale	3–4	Farm produce (road side)	2–3
Bars	6–9	Fish markets, sea foods	3–5
Beauty shops: service	8–15	5, 10, 25c to $2 stores, advt. and	
Bicycles (including repairs)	6–8	non-advt.	4–8
Boats, yachts, canoes	3–5	Floor coverings	4–6
Boilers and furnaces	3–5	Florists—estab. stores, large	
Book stores, circulating libraries	5–8	volume	5–7
Bowling, pool, roller skating	8–10	Foods, health	5–7
Building materials, wood	1–2	Frozen fruits and vegetables	3.5–4
Building materials—misc.	2–3	Fruits and vegetables,	
Business schools	12–15	supermarkets	2.5–4
		small store	6–10
Camera & photographic supplies	4–8	Fruit juices	8–12
Candy, fountain, luncheon	6–9	Furniture: cash, credit, home,	
Cash registers, typewriters, add-		incl. desks, office furn. and	
ing machines	5–7	equipment	4–6
Caterers	6–8	Furs and furriers	6–10
Children's and infants' wear	5–8		
China, crockery, enamelware	7–8	Garages—storage, parking lots	35–50
Cigars, etc., newstand	4–7	Gas stations: 1c to 2c per gal.	
Cleaners and dyers	6–10	Gasoline—wholesale	4–6
Clothes (See Men's and		Gift shops	6–10
Women's Clothing and shoes)		Glass and mirror	5–6
Coal, feed, ice, wood	1–2	Golf ranges	15–18
Cooperage, barrels, boxes	2–3	Groceries, ordinary	3–7
Cosmetics	5–8	Groceries in super markets	
Corsets, girdles, etc	10–12	(self-service)	1–1.5
		Groceries (rural) with apparel,	
Dairy products	2–4	dry goods and general mer-	
Decorating and finishing	4–6	chandise	1.5–2
Delicatessens in super markets	4–5		
Dental laboratories	2.5–5	Haberdasheries	5–8
Department Stores		Hardware	6–9
Less than $500,000	3–4	Heating appliances and oil	
Over $500,000 to $5,000,000	1.5–3	burners	2–4

Type of Business	% of Sale Range in	Type of Business	Range in % of Sale
Hosiery, knit goods and lingerie	7–10	Parking lots	40–50
Hotels (of room rent)	20–25	Pawnshops	4.5–10
Household appliances, incl.		Petroleum products	1–1.5
electric	3–4	Photographs	3.5–6
Ice cream	5–8	Pictures and framing	10–12
Infants' wear	5–8	Plumbing, heating and	
Iron and steel products	1.5–4	ventilating	4–5
Jewelry for cash	5–7	Radio and Television	2.5–6
Jewelry: cheap costume, novelty	7–10	Radio, installment	3–5
Junk dealers	2.5–4	Refrigerators, electric and gas	2–4
Knitting Supplies	7–9	Restaurant supplies	3–8
		Restaurants, cafeterias	4–8
Lamps and shades	8–10	Roofing	2–3
Laundry	8–12	Rugs	4–8
Leather goods, including shoes			
and harness repair	6–10	Scientific and medical instruments and supply, retail	4–5
Liquor, package goods	3–5	Seeds, bulbs, plants and nursery	
Luggage shops	5–6	stock	5–7
Lumber	2–3	Sewing machines	4–6
Lunch counters	5–8	Shoes, men's, women's, children's, varied prices	5–8
Machinery and machine shop	2–4	Shoes, repair	10–12
Mail order house, general mdse.	1–1.5	Sporting goods: athletic and	
Meat markets: in super markets and chains	2–3	playground equipment, specialty, toys and stationery	5–8
Meat market, ordinary	3–5	Stationery	5–8
Men's and boys' clothing	4–8	Store fixtures	4–5
Men's and boys' hats	6–8	Stoves and ranges	5–6
Men's and women's clothing			
cash and credit	4–8	Tailors: cash, credit, custom and merchant	5–10
Men's furnishing	3–7	Teas, coffees, spices	2.5–3
Men's shoes quality	6–8	Theaters, drive-in	3–4
Men's shoes, volume	4–6	Tourist camps	2–5
Millinery, exclusive	10–12	Toys	7–9
Motion pictures, small, large with vaudeville	12–15	Transfer and storage	25
Motorcycles	3–4	Travel bureaus	8–10
Music stores	4–6	Trunk and leather goods	6–10
		Typewriters	3–6
Novelty shops and souvenirs	5–10		
Nuts	8–10	Undertakers	5–8
		Upholsterers	5–9
Office and school supplies	5–7	Women's accessories, incl.	
Optical stores	6–9	lingerie and hosiery	5–8
Opticians and optometrists	7–10	Women's and children's apparel	4–8
Oriental and Russian rugs	5–10	Women's and children's apparel	
Paints, glass, varnishes, specialty lines, wallpaper and		chains	3–5
supplies	6–8	Yardage	4–6

* By Ivan A. Thorson, courtesy of Realty Research Bureau, Inc., 416 West 8th Street, Los Angeles, California, Copyright, 1960.

D-9

LEASE RENEWAL ENDORSEMENT

ATTACHED TO and made part of a certain lease dated........*May 1, 1968*.......
between......*ALBERT D. SIMS*......as Lessor, and......*CHARLES L. STUART*
......as Lessee, covering premises situate and known as..........*201 Conestoga
Street, Omaha, Nebraska*..............

For value received and by mutual consent, the aforesaid lease, of which this Renewal Endorsement is now a part, is hereby extended and renewed for a term
of......*one*.......year, beginning......*May 1, 1969*......., and ending......
April 30, 1970......for a total rental of $......*720.00*....., payable in equal
monthly installments of $......*60.00*....., in advance, plus any and all other
payments required to be made by the tenant as rent or otherwise in accordance
with the terms of said lease. All the terms, covenants, conditions, and stipulations
contained in the original lease, of which this Renewal forms a part, are hereby made
a part of this Renewal and shall be binding on the parties and remain in full force
and effect.

IN WITNESS WHEREOF, The parties hereto set their hands and seals this......*15th*
......day of......*February*..........., A.D. 19....*69*......

WITNESS:
....*PHILIP BAKER, as to both*....   ......*ALBERT D. SIMS*...........
                                                                Lessor
                                   ......*CHARLES L. STUART*.......
                                                                Lessee

OIL AND GAS LEASE

This Agreement, Entered into the 18th   day of   June   A. D. 19 69

Between   ASA P. COURTNEY and MARY B. COURTNEY, his wife

of the District or Township of   Sterling.   County of   Warren   and State of

Pennsylvania,   the party of the first part, Lessor, and   FRED BENNETT,

party of the second part, Lessee.

Witnesseth, That the Lessor, in consideration of_____ one ($1.00)_____Dollars in hand paid, by the Lessee, the receipt of which is hereby acknowledged, ha ve granted, demised, leased and let unto the Lessee, his heirs, executors, administrators and assigns all the oil and gas in and under all that certain tract of land and also, said tract of land hereinafter described, with covenants of general warranty, and that the Lessor ha ve the sole right to convey the premises to the Lessee, with the exclusive right of drilling and operating thereon for and producing oil and gas, and all rights necessary, convenient and incident thereto; such in part as the right to construct and maintain buildings, telegraph, telephone and pipe lines leading from adjoining lands on and across this leasehold and other lands of the Lessor s , and similar rights for roadways and the right to use water, oil and gas from the premises for operating purposes, and the right of removing either during or at any time after the term hereof, all casing, tubing, machinery, buildings, structures and property of the Lessee and his assigns and employees; also, the right of subdividing and releasing all or any part of the premises situate in_____ Sterling

District or Township   Allegheny_____ County and State of_ Pennsylvania _____; on waters of

                    bounded and described, wholly or in part as follows:

On the North by lands of   EPHRAIM GOLDBETTER and ANNA GOLDBETTER, his wife

On the East by lands of   PETER KUEHNER and SARAH E. KUEHNER, his wife

On the South by lands of   Heirs of Fred Rowbottom

On the West by lands of   Heirs of Fred Rowbottom

containing____ seventy (70)_____ acres, more or less, reserving therefrom____ three_____ hundred feet around the present important buildings on which no well shall be drilled by either party except by mutual consent.

It is agreed that this Lease shall remain in force for the term of____ eight____ years from this date and as long thereafter as oil or gas is produced from the premises or as operations continue for the production of oil and gas.

The Lessor   to receive one-eighth part of the oil produced and saved from the premises delivered into tanks or pipe line, in which one-eighth part shall be included any royalty or interest in said oil that may have been heretofore sold, reserved or conveyed by said Lessors or their predecessors in title, and for wells that produce gas only the Lessor s shall be paid for each such gas well while the gas is sold therefrom at the rate of____ One Hundred Eighty ($180.00)_per annum, payable quarterly, while marketed off the premises, and any interest in said gas heretofore conveyed or reserved shall be paid for proportionately out of said amount of gas rental.

It is agreed by the parties hereto that the second party shall have the right to use off the farm for such purposes as it may desire, "Casing Head Gas," (being gas produced from oil wells on the premises) free of all rent or royalty. In consideration whereof, the Lessor s_____may lay a line to any well producing gas on said land to take gas free for____ their____own use for heat and light in one dwelling house on said land, out of any surplus gas over and above what second party, requires to operate the farm and subject to the use, operations, pumping and right of abandonment of the well by second party; Lessor s____to provide and use economical appliances and to use gas at____ their____own risk, and to subscribe to and be bound by the reasonable rules and regulations of said second party, relating to such use of gas.

Second party covenants and agrees to locate all wells so as to interfere as little as possible with the cultivated portions of the farm. And further, to complete a well on the said premises within____ ninety days____from the date hereof, or pay at the rate of____ fifty

($ 50.00____) Dollars quarterly in advance for each additional three months such completion is delayed from the time above mentioned for the completion of such well until a well is completed; and it is agreed that the completion of such well shall be and operate as a full liquidation of all rental under this provision during the remainder of the term of this Lease. All payments may be made direct to the Lessor s   or by check mailed

to Lessors   at   Maple Springs P.O.   P. O.

        Warren   County, State of_ Pennsylvania _____; or in the same who is hereby appointed agent for such purposes.

manner to

It is agreed that upon the payment of   Fifty   his heirs

($ 50.00____) Dollars at any time, by the party of the second part, or by its successors and assigns it or they shall have the right to surrender this Lease for cancellation, after which all payments and liabilities thereafter to accrue under and by virtue of its terms shall cease and determine, and this Lease become absolutely null and void.

All provisions of this Lease shall extend to and be binding upon the heirs, executors, administrators, successors or assigns of the parties hereto.

In Witness Whereof, the parties to this agreement have hereunto set their hands and seals the day and year first above written.

Witness:

HERBERT E. DUNLAP   ASA P. COURTNEY   (SEAL)

                    MARY B. COURTNEY   (SEAL)

                    FRED BENNET   (SEAL)

E-1

POWER OF ATTORNEY *in re* REAL ESTATE

KNOW ALL MEN BY THESE PRESENTS, that I, Henry S. Howard, of the City of Seattle, Washington, have made, constituted, and appointed, and by these presents do make, constitute, and appoint, Jeremiah Richardson, of Seattle, my true and lawful attorney, for me, and in my name, place and stead, to enter into and take possession of all messuages, lands, tenements, hereditaments, and real estate whatever, in *(here describe the lands)* to or in which I am now possessed, seized or am or in any way entitled or interested; and to grant, bargain, and sell the same, or any part or parcel thereof, for such sum or price and on such terms as to him shall seem meet; and for me and in my name to make, execute, acknowledge, and deliver good and sufficient deeds and conveyances for the same, either with or without covenants and warranty; and, to let and demise the said real estate for the best rent that can be procured for the same; and to ask, demand, recover, and to receive all sums of money which shall become due and owing to me by means of such bargain, sale, or lease, and to take all lawful ways and means for the recovery thereof; to compound and agree for the same, and to execute and deliver sufficient discharges and acquittances therefor. Giving and granting unto my said attorney full power and authority to do and perform all and every act and thing whatsoever, requisite and necessary to be done in and about the premises, as fully to all intents and purposes as I might or could do, if personally present; hereby ratifying and confirming all that my said attorney shall lawfully do or cause to be done by virtue hereof.

IN WITNESS WHEREOF I have hereunto set my hand and seal, this first day of March, in the year of our Lord one thousand nine hundred and sixty-nine.

Signed, sealed and delivered in the
        presence of
...... *SARAH E. GLOCK* ......
...... *HIRAM T. GLOCK* ....*HENRY S. HOWARD*....(SEAL)
(Acknowledgement)

E-2

BILL OF SALE FOR HOUSEHOLD ARTICLES

KNOW ALL MEN BY THESE PRESENTS, That ....*we, PAUL LEFFLER AND MAE LEFFLER, his wife* ....of ....*Dallas, Texas*...., for and in consideration of the sum of ....*one ($1.00) Dollar*.... to ....*us*.... in hand paid by ....*Thomas Jarrett and Marie E. Jarrett, his wife*.... of ....*Dallas, Texas*.... at or before the sealing and delivery of these presents, the receipt whereof is hereby acknowledged ha..*ve*.. granted, bargained, sold, released and confirmed and by these presents do grant, bargain, sell, release and confirm unto the said ....*Thomas Jarrett and Marie E. Jarrett, his wife*...., all and singular the ....*following goods and chattels, namely, awnings, four-piece bedroom suite, GE refrigerator, living room rug, stair carpet, and hall mirror*.....

TO HAVE AND TO HOLD the said....*goods and chattels*........................
unto the said ....*Thomas Jarrett and Marie E. Jarrett, his wife, their* ....executors, administrators and assigns, to and for ....*their*.... own proper use, benefit, and behoof, forever.

AND ....*we*...., the said ....*Paul Leffler and Mae Leffler, his wife*...., their executors and administrators, hereby covenant that ....*we are*.....the lawful owner of said goods, chattels and property above referred to, and that the same, and every part thereof unto the said ....*Thomas Jarrett and Marie E. Jarrett, his wife*...., their executors, administrators and assigns, from and against all persons whomsoever, shall and will warrant and forever defend by these presents.

IN WITNESS WHEREOF, ... *we* .... have hereunto set .... *our* .... hand .. *s* .. and seal .. *s* .. the .... *16* .... day of .... *June* .... in the year of our Lord one thousand nine hundred and ...... *sixty-nine* ......
Sealed and Delivered in the Presence of:

.... *ROGER HARRIS* .... *PAUL LEFFLER* .... (SEAL)
.... *CARL B. FRIED* ..   .... *MAE LEFFLER* ..... (SEAL)

On the day of the date of the above Bill of Sale, livery of seizin of the articles above referred to was given by the said .... *Paul Leffler and Mae Leffler, his wife* .... to the said .... *Thomas Jarrett and Marie E. Jarrett, his wife* .....

...... *THOMAS   JARRETT* ......
...... *MARIE E. JARRETT* ......

E-3

AGENCY MANAGEMENT CONTRACT

THIS AGREEMENT made this 15th day of April, A.D. 1969 by and between Evan L. Mercer of Duluth, Minnesota, hereinafter referred to as the OWNER

a
n
d

W. Frank Shook of New York, New York, hereinafter referred to as AGENT, WITNESSETH: That in and for the consideration hereinafter mentioned, the parties hereto have agreed as follows:

FIRST: The Owner does hereby constitute, appoint and employ the Agent as his sole agent and representative for and in connection with the rental, management, direction and operation of the fifteen story brick and concrete office and commercial structure, situate at 1000 Manhattan Ave., New York, known as the Kenmar Building, presently owned by the Owner, for the term of two years, beginning May 1, 1969 and ending December 31, 1971.

SECOND: The Agent agrees to devote his full time, attention, skill and experience to the management, operation and supervision of said building and to act with all fidelity to the Owner.

THIRD: The Owner agrees to pay the Agent the usual and customary commission at the time of making leases for space in said building, as promulgated in the schedule of commissions of the Real Estate Board of New York; if a commercial lease is made by a person or broker other than the Agent, the owner's liability for commission shall be limited to a single commission at the usual and customary rate; all commissions that shall become due hereunder shall be payable at the time the lease is executed; the Owner further agrees to pay the Agent the aforesaid commission on the renewal of any leases negotiated and consummated by the Agent.

FOUR: The Owner further agrees to pay the Agent three per cent of all the rents or monies collected, exclusive of the first month's rent collected under a new lease or the first month's rent under any renewal lease; said commission shall be payable upon the first day of the following month, which shall be deducted each month from the rents and monies due the Owner; the Agent shall render a full statement to the Owner on the fifth day of each month of this agreement, beginning February 5, 1966, showing all rents, income and revenue for the preceding month, less commissions and disbursements, together with a check for the net amount due the Owner.

FIFTH: The Agent agrees to keep a separate Agency account in the Maritime Exchange Bank, where all rents and monies received for, in behalf of, and on account of the Owner, shall be deposited.

SIXTH: It is further understood and agreed that the Agent shall hire and employ such employees as may be necessary for the proper and efficient management of the building, with full authority to hire, supervise and discharge all such employees, to make all necessary purchases of supplies and equipment, advertise space to lease when necessary, contract for and make necessary repairs and alterations, and pay for all supplies, wages, and expenses necessary for the operation and maintenance of the building, for the account of the Owner; provided that the Agent shall not incur any expense, debt, obligation or liability in excess of $500, without the approval of the Owner first had and obtained; all such expenses and disbursements shall be paid by the Agent out of the Agency account, and deducted monthly; the Agent shall attach vouchers for all expenses so paid to each monthly statement submitted to the Owner.

SEVENTH: It is further understood and agreed that the Agent is authorized and empowered to place in the name of the Owner and for his account, any and all insurance of any kind or nature including but not limited to fire, theft, public liability, plate glass, workmen's compensation, and elevator liability, that may be necessary or required in connection with said building, as well as any renewals of such insurance, and to pay the premiums for the same.

EIGHTH: The Agent is hereby authorized and empowered to take any action at law or equity which he may deem necessary, or required for the collection of rents or monies or to repossess any portion of the building premises and to employ counsel in that connection, when necessary; to compromise any rent claim due the Owner before or after suit commenced; and the Owner further agrees to indemnify and keep and save the Agent harmless in connection with any legal action commenced or threatened by or against the Agent as well as from any claim, demand, or action instituted against the Agent by reason of his operation or management of said building.

NINTH: It is hereby agreed and understood that unless written notice is given by either party hereto to the other on or before October 1, 1971, to the effect that it is the intention of said party not to renew the within contract, then and in that event, this agreement shall continue in full force and effect for an additional one (1) year period, and so on from year to year.

TENTH: The parties hereto further agree that upon the termination of this agreement at the end of the term, or by giving notice in the manner aforementioned, then and in that event the Agent shall receive one and one-half (1½) per cent commission upon the rents that may become due or payable under any lease or renewal negotiated and consummated prior to the termination of the Agent's employment, such commissions shall be due and payable as the rents are received; provided, however, that in event any lease is cancelled, terminated or altered voluntarily by the Owner or his Agent, after termination of Agent's employment, then the within Agent shall be entitled to his commission of one and one-half (1½) per cent for the balance of the rental period, forthwith.

IN WITNESS WHEREOF, the parties hereto have affixed their hands and seals the day, month and year aforesaid.

WITNESS:

......KENNETH T. MERCER......   ....EVAN L. MERCER.....(SEAL)
     As to Owner   Owner
........FRANK O. HARPER........   ....W. FRANK SHOOK.....(SEAL)
     As to Agent   Agent

E-4

STANDARD MANAGEMENT AGREEMENT

In consideration of the covenants herein contained:

....(Hereinafter called Owner)
and ....(Hereinafter called Agent)
agree as follows:

1. The owner hereby employs the agent exclusively to rent and manage the property known as:

....
....
....
....

upon the terms hereinafter set forth for a period of ...... years beginning on the ...... day of ......, 19...., and thereafter for yearly periods from time to time.

(a) Owner agrees to pay the agent each month for management ...... per cent of gross rents collected.

(b) Either party may terminate this agreement by serving the other a sixty (60) day notice in writing prior to the expiration date or expiration of any renewal thereof.

(c) Where there is a lease or leases still in effect at the date of termination of this contract the owner agrees to pay the agent for the unexpired term of the lease or leases, at the time of termination or withdrawal of collection, the regular commission as established by the .... Real Estate Board under Withdrawal of Collections.

2. The agent agrees:

(a) To accept the management of the above described premises and agrees to furnish the services of his/its organization for the renting, operation and managing of said premises.

(b) To investigate carefully all references of prospective tenants.

(c) To deposit all collections in an Agency Bank Account, separate from the Agent's personal account. In case of the closing or failure of the bank, the agent shall not be held responsible for loss of any funds.

(d) To render ...... statements of receipts, charges and expenses and to remit balance to the owner, less agent's commission.

(e) To obtain for the benefit of the owner all discounts allowed on purchases of supplies, materials or repairs.

(f) To care for, place and supervise, subject to the owner's instruction, all insurance coverage.

3. The owner hereby gives to the agent the following authority and powers:

(a) To advertise said premises, to display signs thereon, to rent the same, to sign and renew leases, with express authority and power in the agent to execute leases for terms not in excess of ...... years.

(b) To collect rents due or to become due and give receipt therefor.

(c) To save the Agent harmless from all damage suits in connection with the management of the property and from liability for injuries suffered by any employee or other persons whomsoever, and to carry, at his/her own expense, public liability insurance adequate to protect the interests of all parties hereto.

This agreement shall be binding upon the successors and assigns of the Agent and the heirs, administrators, executors, successors, and assigns of the Owner.

In witness whereof the parties hereto have affixed their respective signatures this .... day of ......, 19.....

....(SEAL)
....(SEAL)

SALESMAN'S CONTRACT

(Recommended by Oakland, California, Real Estate Board)

RUSH REALTY COMPANY _____ hereinafter referred to as "Company"

and_____ DOROTHY FISHER _____ hereinafter referred to as "Salesman",

hereby agree, subject to termination at the will of either party, to the following conditions and details of their relationship, namely:

(1) FACILITIES:

Company shall provide Salesman with advertising and with necessary office equipment including space, desk, telephone, signs, business cards and stationery, and shall assist and cooperate with Salesman in connection with his work.

(2) GENERAL CONDITIONS:

(a) Salesman shall read and shall govern his conduct by the Code of Ethics of the National Association of Real Estate Boards, the Real Estate Law of the State of California and the By-Laws of the Oakland Real Estate Board and regulations of Multiple Listing Division of the Real Estate Board, and any future modifications or additions thereto.

(b) The schedule of customary commissions of the Oakland Real Estate Board shall be used in every transaction, and any variation therefrom must first be approved by Company; and Salesman hereby admits knowledge of customary schedules of commissions as published by the Real Estate Board.

(c) Salesman shall furnish his own automobile and pay all expenses thereof and shall carry liability and property damage insurance satisfactory to Company.

(d) Salesman must remain continuously licensed by the State of California to sell real estate as a salesman.

(e) Salesman shall not obligate Company for materials or services without the knowledge and first obtaining consent of Company.

(f) Salesman shall use only such real estate forms as have first been approved by Company.

(g) Salesman hereby acknowledges he is an independent contractor, and is not a servant, employee, joint-adventurer or partner of the Broker. (Note) In some offices, Salesmen are employees of the Broker and (g) may be changed accordingly.

(h) Other Clauses:

(3) COMMISSIONS:

All commissions resulting from real estate transactions procured by Salesman shall be divided between Company and Salesman on a basis of __50__ per cent of the net commission to Salesman. Any expense incurred in negotiating the sale, including listing and Board Multiple Listing commissions, shall first be deducted from the gross commission before such division. No commission shall be considered earned or payable to Salesman until the transaction has been completed and the commission collected by Company.

(4) LISTING COMMISSIONS — SALES — RENTALS AND LEASES:

Sales:

(1) Upon sale of property by other than listing Salesman, he shall be paid out of the commission received by Company, as follows:

a. __10__ per cent on signed non-exclusive listings.

b. __15__ per cent on signed exclusive listings.

c. __15__ per cent of entire commission on signed exclusive listings sold by another Company.

d. __15__ per cent of the gross commission on Board Multiple Listings remaining after payment of the Multiple Listing fee.

(2) Company reserves the right to reject any exclusive listing deemed unsatisfactory and to return said listing to the owner.

(a) Upon termination of Salesman's association by decision of Salesman, Company shall not be liable to Salesman for a commission on any listing procured by Salesman or on any sale of property unless an offer in writing has been obtained from a bona fide purchaser accompanied with a deposit under the listing prior to the termination of association and the same transaction is later completed.

(b) Upon termination of association by decision of Company, Salesman shall receive agreed listing commission on his listings if sold within the life of such listings.

(c) All listings and prospects are the property of the Company.

(5) COMMISSIONS OTHER THAN CASH:

In connection with any type of transaction, if it becomes necessary or desirable to receive all or any part of a commission in property other than cash, then approval of Company must first be obtained.

In such event, Company and Salesman may agree to:

(a) divide such property between Company and Salesman in kind, or

(b) pay Salesman his full share of the commission in cash and retain full ownership in the property so received, or

(c) retain such property in the names of Company and Salesman and thereafter dispose of the same at such time and in such manner as Company and Salesman shall deem advisable. Any profit or loss and any carrying charge or other expense with respect to such property shall be shared between Company and Salesman in the same proportion as their respective interests in the commission involved.

(6) ESCROWS:

Company shall order all title searches and handle all escrows.

(7) ADVERTISING:

All advertising must be first approved by Company before publication; such advertising shall be at Company expense.

(8) TELEPHONE AND TELEGRAMS:

Salesman shall make no long distance telephone calls, nor shall Salesman send any telegrams, without the approval of Company. All messages over $1.00 shall be paid ½ by the Company and ½ by the Salesman for whose benefit the cost was incurred.

(9) LITIGATION

In the event any transaction in which Salesman is involved results in dispute, litigation, or legal expense, Salesman shall cooperate fully with Company and Company and Salesman shall share all expense connected therewith in the same proportion as they would normally share the commission resulting from such transaction without a dispute or litigation. It is the policy to avoid litigation wherever possible, and Company reserves the sole right to determine whether or not any litigation or dispute shall be prosecuted, defended or settled, or whether or not legal expenses shall be incurred.

(10) DIVISION OF COMMISSION:

Any arrangement for division of commission with other brokers must be first approved by Company. In the event that two or more salesmen licensed with Company participate in a commission on the same transaction it shall be divided between the participating Salesmen according to a written agreement or by arbitration.

(11) DEPOSITS, ETC.:

All monies, documents or property received by Salesman in connection with any transaction of Company shall be delivered to Company immediately. All checks must be made payable either to Company, to a title insurance company, or to any other escrow holder.

In the event all or any portion of a deposit is forfeited, disbursement of Company's share shall be the same as though the forfeited amount was a commission received in connection with the transaction.

(12) CORRESPONDENCE:

All letters received and a copy of all letters written by Salesman pertaining to the business or Company shall be turned over to Company for its records. All letters are to be approved by Company before mailing.

(13) OTHER CLAUSES:

Upon termination of salesman's employment, all office material and data, including listings, prospect books and files, office supplies, keys, etc., shall be returned to the company.

The undersigned hereby agrees to abide by all of the foregoing specifications and use his skill, efforts and workmanship in cooperating with Company to carry out the terms of this agreement for the mutual benefit of Company and undersigned Salesman.

Dated this 4th day of
February, 1969

By *William A. Rushton*
ta. Rush Realty Company

Dorothy Fischer
Salesman

E-6

TABLE OF PAYMENTS TO AMORTIZE $1,000 LOAN

Term of years	4% Per Mo.	4% Per Quar.	4¼% Per Mo.	4¼% Per Quar.	4½% Per Mo.	4½% Per Quar.	4¾% Per Mo.	4¾% Per Quar.	5% Per Mo.	5% Per Quar.	5¼% Per Mo.	5¼% Per Quar.	5½% Per Mo.	5½% Per Quar.	5¾% Per Mo.	5¾% Per Quar.	6% Per Mo.	6% Per Quar.	6¼% Per Mo.	6¼% Per Quar.
5	18.42	55.42	18.53	56.77	18.65	56.12	18.76	56.47	18.88	56.83	18.99	57.18	19.11	57.54	19.22	57.89	19.34	58.25	19.45	58.61
6	15.65	47.08	15.76	47.43	15.88	47.78	15.99	48.14	16.11	48.49	16.23	48.85	16.34	49.21	16.46	49.57	16.58	49.93	16.70	50.29
7	13.67	41.13	13.79	41.48	13.91	41.84	14.02	42.19	14.14	42.55	14.26	42.91	14.38	43.28	14.49	43.64	14.61	44.01	14.73	44.37
8	12.19	36.68	12.31	37.03	12.43	37.39	12.55	37.75	12.66	38.11	12.78	38.48	12.90	38.84	13.03	39.21	13.15	39.58	13.27	39.95
9	11.05	33.22	11.16	33.58	11.28	33.94	11.40	34.30	11.52	34.67	11.64	35.04	11.76	35.41	11.89	35.78	12.01	36.16	12.13	36.53
10	10.13	30.46	10.25	30.82	10.37	31.19	10.49	31.56	10.61	31.93	10.73	32.30	10.86	32.67	10.98	33.05	11.11	33.43	11.23	33.81
11	9.38	28.21	9.50	28.58	9.62	28.94	9.75	29.32	9.87	29.69	9.99	30.07	10.12	30.45	10.25	30.83	10.37	31.22	10.50	31.60
12	8.76	26.34	8.88	26.71	9.01	27.08	9.13	27.46	9.25	27.84	9.38	28.22	9.51	28.60	9.63	28.99	9.76	29.38	9.89	29.77
13	8.24	24.76	8.36	25.13	8.48	25.51	8.61	25.89	8.74	26.27	8.86	26.66	8.99	27.05	9.12	27.44	9.25	27.84	9.38	28.24
14	7.79	23.41	7.91	23.79	8.04	24.17	8.17	24.55	8.29	24.94	8.42	25.33	8.55	25.73	8.68	26.13	8.82	26.53	8.95	26.93
15	7.40	22.25	7.53	22.63	7.65	23.01	7.78	23.40	7.91	23.79	8.04	24.19	8.18	24.59	8.31	24.99	8.44	25.40	8.58	25.81
16	7.06	21.24	7.19	21.62	7.32	22.01	7.45	22.40	7.58	22.80	7.71	23.20	7.85	23.60	7.98	24.01	8.12	24.42	8.26	24.84
17	6.77	20.34	6.90	20.73	7.03	21.12	7.16	21.52	7.29	21.92	7.43	22.33	7.56	22.74	7.70	23.15	7.84	23.57	7.98	23.99
18	6.51	19.56	6.64	19.95	6.77	20.34	6.90	20.74	7.04	21.15	7.17	21.56	7.31	21.97	7.45	22.39	7.59	22.81	7.73	23.24
19	6.27	18.85	6.40	19.25	6.54	19.65	6.67	20.05	6.81	20.46	6.95	20.88	7.08	21.30	7.22	21.72	7.37	22.15	7.51	22.58
20	6.06	18.22	6.20	18.62	6.33	19.03	6.47	19.44	6.60	19.85	6.74	20.27	6.88	20.69	7.03	21.12	7.17	21.55	7.31	21.99
21	5.88	17.66	6.01	18.06	6.15	18.47	6.28	18.88	6.42	19.30	6.56	19.72	6.70	20.15	6.85	20.59	6.99	21.02	7.14	21.46
22	5.71	17.15	5.84	17.55	5.98	17.97	6.12	18.38	6.26	18.81	6.40	19.23	6.54	19.67	6.69	20.10	6.84	20.55	6.98	20.99
23	5.55	16.68	5.69	17.09	5.83	17.51	5.97	17.93	6.11	18.36	6.25	18.79	6.40	19.23	6.54	19.67	6.69	20.12	6.84	20.57
24	5.41	16.26	5.55	16.67	5.69	17.00	5.83	17.52	5.97	17.95	6.12	18.39	6.27	18.83	6.41	19.28	6.56	19.73	6.72	20.19
25	5.28	15.87	5.42	16.29	5.56	16.71	5.71	17.14	5.85	17.58	6.00	18.02	6.15	18.47	6.30	18.92	6.45	19.38	6.60	19.84

INDEX

Index